New Mexico in the
Nineteenth Century

New Mexico in the Nineteenth Century
A Pictorial History

Andrew K. Gregg

University of New Mexico Press
Albuquerque

Library of Congress Cataloging-in-Publication Data

Gregg, Andrew K.
  New Mexico in the nineteenth century.

  Bibliography: p.
  1. New Mexico—History—Pictorial works.   I. Title.
F796.G73   1987   978.9′04   87-5915
ISBN 0-8263-1012-5 (pbk.)

PREFACE

THE NINETEENTH CENTURY in New Mexico began with the discovery of copper in a wild corner of a remote Spanish territory and ended with the construction of a new capitol for a territory ready to become one of the United States.

The copper mine at Santa Rita is still in operation. In 1900, although New Mexico had been a territory for over fifty years, it had to wait another twelve to become a state.

Tumultuous times, tremendous growth, economic upheavals, and revolts were all a part of Nineteenth Century New Mexico, yet the rest of the world knew relatively little of what had happened.

In a sense, the image of New Mexico has been distorted by the public interest in its three best-known citizens—Billy the Kid, Kit Carson, and Geronimo. These three captured the stage before the eyes of the world. The rough image they formed continued in countless books, magazine articles, movies, and television shows to shape a picture that the state of New Mexico is still trying both to live down and capitalize on.

Many Nineteenth Century travelers, reporters, and artists wrote and drew what the East expected. They showed a New Mexico full of colorful or savage Indians, cowboys, outlaws, sun-scorched deserts, and sharp mountains.

Sandwiched between the blood and the thunder were archeological reports, ethnological studies, railroad surveys, paeans to the Santa Fe trade, autobiographies, and immigration invitations.

Until the middle 1880s, the rest of the world knew almost nothing about New Mexico. There had been a few obscure books, reports, and autobiographies published. They are well known to historians now, but to the rest of the world from the 1600s until the arrival of the first traders from the East, New Mexico was an unknown land. Charles III, king of Spain, knew so little about his distant territory that in 1775 he asked the Viceroy of Mexico if there were some native New Mexico pelicans available for the royal zoo. (There weren't.)

In 1821, New Mexico and Mexico separated from Spain. In the confusion and opportunistic politicking that followed, violence was a natural outcome. The Pueblo Indians revolted in 1837. When Governor Albino Perez tried to defeat them in battle outside Santa Fe, they lopped off his head and stuck it atop a pole in the capital plaza. A rich ex-sheepherder, who may have started the rebellion, took over the government and put down the revolt.

The East knew nothing of this; Mexico cared little.

At the beginning of the War with Mexico, Kearny's army captured Santa Fe, fought a battle at Brazito, and put down a rebellion at Taos.

The gold fields of California and the Halls of Montezuma got the headlines.

When the Civil War loomed, the South prepared to invade the new territory, then march on to capture the gold in California to finance the Confederate government. Gen. Henry H. Sibley and his army moved north to victory at Valverde, defeat at Glorieta, and then straggled back to Texas in a disastrous rout.

The East worried about the battles of Ft. Donelson, Pea Ridge, and Shiloh.

The Apaches, at first friends of the newcomers from the East, turned against them to become the "human tigers," the Huns of the Southwest.

But now the East and Europe had begun to learn about New Mexico. While the hostiles ravaged isolated areas, settlers poured into the new territory. They were spurred by the hopes of fertile land, new markets, new jobs.

An 1869 guidebook to the West and South warned settlers against the Indians of New Mexico. "The fiendish Apache roams at will over the vast arid plains and among the lonely gorges of a large portion of the territory, ever on the watch for booty and blood."

The postmaster at Santa Fe, however, had a more encouraging view. "In the vicinity of Santa Fe . . . land is very good and can be had at low prices. The climate is healthful, and the seasons mild and delightful. Labor commands from $1 to $5, according to skill." Actually, average agricultural wages in New Mexico at that time were $25 per month without board.

Placid New Mexico boomed. The newcomers brought railroads, oysters, smelters, land grant swindles, longhorns, sorghum, full length mirrors, tuberculosis, and a host of other benefits and plagues.

The boom had been in the making for thirty years.

One of the first to write about New Mexico was Lt. Zebulon Pike. He was sent to the Southwest, probably on a spying mission, in 1806. The following February, Pike and his troops were captured by Spanish soldiers in Colorado and taken to Santa Fe. He got the first guided tour of the area, from there to Chihuahua. There he was held prisoner. He was later released and his pessimistic report, published in 1810, advised that New Mexico be left to the Indians. But his report showed that trade with the area was feasible.

The first traders arrived and found business profitable, if a bit risky. Their stories helped make the Santa Fe Trail a byword in commerce.

A few years later, the East read about the capture of Texas filibusterers in the early 1840s. About 300 had been captured and taken to Mexico. About half survived starvation and disease and were released in 1842. Public indignation, plus the reports of the traders, stirred interest in the acquisition of New Mexico. Then came the Mexican War and Kearny.

With Kearny came the first of many artists to visit New Mexico. John Mix Stanley had come overland with a trading caravan to Santa Fe and found a berth as an army artist. He sketched his way to California and returned to the East where he found fame as a painter of Indians.

Heinrich Balduin Mollhausen, a German, immigrated to the United States in 1849. He toured the Rockies with Prince Paul of Wurttemberg in 1851. The expedition was forced out by Indians, but Mollhausen stayed behind in Nebraska at a lonely river fork when a passing stagecoach, packed full, had to leave him behind. He was snowbound there for two months, gnawed frozen wolf meat, and was almost ambushed by Pawnees. He killed two before he was rescued by friendly Indians. He moved on to Missouri, but the West drew him back. He came to New Mexico as an artist for the Whipple expedition in 1853. He returned in 1857 with Ives' expedition to the Colorado River. Then he went back to Berlin to show his paintings and write hair-raising novels of frontier life.

With the railroads and stagecoaches came magazine artists like W. M. Cary, Theodore Davis, Frederic Remington, and the team of Paul Frenzeny and Jules Tavernier.

The first artists to stay in New Mexico for any length of time came in the 1880s. Charles Craig sketched in Taos in the summer of 1881. The godfather of the Taos Art Colony, Joseph H. Sharp, visited Santa Fe in 1883 and painted at Taos in 1893. He met Bert Phillips and Ernest Blumenschein later in Europe, talked with them and told them of the beauties of the Southwestern scenery—Taos' in particular. Blumenschein visited Taos in 1898 and, later that year, he and Phillips decided to make a wagon trip from Denver to Mexico. They got as far as Taos and stayed.

Men like these helped form the world's image of New Mexico. There were others, too. Unnamed and unknown artists—hacks—labored away to depict the blood and thunder that appeared in the cheaper magazines and dime novels of the day. Some of them knew little about the West and its scenery or customs. A few copied earlier pictures and added embellishments or changed the scenery to fit new plots. They also helped form an image, and their version has proved a strong one. While hundreds saw Stanley's scenes of New Mexico mountains and deserts, thousands saw Remington's dramatic pictures of the chase after Geronimo. Millions are familiar with the simple sketches of Billy the Kid killing his guards at Lincoln and his death at the hands of Pat Garrett.

All these pictures made up the image—the face that the raw territory of New Mexico presented to the world. This is the way the world saw us.

The pictures used in this book are the works of human hands and talent. Some are reproduced from stone lithographs. Others are woodcuts from paintings or drawings. Some are reproductions of woodcuts from photographs. This is not a photo book—there are no halftone pictures of photographs. This is the way the world saw New Mexico in its own time, and with the hand craftsmanship that characterized that time.

For instance, in some of the pictures from *Harper's Weekly* faint white lines may be seen. The *Harper's* engravers, to save time, had a system that called for expert talent and care that has not been seen since. After the original picture was sketched on a large block, it was sawed into squares and passed out to the engravers. As many as thirty-six of them worked on their own blocks. The pieces had to match into one large picture when they finished. The squares were bolted together and a wax mold of the engraving was made. Electrotyping was used to make the final engraving used in the printing.

The halftone screen and photographic reproduction meant the end for the hand engravers. Their days of careful carving and squinting through magnifying glasses were gone.

Because of the time envolved in making a good engraving, and the consequent expense for skilled labor, publishers often borrowed, perhaps stole, woodcuts and other engravings. Some views have been used many times. Sometimes engravers sketched a copy of a picture on a block of wood and cut out all the parts that would appear white. They added their own talent in the process.

The picture source given for a particular scene in this book does not mean that it is the only place where that picture was used.

In general, the old artists and engravers showed a pretty good idea of what New Mexico was like.

Kit Carson was important. He helped open the West. The novels about his life inspired many young men to go west.

Geronimo was important in his time. His depredations helped many a frontier community survive on Army payrolls. (The money spent in fighting Apaches could have bought every warrior a nice plot of land in the Southwest. Yet, in 1877, congress wouldn't be bothered with appropriating funds to pay the army that was serving on the frontier.)

Billy the Kid is probably New Mexico's single top tourist attraction.

But in the days when people remembered and believed in manifest destiny, when a new world was waiting—a world that promised wealth or escape—young men turned toward the West. The Great West! Ho, for the Great West!

Where in the Great West? Well, some place where there is good land, good wages for day laborers, a place where a shrewd trader could make some money. Some wanted to fight Indians, others to forget their name in the states; the lure of the open range and clear sky drew young men.

But they came.

PREFACE TO THE PAPERBOUND EDITION

About the time that the first edition of this book was printed, there was a great increase of interest in the history of the American West. The books and magazines that had provided the illustrations for the first edition became more valuable and scarce. Only a few years later, publication of this collection probably would have been prohibitively expensive.

This paperback edition uses the same illustrations with revisions, corrections, and updating of the text. The viewpoint remains the same. This book shows the way New Mexico was represented to the rest of the world in the nineteenth century. That view may sometimes have been biased, exaggerated, and distorted. Remember that in these pages we see New Mexico through the eyes of past interpreters.

Andrew K. Gregg
January 1987

CONTENTS

(*Land of Sunshine*, July, 1898.)

CONQUISTADORES

THE FIRST Europeans to visit New Mexico were Alvar Nuñez Cabeza de Vaca and three other men. They had been shipwrecked on the coast of Florida. De Vaca led them across Texas, through (some authorities say near) New Mexico and into Mexico.

One of them, Estevan the Moor, returned as a guide for Fray Marcos de Niza in 1539. Estevan went on ahead as they neared Hawikuh pueblo, near Zuni. The natives killed him, reportedly in outrage when Estevan made advances to their women. When Fray Marcos learned of this, he trudged back to Mexico.

Next came Coronado's expedition. It reached Zuni on July 7, 1540. Where Fray Marcos had predicted cities filled with riches, the soldiers found a mud town with hundreds of armed Indians lining the rooftops.

When the Indians showed no signs of surrendering, the Spaniards attacked. Their first assault was met with a barrage of arrows and stones that drove them back. But steel swords and armor were stronger than rocks and arrows. The Indians surrendered in less than an hour.

Sketch of a buffalo (American bison), was drawn by one of Oñate's men, 1599. (Winsor.)

Snarling, curly bison of 1558 has little relation to original animal. (Winsor.)

This early Spanish version looks like a feathered draft horse. (*Land of Sunshine*, July, 1898.)

SEVEN GOLDEN CITIES

WHEN CORONADO arrived in 1540, New Mexico was thought to be a land of riches, of mines of gold, silver, and even quicksilver. And why not? Anything was possible in the New World. Only 20 years before Cortez had plundered Mexico of millions in gold, silver, and jewels.

Seven years earlier, an illegitimate ex-swineherd named Francisco Pizarro had captured the Inca of Peru, accepted a ransom of a room full of gold and then murdered him.

Surely there must be something worthwile in this land of snowy mountains and burning deserts that stretched invitingly north of Mexico.

The story of the Seven Cities of Cibola had begun years before in Europe. The seven cities legend had been shifted from the Antilles to Brazil, to China, and now was placed north of Mexico.

The legend of the treasures of Gran Quivira began as a tale told by an Indian slave at Pecos to lead Coronado's expedition off to starve on the Staked Plains. Coronado reached Quivira in central Kansas, found only a collection of mud huts and promptly executed the slave. He also found that the legend of the seven cities had no basis in fact.

In short, New Mexico as a land of riches was a failure.

The explorers marched back to Mexico, but they had found that land and water were available. The next wave was of colonists. The first try, in 1590, was an aborted one. The leader, Gaspar Castaño de Sosa, did not have authority to colonize.

Don Juan de Oñate did. His army of soldiers and settlers left Mexico in 1598, traveled to San Juan Pueblo and started the first capital of New Mexico.

The colonists had found their land and New Mexico quickly stepped into the modernity of the 17th century.

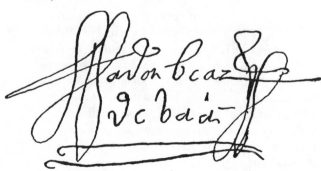

Autograph of Alvar Nuñez Cabeza de Vaca. (Winsor.)

Signature of Francisco Vasquez de Coronado. (Winsor.)

THE MODERNITY of the 17th century included peonage, slavery, the Inquisition, and disease. Life was crude and cruel, but missions, towns, and small haciendas slowly spread up and down the rivers. Some of these sites are almost forgotton today—places like Galisteo and Senecu.

In 1680, a San Juan Indian, Po-pe, led a successful revolt that was the culmination of years of resentment against the Spaniards.

In one sweeping slash, the Indians surrounded and besieged Santa Fe. Outlying settlers and missionaries were killed.

The Spaniards trapped inside the town held out for eleven days. On August 21, they surged out to attack the Indians. They killed about 300 and took 47 captives. The next day the settlers and soldiers, totalling about a thousand, moved out of the capital and began a long and deadly journey to Mexico.

With the Spaniards gone, the Indians fought each other. Po-pe was murdered.

The Spaniards returned in 1692. Don Diego de Vargas and his soldiers took the capital peacefully and raised the banner of Spain again.

Settlers returned the next year to reoccupy Santa Fe and some of the other towns.

Exploration and contacts with the rest of the Southwest began in the 18th century. Trails went out from Santa Fe to the Pacific coast, to western Mexico, and to Texas and Louisiana. By 1792, when Pedro Vial made the first trip to St. Louis, New Mexico was ready for trade with the rest of the country.

First modern horses probably were brought to New Mexico by Coronado in 1540. (*Century*, Jan., 1889.)

Romantic view of de Vaca crossing the Southwest. Actually, the four Spaniards wore deerskins. (*Harper's*, July, 1880.)

Today a super-highway speeds traffic through Apache Pass, once the scene of Indian ambushes on the Arizona-New Mexico border. (Cozzens, 1876.)

Mouth of Night Creek, a tributary of the Gila, is explored by Emory's party. (Emory, 1848.)

SHIPROCK is a spectacular red volcanic neck near Farmington. Rising 1,450 feet above the desert, it reminded early explorers of a sailing ship.

It was an active volcano in the Cenozoic Era some 25 million years ago.

According to Navajo legend, Shiprock is a "rock with wings" that carried their people to these lands from across great seas.

Several dikes extend from the base of the rock. A large one stretches about three miles to the south.

Monument Rock (top) in Santa Fe Canyon in the Sangre de Cristos. (Ritch, 1885.)

Shiprock (center) was never, in historical times, surrounded by lakes as shown in this fanciful sketch. (Thayer, 1888.)

Abiquiu Peak (bottom) near Espanola. This and the Shiprock picture were redrawn from Macomb's work. (Thayer, 1888.)

THE ABIQUIU area is one of the most interesting in the state, with unusual geological features, many fossils, and the nearby Ghost Ranch.

The town of Abiquiu was built some time before 1747 on the site of an old Tewa pueblo. In 1779 the village had 851 inhabitants. Most of them were Indian slaves. The Indian population slowly dwindled while the Spanish population grew. By the time the early Army explorers arrived, the village was almost entirely Spanish with some mixtures of Indian blood.

Fra Cristobal Mountains marked the northern end of the Jornada del Muerto. (Davis, 1857.)

The City of Rocks between Deming and Silver City is now a state park. (Bartlett, 1854.)

THE Jornada del Muerto, or Journey of the Dead Man, began where travelers left the Rio Grande and skirted the east side of the Fra Cristobal Range. They moved south for about ninety miles to rejoin the river near Mt. Robledo. The trip generally took about six days and there was little or no water along the route.

The railroad now follows the old Jornada del Muerto through old cattle towns like Engle and Cutter and past the old Spanish campgrounds.

THE City of Rocks, seen above, is now a state park with running water, a campground and a cactus garden.

The twisted, pitted rocks are of sugarlump welded rhyolite tuff that show millions of years of erosion by wind and water. The rock was formed from small particles of hot lava spewed from the mouth of an ancient volcano. The frothy mass ran over the ground in a thick layer, hardened into a light and porous mass and was covered with ash. The ash dissolved into the tuff and softened it for wind and water to do the carving job seen today.

The Burro Mountains, southwest of Silver City. (Bartlett, 1854.)

Sandstone formations (above) in the Chaco Canyon area appear to be modern buildings and turreted castles. This drawing, from Cozzens, is a copy of a painting made by one of the Kern brothers for Lt. Simpson. Both illustrations are gross exaggerations. (Cozzens, 1876.)

When John R. Bartlett's men surveyed southwestern New Mexico they were captivated by the strange wild country. Here they approach Mule Creek. (Bartlett, 1854.)

The Mogollon mountains (below), rich in minerals, beautiful, and deadly. Gold was discovered here in 1875. Its discoverer, Sgt. James Cooney, was killed by Apaches and is buried in a vault of rock near the town of Mogollon. (Sitgreaves, 1854.)

Lt. Emory's expedition in 1846 moves along the valley of the Mimbres River in south-western New Mexico. (Emory, 1848.)

Indian pictographs were seen by Emory near Red Rock on Gila River. (Emory, 1848.)

Stein's Peak and Stein's Pass near the New Mexico-Arizona border. The pass, along the Butterfield stage route, was a favorite spot for robbers. (Cozzens, 1876.)

Headwaters of the Gila River in the Mogollon Mountains. (Cozzens, 1876.)

A mirage seen on the plateau west of the Rio Grande near Hillsboro. (Cozzens, 1876.)

Volcanic trap dike at Pope's Well, south of Santa Fe. A trap dike is a dense sheet of vertical volcanic rock jutting up to form a ridge. (Newberry, 1876.)

Pinos Altos Mountains near the Santa Rita copper mines were an Apache stronghold for many years. (Dunn, 1886.)

(Below) heading east on one of the first expeditions into the Navajo country, an artist on the Simpson expedition sketched the mountains rising behind Jemez pueblo. (Simpson, 1852.)

View of the Rio Grande below Rincon. (*Harper's*, April, 1886.)

TRAVELERS in New Mexico were often at the mercy of strange elements.

Dust devils that approached tornado force, and occasional tornados, were problems.

Mirages were frequently seen. The most popular story is that of the lake or stream ahead that turns out to be a mirage. However, cities and mountains have also been seen.

Fierce blizzards were apt to roar out of the north. They still are, but the weather bureau is able to give enough warning so that tourists and ranchers are relatively protected.

Wind and dust storms are common, especially in the spring. Early travelers, when caught in a sand storm, holed up as best they could and made themselves as small and tight a target as possible.

Waterholes and springs dried up during droughts. Travelers and even experienced scouts might make a dry march for days to find no water where they had expected some. Indians had various ways of getting water from cactus, carrying it in the intestines of a slaughtered animal or simply carrying a pebble in the mouth to stimulate saliva. Inexperienced white men just died of thirst.

Not a factory smokestack, but a prairie tornado. (*Harper's*, April, 1854.)

"False ponds," mirages as seen by James A. Brewerton in the 1840s. (*Harper's*, April, 1854.)

Cabezon Peak, near the Rio Puerco, stands in a valley that was once Albuquerque's breadbasket. Drought and agricultural over-use turned the valley into a desert. The town of Cabezon, once thriving, is now a ghost town and closed to the public. (Macomb, 1876.)

This exaggerated drawing of a yucca plant shows it to be about forty feet high. The yucca is the state flower of New Mexico. (Drake, 1887.)

Cabezon, sticking into the air like a thick thumb, is the core of an ancient volcano. It is a landmark and was a target for stage coach travelers from Santa Fe to Fort Wingate. (Simpson, 1852.)

THE ORGAN Mountains, because of their distinctive fluted shape, are one of the most spectacular ranges in New Mexico.

They overlooked a section of the Camino Real, where supplies slowly moved north to the capital in Santa Fe and the missions of New Mexico. Later came Baylor's "Buffalo Hunters" to capture Mesilla at the beginning of the Civil War. Next came Sibley's Army of New Mexico. A few months later the remains of his shattered army trudged along the same trail on their dreary retreat south after their defeat at Glorieta.

This view of the Organs does not show the distinctive fluting of the rock formations. (*Harper's*, April, 1885.)

The Organ Mountains and the Rio Grande, near Las Cruces. (Cozzens, 1876.)

The same view, but with a stream and boat (in the desert!) (Bartlett, 1854.)

THE LUSH Mesilla Valley, west of the Organs, was settled early in the 19th century. Mesilla was originally just south of New Mexico Territory after it became part of the United States and the town was settled by Mexicans who didn't want to be part of the U.S.

The valley, along with its prosperous farms and vineyards, became part of Mexico through the Gadsden Purchase.

Mesilla was the capital of the Confederate Territory of Arizona for awhile. Its high point of political turbulence came late in the 19th century, when Democrats and Republicans had rallies on the same day. The two rallies collided on the square in a battle of fists and revolvers that left several dead.

Washington Pass, through the Chuska Mountains of the Navajo country in northwestern New Mexico, was a favorite route of explorers. (Simpson, 1852.)

Mount Taylor, near Grants, is an ancient sacred mountain for the Indians. Lava flows form a *malpais* around much of its base. (Simpson, 1852.)

Some of New Mexico's magnificent mesas inspired sketches such as this. Note the "pueblo ruins" on top of the rocks on the right. (Newberry, 1876.)

Another exaggerated view, this time of the City of Rock near Deming. (Cozzens, 1876.)

Palisades of the Staked Plains in eastern New Mexico. The undulating, grassy plains are bordered by these bluffs near Tucumcari. The plains may have been named for the stake-like bluffs, for the towering yucca stalks growing there, or from stakes driven in the ground to indicate nearby water. (Whipple, 1853-4.)

Lieutenant Emory's troops leave their wagons at the Rio Grande near the base of Fra Cristobal Mountains in 1846. The expedition continued on foot and horseback across western New Mexico and on to San Diego. (Emory, 1848.)

Hot springs near Silver City were well known in the area. A health resort was later established here. (Bell, 1870.)

ONE BIG attraction in New Mexico is the variety of its geologic features. Hot springs and other signs of volcanic activity abound. These include Shiprock, Capulin, the Valle Grande, malpais lava flows, Soda Dam, and others.

New Mexico mountains are volcanic, like Capulin; fault block, like the Sandias, or complex. Nearly every geologic feature, including sea action and continental glaciers, has left some sort of mark in the state.

In the Paleozoic era, northern New Mexico was a shallow island in a sea teeming with long squids and other denizens of salt water.

Continental glaciation brought wet weather and mammoths, camels, and other Pleistocene mammals to New Mexico. Their bones are found in many parts of the state.

In some of the higher areas, Alpine glaciation gouged holes in the mountains and filled tremendous lakes like the one in the Estancia Valley, which stretched from Moriarty to the White Sands.

Scenes of unusual geological formations, some of them very exaggerated, appeared in many early accounts of travel in New Mexico.

"Canon Infierno" is probably Hell's Canyon, a rugged gash that connected Isleta Pueblo with the Manzano mountain towns of Chilili and Escobosa. (Howe, 1852.)

Waterfall on the Rio Bonito. (Ritch, 1885.)

TRAVELERS between Santa Fe and Taos had a rough time in the 1840s.

James Brewerton heard "the sudden report of an escopeta fired by some unseen hand . . . which coupled with the sharp whiz of a ball within anything but a pleasant proximity of my right ear."

Brewerton returned the greetings with a load of buckshot and galloped off to safety.

The road between Santa Fe and Taos as James Brewerton saw it in 1848. (*Harper's*, April, 1854.)

Another scene on the road to Taos. The crosses mark the graves of travelers killed by bandits. (*Harper's*, April, 1854.)

The placer mountains near Golden—the Ortiz and the San Pedros. Gold was mined here many years before the discovery of gold in California. (Simpson, 1850.)

El Morro (Inscription Rock) is now a national monument.
The oldest legible signature is that of Don Juan de Oñate in
1605. (Thayer, 1888.)

The base of El Morro rock is covered with names carved
into the soft stone. Among the many "paso por aqui" entries is that of De Vargas, 1692 shown here as sketched
by an artist on the Simpson expedition. (Simpson, 1852.)

Atop El Morro rock are the ruins of an earlier pueblo, still visible to the tourist who climbs the landmark that is now a national monument. (Whipple, 1856.)

Loaded burros shown here are probably being prepared for a trading trip from Zuni. (*Harper's Weekly*, Jan. 28, 1882.)

BANDELIER
CLIFF DWELLINGS

THE ANASAZI (Navajo for "ancient ones"), were the basketmakers who lived in the cliffs. Their towns thrived by A.D. 500. Droughts in the late 1200 s forced them out of their cliff homes to find dependable water supplies. They became the Pueblo Indians living along the rivers today.

A restoration of the Tyuonyi ruins at Bandelier National Monument. Indians lived until A.D. 1550 in this unusual circular primitive apartment house built of tuff. (Thayer, 1888)

The stone pumas carved in lava were sacred hunting shrines of the Cochiti. They are about five miles from the Rito de los Frijoles on the Potrero de las Vacas. (*Scribner's*, Jan., 1893)

The cliff ruins at Bandelier National Monument. Many other cliff dwellings are scattered around the Pajarito Plateau near Los Alamos. (*Harper's Weekly*, Sept. 7, 1889)

CHACO CANYON

THE great ruins in the Chaco Canyon of
northwestern New Mexico were thriving pueblos
in fertile grasslands in A.D. 1100. They were
abandoned in the 1200s. Hungo Pavi, like Pueblo
Bonito, was a large D-shaped complex of rooms.

Hungo Pavi Pueblo, redrawn from the original sketch in
Simpson's *Report*. (Thayer, 1888.)

Pueblo Pintado, one of the rela-
tively unknown pueblo ruins in the
Chaco Canyon area. (*Harper's*,
Aug., 1882.)

The pueblo of Hungo Pavi (below) as Lt. J. H. Simpson thought it
would have looked in its prime. (Simpson, 1850.)

Ruins of the church at Pecos in the 1840s. It was here that the legend of the Gran Quivira began when an Indian slave was told to lead Coronado's expedition into the desert to die. (Abert, 1847.)

The ruins of Jemez Mission, drawn by one of the Kern brothers. (Simpson, 1850.)

OLD MISSIONS

Many missions were founded at
Indian pueblos in the early 1600s.
Most were abandoned after the
Pueblo Revolt of 1680. The ruins of
the missions and pueblos at Abo,
Gran Quivira, Quarai, and Pecos are
national monuments. The Jemez
mission and ruins are a state
monument. The ruins of Indian
pueblos that had no missions which
are now national monuments are
Aztec, Bandelier, Chaco Canyon, and
the Gila Cliff Dwellings. The ruin
thought to be Kuaua Pueblo, where
Coronado's expedition had winter
quarters, is Coronado State
Monument.

Women getting water from the Rio
Grande. (*Harper's*, April, 1885.)

Ruin of Abo mission, founded in 1629
and abandoned about 1670. It is now a
state monument. (Abert, 1847.)

Ruins of Pecos, re-sketched. (Drake, 1887)

USING one early illustration, later artists redrew pictures for use in books and magazines. The two large pictures on the opposite page were done by John Mix Stanley, artist with Kearny's expedition, and published in Emory's *Notes on a Reconnoissance* in 1848. The changes made in the three small pictures on this page are not enough to disguise their obvious sources in Stanley's work.

(*Harper's*, April, 1854)

An Indian foot race. (*Harper's*, May, 1885)

(*Harper's*, April, 1854)

Ruins of the mission at Pecos Pueblo (above). The mission was started in 1617. The pueblo was abandoned in 1838, when only seventeen survivors of disease and hostile Indian attacks were left. (Emory, 1848)

"Ruins of the Aztek Church" (below). Because of their massive structures and their legend of Montezuma, the Pueblo Indians were first thought to be related to the Aztecs of Mexico. (Emory, 1848)

Quarai mission, established in 1629. It was a village of the Tewas. They abandoned it in 1674 and moved to the El Paso area. (*Scribner's*, April, 1893.)

"THE CITIES that Died of Fear" have become a tourism trademark in New Mexico. The missions and pueblos at Gran Quivira, Quarai, Abo, Tenabo, Tajique, Chilili, and possibly Manzano and Torreon were abandoned a few years before the Pueblo Revolt of 1680 because of drought, disease and harrassment by the Apaches. Some of the towns were later reoccupied. The string of pueblos are generally called the Salines, because of their nearness to the salt lakes near Mountainair.

Gran Quivira. Not the one sought by Coronado in 1541, but a village known as "Las Humanas." (*Scribner's*, April, 1893.)

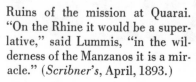

Ruins of the mission at Quarai. "On the Rhine it would be a superlative," said Lummis, "in the wilderness of the Manzanos it is a miracle." (*Scribner's*, April, 1893.)

The watch for Montezuma, drawn by the artistic team of Paul Frenzeny and Jules Tavernier. (*Harper's Weekly*, May 22, 1875.)

PUEBLO INDIANS

MOST OF THE PUEBLOS of the 19th century are still occupied and look much as they did a hundred years ago. But there are some changes. More of the Indians are leaving the pueblos for work in the towns. Schooling is accepted as a part of modern life. Highways have brought tourists to the pueblos to visit and buy both authentic craft goods and cheap gimcracks.

The Pueblo Indians were always willing to integrate or cooperate with the outside world —on their own terms.

The Indians of Acoma and Laguna went to court to solve a problem that would have been settled with arrows and guns if it had been a case of Pueblo against Navajo. The lawsuit involved a painting of St. Joseph that had been brought to Acoma in 1629 and installed in the new mission. It was borrowed by the people of Laguna for help during a drought. It was returned to Acoma, then stolen and taken back to Laguna. The Acomans sued. The case dragged on for five years until the Supreme Court awarded the painting to Acoma in 1857.

The Pueblos continued to be independent or to accept the white man's ways when it suited them.

Taos Indians refused to let meddling whites into their kivas after rumors of immoral practices had been thrown about. The Indians said that when they were admitted to Masonic rites, they might think about letting the whites visit the kivas. In the meantime, there were shotguns to enforce their privacy.

In 1917, Santo Domingo Indians captured state troopers who were looking for rustlers and held them until the Indian agent arranged for their release.

In 1965, Isleta leaders handcuffed and evicted the priest at their pueblo.

All this does not necessarily indicate that the Pueblo Indians are warlike or hostile. They are warm, friendly people who welcome visitors who will respect Indian customs. They have, in fact, put up with many intrusions of privacy, meddling, and intensive anthropological studies that would enrage the average middle-class Anglo. (Would you accept several hundred curious strangers on your front lawn and in your living room while your family had Christmas dinner and opened the presents under the tree?)

There are 18 Indian Pueblos in New Mexico. Some, like Zuni, Taos, and Acoma, are well known and have many visitors. Smaller ones, like Sandia and Santa Ana, are overlooked by the tourists. All the Pueblos welcome visitors, but some are more conservative and have tighter restrictions on pictures, dress, and the areas where the tourists may visit.

Northern section of Taos pueblo. (Davis, 1857.)

Two other views of Taos pueblo are shown in an 1891 guide to the United States. The picture on the right shows the extensive fields at the pueblo.

(Sweetser, 1891.)

(Sweetser, 1891.)

Taos Creek divides the Pueblo into two sections. (Thayer, 1888.)

THE FIRST artists who came to New Mexico lived at Taos and made the pueblo famous. Bert Phillips and Ernest Blumenschein came to New Mexico in 1898. Their wagon broke down near Taos. Blumenschein, taking a broken wheel into the town for repairs, was so struck by the beauty of the area that the two decided to stay. This was the beginning of the Taos art colony, which used the symbol of a broken wagon wheel.

This exaggerated view of Taos pueblo resembles a Babylonian ziggurat. (Peters, 1874.)

The northern part of Taos pueblo as it appeared in 1882. (*Harper's*, Aug., 1882.)

The distinctive features of Taos: doorless walls, ladders and ovens. (Tenney, 1880.)

Indian failing in hunting is chastised by his wife. (Beadle, 1878.)

San Geronimo de Taos, inhabited for more than 600 years, is one of the best known Indian pueblos in New Mexico. (Davis, 1857.)

Indians pressing grapes (below). Traditionally, they did not use wine themselves. Priests had vineyards and wineries and sometimes used Indian labor. (*Harper's Young People*, Dec. 30, 1890.)

The hair style, boots and blanket of
the pueblo women are shown here.
(Wood, 1894.)

A pack train leaving Taos. (Brooks, 1887.)

The Green Corn Dance, held in Taos on the 25th and 26th of July. It is also held at several
other New Mexico pueblos. (Cozzens, 1876.)

San Juan Pueblo, near Espanola, was visited by Onate in 1598. He set up the first capital of New Mexico nearby. It was there for ten years and then moved to Santa Fe. (Ritch, 1882–83.)

Room in Taos Pueblo. This clearly shows roof construction in large rooms. Where the vigas are not long enough to span the whole room, pillars and a pole support shorter vigas in the center. (U.S. Geo. & Geo. Survey, 1881.)

Kearny's army passing San Felipe. This painting was done by John Mix Stanley. (Emory, 1848.)

The mission at San Felipe Pueblo, shown near the center, was built about 1700. (Abert, 1847.)

The Corn Dance at Santo Domingo is one of the Southwest's most magnificent spectacles. This is the clown dancer. (U.S. Census, 1890.)

Female dancer in the Corn Dance at Santo Domingo. The *tablita* or tablet used as her headdress gave rise to the name Tablita Dance, often used to designate the ceremony. (U.S. Census, 1890.)

Male dancer in the Corn Dance at Santo Domingo Pueblo. The feathers, fox tail, gourd, and other accessories are not capricious decorations but have precise traditional meaning. (U.S. Census, 1890.)

The pueblo of Laguna, west of Albuquerque, was named for a nearby lake. (Thayer, 1888.)

The fields at Laguna are shown in this more realistic sketch by an artist who probably worked from a photograph. (*Harper's*, Feb., 1891)

The church of San Jose de Laguna is almost 300 years old, but is still used (*Harper's*, Feb., 1891.)

Houses and carretas at the Pueblo of Laguna. (*Harper's*, Feb. 1891.)

The pueblo of Acoma, near Laguna, sits atop this high mesa. (Abert, 1847.)

IN THE old days, every piece of wood, bit of dirt, and drink of water for Acoma was carried up the steep and narrow path. Before 1629, the only path up was a ladder-like string of finger- and toe-holes gouged out of the rock.

The rugged isolation of Acoma Pueblo shows in this drawing. (Drake, 1887.)

This steep and narrow trail (right) up the mesa was the best path to Acoma for hundreds of years. (Abert, 1847.)

Another early sketch of the famous Sky City pueblo. (Tenney, 1880.)

This church at Santa Clara was built about 1692 and lasted until 1909. (*Harper's Weekly*, Sept. 7, 1889.)

Feast day at Acoma's San Esteban Rey church. Acoma has its annual fiesta on Sept. 1. (*Scribner's*, Dec., 1891.)

Not far from Acoma, the Enchanted Mesa rises precipitous-
ly 430 feet above the plain. A few hardy men have scaled
its height and found a few artifacts but no traces of dwellings. (U.S. Census, 1890.)

The town of San Miguel del Vado was an important stop
for traders along the Santa Fe Trail. Members of Kendall's
Sana Fe expedition of 1841 were imprisoned here before
being sent to Mexico City. (Abert, 1847.)

SINCE the 1840s, when U.S. Army expeditions first visited them, the Pueblo Indians have been subjected to many anthropological studies. Old Spanish records and archaeological excavations have helped fill in their histories.

A quiet corner in the pueblo of Santo Domingo. (Roberts, 1885.)

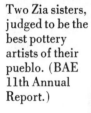

Two Zia sisters, judged to be the best pottery artists of their pueblo. (BAE 11th Annual Report.)

Indian rock carvings are found in all parts of New Mexico. The two examples shown above have a curious history: they were copied in the sketchbooks of expedition artist Richard H. Kern "by some members of the band of Taos Utahs, who killed the old guides, Williams and Dr. Kern, in the spring of 1849." (Schoolcraft, 1856.)

Richard H. Kern, artist with Lt. Simpson's 1849 expedition and brother of the Dr. Benjamin Kern mentioned above, made this painting of Francisco Hos-Ta (The Lightning), governor of Jemez Pueblo. (Domenech, 1862.)

THE INDIANS at Santo Domingo took part in the Pueblo Revolt of 1680. The inhabitants of nearby San Felipe joined with those at Santo Domingo to kill the priests and soldiers at the latter pueblo. In 1837, they allied with other Indians in a revolt, caught Gov. Albino Perez just outside Santa Fe and lopped off his head.

Santo Domingo Pueblo is noted for its jewelry. Its people had lived in several other locations, including Galisteo Creek and the Jemez Mountains. (Ladd, 1891.)

This early view of Santo Domingo apparently was drawn from a written description. (Abert, 1847.)

WITH the coming of the railroad in 1879, tourists poured into the Territory. Visits to Indian pueblos were highlights of their trips. Some stayed for longer periods and brought back large collections of Indian goods. Many of the finest specimens of Navajo blankets, Zuni dolls and other items are now seen in Eastern museums.

Dancers at the Indian pueblos were willing to pose for artists and photographers in the 1800s. (*Harper's Weekly*, Sept. 7, 1889.)

The pueblo of Tesuque is ten miles north of Santa Fe. Each year the pueblo honors its patron saint, San Diego, with ceremonies on November 12th. (Ritch, 1882-83.)

Tesuque Pueblo in the 1880s. The first village, abandoned during the Pueblo Revolt, was about three miles east of the present one. (*Harper's Weekly*, Sept. 7, 1889.)

The saddle cradle is still used in many pueblos. Drawing from a photo by Charles Lummis. (*Harper's Young People*, Jan. 20, 1891.)

Early sketches of Indian warriors such as the one at left were drawn with a classic treatment that made them resemble Greek soldiers. (Domenech, 1862.)

After the coming of the Spaniards, the pueblos adopted the wooden wheeled carreta, oxen, and pack burro. (Ladd, 1891.)

Santa Ana Pueblo, near Bernalillo. Its people first built a pueblo on Black Mesa near San Felipe but moved to their present site in 1692. (Abert, 1847.)

Pueblo Indians such as these, said one 19th century visitor, are "the only native race whose presence on the soil is not a curse to the country." (Bell, 1870)

"Sun, Silence and Adobe," the primitive peace of the Pueblo Indians as eulogized by Charles Lummis. (*Scribner's*, Dec., 1891)

Model of Zuni Pueblo was built at the National Museum in Washington and shown there. (*Century*, Jan., 1885.)

ZUNI PUEBLO

ZUNI is probably the best known Indian pueblo in the United States, despite its conservatism, isolation, and the relatively small amount of publicity it has received compared to Acoma and Taos.

Millions of college students become acquainted with Zuni life and customs through "Patterns of Culture," a book by Ruth Benedict that is used in many anthropology courses.

Studies of Zuni began in the middle of the 19th century when the early Army explorers visited the pueblo and found it almost completely lacking in contact with the white man. Even the Spanish people were viewed with distrust and barred from seeing any of the Indian dances there.

One of the first men to seriously study the Zunis was Frank Cushing, who lived with them from 1879 to 1884. The Zunis distrusted him at first, but gradually adopted him. He eventually became a priest of one of their societies. Articles by or about him appeared in contemporary magazines. His books on Zuni are still republished.

The purity and authenticity of Zuni rituals has attracted anthropologists ever since Cushing's time. They find the Zunis friendly and hospitable, but reticent in explaining old complicated rituals.

Zuni burial was simple and quick. The interment was held outside the pueblo. (*Century*, May, 1882.)

Zuni as shown in one of the earliest New Mexico travel articles. (*Harper's*, Sept., 1858.)

Group of shy Zunis (left) pose for an early maga-zine artist. (*Popular Science*, September, 1874.)

Zuni war party. Warriors who had taken scalps could belong to the Bow Society. (*Century*, May, 1883.)

Frank Cushing in Zuni costume. He was initiated into the Bow Society. (*Century*, August, 1883.) ·

Water is poured on clown dancers before annual trip to sacred lake. (*Jnl. of Am. Eth.*, 1891.)

Zuni maiden carrying water. (*Harper's*, August, 1875.)

DANCES play an important part in the life of the Zunis. They invoke rain, increase fertility, and bring success in war.

Ceremonial games, contests, races, and gambling also are designed to promote the welfare of the pueblo by asking the gods for help.

Priests who perform the rites have received long and arduous training in the intricate steps and prayers they must perform. Moreover, they must prepare themselves by remaining benevolent and continent for several days and undergoing ceremonial washing, taking purgatives, and fasting. Any variance or neglect of these rituals may bring failure to the ceremony, disapproval from the gods, and droughts.

Priests begin their training in childhood and slowly work their way up in their societies until they are ready for their high offices.

Zuni buffalo dancer. (Sitgreaves, 1854.)

Zunis planting corn use traditional sharpened sticks. (*Century*, May, 1883.)

Shalako ceremony is Zuni's best known and most magnificent one. Held each December, it lasts all night. (*Century*, February, 1883.)

Part of Shalako rite is performed in a new home being blessed by the ceremony. (*Century*, February, 1883.)

Street scene in Zuni as a *Harper's* artist sketched it. (*Harper's Weekly*, January 28, 1882.)

Buffalo Dance at Zuni as seen by members of the Sitgreaves expedition in the summer of 1853. The soldiers spent several months there while waiting for Navajo troubles to subside. (Sitgreaves, 1854.)

Zunis mining turquoise at a
sacred spot in the mountains.
(*Century*, February, 1883.)

SORCERY among the Zunis was a capital
crime. The magician might have cast an
evil spell over some person or he might
simply be a scapegoat in a time of trouble.

Cushing tells of one sorcerer, called
"the Bat," (seen on the right), who
hung for more than five hours before he
confessed that he had kept the rain
from falling. He promised to bring rain
within four days.

"Four days passed," wrote Cushing,
"and no rain came; nor did the 'Bat' do
as he had promised, for he returned home
only to threaten revenge on the
priesthood, and since the fifth day no
one outside of that priesthood has ever
seen a trace of the 'Bat'."

Most sorcerers reformed after torture,
said Cushing, but they would be executed
if their victims died or if it was believed
that they caused natural troubles such
as drought or sandstorms.

Sorcerer is tortured by being hanged by
the wrists. (*Century*, May, 1883.)

Around the council fire, where much of the serious business of governing the Indian pueblos takes place. (*Harper's*, June, 1882)

View of Zuni shows prominent stake corrals. (Schoolcraft, 1856.)

Modern (1875) Zuni pottery and shards of old pots. (*Harper's*, Aug., 1875.)

Pa-lo-wah-ti-wa, governor of Zuni pueblo in 1883. Colored headbands were standard wear for all Zuni men. (*Century*, Feb., 1883.)

Zuni street scene. Flat stone on the right is used for making paper bread. (*Century*, Dec., 1882.)

Men and women working or sunning themselves on the terraces of Zuni in the summer. (*Century*, Dec., 1882.)

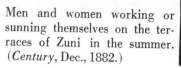

Zuni, (below), its fields and, in inset, a pack train of wood loaded on burros. (*Century*, December, 1882.)

Water for the pueblo was taken from a nearby pool. (*Century*, December, 1882.)

Left, ceremony of planting prayer sticks. Center, Zuni and Thunder Mountain. The Zunis moved to the mountain in times of trouble. (*Century*, May, 1883.)

Flocks of sheep returning to the pueblo. (*Century*, February, 1883.)

Zuni governor (left) and his assistants. (*Harper's*, Aug., 1875.)

Zuni man spinning, drawing the thread from a whorl held by his foot. This was rarely a man's work, but it was done at Zuni. (*Century*, Feb., 1883.)

Zuni woman weaving a belt. The other end of the loom is tied to the central support pillar of the room. (B.A.E. Annual Report, 1882.)

This view of Zuni shows adobe ovens. (*Harper's* August, 1875.)

Shrine at a sacred spring. Shrines are scattered around Zuni at springs, rocks, ruins, and mesas. (Cozzens, 1876.)

Indian and eagle cage. The eagles are kept for their feathers, which are used on masks and costumes in ceremonials. (B.A.E., 1887.)

HOUSEHOLD customs changed little at Zuni. An anthropologist's wife attempted to introduce soap and washtubs in 1879. Her demonstration was ruined because she couldn't wash properly.

"You do not understand that which you wish to teach," said her Indian student, "The missionary's wife, she keeps the water in the tub and does not make a river on the floor."

The Indian showed her how the washing should be done, but the pueblo didn't adopt the practice.

Paper-thin bread, called *hé-wé* at Zuni and *piki* in the Hopi villages, is made for special occasions. (*Century*, Feb., 1883.)

This dramatic view of Zuni emphasizes the height of both the pueblo and nearby Thunder Mountain, or Towayalane. The mountain is three miles southeast of the pueblo and 1,000 feet higher. (Thayer, 1888.)

Rooftops in the pueblos served as living room and workroom, the interior rooms being used for sleeping and storage. Here the potters are shown decorating their wares; each pueblo still has its distinctive designs. (*Century*, Dec., 1882.)

POTTERY was usually baked over dried manure fires for one or two hours.

Zuni mining party camping while on an expedition. (*Century*, Feb., 1883.)

Firing pottery. Anthropologist reported that pottery quality had declined by 1900. (*Century*, Dec., 1882.)

Zuni woman at a window. (*Harper's Week-ly*, Jan. 28, 1882.)

Women grinding corn. The ground stone and corn mixture was hard on the teeth. By the 1890's all Zuni families who could afford it were buying store flour. (*Century*, February, 1883.)

In Kern's lithograph of flour grinding, the women are grinding with almost orderly precision. (Sitgreaves, 1854.)

A ZUNI marriage ceremony had a few simple rituals. The couple decided to wed, they asked permission of the girl's father. The boy ate some of the family's food and worked for them for five days. The pact was finalized with gifts of flour and a deerskin.

Zuni courtship was informal. Couples sat on the rooftops, with girl combing and washing the boy's hair. Marriage and divorce were equally casual affairs. (*Century*, May, 1883.)

Blacksmith shop, supposedly at Zuni, was drawn by one of the Kern brothers and exaggerated by the lithographer. (Sitgreaves, 1854.)

Arch and rock spires near the Zuni reservation. (Whipple, 1853-4.)

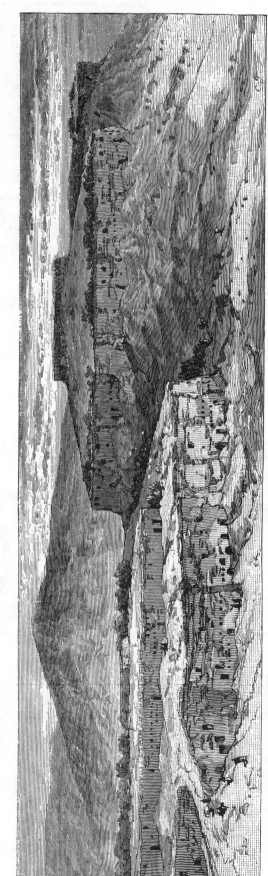

Shrine near the old pueblo of Pin-a-ua was adorned with prayer plumes. (*Jnl. of Am. Eth.*, 1891.)

Sketch of cliff dwellings near Zuni was made from a picture by the photographer who accompanied Cushing and other first Bureau of Ethnology anthropologists to the area. (*Harper's Weekly*, January 28, 1882.)

This romantic view of a Zuni priest blowing pollen at one of the pueblo's shrines was so colorful and dramatic that it was redrawn and used in many books. The painting was originally made by H. B. Mollhausen and published in Lt. Whipple's report. (Top, Cozzens, 1876; below, Cady, 1893.)

STAPLES of Zuni diet included corn breads and mush, eggs, chicken, beef, goats, and mutton. Game included deer, cottontail, and jackrabbits.

Squash was a main vegetable. They also made yucca jam, ate pinon nuts and the fruit of the prickly pear.

The Zunis also enjoyed corn drinks, coffee, and tea.

Women cooking breakfast in the large corner oven. (*Century*, December, 1882.)

Farm houses at one of the small villages outside the main Zuni pueblo. (Thayer, 1888.)

"The Demon of Childhood." Hazing by elders dressed as gods. (*Century*, May, 1883.)

THE ZUNIS wove some blankets, but put no particular emphasis on their craftsmanship. The colors were often from the natural colors of the wool. Patterns were simply wide stripes. They traded with the Navajos for saddle blankets and the ones they wore.

The Zunis also made baskets, pots and beads. Silverwork was introduced by the Spaniards and the Zunis have become famous for this work.

Zuni woman weaving a saddle blanket. (*Century*, February, 1883.)

Artist Kern's exaggeration of Indian life shows a fancier loom. (Sitgreaves, 1854.)

Tablet dancer. (*Jnl. of Am. Eth.*, 1891.)

Ko-ko dancer of Zuni. (*Jnl. of Am. Eth.*, 1891.)

Mudhead, or clown dancer. (*Jnl. of Am. Eth.*, 1891.)

Mudheads dancing in Tablet Dance held each summer. (*Jnl. of Am. Eth.*, 1891.)

Among the New Mexico Indians, the best silver-work today is done at Zuni and Santo Domingo. Most silversmiths have workshops far more simple than the equipment shown here. (*Century*, May, 1883.)

(Below) Zuni Indians threatened to tear up Cushing's sketch pads after he drew dances such as these, but he kept them off with a knife. (*Century*, Dec., 1882.)

ANTHROPOLOGIST J. Walter Fewkes tried to record Zuni songs on wax cylinders in 1891 with an early model phonograph. Attempts to record during the actual dances were not possible because the megaphone used for a microphone would be too far away from the singers and also because they might not approve.

"I thought it best not to imperil the success of my undertaking, possibly the safety of my phonograph, by making such a display." After the dance, priests sang privately for his machine.

Ox train loaded with melons returns to Zuni. (*Century*, Dec., 1882.)

Unromantic view of a pueblo girl. (Chase, 1882.)

THE SEVEN Zuni pueblos that Coronado saw, as well as ten others, are now deserted.

After the revolt of 1680 the Zunis lived on Thunder Mountain. They returned after de Vargas' reconquest in 1692 and built the present pueblo.

The oldest section of the pueblo, on the northwest, is built on the remains of one of the earlier pueblos.

Early sketch of Zuni warriors was copied in other books. (Whipple, 1853-4.)

Emigrants stopping for supplies along the Santa Fe Trail. The "Gin Fiz" sign suggests a touch of refinement in a rough land. (*Harper's*, July, 1880.)

SANTA FE TRAIL

THE FIRST trader over the Santa Fe Trail was a Frenchman, Pedro Vial, who went from Santa Fe to St. Louis in 1792.

The first trading caravan from the U.S., led by William Becknell, arrived in Santa Fe in 1821. Wagon trade over the trail continued until the 1880's.

A caravan of wagons in the circular formation that protected them from Indian attacks. The lead wagon is ready to move out. The others can follow with a minimum of time and effort. (Inman, 1893.)

A caravan arrives in Santa Fe. Early traders were at the mercy of Mexican Governor Manuel Armijo, who charged exorbitant taxes. Traders called him "his obesity." (Gregg, 1844.)

The cattle ranch of Trinidad Romero was five miles below Las Vegas. He was a *rico* of the region, raising fruit and crops as well as cattle. (Mills, 1885.)

New Mexican trader in California. (*Harper's*, Aug., 1853.)

Mail is delivered at a frontier post office. The Butterfield route went along southern New Mexico. Other lines went along the Rio Grande and to other areas of the territory. (*Harper's Weekly*, July 4, 1874.)

Ox-drawn wagons move in a stately procession across the plains. With luck and shrewd bargaining, early traders could make more than a 600 per cent profit. (Gregg, 1849.)

New Mexican "grist mill" consisted of two stones. (Richardson, 1867.)

"Calling for the Relays" was probably sketched directly on a woodblock by Frenzeny and Tavernier. (*Harper's Weekly*, July 4, 1874.)

Conestogas and New Mexican carretas
parked at a village. (Champney, 1888.)

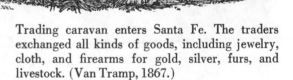

Trading caravan enters Santa Fe. The traders
exchanged all kinds of goods, including jewelry,
cloth, and firearms for gold, silver, furs, and
livestock. (Van Tramp, 1867.)

IN THE early 1800s, trade **routes** went from
Santa Fe to San Antonio, Texas; Tucson,
Arizona; Arispe and Chihuahua, Mexico, and
up into Colorado.

Trading in the more remote villages
was done with mule trains like this.
(Schlagintweit, 1884.)

THE FIRST regular route from Texas to California was the San Antonio and San Diego Stage Company, nicknamed the Jackass Mail. Passengers paid $200 for the ride. For one section a hundred miles west of Yuma, Arizona, they rode the jackasses. The rest of the 23 day trip was spent in a jolting stagecoach. Postage on the Jackass Mail was twenty cents per ounce, but it cost the government $60 to deliver that ounce of mail.

The Butterfield Overland Mail Co. replaced the Jackass Mail in 1858 and continued until the start of the Civil War.

(Top) A flirter is about to be surprised by a rival. (Right) A trading caravan arrives in Santa Fe. (*Harper's*, July 1880.)

Wagons cross the prairie without disturbing a group of placid pronghorn antelope. (*Harper's*, September, 1862.)

Pack train camped in the mountains. The *arrieros*, mule drivers, are getting ready to move out. (Gregg, 1849.)

Aristocratic New Mexican don. (*Harper's*, July, 1880.)

A *baile* (ball) or *fandago* was held on the slightest excuse—or no excuse at all. The dancing, staid by modern standards, astonished some puritan Americans but not the average soldier! (Triplett, 1885.)

"A Saturday Noon in a Southwestern Town", sketched directly on a wood block by Frenzeny and Tavernier for later engraving in the *Harper's* plant. When the artists sketched on wood, a "Z" or "N" was sometimes reversed. In this case, an "N". (*Harper's Weekly*, July 25, 1874.)

NEW TOWNS AND OLD

THE FIRST TOWNS in New Mexico were, of course, the Indian pueblos. When the first Span-ish colonists arrived they settled near the pueblos. Later settlers stuck to the rivers and streams that gave them a dependable water supply. Isolated ranchos grew into small vil-lages and, by the early 1700s towns such as Bernalillo and Albuquerque were scattered along the Rio Grande valley.

When hordes of Anglos arrived after the Civil War, new towns sprang up overnight. Mining towns such as Pinos Altos, Georgetown, Silver City, Chloride, Winston, and others in the southwestern section thrived for years.

In the north, Cimarron, Elizabethtown, Arroyo Hondo, Las Vegas, Bonanza, and others were supported by mines, the stock business, or traders.

Cattle and agriculture boomed Lincoln, Roswell, Tularosa, and other towns in the south-western part of New Mexico.

Some of the old towns had gloriously optimistic names: Acme, Avalon, Park City, Queen, Brilliant. There were also towns named Lizard, Tin Pan, Toboggan Gulch, Hard-scrabble, High Lonesome, and Whiskey Creek.

One town tried both types of names. Badgerville changed its name to Hope. It didn't help. Plans to develop the town failed and it never grew. Today it has a population of about 100.

The Atchison, Topeka and Santa Fe brought new life to the territory in 1879 and a whole new breed of towns—the railheads—were born. As the railroad was built south, and later west, each railhead became a quick metropolis complete with gambling houses, restau-rants on wheels, honkytonks, and hotels. Many of the towns were soon passed by and forgot-ten. Otero, for instance, lasted only six months. Wallace, Waldo, Florida, and other towns had their moment of glory and then were forgotten.

Some new towns began when local landowners held out for high prices. Rather than pay through the nose for land at Las Vegas and Albuquerque, railroad officials bought cheaper lots about a mile from the towns. Railroad stations were built and new business districts grew up about them.

Some of the railroad towns, such as Deming, Vaughn, Alamogordo, and Lordsburg, are still thriving.

Oil and the railroads were important factors in shifting New Mexico's population in the late 1800s and early 1900s. In the 1870s, southwestern towns such as Mogollon, Tyrone, and Shakespeare had relatively large populations. As the mines played out and these towns became deserted, Roswell, Carlsbad, Artesia, Hobbs, and other towns on the southeastern side began to gain population. Cattle and agriculture became more important there as rail-roads provided easier access to the markets.

Then, in the 20th century, oil and potash were discovered. Except for Albuquerque and Santa Fe, the southeastern cities are now generally the most populous in the state.

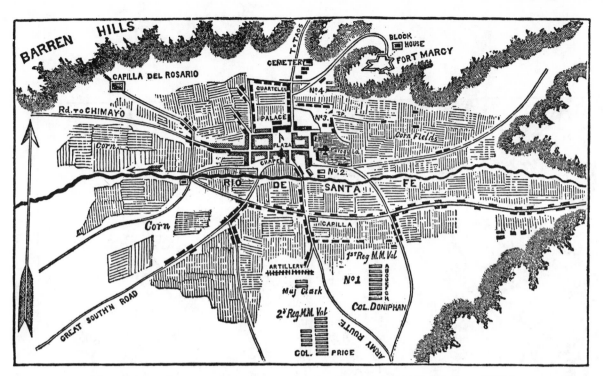

Map of Santa Fe just after its occupation by Kearny in 1846. (Hughes, 1850.)

Santa Fe as it was just after the American occupation. The new Fort Marcy is on the low hill where the flag is seen in this picture. (Abert, 1847.)

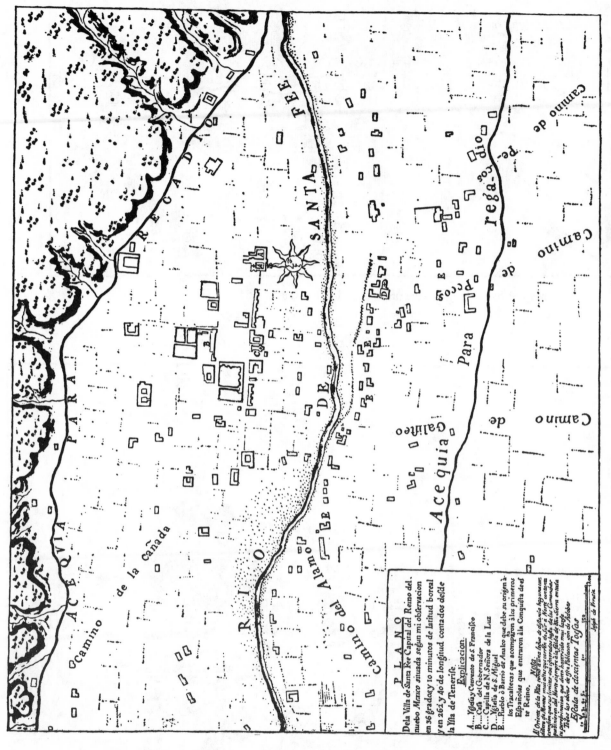

The earliest known map of Santa Fe, drawn by Jose de Urrutia, around 1766-68 (Adams.)

Santa Fe is a placid agricultural town in this old drawing. (*Harper's Weekly*, Sept. 13, 1879.)

South side of the Santa Fe plaza. (Beadle, 1873.)

Stagecoach arrives at the Exchange Hotel on San Francisco street. (*Harper's*, April, 1880.)

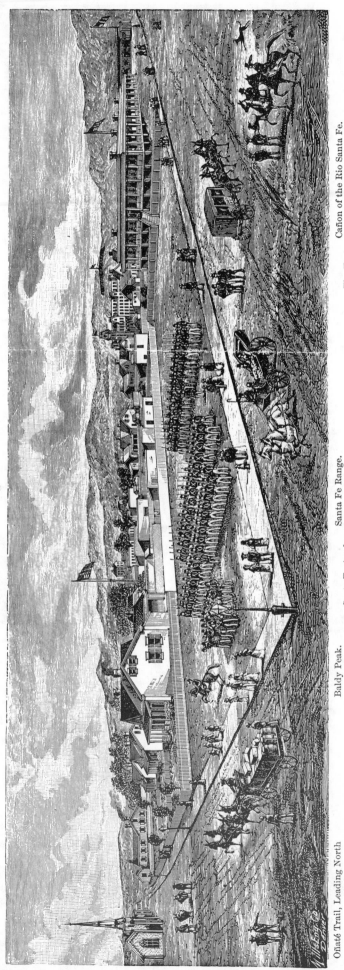

Oñaté Trail, Leading North

Baldy Peak.

Cañon of the Rio Santa Fe.

Presbyterian Church.   Hospital.

Santa Fe Academy.   Santa Fe Range.

Palace Hotel.   The Fort.   Old Spanish Government Palace.

Officers' Quarters.

Soldiers' Barracks. H'dq'rs of the Post.

Residence of Gen. L. P. Bradley, Com'dg Dist.

Grant Street, looking North.

Officers' Quarters.

General Offices.

Palace Avenue, looking East.

The further of the three residences facing Grant Street was the quarters of Ex-President Grant and family, when they visited Santa Fe, in 1880.

HEADQUARTERS MILITARY DISTRICT OF NEW MEXICO.

FORT MARCY. (Santa Fe.)

Map of the Military District of Santa Fe. Few of the buildings shown here are still standing. (Ritch, 1885.)

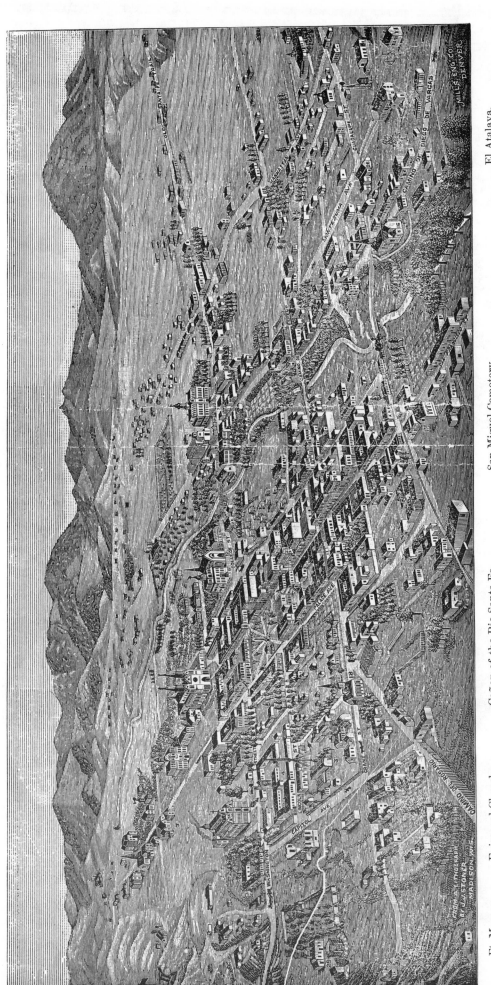

Ft. Marcy.   Episcopal Church.   Cañon of the Rio Santa Fe.   San Miguel Cemetery.   El Atalaya.
St. Vincent's Hospital.   Cathedral San Francisco (See of Santa Fe.)   Bishop's Garden.   Camping Ground U. S. Army, Aug. 18, 1846.   Santa Fe Trail.
Palace Hotel.   Academy and Convent Sisters Loretto.   San Miguel Church and College.   Rio de Santa Fe.
Masonic and Odd Fellows' Cemetery.   Spanish Government Palace.   Plaza and Center of Business.   Territorial Penitentiary.
Gas Works.   State House Grounds.   U. S. Military Reservation, H'd Qrs. Dist. N. M.   Congregational Church.
Tri-Centenary Celebration Grounds, 1883.   Presbyterian Church.   Texas, Santa Fe and Northern R. R.   Guadalupe Church.   A. T. and S. F. R. R. Depot.
Methodist Church.   U. S. Indian School. (Gov. Vigil Place.

CITY OF SANTA FE, NEW MEXICO.

(COPYRIGHTED.)

Presented by the Bureau of Immigration, New Mexico.

Birds-eye view of Santa Fe in 1882. The general layout of the town may still be recognized and some of the buildings identified are still there. (Ritch, 1882-3.)

One of Santa Fe's most popular subjects for visiting artists is this adobe house, said to be the oldest inhabited one in the U.S. Part of it may have been built by the Indians who lived in Santa Fe before the Spaniards arrived, but other parts were added later. (*Harper's Weekly*, Sept. 13, 1879.)

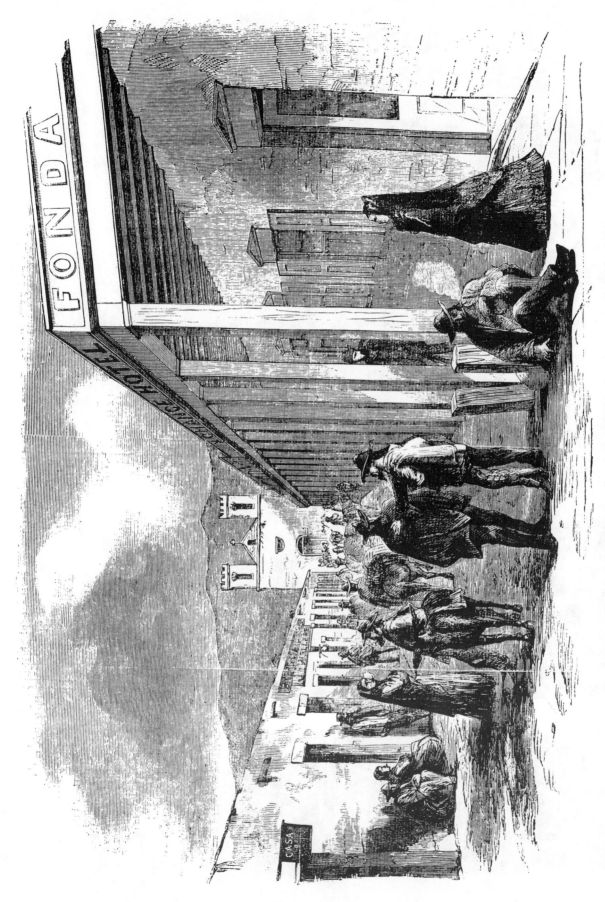

San Francisco Street in Santa Fe has changed since this drawing was made in the 1880s. St. Francis Cathedral looks about the same, but the Exchange Hotel has been replaced by La Fonda. (*Harper's Weekly*, Apr. 21, 1886.)

Pencil sketch of the Palace of Governors was made by Gov. Lew Wallace. (Wallace, 1889.)

GAMBLING was one of Santa Fe's main industries, and monte its most popular attraction. Dollars, pesos, Spanish doubloons and gold dust were all legal tender. Players habitually kept a bowie knife or pistol handy to satisfy any complaints.

Dona Tules (Gertrudes Barcelo,) Santa Fe's foremost lady gambler. (*Harper's*, April, 1854.)

Patrons in the gambling house of Dona Tules in Santa Fe. (*Harper's*, April, 1854.)

This view of Santa Fe (right) makes it appear very populous. Design of the Palace of Governors shows brickwork front. (Thayer, 1888.)

Palace (center) in the 1890's in territorial style. (*Harper's Weekly*, July 19, 1890.)

Palace and Santa Fe's tree-shaded plaza. The palace has since been remodeled to its more original Pueblo form. (Ladd, 1891.)

Catron Building on the east side of Santa Fe Plaza is still used by the Catron law firm and the design of its upper story remains unchanged. (Frost, 1894.)

Street scene in Santa Fe, 1885. A stagecoach turns from what is today Shelby street onto San Francisco street. The Exchange Hotel is now La Fonda. Seligman's store has gone, but its successor recently rebuilt the *portal* or roof over the sidewalk. (Ritch, 1885.)

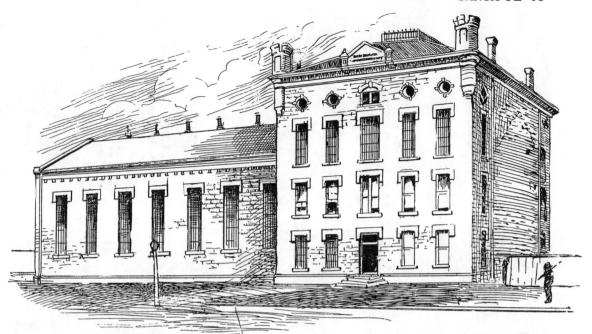

The old Territorial Penitentiary (above) was near Cerrillos Road and Cordova Road in Santa Fe. It was recently torn down. Santa Fe was given its choice of the penitentiary or the state university; it chose the prison. (Frost, 1894.)

Caramba! A burro can be ornery at times! (Beadle, 1873.)

The Presbyterian Mission School (below) was a Santa Fe landmark. (Frost, 1894.)

Gambling in Santa Fe was both popular and legal. (Richardson, 1867.)

State capitol was started in 1900. It is now part of the state office building. (State letterhead, 1917.)

THE TERRITORIAL style of architecture popular today is a mixture of pueblo adobe and Californian. It is a relatively late blending of traditional materials and modern methods.

Most of the larger buildings built during territorial days were inappropriate-looking but relatively functional buildings in Victorian.

Family making tortillas. (Gregg, 1849.)

Class building of St. Michael's College on College St. in Santa Fe. (Frost, 1894.)

Easterner who married a New Mexican girl introduces a friend to his new horde of relatives. (Beadle, 1873.)

New Mexico's capitol from 1884 to 1892. (*Ladd*, 1891.)

This is apparently the architect's drawing for the capitol authorized by the Territorial Legislature. Only the section on the right was built. (Ritch, 1885.)

Old Federal Building on South Federal Place (above) was built shortly after the Civil War. (Frost, 1894.)

This early sketch of Santa Fe was probably drawn by one who had never seen the town. (Frost, 1851.)

Indian School in Santa Fe (below) is now the New Mexico School for the Deaf. (Frost, 1894.)

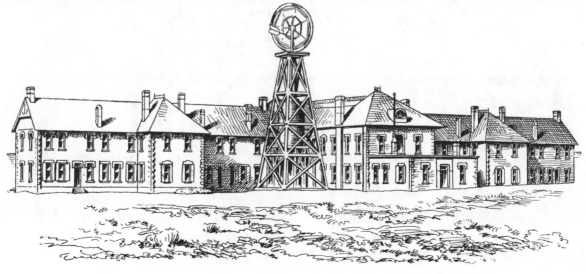

A bustling Santa Fe street. (Higgins, 1896.)

J. GOLD'S FREE MUSEUM (below,) is one of the older surviving buildings in Santa Fe. The city attempts to save its old buildings through historical zoning, but some buildings outside the zones have been torn down.

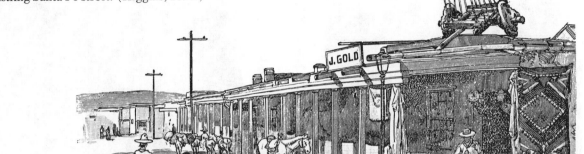

San Francisco Street in the 1890s. The "Free Museum" is now a trading post. (*Harper's Weekly*, July 19, 1890.)

Santa Fe in the 1890s. The large building on the right was New Mexico's brand new capitol. It burned down a year after this picture was published. (Ladd, 1891.)

Early home of the First National Bank, Santa Fe, founded by Lucien Maxwell and others in 1870 as the first bank in New Mexico. (Ritch, 1882-3.)

The Spiegelberg Building in Santa Fe. (Ritch, 1885.)

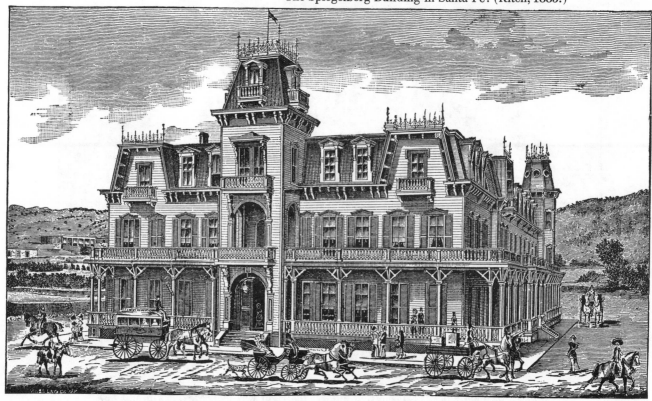

Palace Hotel in Santa Fe stood near today's City Hall on Washington Ave. (Ritch, 1885.)

Santa Fe was a cosmopolitan city in the 1880s and '90s. The hotels were prosperous and ornate. The best food was shipped in by rail. Beautiful furniture, statues, pianos, and other symbols of gracious living were all in evidence in the better homes. The stores sold an amazing variety of goods, from pins to wagons. Bacon was about 11 cents per pound. Coffee mills sold for $5.50 per dozen. Mixed and fancy candy was 17 cents per pound.

The home of Abraham Staab on Palace Avenue has had its face lifted since the 1800s. It is now a large motel, but some of the interior remains the same. (Ritch, 1885.)

DeVargas Street and San Miguel Church. (Ritch, 1885.)

Pioneer merchant Levi Spiegelberg hosted President Rutherford B. Hayes at this home in Santa Fe in 1880. (Ritch, 1885.)

ARCHBISHOP LAMY and the St. Francis Cathedral gained national recognition through Willa Cather's novel *Death Comes for the Archbishop.*

Religious ceremony in the streets of Santa Fe. (*Harper's,* July, 1880.)

Archbishop Lamy and the St. Francis Cathedral as he originally planned it. The tall towers were never finished. (Ritch, 1885.)

View of Santa Fe from Fort Marcy. (*Harper's Weekly,* July 14, 1883.)

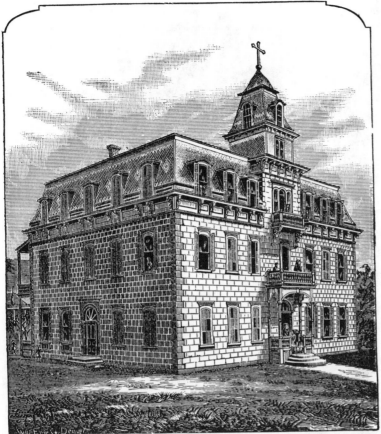

Loretto chapel has famous miraculous circular staircase. (*Harper's*, April, 1880.)

Loretto Academy, founded in 1853, closed in 1968. (Ritch, 1885.)

Interior of St. Francis Cathedral. (*Harper's*, April, 1880.)

Roof of St. Francis Cathedral during its construction. (*Harper's*, April, 1880.)

San Miguel Church.
(Sweetser, 1891.)

SAN MIGUEL church has been changed
several times since it was built. Triple-
stepped tower atop it was destroyed by a
storm in 1872.

"Oldest House in Santa Fe." (*Harper's Weekly*, Sept. 7, 1889.)

San Miguel Church as it appeared in the
1870s. (Roberts, 1885.)

Wooden-wheeled carreta was drawn by oxen. Probably no working example of either is left in New Mexico. (Peters, 1874.)

San Miguel Church and College Street
in the 1880s. To the right, with cu-
pola, is St. Michael's College. (*Harper's Weekly*, July 14, 1883.)

View of Our Lady of Guadalupe Church, from the side. The figures are walking down what is now Agua Fria St. (Schlagintweit, 1884.)

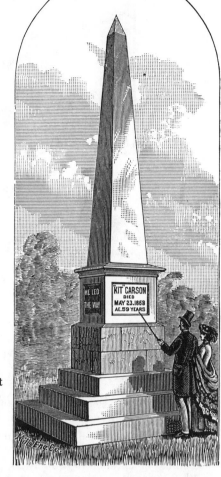

Monument to Kit Carson still stands in front of the old Federal Building. (Ritch, 1885.)

Soldier's Monument to Civil War veterans is in the Santa Fe plaza. (*Harper's Weekly*, July 19, 1890.)

San Miguel Church and DeVargas St. A state office building now stands where the building on the right is in this picture. (Frost, 1894.)

IN THE last years of the 19th century, Santa Fe settled down to outgrow its earlier, rowdier days.

Business blossomed. The town had a population of 6,038 (excluding Indians) in 1890. It was the largest single town in the territory.

One highlight in those days was the tertio-millennial celebration held in 1883, supposedly because the city was a third of a thousand years old. (1550 had been arbitrarily picked as its birth date.) Chartered Pullman cars brought visitors from as far away as New England. The fiesta was considered a great success, though its backers lost money.

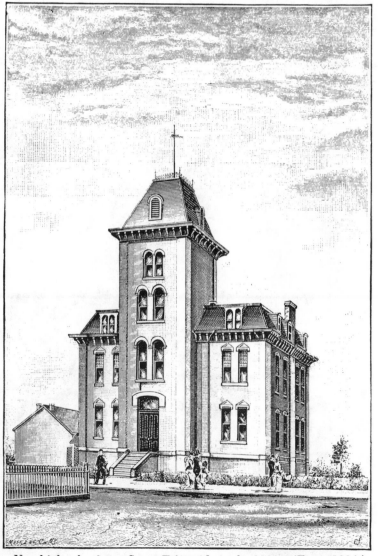

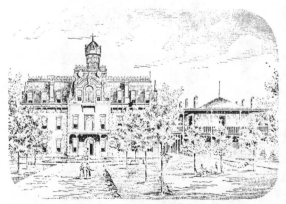

St. Vincent's Sanitarium, founded by Archbishop Lamy and the Sisters of Charity of Cincinnati. (Frost, 1894.)

New high school was Santa Fe's pride in the 1890s. (Frost, 1894.)

St. Catherine's Indian School
in Santa Fe. (Sweetser, 1891.)

Outdoor market near the plaza
in Santa Fe. (*Harper's*, April,
1880.)

Students listening to the padre.
(*Harper's*, April, 1880.)

THE SANTA FE plaza has been
the scene of both peace and
action for more than 350
years. In 1680, besieged
Spanish colonists slowly
trudged out of the plaza to
escape the rebelling Pueblo
Indians. Religious and
patriotic celebrations here
marked Mexico's indepen-
dence from Spain in 1821. The
plaza was the busy end of the
Santa Fe Trail for many years.
It is now a quiet oasis in the
midst of bustling auto traffic—
but still the cultural center of
Santa Fe.

A bustling spring morning on
the plaza in Santa Fe. (*Harper's*,
April, 1880.)

Early sketch of Santa Fe, with mission in foreground. Flag in the distance is atop Fort Marcy. Right foreground is now the site of an urban renewal project. (Davis, 1857.)

Wood peddlers brought burro-loads of fragrant piñon logs to market in Santa Fe's plaza. (*Harper's*, April, 1880.)

When the first traders came over the Trail, Santa Fe was the largest town in New Mexico. (Howe, 1852.)

Described as the only Protestant Church in Santa Fe in the 1870s. (*Harper's Weekly*, Sept. 13, 1879.)

San Miguel Church was built in the Barrio de Analco (the ward beyond the river) for Indian servants from Mexico. It is claimed to be the oldest church in the U.S.

View of Santa Fe from the roof of St. Michael's. (Sweetser, 1891.)

San Miguel Church after one of its restorations. (Drake, 1887.)

First Presbyterian Church was built in 1881. (Ritch, 1885.)

A "grand entree into Santa Fe" was the description given for this vignette by an early traveler. (*Harper's*, April, 1854.)

Making cane seat chairs. Most of the things made in early 19th century New Mexico would be considered the products of crafts rather than industries. (Higgins, 1896.)

Seal of New Mexico. Left, early Historical Society seal; center, an elaborate seal from the Blue Book of the territory, 1882; right, modern seal, adopted after statehood in 1912.

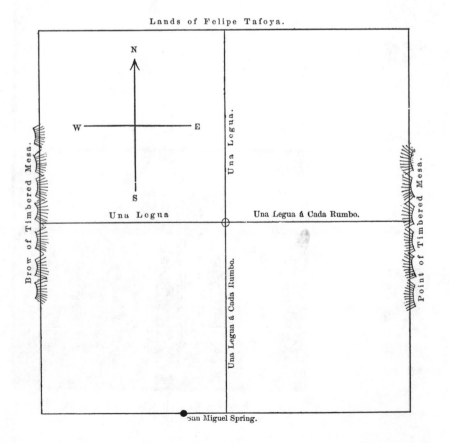

Spanish land grants in New Mexico were made by the governor at Santa Fe in the name of the king, with final title retained by the king. After annexation by the United States, a legal procedure was established by which old titles could be validated and continued. Sketch map here shows boundaries of the "San Miguel grant, in the province of Navajo." Later known as the Bartolome Fernandez Grant, it is now part of a big ranch owned by Floyd Lee at San Mateo, near Grants. (U.S. Govt. Doc., 1874.)

Sleepy plaza of Albuquerque in the 1850s. This plaza was actually to the west of today's Old Town Plaza. (Davis, 1857.)

ALBUQUERQUE

San Felipe Church looks much the same today, but Sister Blandina's convent has been added, and a different wall built. (Sweetser, 1891.)

Wall around the plaza was added later. (Sweetser, 1891)

This building housed the St. Elmo and the White Elephant saloons. It was where the Sunshine Building on Second and Central is today. (Ritch, 1885.)

One of several old haciendas in Albuquerque. (*Harper's*, April, 1885.)

MANY of Albuquerque's older residents, like the Hunings, Armijos, and Blueher's, lived in Old Town but had businesses in New Town. Visitors from New Town to Joe Badaracco's Summer Garden and the county offices on the plaza were common. In the 1880s, a horse-drawn trolley operated between the two areas.

Franz Huning's home was a showplace of Albuquerque. It stood near 14th and Central until the 1950s. Some of the lumber for the house came from Illinois, other materials were brought from England. (Haines, 1891.)

View of the mesa at the mouth of Tijeras Canyon, with insets showing Albuquerque scenes, was sketched for a local humor magazine. (*Adobeland*, Aug., 1891.)

Early view of Albuquerque and the Sandia Mountains. (Whipple, 1856.)

New Mexico carreta. (Chase, 1882.)

First bridge across Rio Grande at Albuquerque was 1,600 feet long. (Ritch, 1882-3.)

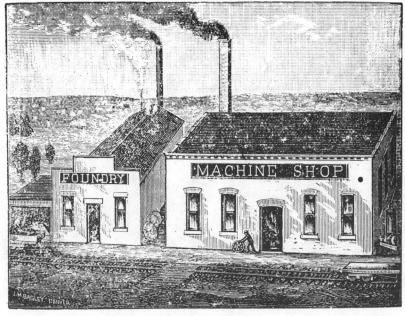

Albuquerque Foundry and Machine Shop were at the east side of the railroad tracks, south of Central Ave. (Ritch, 1882–83.)

Bernalillo County Court House was just off Central Ave. (then Railroad Ave.) near Old Town. (Letterhead, 1891.)

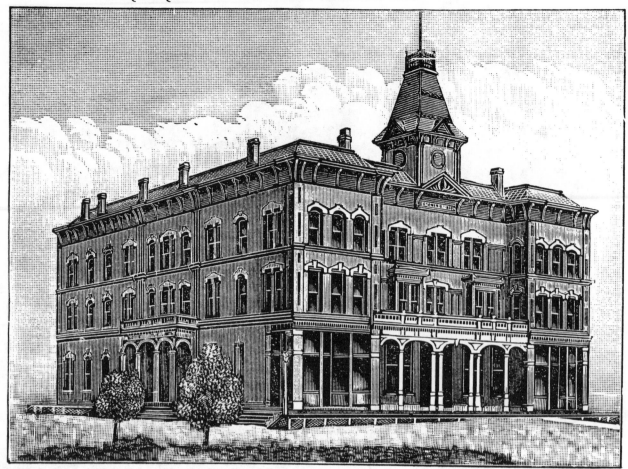

San Felipe Hotel stood on the corner of Fifth and Gold, where the newest Federal Building is today. (Haines, 1891.)

NEW TOWN sprang up like grass after a desert rain when the railroad arrived in 1880.

Hill St. (now Elm St.) marked the eastern edge of the town in the 1890s and there were hardly more than two dozen houses between Tenth Street and Old Town.

This Victorian mansion in Los Lunas, built in the 1880s, home of Solomon Luna, later of the Otero family, has been restored. (Carruth, 1897.)

Commercial Club was on the corner of Fourth and Gold in Albuquerque, where the Simms Building is today. (Frost, 1894.)

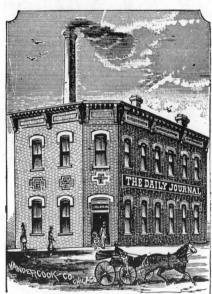

The old Albuquerque *Morning Journal* office was at 312 Gold SW. (Ritch, 1885.)

A flour mill, "Molino de la Glorieta," stood near the Huning home. It was near the corner of today's Central and Laguna Blvd., SW. (*Harper's*, April, 1885.)

Original building of the present University of New Mexico. Remodeled, it is now Hodgin Hall. (Frost, 1894.)

The women of Albuquerque who lived on the west side of the Rio Grande didn't wait for the small ferry when they wanted to cross the river to attend Mass. They simply pulled up their skirts and waded across. (Beadle, 1873.)

The latest Victorian gingerbread and a widow's walk decorated the M.A. Otero home in Bernalillo. (Ritch, 1885.)

LAS VEGAS

LAS VEGAS began with the awarding of a land grant to Don Luis Maria Cabeza de Baca and his seventeen children in 1823. The family was soon driven out by hostile Indians.

In 1832, Santa Fe trader Josiah Gregg noticed one small hovel where the town stands today. In 1835, 29 men petitioned for the grant title formerly held by the de Bacas.

The town they built was a monotonous collection of mud huts that made a poor impression on travelers seeing New Mexico for the first time.

When Kearny's Army of the West reached Las Vegas in 1846, one of his first acts was to climb atop one of the houses on the plaza and read a message proclaiming New Mexico part of the U.S.

In 1879, Manuel Barela and Giovanni Dugi were hanged from the windmill on the plaza. Barela had killed a couple of men while testing his marksmanship by shooting off their coat buttons—from the front. Dugi had killed two men "by accident" he said, when his revolver fired when he demonstrated the road agent's spin.

When the local vigilantes lynched the two, they pinned a note to Dugi's coat. "This was no accident."

The new, raw town of East Las Vegas was built and ready for the first railroad train when it arrived on July 4th, 1879.

The railroad helped boom the new town. It also brought a gang of killers, con men and robbers who ran the town for about six months. They decamped before the vigilantes could use them to decorate tree limbs.

The new town then settled down and began to thrive. The two towns, East and West Las Vegas, remained separate until 1968, when the citizens voted to combine them.

First house in Las Vegas was built by Manuel Romero in 1833. (Wilson, 1880.)

Old Catholic church at Las Vegas was on the northwest corner of the plaza. (Wilson, 1880.)

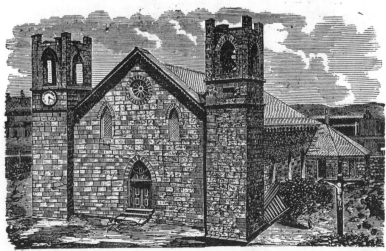

Our Lady of Sorrows Church in old Vegas had no heat, was called a "magnificent refrigerator." (Wilson, 1880.)

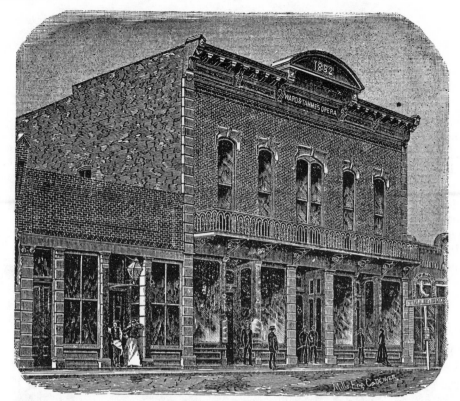

First National Bank building on the Old Las Vegas plaza is still there, but the other buildings shown on this page are now gone.

Ward and Tamme's Opera House was at 320-2 Railroad Ave. (All pictures on this page show Las Vegas, from Mills, 1885.)

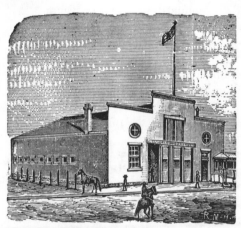

Street car stables were on the west corner of Main and 12th streets.

Wells, Fargo and Co. express office was on Lincoln between Grand and Railroad.

Optic Building was on Lincoln near the corner of 7th and Grand.

LAS VEGAS got its first growth through the Santa Fe trade. Mining, stock raising and agriculture later brought more business. In the 1880s, Las Vegas rivaled Santa Fe and Albuquerque in size and importance.

West Las Vegas as it looked in 1880. (Wilson, 1880.)

Main store of the Ilfeld Co., on the Plaza in Las Vegas. (Letterhead, 1899.)

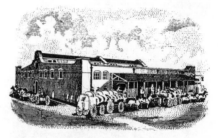

Ilfeld's wholesale warehouse. This firm was one of the largest in the territory. (Letterhead, 1899.)

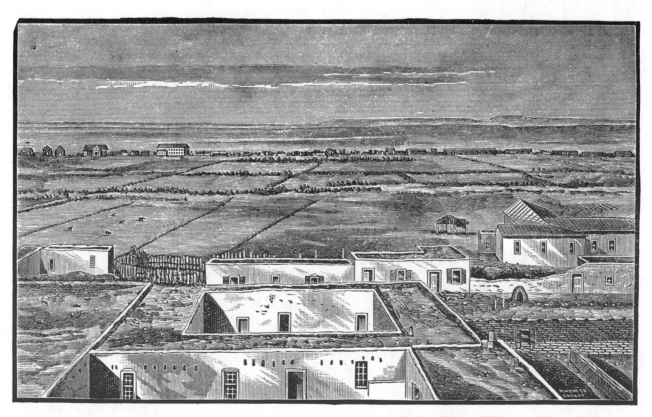

Las Vegas in 1880. In the background is the new town, East Las Vegas. (Wilson, 1880.)

Burros carried everything and everybody along rough New Mexico trails and through crowded streets. (Wilson, 1880.)

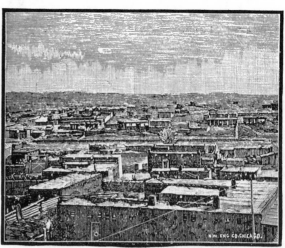

Adobe homes in the southern section of Old Las Vegas. (Wilson, 1880.)

Haciendas owned by *ricos* were often shaded by surrounding cottonwoods. (Ladd, 1891.)

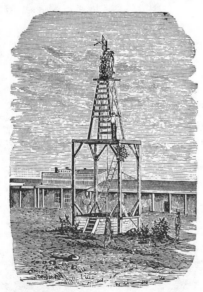

Windmill stood in the Old Las Vegas Plaza. It was torn down in 1880 after citizens complained that the men hung from it might have contaminated the water. (Wilson, 1880.)

The burros in this exaggerated drawing seem to be doing a balancing act—carrying barrels, wood, and tremendous loads of hay without pack saddles. No burro would submit to such an indignity. (Richardson, 1867.)

LUXURY SPA OF THE WEST

NEW MEXICO has been a mecca for health seekers for many years. Fifty years ago the high towns such as Las Vegas, Santa Fe, and Albuquerque had small suburbs of tents where "lungers" waited either to die or recover. Many who came west for their health, including Sen. Clinton P. Anderson, lived to become prominent citizens. Other famous health seekers included Gov. William Thornton, Sen. Bronson Cutting, and Dr. John H. (Doc) Holliday.

THE MONTEZUMA Hot Springs Hotel was started in 1879 and sold to the Santa Fe Railway in 1880.

VISITORS at the hotel included Generals Grant and Sherman, President Hayes, and Jesse James (who said he was a railroad man.)

The Montezuma burned down in 1884 and was replaced by the Phoenix, but even the new hotel was locally called the Montezuma.

The magnificent old Phoenix still stands in a wooded canyon near Las Vegas. It became a seminary for Mexican priests, then an international secular college.

Old Phoenix Hotel looks about the same today as it did when this was drawn eighty years ago. (Thayer, 1888.)

Fountains and spacious grounds were laid out in front of the Phoenix. (*Las Vegas Hot Springs*, n.d.)

Porches at the Phoenix overlooked the green Gallinas Canyon. (*Las Vegas Hot Springs,* n.d.)

Fireplace in the Phoenix lobby had identical copies on the second and third floors above it. (*Las Vegas Hot Springs,* n.d.)

Plush dining room at the Phoenix offered trout, venison, partridge, grouse, duck, crab, turtle, shrimp. (*Las Vegas Hot Springs*, n.d.)

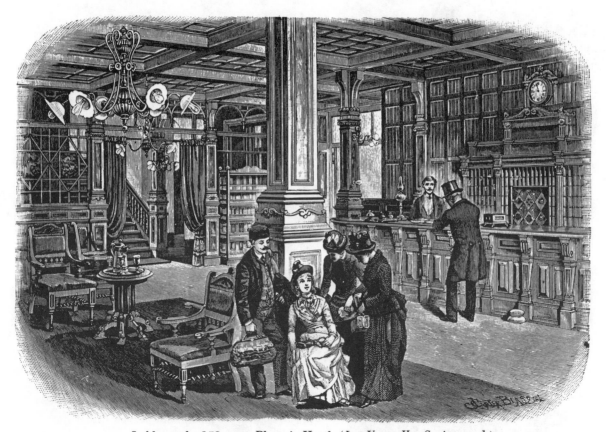

Lobby at the 172-room Phoenix Hotel. (*Las Vegas Hot Springs*, n.d.)

Gallinas Canyon, west of Las Vegas, seen from porch of the Phoenix Hotel. (*Las Vegas Hot Springs*, n.d.)

Phoenix Hotel nestled in the canyon. It was surrounded by pines, bath houses, bridle paths. (*Las Vegas Hot Springs*, n.d.)

Don Fernando de Taos, the Spanish town of Taos, was settled in the 1700s. The tradition of trading began early, when Taos Pueblo Indians bartered with the Apaches, Utes, Navajo, Comanches, and Pawnees. The rendezvous of the early fur trappers and mountain men at Taos were riotous annual events. (Davis, 1857.)

TAOS

Ruins of the Catholic mission at Taos Pueblo. It was burned during the 1847 Taos Revolt. (Schlagintweit, 1884.)

A fanciful sketch of "Kit Carson's home in Taos." The home, now an excellent museum, probably never looked like this, nor did the town behind it. (Peters, 1858.)

The town of Socorro nestles at the base of Socorro Mountain. The town began in 1628 when a mission was built at a Piro pueblo there. Socorro has seen the Pueblo Revolt, the Civil War, cattle drives, and the violence of frontier life. The nearby mines are closed, but the town survives on trade and agriculture. (Ritch, 1882-3.)

The smelter at Socorro processed silver from the mountains. The silver was discovered in 1867, and the town soon boomed to become the biggest in New Mexico in the 1880's. (Ritch, 1885.)

Mora courthouse, now gone. (Letterhead, 1890.)

Chaves County courthouse was built in 1890. It has since been replaced. (Letterhead, 1891.)

San Miguel County courthouse in Las Vegas' new town. (Letterhead, 1889.)

Windsor Hotel in Socorro was on East Manzanares St. (Ritch, 1885.)

Original building of New Mexico School of Mines at Socorro. The school opened in 1892. (Letterhead, 1894).

Another view of the School of Mines, now the New Mexico Institute of Mining and Technology. (Frost, 1894.)

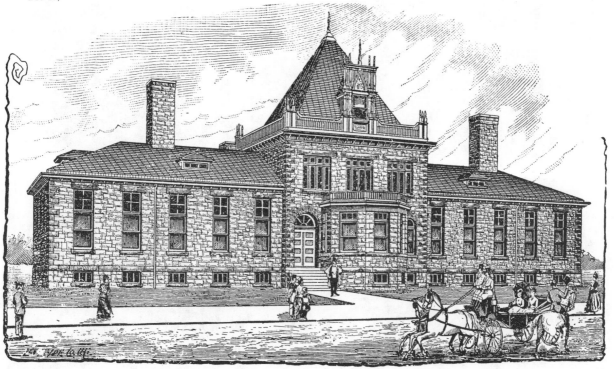

The town of Cubero, near Laguna, as it was in the 1850's. (Davis, 1857.)

A street in the village of Los Lunas. (Frost, 1894.)

Wool warehouse at Springer. (Ritch, 1882-3.)

Upper Cubero. The pillar in the background is, like Cabezon and Shiprock, the core of an ancient volcano. (Davis, 1857.)

Peaceful town of Algodones. The town is still peaceful, but no longer on the main trail to Santa Fe as it was in the 1800s. (Beadle, 1873.)

Old mill at Chamita, near Abiquiu. (Sweetser, 1891.)

Raton, seen from Goat Hill. (Sweetser, 1891.)

Ojo Caliente resort above Espanola. The springs had been used by Indians for many years before the Spaniards arrived. (Ritch, 1885.)

The town of Eddy, organized in 1889, is now
Carlsbad. (Ladd, 1891.)

First school building in Carlsbad. (Frost, 1894.)

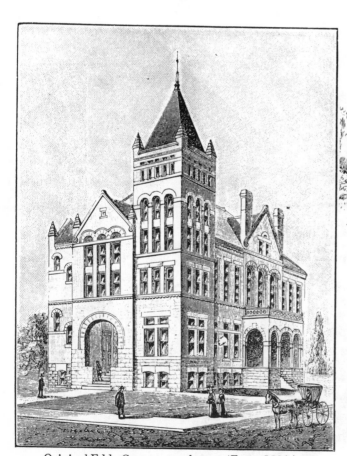

Original Eddy County courthouse. (Frost, 1894.)

Irrigation projects at Carlsbad. (Sweetser, 1891.)

Sierra County courthouse was built in Hillsboro in 1892. It is now one of the ruins in that ghost town. (Sierra County letterhead, 1900.)

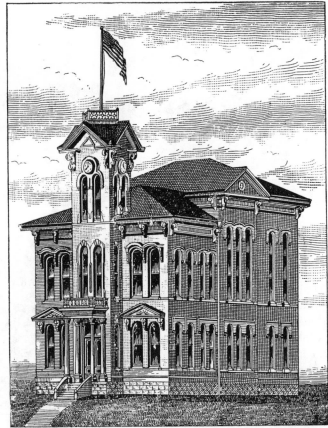

First agricultural college building at Las Cruces, built in the early 1890's, was Hadley Hall. It was named for the founder of the college. (Frost, 1894.)

Irrigation ditches bring water to the crops. (Wood, 1889.)

Beehive shaped oven, or *horno*, is seen at Indian pueblos. (Thayer, 1888.)

Grist mill. One of the few examples left in New Mexico is the large and historic old mill at Ruidoso. (Ritch, 1885.)

The gardens of Isleta, a peaceful oasis along the Rio Grande. (*Harper's*, April, 1885.)

TRADITIONAL adobe homes, such as the one shown on this page, sometimes had walls three feet thick. Adobe is a fine insulation, keeping the house warm in winter and cool in summer. Long vigas support layers of smaller branches and twigs. Adobe is piled on top for the roof. Carved beams instead of vigas and ornate corbels were sometimes used for their decorative qualities.

Square adobe houses enclosed a large, cool central plaza in typical New Mexican homes. (*Harper's*, April, 1885.)

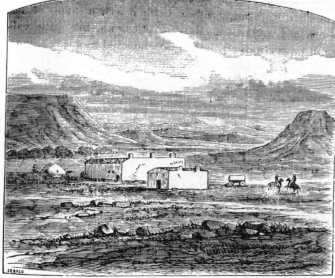

The town of Bluewater, near Grants, was an isolated village until the 1880s, when a railroad was built from Albuquerque to the West Coast. (Beadle, 1873.)

Colonists with deVargas settled the village of Villa de Santa Cruz de la Cañada in 1695.

Two small battles were fought near Santa Cruz, one in the revolt of 1837 against Gov. Perez and another during the Taos Revolt of 1847.

Some settlers lived in dugouts covered with dirt or pieces of dried marsh grass. (*Harper's Weekly*, Sept. 7, 1889.)

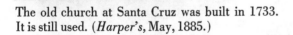

The old church at Santa Cruz was built in 1733. It is still used. (*Harper's*, May, 1885.)

Emigrant to New Mexico is "out here for his health." (Chase, 1882.)

Church and shrine at Santa Cruz stand on the main plaza. (Ritch, 1885.)

Wild fandango at Santa Fe. (Beadle, 1873.)

The town of Valencia, south of Albuquerque, and a nearby lava-topped mesa named Tomé Hill. (Emory, 1848.)

Settlers were induced to come to New Mexico by land offices brochures showing pictures of a "modern agricultural ranch" such as this. Railroads, rivers, and forests were emphasized. (Ritch, 1885.)

GHOST TOWN

LAKE VALLEY began early in the 1880's when miners found gold in the area. It grew quickly from a crude camp to a prosperous town. The ore was worth as much as $1,000 a ton. The veins of gold, silver, lead, and manganese were usually at a depth of only forty feet or less.

   The town died in the financial panic of 1893.

Smelting works at Lake Valley. The Bridal Chamber mine there once produced $3 million in horn silver ore in six months. (Thayer, 1888.)

The mines around Lake Valley were lode mines, unlike the open pit copper mines at Santa Rita. (Ritch, 1885.)

The town of Lake Valley, west of Hatch, is one of several old mining camps in that area that are now ghost towns. (Ritch, 1882-3.)

Soldiers in the Mexican War had no travelling laundry; instead they halted for a "camp washing day" as in this sketch from the journal of William H. Richardson. (1848.)

Bent's Fort on the Arkansas River was not in New Mexico but it was the principal stopping place on the Santa Fe Trail. It is now being restored by the National Park Service. (Inman, 1893.)

Members of the Texan Santa Fe expedition of 1841 are marched south to Mexico City after their capture. (Brown, 1906.)

Members of Col. Jacob Snively's 1843 Texan expedition to Santa Fe find their horses stampeding through their camp. The 107 men were captured by Capt. Philip St. George Cooke of the U.S. Army near today's Dodge City. (Sage, 1854.)

WAR WITH MEXICO

AN UNPOPULAR WAR between the U.S. and Mexico began on May 13, 1846. Generals Zachary Taylor and Winfield Scott moved on Texas and Mexico City. Gen. Stephen Watts Kearny and his Army of the West headed for New Mexico.

The army arrived in Las Vegas on August 15th. Kearny climbed atop a roof on the plaza and proclaimed New Mexico part of the U.S. Three days later, after Gov. Manuel Armijo had placed his troops for battle and then escaped south to Mexico, Kearny marched through a dispersed Mexican army and took Santa Fe.

Kearny marched on to California. He left Col. Alexander Doniphan in charge. Doniphan took on the Navajo and forced them to sign their first treaty of peace with the U.S. When Col. Sterling Price and his volunteers arrived from Missouri, Doniphan moved south to the Battle of Brazito and on to Chihuahua.

Price put down a rebellion at Taos, fought Indians and slowly brought a troubled peace to the new New Mexico Territory.

In the meantime, Lt. Col. Philip St. George Cooke forged a trained group of soldiers from Mormon immigrants and led the Mormon Batallion across southern New Mexico to California.

One of Kearny's soldiers. (Frost, 1851.)

Common soldiers were more informal in both dress and mounts. (Hughes, 1850.)

Col. Alexander Doniphan led troops south to Brazito and Chihuahua. (Hughes, 1850.)

Doniphan's troops marching through the Jornada del Muerto. (Richardson, 1848.)

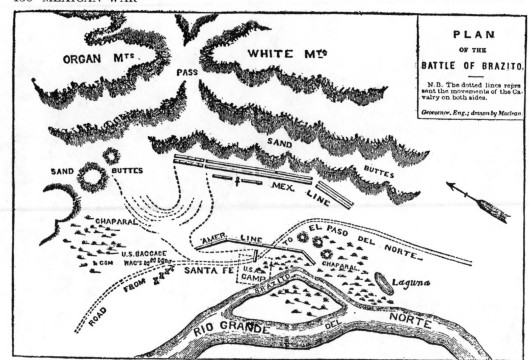

Battle of Brazito was the only battle of the Mexican War fought in New Mexico. (Hughes, 1850.)

DONIPHAN's troops were camped at Brazito, nine miles below Las Cruces, when 1,000 Mexican soldiers approached. Doniphan's 856 men prepared their long rifles and, when the Mexicans were close, poured a heavy and accurate rifle fire into them. The Mexicans retreated, and many were killed by Apaches who had been watching the battle from nearby hills.

Part of Doniphan's mule train. (Frost, 1851.)

Sterling Price, an officer with Doniphan, later became a Confederate general. (Dunn, 1886.)

Kearny's troops crossing New Mexico mountains. (Harper's, July, 1880.)

Kearny's troops on their march through New Mexico. (All pictures on this page from Frost, 1882.)

Doniphan's men camped at the base of the Fra Cristobal Mountains. They marched on to meet Mexican troops at Brazito.

Capt. James Burgwin was killed during the storming of the Taos Church.

Doniphan's soldiers meet Mexican traders along the route south to Chihuahua.

Kearny's officers attend a baile at Santa Fe a few days after the town is taken.

Kearny's men camped at Valencia. The locals took advantage of army needs and charged 25¢ a stick for firewood.

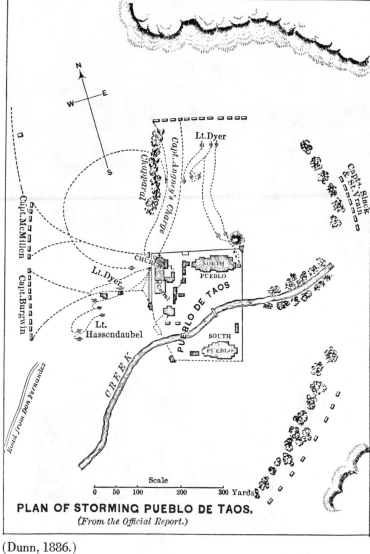

PLAN OF STORMING PUEBLO DE TAOS.
(From the Official Report.)

(Dunn, 1886.)

The Taos Revolt started on January 19th, 1847. Townsmen and Indians killed Gov. Charles Bent and other Americans in Northern New Mexico.

Col. Sterling Price and his Missouri Volunteers marched on Taos. They found most of the rebels barricaded inside the old mission at the pueblo. They bombarded it for two hours and returned the next day for a direct assault. Soldiers chopped holes in the walls and threw artillery shells inside.

At least 150 rebels were killed and the survivors surrendered the next day. Several of the leaders were executed and the revolt was over.

The Volunteer. Originally drawn to represent J. W. Patton immediately after first being under fire at Brazito. (Hughes, 1850.)

Doniphan's men met rancheros such as these while on the way to Mexico. (Hughes, 1850.)

Fort Fillmore in 1884. (*London Illus. News*, Dec. 2, 1854.)

CIVIL WAR

FORT FILLMORE, built in 1852, was a small post along the Rio Grande near Mesilla. It was the first target of Col. John R. Baylor's troops in the beginning of the Civil War.

Baylor's men reached Mesilla late in July, 1861. On July 25th they confronted the Federal soldiers. After a short exchange of cannon balls and musketry the Union commanding officer, Col. Isaac Lynde, ordered a retreat to Fort Fillmore. The next day he ordered the fort abandoned.

The 800 Union soldiers were to surrender the fort to only 250 rebels. Lynde's officers were obedient but outraged.

The fort was abandoned and the soldiers trudged toward Fort Stanton. Baylor's troops, following behind, picked up stragglers by the dozens. Lynde surrendered his entire command to Baylor at St. Augustine Springs.

He was later dropped from the Army rolls amid charges of treason and cowardice.

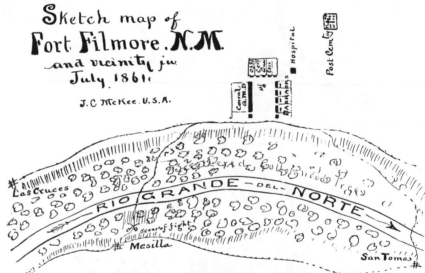

Plan of Ft. Fillmore, sketched by Maj. James McKee, a surgeon at the post in 1861. (McKee, 1878.)

Fort Cummings was built in 1863 on the Mesilla-Tucson stage road. (Bell, 1870.)

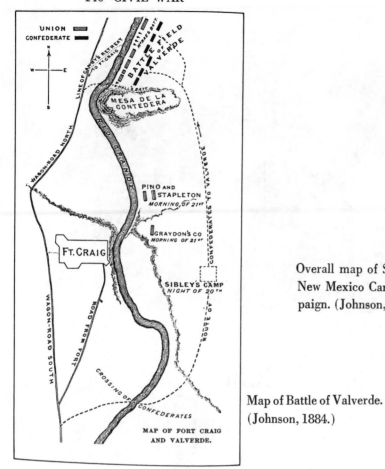

Map of Battle of Valverde. (Johnson, 1884.)

Overall map of Sibley's New Mexico Campaign. (Johnson, 1884.)

The ford on the Rio Grande near Fort Craig was the scene of the Battle of Valverde.　(Abert, 1847.)

Col. E. R. S. Canby was commander of the Union troops during the Civil War action in New Mexico. (Lossing, 1877.)

Gen. Henry H. Sibley headed Confederate Army in New Mexico. (Lossing, 1877.)

One of Sibley's "Texas Rangers," according to a Civil War historian. (Lossing, 1877.)

A more realistic view of one of Sibley's rangers. (Lossing, 1877.)

This first drawing of a Texas ranger appeared about a year before Sibley's invasion and was of one of Ben McCullough's Rangers in Richmond. The artist who made the later drawing (at left) probably copied directly from this woodcut, which explains the reversed sketch. (*Harper's Weekly*, July 6, 1861.)

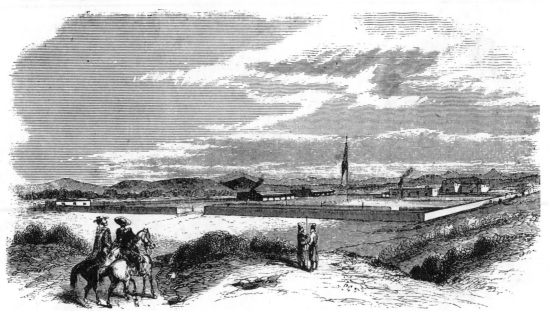

Fort Thorn, near Hatch, was established in 1853 and abandoned in 1859. (Davis, 1857.)

FRONTIER FORTS

U.S. ARMY forts stretched along the Rio Grande to protect the Camino Real and across southern New Mexico to guard the Butterfield Trail. Fort Union took care of the Santa Fe Trail. Fort Bascom protected eastern New Mexico from the Comanches. Forts Stanton, Sumner, Lowell, Wingate, and Tularosa guarded Indian reservations.

A scene along the Jornada del Muerto (Journey of Death) in southern New Mexico. (Richardson, 1867.)

The mountain men opened the west by trapping beavers for the beaver hats popular in the early 1800s. (*Century*, January, 1889.)

When Fort Defiance was built in 1851, it was in a part of New Mexico that was later given to Arizona. Abandoned in 1861, it was reactivated in 1868 as a Navajo Indian Agency and still serves that function. (Dunn, 1886.)

"We closed at full gallop" was dime-novelist Mayne Reid's caption for this drawing. The reata looped above the Indian's head was actually used as a weapon during combat. (Reid, 1863.)

Navajo Indian (left) wearing a silver concho belt and other ornaments. The ornament resembling a crucifix was said to be a Navajo design for the morning star. (BAE *Report*, 1881.)

Fort Union lasted from 1851 to 1891. The fort itself never was the scene of any action, but it was an important personnel and supply depot for the military district of New Mexico. It is now a national monument. (Davis, 1857.)

The use of poisoned arrows by hostile Indians was a common myth. Hardly any of the North American tribes used poison, but unsanitary conditions often brought on blood poisoning in an arrow wound. The Indians of New Mexico did not, as shown here, use rattlesnake venom. (Tenney, 1880.)

Survivors of a forced march in winter reach Fort Massachusetts after a gruelling trip from Fort Bridger, Wyoming, in 1858. Capt. R. B. Marcy was in command. (Marcy, 1866.)

THE FRONTIER FORT was a prominent feature of New Mexico for fifty years. Except for Fort Marcy, built during the Mexican War, troops were at first stationed in rented barracks at such places as Rayado, Abiquiu, Cebolleta, and Socorro. After the first chain of forts had been built, locations were changed for reasons of health or convenience. Only a few of the forts were completely walled; most were clusters of buildings, usually adobe. A few temporary hay camps or other casual spots have been misnamed forts on some maps. Today the remains of some forts are being considered as possible sites for restoration.

Fort Massachusetts was established in 1852 in a strip of land that later became part of Colorado. This northernmost outpost in New Mexico was closed in 1858. (Peters, 1874.)

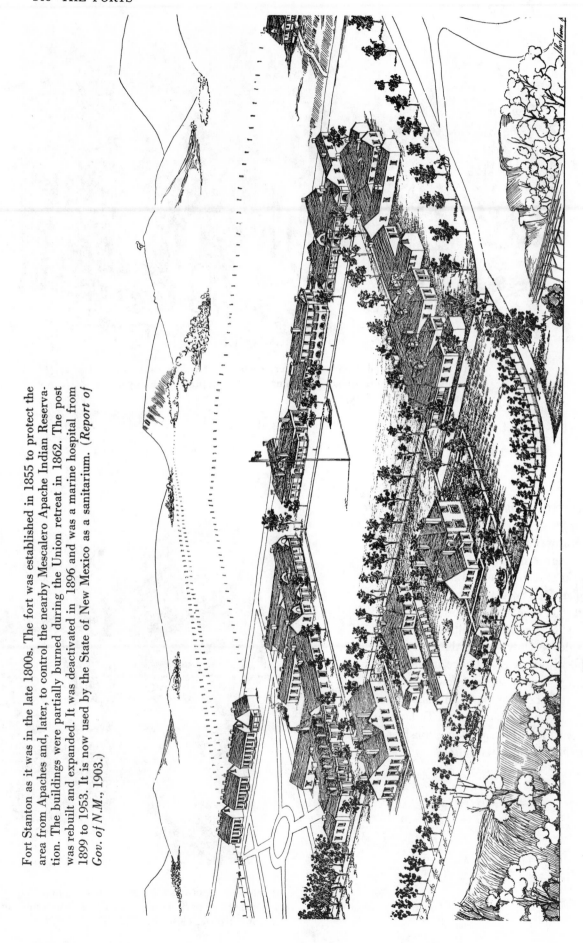

Fort Stanton as it was in the late 1800s. The fort was established in 1855 to protect the area from Apaches and, later, to control the nearby Mescalero Apache Indian Reservation. The buildings were partially burned during the Union retreat in 1862. The post was rebuilt and expanded. It was deactivated in 1896 and was a marine hospital from 1899 to 1953. It is now used by the State of New Mexico as a sanitarium. (*Report of Gov. of N.M., 1903.*)

Dismounted cavalry drill, a new tactic, is tried by troopers at Fort Bayard. Soldiers sometimes used a breastworks of horses during a skirmish, but the horses had usually been killed in an ambush and not trained to lie down. This painting was made by one of the West's best-known artists, T. de Thulstrup, from a photograph made by pioneer photographer Christian Barthelmess. (*Harper's Weekly*, April 4, 1885.)

"The Apaches are coming!" A New Mexican Paul Revere spreads the news to isolated *ranchos* in this dramatic early drawing by Frederic Remington. (*Harper's Weekly*, Jan. 30, 1886.)

A cavalry trooper hoists the guidon to signal the main command during a scout after Apaches in the Arizona-New Mexico desert. (*Harper's Weekly*, July 17, 1886.)

The relaxed gentleman in the center is Nana, one of Geronimo's sub-chiefs. The engraver removed some wrinkles. Nana, by this time, was over eighty years old. The picture was taken in Mexico when he and Geronimo were preparing to surrender to Gen. George Crook. The engraving was made from several photographs taken by an enterprising photographer, Frank Randall, who accompanied Crook's expedition. (*Harper's Weekly*, April 17, 1886.)

INDIAN WARS · 151

Mescalero Apache leaders. Left to right, head chief San Juan, medicine man Gorgonio, and head war chief Nantzilli. (*Harper's Weekly*, May 29, 1886.)

GERONIMO!

GERONIMO, last leader of the "human tigers," hated Mexicans and Americans. He fought until 1886, when he surrendered for the last time and was sent to Florida.

He mellowed in later years and joined the Dutch Reformed Church.

Geronimo in captivity.
(*Century*, May, 1889.)

Geronimo just before his surrender to Gen. Miles, from a photograph taken during an earlier conference with Gen. Crook. (*Harper's Weekly*, April 10, 1886.)

Charles McComas, son of Judge H. C. McComas. His kidnapping was the beginning of an Apache raid into New Mexico in 1883. Army troops followed the Apaches into Mexico until Geronimo surrendered. (*Harper's Weekly*, April 28, 1883.)

Gen. George Crook commanded troops in Arizona from 1871-5 and from 1882-6. (*Harper's Weekly*, August 4, 1883.)

William Waldo holds off hostile Comanches and Kiowas during an attack on the Bent brothers trading party near Taos in 1829. (Triplett, 1885.)

Officers' quarters at Fort Wingate. The fort was originally established at San Rafael, near Grants, in 1862 and moved to its present location in 1868. It was deactivated in 1911, but kept as a storage depot. (Beadle, 1873.)

APACHES had been raiding isolated ranches in New Mexico and Mexico for many years before they turned against the Americans in 1851. In that year, Mangas Colorado was flogged by miners at Pinos Altos and 35 years of war began. Mangas led raids in New Mexico until he was murdered in 1863 at Fort McLane.

Victorio, Loco, Cochise, Nana, and Geronimo continued the fight.

All sides, Army, Indian, civilian, and Mexican alike, indulged in massacres, ambushes, atrocities, and treachery during the Apache wars.

Geronimo discussing peace terms with General Crook. (Kelsey, 1901.)

GENERAL CROOK's tactic was to use Apache scouts to help find and fight renegade Apaches.

"Flying columns" were organized by General Miles to pursue the hostiles relentlesly. His orders were, "Commanding officers are expected to continue a pursuit until capture."

Army life in New Mexico was often lonely and dangerous. Courier duty, shown above, was more so than most other jobs. Stagecoaches, telegraphs, and heliographs carried many messages, but the courier was needed to carry messages and warnings between the isolated camps or forts and troops in the field. (*Harper's Weekly*, October 9, 1886.)

Apache mother and child. The child is on a cradle board that can be slung on the back. (*Century*, May, 1887.)

Geronimo is shown a heliograph that could relay messages quickly across the desert. It was an important factor in ending the Apache wars. (Miles, 1896.)

A common marker in the Southwest. (Cozzens, 1876.)

Apache braves in summer dress. (*Century*, May, 1887.)

Apaches scalping soldiers. This drawing is another that has been used many times. As originally published in *Harper's Weekly*, it showed Modocs scalping Gen. Canby in California. (Miles, 1896.)

CAPT. CRAWFORD.

The body of Capt. Emmett Crawford is brought to Lang's ranch near Cloverdale. When U.S. troops were chasing Geronimo in Mexico, Mexican soldiers thought Crawford's Apache scouts were hostiles and fired on them. Crawford stepped out to tell them to stop and was shot in the head by a Mexican scout. (*Harper's Weekly*, April 10, 1886.)

Apache scouts sent out to catch renegades sometimes brought back a head as proof of their efficiency. (Miles, 1896.)

Victorio, one of the greatest Apache war chiefs, was killed in an ambush in Mexico in 1880. (Ladd, 1891.)

Almost 300 Chiricahuas surrendered to Gen. Crook in 1886. Geronimo followed, saying "Once I moved about like the wind. Now I surrender to you and that is all." The next night, however, he got drunk and escaped with 40 followers. He remained hostile for another five months before surrendering to Gen. Miles. (Kelsey, 1901.)

A Comanche buffalo dance. The bison was important to
Comanche life, providing the tribe with food, clothing,
utensils, string, teepee covering and almost everything
else the Indians needed. They bartered the skins for cloth,
beads, and guns. (Eastman, 1874.)

Comanche on horseback, from an early
drawing. (Goodrich, 1849.)

Apache wickiups spread along the valley of the Mimbres
River. The domed huts were covered with brush or skins.
(Cozzens, 1876.)

Scout inspects deserted wickiup. (Whipple,
1853-4.)

Trouble near Fort Selden—a cowboy, insulted when an owner demanded a disputed steer be cut out of the herd, chases him off with a few bullets. (Powers, 1872.)

Comanches were a menace to travelers on the plains. Here they are preparing to attack a wagon train. (Cardona, 1892.)

Traveler Stephen Powers, who toured alone from coast to coast, is captured by Apaches near the New Mexico-Arizona border. (Powers, 1872.)

THE NAVAJO

THE NAVAJO TRIBE celebrated the 100th anniversary of its return to its homeland in 1968. Hundreds of Indians gathered at the Bosque Redondo and re-enacted the signing of the 1868 peace treaty and then made a symbolic march home. The Indians wore historic costumes and used traditional means of transportation while passing through the towns, but they rode a bus between cities.

Navajo braves in Santa Fe to discuss a truce with Comanches who were raiding the Bosque Redondo reservation. (Bell, 1870.)

Navajo in their best clothes make their way toward the agency for a head count and monthly rations. (Beadle, 1878.)

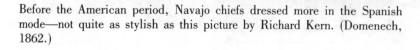

Before the American period, Navajo chiefs dressed more in the Spanish mode—not quite as stylish as this picture by Richard Kern. (Domenech, 1862.)

FOR THE FIRST HALF of the 19th century, the Navajo roamed and raided as they had for hundreds of wears. In 1846, after New Mexico had been taken by Kearny's troops, Col. Alexander Doniphan marched out of Santa Fe with several hundred soldiers. His target was the Navajo tribe to the west. One column moved to the San Juan area and swept south. Another went up the Puerco River. Between them, they pinched a good part of the Navajo and collected them at Big Bear Springs, where Fort Wingate is today. There the Navajo signed the first of their treaties with the U.S. government.

The Navajo sweathouse is a primitive sauna. Water is poured over heated rocks; steam rises and fills the small, insulated hut. After an hour or two of sweating and singing, the Indians dash out and leap into a snowbank or stream. (B.A.E. *Report*, 1886-7.)

Navajo woman weaving a saddle blanket. The size of the loom determines the size of the finished work. Saddle blankets on this type of loom can be made with a minimum of work. Larger looms for rugs mean that the weaver must move around to pass the shuttle through the wool. (B.A.E. *Report*, 1882.)

The Navajo arrived in the Southwest about 500 years ago and began raiding the peaceful Pueblo Indians. The Apaches first appeared in Texas in the middle of the 16th century and were driven west into New Mexico by the Comanches.

This weaving scene of the 1870s would be the same on many parts of the Navajo reservation today. (*Harper's*, August, 1876.)

This drawing of a train was made by Choh, a young Navajo living near Fort Wingate. The sketch was made from memory and shows an unusually realistic style. (*Mag. of Am. Hist.*, Dec., 1889.)

Workshop of a Navajo silversmith. The Navajos learned the craft at the Bosque Redondo reservation near Fort Sumner. They began by counterfeiting metal ration discs issued by the army. They switched to silver work after they returned to their homelands. (Bur. of Eth. Report. 1890-1.)

THE NAVAJO · 163

Navajo shepherdess tends her flock in solitude on the reservation. (Brooks, 1887.)

Navajo woman (below) weaving a belt. (*Bur. of Eth. Report*, 1881-2.)

THE NAVAJO learned weaving from the Pueblo Indians in the 17th century. By the beginning of the 19th, they were the best weavers in the Southwest.

The same types of looms and spinning sticks have been used for 300 years.

The patterns used today were introduced by traders in the 1870s, and analine dyes supplied by them gradually replaced duller vegetable dyes. By 1890, the Navajo were selling all of their weaving.

William Arny, the bearded one, led this group of Utes and Jicarilla Apaches and their agents on an exploration of the area between the San Juan and the Colorado rivers. (*Harper's Weekly*, Aug. 22, 1868.)

KIT CARSON was born in Kentucky and came west at the age of 17 in 1826. He hunted and trapped from Chihuahua to Montana, drove sheep to California, and gained fame as John C. Fremont's guide on two expeditions. A colonel during the Civil War, he rounded up the Navajos in a winter campaign in 1863-4. He died in Fort Lyons, Colo., in 1868.

He was a small, sandy-haired modest man. When shown a dime novel with a picture of him holding a swooning woman and fighting off Indians, he stared at it for a long moment and said, "This here might have happened, but I ain't got no recollection of it."

Romanticized Carson was the basis for dime novels, TV shows and movies. (Above, Cozzens, 1876. Below, Beadle, 1878.)

Authentic sketch of Carson from a photograph. (Richardson, 1867.)

Carson in Union army uniform, from a photo. (Conard, 1891.)

Lt. Zebulon Pike led spying expedition into New Mexico. He was captured in Colorado in 1807 and brought to Mexico. His report helped start the Santa Fe trade. (Dunn, 1886.)

THEY LED THE WAY

Ceran St. Vrain partnered with the Bent brothers, brought Kit Carson west, lived in a lavish hacienda in Mora. (Conard, 1891.)

James P. Beckworth, a mulatto, trapped in New Mexico and later became chief of the Crows. (Beckworth, 1856.)

Richens Lacy "Uncle Dick" Wootton came to New Mexico in 1838, built 26 miles of toll road in Raton Pass in 1860. (Conard, 1891.)

Don Jesus G. Abreu, a Santa Fe boy, clerked in a Kentucky store, then moved to Missouri while he attended school on the savings he had garnered out of his wages of fifty cents a day. He returned to New Mexico and become a merchant at Rayado. (Haines, 1891.)

Solomon Luna was a prominent sheep owner. The Luna family once owned 150,000 head of sheep. Los Lunas is named for the family. (Haines, 1891.)

Rep. Stephen Elkins delayed statehood for New Mexico for 39 years by alienating Southern congressional votes. (*Leslie's*, Oct. 25, 1884.)

Col. J. Francisco Chaves, soldier, politician, attorney, educator, was murdered at Pinos Wells in 1904. (Haines, 1891.)

L. Bradford Prince came from New York in 1878 when he was appointed chief justice of the New Mexico supremè court. He served until 1882 and was appointed governor of the territory in 1889. (*Adobeland*, Aug. 1, 1891.)

Chief Narbona of the Navajo was killed by U.S. troops during a short fight while arranging a treaty between the two forces in 1849. (Simpson, 1850.)

Michael Cooney was the brother of James Cooney, who found gold in the Pinos Altos Mts. Michael took James' interests after he was killed by Apaches and became a leading figure in southwestern New Mexico. (Haines, 1891.)

Henry Lambert, a former chef for Presidents Lincoln and Grant, built the St. James Hotel in Cimarron in 1872. The hotel has had a lively history and is still in business. (Haines, 1891.)

Judge Warren Bristol came to New Mexico in 1872 from Minnesota to become a justice of the territorial supreme court. He presided at the trial of Billy the Kid in Mesilla. Bristol moved to Deming in 1885. (Haines, 1891.)

L. M. Keithley was the first Anglo settler in Las Vegas. He arrived there in 1839 and started a store and trading post. (Wilson, 1880.)

Nestor Armijo was born in Albuquerque and educated in St. Louis. He was a banker in Chihuahua, Mexico, until he escaped during the revolution of 1872 and moved to Las Cruces. (Haines, 1891.)

Lucien Maxwell owned the largest land grant in the world. It stretched from Springer to the Las Animas River, Elizabethtown to Raton—1,714,764 acres. (Conard, 1891.)

THE COMING OF COMMERCE

TRADE IN NEW MEXICO began in prehistoric times when Indians bartered at established centers like Taos Pueblo and the pueblo of Las Humanas that is now Gran Quivira.

New Mexico has always had relatively little industry and has depended heavily on trade and commerce. Supplies and goods traveled up the Camino Real to Santa Fe and along other primitive trails to other parts of the West. Heavy trading with the Midwest began in the 19th century when great wagons rumbled over the Santa Fe Trail. The traders fought bad weather, Indians, and dry-land pirates to bring their goods to Santa Fe.

Rich veins of gold were discovered at about the time of the Civil War, but nothing could be done with them because of the isolation of the areas and the danger of hostile Indians.

Then the Army moved in to protect the miners and settlers. Large cattle ranches started in the 1870s to supply the soldiers and a cycle of commerce began that is still going.

The railroads arrived to bring immigrants and settlers to take the open land, work the mines and swell the territory's population from 91,874 in 1870 to almost 200,000 by 1900. With the railroads came would-be cowboys, foreign remittance men, gamblers, tourists, tubuculars—just about every example of the human species.

New Mexico has always received much of its income from tourism and government spending.

The early reports on the area, from Cabeza de Vaca's to Zebulon Pike's, helped promote New Mexico. During the last half of the 19th century, many magazine articles, books, and government reports boosted the territory with tales of fertile land, rich gold strikes, buried treasure, fantastic scenery, a healthy climate, and the two subjects that have probably been most important to New Mexico tourism: cowboys and Indians.

Though many of the reports were fanciful, they brought the people who turned New Mexico into a thriving state.

The U.S. government, like the Spanish and Mexican ones, has had an important part in New Mexico's economy. The military arm, especially, has always had a big stake in the area since the days of matchlock muskets when careful soldiers waited patiently for a burning cord to ignite a flash pan of powder to fire their gun and hoped that the ball and powder hadn't fallen out of the barrel. Now New Mexico plays an important part in future flights into space.

THE SPANISH conquistadores were disappointed in their search for gold, silver or quicksilver. Except for the copper mines at Santa Rita, there are few records of mining activity until gold was discovered in the Ortiz Mountains in the 1820s. Though hampered at first by crude mining methods and land grant problems, the mines blossomed in the late 1880s to produce millions in gold and silver.

Gold strikes were made in most of the mountainous areas of New Mexico. Mining camps sprang up in the Mogollons and the Black Range in the 1870s. The towns were plagued by Apaches, but they survived to produce more millions in gold.

Ore was crushed in stamp mills such as this. A drive wheel lifted the vertical hammer rods, letting them fall to pulverize the rock. The thunder of these old mills rumbled across the valleys, and the foundations of these mills still can be seen in abandoned workings (Bell, 1870.)

Arrastra, powered by horse or burro, was used to grind ore under a heavy stone pulled around in a circular trough. (Drake, 1887.)

According to legend, Indian slave labor was used in the old Spanish mines of New Mexico. Actually, very little mining was done in those days. Simple ladders (right) made of notched logs were used in Indian pueblos and, later, in pit mines. (Ritch, 1885.)

Valley of the Santa Rita mines. (Bartlett, 1854.)

Triangular fort at the mines was built in 1803 by Francisco
Manuel Elguea. (Bartlett, 1854.)

Stoping in a mine. This method is not used in a strip mine such
as Santa Rita. (Thayer, 1888.)

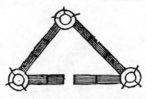

Plan of the presidio at Santa Rita. Fort Webster
was later built near this spot. (Johnson, 1848.)

FAMOUS MINES

COPPER was discovered at Santa Rita by Lt. Col.
Manuel Carrisco in 1800. Mining started in 1803
and for 34 years the mule trains carried ore
south to Mexico City for coinage at the royal mint.
Lt. Zebulon Pike, taken on a tourist's journey in
captivity through New Mexico, reported the mine
was producing 20,000 mule team loads of copper
each year.

Though the Apaches were not happy about
having a copper mine deep in their territory, the
area was relatively peaceful until 1837. In that
year the State of Chihuahua put a bounty on
Apaches. A warrior's scalp was worth $100, a
squaw's $50 and the death of an Indian child
was worth exactly $25 in gold pesos.

Two American entrepreneurs, Johnson and
Gleason, took advantage of this business
opportunity to stage a party at the dry lakes south
of Santa Rita. They invited the local Apaches
and their leader, Juan Jose. When the Indians
had gathered around presents piled in the desert,
a hidden howitzer loaded with slugs, nails, and
chains was fired into their midst. When Johnson
and Gleason and Mexican soldiers from the
presidio at Santa Rita finished their business,
some 400 Apaches were dead.

Juan Jose was one of the dead. Leadership of
the tribe now fell on the shoulders of a vengeful
firebrand called Mangas Colorado.

Under his guidance, the tribe cut off the
supplies from Chihuahua to Santa Rita. When
food ran short, the people of the town packed
their belongings and moved south. Somewhere
along the old trail to Chihuahua they were
ambushed and slaughtered.

Greed and revenge had begun a blood bath
in the Southwest that was to last for fifty years.

Lode mining works veins of ore to be processed above ground. (Thayer, 1888.)

Panning gold in the mountains near Cerrillos. (Gregg, 1849.)

METHODS of mining vary. Panning or washing separates gold from sand by running water which washes away the sand and leaves the heavier gold. Panning is used to find gold in stream beds and also to help locate veins of it in bedrock along the stream.

With lode mining, ore is taken from tunnels and sent to a mill for processing. Crushed ore is treated with acid to dissolve the gold for later recovery.

Lt. Emory's detachment, on reconnoissance, were among the first Anglos to pay an official visit to the Santa Rita mines. (Emory, 1848.)

NARROW GAUGE LINES

THE FIRST railroad entered New Mexico in 1879 after a dramatic stand by toll road owner Dick Wootton and engineer Ray Morley in Raton Pass. They and volunteers from Wootton's inn held off workmen of the Denver & Rio Grande line and saved the right of way for the Santa Fe line.

The Santa Fe went on to Las Vegas, Albuquerque, Socorro, and El Paso. Another line branched off from Belen west to California. Another, now abandoned, went west from El Paso through the Hermanos and Peloncillo Mts. into Arizona.

The Santa Fe railroad uses switchbacks to climb Raton Pass. The pass is at an elevation of 7,834 feet. (Thayer, 1888.)

Toltec Tunnel (left) bores through the mountains along the Denver & Rio Grande narrow gauge railway near Chama. (Ritch, 1885.)

The "Chili Line" railroad in the 1880s went from Santa Fe, past Embudo (above), and into Colorado. (Ingersoll, 1889.)

Portal to the tunnel at Toltec Gorge on the Denver & Rio Grande railroad in northern New Mexico. Efforts are being made to preserve this narrow-gauge line. (Ritch, 1882-83.)

The first railway train into New Mexico, from an old sketch. The railroad doomed the Santa Fe Trail. (Inman, 1893.)

Lucien Maxwell's magnificent home at Cimarron was always open to guests, including many noted travellers. (Inman, 1893.)

Starvation Peak towers above the village of Tecolote near Las Vegas. According to legend, about 120 Spanish colonists were besieged by Indians on the peak and starved to death. Hermit's Peak, in the vicinity, is another landmark with a legend. (Higgins, 1896.)

An early cattle ranch in San Miguel county, owned by Mrs. S. B. Davis. (Ritch, 1885.)

OPEN RANGE DAYS

THE CATTLE business in New Mexico, as in the rest of the West, was once considered a get-rich-quick scheme. The idea was to lease, buy, or steal a piece of lush prairie, turn a few cows loose and let them breed into a fortune.

Things were not that easy.

Weather and diseases were highest on the list of pitfalls. A dry year, a snowstorm, or an epidemic could wipe out a ranch.

Rustlers were usually no menace, but occasional thieves, homesteaders, or cowboys would help themselves to a beef. The total was sometimes high.

Mismanagement and ignorance were other good reasons for going broke. Some ranches were owned by Easterners or foreigners who misplaced their trust in foremen and employees who had no loyalty to faceless bosses.

Overhead was also important. There were no rich cowboys, but a lot of hungry ones ate into the profits.

With all these drawbacks, fantastic profits still could be made by a rancher with good luck and experience.

New Mexico cattleman Charlie Siringo once estimated that a cow cost $4.75 to raise and $5.75 to get it to Chicago, where it could be sold for about $28.50—a profit of $18.

A cowboy trying to rope a steer this way, without dallying the lariat around his saddle horn, would lose either his rope or his arm. (Siringo, c1886.)

Any cowboy would be amazed to see such a neat, orderly column of cattle as drawn by this Easterner. (Siringo, c1886.)

Lambs in a corral on a ranch near Santa Fe. The sheep business in New Mexico is an old and respected one, with little of the friction with cattlemen that was seen in other parts of the West. (*Special Report*, 1892.)

Wool from one clipping on a New Mexico sheep ranch is shown ready for shipment. Profits on sheep could be high, but the business was plagued by the same troubles, including rustling, as the cattle business. (*Special Report*, 1892.)

PENITENTE BROTHERS

THE THIRD ORDER of St. Francis was founded in 1218 when painful penance was common.

It was introduced into New Mexico in 1598. Don Juan de Onate and his soldiers celebrated Holy Week with penance and scourging.

Though the custom died down in Europe, it continued in New Mexico. A group related to the Third Order became the Penitentes, or Brothers of Light. The Penitentes were sometimes the only religious organization in remote mountain villages that saw a priest only a few times a year.

In 1828, the new Mexican government expelled most Franciscan priests from Mexico and New Mexico. The Brothers of Light were left without leadership and sponsorship. They became an underground organization, unrecognized by the Catholic Church. While the Church ignored them, the Penitentes continued their old rites in a sort of open secrecy.

This scene (left) appears to be a masochistic frolic rather than a solemn religious rite. (*Harper's*, May, 1885.)

Night procession of hooded penitentes is led by the "pitero", whose shrill piping may be heard for miles in the high New Mexico mountains. (Darley, 1893.)

IN THE 19th century, Penitente ceremonies were more open and common than today. Early traders, usually Protestants, wrote scathing accounts of the Holy Week rites without mentioning or understanding the religious motives of the Brothers of Light.

Charles F. Lummis, in 1888, was the first to photograph the crucifixion. He did this with the protection of armed friends and later was almost murdered.

The Penitentes became more secretive toward the end of the 19th century. Few Anglos were invited to see ceremonies. Uninvited ones were turned away, sometimes beaten, sometimes killed.

Magazine writer Carl Taylor took pictures of Penitente ceremonies near Tijeras in 1936. Before he could mail off his pictures and story he was found shot to death in his lonely cabin. The pictures were gone.

A Penitente is crucified on Good Friday. Today he is bound to the cross on the local Calvary. In many villages in the last century he was actually nailed to the cross. (Darley, 1893.)

Many Anglos saw the Penitente rites including, shown above, Alex Darley, who wrote a lurid account of them. (Darley, 1893.)

The reata torture as depicted by Alex Darley. Methods of penance included scourging with cactus whips, cactus bound around the chest and head, and legs bound with cactus, rawhide, or chains. (Darley, 1893.)

Procession of Penitentes at San Antonito, a small village in the Sandias. (Harper's Weekly, Sept. 7, 1889.)

Penitentes on their way to the local Calvary. (Darley, 1893.)

LEYES

para

EL GOBIERNO DEL TERRITORIO DE

NUEVO MEJICO.

TESTAMENTARIAS.

SECCION 1. Las leyes hasta ahora vigentes relativas á herencias, repartimientos, ultimas voluntades y testamentos segun estàn contenidas en el tratado sobre estas materias escrito por Pedro Murillo de Lara, quedaràn vigentes en todo lo que son conformes con la constitucion de los Estados Unidos y estatutos tambien vigentes

2 Los Prefectos concederan letras credenciales para testamenterias y para Abintestatos.

3 Las latras para testamentarias y Abintestatos serán concedidas en el condado en qu el hogar ó lugar de residencia del difunto estubiere ubicado. Si no tenia hogar ó lugar de residencia al tiempo de su muerte y poseyera tierras las letras credenciales se concederán en el condado en s tierras ó parte de ito no tenia hogar ó cia y no poseia tierdrán concederse en m ir'ò ó donde etuarte de sus bienes. Si

LAWS

for

THE GOVERNMENT OF THE TERRITORY OF

NEW MEXICO.

ADMINISTRATIONS.

Section 1. The laws *heretofore* in force concerning descents, distributions, wills and testaments, as contained in the treatise on these subjects *w* itten by ·Pedro Murillo De Lorde, shall remain in force so far as *they* are in conformity *with the* Constitution *of the* United States and the State laws in force for the time being.

2 The prefects shall grant letters testamentary and of administration

3 Letters testamentary and of administration shall be granted in the county in which the mansion house or place of abode of the deceased is situated. If he had no mansion house or place of abode at the time of his death, and be possessed of lands, letters shall be granted in the county in which the lands or a part thereof lies.

If' the deceased had no mansion house or place of abode, and *was* not possessed of lands, letters may be granted in the county in which he died or where the greater part of his .

Page from the Kearny Code (above), the first book printed in New Mexico after U.S. occupation. Done in 1846, it was the initial code of laws for the new territory, with text in Spanish and English. Printing was done on the old hand-press brought by Josiah Gregg in 1834 and owned by Padre Martinez at the time of the invasion. (From original in Museum of New Mexico.)

CUADERNO

DE ORTOGRAFIA.

DEDICADO A LOS NIÑOS DE LOS SEÑO-

RES MARTINES DE TAOS.

Santa Fe 1834 Imprenta de Ramon Abreu á Cargo de Jesus Maria Baca

BOOKS AND THE LAWS

The first book printed in New Mexico was a small spelling book, or *cuaderno de ortografia*, printed at Santa Fe late in 1834. Ramon Abreu owned the press at that time and Jesus Maria Baca was the printer. Padre Martinez wrote the little book, shown here in actual page size, and later owned the press. (Museum of New Mexico.)

THE BAD AND THE BRAVE

NEW MEXICO'S BEST KNOWN OUTLAW, Billy the Kid, overshadows the many others who visited or operated in the Territory.

Not that New Mexico was a paradise for outlaws. It was a crossroads, a sort of stopping place for the famous and infamous. Some stayed; others passed through on their way to safety or fame—as their own case may be.

Clay Allison was one of the West's deadliest killers. He liked to get drunk and ride the streets of Cimarron dressed in a gun belt, boots, and hat—nothing else.

Marino Leyba and his men robbed travelers in the San Pedros until the gang was captured, one by one, and taken to Albuquerque where they were quickly lynched.

Charles Kennedy kept an unusual inn high in the mountains near Elizabethtown in the early 1870s. Some of his more affluent customers didn't leave the place. Outraged citizens found human bones buried in his yard and hanged him, appropriately enough, in a slaughter house.

Many other well known Western lawmen or outlaws not generally associated with New Mexico spent time in the Territory. Doc Holliday had a dental office in Las Vegas while he dabbled in stage robbery and murder. Jesse James visited the town in its toughest days to see if there was room for him. He put up at the Montezuma Hotel and said he was a railroad man. He decided Las Vegas was too tough for him and moved on. Wyatt Earp had a profitable bunco game in Albuquerque's Old Town in 1882 until forced to move on.

Roy Bean lived in Mesilla before he was Law West of the Pecos. Bob Ford, killer of Jesse James, had a saloon in Las Vegas in 1889. Soapy Smith, king of the Yukon confidence men, learned many of his tricks in New Mexico. Buffalo Bill Cody recruited cowboys and Indians for his wild west show in the Cimarron area.

Tom Horn was an Army scout in New Mexico before becoming a hired killer in Wyoming. Butch Cassidy and his Hole-in-the-Wall Gang hid out in New Mexico when things were too hot for them in Wyoming. Lou Blonger, Denver's crime king of the early 1900s, was a deputy marshal of Albuquerque in 1882. Burton C. Mossman, founder of the Arizona Rangers, grew up near Las Cruces and returned to the Pecos area to settle after travels in Arizona and Montana.

Bill Tilghman, Mysterious Dave Mather, Long Haired Jim Courtright, Bat Masterson, and even (so early biographies say) Wild Bill Hickock visited New Mexico.

But New Mexico was no haven for badmen. Justice was often fast and final, and if not swift enough by legal means, the citizens were willing to uncoil a rope.

Colorado bandit Charles Allison and his gang were captured by detective Frank Hyatt at a livery stable at 115 First St. in Albuquerque in 1881. Allison had specialized in stage and train robberies. He was sentenced to 37 years in the Colorado pen.

Filomeno Gallotti (below) and several others murdered four of his countrymen in Denver in 1875. He was tracked to Taos by detectives W. Frank Smith (left) and James Lewis, who grabbed Gallotti's gun hand to avoid trouble.

A local man named Thaw (right) had posed as a sheep buyer to lure Gallotti into the trap. (Both pictures from Cook, 1892.)

Slap Jack Bill (The Pride of the Panhandle) and Bull S. Jack were arrested for the robbery sketched below. They are shown being questioned by a U.S. Marshal in Santa Fe. (Hayes, 1880.)

NOTICE!
TO THIEVES, THUGS, FAKIRS AND BUNKO-STEERERS,
Among Whom Are

J. J. HARLIN, alias "Off Wheeler;" SAW DUST CHARLIE, Wm. HEDGES, BILLY THE KID, Billy Mullin, Little Jack, The Cuter, Pock-Marked Kid, and about Twenty Others:

If Found within the Limits of this City after TEN O'CLOCK P. M., this Night, you will be Invited to attend a GRAND NECK-TIE PARTY,

The Expense of which will be borne by

100 Substantial Citizens.

Las Vegas, March 24th. 1882.

FOR SOME SIX months, an infamous group of thieves, killers, and con men called the Dodge City Gang ruled the new town of East Las Vegas. Their leader was a dapper gent known as Hoodoo Brown. A justice of the peace, Brown held court in a saloon and rapped for attention with his Winchester.

The gang fled Las Vegas in March, 1880, after one of its members, policeman J. J. Webb, killed and robbed a rancher.

A warning poster was distributed by the Las Vegas vigilantes. Many copies of this poster, usually altered, have been printed. In some copies the date has been changed to 1881 because Billy the Kid was not alive in 1882. However, the Billy mentioned in this original was counterfeiter William Wilson. (Las Vegas, 1882.)

THE HOLDUP shown on the right happened in September, 1879, just a few miles out of Las Vegas. The stage to Santa Fe was stopped at Tecolote. The passengers filed out and were ordered to sit on a nearby log. Ex-Gov. William Arny had hidden his money. One of the bandits, possibly Doc Holliday, suggested that they search "the antedeluvian gentleman" again. The money was found on the second try.

Some of the hold-up men were members of the Dodge City Gang and the Las Vegas police force. Slap Jack Bill and Bull S. Jack were turned loose.

"Road Agents at Work" was drawn by Harper's artist W. A. Rogers, who was either an eyewitness or talked with the robbery victims the next day. (Hayes, 1880.)

A quarrel over cards at a New Mexico ranch as sketched by Frederic Remington. Time went slowly during winters on the ranches. There was little work and tempers were short. Scenes like this were common. (*Harper's Weekly*, April 23, 1887.)

Billy the Kid is killed by Sheriff Pat Garrett in Pete Maxwell's
bedroom at Fort Sumner. (Garrett, 1882.)

BILLY, THE KID

Best known picture of Billy the Kid. (Garrett,
1882.)

Pat Garrett had a controversial life. He was murdered in 1908.
(Garrett, 1882.)

Billy the Kid escaped from the Lincoln County jail in the courthouse on April 28, 1881. He shot one guard on the stairs, grabbed a shotgun and shot the second guard in the street. He found a horse, leaped into the saddle, fell off, jumped on again and rode off. (Garrett, 1882.)

Billy, Dave Rudabaugh, Billy Wilson, and Tom Pickett were captured on December 23, 1880, when they were hiding in a stone shack at Stinking Springs, near Ft. Sumner. Garrett and his posse killed Charlie Bowdre and cut off the fugitives' food supplies until they surrendered. (Garrett, 1882.)

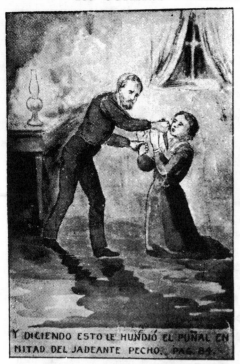

Vicente Silva lured his wife to their ranch north of Las Vegas and stabbed her. (De-Baca, 1896.)

Gabriel Sandoval, Silva's brother-in-law, was killed and buried in an abandoned cesspool. (DeBaca, 1896.)

THE FORTY BANDIDOS

VICENTE SILVA, saloonkeeper, operated in the Las Vegas area for about 15 years. He arrived in old Las Vegas in about 1875 and set up a saloon, the Imperial, that ran day and night.

He moved outside the law in about 1888. His gang, called the 40 Thieves, specialized in murder and rustling. By 1891 the town was ruled by thieves. In 1892, the owner of some stolen horses persuaded one of the gang, Patricio Maes, to show him where the horses had been hidden at one of Silva's ranches.

Informer Patricio Maes was tried by the gang and hanged from a bridge. (De-Baca, 1896.)

Cecilio Lucero murdered his cousin and a shepherd, tied the bodies behind two burros and let them remove the evidence. (Debaca, 1896.)

JIRÓ EL ESCOTILLÓN CON RUIDO ESPANTOSO Y CONMOVEDOR. PAG.112

Two of the 40 Thieves were hanged for murder. (DeBaca, 1896.)

Vicente Silva. (DeBaca, 1896.)

SILVA was an outlaw after the discovery of the stolen horses. He sneaked back to Las Vegas to order the execution of the informer, Maes, and then killed his brother-in-law and wife.

After her burial, one of the members of the gang stepped up behind him, put his revolver behind the leader's ear and fired. Exit Silva.

SILVA CAYÓ AL SUELO COMO HERIDO POR EL RAYO, PARA NO LEVANTARSE MAS. PAG. 87.

The end of Silva—murdered by his own henchman. (DeBaca, 1896.)

TODOS CLAMABAN LA VENGANZA. PAG. 96.

Cecilio Lucero was lynched for his crimes. (DeBaca, 1896.)

CON BASTANTE TRABAJO Y Á FUERZA DE PALANCAS É INGENIO LO PUSIERON EN UN CARRO. PAG. 52.

The gang stole a safe from a Los Alamos store and found only $40 and postage stamps in it. (DeBaca, 1896.)

A HERITAGE PRESERVED

THE END OF THE NINETEENTH CENTURY saw rapid improvements in New Mexico's life and economy. The first telephones in New Mexico were used in Santa Fe in 1881. Graded, quality cattle replaced the wild longhorns. Cattle growers supplemented their stock with once-hated sheep. Albuquerque was lit by electricity in the 1890s.

The Twentieth Century brought more changes. New colleges began. Oil was discovered in Eddy County in 1909. Statehood came in 1912. Oil wells blossomed at Artesia and in the San Juan country in 1922. In 1945, almost a hundred years after Kearny's troops marched into New Mexico, the world boldly threw itself into the Atomic Age in one tremendous explosion near Alamogordo.

By this time the old *torreóns* in the Manzano Mountain towns were gone. Drought and mismanagement had turned plains into deserts. Vandals and treasure hunters with picks, shovels, and sometimes dynamite had worked over ghost towns and forts.

Many of the old landmarks are gone. Huning Castle was torn down in 1955. Not even a modern supermarket or parking lot marks its site. One historic house in Santa Fe was razed in 1968 as part of an urban renewal program. The old Palace Hotel in Cerrillos was burned by vandals in 1968.

But not everything has been lost. The New Mexico Historic Sites Program was started as an ambitious project to benefit the state and its communities. Not only would historic sites be recognized and protected, but the work would generate more business, wages, and tourism. There was a long list of projects and possibilities—the preservation of Fort Sumner, Fort Cummings, the ghost towns of Mogollon and Shakespeare, Santa Fe's Barrio de Analco and, in the Taos area, the town plaza, Turley's mill, and several *torreóns*. The old plazas at West Las Vegas, San Miguel del Vado, the towns of Mesilla and Santa Cruz, and areas like the Galisteo Basin were other possibilities. Even while plans were going on, historic buildings were going down, including several old hotels in Albuquerque and whole blocks of buildings erected there when New Town was formed in the 1880s. But some projects were finished, and many buildings were saved and restored.

Other state and local organizations have carried on the work, not only with old buildings, but in projects in oral history, local history publications, museum collections and displays, and in other ways.

There has always been an interest in the history of New Mexico and the Southwest, but in recent years it seems that there has been a new awareness of what can be done to preserve our heritage, and of the educational and economic benefits that follow.

New Mexico's heritage has not been forgotten, and steps are being taken to keep it alive for the future.

SOURCES

ACKNOWLEDGMENTS

The pictures in this book came from nearly three hundred books, newspapers, or magazine articles. Many people suggested sources, found books, or gave access to rare items. These persons included David Otis Kelley, University Librarian, and Philip H. Fangman, Special Collections, University of New Mexico; Dr. John Polich, Mrs. Julia K. Shishkin, Mrs. J. R. Derryberry, and Nancy Gardetto, Museum of New Mexico; Jack D. Rittenhouse (who suggested and supervised this book), University of New Mexico Press; Dr. Myra Ellen Jenkins, New Mexico State Records Center and Archives; Mrs. Alys Freeze, Denver Public Library; Katherine McMahon, Albuquerque Public Library; Robert K. Dauner, University of New Mexico Photo Services; Phil Cooke, Press of the Territorian; Dale F. Giese; and Gil Campbell, U.S. Air Force Academy.

PICTURE SOURCES

Pictures have been reproduced from the source cited under each illustration, listed below in detail. Readers who wish to verify a fact in a caption will not necessarily find it in the same source as that of a picture.

Abert, Lt. James W. *Report of a Military Reconnoissance of the Arkansas, Rio Del Norte and Rio Gila,* Washington: 1847.

Adobeland. Albuquerque: 1881.

Adams, Eleanor. *The Missions of New Mexico, 1776.* Albuquerque: 1956.

Agriculture, U.S. Dept. of. *Special Report on the Sheep Industry.* Washington: 1892.

Bartlett, John R. *Personal Narrative of Explorations and Incidents in Texas, New Mexico, California, Sonora and Chihuahua.* London: 1854.

Beadle, John H. *The Undeveloped West . . .* Philadelphia: 1873.

————. *Western Wilds . . .* Cincinnati: 1881.

Beckwourth, James P. *My Life and Adventures.* New York: 1856.

Bell, William A. *New Tracks in North America.* London and New York: 1870.

Bourke, John. *Snake Dance of the Moquis.* London: 1884.

Brooks, Eldridge S. *The Story of the American Indian.* Boston: 1887.

Brown, William Horace. *The Glory Seekers.* Chicago: 1906.

Cady, Annie Cole. *The American Continent and its Inhabitants Before Columbus.* Philadelphia: 1893.

Cardona, Adalberto de, *De Mexico a Chicago y Nueva York.* Mexico: 1892.

Carruth, J. A. *Business Directory of Arizona and New Mexico.* Las Vegas: 1897.

Census, U.S. Bureau of. *Report on Indians Taxed and Indians Not Taxed.* Washington: 1890.

Century Magazine. New York: 1882-98.

Champney, Elizabeth W. *Great Grandmother's Girls in New Mexico.* Boston: 1888.

Chase, Charles M. *An Editor's Run in Colorado and New Mexico.* Montpelier, Vermont: 1882.

Conard, Howard L. *Uncle Dick Wootton.* Chicago: 1891.

Cook, David J. *Hands Up.* Denver: 1892.

Cozzens, Samuel W. *The Marvelous Country.* Boston: 1876.

Darley, Alex M. *The Passionists of the Southwest.* Pueblo, Colo.: 1893.

Daunt, Achilles. *With Pack and Rifle in the Far Southwest.* London: 1886.

Davis, W. W. H. *El Gringo.* New York: 1857.

De Baca, Manuel, *Vicente Silva,* Las Vegas: 1896.

Domenech, L'abbe Em. de. *Voyage Dans les Grands Deserts.* Paris: 1862.

Drake, Samuel Adams. *The Making of the Great West.* New York: 1887.

Dunn, J. P. Jr. *Massacres of the Mountains.* New York: 1886.

Eastman, Edwin. *Seven and Nine Years Among the Comanches and Apaches.* Jersey City, N.J.: c1873.

Ellis, Edward S. *History of Our Country.* Cincinnati: 1900.

Emory, W. H. *Notes on a Military Reconnoissance from Fort Leavenworth to San Diego.* Washington: 1848.

————. *Report on the U.S. and Mexican Boundary Survey.* Washington: 1859.

Ethnology, U.S. Bureau of. *Annual Report.* Washington: 1880-90.

Frost, John. *History of Mexico and its Wars.* New Orleans: 1882.

————. *Indian Wars of the United States.* Auburn, N.Y.: 1851.

————. *Thrilling Adventures Among the Indians.* Philadelphia: 1851.

Frost, Max. *New Mexico.* Santa Fe: 1894.

Garrett, Pat F. *Authentic Life of Billy the Kid.* Santa Fe: 1882.

Goodrich, Samuel G. *Manners, Customs and Antiquities of the Indians.* Boston: 1849.

Gregg, Josiah. *Commerce of the Prairies.* New York: 1849.

————. *Scenes and Incidents.* Philadelphia: 1856.

Haines, Helen. *History of New Mexico.* New York: 1891.

Harper's Magazine. New York: 1853-91.

Harper's Young People. New York: 1889-91.

Harper's Weekly. New York: 1861-96.

Hayes, A. A. *New Colorado and the Santa Fe Trail.* New York: 1880.

Higgins, C. A. *Guide to the Pacific Coast.* Chicago and New York: 1896.

Howe, Henry. *The Great West.* New York: 1852.

Hughes, John T. *Doniphan's Expedition.* Cincinnati: 1850.

Illustrated History of New Mexico. Chicago: 1895.

Ingersoll, Ernest. *The Crest of the Continent.* Chicago: 1889.

Inman, Col. Henry. *The Old Santa Fe Trail.* New York: 1897.

Ives, Lt. Joseph C. *Report Upon the Colorado River of the West.* Washington: 1861.

Johnson, R. V. and C. C. Buel, eds. *Battles and Leaders of the Civil War.* New York: 1887.

Johnston, Abraham. *Journal.* Washington: 1848.

Journal of American Ethnology and Archeology. Boston and New York: 1891.

Kelsey, D. M. *History of Our Wild West.* Chicago: 1901.

Ladd, Horatio. *The Story of New Mexico.* Boston: 1891.

Land of Sunshine. Los Angeles: 1894-8.

Las Vegas Hot Springs. Chicago: 1887.

Leslie's Illustrated Weekly. New York: 1877-94.

London Illustrated News. London: 1854.

Lossing, Benson J. *Pictorial Field Book of the Civil War in America.* Hartford: 1876-8.

Macomb, John H. *Report of the Exploring Expedition from Santa Fe, N.M. . . .* Washington: 1876.

Magazine of American History. 1889.

Marcy, Randolph B. *Thirty Years of Army Life on the Border.* New York: 1866.

Mayer, Brantz. *Mexico.* Hartford: 1852.

McKee, James C. *Narrative of the Surrender of . . . U.S. Forces at Fort Fillmore, N.M.* Prescott: 1878.

Miles, Nelson A. *Personal Recollections.* Chicago and New York: 1896.

Mills, T. B. *San Miguel County, Illustrated.* Las Vegas: 1885.

Mollhausen, Balduin. *Diary of a Journey from the Mississippi to the Coasts of the Pacific.* London: 1858.

Newberry, J. S. (See: Macomb.)

New Mexico, *Report of the Governor.* 1903.

Peters, DeWitt C. *Kit Carson's Life and Adventures.* Hartford: 1874.

————. *Life and Adventures of Kit Carson.* New York: 1858.

Popular Science. New York: 1874.

Powers, Stephen. *Afoot and Alone.* Hartford: 1872.

Reid, Mayne. *The Scalp Hunters.* New York: 1863.

Richardson, Albert. *Beyond the Mississippi.* Newark: 1867.

Richardson, William H. *Journal.* New York: 1848.

Ritch, William. *Official Report of the Territory of New Mexico.* Santa Fe: 1882-3.

————. *Aztlan.* Boston: 1885.

Roberts, Edward. *With the Invader.* San Francisco: 1885.

Sage, Rufus. *Scenes in the Rocky Mountains.* Philadelphia: 1854.

Santa Fe New Mexican. Santa Fe: 1881-2.

Schlagintweit, Robert von. *Die Santa Fe und Sudpacificbahn in Nordamerika.* Cologne, Germany: 1884.

Schoolcraft, Henry R. *Information reporting the History, Condition and Prospects of the Indian Tribes of the U.S.* Philadelphia: 1856.

Scribner's Magazine. New York: 1891-3.

Simpson, James H. *Report.* Washington: 1850.

Siringo, Charles. *A Texas Cowboy.* Chicago: c1886.

Sitgreaves, Capt. Lorenzo. *Report of an Expedition Down the Zuni and Colorado Rivers.* Washington: 1854.

Speer, William S., ed. *Encyclopedia of the New West.* Marshall, Tex.: 1881.

Steele, James W. *Rand, McNally and Company's New Overland Guide to the Pacific Coast.* Chicago and New York: 1888.

Sweetser, M. F. *King's Handbook of the U.S.* Buffalo: 1891.

Taylor, Benjamin F. *Short Ravelings from a Long Yarn.* Chicago: 1847.

Tenney, E. P. *Colorado and Homes in the New West.* Boston: 1880.

Thayer, William. *Marvels of the New West.* Norwich, Conn.: 1888.

Triplett, Col. Frank. *Conquering the Wilderness.* New York and St. Louis: 1885.

U.S. Geographical and Geological Survey *Report.* Washington: 1881.

U.S. Govt. Doc., 1874: 43rd Cong., 1st Sess., H.R. Ex. Doc. No. 206, on private land claims.

Van Tramp, John C. *Life in the West.* Columbus, Ohio: 1867.

Wallace, Susan E. *The Land of the Pueblos.* Troy, N.Y.: 1889.

Whipple, Lt. A. W. *Report.* Washington: 1856.

Wilson, H. T. *Historical Sketch of Las Vegas.* (Chicago: 1880.)

Winsor, Justin. *Narative and Critical History of America.* Boston and New York: 1886.

Wood, Stanley. *Over the Range to the Golden Gate.* Chicago: 1889.

INDEX

CHIEF JOSEPH & THE FLIGHT OF THE NEZ PERCE

CHIEF JOSEPH

& THE FLIGHT OF THE NEZ PERCE

The Untold Story of an American Tragedy

Kent Nerburn

HarperSanFrancisco
A Division of HarperCollinsPublishers

For Larry O'Neal
who has labored so selflessly for a people not his own and

for all the children of the Lapwai and the Colville
in whose hands the Nez Perce future lies

Contents

Part 3

A Time of Betrayal and Exile

Introduction

Searching for Joseph

History is but a tapestry of stories, imperfectly woven.

O N NOVEMBER 20, 1903, a tired, stoop-shouldered man with chestnut brown skin stood on the sidelines of a football game at the University of Washington in Seattle. He understood little of what was going on, but he followed the action with keen interest, enjoying the efforts of the young men and nodding approvingly whenever the ball carrier emerged unscathed from the pile of bodies after a tackle. His presence at the game so fascinated the other spectators that they seemed almost as interested in him as they did in the game itself.

This man, so seemingly engrossed in a game about which he understood little, was a sixty-three-year-old Nez Perce Indian named Hin-mah-too-yah-lat-kekht, or Thunder Rising in the Mountains. But to the American public he was known as Chief Joseph, "the Red Napoleon," the man who was reputed to have masterminded one of the most cunning military retreats in American history and to have outfoxed and outmaneuvered the best that the American army had to offer. He was America's greatest living Indian celebrity.

Joseph had come to Seattle at the request of Sam Hill, son-in-law of the railroad magnate James J. Hill, to give a speech in the Seattle Theater. It was but one speech of many he had given around the country over the previous decade in an effort to gain the return of his small band of Nez Perce to their homeland in the high Wallowa Valley in the mountains of eastern Oregon.

As at all his speeches, Joseph's Seattle appearance was a great civic event—a chance to see the man Buffalo Bill Cody called "the greatest Indian America ever produced" and whom photographer Edward Curtis praised as "one of the greatest men who ever lived." The auditorium was packed and the press and local dignitaries were in full attendance.

Most had heard of his previous speeches, in which he had recounted how his people had been forced to leave their land as part of a treaty his band had never signed; of the great exodus they had undertaken across the mountains of Idaho and Montana in search of freedom; of the sad exile they had endured in Kansas and Oklahoma; and of their continued exile on land not their own in the northeastern part of Washington on the Canadian border.

They had heard of his eloquent pleas for just treatment by the government, asking only that his people be treated as free men and women—free to travel, free to trade, free to talk and act and worship in accordance with their own conscience; his almost prayerful petition that the spirit of brotherhood might wash away the bloodstains that soaked the earth, that all people might live as one, smiled upon by the Creator, common children of a common land, living together beneath a common sky.

They sat in rapt anticipation, waiting for the legendary Indian leader to emerge and galvanize them with his rhetoric.

But the person who took the stage seemed anything but a noble orator. He was a worn and weary man, bent and bowlegged, dressed in full headdress and traditional chieftain regalia. He seemed more tragic than noble, more anachronistic than imposing.

Taking a drink from a glass of water and leaning heavily against a table, he began to speak, his words translated instantly by the interpreter who accompanied him. "I have a kind feeling in my heart for all of you," he said. "I am getting old and for some years past have made several efforts to be returned to my old home in Wallowa Valley, but without success.

"The government at Washington has always given me many flattering promises," he continued, "but up to the present time has utterly failed to fulfill any of its promises." He told of how he was not surprised because his life had been filled with broken promises, and of his dream to be buried by the side of his father and children.

"I hope you will all help me to return to the home of my childhood where my relatives and family are resting," he concluded. "Please assist me. I am thankful for your kind attention. That is all." Then he sat down.

The audience was respectful, even touched. But they were also stunned. This was not the speaker they had been led to expect, the man who had been favorably compared to the great orators of the Roman senate. The local paper even mocked his presentation, recreating his Indian language as "Um-mum-mum-halo-tum-tum-um-mum" and describing his appearance as "looking like a turkey cock on dress parade." They characterized his speech as "grunts" and implied that any meaning in the words had likely been invented by the translator.

The chief accepted all this with equanimity. He was used to both the adulation and vilification of the white public and government. But none of that was important to him. All he cared about was the fragile hope that he and his people someday would be allowed to return to their beloved Wallowa, the land that the Creator had given them and the earth that held their ancestors' bones.

He remained several more days in Seattle, signing autographs, posing for photographs, and visiting the University of Washington. Then he quietly returned to his home on the Colville Reservation, 350 miles from the city where he had just spoken and 200 miles from the Wallowa, where he hoped to spend his final days.

He lived on for less than a year, passing away quietly on September 21, 1904.

The agency doctor, who attended him in his illness, declared simply that the chief had succumbed to a "grief which ended in death."

He was never allowed to return to his homeland.

Joseph's story, and the story of the Nez Perce, has become part of the standard lore of the American Indian. Its outline has been presented to students by caring teachers and professors for years: Joseph, the Nez Perce chief, led 800 men, women, and children on a 1500-mile retreat after having been illegally forced from their homeland in Oregon by a U.S. government that was hungry for land and unwilling to meet its treaty obligations.

In the course of this journey they outmaneuvered five U.S. armies, assisted white travelers they met along the way, and managed to elude the best and brightest that the U.S. military had to offer. Finally, only forty miles from the Canadian border and freedom, the tired Nez Perce, slowed by their wounded and weary, were surrounded by the U.S. forces. They could have escaped by leaving the women and children and injured and elderly behind, but this Joseph was unwilling to do. Wrapping his blanket around his shoulders against the frigid winds of an approaching high plains Montana winter, he walked across the snow-swept battlefield and handed his rifle to the commanding officers of the U.S. military, speaking that now-famous sentence: "From where the sun now stands, I shall fight no more forever."

A fine story, full of pathos and nobility and all the poignancy of the American Indian struggle. A fine story, but false. Or, to be more accurate, only half true.

The real story, the true story, is every bit as poignant and every bit as dramatic. But it is obscured by the myth because the myth is so powerful and so perfectly suited to our American need to find nobility rather than tragedy in our past. It is also a myth of our own devise, and therein lies a story.

I first encountered the story of Chief Joseph fifteen years ago when I was working on the Red Lake Indian Reservation in the woods of northern Minnesota. I had been hired to lead a group of students in collecting the memories of the tribal elders.

My students were good, caring people who wanted to do right by their parents and grandparents. But they had no context from which to work. Many were poor readers and few knew anything about their own tribal history, much less the history of other tribes in America. In order to understand what their grandparents and great-grandparents had experienced, they needed to learn something about the lives of the native peoples who have lived on this land.

I knew I could not give them standard textbooks, nor did I want to. Instead, I wanted them to learn from the voices of native peoples without the intervening interpretive lens of non-native authors or a non-Indian teacher. So I decided to put together a small book containing the words of Indian leaders and thinkers. I was confident that, with careful research and proper framing, I could create something that would educate the students and prepare them for the undertaking before them.

I set about my task with cautious determination. I read through old documents and parsed arcane anthologies. I looked at old treaties and old diaries. I found voices, common and obscure, and collected them together into a document that seemed to represent the best of Indian expressions about what it meant to be a native person on this American continent.

The students were fascinated, but I were transfixed. In these native voices, I discovered a clarity and dignity that far surpassed anything I had ever encountered. It was as if I were hearing the most measured, well thought, and heartfelt oratory of which a human being is capable. It brought to mind the comment of the famous western sculptor, Frederick Remington: "There is a dignity about the social intercourse of old Indians which reminds me of a stroll through a winter forest."

And the oratory that touched me most deeply was the story told by Chief Joseph of the Nez Perce in a long, heartrending speech given to an assemblage of dignitaries in Washington, D.C., in 1878.

In his words I caught a glimpse of the true tragic dimensions of the Native American experience since the arrival of the European on these shores and of a quality of heart and dignity of spirit that we, as a nation, are poorer for having lost. Here was a man who embodied all that I believed about compassionate leadership, the kind of person I could gladly hold up as a model of worthy manhood to my students or my son.

Over the next fifteen years I continued to work on Indian issues. I published several books, continued to work among Indian people, speak on Indian subjects, and learn. It was more than an interest; it was almost a calling. In my corner of northern Minnesota, where nature dominates culture and the presence of the first people is strong, I grew, day by day, to believe that it is in the native people of this continent that some fundamental truth is vested. And all of this served only to deepen my respect and admiration for the man whose words I had transcribed for my students those fifteen years before.

So when the opportunity arose to do a book on Chief Joseph, I was excited. But I was also apprehensive. My time among native people had shown me that there is little they hold in greater disdain than non-natives dabbling in Indian issues for fun and profit. I did not wish to be the next person in this unsavory tradition. Still, I believed that Joseph was a man whose life and character should be better known and whose story was important—even central—to an understanding of who we as a nation are and who we might yet be. I wanted that story to be told—honestly, accessibly, and with compassionate sympathy. So I accepted the challenge.

The task was daunting. I could not claim to see through a native person's eyes, but neither did I wish to write a bloodless, analytical history. I wanted the story to have a heartbeat, and I wanted it to be written in such a way that native people who read it would say, "Yes, this *wasichu*, this *Soyapo*, this *jamokaman*, understood. This white man has done a good job."

So I armed myself with every book I could find, every monograph that could be extracted from every library I could access, every newspaper account I could dredge up from every publisher's morgue, and every personal testimony, both native and white, that existed in every archive, and interred myself beneath the material, hoping to read my way to the surface with some kind of understanding.

But, try as I might, something was wrong. Though the story was becoming clear, it was not coming to life. I was missing something essential. I needed to find a way to bring the reader closer to the heartbeat of the man and his experience. I needed to go to Nez Perce country, meet the people, feel the pulse and lifeblood that lay beneath all my research.

And so it was that I found myself several thousand miles from my home, wandering through some of the most beautiful, intimidating, and awe-inspiring country I had ever confronted, in search of a man I did not know how to find. My hope was to hear the story of Joseph from the Nez Perce themselves and to feel the presence of the earth they held so dear. For I knew that no Indian can be understood apart from the land of his or her birth and that to understand Joseph I needed to understand the heart and spirit of the land from which he had come.

This land the Nez Perce called their own—the land where Joseph was born and raised—is known as the Columbia Plateau. Now, as when the Nez Perce first encountered Lewis and Clark, this great broad continental shoulder between the Cascades and the first outcroppings of the mountains that will become the Rockies is almost unknown to the general population.

It is "fly-over" country, a blank spot on the map, a transition zone meant to be shot through or over or across by the fastest, most expeditious means possible. A few names might strike a momentary shiver into the hearts of people familiar with the West: Selway-Bitterroot Wilderness, Hells Canyon, River of No Return, even northern Idaho itself. But to anyone other than smoke jumpers and the smattering of residents who call the isolated cities and towns home, this essentially roadless wilderness area is a dark and woolly terra incognita where small-engine planes disappear in small poofs against inaccessible mountainsides, and forest fires sweep across expanses as vast as the state of Rhode Island.

Wandering through this landscape, I did not find those characterizations to be far wrong. It was a land of hillsides so vertical that a person must climb them on all fours, of the deepest gorge on the North American continent, where a person standing on the top looks down more than a mile to a tiny silver ribbon of water that, in fact, is a cataract roiling over boulders the size of houses. It was a land of sudden precipices, of high mountain meadows and cobalt blue lakes, of bald, dun-brown hills that roll like rumpled carpet until they disappear into a hazy, purple horizon.

Everywhere I went I was overwhelmed with the presence of the forces that had created this landscape. The dry river courses with cataracts larger than Niagara, now only echoes of the water that once roared over their surface. Mountains shoved up on impossible angles, a tectonic wreckage stretching for miles and covered now with endless expanses of dark green forest. Dried lava flows. Deep, impassable river gorges that cut like knife wounds into the flesh of the land. Rolling, grass-covered beds of long-forgotten seas.

I drove through these misted valleys, high mountain meadows, and dizzying gorges with something approaching awe. I could not help but feel a hint of what the white soldiers of the 1860s and '70s—fresh recruits from somewhere back east or foreign-born young boys trying to make their way in the new country—must have felt in the presence of this landscape. It was a sensation bordering on terror—a terror of scale, of vastness, of indifference; of knowing that you could be swallowed up in this land and disappear without a trace.

These were spaces of such greatness and emptiness that a wrong turn and an hour of walking could get you so lost and so far from rescue that your loudest cries for help could go unheard, your signal fires and gunshots to draw attention washed into silence by the rustling of the trees and the great, empty howlings of the wind. There was no doubt in my mind that the bones of many soldiers and trappers and miners lie unburied on these forbidding hillsides and will remain there undiscovered forever. And the thought that settlers dragged their wives into this country and told them to set up households in rude shacks and rough-hewn cabins made me shudder with a kind of shapeless dread.

Yet this was the land the Nez Perce called home. It was the place where they developed the most dominant culture in the native Northwest, ranging out from their home villages on the Plateau as far as the Pacific Ocean to the west and the pipestone quarries of Minnesota to the east. It was on their trails that Lewis and Clark fumbled their way across the mountains from buffalo country, in their canoes and with their guarantee of safe passage that the Corps of Discovery made its way down the Columbia toward the great western sea.

These were the people who felt such confidence in their life and ways that they opened their hearts and minds to anything brought in from the outside. They were the people who figured out how to make the strongest and most accurate bows of any native people; who learned how to geld horses using sharpened rocks, and could do so with such precision that Lewis and Clark said their facility at the task exceeded that of white men with their finely honed knives. They were the people who would make a cradle board with a hundred thousand beads on it, who would swim across the ice-laden Salmon River every day all winter to keep their bodies strong.

They were the tribe whose men often stood well over six feet while the American soldiers of the same era were averaging five feet six or five feet seven inches in height, whose women owned the lodges and food sources of the people and were empowered to sell them for their own profit, while white women of the time were told to subjugate themselves to the will of their husbands and submit to them in all things under the control of God and man.

I was in a land of giants, and, like every white interloper since the time of Lewis and Clark and the fur traders, I had to either grow to meet the experience or shrivel to my quivering, domestic scale, turn tail, and run. In spite of strong inclinations to the contrary, I decided to grow into the task. I would traverse this landscape, meet the people, take the chances at rejection and downright hostility, speak the truth, show my heart, and see what emerged.

I am no stranger to the reality of contemporary reservations. My time among native people in northern Minnesota and the Dakotas has disabused me of any naive romantic notions. I did not expect to find bronzed men towering over me on horseback or women running onto battlefields to attack advancing warriors with hatchets. But I did expect to find men and women who shared some of the basic characteristics of their ancestors. And I was not mistaken.

From my first contact, I sensed that these people were different from the other native people I have known. They did not seem wounded by the dominant American culture so much as masters of it. It was not that they had become the proverbial "apples"—red on the outside and white on the inside. Rather, they had figured out what American culture offered and had accepted it with a kind of contemptuous indifference as if, though it had emerged victorious, it was an adversary not quite worthy enough to merit the expenditure of any emotional or spiritual energy. To put it a different way, they seemed bigger than the cultural battle they had lost.

I don't want to put too fine a point on this. The primary reservation town of Spalding, just outside of Lewiston, Idaho, was the usual tragic assemblage of decaying houses with abandoned cars propped up on concrete blocks. It was unemployed men hanging around a gritty, cinder-block supermarket, too many government vehicles and workers driving on too-dirty streets, kids wandering around in oversized jackets, too many of them smoking, too many of them too young to be doing so.

But there was something else going on—something I couldn't put my finger on—and I confronted it every time I stopped in a store or on a corner or to pick up a hitchhiker. It had to do with a willingness to meet me eye to eye, a "who are you?" that had an honest openness to the possibility that I might be a good man, notwithstanding my whiteness, and that my skin color and *auslander* status would not necessarily be held against me.

Conversations did not get shut down with one-word answers. A request for directions did not get shunted aside with a muffled "I don't know" followed by a hurried exit. The people met me as I had hoped to be met: with a cautious skepticism and a willingness to listen. In some strange fashion, I felt like I was beginning to get a grasp on the character of the people from whom Joseph had sprung.

But none of my growing confidence and understanding prepared me for the response I would get when I mentioned the man himself. Eyes darkened. Body language changed. People glanced around as if worried that they were being observed. Some of this was clearly discomfort with the prospect of another white man come in search of the legendary Joseph. But there was something deeper here, something more personal. Joseph touched a chord in these people that resonated far below my understanding, and it was not some bright, sunlit, major-key harmonic.

All through the reservation I confronted this—in the Nez Perce interpretive center at Lapwai, in the reservation headquarters town of Spalding,
in the small village of Kamiah, where the strange mound of land called the
Heart of the Monster marks the spot where Coyote is said to have created
the Nez Perce from drops of a monster's blood. Everywhere I went, the
openness and friendliness became a hooded reticence when I mentioned
the name of Joseph.

Confused and troubled, I left the reservation and headed north toward
the town of Nespelem on the Colville Reservation, two hundred miles
to the northwest near the Canadian border in Washington. It was there on
the Colville Reservation that Chief Joseph and a small remnant of the tribe
had been forced to settle after their return from exile in Oklahoma and
there that Joseph himself is buried. I thought that perhaps I could get
some answers in this isolated, rolling country where Joseph's direct ancestors still live today.

Nespelem is far different from Spalding. Spalding is a Nez Perce town.
But Nespelem is the center for twelve tribes that were shoehorned together
by the U.S. government in the 1800s in an effort to amalgamate the native
peoples and reduce their landholdings to as small an area as possible. The
Nez Perce are just one of these twelve, and they reside here in an uneasy
peace with the eleven other tribes, many miles from their aboriginal homeland.

Over the years they have made this their home, and they are proud of
it. But it hurts and angers them that all the notoriety—and all the attendant benefit—resulting from their famous chief seems to accrue to the
Lapwai branch of the tribe, despite the fact that the Colville people are his
true heirs and inheritors and that it is near Nespelem that Joseph lived out
his later years and is buried. But if they feel slighted, they also feel protective. They are even more skeptical about "Joseph seekers" than their Nez
Perce brothers and sisters two hundred miles to the south.

After a few stops at gas stations and a few cautious inquiries, I was directed to some of the people in charge of the Nez Perce legacy in Nespelem.
These encounters proved to be even more disconcerting than the encounters at Lapwai. In short order I was measured, parsed, and dismissed with
ominously coded messages about seeking contact with people without
tribal approval. I left chastened and sobered and wondering about the
wisdom of my entire enterprise.

There was only one stop left. It was the town of Joseph, Oregon, two hundred miles south of Colville and a hundred miles from Lapwai across the jaw-dropping grandeur of the Snake River gorge. Far outside the borders of any contemporary reservation, the town stands on the aboriginal land where Joseph's band once lived and where the chief himself was raised. It is situated in the stunning, high mountain Wallowa valley, surrounded by tall, snow-covered peaks and graced in its center by a blue jewel of an alpine lake. It is easy to see why Joseph said, "I love that land more than all the rest of the world." Anyone who grew up here would feel the same.

Unlike Spalding, with its cinder-block grocery store and worn-down reservation housing, or Nespelem, with its few small gas stations and reservation stores, Joseph is a western, single-main-street tourist town filled with gift shops and massive post-and-beam bed-and-breakfasts and a plethora of boutique bronze casting foundries and their attendant galleries.

Large, representational bronze sculptures line the streets—high-quality, high-dollar, Charles M. Russell kinds of works, all depicting cowboy and Indian themes. The town is awash in romanticized Americana, all focused on frontier themes, all directly or indirectly related to Chief Joseph or his time. "The Chieftain Visitors Guide." "The Chief Joseph Days Rodeo." Cowboy bronzes, Indian jewelry. It's "the town that Joseph built," right in the middle of the beautiful, isolated, Switzerlandlike ancestral homeland of Joseph's band. Here Joseph is not a historical figure but a cultural commodity, a brand name, a hood ornament on the vehicle of American tourist enterprise.

But what struck me most was that the name Nez Perce, with its clumsy anglicized French origins, was nowhere to be seen. While the man who signified the tribe in the public imagination was memorialized on almost every sign and storefront, the tribe itself was almost nonexistent.

Slowly, I began to understand the Nez Perce ambivalence toward Joseph and their reticence toward me when I asked about him. The man was a conundrum that they could not easily resolve. White culture had elevated him to heroic, even iconic, status—after all, why was I there if not to continue the cultural canonization of Joseph?—while effectively expunging the Nez Perce people themselves from the national historical consciousness. This sort of hero worship fit perfectly with the American penchant for glorifying the individual, but it stood in direct opposition to the fundamental native belief that the group is more important than any individual member. Yet it was only through Joseph that the Nez Perce retained any cultural status or visibility. Without him, they would slip into the same cultural invisibility as the Potawatomi or the Lemhi or the Gros Ventres.

But I knew that this was only half the story. Sitting Bull and Crazy Horse are elevated by the Lakota people and, to a large extent, give the Lakota their identity within the larger context of American culture; Tecumseh is held in proud regard by the Shawnee; Geronimo is highly praised and revered among the Apache. Each of these tribes holds a similar cultural bias against celebrating the individual over the group, yet these men are proudly held up by their respective peoples and seen as a source of pride. Why would the Nez Perce feel any different about Joseph?

It took breakfast with a Nez Perce man in a small roadside café on the outskirts of Lewiston, Idaho, to lead me toward an answer. There, over Denver omelets and cups of coffee, he began talking about the astonishing, tragic journey that his people had undertaken in 1877—the very same journey that had initially fired my fascination with Joseph back when I had been compiling the book of native voices for my students on the Red Lake Reservation.

"What people don't realize," he said, "is that in the flight—the only thing that any white person knows or cares about us—Joseph was a bit player. He just took charge at the end because the other chiefs were gone. He didn't even want to go. But you look at the history books, it's all 'Joseph's journey,' 'Joseph's retreat.' Many of our people even see him as a coward and a traitor for surrendering. But without him no one pays any attention to us."

He gestured vaguely in the direction of the Bitterroot Mountains, which begin their ragged ascent just a few miles to the east of the restaurant where we were sitting. "Right now the National Park Service is up there widening the traditional trail our people used to travel to buffalo country—the same one we used to escape from the soldiers. But they're not doing it to commemorate us, they're doing it to commemorate Lewis and Clark."

He put his fork down and looked out the window in the direction of the mountains. "We made that trail. We'd been traveling across it for centuries. Lewis and Clark just used it. If that trail hadn't been there, they would never have made it across. There wouldn't have been any Lewis and Clark to celebrate. But no one cares about that. We're just a footnote, a curio, like we've always been. If it wasn't for Joseph we wouldn't even be on the historical radar. We'd just be roadkill on the Lewis and Clark superhighway."

Suddenly, the whole picture began to fall into place. In the great shadow of the national orgy of self-congratulation over the journey of Lewis and Clark, the Nez Perce people had undertaken another journey, one far more difficult, far more taxing, far more tragic, and every bit as much a part of the American experience as that of the two celebrated explorers. But their journey was almost unknown, almost ignored. The only reason it was kept alive at all was because of a man who, until the last moments, had been a "bit player."

Far from being the "Red Napoleon" or a towering figure of central leadership, Joseph had been a simple camp chief who had achieved his legendary status as much for being "the last man standing" as for anything he did during the journey. And he had done nothing to debunk the myth that built up around him in the subsequent years. Yet it was by letting that myth be built that he had kept the Nez Perce people alive in the national historical consciousness.

Small wonder, then, that the Nez Perce held conflicting views about the man. And small wonder that they looked with a jaundiced eye on writers like me who wanted to tell his story. We kept the flickering light of their cultural presence alive, but we did it by perpetuating a myth that distorted their history while ignoring a story that was every bit as worthy of being told.

At that moment, I knew what my literary task would be. I would try to unravel that myth, to put the story of Joseph in its proper perspective, to tell the story the way that it needed to be told.

This book is the result of a four-year effort to accomplish that task. It is also the endpoint of a profound personal journey. In those four years I traveled and retraveled the route of the great Nez Perce exodus, being awed by the distances, intimidated by the mountain passes and impassable terrain, astonished at the rock slides the men, women, and children navigated as they were chased first by one army, then another, in their desperate run for freedom.

I spent days and nights on the bleak Bear's Paw surrender site, wandering the hillocks and creek beds, shivering with cold on the edge of the shelter pits that the women dug with frying pans to protect their families from soldiers' bullets and the snow-driven high-plains Montana winds. I journeyed across the emptiness of the Dakotas, where the wounded and defeated captives were marched on their way to exile in the distant Indian Territory of Oklahoma. I walked the river bottoms of Kansas and the cruel flatlands of Oklahoma, where the pitiful survivors were detained and resettled like prisoners in our great, free, American land. By the end, there was not a foot of this journey that I had not traveled or at least shadowed.

In the course of that time I became intimate, as only a solitary traveler can, with the people who made that journey. White Bird, the seventy-year-old chief who would not trust white promises and continued the flight into Canada while Joseph surrendered; Sees Koo Mee, who in his youth had lost both feet and a hand to frostbite but still made the journey and fought by rolling and dragging himself into position; Noise of Running Feet, Joseph's twelve-year-old daughter, who was sent off alone across the snowy Montana plains in a desperate run to escape capture; Chief Looking Glass, the complex man of compassion and arrogance whose motives for leading the people slowly in the face of danger were never completely clear; and, of course, Joseph himself, the quiet leader and man of peace who allowed himself to be elevated to a cultural icon after the surrender in order to keep the nation's attention focused on the tragic plight of his beleaguered people.

As much as I could, through research and sympathy, I lived their life, knowing well that what I experienced was only a pallid and distant reflection of the searing emotional truth that was theirs and theirs alone. But I gave myself to the journey with all that was in my heart and mind.

And what I found was something far greater than I had ever imagined. I found a humbling, ennobling, tragic story that is almost unmatched in the annals of the American experience. I found a story of grandparents, too weary or wounded to continue the flight, who were given blankets and pitiful portions of food, then left behind by tearful family members to die on the side of the trail. I found a story of a young mother forced to kill her baby in order to stop the incessant crying, which would give away the fleeing people's location to the pursuing soldiers. I found a story of Nez Perce women giving water to terrified young American soldiers who lay wounded on the battlefield. And, yes, I found the story of Joseph, a man whose true greatness for more than a hundred years has been obscured by myth and shrouded in legend.

It is my hope that in this book I can give you, the reader, some feel for the sweep and scope of this little-known American story. It is a truly American saga, as much a part of who we are as any pioneer journey or grand exploration. To understand it is to understand better who we are as a people and at what cost we have made ourselves the nation that we have become today. We owe it to ourselves, and to those we have mythologized and silenced, to make sure that this story is heard.

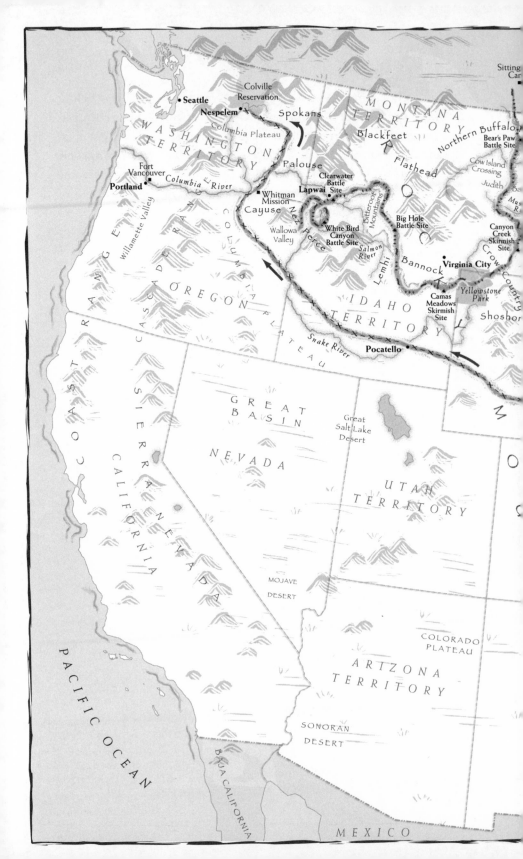

CANADA (OLD WOMAN COUNTRY)

Fort Buford

Yellowstone River

Milk River
Peaks
Missouri

Tongue River
Cantonment/
Fort Keogh
Little
Horn
Site

Cheyenne

Bismarck

Fort
Abraham
Lincoln

MINNESOTA

St.
Paul

WISCONSIN

GREAT

Sioux/Lakota

DAKOTA
TERRITORY

Missouri River

Black
Hills

WYOMING
TERRITORY

Cheyenne

CENTRAL
LOWLAND

IOWA

Mississippi River

NEBRASKA

PLAINS

High Plains

Denver

COLORADO

KANSAS

Fort
Leavenworth

St. Louis

MISSOURI

Ozark Plateau

Arkansas City

Ponca/
Oakland Agency

Quapaw
Agency

NEW
MEXICO
TERRITORY

P
L
A
I
N
S

INDIAN
TERRITORY

ARKANSAS

TEXAS

0   200 miles

The Flight and Exile of Chief Joseph
and the Nez Perce People, 1877–1985

...~... Route of the Nez Perce
×–×–× Post–Surrender Route

Part One

A Time of Hope

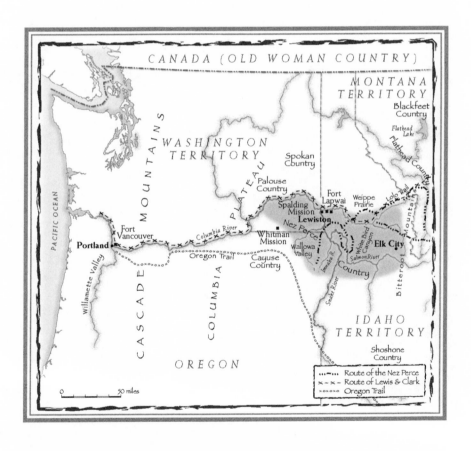

"We Thought They Might Be Descended from Dogs"

THE NEZ PERCE first encountered the European world, and the
Europeans first encountered theirs, in a wide, pine-rimmed meadow
in the foothills of the Bitterroot Mountains on a sunlit day in the autumn
of 1805. There, in a flower-covered field called the Weippe Prairie, in the
state we now call Idaho, three young Nez Perce boys were lazily playing
with sticks and bows while their mothers and grandmothers dug camas
roots on the far side of the clearing. It was the autumn gathering time, and
the roots they dug would be dried and pulverized and made into meal for
bread. A good harvest meant a good winter, and this year the harvest was
good.

Smoke rose from fires near the buffalo-skin teepees, which were set in
the same places they had been set for as long as anyone could remember.
Each family had its own spot, each band its own area. The gathering had
the gentle grace of a yearly ritual, when the different bands of the tribe
came together from their distant homelands to share in the harvest, to
meet family and friends, and to offer the firstfruits of the camas gathering
in thanks to the earth for the bounty she had given.

Only women and children and elders were in the camp. The younger
men had gone off across the rugged hills toward the south to confront the
Shoshone, who had killed three Nez Perce peace emissaries the season
before. It would be some time before they would return, and by that time
the harvest would be finished and the bands would be ready to return to
their respective wintering grounds in the lower valleys, where the snow

seldom reached and the waters seldom froze. The sun was warm, the digging was good, and the day had an air of quietude and peace.

Through this golden autumn peace the three boys heard the snorts of horses and saw a glint of movement in the woods on a nearby hillside. Soon a figure emerged, then another and another, all on horseback, all unlike any the boys had ever seen. They had arms like men, legs like men. But their faces were covered with fur, like dogs. One of the figures had hair the color of sunset. Another was black and had hair like a buffalo. He looked like a warrior painted for night battle, except that the blackness was not paint but skin itself.

The boys tried to run, but the creature with the sunset hair caught up with them. He made gestures of peace with his hands and gave them lengths of red ribbon. He motioned for them to return to camp and bring back the leaders of the people.

The boys arrived at the lodges breathless and terrified. They pointed to the field and told of the pale beasts with the hairy faces and held up the ribbons they had been given. In the Nez Perce fashion, the youngest boy was asked to deliver the worst news about these beasts they had encountered. He huddled with the other boys for a moment, then turned and spoke solemnly. "They all had eyes like dead fish," he said.

The strangers were led back to camp, where everyone gathered around them. They seemed by all accounts to be men, though not of any tribe that had ever been seen before. Their language was not recognizable and their condition was barely above that of animals. They were filthy and squalid and gave off a repulsive odor. With their hairy faces, there was some thought that they might be descended from dogs.

The "sunset hair" acted as the leader. He seemed friendly and offered gifts. Most important, he and the others with him carried guns with long barrels, a mysterious weapon of which the Nez Perce had only recently learned. Earlier that year, a band of hunters who had gone across the mountains to the buffalo country had traded for six of these strange weapons and brought them back to the Nez Perce villages. They spoke in awe of what these guns could do—about the terrific noise they made and how a ball placed in the long barrel could kill an animal from a distance far greater than that reached by an arrow.

The Nez Perce had long been known as the makers of the finest bows and arrows of any tribe, having learned to steam the horn of the mountain ram until it softened, then to shape it into a bow and strengthen it with rawhide attached with the boiled blood of the sturgeon or the grease from the skin of the salmon. Once hardened, these bows were powerful enough to launch an arrow completely through the body of a deer. All the tribes with whom the Nez Perce traded were hungry to obtain them.

But these long-barreled guns were even more powerful—perhaps not as efficient for warfare, but well able to pierce the leather shields of enemies and quite capable of stopping attackers and terrifying horses at a great distance. That these beings had these guns spoke of great power and influence, whether in fact they were men or beasts.

The dog-men were led down the hill to the camp of Twisted Hair, a chief who had been too old to go off on the raiding party against the Shoshone. Though frightened, he greeted the strangers with hospitality, feeding them a meal of camas roots and salmon. They seemed both appreciative and friendly.

While the strangers ate and slept, the situation was discussed in council. There was some thought to kill them, because stories had long been told about strange, pale-skinned men coming from the east who would bring sickness and ruin. But one old woman called Watkueis, or "She Who Had Returned from a Far Country," spoke to spare their lives. Years ago she had been captured by Blackfeet while in buffalo country and had been passed from tribe to tribe until she had escaped and been taken in by some of these pale-skinned people who were living north of the Hidatsa country many weeks' journey to the east. They had treated her kindly and let her stay with them. She called them "Soyapo," or "Crowned Ones," because of the strange hats they wore on their heads. If these beings were Soyapo like those people among whom she had stayed, they deserved not only to keep their lives but also to be honored as guests. The Nez Perce accepted the counsel of this old woman and decided to welcome these strangers.

Soon more of these dog-men emerged onto the prairie—almost forty of them, also bedraggled and foul smelling. They all had strange and appalling habits, like the willingness to eat puppies. But they possessed objects of great power, like the guns, and objects of great beauty, like cloth and beads and flags of many colors. They also carried mysterious objects the Nez Perce had never seen, like glass that could gather the sunlight to make fires. They were on a journey in search of the great bitter-tasting water in the direction of the sunset and had been trapped in the mountains, almost starving, until the first group had worked its way out into the Weippe and found the three boys playing.

They were very appreciative of the kindness shown them and lavished many gifts upon the Nez Perce. They called themselves the Corps of Discovery. Their leader was a man named Captain Lewis, and the sunset-haired man was known as Captain Clark.

The Nez Perce soon grew fond of these dog-men. They were friendly and generous, and possessed many miraculous objects. For their part, the dog-men found the Nez Perce to be among the fairest and most honorable of the native people that they had encountered in their long journey from the East. Clark wrote that the Nez Perce showed "greater acts of hospitality than we have witnessed from any nation or tribe since we have passed the rocky Mountains."

The Nez Perce accompanied the dog-men down from the Weippe to the river that they knew led to the great bitter-tasting water. They took them to their canoe-making spot where trees grew straight out from the banks of the river before curving upward toward the sun. They helped the men of the Corps fell these trees and showed them how use the natural curve of the trunk to create canoes with the grace needed to navigate the fast rivers they would soon be traveling.

Then they drew a map on a white antelope skin and sent the men on their way down the rivers toward the great bitter-tasting water. Twisted Hair and another chief named Tehoharsky accompanied them as far as the great falls where all the different tribes came to trade, to make sure that they would be treated well by the tribes farther down the rivers.

The kindness and honesty of the Nez Perce people so impressed Lewis and Clark that they left their horses and saddles with them, accepting the chiefs' words that when they returned after the winter snows their goods would be safe and their horses would be strong and well nourished. In exchange, the explorers gave the chiefs two more of the long-barrel guns and a hundred of the round balls that the guns used as ammunition.

When the Corps of Discovery returned in the spring, they found that the Nez Perce had kept their word. Only several horses had been ridden, and the chiefs showed great anger at the fact that this had been done. An American flag that Captain Lewis had given as a gift could be seen flying over the lodge of one of the chiefs, and the people greeted the returning travelers warmly. They even brought out two canisters of gunpowder that they had rescued after their dogs had dug them up from the place where the Corps had buried them the previous fall.

Because the winter had been long, the passes across the mountains were not yet open. After it became apparent that their horses' hooves would break through the snow if they tried to navigate the passes too soon, the Corps decided to stay among the Nez Perce until the snows had melted and the trails had cleared.

The Nez Perce made room for the travelers in their camp. Their winter dwellings were long, skin-covered shelters made by leaning two poles against each other, teepee fashion, and connecting these with ridge poles that ran in a line across the top. Some of these lodges could reach a hundred and fifty feet in length, and inside many families would have individual spaces, each with a small fire for warmth and cooking, with the smoke rising up and going out an opening along the ridge pole at the top.

Perhaps because of this, perhaps for some other reason, the Nez Perce were widely afflicted with a soreness and swelling of the eyes. Captain Clark, wishing to alleviate their suffering, began ministering to them with eye washes, which cured the affliction in a way that the Nez Perce considered miraculous. He also was able to cure their stomach ailments with a purgative that he had received from a doctor who had given him some rudimentary medical training before the Corps had departed from the East. It was volatile and brutal, but it emptied a man or woman in short order and gave a relief greater than the discomfort caused by the treatment itself.

Soon Captain Clark was besieged by Nez Perce seeking relief from various ailments. He often found himself staying up late into the night treating the sick and injured who lined up outside his tent. In one instance, he was able to cure a chief who had been unable to move his arms and legs for years. Prescribing sweat baths and plying him with laudanum, cream of tartar, and sulfur, he somehow made the man able to walk. This act of magical power, combined with the miraculous objects his men possessed, like the bar that could draw metal to it and the long tube that made far things seem near, made the strangers seem more powerful to the Nez Perce than any people they had ever met.

When the passes finally cleared and the Corps was able to go on its way, the Nez Perce clasped hands with the men, saying that for all times the Nez Perce people and the Soyapo people would be friends.

It was a promise that in the keeping and in the breaking would shape the lives of the Nez Perce forever.

The Nez Perce had always been a supremely confident and open-minded people. They lived in a lordly isolation on the high shoulder of land that ran north and south along the western base of the Bitterroot Mountains, the first craggy outcroppings that foreshadow the coming of the Rockies. To their west lay the people of the coast, to their south, the people of the desert, and to their east, over the mountains, the people of the plains. The Nez Perce were familiar with them all and ranged freely in all directions, trading their highly prized bows and arrows and beautifully crafted clothing and domestic goods for objects of value that the other peoples had to offer.

The Nez Perce were not a warlike people. Their land provided all they needed, and their interest in casual tribal warfare was almost nonexistent. As with all peoples, they had neighbors with whom they were on better terms and neighbors for whom they had no good feelings. But their land was big, their lives were good, and the Creator had blessed them with a place on the earth that provided them with all the material wealth they needed. Their only consistent clashes were with the Shoshone and Paiute to the south, who often encroached upon Nez Perce hunting and gathering lands. But even these clashes were sporadic and episodic and seldom engaged in except to redress grievances or as means by which young men could achieve personal honor or increase their status as warriors. Beyond these encounters, the Nez Perce were content to let all people live in peace where the Creator had placed them, and they expected others to do the same.

The tribe itself, which numbered about 4000, was spread out over a vast country that stretched over thousands of square miles. They lived in small, isolated bands separated from one another by the difficult terrain of the Plateau country. Some of the bands, like the Wallowas, lived in high mountain valleys surrounded by snow-covered peaks. Others lived far below along curving, twisting rivers. Travel between villages could be arduous, many-day journeys along switchback trails and across rushing, dangerous rivers. A traveler not familiar with the pathways could become hopelessly lost on a forested mountainside or end up standing at the rim of a canyon so dizzyingly deep that people or animals moving along its bottom would seem to be no more than tiny specks.

The difficulties of travel and the unique nature of the landscape in which each band lived kept the people separate except for the several times each year when they gathered at the sites where the bounty of the earth provided sustenance in which they could all share. Salmon runs, kouse and camas prairies, and places where game was plentiful became their common sacred sites and meeting places because it was in such places that the Creator had placed the richest gifts of life. Otherwise, they stayed to themselves, moving back and forth from high country to the river bottoms as necessary to follow the game or avoid the cruelties of a harsh seasonal climate.

Some bands even made forays over the mountains into the buffalo country, following animal trails that had, over the centuries, become well known and established routes of human transit. But even when they joined together for common causes such as buffalo hunts, each band was its own master with its own leadership, and each was free to make its own choices in matters affecting the welfare of its own people.

This same fierce independence was bred into their personal character. No one would presume to tell another how to believe or live, and none could speak for another unless appointed to do so. Women were free to leave their husbands if they so desired and were able to own their own property and have their own wealth. Children were taught the traditional skills attendant upon the responsibilities of their sex, but each child was encouraged to go out at a young age to fast and pray in order to find a personal guardian spirit, or *wayakin,* which would provide them with powers and abilities that were theirs alone. This *wayakin* could then be called upon for assistance throughout the person's life, so long as the *wayakin* was treated with honor and respect. The only great collective responsibility was to use whatever skills or talents a person developed for the good of the tribe in situations of need.

As a people, the Nez Perce were clean, fastidious, upright, and moral. They were impeccable in their personal behavior and generous to those who came among them, but uncompromising in their conviction that their place on the earth had been given to them by the Creator. Yet they were also extremely adaptable and open to the ways of others. They took great pride in the way they had received the horse from the Shoshone and had quickly learned how to breed their stock into the best of any horses owned by any people. From the plains Indians across the mountains they had learned of the use of the teepee and the rich gift of the buffalo. From the tribes to the west they had taken much of their personal decoration and adornment. It was their belief that the Creator had given each people special skills and gifts, and it was their right and privilege to acquire the skills and gifts possessed by others and adapt them to their own needs.

With the departure of Lewis and Clark and their Corps of Discovery, the Nez Perce quickly returned to their normal ways. But the strange, gift-giving dog-men who had come among them with such miraculous powers had opened them to the possibility that there was another way to live, well favored by the Creator and far different from the ways of any other tribe they had met. In these passing strangers they had seen a people with a power that exceeded even their own. They were determined to get that power for themselves.

Their first opportunity came several years later, with the arrival of the people called the "mountain men." Before departing, Lewis and Clark had promised to send other Soyapo to set up places where tribes could meet and trade in peace, both with each other and with the Soyapo. This seemed good to the Nez Perce. They were not inclined toward conflict and took no real pleasure in fighting with other tribes. A place of peaceful trading would provide the opportunity to exchange their various goods without long, exhausting travel and the difficulties of passing through lands of hostile bands. It would also allow them to gain the goods, and maybe the secrets, that had made the Soyapo so powerful.

But when new Soyapo arrived several years later, they were very different from Lewis and Clark and the men of the Corps of Discovery. Lewis and Clark had been respectful and interested and generous with gifts. These new Soyapo men showed no interest in the Nez Perce beyond their women and a desire for the fur of the beaver.

The Nez Perce had no interest in trapping the beaver. Its tail was a great delicacy, but the beaver also had strong spirit power. It did not seem wise to kill them only to gain their skins. Besides, the Nez Perce had always been a riding and hunting and fishing people, accustomed to running down large game on horseback and bringing back food enough for many people to eat. They had no desire to spend their time squatting in cold streams waiting to trap small animals. Such things were for young children playing at the game of the hunt.

Nonetheless, the Nez Perce reached out their hands in friendship to these new Soyapo, as they had promised they would. But when the mountain men discovered that the Nez Perce would not trap beaver, the relationship cooled. Occasionally, a Soyapo trader would show up trying to purchase beaver pelts, and the Nez Perce would offer him a bearskin or the pelt of a rat. This simply angered the mountain men and made them keep a farther distance from this tribe that seemed so arrogantly indifferent to the realities of profitable exchange.

But the Nez Perce desperately wanted the goods these Soyapo had to trade. These men had guns and kettles and arrowheads made of steel, and cloth that could be made into clothes that dried quickly and weighed almost nothing. The neighboring tribes, those willing to trap the beaver, were beginning to gain these things, and with their new guns they were beginning to threaten the power and dominance of the Nez Perce. The Nez Perce needed to find a way to gain the Soyapo guns and goods that were falling into the other tribes' hands. And that way had to be something other than trapping the beaver.

What the Nez Perce had to offer were their horses. They had seen the mountain men's horses—a slow and plodding lot, good for carrying loads but not for swift travel and long riding. Long ago, with their skills of gelding and breeding, they had bred speed and stamina into their stock. Their herds were abundant, some of the largest on the continent. Many of the richer Nez Perce had herds numbering in the thousands. They knew that a man without a good horse in their country was doomed to live a small life. If they were patient, they reasoned, the trappers would have to come to them for mounts. Then they could make hard bargains and gain the goods they desired.

Eventually, this attitude created bad feelings. In one instance the Nez Perce refused to assist a huge mountain man named MacKenzie when he came into their country seeking beaver. They offered horses for his goods, but he wanted only pelts. So he made camp nearby and put his own men to work setting traps. Lacking knowledge of the streams and animals, the men spent an entire summer trapping without success. The Nez Perce mocked them, saying that Brother Beaver saw the stinginess of the Soyapo trappers and decided to be stingy with his skin.

By autumn, with winter coming and the streams starting to freeze, MacKenzie and his men were almost out of supplies. They approached the

Nez Perce, offering finally to trade goods for horses so they could use them for food. The Nez Perce agreed to trade, but only at exorbitant rates. This so irritated MacKenzie that he decided to leave for the winter rather than meet the Nez Perce demands. He placed his trade goods under a tarp and announced that he would return for them the following spring.

When spring came and he made his way back into Nez Perce country, he found his tarp almost empty. He became enraged and went to the nearest village and began tearing apart every lodge. Among the Nez Perce, a hungry person could always go into another's lodge in search of food, but it was a grave insult to enter someone's lodge without respect. MacKenzie was not only showing no respect, he was ripping up tents and packs with daggers.

When he had finished his ransacking and regained his goods, he announced he was now ready to trade for horses. But the Nez Perce wished nothing more to do with him and turned away. So he began shooting horses, one by one, and leaving a pile of goods equal to the value of the horse next to the severed head of each animal he killed. In this way he procured the horsemeat he needed, then left.

Such situations were common, and many were far worse. One Nez Perce man was bound hand and foot and hanged in front of his people because the trappers were convinced he had been stealing their goods. Many others were shot. And though the Nez Perce developed warm friendships with many of the mountain men, even to the point of letting them live among them and marry Nez Perce women, this did not gain them access to the trade goods they so desperately desired.

Meanwhile, more places were being set up for the trading of goods—the kinds of places promised by Lewis and Clark—and they were all being built along rivers in the lands of the tribes that were willing to trap the beaver. By refusing to change their lives to meet the demands of the trappers, the Nez Perce were falling far behind the other tribes in their quest to gain Soyapo goods and power. They needed to find another way to bring the Soyapo and their power among their people.

That way came in the form of a small black book that the Soyapo called the "Book of Heaven."

2

A Harvest for the Lord

WHILE LEWIS AND CLARK had lived among them, some of the Nez Perce had seen the men of the Corps of Discovery staring at a small black book. This book contained many pages covered with strange markings that the men said were the same as words that came out of a man's mouth. The Nez Perce could not make sense of these markings because they were not in the shape of anything they recognized. But the men said they were the words of the Creator and told the Creator's secrets. They called this book the "Book of Heaven."

The Nez Perce had always understood that the Creator put his teachings in the animals and the earth. They could see the arch of stone where Coyote had frozen Ant and Yellow Jacket into rock as eternal punishment for their endless arguing with each other. They could see the sacred hill down by the homeland of the Kamiah band, where the monster's heart lay after having been ripped out by Coyote as he formed all the peoples of the earth from different parts of the monster's body. They could look at the animals and know the stories from before the time of people when the Creator gave each animal its skills and power. But they had never imagined that the Creator would put the secrets of his power in a book that he would give to these strange, bearded men from the east.

They had asked the mountain men about this book. Some of them had heard of it, though few seemed to care much about it. Some of the Indian scouts who traveled with the trappers—people called the Iroquois from far in the direction of the sunrise—had also heard of it. They had seen Soyapo spirit law teachers in their own country and had heard them tell of the se-crets in the book.

The Iroquois told the Nez Perce what they remembered—something about a strong spirit power named Jesus and a place of fire where bad people went when they died. They showed the Nez Perce special ways to make signs by touching their head and shoulders and heart to give them-selves spirit power. They even hinted that the Nez Perce might be failing in hunts and warfare because of their failure to possess the white man's spirit power. If this book truly held the secrets of Soyapo power, the Nez Perce needed to get it.

This feeling was only increased by events taking place among their sister tribes of the Spokan and Flathead. The Spokan lived just north of the Nez Perce in rolling, open hill country. The Flathead, or Salish, lived just to the east of the Spokan. Both of them were friendly with the Nez Perce, and both had more contact with the Soyapo because both were more willing to hunt the beaver, and both lived in country where it was easier for Soyapo traders to travel. It was through these sister tribes that the Nez Perce learned much of what they knew about Soyapo ways.

Twenty winters after the coming of Lewis and Clark, some British Soyapo came among the Spokan and Flathead talking about the Book of Heaven. As all the Indians in the area had learned, there were two great tribes of white men in the East who competed with each other for furs. One was called the British, and the other was called the Bostons, or the Americans. The mountain men would work for either of them, but each of them set up their own trading forts where the mountain men and Indians went to exchange their furs for goods.

The Bostons were more easygoing and easy to trade with, while the British were more formal and less willing to bargain. But beyond that there was little difference until one of the British Soyapo had begun to speak about things of the spirit. He said he wanted to take a young boy from the Spokan and one from the Flathead and bring them east to teach them about Soyapo ways.

At first the Spokan chiefs had become angry, saying they were not like dogs who willingly gave up their children whenever anyone wanted to take them. But when these men said the boys would be taught the Book of Heaven and the secrets of the Creator's power, the chiefs not only were happy to let them go, they insisted the men take the chiefs' own sons.

The boys were gone for three winters. When they returned, they wore clothes in the white man's manner, their hair was cut short, and each had a Book of Heaven. They had learned the Soyapo tongue and in many ways seemed to be more like Soyapo than like their own people.

The boys, who were now in their middle teens and able to speak with the authority of men, gave many talks about the white man spirit laws they had learned and about a spirit power named Jesus, who was stronger than all other spirit powers. They told about a place where people who followed the spirit laws went after they died, and another place of endless fire, where those who did not follow the spirit laws were sent when they died. All of this, they said, was written in this Book of Heaven.

Many Nez Perce who were in the area went to hear the boys talk and came away amazed. This confirmed all they had been hearing from the trappers and the Iroquois. The Soyapo truly did have special knowledge from the Creator, and that knowledge was all contained in the secrets of the Book of Heaven. If the Nez Perce could get that book, perhaps they could get that knowledge for themselves and would not have to hunt beaver to trade for Soyapo power and goods.

The Nez Perce met in council and decided to send some men in search of the book. With their Flathead friends they created a hunting party of seven men and sent them off to Soyapo country. They decided to go to the place where Captain Clark was now the head chief, a place the trappers called St. Louis. It was in American country, many weeks' journey far over the mountains on the other side of the buffalo plains, in a place where the Nez Perce had never been. They had considered going north to the British Soyapo country where the two boys had received their books, but that would have meant traveling through the country of the murderous Blackfeet, and none wished to take this risk. Besides, Captain Clark had been generous to them before. If he had one of these Books of Heaven, he would surely give it to them.

The seven men set off with a group of mountain men who were returning to the land of the white man to trade for goods. Their journey took them over the mountains and across the great rolling buffalo country farther toward the east than any of them had ever traveled. Three of the men became afraid and turned back before reaching St. Louis. But the others made it safely and found themselves in an encampment unlike any they had ever seen.

There were lodges made of wood and stone that stood as high as trees. These lodges had walls made of something as thin and clear as river ice so a man could see out and the light of day could come in. There were horses pulling boxes that moved on rolling circles, and in the rivers were boats as long as the great lodges the Nez Perce lived in during the winter. All the buildings had doors made of flattened trees that would not open unless you put a piece of metal in a small hole and turned it around and around. Everywhere you looked were tools and weapons made of steel. It was truly a place of power and magic.

The men found Mr. Clark, who greeted them warmly. Though they could not speak each other's languages, they could make themselves understood through signs and gestures. They were taken to a great stone building filled with candles and wooden figures of bearded men. There they met spirit law teachers and were given crosses and the Book of Heaven. They had succeeded in their mission.

But two of the men soon became sick and died. Something in the white man's world was not good for their health. They were buried in that place, far from their land and their people. Then the others took the book and began the journey home.

Sadly, they too died before returning, and the book they carried with them was lost. So the Nez Perce remained without the Book of Heaven and the power it possessed.

But their hunger for it did not decrease.

While in St. Louis, the Nez Perce messengers had created a great stir. Walking the streets in their tribal dress, in an apparent quest for the Christian gospel, they represented everything the American people wanted to believe about the hunger of the Indian people for deliverance from their savage ways.

The year was 1831, and the young American nation was in the throes of a great religious revival. The conviction that a person could be saved from hellfire only by God's whim was being replaced by a belief that God's touch, earnestly sought, could change a person's heart and place that person among the saved. Faith in this power of conversion was sweeping the land.

To those who felt they had already been saved, no task was more important than bringing the word of God to others who were still living in darkness. Missionaries were setting sail for Africa, Asia, the Pacific Islands, and anywhere else that the gospel had not yet been preached.

When word reached the churches back East that a group of Indians from deep in the uncharted West had been seen wandering the streets of St. Louis in search of the word of the Lord, the effect was instantaneous. A call was put out for men who would endure the hardships of the unknown mountains and deserts and forests of the West to bring Christian teachings to these untutored children of the wild.

Among the men who answered that call was the Reverend Marcus Whitman, a Presbyterian minister and physician from Ithaca, New York. Along with another intrepid missionary, Samuel Parker, he came west to St. Louis in the summer of 1835, four years after the Nez Perce had made their journey in search of the book, and declared his intention to travel across the plains to the annual gathering where trappers from the western interior rendezvoused with traders from the east to exchange furs for goods. From there, he announced, he and the Reverend Parker would continue across the mountains to the unknown interior to seek out the tribes that had shown such an earnest hunger for the word of the Lord.

The rendezvous were great, raucous gatherings held each year at a predetermined site on the eastern edge of the Rockies after the snows had melted and the passes had cleared. The trappers came with furs they had harvested or purchased from the Indians to exchange for goods and supplies brought in on wagons from St. Louis and cities in the East. Many Indian tribes—some hoping to make deals directly with the traders, others simply wishing to partake in the camaraderie and revelry—came with their own goods for bartering. A general armistice was put in effect, and smoke from a thousand fires filled the sky while Indians and whites alike fought, gambled, traded, and drank far into the night.

The Nez Perce often participated in these events. Many of them spent long periods—sometimes years at a time—living in buffalo country hundreds of miles across the great mountains from their ancestral homelands, and the horses they owned and the buffalo skins they gathered were valuable objects of trade. It was the one time when their failure to trap the beaver did not put them at a disadvantage in gaining the white man's goods.

The debauched nature of the rendezvous was legendary, and it did not make missionaries welcome guests. But the Reverend Parker and Dr.

Whitman knew that this was the one place where they could make the connection that would get them to the tribes who had come to St. Louis seeking the light of Christian truth. So they joined with a trading caravan and made the long journey across the plains to the broad valley where the drinking and gambling and horse racing were already fully under way.

Their arrival was met with something less than enthusiasm by the reveling mountain men. But the Nez Perce in attendance were overjoyed to see these Soyapo teachers of spirit law. More than white man's goods, the Nez Perce desired the secrets of the white man's power. And here at the rendezvous were men who knew that power.

When the Reverend Parker and Dr. Whitman realized that there were men at the rendezvous from the tribes that had sent their messengers to St. Louis, they too were overjoyed. They willingly agreed to travel back with them to their country to begin establishing mission sites and teaching the ways of the Christian faith.

The Nez Perce watched the men closely. It was important that they be men of strong power who could assist the people in gaining Soyapo secrets. Dr. Whitman soon showed that he was such a man. He cured many of the mountain men of a violent stomach sickness and removed an arrowhead from deep in the back of one of the trappers. He reminded the Nez Perce of Captain Clark with his miraculous powers of healing.

But Dr. Whitman disappointed them by announcing that he had to return to the settlements of the whites to gather more goods and people. The Reverend Parker, however, agreed to travel back with the Nez Perce to their homeland.

The Nez Perce did all within their power to show Parker the highest respect during the journey. The women brought him fresh strawberries and placed fragrant leaves on the ground beneath his bedding, and the chiefs let him ride in the place of honor at the front of the travelers so he and his horse would always be walking on fresh ground.

Parker rewarded the Nez Perce kindness by giving instruction in spirit law during the travels, teaching each of the various chiefs one of the ten commandments so he could memorize it and pass it on. With the assistance of Indians who knew a few words of English, he also gave sermons to the people in long lodges that the Nez Perce constructed for the purpose, placing their finest animal skins on the ground for the Reverend and waiting patiently on their knees for his teaching to begin.

Parker intended to stay with the Nez Perce and continue his ministry. Unfortunately, he developed severe headaches and chest pains during the journey, and after a short stay, was forced to leave. But before he departed he promised that Dr. Whitman and other spirit law teachers would soon follow to continue instructing the people in the Soyapo Book of Heaven and the secrets it contained.

The following summer, in 1836, the Nez Perce traveled back to the rendezvous in the hope that they might meet Dr. Whitman there. It was a source of great joy when they first heard the creaking of wagon wheels and saw the carts emerging in the distance carrying men with huge beards and shirts as white as fresh mountain snow. But the joy turned to amazement when they saw these carts also carried two Soyapo women.

The Indians had never seen white women before. They seemed as slight as twigs, and their skin was as pale as morning sunlight. They looked unfit for any work and likely to break at the slightest touch of a man's hand.

The Nez Perce women ran and kissed the white women, as the mountain men had instructed them to do. At first they had to contend with these mountain men for the women's attention, but they soon discovered that their real struggle lay with the women of the other tribes. All tribes wanted the prestige of having the spirit law teachers settle among them, and the women of the Cayuse and Nez Perce almost came to blows in their efforts to gain the favors and attention of these two pale-skinned Soyapo.

The Indians soon learned that, despite their frail appearance, these Soyapo women had strong hearts. One, the wife of Dr. Whitman, had long, flowing hair the color of red sunlight and was, to the Indians, beautiful beyond measure. The other, the wife of a hard-eyed man named Reverend Spalding, had a rough voice and hair the color of mud. But she showed deep concern for the Indian wives, even trying from the first day to learn some of their language. The Indians soon opened their hearts to both women.

When the rendezvous was over, the Spaldings and Whitmans and the others in their party set off with the Cayuse and Nez Perce across the plains and mountains back to the Plateau country. It was slow traveling because the ministers insisted on bringing wagons on the small trails, since they did not think it fitting for women to ride on the backs of horses. The Indians found this strange, but they did not wish to question Soyapo ways. So they continued to cut brush and remove rocks so the trail would be wide enough to allow passage of the women's horse-drawn carts.

All through the journey the Nez Perce and Cayuse women continued their bickering about where the missionaries should settle. All knew that any tribe and band that gained their presence would increase greatly in prestige. Eventually, at journey's end, Dr. Whitman announced that he and his wife would settle among the Cayuse instead of the Nez Perce. His examination of the land in Cayuse country had convinced him it would more easily yield to the plow and would more quickly bear fruit than the mountainous ravines and canyons and barren hillsides of the Nez Perce homelands through which they had just traveled.

This saddened the Nez Perce, who had watched him cure the sick at the rendezvous and believed him to be a man of great medicine power. But when the Reverend Spalding announced that he and his wife would settle among them, the Nez Perce were greatly relieved. Since he too knew the Book of Heaven, they would still be able to gain its knowledge. They also would have the favor of his kind and caring wife.

At first the Reverend Spalding could find no place in Nez Perce country that pleased him. The high cliffs and narrow river valleys offered little in the way of tillable land, and where the hills opened, they became bald and treeless—harsh, waterless places that would be almost unlivable under the relentless summer sun.

Finally, after long searching, the Nez Perce found a place on one of their creeks that met with the Reverend's approval. It had good soil, took in enough sun for growing, and had a flowing spring nearby. When he announced that he and his wife would settle there, the Nez Perce were overjoyed.

The Reverend told the Nez Perce that he wished them to build him a lodge made of logs piled on top of each other. They found it strange that a man would want to live in a house that could not be moved. The animals moved, the seasons changed. To follow the animals, people also needed to move. It made no sense to live in a house made of logs when a light, easily dismantled lodge made of poles and skins would do. But because the Nez Perce wanted to please the Reverend and his wife, they acceded to his request.

The logs the Reverend wanted for his lodge were from a river two miles distant. Some were as big around as a man and as long as two men standing on each other's shoulders. The Nez Perce men did not relish the task of carrying tree trunks several miles. Carrying was women's work. But the task was too demanding for the women, so they undertook it themselves, working without complaint.

The Nez Perce women, meanwhile, were enlisted to use the Reverend's ax to shape the trees, since the men were unused to using cutting tools and handled them poorly. Once the logs had been squared, the men hoisted them on their shoulders and carried them to the new location, where the logs were piled on top of each other until they became walls too heavy to be lifted by all the men of the tribe.

By midwinter, the strange dwelling was completed, and the Reverend and his wife were able to move into a log home that the Nez Perce felt would have been big enough to house a dozen or more of their own families. However, the following summer, the Reverend Spalding declared that the place he had chosen for his lodge was not to his liking. It was too hot and had too many biting bugs. He told the Nez Perce he wanted to have his house moved back down to the river, right by the spot where they had gathered the logs.

It was a fine piece of land, low and flat and covered with shade trees. The Nez Perce knew it as the Lapwai, or the Place of the Butterflies, because it was here that the butterflies gathered each spring, filling the sky with their color and movement. They only wished that he had chosen that spot for his home in the first place.

The Nez Perce men dismantled the house and carried the logs, one by one, back to the spot they had come from. But this time the men did not work so willingly. If the Reverend had wanted a lodge that could be moved, he should not have built such a log dwelling in the first place.

But the Reverend Spalding overcame their resistance by kicking and whipping them if they worked too slowly. This was a hard insult for the Nez Perce to endure. The whip man was an honored position in the tribe, hired by parents to correct children's bad behavior. But he never whipped adults. By acting as a whip man and whipping the grown men, the Reverend Spalding was treating them like children. It was not an offense easily forgiven or forgotten.

Despite the Reverend's harsh ways, the Nez Perce soon learned to have great respect for him. He worked harder than any man they had ever seen, laboring from first sun until long past dark. He dug the earth and coaxed plants to grow in straight rows; he built fences; with the help of the Nez

Perce men he dug a long trench from the river that allowed water to come into his camp. At first the Nez Perce were confused. But when he built a wheel that was turned by the water and attached it to a heavy stone that could grind seeds to powder, they began to understand. The river now became their hands, just as the horse had become their legs. They were learning the secrets of the Soyapo way, just as they had hoped.

He did many other miraculous things as well. He built another wheel that would move a metal blade with fishlike teeth up and down to cut trees into boards. He made a large bag that would blow on fire and make metal so hot that it turned the color of the sun and ran like water. With this he fashioned tools for cutting and digging into the earth.

Though most of the Nez Perce were amazed, a few were uneasy. It was not good to rip the mother's flesh, they said, not good to make the river go where the Creator had not sent it. But the Reverend Spalding told them that this was the Creator's new way, as told in the Book of Heaven. The Creator, he said, wanted them to make the earth work for them, just as their human mothers worked for them.

To prove this, he brought out small brown root bulbs that he called potatoes. Some he gave to people who were open to the Book of Heaven. Some he gave to those who wished to stay with the old ways. He instructed them all to put their bulbs in the ground and cover them with earth.

The next summer, the bulbs planted by the people who had accepted the book had grown into new plants with new bulbs. Those planted by the followers of the old ways had not grown at all. There had been no difference between the two except for white dots on those he had given to the people who had become followers of the book. The Reverend Spalding said that this showed that the Creator gave his favor to people who accepted the Creator's new way. To most of the Nez Perce, this was even more proof of the Soyapo's mysterious powers.

Soon many bands were sending people from their villages to learn the magic of the Soyapo ways. Each day the Reverend Spalding would gather everyone together and speak of the book and its secrets—once just after sunrise and again just before dark. He was not able to speak the people's language, but with hand signs and the help of Nez Perce who had learned some of the Soyapo tongue, he made himself understood.

He told of them more about this Jesus who had the strongest spirit power. He told of how Jesus had died and stayed dead for three days, then had come back with spirit truth. He told how Jesus was the Creator who had assumed human form.

All of these things the Nez Perce could easily understand. Many of their strongest medicine people would fall into death sleeps in which the breath stopped and the body became cold, then would wake after several days with messages from the spirit world. They knew too that those with great medicine power could readily assume many forms. If the Creator himself had taken on the form of Jesus, this Jesus must have the greatest medicine power of all.

Day after day, the Reverend Spalding continued his teachings. Much of it was confusing and difficult for the Nez Perce to understand. But the heart of the message was clear: Jesus was the greatest *wayakin*, greater than all their *wayakin*s, and if people believed in him, their spirits would live forever in the good place. If they did not, after they died their spirits would go to a place where fire burned forever and they would feel the pain of burning for as long as the sun was in the sky.

All had burned their hands in fire, and none wanted to feel such pain forever. If the Book of Heaven said they must choose between living with Jesus in a good spirit place after they died or burning forever in a place with flames as hot as those that melted the Reverend Spalding's metal, it was not a hard decision to make. They would choose to live with Jesus.

Among those most eager to learn these new spirit ways was a man named Tuekakas, head chief of the Wallowa band, who lived in a high mountain valley several days' journey from the Lapwai. In the winters he and his people would move down to the river bottom of the Snake and set up camp a day's ride from where the Reverend Spalding had built his mission.

The Wallowa Valley was among the Nez Perce lands most blessed by the Creator. Its streams were rich in fish, and its grazing meadows were filled with grass that grew as high as a horse's flank. In its center was a great blue lake that reflected the clouds passing in the sky. All around were high, snowcapped mountains and rolling, forested hills.

The Wallowa people were isolated from the other bands by the surrounding mountains and the deep river gorges. To travel to or from their country meant several days' journey along steep mountain trails and across fast-moving, treacherous rivers. In many ways they had more in common with the Cayuse people who lived to the west than with the Nez

Perce bands, who lived across the Snake and Salmon and traveled over the mountains to buffalo country. But in language and heart they were Nez Perce, and always they would attend the common Nez Perce feasts and participate in the gatherings where offerings were made to the Creator. And always they took part in the councils where issues that affected the Nez Perce common good were decided.

Tuekakas, their leader, commanded great respect from all the bands. Though a Cayuse, he had become part of the Nez Perce by marrying into the tribe and choosing to live among them. He was a proud man, holding himself and those around him to strict account. It was said that his word was his bond and that he would never be the first to break an agreement.

The arrival of the Reverend Spalding was of great interest to Tuekakas. Years before, when the Nez Perce were just beginning to hear about the Book of Heaven, a strange Soyapo named Bonneville had wandered into the wintering grounds of Tuekakas and his people. This Bonneville had become trapped in the narrow, snow-filled canyons and had tried to make his way to safety by walking along the perilous, thin ice on the edge of the half-frozen, fast-moving Clearwater River. When he had chanced upon Tuekakas's winter camp, the chief had willingly taken him in. Bonneville had quickly shown himself to be a man of great heart. He had torn up his own coat and wound strips of its colored cloth into hats for the women. He laughed easily and respected the Nez Perce ways. He amazed the people because he had no hair on his head, which made him powerful against scalping. He spoke often of the book that contained the Creator's teachings.

When Tuekakas heard that a new Soyapo spirit law teacher had come to the Lapwai with the book, he was intent upon meeting him. He traveled down the mountain passes and through the deep gorges to the Lapwai to take this man's hand in friendship.

Tuekakas and Spalding quickly formed a strong bond. Tuekakas recognized in Spalding a man who shared his own sense of honor and personal rectitude. Spalding saw in Tuekakas a man of piety and strong moral character. It was not long before the chief was bringing his band to winter at the Lapwai mission to learn the ways of the missionary and the teachings of the book.

Tuekakas took to Spalding's teachings almost more readily than any other Nez Perce. With the assistance of Nez Perce who knew a few words of English, he listened with diligence as the Reverend spoke of the book and the miraculous powers of Jesus. Then Tuekakas would speak for hours to his own people in their own language about the great teachings he was learning.

The teachings were hard for the people. They surely did not wish to go to a place to be burned forever in a fire, but many of them became upset when the Reverend said they had to take Jesus as their only spirit guide and speak out against their own spirits, saying aloud, "I believe in you no longer." It seemed dangerous to dishonor their own spirits, and some privately wondered if perhaps the Creator had given different spirit guides to different people.

But Tuekakas remained strong in his acceptance of these new teachings. He even received the Christian spirit bath that washed a man clean of his old ways. He accepted the gift of a Christian name, Joseph, and remarried his wife in the Christian fashion. She too was given a new name, Asenoth. As their children were born, they too were given Christian names and given the spirit bath that would let their spirits live forever with Jesus.

Among these children was a boy born in a cave a day's journey from the Reverend Spalding's mission. Like his father, he was given the Christian name of Joseph.

3

A Child of Two Worlds

YOUNG JOSEPH was born in the year 1840, four years after the Reverend Spalding had arrived and just when the missionary was at the height of his power and influence. Because of his father's friendship with the Reverend, Joseph was accorded a privileged status at the mission.

While his father sat at Spalding's side learning the ways of the Book of Heaven, young Joseph was given the freedom to play with the white children, often being pulled around the mission grounds in the same wagon with the Spaldings' son.

With a free and innocent curiosity, he was able to drink in the strange, almost magical reality of this Soyapo settlement with its heavy wooden buildings and great, groaning grinding stones and fire-breathing bags that melted metal. Though he was too young to understand what he was seeing, he knew from the first that there was a world different from the Wallowa and that the people in this other world, with their strange ways and different skin, had magical powers and treated him with kindness

Then, each spring, when the mountain snows began to melt, he would travel back with his family up the long trails to the Wallowa, where he was trained in the old ways, learning the medicine power of the plants, the names and powers of all the animals, and the language of the birds.

It was an idyllic life for a child. But for the Nez Perce people themselves, who were also living these separate lives, it spoke of a tension in their spirit that was becoming increasingly difficult to resolve. They had willingly embraced the presence of the Reverend Spalding when he had first arrived because he had brought new knowledge that they could use to help their people, just as they had used the knowledge of the horse and the ways of the buffalo people and the weapons and tools of Soyapo strangers who had come before. But they had not expected to be told to give up their old ways in order to gain this knowledge. Now they were being told they had to choose, and they were unsure what to do.

Some of the bands, especially those whose home villages were nearest the places of the missionaries, gave themselves over completely to these new ways, as the Reverend demanded. They cut their hair, adopted Soyapo clothes, raised Soyapo sheep and pigs and cattle, and dug into the earth with metal blades. They marked off squares on the earth and taught different plants to grow in straight lines. They lived in heavy wooden houses, attended church, and sold the food they did not need instead of giving it away to others.

They said that this new way was better for the people—that it allowed them to take better care of the elders and the children, that it meant less time of empty bellies. Soyapo livestock freed them from the need to cross the mountains to hunt buffalo. Planting gardens in the Soyapo manner meant they no longer had to make seasonal pilgrimages to the camas and kouse grounds. They had apple trees for fruit, corn and potatoes for grain, and solid houses for protection against the weather. By learning the Soyapo tongue they could now read the Book of Heaven and could understand the ways of Jesus. They were on the good path, and their people were prospering. They did not want to burn forever in a place of endless fire.

But other bands were not so sure. Much of what the Reverend Spalding taught went against the teachings of the ancestors. It was not good to dig into your mother's flesh or cut her hair. It was not good to forget the old practices of offering the spirits the firstfruits of the harvest. And they could not believe that the Creator wanted them to abandon the teachings he had placed in the earth in favor of a strange book about a man who lived far away in a desert.

By the time Joseph was five, the heart of the Nez Perce had begun to split. Two years before, in 1843, another Soyapo had come among them, a Dr. White, and he had given them new, harsh rules that he said were from the same white fathers who had sent Lewis and Clark. But these laws were more about what people could not do than about what they should do. The Reverend Spalding supported Dr. White, even placing a metal ring in a tree at a height higher than a man's head so people's hands could be tied to it while they were lashed for acts that went against these new Soyapo laws.

Old men were being lashed for going into another's lodge for food when they were hungry; children were being lashed for taking ears of corn from the garden of another. If you rode a horse that belonged to another or touched another man's goods, you were lashed. If you burned another man's building, you were hanged. There was even a law that told who could own dogs and who could not.

Most troubling of all, these new laws did not seem to apply to the white people. When the son of a Walla Walla chief was killed by Soyapo who had falsely accused him of stealing, the white leaders would not kill the murderers, even though the first law on the list Dr. White had given them was, "Whoever willfully takes the life of another shall be hung." If the laws were not followed by the Soyapo, why should they be followed by the Nez Perce and the other tribes?

But what most turned the hearts of many Nez Perce against the Soyapo was the decision by the white law officials to make one man, Ellis, the head chief over all the Nez Perce bands. It went against the Nez Perce way to place one chief over all the others. Decisions of importance were to be made in council, and Ellis, though wealthy, had never won great distinction in hunting or warfare and was favored by the Soyapo only because he had been sent to study among the whites and could speak their language. To call him the head chief over all the people showed that the Soyapo had no respect for Nez Perce ways.

Eventually trappers who had taken Nez Perce wives also began speaking against the missionaries. They pointed out how the Reverend Spalding made the Nez Perce pay for seeds and plows but did not pay them for their land and air and water. The hunters returning from the buffalo country also brought disturbing news. While on the buffalo plains they had met many men with Soyapo fathers and Indian mothers. These half brothers had told them that Soyapo with the Book of Heaven spoke with split tongues.

It would happen like this, they said. First the missionaries would come, talking spirit law. But soon others would follow who would use that law to take what belonged to the Indian. These men would hold the Book of Heaven in one hand while stealing Indian land with the other. They would divide everything into "mine" and "yours." They would make the Nez Perce pay for goods while taking what they wanted for their own. Soon they would own everything and the Nez Perce would be left with nothing.

This was too close to what the Nez Perce were seeing with their own eyes. The angriest among them began to harass Mr. Spalding and his people. They stopped going to hear him teach spirit law and threw rocks at the school building and spit through the doors and windows at his wife. They broke down the fences and smashed the mill and cut off the ears and tails of his cattle.

Those in the tribe who now lived by the Soyapo ways spoke out against this, saying that Nez Perce who were afraid of the new law were like boys who were afraid to become men. They reminded them of the many gifts they had received from other strangers, like the horse, the ways of the buffalo, and the guns and tools and cooking pots. The new ways of the Spaldings were no different. And by doing violence to the Reverend and his family, they were betraying the promise of friendship their ancestors had made to Lewis and Clark.

But the angry ones refused to listen. These men are not like Lewis and Clark, they responded. Lewis and Clark brought gifts, not laws. Lewis and Clark did not make the Nez Perce wear different clothes. Lewis and Clark did not make them cut their mother's flesh to place seeds in the earth so lazy men could get food without going on the hunt. Lewis and Clark did not ask them to become a nation of old women who sat watching plants grow and slow cows walk while Soyapo told them where to live and how to dress and what to eat and how to worship the Creator.

In exchange for a life of ease, they said, the Soyapo had given them a life of fear. Already, many among them were more concerned about not going to the land of fire than they were about honoring the ancestors and serving the good of their people.

Why too, they asked, did the Soyapo fight among themselves about the path of heaven? The Reverend Spalding was constantly speaking angrily against the Black Robes who had come among the Cayuse and taught a different spirit law from his. And he was always arguing with other Soyapo at the mission about the Book of Heaven. Their grandfathers had taught them that people should not fight about religion because all people were free to find their own path to the Creator.

Gradually, the Nez Perce were becoming a people divided.

All these questions were reduced to nothing during the winter of 1846, when the Creator finally spoke. And he did it in the old way, through the voice of the earth.

That year the snows came early and deep, and went down low into the valleys and canyons, covering the ground where the horses and cattle grazed. The winds blew so cold that a strong man could not remain outside without cover. The rivers and the streams froze. No one alive could remember such a winter.

Unable to find food, the horses and cattle began to die, and the plants that the Reverend Spalding had taught the Nez Perce to harvest froze and became worthless. A great hunger came upon the land and the people.

The medicine men, who had long spoken against the ways of the Soyapo, said that this was the Creator's punishment for the Nez Perce's having abandoned the ways of their grandfathers. This was no longer the voice of some Soyapo spirit teacher speaking to them, they said. It was the voice of the Creator himself. The disagreements among the people were only a reflection of the confusion of their spirit. There was only one way to set things right. The ways of the Soyapo must be abandoned and the teachings of the old ways restored.

Tuekakas listened closely to the counsel of the medicine men. They had the wisdom of the ancestors, and their words were not to be discounted. But neither could he discount the words of his friend, the Reverend Spalding, and the truth that was contained in the Book of Heaven.

Night after night he read the words in his copy of the book that the Reverend had given him as a gift, hoping to find answers to what was happening to his people. It was in his hands to lead, and if the way was clouded, it was up to him to find a clear path.

He conferred too with his brothers among the Cayuse, who lived a few days' journey to the west in the country where Dr. Whitman had settled and built his mission. What he learned from them was unsettling.

Dr. Whitman had once been a caring father, they said, but lately he had seemed more concerned with bringing Soyapo to the land than in teaching spirit law to the people. Several summers before, he had gone back to the East and returned with over a thousand Soyapo. The travelers had stayed only a few days, then gone on toward the great water, but while they were at the mission they had been allowed to camp in Dr. Whitman's yard and come into his house, while the Cayuse were kept at a distance. Such an insult, they believed, spoke of the doctor's true heart.

Now, each year, great numbers of Soyapo were coming in large wagons with billowing cloth tops, carrying not just men, but families. And they were not just passing through. They were building fences and marking off lands. They were turning the mission into a Soyapo village, and the doctor was favoring them in all things, from trading to the time he spent teaching them spirit law.

Perhaps most troubling of all was what the Cayuse had been learning from the Black Robes. The Black Robes were men who taught a different spirit law than the Reverend Spalding and Dr. Whitman. They wore long black robes and hung crosses around their necks. They gave the people medals and coins like those that had been given by the great men, Lewis and Clark. They had beads to help the people pray and crosses to keep away the evil. They rang bells and lit candles and had strong ceremonies that brought curses if they were not followed. They were strong like warriors and did not need women. These Black Robes had said that the Reverend Spalding and Dr. Whitman were teaching the Book of Heaven falsely. By following that false path, they said, the people would be led to the place of endless fire.

To save them from that place, these Black Robes gave the people the gift of the new life from pure water as soon as they came among them. They were not stingy with spirit gifts like Dr. Whitman, who would let people burn forever rather than give them the gift of the saving water if he did not think they were worthy. Because of the big hearts of the Black Robes, many of the Cayuse people had begun to listen to their words and to ignore the words of Dr. Whitman.

What Tuekakas learned from the Cayuse supported what he was learning with his own eyes and ears. He had seen that the Reverend Spalding was spending more time speaking against the Black Robes than he was teaching the way of the good path. And he was, indeed, stingy with the gift of saving water, giving it to very few rather than to anyone who needed it. The Black Robes, his Cayuse brothers had told him, came to the bedside of any Indian who was close to death and gave them the gift of the water if they asked for it, so they could go to the good place with Jesus. But the Reverend Spalding would not do this. And he was charging the Nez Perce for the tools and cattle, yet he still would not pay the Nez Perce for the land on which he had placed his own house and garden. His way was indeed less generous than the way of the Black Robes, if what the Cayuse said was true.

With such confusion surrounding him, Tuekakas decided it was time to withdraw his people from the influence of the Soyapo ways.

Tuekakas had actually begun his withdrawal from the Soyapo world several years earlier. He had not taken kindly to the decision to appoint Ellis head chief, and he had not looked favorably upon the intrusive, punitive Soyapo laws and the unseemly glee with which some of the other Nez Perce had embraced the whip as a way of enforcing them. He still valued his friendship with the Reverend Spalding and counted his Book of Heaven as among his most prized possessions. But when the Soyapo leaders had begun speaking more of laws than things of the spirit and had begun to demand that the people give up their old ways in order to accept the new, he had lost faith in their goodness.

But it was a government act, not an act of Reverend Spalding or the other teachers of spirit law, that finally led him to make the decision to leave. During a distribution of goods a man from the Soyapo government presented him with a tattered blanket in the presence of his own people. For a man who believed that a gift was a statement of a person's heart, this blanket was an insult too great to ignore. He threw the blanket at the man's feet and declared, "I am not a poor man. I have no need of your gifts. Why do you make fun of me before my own people by giving me a rotten blanket? You put shame on me in the eyes of all the chiefs." Then he withdrew his people from the mission and vowed that they would have no more to do with the Soyapo and their insulting ways.

For several years he was able to keep this vow. His people returned to their traditional practices, wintering in the deep folds of the Imnaha Canyon near the banks of the Snake, then returning each spring along the narrow mountain trails to the high, mountain-rimmed Wallowa Valley. There they carried on life in the old way, respecting the traditions that had been taught to them by their ancestors. Aside from occasional visits to meet with relatives and friends who lived near the mission, they had little more to do with the Soyapo world.

But with each passing year it became increasingly difficult to keep out the influence of the Soyapo ways. More and more settlers were traveling through the low valleys on their way to the coast, and more and more contact was becoming inevitable. Roving bands from the Wallowa would ride down from their high mountain homeland, bringing horses grown strong from good breeding and feeding on the rich mountain grasses, and trade one healthy horse for two or more of the weary horses of the travelers. They would then take these worn-down mounts back to the Wallowa, fatten and strengthen them, and return the following year to trade them to new Soyapo travelers. In this way some families had been able to increase their herds to over 1500 horses. They had also been able to trade for oxen, guns, ammunition, and beef cattle.

But this wealth was coming at a price. Alcohol too was making its way into the Wallowa, and there were those among the people who behaved as if they were not in their right minds when they drank this Soyapo spirit water.

Tuekakas reminded the people to keep their distance from the white settlers. Raise horses, eat things that grow of their own, and come and go as you please, he said. But beyond trading for that which is good, do not get involved in Soyapo ways.

By and large, the people followed his advice. They continued to dress in the old manner and to keep their faith in the old truths. The young men wore their hair long, with braids at their right or left temple to designate their status as a favorite son or grandson. Families with a daughter as the firstborn raised her to be a basket hat woman, who could advise the men of the tribe when she grew to maturity. They kept to the sweats and the strict ways of the longhouse. They made their seasonal pilgrimages to sacred hunting grounds and fishing spots and gathering places and offered the firstfruits of any harvest to the Creator in the prescribed manner. In all ways they were becoming once again children of their ancestors rather than children of Jesus, if they could just stay free of Soyapo ways.

But Tuekakas could sense dark clouds gathering on the horizon. From the people who traveled to the great bitter-tasting water he had heard of new outbreaks of the sickness with the killing spots. Soyapo towns were springing up on Indian lands in the coastal valleys, and soldiers were arriving in increasing numbers to protect Soyapo travelers and enforce Soyapo laws.

Slowly but inevitably, the people were being surrounded by Soyapo. The river of settlers, traveling through the valleys, was quietly becoming a sea.

———————

None of this had any immediate impact on young Joseph, who was now in the fullness of youth. Because he was now living in only the Wallowa and the Imnaha, his life was being shaped in all manner by the traditional ways. He bathed every morning, drank water as purification before eating, learned to honor each season and each gift of the Creator. He received training in the boyhood skills of riding and bridle making and caring for horses and was taught the deeper knowledge of the ways of the animals and the messages in the waters and winds.

But as the son of a chief, he was also being raised as a chief in the making. He was dressed differently and kept apart from the others in times of raucous play so he would learn the qualities of dignity and distance that must be reflected in a chief's character. If his playmates got into trouble, it was he who was punished, for it was imperative that he be taught to take responsibility for the actions of everyone around him. In all his words and behavior, he was held to strictest account, reminded constantly that he must think first of the people and only then of himself, and that he must never do anything unworthy of the best vision of the person he was expected to become.

None of this was hard for the young boy because by temperament he was a quiet and thoughtful child. Holding his tongue and shaping his thoughts came naturally to him, as did resisting the impulse to anger and rash actions. Even at this young age he commanded respect and demonstrated the clear, self-contained strength that would be needed in a leader of the people.

His closest companion was his brother, Ollokot, three years his junior. Ollokot was as fun loving and gregarious as Joseph was taciturn and watchful. Unlike Joseph, Ollokot was encouraged to run with the other boys because he was being raised to assume the important post of war chief, and it was essential that he learn to inspire loyalty and friendship. What was crucial in his upbringing was that he always be required to take a leadership role in group activities and that he learn to take decisive action in times of stress and crisis. With his strong physique, courageous attitude, and winning smile, he too seemed ideally suited to his task.

Together these two brothers—Ollokot, the fun-loving youth who inspired loyalty, and Joseph, the taciturn, thoughtful youth who commanded respect—offered promise and hope for a new generation of Nez Perce leadership that could keep the Wallowa people secure and free.

Then, in Joseph's seventh year, the year the whites called 1847, a great crisis erupted that brought that promise and hope into question. Some of the Cayuse rose up and murdered Dr. Whitman, his family, and many others at the mission.

There had been anger at the way the doctor had been favoring the Soyapo and anger at the way the Soyapo were now filling up their land. But more than that, many of the Cayuse people had begun to question whether his spirit power was good or evil or whether he even had spirit power at all.

Recently, the sickness with black spots had come among them, killing their elders and their children. Not only did the doctor's medicine not make them well, but many felt it was the medicine itself that was causing the illness and that it was part of the doctor's plan to kill the Cayuse so the Soyapo could have their land.

There had been other things too—the melons from the Whitmans' garden that had made people sick; the young boy who had choked to death on a piece of meat after Dr. Whitman had spoken angrily to him and touched him on the shoulder. For those who had eyes to see, it was clear that Dr. Whitman might be much worse than a false medicine man. He might be an evil spirit.

Even those among the Cayuse who doubted this could not deny that the doctor's medicine was weak. The great power shown them all by Lewis and Clark, the power they sought and for which they had given up their old ways, did not lie in the doctor's hands. Maybe the Black Robes were right. Maybe the medicine men were right. It did not matter. What was important was that the ways of Dr. Whitman were not right. And maybe they were something far worse.

So the angriest and most fearful members of the tribe had attacked the doctor's house, bludgeoned him to death with a pipe tomahawk, wounded his wife, then dragged her outside, where they threw her in the mud, shot her repeatedly, and whipped her as she died. They then went on a rampage and killed eleven more white people while taking forty-seven captives and burning all the mission buildings to the ground.

Such a savage attack spread fear throughout the entire Columbia Plateau. Many of the remaining settlers fled for their lives, and the tribes prepared for what they knew would be harsh retribution. Even those who had taken no part knew that whites did not differentiate among Indians when punishment was meted out and that a dark skin would mean a dark fate when the soldiers and settler fighters arrived to exact vengeance for the killings.

For some on both sides, however, the killings represented an opportunity. It was a chance, they believed, to come to a final resolution on ownership of the land. The whites who had long feared a great uprising saw this as a chance to annihilate all the Indians so the settlement of the Plateau could continue unimpeded. The Indians who had doubted the Soyapo ways and had become alarmed at the increasing Soyapo presence saw this as the opportunity to drive the settlers from their land and reclaim it for themselves and their children.

Those caught in the middle—the settlers who had become friends with the Indians and knew that these were the actions of a few individuals, and the Indians who had taken to white ways or believed that coexistence was the only route to peace—were forced to act quickly. The government was already mustering a military force made up of angry settlers and soldiers from as far away as San Francisco. They would soon ride into the Plateau, and a plague of violence would be unleashed that none on either side would be able to control.

At this point, a British trader the Indians respected came among them with an offer to exchange the forty-seven white captives for a ransom of blankets, bullets, guns, and tobacco. Though he pointedly refused to make any promises, the Indians agreed to the exchange in hopes that it would forestall any violent retribution.

But the freeing of the prisoners only exacerbated the situation. Once back in the white settlements by the coast, the captive settlers gave graphic descriptions of the skull-smashing and mutilating that had taken place at the Whitman mission. Any willingness to stay the hand of justice now ceased to exist among the whites.

Over the next several months, conditions deteriorated. Isolated clashes took place between belligerent Indians and groups of settlers and soldiers all throughout the Plateau. The situation was threatening to break out into full-scale war. The Reverend Spalding, who had run for his life with the rest of the settlers, sent a passionate plea to his friends among the Nez Perce to stay far from the violence. He entreated them to meet with a group of government representatives who were preparing to travel from the coastal regions into the Plateau. "With good hearts they meet you," he wrote in his stilted prose. "The good are not to be punished. . . . Very many Americans are going to seek the bad Cayuses. . . . There will soon be large ships from California."

The Nez Perce had no faith in these promises, but even those who were opposed to the Soyapo ways had no desire for this war that the Cayuse had started. They were willing to meet with these government men to express their desire to avoid conflict.

Unfortunately, the government representatives, who were coming from the Willamette Valley 250 miles away, were not traveling alone. Though the men had been instructed to travel with a minimal military presence in order to avoid increasing the tensions, the military man among them, a Colonel Gilliam, had insisted on bringing his entire contingent of 400 soldiers and armed volunteers. By the time they met with the Nez Perce, these soldiers had been involved in serious clashes with the Cayuse, and the Nez Perce were prepared for the worst.

The meeting took place at a camp that the soldier leader had set up on the site of the burned-out Whitman mission. The Nez Perce rode in 250 strong, showing no fear. Bypassing Ellis, they had designated Tuekakas to be their spokesman. His respect among the Nez Perce, his Cayuse blood, and his long-standing friendship with the Reverend Spalding made him the person most likely to be able to broker a peace, if there was peace to be had.

Tuekakas held up his Book of Heaven, given him by the Reverend Spalding. "It is my light," he said. "I speak for all the Cayuses present, and all my people. I do not want my children engaged in this war. . . . You speak of the murderers. I shall not meddle with them. I bow my head. This much I speak."

After the other chiefs had spoken, the government representatives were somewhat mollified. The Nez Perce, the most numerous and potentially dangerous of the Plateau tribes, seemed pacified. Without Nez Perce participation, there was little likelihood of an all-out war. In gratitude, they appointed one of the mountain men who had married a Nez Perce woman to serve as Indian agent to the tribe and promised that no more white people would ever be allowed to settle in Nez Perce lands.

Tuekakas went back to his distant Wallowa Valley, convinced that he had brokered a successful peace. His children, indeed, would not have to become engaged in a violent and fruitless war.

4

A Tide of Laws and Men

THE EFFORTS OF Tuekakas and the other chiefs were partially successful. The Plateau did not break out into full-scale war. But some among the whites were still intent on finding the killers, and some among the Indians were intent upon keeping them hidden. As a result, skirmishes continued.

By and large, these skirmishes amounted to nothing. In a great landscape of green, rolling hills, deep canyons, and heavily forested, craggy mountain ranges stretching for hundreds of miles, it was impossible for the small numbers of whites to mount any concerted military action. And there was no common sentiment on the part of the various tribes as to what kind of stand to take in relation to white demands. So the encounters generally devolved into unfortunate incidents where white volunteers, coming upon a wandering band of peaceful Indians, shot them without provocation, or where old men were killed for protesting the confiscation of their cows.

It was a war of attrition, with neither side having the heart to do what was necessary to achieve all-out victory. Eventually, the soldiers and citizen volunteers, unable to either catch the killers or root out pockets of resistance, withdrew to the safer, more settled areas back in the Willamette Valley toward the coast. In leaving, they told the tribes that all could live in peace if the killers were handed over but that the Cayuse, because of their continued warlike behavior and stubborn refusal to assist in identifying the killers, had forfeited all rights to their land. It would now be open to settlement by the whites.

This angered the tribes, especially the Cayuse, because many of them had remained friendly toward the whites and had wanted the killers turned over for punishment. Now they too were being punished for the actions of a few.

But in reality, this edict had little practical effect because few settlers were willing to brave the dangerous wilds of a country that had seen a God-fearing man like Dr. Whitman suffer such a cruel and savage fate. So when five men purported to have been the killers were seized and hanged for their misdeeds on June 3, 1850, a kind of peace settled over the Plateau. The missionaries had fled, the white settlers had left for less dangerous territory, and newcomers traveling on the wagon trails wanted to do nothing more than pass through as quickly as possible. The punishment of the supposed killers had satisfied all but the most bloodthirsty of the whites, so there was little reason for military presence among them. The Nez Perce, the Cayuse, and all their kin seemed once again to have found peace in their own country.

But this peace could not last forever. In 1848, a year after the massacre and two years before the killers were hanged for their crimes, an event had taken place hundreds of miles away that would shape the world of the Plateau people for generations to come.

Gold had been discovered in California.

At first, the discovery worked to the advantage of the Indians in the Northwest because the troubling tide of immigrants into their country almost completely dried up. There was precious little reason to brave uncertain Indian Territory when there was wealth for the taking in the streams and creek beds of the country seven hundred miles to the south.

But it took only the end of the Gold Rush dream to turn the attention of the travelers back toward the north. By the early 1850s, wagon trains from the East were hearing from returning stragglers that the gold boom was over, and they suddenly looked with more favor upon the old Oregon Trail, which had been almost forgotten in the frenzy to get to the California gold fields. Wagons began diverting at the cutoff near Salt Lake City and heading toward the Northwest and the more reasonable, if less sensational, promises of riches in ranch and farmland. At the same time, disenchanted, destitute miners from California headed north in hopes of salvaging something from a dream that had turned to dust.

All manner of immigrant and American-born dreamers who had left their homes for the promise of wealth headed toward the Pacific Northwest. Oregon Territory, so long the woolly domain of fur trappers and proselytizers, was suddenly in the sights of miners, claim jumpers, hustlers, laborers, landless former farmers, entrepreneurs, prostitutes, and all manner of humanity who had been drawn to the promise of easy riches in California.

At first these newcomers were interested in only the fertile coastal valleys. But as those valleys began to fill up, settlers cast their eyes over the Cascade Mountains and across the dry high-country desert toward the rich grazing lands of the distant eastern Columbia Plateau. For emigrants who had not been part of the Whitman massacre or its bloody aftermath, the land seemed more promising than dangerous. The isolated and rugged terrain and fear of hostile Indians, which for several years had acted as a barrier to the whites and a protection of the native peoples, once again seemed like no barrier at all.

It was at this point that the government edict regarding the opening of the Cayuse country for settlement began to affect the tribes. It was exacerbated by a political act that had taken place shortly before the Whitman massacre and about which the Indians had no understanding at all.

Since the time of the first white incursions into the Northwest, the area had been almost without government. The British and Americans had shared it under an uneasy truce of joint occupancy, leaving it mostly to its own devices. It was too far removed from any centers of power, too sparsely populated, and of too little economic interest to merit the expenditures of will and finances necessary to bring it under government control. Such order as existed had been maintained by the fur companies, the various missionaries, and shadowy opportunists who got themselves appointed to vague roles as Indian agents or liaisons. But all of this had amounted to nothing. People had done what they chose and solved their problems between themselves by whatever means they had at their disposal.

But as Britain and the United States had begun to see the economic and strategic value of the area, it had become an object of greater political contention. Each nation wanted ownership in order to claim the resources and seaports, but neither could afford to expend military or financial resources in an attempt to control it. So, rather than engage in armed conflict, settlers had been encouraged to move into the territory and stake their claims so ownership could be taken by a kind of tacit eminent domain.

Dr. Whitman's journeys back east, ostensibly to get supplies for the continued effort to bring the gospel to the natives, had been as much about bringing new American settlers to the West as they had been about replenishing depleted supplies. New settlers would increase the American (and Protestant) presence and would help establish the right of ownership when the time of decision came.

When that decision had finally been made by the Oregon Compromise agreement of 1846 and the country below the 49th parallel was granted to the United States, the fate of Indian people took a turn that would influence them forever.

The United States had evolved its practices regarding Indians during the settling of the East and had begun shaping these practices into national policy. Under this policy, Indian tribes were to be dealt with as separate nations. Treaties were to be made, and both signatories were to be bound to certain behaviors and limits by the terms of those treaties.

This rule of mutual legal compact, with its European roots, had no precedent among the individualistic native peoples of the continent. No concept of "tribe" as a political unit even existed among them. They were bound together by language, family, and cultural affinity. You knew who your people were, but there was no formal line by which someone was designated in or out. People married into a group based on custom or circumstance; people lived with and became part of other groups with whom they had friendly relations. And within the groups, no person spoke for the rest in all matters, and even consensus did not bind those who had not given their consent. If you disagreed with a decision, you simply were not bound by the agreement. Your decisions were your own, based on your own sense of honor and responsibility, and these were governed not by external laws but by the obligations you felt to spiritual forces, your ancestors, and the people whose care you felt had been entrusted to your hands. If you did not agree with the decision of a leader, you simply moved away or refused to comply.

In addition, the idea of land as personal property, a key principle on which the United States was basing its treaties, was alien to the native people. How could one "own" the land? You were born from the land, nurtured by it. It was your mother, and you could no more buy or sell it than you could buy or sell your birthright as a child of your mother. Agreements based on hard lines of land ownership lay beyond both understanding and any acceptable practices of moral responsibility toward the earth.

Prior to the actual establishment of a border between Canada and the United States in 1846, this had not been an issue because even the whites in the vast territory of the Pacific Northwest had operated on the more amorphous principles of usage and occupation. But the conclusion of the border agreement changed everything. America could now expand without resistance into the previously ungoverned Pacific Northwest, and it could do so under its own self-defined rules of ownership and legally binding treaties.

Suddenly, the tribes—people with no tradition of a single, dominating leader, no belief in the actions of one binding the behavior of all, and no precedent for establishing hard, arbitrary lines of property ownership—were being asked to make legally binding decisions about who owned what and who could go where and under what circumstances. The earth, which had once been understood as a spiritual gift and birthright, had become a negotiable legal entity. Land had become property.

This was a recipe for disaster for all Indian people, but especially for tribes that ranged freely, like the Nez Perce. They moved with the seasons, wandered hundreds of miles, and sometimes would leave their home territory for years at a time to travel to buffalo country. But in their minds, they were bound to those homelands like one is bound to a family, or the salmon is bound to the waters of its birth, and their presence or absence did not in any way change or compromise that bond.

But to settlers, and to the country that now was claiming the right to define the rules of settlement, nonoccupation meant nonownership, and inefficient usage reflected moral failure. Christian scriptures commanded people to subdue the earth and make it fruitful, and the United States was a country that believed itself founded on scripture. People who did not occupy land or who used it inefficiently could be demanded to move, and the land could be given over to more industrious sorts who would fulfill the biblical injunction to make it yield and bear fruit. At minimum, the amount of space claimed by wandering people could be cut down to more realistic size based on practices of efficient agrarian usage, which, it was assumed, they would eventually adopt.

So roaming tribes like the Nez Perce presented a real problem. The only way to work a viable agreement with them was to put all the lands they claimed as their homelands inside the area reserved by the treaty and to allow them hunting and fishing rights in their traditional migration patterns, or to pay them handsomely to accept less.

This was what the earlier treaties with Indian peoples in the East, at their best, had tried to do. And this was what the government hoped to do with the tribes in the Northwest. However, since the ultimate purpose of the treaties was not fairness and equity but control and containment that enabled white settlement to continue unrestricted and unabated, all legal and extralegal measures necessary to ensure this had to be taken. If bribes had to be offered, lies told, or conditions abrogated in order to meet changing circumstances or to overcome Indian obstinacy, so be it. If, ultimately, Indians had to be removed by force and resettled in distant lands, so be that as well. The flood of white settlement, it was believed, could not be stopped. It was both a physical and historical inevitability. The white race was destined by nature to overrun the Indian people, and any concessions made to protect these unfortunate souls were understood by settlers and the government to be acts of unnecessary generosity.

Consequently, when the post–Gold Rush tide of settlers began to flow in from California and the East, the Nez Perce and the other Plateau tribes found themselves facing a very different set of circumstances than they had confronted even a few years before. Now they were being overrun by people who sought not to share the land, but to take it. And these people had a government behind them to enforce their right to do so.

Tuekakas watched all this from his hawk's eye vantage point in the high, mountainous Wallowa. Visitors from the tribes near the coast were telling of white settlers flooding into their land, going where they would, doing what they wished, killing native people, and bringing new sicknesses that could not be cured. They were drawing lines and building fences and shooting Indians who ventured across. Their numbers were so large that Soyapo leaders could not hold them back, and even when they could, they chose not to.

The coastal chiefs were being told that the only way to survive was to choose a small piece of land and to move onto it so the government soldiers could protect them. This met with no one's favor. No person had the right to tell another where to go or not go. No one could claim to make laws about the land that went against the teachings of the Creator.

From across the mountains toward buffalo country, stories were filtering in of new forts being built on rivers and new Soyapo towns growing up in places that native peoples had always known as their own. Even in the Nez Perce's own country, the trails were now alive with the groaning wheels of white-topped Soyapo wagons moving in formation across the hills and along the river valleys.

Most disturbing of all was the rumor of a white chief from the East who was coming with soldiers to buy Indian land and open it to white settlement.

The "chief" to whom these rumors referred was Isaac Stevens, an energetic whippet of a man who had gotten himself appointed as the governor of Washington Territory, a new jurisdiction carved out of the vast original Oregon Territory. Stevens was an impetuous man, impatient with obstacles and wasted time. In addition to being appointed governor, he had convinced the Department of War to make him head of a survey team that would try to find a potential railroad route to the Pacific. In his efforts to learn the best trails and pathways he had hired Indian guides who had passed the word of his coming from band to band until it had crossed the mountains and reached the ears of the Yakima, and then the Palouse and Cayuse and Nez Perce.

With forces gathering around them, the chiefs of the Plateau tribes determined that they needed to take preemptive action. They met in grand council and decided that none would act alone to make agreements with this new white chief and that if they had to draw lines around their land to keep the white settlers out, all the land that the Creator had given to each tribe must be protected by those lines.

Though the sentiment for protecting the land was universal, opinions on how to achieve this were not. Many among the Nez Perce, and some among the Cayuse, had embraced the ways taught by the now-departed missionaries. They had no quarrel with the white newcomers, only a desire to protect the land that the Creator had given their people as a birthright, and a healthy fear of the diseases that the white settlers brought in their wake. Others, like Tuekakas, wished to remain on friendly terms, even if they did not wish to embrace the white people's ways. Then there were those who still harbored ill will toward the white invaders and happily would have taken up arms against the interlopers who demanded land, fealty, and abandonment of the old ways as taught by the ancestors. Many of these were followers of Smolholla, a diminutive, hunchbacked man from the Wanapum tribe that lived on the edge of the Columbia River in the dry country west of the Nez Perce.

Smolholla was a person of great spiritual power who had fallen into a death state and awakened three days later with a vision from the spirit world. In his vision, he had been told that the white ways were bad for Indian people—that they caused sickness and confusion and that all the strife in their country and in their people's hearts was because they had abandoned the old ways and begun cutting the earth and living in a manner displeasing to the Creator.

His message spoke not only to those who had been opposed to the missionaries but also to many who had begun to have doubts about the suitability of the Christian way for Indian people. Just as they had accepted Jesus because he seemed to embody many of the traditional ways of the people, they now listened to Smolholla because his experience seemed to reflect the experience of Jesus while reclaiming those traditional ways. He and his followers were known as "Dreamers."

With these different points of view, the members of the Plateau tribes—Christians, Dreamers, and followers of the seven-drums longhouse ways of their ancestors—prepared to meet in council with the new law chief, Stevens, to see what sort of guarantees they could gain regarding the protection of their land and the continued freedom and safety of their people.

Stevens was more than willing to meet with the tribes. He wanted issues settled as quickly as possible so he could get on with the business of developing the country. He did not wish to have any trouble either with or from the Indians and was prepared to provide each tribe with a reasonable amount of land in the form of a reservation. But if the Indians were too obdurate or too excessive in their demands, he intended to take what he wanted on whatever terms he chose.

Stevens had no taste for long negotiations or equivocation, but he knew that long negotiations were part of the Indian way of arriving at decisions. Discussions went back and forth, with extended formal prologues, oblique references to issues, constant revisiting of points, and grand rhetorical soliloquies by various leaders, all in the effort to reach a meaningful consensus. He was willing to endure this, but in his mind the outcome was already decided: he would have their lands. The only issue was on what terms.

In late May 1855, Stevens set up an arbor in a grove of trees just down the river from where the Whitman mission had stood, and prepared to meet the Indians with feasts and gifts. When the Nez Perce rode in first, over 2400 people strong, and circled his 100 men with 1000 stripped, painted, shield-thumping warriors, it became abundantly clear that the negotiations would have to be handled delicately. The Nez Perce had intended no threat, only a grand ceremonial entry, and Stevens understood this. Nonetheless, their numbers were daunting.

The demeanor of the Cayuse and Walla Wallas and Umatillas, who arrived shortly thereafter, however, spoke of a different attitude. They did not make a grand entry but merely camped sullenly behind a distant grove of trees, refusing to acknowledge Stevens or to accept any gifts or provisions. But Stevens was undeterred. He had stocked a wooden storehouse with gifts for the various tribes, and he believed that his feasts, gifts, and promises would eventually bring all the people to his side.

When all the tribes had arrived, he began his council. Despite rumors of threats against him and his men, he bravely stood his ground in the face of some 5000 assembled Indians, constantly and even brazenly making the case for the benefits of reservation life.

In the course of the next twelve days, he told them that the reservations were the only way the Great Father back East could protect them from the incursions of whites flooding into the area; he made outrageous claims that the Cherokee removal far to the east had resulted in prosperity for the Cherokee people; he promised more schools, more tools, more cattle, more money; he insisted that the government would keep white people off the reservations while Indians would have the perpetual right to hunt and fish on all their traditional grounds, whether within or beyond the boundaries of the reservations.

He even claimed that the Nez Perce would be free to continue their wide-ranging journeys across the mountains into buffalo country and that the government would assist in bringing a lasting peace between the Nez Perce and the Blackfeet. There was hardly a promise he would not make so long as the Indians accepted the basic premise that they be limited to living on a designated piece of land. This same model of negotiations had been used successfully in the East, and if the end result was betrayal of promises, that was of less import than the immediate need to get the tribes to accept the premise of confinement on well-defined pieces of land.

To those people and tribes who were positively disposed toward the whites, his offer was tempting, so long as all their traditional homelands were included in those designated reservations. But to others who mistrusted white promises or who were being deprived of their lands, these offers rang hollow. And to those, like the Dreamers of Smolholla and the strict followers of the seven-drum way, who believed that the earth was the living, breathing mother from whom they had been born, such talk of buying and selling parcels of the earth was spiritually repugnant.

In the course of the lengthy negotiations, Lawyer, one of the Nez Perce chiefs who long had been a friend of the whites, ingratiated himself with Stevens by moving his teepee near the governor's camp, ostensibly to protect the governor from a murder plot that some of the disaffected Indians were said to be hatching. Lawyer was a practicing Christian and a convert to white ways as well as an advocate for accommodation, so it was not clear that his move wasn't really an attempt to place himself and his family closer to the governor in order to gain protection from the less conciliatory Nez Perce. But his apparently magnanimous gesture as well his facility with English and his fervent Christian prayer sessions, which took place within earshot of Stevens, immediately made him a favorite of the governor. Stevens soon designated him as the head chief and spokesman for the Nez Perce people.

This designation was met with derision and contempt by the other Nez Perce leaders, who knew that Lawyer held no such authority. He was no more the chief over all the people than Ellis had been, and Lawyer himself knew it. But, both for self-serving purposes and because he believed he could use his English to negotiate the best conditions for the Nez Perce, he accepted the mantle with relish. He had been intimately involved in the negotiations to turn over the Cayuse responsible for the massacre at the Whitman mission and felt that he had a better understanding of the white man and the white man's laws than any of the more traditional chiefs.

The negotiations went on for eighteen days. The tribes were of varying minds and had varying concerns. Some did not like the proposed boundaries. Some were skeptical of white motives. Some were offended by the greater level of favors that seemed to be being promised to the most conciliatory or overtly Christian of the bands and tribes. Some simply opposed the process or the very concept itself. And some were resistant because all the affected tribes of the Plateau were not even present at the gathering.

In the end, after two and a half weeks, Stevens had made his case sufficiently to bring all those present, either willingly or reluctantly, to the brink of signing an agreement. But on that day, Chief Looking Glass, the seventy-year-old patriarch among the Nez Perce chiefs, rode into the assembly. He had been informed of the council while he was across the mountains in buffalo country and had ridden almost without stop in order to arrive at the gathering before the bands acted.

Because of his age, experience, and stature as a warrior and buffalo hunter, he was the closest thing the Nez Perce had to a head chief. He certainly commanded more respect than Lawyer. Without even getting off his horse, he berated the assembled Nez Perce and told them to go back to their lodges. "I will talk to you," he said. His brusque manner and insulting lack of ceremony in the presence of Stevens could not be misinterpreted.

But during the ensuing discussions with his people, Looking Glass inexplicably had a change of heart. There was some speculation that he and Lawyer had staged the entire event to extract more concessions from Stevens, but the enmity between the two men made that unlikely. Nonetheless, two days later, all the Nez Perce representatives, along with those of the Cayuse, Umatilla, Walla Walla, Yakima, and minor assembled tribes, all acceded to the agreement.

But it was not clear to what they had agreed. Though Stevens had made many grand promises during the negotiations, it was not clear exactly what was in the treaty itself. Translation of terms was an arduous process, going from one language to another, and none could be sure that the translations were accurate. Then, in the actual signing, some of the chiefs merely touched the end of the writing implement while white scribes marked Xs next to their name, and in more than one instance they claimed they believed that they were agreeing only to friendship with the whites.

With the exception of Lawyer, even those who were able to sign their names were not permitted to do so, leaving a document with only Xs as proof of the Indians' agreement to its terms. There was also talk that Stevens had visited the tribes separately and in private and told those who did not sign that their people would soon find themselves walking "knee-deep in blood."

But, whatever the forces were that drove the decision, on Monday,

June 11, 1855, the document was completed and sent to Washington to await Senate approval and presidential signature before becoming a legally binding agreement between the United States and the tribes of the Columbia Plateau.

The Nez Perce had accepted this treaty in no small part because all their lands were contained within its designated boundaries. Many among them were devout Christians and willing converts to the white way of life. To such people, and even to those who did not look so fondly on white culture, the promise of schools, plows, grist mills, lumber mills, teachers, blankets, clothing, and money seemed a worthy return for an X on an agreement that otherwise seemed to have no impact on them.

But the Nez Perce, by signing, had agreed to much more than they knew. They had given tacit acceptance to the idea of land as something salable and negotiable and had allowed the white government to set the terms by which the two peoples thereafter would come to agreements. They had also established themselves unwittingly as a unitary group for the purposes of negotiation. If they did not now realize this, or did not appreciate its full implications, they soon would.

Tuekakas had played no large part in the negotiations. Though he was one of the most respected chiefs and the government representatives had eagerly sought his agreement, he had stayed in the background, secure that his distant Wallowa was of no interest to whites and concerned only that the final boundaries include all his traditional land. Since they did, he left the treaty proceedings satisfied that the real effect of the new agreement was not to limit the place of his people on the earth, but to protect that place from white incursions. In his mind, he had signed as the representative of the Wallowa band, and his signature was binding only in regard to the Wallowa band and its lands.

Young Joseph had accompanied him to the proceedings and had watched with great interest. Though only fourteen, the boy was already being groomed for leadership, and this was an opportunity to observe the art of negotiation and the ways of the whites. And it had been time well spent. He had heard different arguments, different ways of expression, different positions, and different points of view. He had been able to observe not only the Nez Perce, but also the white government officials. And he had heard firsthand that to which the U.S. government and his people had agreed.

Young Joseph was very different from his father. Though Tuekakas was a man of traditional roots, he still read his Book of Heaven and honored the teachings of the Reverend Spalding. Young Joseph had learned a common human respect for the whites as people while a child at the Lapwai, but he had been too young to be deeply immersed in the beliefs that the Reverend espoused. As a result, he had grown to manhood with both a more singular sense of the old ways and a more conciliatory attitude toward whites than his father now possessed.

Young Nez Perce boys traditionally kept a distance from their fathers in order to foster an attitude of respect, and young Joseph, though being groomed to take his father's role as chief, was no different. He had received much of his training about manhood from favorite uncles and had been taught the ways of the longhouse and the important feasts from the elders. His childhood learning had come at the hands of the grandmothers, and his understanding of the animals and birds and plants had been given him by those with medicine knowledge. His father's role was to embody the principles of leadership and pass them on to his son through example. But the character and spiritual formation of the boy had been guided by others in accord with the strict requirements for the raising of a future leader.

By the time Joseph had gone with his father to the treaty gathering, he was truly a child of the old ways. He had been on his *wayakin* quest and had met the spirit power that would be his guide throughout his life. He had learned the song that the spirit guide had given him and had revealed his newly given name to the tribe at the autumn feast where such announcements were made. Young Joseph, son of Tuekakas, was now Hin-mah-too-yah-lat-kekht—Thunder Rising over Distant Mountains—and his character as well as his demeanor were well reflected in this name.

The treaty that resulted from the proceedings young Joseph had attended was an uneasy agreement at best. Most of the tribes were unclear about the agreement, and scratches on paper did not bind an Indian heart when it felt it had been wronged.

Unknown to the Indians when they had signed the agreement was a prior law, made at the time the Pacific Northwest had come into American hands, that any white man could claim for himself 320 acres of land in this new territory and another 320 acres in the name of his wife. The broad and sometimes imprecise boundaries negotiated with the various tribes meant little to the incoming settlers, and the government was almost completely unable to enforce even those boundaries that could be defined. Add in the dissatisfaction many of the tribal members felt with the conditions of the agreement, the favoritism shown to those tribes and leaders who were most compliant with white wishes, and the venality and criminality of many of the whites who were coming north from the gold fields, and it was inevitable that the fragile peace would not hold.

Soon the Plateau was once again riddled with war. Bloody encounters were taking place between government soldiers and various disaffected tribes who felt betrayed by the treaty conditions. White men were having their throats cut and their bodies burned by marauding bands of warriors, and white soldiers were killing elderly Indian men, cutting off their fingers, and using strips of their flesh for razor strops.

It did not help that the U.S. Senate was dragging its feet on ratification. The tribes were watching their homelands fill up with settlers while seeing none of the proposed benefits from their agreeing to government terms. No money was forthcoming; neither were the promised goods, schools, mills, cattle, or tools. Those tribal leaders who had argued most strongly for accepting the white conditions were now losing prestige most rapidly. And those who had opposed the treaty were finding their influence growing.

Stevens and the other government officials were counting on the Nez Perce to be the voice of reason. They numbered around 4000, making their population equal to all the other tribes combined. They had always been friendly toward the whites, and some had even shown great promise, as the white leaders saw it, in "abandoning their Indian ways to become productive members of society." They also had been given the most of what they wanted in terms of land, and that land, with its rocky inclines, deep gorges, and deep winter snows, was the least desirable to white settlers of any land in the Plateau. If being left alone constituted the desired outcome of the treaty, the Nez Perce had received the greatest benefit of any of the signatory tribes.

But the failure of the government to deliver on its treaty promises of goods and amenities was fracturing their seemingly solid front. While some Nez Perce stood so loyally by the whites that they donned soldiers' uniforms and served as escorts for government officials traveling around the Plateau, others were beginning to have serious doubts about the agreement. Lawyer was being openly ridiculed by other tribal leaders for his naive trust in the good offices of the whites, and Tuekakas was brooding over the massacre of twenty-seven Cayuse women, elders, and children who had traveled to his country to visit their relatives. What had been a difference in philosophy about how to deal with the whites was becoming an actual rift in the tribe.

In general, the rift was following familiar lines. The Christian bands—those who had lived along the river edges and had been visited most easily by missionaries—were standing by the white government and the treaties. Those who had traditionally lived far from the sites of white visitation and had not had Christian missionaries actually live among them were turning away from the empty promises of the government. Among this latter group were the people of Tuekakas, who lived in closer proximity to the Cayuse than to the Christian Nez Perce, and Looking Glass, who spent much of his time across the mountains in buffalo country.

Unlike their Christian brothers and sisters, these more disaffected bands had not taken to sedentary living and had not experienced the material benefit of shifting to a life based on raising crops and domestic animals. They even began insisting that they had not understood the conditions of the treaty and wished it to be revisited. Lawyer stood strong against them, even becoming a spokesman for the government, publicly declaring that all fifty-eight men who had signed the treaty had been well aware of its contents and had signed of their own volition.

This fracturing of the fragile peace, and the relationships behind it, was taking place all across the Plateau. Not only were the benefits of the treaty not forthcoming, its protections were not being upheld. White men, with little interest in Indian claims and points of view, were moving into the land to claim the acreage they felt was their due under the new territorial laws. They had no interest in the niceties of governmental treaties, especially those that had not been ratified by the Senate and signed by the president, which this one had not. The government itself was powerless to stop them. Its military presence was too small and spread out, and even if the soldiers had chosen to act, their authority was limited as long as the treaty remained unratified.

Meanwhile, the land-hungry settlers poured onto Indian lands. Like the Indians themselves, these settlers valued areas with ready sources of water and good farming and grazing sites. Lands that were highly valued by the tribes and that lay clearly inside the boundaries of the treaty lines were being brazenly occupied and claimed by white intruders.

Some of the tribes remained peaceful, hoping that the white government would stand by its promises. Others, convinced they had been wronged, engaged in direct confrontation. Still others took advantage of white land hunger to sell some of their own lands and to find employment as scouts or ferrymen.

At first the Nez Perce were not deeply affected by these intrusions. Their land, being craggy, cold in the winter, and far to the east on the edge of the mountains, had not initially drawn many of the white settlers. The biggest issues they were facing were the nonperformance of the government in meeting its terms of payment of goods and money and the spillover of outrages such as the one Tuekakas's visitors had suffered.

As to the white settlers themselves, most of the Nez Perce remained on friendly terms with them. Since the departure of the missionaries, the Christian bands had taken on the governance of their own people and had developed settlements that mirrored white settlements in appearance and in practices. They were quite happy to see the return of white goods and opportunities. Bands of a more traditional bent simply kept their distance.

But many of the white immigrants flooding north were not interested in becoming settlers. They had not lost the gold fever that had brought them west, and they still sought the big strike. They knew how to read landscapes for telltale geological signs as well as what to look for in hillsides and creeks. They also knew what to ask when they spoke with Indians and what to watch for as they surveyed tribal handicrafts and decoration. And when they saw evidence of gold, they knew what to do.

Many of the Nez Perce who were friendly to the whites were happy to show off their gold. To them it was simply a beautiful adornment with no more or less intrinsic value than an abalone shell or a sky-colored bead. Its greatest value, they felt, was as a trade good with the white people, who obviously valued it far beyond its reasonable worth.

Soon stories abounded of gold in the hills and streams of Nez Perce country, and white adventurers were wandering the reservation lands in search of the metal. This did not meet with great favor among all the tribal members, but as long as the intruders kept to trails near the rivers and continued to enrich the Nez Perce through trade, they could be tolerated.

Then, in February 1860, an intrepid miner named Pierce convinced one of the Christian Nez Perce to assist him and his party in their search for the metal. Their preliminary pannings and makeshift sluicings produced eighty dollars in gold dust. Word spread quickly, and the people who had drifted north from the gold fields of California once again had a focus for their gold hunger. They poured into Nez Perce country on foot, on horseback, or by any means they could. The rush was on.

The Treaty of 1855 had finally been ratified the previous year, so the miners now were trespassing on land that officially belonged to the Nez Perce. But gold fever knew no boundaries. Soon ferries filled with prospectors were churning up the Columbia to its junction with the Snake, then heading up the Snake toward Nez Perce country. Ferries could go only as far as the bend where the Snake met the Clearwater, so the men coming from the coast disembarked at this point. It was only several miles down the river from the Lapwai and lay well within the boundaries of the reservation.

Lawyer, who felt himself in charge of this territory, agreed to allow several buildings to be built as storehouses for goods for soldiers who would enforce the treaty provisions. But the miners quickly built tent shelters and canvas lean-tos and began turning this drop-off point into their base of operations. They named the place Lewiston, but it was better known as Ragtown, and before a short month was out, it was the site of a shabby makeshift village of more than 1200 inhabitants.

Soon the area was overrun with prostitutes, liquor peddlers, hardware outfitters, and land speculators all plying their trades from the confines of their tents and shelters. Newspapers from the larger settlements like Portland printed overblown stories of gold fields bigger than those in California in hopes of drawing a larger population base and thus more economic opportunity to the sparsely settled Northwest.

Many of the Christian Nez Perce from nearby Lapwai and Kamiah saw opportunity as well. They could sell foodstuffs and horses and could serve as ferrymen and guides. The white incursion, though in violation of the treaties, seemed as much a boon as a problem so long as the miners did not establish permanent settlements and contributed to the Nez Perce economy through their purchase of goods and services.

By 1861, the goods promised by the Treaty of 1855 finally began to flow in, albeit at a trickle. Lawyer believed that they should go to the burgeoning riverfront Christian villages to aid in bringing the Nez Perce the economic benefits of American society. But the outlying distant tribes felt otherwise. They too had signed the treaty, and they felt that they too should benefit. At a minimum, they should be repaid for the horses they had supplied to the U.S. government during its clashes with more belligerent tribes.

But if there was any chance of this happening, that chance disappeared when the attack on Fort Sumter took place thousands of miles away on the Atlantic seacoast of America. Suddenly the nation's interest, as well as its finances, all headed East. Promises to ragged Indian bands in the West would have to be put on hold. Such goods as were promised came in slowly and were of mediocre quality. Blankets held together by glue rather than stitching, and hoes made of iron rather than steel were typical of the violations of the treaty. Promised buildings were erected as shells, if at all, and unscrupulous agents claimed thousands of dollars for fences that were never built.

Soldiers too were suddenly at a premium. Men were needed back East to preserve the Union, and those who originally had hailed from the South felt compelled to go home to fight for their cause. The Columbia Plateau, in the throes of a chaotic population explosion where beliefs, cultures, gold, and land were being stirred into a volatile mix, was left largely without an army to keep that mix under control.

By 1862 the chaos had become incendiary. There were more than 18,000 whites in the Nez Perce country, and precious few of them were broad-minded civilization builders. They were criminals, hustlers, down-and-outers, desperate family men who had seen their California dreams turn to dust, foreigners seeking opportunity, and all manner of miscreants and idiosyncratic individualists for whom life in an unsettled frontier seemed more appealing than a sedate life in a growing, orderly country. Vigilante justice was the order of the day, and claim jumping, thievery, and murder were common. White settlement that had originated in the service of the Lord was now operating on the fuel of alcohol and greed.

It went without saying that the Dreamers and other Nez Perce who held to the traditional belief in the sanctity of the earth were appalled at the violation of the land. But even those less committed to the old ways were outraged by the white men taking their land, raping their women, hanging their sons and brothers and fathers and friends, and turning the weak among them into beggars for drink.

To be sure, good families also entered the territory, and these the Nez Perce befriended, offering help with crops and caring for their children. But even the most morally upright of these newcomers had taken up residence in spite of, not because of, the Indians. The Nez Perce were, at best, a useful service population; at worst, they were an impediment to the newcomers' designs upon the land and its wealth.

Because the white towns followed the reports of gold, they had become floating, violent settlements. Whenever a miner entered a settlement like Lewiston with gold in his pockets, a stampede of men would set out for the place where he had filed his claim. The traders and prostitutes and peddlers with their barrels of whiskey would pack up and follow, and a rude, lawless town would spring up on the spot, no matter how distant or unlikely.

Elk City was typical. In the early summer of 1861, Elk City was nothing more than a forested mountainside deep in the foothills of the Bitterroots on the eastern edge of Nez Perce country. But when a prospector arrived back in Lewiston bragging about a potential strike, a thousand miners ran, rode, and scrambled their way up the hillsides toward the location. Within two weeks, the brush huts of those who had found the spot were replaced by twenty log buildings. By the end of that month, forty-six buildings straddled a crude main street, selling mining goods, alcohol, and the favors of women.

Though Elk City remained in existence after the gold was extracted, many similar settlements did not. When a vein dried up, towns were abandoned as quickly as they had been created. But while there was money to be made, the miners forced their way past all Indian resistance, bought the Indians off, or "pacified" them with liberal amounts of liquor.

As the strikes continued, the miners forced their way ever deeper into Nez Perce territory. The bands now being affected were not Christian bands positively disposed toward white settlement, but bands that had sought to avoid involvement or contact with whites. They were also bands who had received none of the purported benefits of the Treaty of 1855. Now the one benefit they had received—freedom from white intrusion—was being withdrawn.

It quickly became evident to government officials that the encroachment on Indian lands could not be stopped. So, instead of trying to enforce the provisions of the Treaty of 1855—an effort for which they had little heart in the first place—they tried to renegotiate its conditions and boundaries.

Stevens once again called the tribes together in council. Few of the Nez Perce even wished to attend. They well remembered Stevens's standing before them in 1855, grandiloquently proclaiming the sanctity and inviolability of the treaty boundaries for as long as the sun should shine. They remembered the promises of houses, tools, schools, hospitals, and annuities, none of which had been forthcoming. They saw no reason to meet with a man whose words sounded good but meant nothing. Consequently, many of them stayed home or kept far back from the proceedings.

Lawyer, however, and Timothy, the other most loyal and devoutly Christian of the leaders, did attend. They had been subject to ridicule for their naive trust in the whites and their promises, and they needed some explanation and reassurance that the situation was changing. They also saw the astonishing numbers of whites flooding into their country and realized that it was only through government assistance that this tide could be controlled at all. Better, they thought, to meet with the government and gain some promises and advantages than simply be overwhelmed by the lawless white settlers and their world of violence and alcohol. A new treaty might not get them back the lands they had lost, but perhaps it could stop further intrusion by limiting the settlers and miners to the towns they had already established and keeping them to the trails along the river bottoms while they moved back and forth in search of gold.

By this time, many of the chiefs who had been part of the initial treaty were getting older, and their sons, often men honored with the same names as their fathers, had come along to observe or participate. Young Looking Glass, young Lawyer, and young Joseph were among them. All were men of considerable character and personal magnetism in their own right. They had all grown to adulthood since the arrival of the whites, and it was not the handshake with Lewis and Clark that had influenced them most but the relationships with the subsequent white intruders.

If the chiefs were skeptical at the prospect of the treaty, they were astounded at what was actually offered. Far from asking only for a few towns and safe passage for miners, the government negotiators proposed that the Nez Perce give up all their land except for a small area around Lapwai and Kamiah and that they be paid for their forfeited country with small individual plots of land within these boundaries.

The presumptions on which this offer was based were astonishing to the chiefs. It presumed they would all become farmers and live on small bits of land; it assumed they would all give up their homelands that had been given them by the Creator and from whose soil their very bodies had been made; and it assumed that independent peoples, living far apart with their own leaders, their own cultural practices, and their own relationship to the animals and plants of the earth, would now be willing to blend together into a community of garden plots and farm animals. Even if the government could provide this—and previous experience indicated it could not—such a way of living was an affront to everything the people had believed since the Creator had put them on earth. It also was a direct violation of that to which they had agreed only a few short years before.

The negotiators tried to sweeten the offer by doubling the size of the land and throwing in promises of schools and teachers and mills. They even had the effrontery to say that this treaty would guarantee the payments that had been negotiated under the last treaty but thus far had not been received.

Any chief who had any relationship to the old beliefs or whose property lay outside the proposed boundaries or who had reason to doubt the good offices of the government simply refused to participate further. Even Lawyer was disgusted and threatened to leave.

The negotiators persisted, darkening their offer with threats. The chiefs then met in council to discuss the situation. There still was no unanimity among them as to whether they had acted as a group or as individuals representing only their own bands in signing the Treaty of 1855. And they saw no reason why the conditions of that treaty should not be upheld. "As long as the sun shall shine" did not mean "until the white man changes his mind."

After a long, emotional council at which the many points of view were discussed, the Nez Perce made a momentous decision. If bands like Lawyer's wished to make agreements with the U.S. government on such terms as were proposed, they were free to do so. The others would stay together and speak with a common voice, refusing any further involvement with the white man and his promises. The Nez Perce nation, so long bound together by their common language and their common origin from the Creator, would cease to exist. From this point forward, they would be two distinct peoples.

The men from the two sides then shook hands, and those who wished no involvement with the treaty process withdrew.

The five major chiefs who had withdrawn from the negotiations then left the treaty proceedings and returned to their own lands. Tuekakas, who was among them, was so upset by what he had seen that he returned to his beloved Wallowa and built cairns of rocks on the tops of the ridge that marked the end of his land. Inside this line was the part of the earth that the Creator had given to his people, and neither governments nor other bands in the tribe would ever cause him to abandon it.

But after the dissatisfied bands departed from the treaty gathering, Lawyer made a dangerous and momentous choice. He signed a treaty giving all the Nez Perce land outside the proposed boundaries to the United States in exchange for the goods and benefits that the government offered.

It was not clear to all that he believed he was signing for more than his own people and making an agreement that affected more than his own land, but in the eyes of the government he was the head chief, and this made him the spokesman and representative for all the Nez Perce. His signature was their signature, and to make sure of it, they had him round up fifty-one other men to make Xs on the paper. The commissioners' thinking was simple: no one in Washington knew or cared who the actual chiefs were. If the number of signatories looked the same as the number on the Treaty of 1855, it would look like there had been universal accord.

With this piece of paper, they could claim that the Nez Perce had agreed to be settled on a tiny piece of land in Idaho and, in exchange for a few favors, had agreed to give away land that covered much of eastern Oregon, part of southern Washington, and all of Idaho Territory up to the edge of the mountains. Governor Stevens had achieved his goal, and the chiefs who had left the treaty proceedings were now, in the eyes of the government, living on land to which they had no claim.

Meanwhile, back in his distant Wallowa Valley, Tuekakas remained so incensed by what he had seen that he tore up his prized Book of Heaven, which the Reverend Spalding had given him. If the government's duplicity reflected the Christian way, he no longer wanted any part of it.

All this was observed by his sons, Joseph and Ollokot, who were now grown men. It was they who would have to deal with the fruits of this "thief treaty" when the mantle of leadership passed to them.

The mining boom soon passed, and the most craven of the opportunists left for greener pastures. What remained was the residue of white settlement in the form of towns, ranches, and farms. The residents of these white settlements were now firmly rooted in the area, mostly in the vicinity of the Nez Perce who had signed the treaty.

The white settlers had built homes and businesses, planted orchards, tilled land, and fenced gardens and livestock ranges. They had started newspapers, banks, theaters, and concert halls. Their children had been born here; their sweat had built lives here. They were Oregonians, Idahoans, or Washingtonians. Above all, they were Americans, and in their minds this was America.

The remaining Indians, whom they now greatly outnumbered, were little more to them than a nuisance or an impediment. They were simply a remnant, destined to disappear either by extermination from disease and alcohol or by acculturation to white ways. Some of the settlers made friends with the Indians, some simply used them. Others continued to live in fear of them and regarded them as animals or spoke out for their eradication. But in no way were they accorded respect as the legitimate owners or spiritual inheritors of the earth on which they all were living.

Many of the Nez Perce, especially those who had embraced Christian ways, willingly accepted this condition. Having survived the onslaught of the lawless gold seekers, they were now free to continue their own progress toward a more settled and civilized life. Many still kept to some of their old ways, living in skin shelters and traveling occasionally to buffalo country, but their impulse and trajectory lay toward the white way of living. There was good money to be made in trade with the whites, and they could avail themselves of schools and goods and modern practices of agriculture and animal husbandry. They dressed like whites, sought out white teachers and preachers, and tried in their own fashion to imitate and replicate white practices whenever possible.

Their only real difficulties arose when there was a confrontation with whites over property or behavior. Then the white voice was always heard above the Indian's. When those among the lawless element—and there were still many left over from the Gold Rush—killed or raped or stole from an Indian, the Indian had no recourse. But when an Indian committed a crime against a white, retribution was swift, often directed against any Indian who happened to be nearby.

The Nez Perce complained endlessly about this situation, but official corruption was rife. The agents appointed to protect them as often as not took the money designated for Indian projects and disappeared. One agent at Lapwai absconded with ten thousand dollars earmarked for teachers' salaries when there were not even any schools in existence. Justice, such as it was, remained vigilante justice for crimes committed by Indians, while Indians could expect no justice for crimes committed by whites.

Still, the treaty Nez Perce kept their faith in the white ways. Simply because some among the whites were unable to live up to the standards of their own culture and religion did not mean that those standards were wanting. There were weak and venal men among every race, and the Nez Perce had always taken the ways of others, perfected them, and practiced them with a sense of excellence that exceeded that of the people from whom the new knowledge had come. With regard to white religion and civilization, they intended to do the same.

With the exception of White Bird, the chief of the band whose canyoned and furrowed homeland had been overrun by miners, the nontreaty chiefs, by and large, had remained untouched by the white incursion. Their homelands had held little long-term interest for the gold seekers, and any arable land they possessed lay too far from main settlements to attract any but the most intrepid of the settlers. It was only after the gold began to dry up and the ranchers and other settlers began to fill up the areas of easy access that these outlying areas became more appealing. Then difficulties began to multiply.

The traditional camas-gathering places, though distant from the main settlements, were wide, flat expanses, attractive to the plow and the fence. The broad grazing prairies used by the Nez Perce for their horse herds offered promising possibilities for cattle raising. As white settlers began to move toward these areas, they moved directly into the paths, and into the lives, of those Nez Perce who specifically and pointedly had turned away from white culture and gone off to live in their traditional manner. Soon, a band entering its traditional camas grounds was as likely to find it destroyed by settlers' pigs as to find it full of the Creator's bounty of roots and beautiful purple flowers.

Tuekakas's high and distant Wallowa Valley was among the lands that had remained free from settler intrusion. The trail in was difficult, there was no viable way to enter with wagons, and the deep snows of winter made it unsuitable for year-round habitation. But as settlers filled the arable river valleys and accessible meadows in the lowlands, newcomers began to turn their thoughts toward this inaccessible valley, reputed to be more beautiful than any in the Sierra and the Rockies and to have grazing grass as high as a saddle's stirrup.

Even before any settlers arrived, Tuekakas could see what was coming. White men's surveying teams were making their way over the mountains during the summer and piling up stones to mark out divisions on the land. He and his band dismantled the mounds, but they knew well what such incursions portended.

With his own health failing and his eyesight almost gone, Tuekakas took Joseph aside and began to instruct the young man in dealing with the whites. "Never accept any gifts," he said, "or they will say that you have sold something." Take no pay, sign no paper, do not even touch a white man's paper with your hand, or they will say that you have agreed to what it contains.

He reminded Joseph that it would soon fall upon him to assume leadership of the three hundred people of the Wallowa band, and it would be his duty to protect the their land. "A few years more, and white men will be all around you," Tuekakas said. "You must stop your ears whenever you are asked to sign a treaty selling your home. This country holds your father's body. Never sell the bones of your father and your mother."

Joseph, who by now had been well schooled in the traditional ways and had drunk deeply of the teachings of Smolholla regarding the spiritual presence of the earth, heard well. As his father lay dying, he took the old man's hand and swore that he would protect the valley with his life.

On a warm August day in 1871, with a blue sky vaulting overhead, old Tuekakas died. Joseph and Ollokot buried him in the valley that he had loved so well. They placed the skin of his favorite horse on a frame above the grave so the man and his horse could ride together in the spirit world, and they placed a small bell on a painted branch nearby so the breath of the wind could sing its small and mournful note to the memory of the man who had given so much to the land and the people of the Wallowa Valley.

Then they turned their hearts toward the task of upholding the promise they had made to never give up the land that held their father's and mother's bones.

5

"We Will Not Give Up the Land"

JOSEPH WAS NOW the head chief of the Wallowa band, a position for which he had long been prepared. He was thirty-one, strong, reserved, and watchful. He had not been a warrior, had not won praise as a hunter—he had only once traveled across to buffalo country—and he did not seek to draw attention to himself. He had the good fortune to have Ollokot, his younger brother and best friend, to serve as the leader of the young men of the tribe in matters of hunting and war.

For his part, Joseph was content to lead with the firm strength he had inherited from his father and to keep his heart to the issues of protecting the people and the land. He had a seven-year-old daughter, he loved his family, and he loved the earth on which he lived.

In all things he followed the old ways and encouraged his people to do so as well. They rose early, drank water in praise of its clear gift of life, and took their morning sweats to purify their bodies and spirits. The young boys tended the horse herds, made bridles from leather and grasses, swam the rivers, toughened their bodies. The young girls were trained in crafts and life skills by the grandmothers.

Women sang their root songs, gathered berries, tanned hides, and kept the camp. Men hunted, smoked, met in council. The strict ways of the longhouse were observed, where the first catch, the first harvest, the first gathering, was offered to the Creator before any were allowed to partake of it.

Life was lived in accord with the seasons—spring, summer, and autumn being the times of gathering and preparing and winter the time of reflection and storytelling. All actions were performed in a counter-clockwise manner to reflect the transit of the sun.

From the songs to the ways of raising children to the teachings of the elders about the plants and animals, the people lived in accord with the teachings of the earth handed down from the ancestors. They were safe in their beloved Wallowa Valley and had left the ways of the white teachers and missionaries behind.

There were still doubts and concerns. When they visited their relatives in the distant villages where Christian ways were practiced, they could not help but see the wealth that their brothers and sisters had amassed by following the white ways. They were not blind to the abundant lives that came from raising crops inside of fences and animals inside of pens; neither were they immune to the barbs thrown their way when their Christian relatives showed how they could read markings in books and write sentences that others could read.

But all of this had come at a price. The Christians had given up the old ways. With their short hair and white dress, they could no longer tell who was a favorite son or grandson by the way the hair was braided. They could no longer communicate by pulling the blanket over both shoulders to indicate in council that their point of view had been expressed. They might know about spirit powers in the sky or in the Christian book, but they no longer spoke with the trees or knew the different messages in the wind or had the protective power of the *wayakin* spirit, which came only from fasting and seeking until the spirit decided to show itself to you.

It was to the Wallowa people and to other bands who had not signed the treaties and had stayed away from white ways that these old powers still came. It was to them that the earth and the grandfathers still spoke.

Joseph held no ill will toward the Nez Perce who had chosen to go with the white ways, nor did he feel any animosity toward the white settlers themselves. He wished only to have his people left alone to live in the old manner as the ancestors had prescribed. He intended to lead them in this manner for as long as the Creator and the people wanted his guidance.

But shortly after his father's death, this simple wish was tested.

Even as his father lay dying, stockmen, lured by the glowing descriptions of the surveyors, had been riding over the pass, disregarding Tuekakas's stone boundary markers and probing the valley to see if it was worthy of further exploration. What they discovered was a land of abundant game, fish-filled creeks, meadows of lush grazing grass as high as a man's shoulders, snow-covered peaks, evergreen-studded hillsides, and a great lake as blue as the sky. It was a paradise for homesteading, made difficult only by its relative inaccessibility, snowy winters, and a few hundred wandering savages who didn't even occupy the land for the entire year. The stockmen's minds were quickly made up.

That winter of 1871, as Joseph and his people made their traditional journey down the mountain trails to the Imnaha Valley lowlands by the Snake River sixty miles away, these men drove their stock over the pass into the valley and began staking claims. When the Nez Perce returned in the spring, they found white men living in cabins on the creeks, at the head of the lake, and in many of the places the Nez Perce traditionally made their camps. These white men announced that the government had opened the land to settlement and these were now their homes.

Joseph politely but firmly explained that his father had never sold this land and that the government had made a treaty long ago promising it to his people forever. He bore no ill will toward white people, he said, but would not give up his land. He gently but firmly requested that they leave.

The settlers, however, insisted on staying, pointing to the treaty that Lawyer had signed in 1863 as proof of their right to be there. Joseph explained that this treaty was not valid, that his father had never signed it, and that it was the old Treaty of 1855, guaranteeing the Wallowa people their valley for all time; that was the law by which this land was governed.

The white settlers were impressed and even a bit intimidated by the chief's clarity and civility. But they had no intention of leaving their new homesteads because a small band of savages claimed it had been given to them for all times in an outdated treaty or, even more absurdly, by some spiritual promise of the Creator.

By the middle of the summer following Tuekakas's death, the situation had become critical. Both the whites and the Indians were remaining civil, but they had come to an impasse. Both groups decided to appeal to the Indian agent, a well-intentioned Presbyterian man named John Monteith.

Monteith had been appointed Indian agent over the region under President Grant's new Peace Policy. According to this policy, put in place in 1868, the control over Indian tribes would be given to various religious denominations, which would be responsible for administering treaties and bringing the Indians along the inevitable path to civilization. It seemed a far preferable course to the difficult, expensive, and inflammatory policy of having the military oversee the Indians. The churches could guide with a gentler hand, and they would save the government money. The Nez Perce had been assigned to the Presbyterians, and Monteith was their representative.

Monteith was not a bad man, at least compared to the previous Indian agents. But, like all good Christians, he saw the Indians as people trapped in a childlike stage of human development who needed, both for their own survival and for the salvation of their eternal souls, to advance toward civilized ways and Christian truth. To him, bands like Lawyer's and Timothy's were the successes. Joseph, no matter how clear thinking, well spoken, and honorable, was a man of the past. He and his people had to move forward.

Monteith tried to broker meetings between the settlers and the Wallowa Nez Perce, offering all kinds of suggestions and compromises. But there was little place for compromise when the land was at stake.

Eventually, Joseph agreed to allow the settlers to remain so long as they stayed inside the small plots of land they had chosen. There were not many of them, and if they stayed to themselves, conflict could be avoided.

But the settlers did not stay to themselves. Their animals wandered, their presence brought whiskey peddlers into the area, and conflicts inevitably ensued. Tensions rose, and the government had to step in. Again, Joseph spoke with clarity about the misunderstanding that had brought them to this impasse. The Nez Perce, he said, were not a single people under a single chief, no matter what the white men wanted to believe. They were made up of many bands, and each band had its own leader and was free to make its own decisions. When Lawyer and those other men had signed that treaty ten years ago, they were signing only for themselves and the members of their bands. The chiefs who did not sign—and Joseph's father had been among them—were no more bound by that treaty than they were by some treaty signed by the Iroquois or Lakota or some foreign government.

The government was flummoxed. It had opened the land to settlement, and under the terms of the Homestead Act of 1862, settlers were claiming 160-acre parcels but were required to make improvements to validate their claims. Stopping these settlers meant stopping their improvements and putting their claims in jeopardy. But allowing the settlement and the improvements meant permitting white intrusion on land that may not even have been included in the 1863 treaty. The agents pushed for compromise and eventually convinced both Joseph and the settlers to accept a division of the valley with protections for each group.

But somehow, in the transcribing, the designated areas got mixed up, and the Nez Perce were given the land on which the settlers had built their homes, and the settlers were given the Nez Perce grazing land. Once again, trouble brewed.

Some of the settlers, weary of the strife, packed up and left. Tensions were growing between the Modoc tribe and the whites a few days' journey south near the Oregon-California border, and they wanted no part of any Indian war. They abandoned their claims, as Joseph had initially requested, and went back to the valleys.

This action, however, only enraged many white settlers who lived outside the Wallowa. The idea that Indians could intimidate white people and drive them out of their lands was simply unacceptable. Indians needed to be taught a lesson, and they needed to be kept in their place. Driven by principle and fueled by alcohol, these settlers were ready to show the arrogant Nez Perce the power and wisdom of white justice.

By this time more than homesteads were at stake. Road-building companies had secured contracts to create access to the valley. Land speculators were busy. Ditch diggers were crisscrossing the land with irrigation canals. The loss of the valley would mean the loss of business to white concerns. They began speaking out in the newspapers and government offices until the clamor reached the Oregon statehouse in Salem, then all the way to the Department of the Interior. Through silver-tongued oratory, adamance, and guile, they said, this Chief Joseph was resisting the rightful course of progress, and the local Indian agents were falling for it.

For three years, confusion reigned and tensions escalated. Joseph was convinced that he had been given the right to his land as a reservation, and the few whites were to be contained and constrained into small areas. But the edict from the government inverting the areas of ownership had turned that into chaos. The white settlers saw the Indians leave every winter, then come back like wanderers in the spring, making it seem that Indians mistook roaming for owning, and they set their own stock free to graze in traditional Nez Perce grazing areas. The rabid anti-Indian whites, of whom there were many throughout the West, saw capitulation to any Indian wishes as weakness. The politicians in Washington, wishing to keep the support of the people in the West so they could gain their votes on important issues, listened to whichever voices spoke the loudest. And white settlers all through the Northwest, influenced by rumor and inflammatory newspaper articles, began to fear that a great Indian uprising was in the offing. Add in the disastrous effects of alcohol on the behavior of both Indians and settlers, and conflict was inevitable.

The man who found himself front and center in dealing with this potential conflict was General Oliver Otis Howard. In 1874 he received appointment as the head of the army's Department of the Columbia, which stretched south to north from California to the Canadian border and west to east from the ocean to the crest of the Bitterroots. It also included Alaska and contained within its boundaries all of the lands of the Plateau tribes, including the lands of the Nez Perce.

Like most men in a position of authority in the Northwest, Howard was a Presbyterian, and in his case this was no insignificant fact. He had been a highly decorated officer during the Civil War and had even lost his right arm in battle. But he was, at heart, a man of peace who at this point in his life preferred teaching Sunday school in Portland to soldiering. He had served as head of the Freedman's Bureau and had been a champion for the freed slaves after the Civil War, and he had been able to broker peace with the Apaches in the Southwest prior to his posting to the headquarters of the Department of the Columbia at Fort Vancouver, directly across the Columbia River from Portland and 360 miles west of the Nez Perce reservation at Lapwai.

There were many who felt that the general's overtly Christian manner compromised his military decisions. But he himself was confident that though he preferred peace to a sword, he had the mettle to make the hard military decisions when such decisions were necessary. His success during the bloody Civil War had proved this.

As a part of the continuum of Presbyterian presence in the area, stretching from Spalding to Monteith to Howard himself, Howard understood his task as to be the military arm of the Christian peace process to which his denomination had committed itself. The rabble of the miners and politicians and warmongers of various stripes was less important to him than doing the bidding of his God in bringing the savages of the area to a proper relationship with the Lord and civilization.

When word came to him that the troublesome Chief Joseph wanted to meet with him to discuss the situation in the Wallowa, he immediately agreed. The Wallowa was an insignificant issue in his overall command, but he wanted to take the measure of this increasingly notorious chief and ascertain exactly how much potential for problems he represented.

The two men met on the Umatilla Reservation in the spring of 1875. Joseph had been leader of the Wallowa Nez Perce for almost four years, and Howard had been head of the Department of the Columbia for nearly six months. Joseph approached the general and fixed him with a clear-eyed, penetrating gaze. He wanted to know if Howard had any message for him and his people about the ownership of their land. Howard had none and told Joseph so. But in the meeting he fancied that he and Joseph had experienced a meeting of minds and, in some unspoken manner, had established the foundation of a deep understanding and friendship.

Shortly thereafter President Grant officially rescinded an order that had given Joseph part of the Wallowa as a reservation and opened it instead to white settlement. Agent Monteith informed Joseph, who took the news badly. But his response was mild compared to that of his young warriors, who immediately started clamoring for war.

Not wishing to run the risk of a fight with the U.S. Army, Joseph called a gathering of all the nontreaty chiefs. The meeting took place in the early summer of 1875 in Joseph's Wallowa Valley. In attendance were Eagle from the Light, who lived far toward the Bitterroot Mountains and was disgusted with the entire white presence; Looking Glass, son of the revered chief of the same name, who lived on a distant river bend many miles south of the white settlements and wished only to have his people be free to tend their gardens and travel to buffalo country to hunt in the old way; White Bird, whose craggy lands had been overrun by miners and whose people were suffering endless cruelties and indignities at the white intruders' hands; and Toohoolhoolzote, a strong follower of the ways of Smolholla and adamant believer that the earth would not long tolerate the cruelties and desecrations being visited upon her by the white settlers and those Indians who had chosen to follow the white man's ways.

Toohoolhoolzote, White Bird, and Eagle from the Light argued for war. Each, for his private reasons, had reached the breaking point. Joseph and Looking Glass counseled for prudence and restraint. Such a war, they believed, was unwinnable and would only bring the full force of the U.S. government down upon their people. Better to continue seeking a peaceful resolution to these endless white encroachments.

Because the tribal spiritual leaders agreed with the moderates, the cause of peace carried the day. But the pressure for action was now building within the bands, and their frequent gatherings and obvious dissatisfaction were not going unnoticed by the whites.

On all fronts, the situation was accelerating and deteriorating. From this point forward, every small encounter was fraught with significance. An old Indian man shooing some settler's horses away from his herd was accused of driving a white man's horses from their rightful grazing grounds. Tribal members who traveled to visit distant relatives were suspected of gathering to hold war councils. White men, frustrated with the government's indecisiveness, began moving into the Wallowa, taking over pasturage, and even building a toll road right past Tuekakas's hallowed stone barriers.

Finally, in June 1876, one of Joseph's close friends was shot and killed in an altercation with several white men who were convinced he had stolen their horses. Many versions of the story floated about, but the central issue was that Joseph's friend Wind Blowing was dead, and one of the most hated of the white men, a whiskey-peddling young thug named McNall, was alive and boastful and subject only to white justice.

McNall was well known for his arrogance and belligerence, and his family was notorious for castrating Nez Perce horses they found near their herd. Wind Blowing, in contrast, had always been a reasonable and honest man. When the supposedly stolen horses were found several days later grazing contentedly near the home of their owner, the more belligerent tribal members were ready to act. The time, they said, had come to exact justice in a Nez Perce fashion. But Joseph, again, stayed their hand. It was a white man's crime, and it should be dealt with by white man's justice, just as a Nez Perce crime should be dealt with by Nez Perce justice.

The potential for conflict was obvious, and the whites in the Wallowa feared violence, so they sent for government assistance. In short order the issue landed in Howard's lap. From his distant post in Fort Vancouver, he dispatched some of his most trusted aides to meet with Joseph and his followers at the Lapwai.

Joseph arrived with his brother, Ollokot, and forty of their people. If

Howard's representatives had expected belligerence, they were pleasantly surprised. Joseph proved from the outset to be both conciliatory and thoughtful. Wind Blowing was a quiet, peaceable man, he said, and the white men who had killed him were known to be quarrelsome troublemakers. There was no need for war, but there was a need for justice to be done.

The government officials nodded in quiet agreement at the reasonable nature of this powerful chief. But then Joseph took his argument in an unexpected direction. The death of his friend, he explained, though unfortunate, was now a fact. But it was also a fact that his body had been buried in the Wallowa and his spilled blood had made the earth in that valley ever more sacred to the Nez Perce. Let the death of Wind Blowing hallow that land ever further in the minds of white men and cause them to commit themselves even more to preserving it for the Nez Perce for all time to come.

Howard's men were stunned. This was a serpent's logic—clear, efficient, and deviously lethal. It took the high-minded position of calling for peace rather than punishment—exactly what the white officials wanted—but it made the price of that peace exactly what the white officials could not give up. No member of the ancient Roman senate could have been more eloquent, no highly skilled barrister more guileful and succinct. It was clear that Joseph was a formidable presence, both in the power of his character and the quality of his mind. As one of the government representatives in attendance put it, he displayed "an alertness and dexterity in intellectual fencing . . . that was quite remarkable."

Occasions like this only served to enhance the chief's reputation among the whites. To some, it marked him as a reasonable and eloquent man, far different from the other Indians they had known, while to others it further established him as a dangerous, wily adversary.

General Howard and his military subordinates were among the former. For them, it was a relief to be dealing with a peace-loving chief who was conciliatory in outlook. Howard immediately set out to bring the murderers to trial and to find an amicable solution to the impasse regarding the disputed Wallowa Valley.

But the agents and local residents resented the intrusion of a military man into civil affairs. To them, Howard had no investment in the outcome beyond peace, and he was far too willing to be conciliatory toward obdurate savages.

Months passed, and the killers were not even arrested. Their presence as free men wandering the Wallowa galled the Nez Perce, who began holding all-night dances with drumming and singing, and riding prominently along the ridgetops, stripped and painted for war. Joseph himself showed an ominous change of heart when he announced that since white men tried Indians who committed crimes, it was only right that Indians should try white men who committed crimes, and he demanded that the killers be turned over.

Tensions were escalating quickly. One of the young braggarts among the white settlers announced to some Indian women that he and his friends had taken about all they could tolerate and were going to kill and scalp all the Indians. He announced that he, personally, intended to kill Joseph and wear his scalp on his bridle. For their part, the Nez Perce warriors set up targets near the home of one of the men involved in the initial shooting and began engaging in very public displays of target practice. It was a strained situation. The wrong move, the wrong signal, and the entire valley would be engulfed in a bloody war.

Neither Joseph nor Howard wanted this. But Joseph's patience was wearing thin, and Howard was hundreds of miles away in Fort Vancouver. Finally, on September 2, Joseph and his people issued an ultimatum. It had been almost three months since the murder, and no white man had been arrested. The time had come for the settlers to turn over McNall and Findley, the two men the Nez Perce held responsible for the killing, then leave the Wallowa Valley. If this was not done by the following Sunday, Joseph's men would ride through the valley and burn down all the settlers' homes.

Some of the settlers left; others barricaded themselves in cabins. The Indians again stripped for war and stationed themselves on promontories. It seemed that an armed confrontation was inevitable.

But Joseph still did not want armed conflict. When some of the more reasonable settlers convinced him that all the threats to the Indians were coming from well-known hotheads and troublemakers, he again prevailed upon his warriors to harness their anger. Eventually, a small force of soldiers arrived from Fort Walla Walla. Their leader, who had been convinced by Howard that Joseph was a reasonable man, assured Joseph that the murderers would be turned over for trial and asked Joseph to stay on one side of the valley except to come to town for supplies. Joseph agreed and, to show good faith, made all his warriors dump their bullets on the ground as a symbol of their willingness to keep the peace.

Eventually the two men were turned over and tried, but because no Indian was willing to swear an oath in the white man's fashion, no witnesses were heard who contradicted the men's claims of self-defense. McNall and Findley were exonerated based on their own testimony.

But it was not this injustice that ultimately set the course of trouble for Joseph and his people; it was a promise made by General Howard during the time of escalating tensions. He had determined that a commission of reasonable men, sitting together, could come to a reasonable resolution to the problem of ownership and settlement of the Wallowa Valley, and he had sent word of this idea to Joseph.

Joseph, as always, was willing to seek a peaceful solution to problems that might lead other men to war, and he had used the promise of this commission to keep his young warriors in check. Now that the problem of the killing of Wind Blowing had been put to an uneasy rest, it was time to seek this peaceful solution.

But Howard's idea of a peaceful solution was far different from Joseph's. He acknowledged that the Indians and the white settlers could not share the Wallowa without constant trouble. But rather than remove the whites or establish hard boundaries between the two, his solution was to remove the Indians. He believed that since there was already a place set aside for the Nez Perce down by Lapwai, and since it was inevitable that the Nez Perce would accept the ways of progress and civilization, the only reasonable solution was for Joseph and his people to abandon the Wallowa and make their permanent residence on the distant Lapwai reservation among the settled, short-haired, Christian, farming Nez Perce. His commission of reasonable men was really just a forum in which he could deliver his preconceived "reasonable solution" to Joseph and the Nez Perce.

Howard's council did not prove successful. Three of the five men representing the government came from Washington, D.C., and they neither understood nor felt sympathy for the Indian situation in the West. They arrived in Idaho on November 7 and soon found themselves sitting in the lonely and isolated confines of the Lapwai while Joseph made his way at a leisurely pace from his home in the distant Wallowa Valley. When the chief finally arrived six days later with sixty warriors, he wasted no time in explaining his position. In a clear, measured, and well-reasoned manner, he declared that neither he nor his father had ever sold the Wallowa and that claiming they had was as absurd as if a neighbor sold your horse and then said you were responsible for delivering it to the purchaser. He refused to even discuss the possibility of moving to the reservation.

"What shall we tell the president when we get back?" the commissioners asked him.

"All I have to say is that I love my country," Joseph responded. "We will not sell the land. We will not give up the land."

Without giving even an inch from his initial position, he exited the council and returned to his home country.

Once again, Joseph's clarity and lack of rancor left the government representatives confused and frustrated. By every measure Joseph was a good and reasonable man, and his case for remaining on his land was not without legal merit. The Treaty of 1863 was still suspect, and every decision that had been made since that time was clouded with legal uncertainty. It was only the irreversible flow of white settlers that made the movement of the Wallowa Nez Perce onto the reservation seem necessary and inevitable.

But a fateful encounter on the plains of Dakota Territory five months before had put every military man in the West on edge. There, at a creek called the Little Bighorn, a large contingent of Lakota warriors under the leadership of Sitting Bull and Crazy Horse had overwhelmed U.S. troops led by the vaunted Indian fighter, George Armstrong Custer, and murdered the soldiers in most hideous fashion. The gruesome murders and mutilations had imprinted themselves on the minds of every man who saddled a horse or picked up a gun in service of the United States, and the strategic success of the Indians had put every commander in the West on notice that large numbers of Indian warriors were nothing with which he wanted to trifle.

Consequently, the more reasonable and charismatic Joseph appeared, the more dangerous he became. In the government's eyes, it was just such a man who could galvanize Indian resistance in the Plateau and knit the many tribes and factions into a formidable, perhaps unbeatable, military force.

This danger was increased by the belief that Joseph was under the influence of Smolholla, who by now was teaching of an Indian messiah and the resurrection of the dead. Convinced that Joseph was being manipulated by a man they considered a "wizard," the negotiators issued their report asserting that the entire affair had to be brought to an end—militarily, if necessary.

The treaty Nez Perce, now led by a man named James Reuben, were quick to support this idea. Almost more than any white person, these Christian Nez Perce, with their historic commitment to the spiritual significance of life, had taken their Presbyterianism to an extreme of piety. To them, Smolholla was the purveyor of dangerous falsehoods. His pernicious brand of belief was harmful to their people and threatened to ensnare those among them who were not strong in their Christian faith. In their minds, Smolholla had to be stopped.

It mattered little that Joseph was not a direct follower of Smolholla—that the two men were simply following different tributaries of the traditional seven-drum belief in the living, life-giving power of the land and all its creations. To those among both the whites and the Nez Perce who followed the Christian path, the Wallowa chief and the hunchbacked prophet from Palouse country seemed as one, and all knew that men under the spell of a messianic spiritualism were as dangerous as men under the influence of alcohol.

So during the winter of 1876, while Joseph and his people camped in their traditional wintering grounds down in the Imnaha Valley near the confluence of the Snake and Clearwater rivers, plans were being made to occupy the Wallowa with troops and to demand that the chief and his band move onto the reservation at Lapwai by April 1. There they could be contained, controlled, and kept from fomenting dissatisfaction. With them out of the way, the rich Wallowa could finally be opened to white settlement without fear of violence or Indian resistance.

In an attempt to forestall violence, the treaty Nez Perce sent a delegation of four men down to the Imnaha to meet with Joseph and ask him to come onto the reservation peaceably. Joseph once again refused. Why was it, he asked them, that white men could not understand that the land had been given to his people by the Creator and that he had sworn a sacred trust to his father never to abandon it, no matter what was offered or threatened? His body was of that land. He could not leave it, he could not sell it, he could not betray his father's dying words.

The four men went back to the government officials with the news, and the stage was set for a potentially ugly confrontation. But General Howard still wanted to avoid bloodshed. He had no interest in harming Joseph or his people. He still believed that more reasonable minds could prevail, and in his heart he knew that Joseph's argument had both moral and legal merit. But orders were orders, and he was perilously close to having to remove Joseph from the Wallowa by force.

Over the next few months he tried talking with the other nontreaty bands of the tribes in the Plateau. If he could convince some of them to accept reservation life, there would be pressure on the others to acquiesce, and the danger of concerted opposition would be minimized. His goal was to get them all to move onto existing reservations without bloodshed. The time was long past for talk of compensation or sharing of the land.

Still, Joseph towered head and shoulders above all the other leaders in Howard's thinking. His eloquence was unparalleled among the chiefs, his quality of mind beyond reproach. He also exuded a forthrightness and clarity that drew others to him. In Howard's mind, he was an oak tree among reeds and willows.

In addition, it was his land that had become the center of the controversy. The other nontreaty Nez Perce lived farther to the east in less contested areas and amounted to little in terms of opposition. White Bird, Looking Glass, Toohoolhoolzote, and the others were secondary concerns. Likewise, the various Cayuse and Palouse chiefs were once again more nuisances than adversaries. Their lands were not as highly sought, their opposition not so closely followed in Portland and Washington, D.C., their personal characters not so dynamic. It was Joseph who embodied the problem, and it was in dealing with Joseph that any solution must ultimately lie.

Howard understood this, but he consistently undermined his own efforts by making error after error in protocol in dealing with the Nez Perce. In one instance, he sent an underling to represent him at a meeting he had promised to attend, thus insulting Ollokot, who had gone as the chief representative of the Wallowa Nez Perce and had no interest in dealing with what he called one of General Howard's "boys." In other instances, he spoke abruptly, denying the Nez Perce their normal manner of discourse in discussing issues of importance. But in no case did he so underestimate and miscalculate as in the meeting on the grounds of Fort Lapwai in May 1877, the meeting that came to be known as the council where General Howard "showed the rifle."

6

"I Am a Man; You Will Not Tell Me What to Do"

FORT LAPWAI WAS NOT a fort in the sense of a barricaded enclave. It consisted of a few whitewashed buildings rimming a parade area, with barracks for men, stables for horses, and the usual storage buildings, officers' quarters, and rooms to serve as jail cells, laundries, and medical quarters. It sat lonely and isolated along the side of a creek amid the barren, bald hills that had so depressed the Reverend Spalding upon first arriving in the country.

The soldiers who manned the fort were mostly ill-trained remnants of the post–Civil War army—immigrants, down-and-outers, and young boys with no families and no prospects who had joined the military as a way to advance in a world that offered them few opportunities. Many spoke little or no English. Those who had any skills at all were more likely to be blacksmiths, carpenters, and clerks than men with experience at soldiering.

There were a few seasoned officers but little in the way of equipment. The soldiers had few decent weapons and had received almost no training. Howard had not wished to waste his limited budget on bullets for target practice, so the troops were poor shots as well as poor riders.

It was this crude collection of 120 men that was charged with the responsibility of keeping order in the broad Columbia Plateau, and these men now found themselves responsible for keeping the Indians in line during the council that Howard had called in order to issue a final ultimatum to the nontreaty Nez Perce.

Howard had invited all the leaders—Joseph, White Bird, Looking Glass, Toohoolhoolzote, and any others who chose to come. He was no longer in a mood to compromise or discuss. All that interested him was informing the recalcitrant Nez Perce, in no uncertain terms, that they would have to give up all claims to their traditional lands and move onto the reservation at Lapwai with the treaty Nez Perce. He would listen to their usual rhetoric about the land as their mother and the misunderstandings about the treaties, but he would give no quarter. This was the final council; this was the concluding act to the long, agonizing battle that had resulted from the misunderstandings and missteps by the government and the Indians alike. At its conclusion the matter would be resolved and the Indians would be given a timetable for completing the move. The only issue was how best to accomplish this without violence from the more belligerent elements among the nontreaty factions.

The meeting took place under a pall of tension. Joseph and his people arrived first, and Howard tried to begin the treaty proceedings immediately. In his mind, instructions for all the bands were going to be the same: give up your resistance and come onto the reservation, or be moved there by force. It mattered little if he told this to them as a group or to each band individually.

But Joseph refused to listen until the other bands arrived. They needed more time to traverse the snow-covered mountain trails, he said, and he would not speak without their being present. Reluctantly, Howard agreed. But the mood was anything but cordial. Even the usually gregarious and good-natured Ollokot grumbled that he was sick of being treated like a dog and wondered aloud why there should not be one law for all men rather than rules for Indians and special treatment for white men.

When the other tribes arrived, it became obvious that this meeting was going to require delicacy. Howard and his small outpost of soldiers found themselves watching nervously as hundreds of warriors, arrayed in full battle dress with their faces painted a blood red vermilion, paraded slowly around the perimeter of the small, unprotected Fort Lapwai garrison.

The Nez Perce, however, were not in a violent mood. They merely had no further patience for equivocation and misrepresentation. They had met previously and decided that Toohoolhoolzote should serve as their spokesman. He was a man of powerful medicine and a committed follower of Smolholla's teachings about the living spirit of the earth. It was he who would be charged with the challenge of finally getting through to this hardheaded general regarding the issue of the land. He would speak as long as was necessary to get across the people's feelings about the sacredness of the earth.

The council began poorly, with Howard adamantly stating that there was only one possible outcome—the nontreaty bands were going to have to move onto the reservation. This struck the Nez Perce as not only disingenuous but also insulting. They had been called to council, not to a lecture. They had not traveled on difficult, slippery trails and across treacherous, snow-swollen spring rivers only to be treated like children.

Chief White Bird sat silently, his mouth obscured by an eagle wing that he held in front of his face. The other nontreaty chiefs stood by impassively, listening to the white agent Monteith and the one-armed General Howard talk as if the Indians had no rights and no point of view. The treaty Nez Perce, who were also in attendance, kept a careful eye on their nontreaty brothers, making sure to note any potentially dangerous comments or actions that they could pass along to the government officials at the end of the day's proceedings.

On the second day, Toohoolhoolzote took the floor to fulfill his role as spokesman for the people's position. He was a gruff man with a guttural voice—"a cross-grained growler" in Howard's estimation—but he was an eloquent spokesman for the people's love of the land. He was also a man whose hatred for the white intrusion was impossible to miss.

He chided Howard for treating them like children and spoke derisively about this "Washington" to which Howard and Monteith constantly referred. "Is he a chief or a common man, a house or a place?" he asked. "Leave Mr. Washington—that is, if he is a man—alone. He has no sense. He does not know anything about our country."

He derided Howard's constant threats of military force and challenged him to speak man to man. Then he began, in his most fervent oratory, to explain to Howard that the earth was alive, that the earth was their mother, that you do not sell your mother, you do not negotiate about your mother, you do not dishonor your mother by cutting her hair or digging in her flesh, and you do not feel compelled to change her to suit your own selfish and shortsighted needs. He had no interest in the kinds of bargains that the treaty Nez Perce had made, and none of the chiefs who had come to this council had ever made such bargains, nor would they in the future.

Toohoolhoolzote was carrying the day. The other chiefs and warriors were nodding their assent and raising excited murmurs of approval whenever he made a particularly eloquent point in their behalf. The treaty Nez Perce could see that throughout the gathering men were pulling their robes over their shoulders, indicating that the words of Toohoolhoolzote spoke for them.

Joseph and Looking Glass, more than the other assembled chiefs, were wary of the potential for violence. Joseph knew well that only a small spark was needed to set off a massacre that would leave all the white men dead. Though this might bring some satisfaction to the angry and frustrated young warriors, it would eventually result in the annihilation of all the Nez Perce when the full force of the U.S. military was brought against them.

As the atmosphere in the room became ever more tense and agitated, he proposed an adjournment. Howard quickly agreed, even offering to postpone the meeting for the entire weekend, ostensibly to allow people time to reflect and to give the recent arrivals time to rest up from their arduous journey. But in fact, Howard's purpose was to allow the troops he had sent for more time to make their way into nearby positions. His few frightened young men, standing with their rusty rifles just out of sight in the adjacent buildings, did not engender confidence in the face of the growing restiveness and belligerence of the nontreaty warriors.

When the meeting resumed on the following Monday, Toohoolhoolzote picked up where he had left off. Brushing aside Monteith's opening statement about how the Nez Perce would be able to continue their traditional religious practices while living on the reservation, he launched into another impassioned explanation of the sacredness and motherhood of the land. By now more nontreaties had arrived, and his audience was ever more supportive.

After allowing the chief to go on at some length, Howard decided he had heard enough and abruptly informed Toohoolhoolzote that twenty times over he had listened to this talk about the motherhood of the land and the chieftainship of the earth, and it was now time to speak of practical things.

Unaccustomed to being interrupted, and insulted by Howard's arrogant dismissal of his argument, Toohoolhoolzote lashed out at the general. "Who are you to tell me what to do? What person pretends to divide the land and put me on it?"

"I am that man," Howard answered.

Toohoolhoolzote flew into a dark rage. "I am chief here," he said. "No man can come and tell me anything I must do. Go back to your own country. Tell them you are chief there. I am chief here."

The tension in the tent was becoming dangerous. Howard had lost all patience, and Toohoolhoolzote was on the edge of violence.

"My orders are plain and will be executed," Howard said. "You will go onto the land, or I will send soldiers to put you on it."

Toohoolhoolzote had reached a point of almost uncontrollable anger. "I am a man," he said. "I have a prick. You will not tell me what to do."

Howard's spine stiffened. Toohoolhoolzote not only had demeaned his authority, he had offended his Christian sensibility.

"Take him to the guardhouse," Howard commanded.

A tall soldier stepped forward and pushed Toohoolhoolzote backward, causing him to fall over some of the other men. Toohoolhoolzote was a man of legendary physical strength—he had been known to return to camp after a hunt carrying a deer on each shoulder. It was all Joseph and the other chiefs could do to keep the meeting from breaking into violence.

Eventually Toohoolhoolzote was convinced to accept the incarceration. The other chiefs knew that numbers were on their side and that it was unlikely Howard would dare inflame the situation further by keeping their chosen speaker imprisoned for long.

But unwittingly, Howard had committed a crime against Indian protocol that was almost more grievous than the insult he had visited upon Toohoolhoolzote. When the chiefs had arrived, they had left their weapons outside the tent, which was the traditional Indian statement that no belligerence would be exhibited during the discussions that took place inside. To violate this rule of decorum by even the slightest mention of violence was to "show the rifle," and it was among the greatest violations of the universal Indian code of conduct. By threatening to use force to remove the bands from their lands, and by laying hands on Toohoolhoolzote, Howard had "shown the rifle" and established himself as an untrustworthy, dishonorable adversary, worthy from this point forward of neither respect nor consideration.

The council was in shambles. Rumors flew on both sides. The treaty Nez Perce reported that they had heard war songs being sung in the nontreaty camp on previous nights. Joseph had been informed by messenger that while the council was taking place, troops had entered the edge of the Wallowa, where women and children of his band remained at home unprotected. No one knew exactly what was transpiring. But it was clear to the nontreaty chiefs that these white men were a cruel and devious lot, as numerous as locusts and as powerful as grizzlies. The time had come for the chiefs to make a difficult decision.

For the next several days, they listened to the talk of the white men. The young men of Toohoolhoozote's band were prepared to fight and die for the honor of their chief, who remained in the guardhouse. This feeling only increased when Toohoolhoolzote was finally released wearing a fresh white shirt, the symbol of a bride, which none failed to recognize as a pointed indignity visited upon him in response to his comment about his manhood.

White Bird's young men too were ready to fight. Their land had been the most overrun by the miners, who were the worst of the white men—greedy, rapacious, untrustworthy, dissolute. For over a decade they had put up with rapes, murders, thievery, and all manner of indignities. They had seen their mothers and grandmothers shortchanged and cheated in trade by the white shop owners. They had seen acts of unconscionable cruelty and cowardice, as when half-blind Eagle Robe had been shot by a miner after the old man had complained about a fence that the miner had built across his garden.

They had seen the old woman Eye-a-ma-koot hacked to death with a pick by a miner who was upset that their dogs had gotten into a fight. They had seen the white man Harry Mason beat people with a bullwhip if they approached too near his cabin.

They had endured all they could take of their elders fawning before the outrages of the white man. This was not the way their ancestors had behaved; this was not what it meant to be a Nez Perce. They were prepared to fight, and they were prepared to do it now.

But Joseph and White Bird managed to keep the angrier factions in check. They were proud of the fact that their people had never broken the trust made with Lewis and Clark, and they saw clearly the physical numbers of the whites. Honor went only so far. The massacre of women and children and elders, which would surely occur in an all-out war, would violate their sacred trust to protect the people. Killing white men was like trying to remove grains of sand from the shore one by one. Better to acknowledge the reality of the situation and try to make the best of the circumstances.

The young men's anger festered, but reluctantly they agreed. Their hands would be stayed. But if more indignities were visited upon them by this arrogant one-armed general with his talk of Washington and Great Fathers and Jesus, they would bypass the peace-talking chiefs and do what Nez Perce honor required.

Joseph's concern, however, went beyond issues of warfare and honor. In the course of the council, Howard had announced that the bands would have thirty days in which to gather their belongings and report to the reservation. Such a demand was as heartless as it was impossible. The band's horses and cattle were still wandering the hills and valleys of their winter pasturage, and the trails were still covered with snow.

Surely Howard had seen that White Bird's band had not even been able to arrive at the council at the appointed time, and this while traveling without household goods or animals or the sick and elderly. The journey Joseph's people would have to undertake was even more perilous. They would have to gather their stock, prepare the sick and crippled and elderly for travel, navigate the slippery, slushy mountain trails from the Wallowa, and cross rivers swollen by winter runoff. Even if they abandoned all their goods, their chances of success were slim.

Joseph confronted Howard with this. Even if his people agreed to move, he said, what Howard was demanding was impossible. He pointed out that the U.S. soldiers, packing lightly and traveling without women and children, took days to cross even the smallest rivers. Why should his people be subject to such impossible demands if Howard's own men were unable to comply with similar conditions?

But Howard no longer had patience for such arguments. Be on the reservation in thirty days, he said, or be prepared to be moved there by military force. Once again, he was brandishing the rifle in a council that was supposed to be a meeting in search of peace.

Eventually the council broke up with Howard's having given no quarter. He fancied that he had carried the day with his "fearless sternness." He even convinced White Bird, Looking Glass, and Joseph to accompany him on a long ride through the proposed reservation area to look for suitable areas of residence. Though Joseph indicated that he did not wish to displace whites who had already established homesteads there, Howard felt the journey was a great success. He paid little note to White Bird's measuring the speed of their best horses by challenging Captain Wilkinson to a race or to White Bird's punctual arrival at the parade field every morning to sit silently on his horse watching the fort's soldiers drill.

Part Two

A Time of War

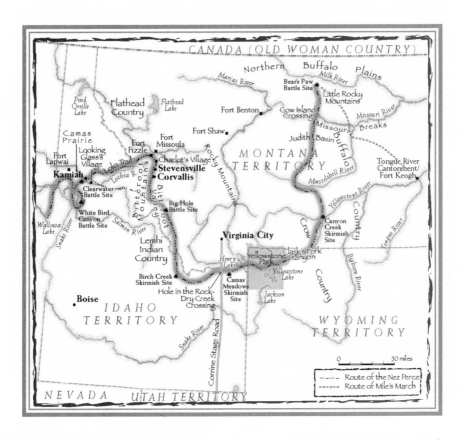

7

"There Have Been Killings"

IN EARLY JUNE 1877, three weeks after the conclusion of Howard's council at the Lapwai, Joseph's people rode solemnly down the narrow trail from the Wallowa toward the turbulent Snake River. It was a steep, vertical descent of almost a mile on narrow winding paths. The footing was still treacherous from the winter snows, and it got only worse as the heavy hooves of the cattle and horses churned the earth into a viscous, slippery mud.

Howard's heartless timetable, which required them to be on the reservation by June 14, had made it impossible for them to gather all their stock from the wide prairies and hills. It had also assured that the newly born calves and colts would have little chance of surviving the journey. Even if they made it down the slippery, perilous trails, they would surely drown as they tried to cross the half-mile-wide Snake River, which was roaring with its winter runoff.

Joseph had made the hard decision. He had chosen to abandon the land that held the bones of his father and mother in order to save the lives of the people who had been entrusted to his care. The violation of his oath to his father weighed heavily upon him, but it was to the living that he knew he must be responsible. To do otherwise was to violate the sacred trust of leadership.

Though the people were long practiced in making bull boats by building frames of willow and covering them with buffalo hide, these small, bowl-like boats were good only for carrying people and a few household goods. They would be of no service in getting the cattle and horses across.

The only hope was the people's knowledge of the currents and water patterns. By entering the river at the right point, they could literally allow themselves to be carried across to the other side by the eddies and current. But once outside these hidden passageways, any boat or animal would be swept to its destruction in fast-moving turbulence. Even with the young boys leading the horses across with ropes, many would be carried away to be crushed against the rocks. And the cattle had almost no chance. They were poor swimmers and panicked easily. Only by sheer luck would any of them survive.

As to the people, most would make it to safety. But it was cruel to see the blind being led by ropes down the trails and the infirm elderly trying to hobble with the aid of sticks and tree branches.

Goods that could not be carried had been cached in holes and hollows and covered with earth and furs. But all knew that the whites were watching and would steal everything as soon as the Indians had crossed the river, just as they had stolen the people's horses and cattle when they found that the Nez Perce were being forced to leave.

The sad truth was that the people were leaving their homeland for the last time, and all felt it in their hearts.

The bands had decided to meet one final time in the broad Camas Prairie far across the Snake and the Salmon, near the place where the new reservation began. There they could hold one final gathering in the old way, with dancing and feasting and the harvesting and drying of camas roots. It would show the children how the old ways had been and allow the elders to experience the good days one last time.

The people's spirits were heavy and filled with doubt. Had the Creator abandoned them? The treaty bands were prospering; they had experienced no dark punishment for gouging the earth's skin and cutting her hair. Was it possible that theirs was the way by which the Creator wanted all people to live?

Still, none wanted to abandon the teachings of the ancestors. Perhaps it would be possible to live with their Christian brothers and sisters but keep to the old ways in those things that mattered.

Even so, there would have to be changes. The reservation that had been set aside was too small to allow all the bands' horses and cattle to graze freely. And the treaty bands would surely be more favored by the white government and given more privileges and authority. Still, this could be tolerated if the people were allowed to keep to the old ways—hunting and fishing in the old places, going across to buffalo country if they so wished, making their seasonal journeys to the harvesting grounds of the kouse and the camas at the time appointed by the Creator.

What was most troubling was the betrayal of their land. None could say if the land, angry at its abandonment, might not visit harm upon them. Would the spirits of their ancestors be angered at having their bones abandoned to the white man's picks and plows? Would their *wayakin* spirit guides abandon them in return? Did they simply lack the courage to fight for the mother who had given them birth? Should they have stayed and resisted rather than turning the land over to the false ways of the whites?

With such questions in their minds and hearts, the people made their way across the turbulent Snake, over the rugged mountain paths, across the raging Salmon, and up from the river to the blue-flowered Camas Prairie for this final gathering of freedom.

Most of the cattle had been lost at the Snake crossing. By the time they reached the Salmon, it was clear that the remainder would drown in another river crossing, so they were left behind to be slaughtered by the men during the time of the great gathering. That at least would provide the people with food for some of the winter while the stock was replenished and some means of subsistence established.

This was especially important to Joseph. His responsibilities were complex. Though he had been forced to betray his promise to his father to protect the land with his life, he did not wish to ignore his father's admonition to take no gifts from the white man lest you be said to have made promises and trades that bound your people to things to which you did not agree. He wanted his families to enter the reservation with their own food, their own shelter, their own camp goods, their own lives. They might have given up their land, but they would not give up the ways of their ancestors. With the help of the beef from the cattle, perhaps they could make it to spring without relying on the dangerous practice of accepting food and supplies from the white agents and government.

His wife, Springtime, was due to give birth in a few days. She and the others like her, as well as the elderly, needed nourishment after this hard journey. And he needed to show respect for the old ways and old promises. One of the elderly men of the tribe had bequeathed him the beef from some of his cattle before his death, and Joseph needed to honor that bequest by securing that beef rather than letting the cattle drown wantonly in the raging current of the Salmon.

So after he had seen his people comfortably settled in the wide beauty of the Camas Prairie, he went back to the Salmon with some of the others to slaughter such beef as they could, both in memory of the old man and for the future nourishment of the people.

It was as he was returning from the slaughter that he first realized something must have gone wrong at the camp. Two Moons was riding toward him in an agitated manner.

There have been killings, Two Moons explained. Some of the young men have ridden off. Others have followed. They say many white people have lost their lives.

It was everything Joseph had feared. When he had left the camp, there had been thousands of horses grazing contentedly in a purple sea of camas flowers amid hundreds of teepees with thin ribbons of smoke curling into the blue cloudless sky. The old women had been laying out the bulbs on blankets to dry, and the old men had been gathered in circles, smoking their pipes and playing at dice and cards. The camp was alive with children's laughter. It was as he had wanted it to be, as it should be.

But now something had changed.

The scene that greeted him as he rode back into the prairie was dark and chaotic. People were running everywhere. The camp was half dismantled; many of the bands had already left. Children were crying, and women rushed about trying to gather such goods as they could in preparation for departure. The remnants of the other camps littered the ground. A sense of panic filled the air.

Joseph tried to piece together what had happened. It had begun with Wahlitits, the young man of White Bird's band whose father, Eagle Robe, had been killed by the squatter who had built fences across the old man's property.

As the old man had lain in his bed dying a slow and painful death, he had exacted a promise from his son that there would be no acts of retribution or vengeance. "Do not bother the white man for what he has done to me," he said. "Let him live his life." And Wahlitits, being a good son, had agreed to abide by his father's wishes.

But it had been hard. Wahlitits was a child of the old ways. He was known as one of the best of White Bird's young men—strong and forth-right, a protector of the weak and defender of all in need. It was said he could climb a cliff straight up and that no man had ever beaten him in a footrace. He swam the icy waters of the Salmon every day of the year to toughen his body and was legendary for tying two wild horses to ropes around his waist and standing fast while they tried to escape. His father's demand had flown in the face of all he had been raised to believe about a worthy manhood and a warrior's sense of honor. But he had swallowed his pride in order to respect the wishes of the man who had given him life.

Apparently, during an evening parade through the camp—something the young men liked to do to impress the women and to show themselves as warriors—Wahlitit's horse had stepped on a blanket where Yellow Grizzly Bear's wife had been drying kouse roots. Yellow Grizzly had chided Wahlitits, telling him that if he were so brave, he should avenge his father's death rather than staging mock war parades and spoiling the hard work of old women, who at least were doing something of value for the people.

The criticism had stung Wahlitits deeply. After a night of tearful inde-cision, caught between his promise to his father and the insulting chal-lenge of Yellow Grizzly, he had gathered his two cousins and ridden off in the direction of the cabin where the man who had killed his father lived.

Now the whole valley was choking in blood.

There was talk that alcohol had been involved. Joseph knew well what alcohol did to his people, especially when it freed a deep rage that they were keeping inside. But even if there had been no alcohol, Joseph could sympathize with Wahlitits. He knew the difficulties of keeping a promise to a father in the face of mounting insults and indignities. And he under-stood the young men's rage at being stopped from acting as warriors and meeting the insults in the ways of the ancestors. But the stories of mur-ders—if they were true—had set the bands on a course of bloodshed that no quest for honor could justify.

"We must remain here," he told his people. "If we leave, it will look like we were part of the killings. We must wait until we see what the soldiers will do. Perhaps we can explain to them."

But the people were frightened. White law never listened to an Indian. When one committed a crime, all were guilty. Worst of all, one of the young men who had followed Wahlitits had been from their band. To remain in this place was to choose to join the camp of the dead.

Joseph managed to calm them enough to stay the night. But in the darkness, a bullet from an unseen gun ripped through one of the Nez Perce lodges. This was message enough. The time had come to follow the other bands to safer ground.

Howard stood in stunned disbelief as he read the note that had just been passed to him. He read the words slowly, deliberately, first to himself, then to his assembled officers. "The people of Cottonwood undertook to come here during the night . . . all wounded or killed . . . we have reports that some whites were killed yesterday on the Salmon River . . . fear that the people are all killed. . . ." The whole dispatch was a confused litany of secondhand information and desperate hearsay. But the words in the center of the communiqué could not be ignored: "One thing is certain; we are in the midst of an Indian war."

Howard was at a loss. He had thought matters were under control. Joseph and the other bands had agreed to enter the reservation and, as far as anyone knew, had been gathering peacefully in the broad Camas Prairie in preparation for doing just that. But this communiqué from the small settlement at Mount Idaho on the edge of the prairie told otherwise.

Shortly after reading this message, he was handed a second dispatch. Unlike the first, it had specifics. ". . . the wounded have come in. Mr. Day mortally; Mrs. Norton with both legs broken; Moore shot through the hip; Norton killed and left in the road." He tried hard to keep a cool demeanor. He felt it essential that a commander of men always present a poised and self-possessed front to those around him. But this spoke of the Indian outbreak so many had predicted and all had feared.

He contemplated what had gone wrong. He had heard all the rumors—that the Nez Perce were paying exorbitant prices for gunpowder and trying to trade horses for guns; that women were curing more jerky than usual in preparation for a long siege against the whites. He had listened patiently to breathless stories of runners being dispatched to the Coeur d'Alenes and Spokans telling them to prepare for war and to all the hearsay about the war parades taking place on Camas Prairie.

But he had taken none of this seriously. Rumors were always rife when great groups of Indians gathered together, and the gathering on the Camas Prairie probably numbered close to eight hundred. To white settlers, ever nervous about Indian motives and activities, the horse races and war games and painted faces naturally might have seemed to be a prelude to battle. But Howard understood Indian ways. The presence of the women and children were a sure indication that this was not a gathering dedicated to war. By every indication this had been just one final bittersweet celebration before the remnant bands made their way onto the reservation. And why should he have assumed otherwise? After all, Joseph and the other chiefs had given him their word at the Lapwai council. In fact, during the ride through the reservation country in search of places to settle, they had seemed almost positively disposed toward the move.

But now he was forced to ask if perhaps he had been too trusting. Joseph's increasing adamance had been a concern to him, but the chief had always counseled peace to his young men, even in the most trying of circumstances. Yet now there were rumors of Joseph's being right in the middle of the bloody killing. There was even a report that he had stabbed one of the settler women in the heart down on Slate Creek.

It was difficult to get a clear picture of what had actually occurred. There were reports of rapes and torture and babies' tongues being cut out. Houses had been burned; miners' goods had been stolen. There was the appalling story of a brave placing a young child's head between his knees and squeezing it until the skull cracked. Everything was one great swirl of horror, hearsay, and, quite likely, hysterical fabrication. But how to sort fact from fiction? He did not wish to send troops, especially raw troops such as his, into battle based on rumor.

And, truth be told, even if his men had been well equipped and well trained, the Nez Perce were not a foe he was anxious to engage. They were seasoned, open-country fighters whose horses were far better than any possessed by his cavalry. To see their young warriors galloping across the prairies, as if the horse were an extension of their bodies, was to realize how rudimentary were the riding skills of even his best men.

And this was not terrain congenial to infantry fighting. Though the fifty miles down to the Camas Prairie and Mount Idaho were relatively easy to traverse, beyond there, down in the canyon of the Snake where much of the killing had taken place, the land became like the spine of a great animal. The angles of the hills became so acute that you had to traverse them on laborious switchbacks or climb them on all fours. Weather changed with the altitude and could go from frigid to scorching in a matter of a few miles. Storms were so severe as to wash out passes in a single rainfall; rock slides and timberfall were common, rendering trails impassable; and forests grew so dense that you had to break fresh trail to get supply wagons and artillery through. Even if you knew the trails and passages—knowledge decidedly in the Indian's favor—there were other, less manifest dangers. The sun was deceptive and hard to gauge. Outside the river valleys, water was often hard to find, and dehydration was a constant threat.

And then there were the rivers themselves. Joseph had been quite right about the difficulties in crossing them. While the Indians had generations of experience with currents and building bull boats, Howard's men were reduced to sending a good rider across with a rope, fastening it to a tree on the other side, then dragging themselves across on horseback or rafts, if they could even find the lumber necessary to build them. If they chose wrongly, they were swept to their deaths, and even if they successfully navigated the treacherous currents, their ammunition and artillery were often rendered useless by the soaking they took in the crossing.

Howard silently cursed his naiveté. How blind he had been during that sun-blessed ride with Joseph, Looking Glass, and White Bird during the search for homestead sites on the new reservation! It had never crossed his mind that the good-humored horse race proposed by White Bird might really have been a way to assay the speed and agility of the military's best horses and riders. Likewise, it had never occurred to him to question the purpose of White Bird's daily visits to the parade ground to watch the men drill. Now each moment of the treaty negotiations, each corner of the post that the Nez Perce had been allowed to observe, each casual comment made on those comradely rides up and down the length of the Lapwai and the Clearwater became a moment of vulnerability.

He might not have pursued this line of thinking, might have written it off as idle speculation and unprofessional second-guessing, had not a single memory kept creeping into his mind. During the council meeting the previous month at Fort Lapwai, he had shown the chiefs a petition sent by the settlers along the Salmon River outlining their grievances against the Nez Perce. The people who had signed it were solid citizens, not prone to fabrications or self-serving claims against innocent Indian people. He had hoped, by showing this to the Indians and reading the names of those who had signed, to make them realize that good people had legitimate complaints about the behavior of some members of their tribe.

Now those same names of those same good people were coming back to him in a different context. They were the names of the settlers who were being murdered and raped and tortured in the deep canyons of the Salmon River and White Bird Creek sixty miles to the south.

The war that few had wanted now raced like cloud shadows across the landscape. The Norton family, trying to escape through the Camas Prairie at night, had been run down and killed by Nez Perce. John Chamberlain, who had been bringing a wagonload of flour to Lewiston, was found dead a few hundred yards from his wagon. He was cradling the lifeless body of his three-year-old daughter, while his youngest child, barely a toddler, was discovered lying beneath the bodies of her father and sister with a gaping knife wound in her neck. Chamberlain's pregnant wife was found wandering incoherently about a mile away, still alive but hysterical from repeated rapings and an arrow wound in her breast.

All across the wide Camas Prairie and over the ridge along the creeks and rivers of White Bird Canyon, the scene was being repeated. None of the settlers knew what was happening or why. All they knew was that eight hundred Nez Perce and all their horses had been gathered on the Camas Prairie and that Indians were now attacking settlers in their homes. Families were frantically gathering in small groups and standing logs on end in trenches to build makeshift forts against attack. From their hiding places they could see smoke from burning haystacks and homestead cabins filling the sky.

The Nez Perce too were desperate. Most of them had not wanted this war. They had feared it perhaps even more than had the white settlers. All knew that there had been divisions within the tribe. Much talk had been taking place even in the great gathering on the Camas Prairie as to whether or not the people should move onto the reservation, but few had thought that an attack on the whites was a right course of action.

The chiefs met in hurried council. This was an unprecedented situation. They were used to long deliberations where each spoke until finished while all others took such time as they needed to consider the arguments put forth. But there was no such luxury now. They were now a hunted people, traveling with all their earthly goods, all their horses, all their children, and all their elders.

After short deliberations they had decided to move the people off the open Camas Prairie to a protected rock overhang several miles back toward the passage down to the Salmon River. At least there they would be safe until they decided what to do.

But the young men were not finished. The initial wave of killings had only whetted their appetite for blood and vengeance, and their pent-up anger could not now be contained. Other warriors both young and old joined them. This was the war their fathers had not had the courage to fight. This was the chance to reclaim the honor of the Nez Perce and show the spirits of the ancestors that the Nez Perce would not abandon their land.

While the families huddled in the place of the overhanging rocks, the young warriors rode in and out of camp, shouting and brandishing weapons they had found in settlers' cabins. It was clear now that they were out of control. They had found an ample stock of alcohol during their raids of settlers' homes and stores and wagons and now were crazed beyond all possibility of reason. Young men who had been raised to look upon rape as an offense punishable by death and had been taught that the murder of a woman or a child was an act of supreme cowardice were now moving across the landscape raping and murdering with an almost gleeful abandon.

Once Joseph and his people arrived, it was determined that the whole group should move over the ridge into White Bird Canyon. Since there was only one way into the canyon, it could be guarded easily by a handful of warriors. When the soldiers arrived, and they surely would arrive, perhaps a group of men sent forth under a flag of truce could forestall any further violence. It was worth a try, and surely preferable to an all-out war with soldiers and enraged settlers who had now seen their families murdered and their homes pillaged and burned.

Only Looking Glass disapproved. His men had played no part in this attack, and his women had already planted their gardens back at home. He wanted no involvement with the whites for himself or his people. The other bands could do what they wished, but he and his band would return to their land along the Clearwater.

This left four bands—Joseph's, White Bird's, Toohoolhoolzote's, and the Palouse people led by Hahtalekin and Husis Kute. Of these chiefs, Joseph was the youngest and most conciliatory. All knew that his heart was in the Wallowa and that he would do what was necessary to reclaim his distant homeland. Talk had passed that he had been ready to join the religion of the Black Robes if it would help his people keep their land. There was even some doubt about his motives for staying back at the Camas Prairie when the others had left after the initial killings. Perhaps it had been as a rear-guard lookout, as he had said. But perhaps it had been to make private deals with the soldiers and government.

So despite the high regard in which he was held as a spokesman for the Wallowa people, he was now looked upon with a shadow of suspicion. His counsel would be valued, but it would not be heard with a completely trusting ear.

General Howard tried to quell the hysteria. He did not know what had happened, but he knew if the Nez Perce really had gone on the warpath, the scattered families of settlers had no realistic possibility of defending themselves without military assistance. He had no choice but to act.

He decided to send out a force of about a hundred men under the command of Captain David Perry, a seasoned Indian fighter who had exhibited great bravery and skill in the fight against the Modocs in the California lava beds four years before. Despite the rawness and lack of training of the Lapwai troops, he fully expected that these men, under Captain Perry's able leadership and assisted by treaty Nez Perce scouts, could bring the situation under control, either through negotiation or confrontation. Howard himself would remain at Lapwai until reinforcement troops he had summoned from the Wallowa Valley arrived.

For the next two days he followed Perry's progress in reports delivered by riders. He had every reason to believe that his troops would soon have the situation in hand. But on the afternoon of the second day, when two of Perry's men came riding into camp frightened and disoriented, he began to sense that all might not be right. On the third day, a dispatch from Perry himself arrived, and the reality of the situation began to sink in.

"The fight resulted most disastrously to us," it read, "in fact scarcely exceeded by the magnitude of the Custer massacre in proportion to the numbers engaged."

The mention of the Little Bighorn debacle and the images of its 250 murdered and mutilated soldiers sent chills through the general's heart. To use that battle in reference to an engagement meant that something

dreadful had happened. Howard now knew that this was no isolated erup-
tion of small dissatisfactions. He was facing the possibility of an Indian
war that might involve all the tribes of the Columbia Plateau.

For the Christian treaty Nez Perce living in the white manner at Lapwai
and Kamiah this was the fulfillment of their worst fears. Though many of
the Nez Perce women cared for the children of the whites and the men of
both races traded together and farmed together, this kind of outbreak was
sure to make the worst among the whites turn against all people of brown
skin, and maybe even bring the wrath of the government down upon all
Nez Perce.

The nontreaty bands were their brothers and sisters, and many had relatives living among them, but they knew they had to distance themselves as
much as possible in order to save their own homes and families. Their choice
of loyalty—to blood or belief—now became a matter of personal survival.

Meanwhile, sixty miles away in White Bird Canyon on the banks of the
Salmon, the nontreaty Nez Perce were now in a quandary. The soldiers had
indeed come, as they had expected. A group of six warriors had ridden out
to greet them with a white flag held high, hoping to work out some kind
of peaceful accord. But one of the settlers whom many of them knew, a
hotheaded coward and bully named Ad Chapman, had begun firing at the
warriors. The six emissaries had quickly raced behind the hills and made
their way back to the camp. The warriors who were able to fight then
mounted their horses and prepared for battle.

It was not a strong force that the Nez Perce sent out against the soldiers. Many of the best warriors had been involved in the raids on the settlers' stores and wagons and had spent the previous evening drinking
themselves into a stupor on the whiskey that was one of the key spoils of
those attacks. By the early dawn, many of them had been too drunk to even
stand.

Nonetheless, the battle had been short and surprisingly easy. The
young soldiers who had come from the Lapwai had been exhausted from a
thirty-hour ride with almost no sleep. They had seemed poorly trained and
unaccustomed to both riding and shooting. Many of their weapons had
jammed when they fired, and their horses, unlike those of the Nez Perce,
were skittish in the presence of gunshots. They had shown no stomach for
the fight, and their tactics had been clumsy and flawed.

The Nez Perce had simply waited behind some of the rolling hills in the canyon while the soldiers came over the ridge, then ridden out and struck the army in the flank. The troops who had not been killed outright had been scattered and sent into a panicky retreat. Though the Nez Perce had been fighting mainly with bows and arrows and ancient rifles, their skills on horseback had given them a great advantage. From their youngest days they had been raised on horses, often even sleeping strapped in the saddle on family journeys.

Their childhood war games had involved riding full speed in circles around a post while hanging off the side of their horses and firing arrows at the post from beneath the animal's neck. By the time an actual battle came, they could ride full speed while loading and unloading rifles or preparing an arrow for flight, and they could fight from their saddle with a skill far beyond any possessed by the soldiers. Their marksmanship was deadly because they could roll off their horse, fire a rifle shot, and remount in a single motion, allowing them the steady accuracy of firing from a stationary position while still retaining the fluid mobility of mounted warfare.

They also understood white fighting techniques. It was not without purpose that White Bird had sat on his horse, day after day, at the edge of Fort Lapwai watching the soldiers drill. They knew that white soldiers fought under command, not singly. So the first act had been to shoot the bugler because they knew that a white army without a voice was an army without a mind. Next, they had sought to kill all soldiers who wore stripes because they knew that without commanders the men would be disorganized and helpless. White soldiers were not like the Nez Perce—trained to fight alone and able to signal each other with animal calls and blankets.

The battle had been over in a matter of hours. When it was finished, thirty-three soldiers lay dead, and the Nez Perce had suffered only a few minor injuries. But for many of the people it had felt like a hollow victory. There was no glory in killing young men who had died holding their hands over their faces and crying for their mothers.

But for the young warriors who had started the fight, and those who had gotten swept up in the battle, it was a time of great celebration. They had been outnumbered two to one, had been fighting with far inferior weapons, and still had defeated the white soldiers with ease. They had earned their manhood and had done what their chiefs had lacked the courage to do. To be a Nez Perce no longer meant to cower like old women. With the sixty rifles they had captured during the fight they could drive the settlers out of their land and reclaim the country that their grandfathers had been given by the Creator. With the help of their *wayakin* powers they would restore the honor of the Nez Perce. They would make the spirits of their ancestors proud.

But the older men saw danger. They knew now that all-out war was coming, and it would be war without victory. If they did not escape quickly, everyone from the youngest children to the blind and crippled elders would die at the soldiers' hands.

The entire camp had descended into chaos. Mothers were gathering their children. Young boys were running excitedly in hopes of being able to join in the fight. Some of the warriors had resumed their drinking while others were solemn and cold-eyed, readying themselves for sacred battle. The women were hurriedly stripping the bodies of the dead soldiers of their weapons and ammunitions. Some of the basket hat women were covering the bodies of the young soldiers with their best blankets. They wished to show that the Nez Perce had wanted no part of this fight.

There was no overall leadership, no overall control. Even the chiefs were unsure what to do. How were they to fight with women and children and elders among them? How were they to control young men who were beyond the reach of reason and convinced that they were serving the honor of their ancestors? How were they to flee with thousands of head of horses and all their household goods? They had packed for moving, not for battle or flight.

All they knew for certain was that the soldiers would now come, and they would not come in small numbers and with few weapons. Joseph had told the people that the whites were like grizzlies and the Nez Perce were like deer, and his conviction was about to be tested. The grizzly had been awakened.

Joseph himself sat exhausted in his lodge. With an infant daughter only a few days old, he had not wanted this fight. But once the shooting had started, he had gone into the battle, taking no lead but doing his part, always warning the warriors to be careful not to kill one another by mistake. He was still opposed to war. He did not see how it could come to good. He was still willing to go on the reservation, to try living among the whites and the Nez Perce who had accepted the Christian way. His people had done so when he was a child. Perhaps they could do so again. But if war had come and they must now all die, he wanted his death to come in his own beloved Wallowa, where his parents were buried and the land knew his name.

The other bands, however, were not of similar mind. Toohoolhoolzote still smarted from the insult done to him by Howard at the peace council, and his young men were ready to fight. White Bird too had a group of young warriors who had smarted too long under the indignities and injustices of the white intruders. The Palouse chiefs, Hahtalekin and Husis Kute, were Dreamers from the country of Smolholla and looked with no favor upon conciliation. Looking Glass, who had been the only other voice of moderation, had returned to his own country and disavowed himself of any involvement in the situation.

In hurried discussion, the chiefs decided that the people should cross back over the Salmon River to the west. The hills on the opposite side rose almost vertically and opened into rough mountainous country where the soldiers would have difficulty traveling with their heavy weaponry, and ambush by the warriors would be a real possibility. It also took them back across the river.

Rivers were the Nez Perce's best allies. The people knew the waters of their country like they knew the folds of the land. Just as Joseph and his people had been able to cross the thunderous Snake by allowing themselves to be carried by unseen eddies and currents, the assembled bands could use their knowledge of the Salmon to cross safely to the other side. The soldiers, who were ignorant of the character of the river and burdened with heavy equipment, would have a difficult time following. They would have to construct rafts, send men across on horseback to secure guide ropes, then put themselves at the mercy of currents they did not understand. Even if they were successful, it would put them far behind the people. If they were not, it was all the better. A soldier swept away in a strong current was as lost to the fight as a soldier felled by a bullet or an arrow.

Joseph supported the plan because it moved him back toward the Wallowa. Once they were through the rumpled mountains on the other side of the Salmon, there was only the Snake to cross in order to return to the trails that led up to his homeland. It was his hope that this crossing back over the Salmon would be the first step on the trail back to the Wallowa.

But the other chiefs and warriors were not looking at it as a chance for retreat. They saw it as part of a larger strategic action. Forcing the soldiers to do the one thing that they did most poorly—fording fast-moving waters—would allow the people to gain time. A few warriors would stay close to the river and goad the soldiers to cross, then hold them back with sporadic gunfire while the people and animals climbed the rugged hills and made their way north to another crossing point back by the Camas Prairie. There they could cross back to the side they were now on and make a run for the eastern mountains on the far side of the prairie. Then, if they so chose, they could make their way across the Lolo Trail to Montana and freedom among their friends and brothers, the Flatheads. Meanwhile, the warriors could scour the prairie and destroy any supply wagons coming down from Fort Lapwai to provide ammunition and supplies to the troops.

The strategy worked to perfection. Howard arrived at the Salmon River with his troops and his treaty Nez Perce scouts, only to find the nontreaty Nez Perce warriors across the river, taunting him. "You are getting fat eating government food," they shouted across to James Reuben, who had joined up with the military to serve as one of their scouts. "Come and get us. We will take your scalps."

Every time the troops tried to cross, a few gunshots sent them hurrying back to cover. The river too proved impossible to cross. Howard's men were incapable of navigating its currents without assistance, and all efforts to string a rope across the river to serve as a guy line ended in failure.

Between the gunshots, the river, and Howard's soldiers' newfound fear and respect for Nez Perce fighting skills, the troops were held at bay for four days. Meanwhile, the families moved far up into the ragged hills on their side of the river. Had they not been hidden from view by the rugged terrain and heavy stands of pine, Howard could have seen the long line of people and horses moving like small specks along the ridgetops, heading back north, where they did indeed cross the river twenty-five miles downstream, ending up back on the same side as Howard now stood.

Once the rear-guard warriors retreated and allowed Howard to proceed, the general sloshed his troops across, dragged his heavy supply wagons up to the ridgeline, and set out in clumsy pursuit. What he confronted was a landscape uninhabited by whites and unknown to the soldiers. As one of Howard's men wrote, it was "broken beyond my power of description—a perfect sea of mountains, gullies, ravines, and canyons."

By the time they reached the Nez Perce's second crossing point, the Indians had crossed the river again and were moving toward the east, over the very same Camas Prairie where they had been camped prior to the attacks on the settlers and through which Howard and his men had marched only a few days before.

To make matters worse, this second fording spot proved more difficult than the first to Howard. After stopping to build a raft by dismantling a cabin owned by one of the treaty Nez Perce, he found that his men were incapable of getting it across the churning, roiling, winter-swollen river. He ended up leaving the turbulent waters and retracing his steps to the original fording place, thus leaving himself with a cold trail and the Indians with a much greater lead.

Meanwhile, the main body of the Nez Perce was now making its way across the broad, flat, fifty-mile-wide expanse of the Camas Prairie. It was a risky transit, for there was little cover other than low hills and swales. Though the white settlements were few and scattered, often consisting of nothing more than a few houses huddled around a grain storage building, movement across this broad open area left the people exposed to attack from soldiers or settler volunteers.

And such attacks were coming. The chaotic situation and rumors from soldiers, settlers, and nontreaty Indians alike had convinced the frightened settlers that a great Indian war was now upon them. Lacking any clear indications of the Indians' destinations or intent, they had formed into loose groups and set out in search of the renegades to kill them or drive them away from their land. All across the prairie, brief encounters and skirmishes were taking place between roving bands of warriors, intent upon protecting their people from the whites, and groups of military and settlers, intent upon protecting the white families from the Indians.

Mostly, the Indians prevailed. The young men were taking their new-found status as warriors seriously, and because of the guns and ammunition they had taken from the dead soldiers at White Bird Canyon, they were now well equipped for combat. With their superior skills of horsemanship and marksmanship, they were easily able to protect the people from the attacks.

But the chiefs still hoped to avoid an all-out war. They called off the warriors whenever approaching soldiers or volunteers halted their advance. With many blind, crippled, and sick among them, their only desire was to hold back the white attackers while the people made their way across the Camas Prairie country toward the base of the Bitterroot Mountains at the Clearwater River. There they would be at the foot of the trail over to buffalo country, and there they could hold council so each band could decide if it wished to run, fight, try to counsel with the whites, or surrender to an uncertain fate at the hands of white justice.

Joseph and the elderly White Bird had taken responsibility for caring for the people and assisting them in setting up camp and preparing for travel. As camp chiefs, they had organized moves before, but never under circumstances of flight. Helping the elderly, choosing camp sites, making sure that the younger boys kept the horses safe and fed, protecting the women when they went out to gather wood and food, and simply organizing so many people to move was a difficult task. Horses, dogs, camp gear, food, infants, sick and wounded, and elderly adults had to be watched over. With no overall leadership and each family able to act according to its own intentions, convincing all to follow a common purpose was a delicate task. But the need for defense made it essential that the group stay together.

With the young warriors at least momentarily under control and satisfied to serve as advance scouts and outriders, the mass of people and animals moved across the great bowl of the Camas Prairie and dropped down into the valley of the Clearwater River, just a few miles from the start of the Lolo Trail, which wound across the mountains into buffalo country. Here they made camp only a short ride away from the Weippe Prairie where their ancestors had first encountered Lewis and Clark, and only several miles up the river from where Looking Glass and his people were living peacefully, unwilling to be part of the hostility that was rapidly growing around them.

8

"We Are Living Here Peacefully and Want No Trouble"

NONE AMONG THE NONTREATY Nez Perce assumed that Looking Glass would play any part in the decision making or even be part of any meeting held by the chiefs. He had upbraided them all after the first killings and had sworn to stay far from any confrontation. But Howard had heard from various treaty Nez Perce that the chief was letting his young warriors join the renegades, so he had dispatched a group of soldiers and settler volunteers to Looking Glass's camp to stop him from assisting the belligerents.

Though Looking Glass's band had not adopted Christianity, they had adopted many of the white farming ways. Their little village on the banks of the Clearwater River included gardens of potatoes, corn, beans, squash, cucumbers, and melons as well as a few milk cows and beef cattle. It was a quiet, idyllic setting, with teepee lodges, split rail fences, and herds of horses grazing contentedly in nearby meadows.

When he learned that soldiers were coming, he placed a white flag on a pole in the direction from which they would arrive and sent a messenger out to meet them. "Tell them to leave us alone," were his instructions to the messenger. "Tell them we are living here peacefully and want no trouble."

But the soldiers, well fortified with liquor, refused to listen to the messenger and rode into the village, shooting and rampaging and looting. They trampled the gardens and smashed the women's cooking pots, then tried to set the teepees on fire.

The people became so frightened that one woman tried to escape across the river with her baby strapped to her back. She was swept away and the baby was never found. Others were wounded as they fled into the woods in panic.

The soldiers and volunteers continued their looting, taking buffalo robes and bags of powder and anything that looked like it might be of value. Then they destroyed what remained. They drove off all the horses and cattle and shot randomly at anyone they saw. Several of Looking Glass's people were injured, and the band lost almost all of its food and possessions.

By the time the other nontreaty bands had completed their successful crossing of the Camas Prairie, Looking Glass's people were staring at a decimated, leveled campsite with uprooted gardens, scattered and smashed household goods, and almost no shelters.

Unaware of this tragedy, the other nontreaties made their camp several miles away in a wide valley at the base of a high, almost perpendicular bluff. The same Clearwater River that ran by Looking Glass's ravaged village flowed through the center of the campsite, affording good water for the people and the horses and offering a fine, wide area for camping and grazing.

Here the chiefs and warriors and influential basket hat women took time to rest and continue their discussions. Should they flee across the mountains, then continue east to buffalo country? Should they cross the mountains, then turn north to the Old Woman Country the whites called Canada, where they heard that Sitting Bull had been allowed to settle in peace after the fight at the Little Bighorn? Should they surrender? Should they send the women and children into hiding while the men stayed back to fight? There was no easy answer because no one knew the number or intentions of the soldiers, and no one knew the full extent of the complicity of the treaty Nez Perce.

Whatever direction the various speakers were leaning, it all became moot when Looking Glass rode in with a dark and ominous message. "Two days ago my camp was attacked by the soldiers," he said. "I tried to surrender in every way I could. My horses, lodges, and everything I had were taken away from me. Now, my people, as long as I live I will never make peace with the Americans. I am ready for war."

Any remaining sentiment to trust the honor of the American soldiers and government now disintegrated. They had to fight or flee.

But while the people were discussing their choices, unbeknownst to them, Howard's soldiers were moving along the top of the bluff several miles back from the crest that towered over their campsite. He had made it across the river, losing several horses in the process, and had consolidated the forces that had been spread out over the prairie. He was now moving with a force of almost five hundred men. He had also picked up an intrepid war correspondent named Thomas Sutherland, who had recently graduated from Harvard and was trying to make a name for himself by reporting directly from the front, an idea considered novel and daring for the time. The two men had struck up such a good friendship that Howard had begun including the young correspondent in his command retinue.

So with his own soldiers, the remnants of the command that had been decimated at White Bird Canyon, a motley group of settler volunteers, and his own personal war correspondent who was issuing dispatches to the *Portland Standard,* the *New York Herald,* and the *San Francisco Chronicle,* Howard had begun moving to the south in an effort to loop around the renegades and catch them unawares. His march along the top of the bluff, with his supply wagons trailing far behind, was merely part of this positioning.

But one of the settler volunteers who happened to be wandering along the top of the bluff a ways off from the main command made a discovery that immediately altered the military's plans. Far below, on the flats across the river, the man saw what looked to be almost seventy teepees and hundreds of horses. Young Indian boys were engaged in horse races, and women were bathing in the river. Clearly, these were the hostiles, and clearly, the camp was not prepared for war. He immediately hurried back and informed General Howard.

Howard had assumed the Indians were in the area, but this was a stroke of unexpected luck. He now had not only the strategic advantage of high ground but also the incalculable advantage of surprise. Unfortunately for him, however, that surprise was not total. Indian lookouts had caught a glimpse of the settler as he peered down on them and had shouted to the others to mobilize.

The terrain too proved to be less of an advantage than Howard had hoped. Only two long, narrow wooded ravines snaked down from the high bluff, so any attackers had to either ascend or descend through those passages.

The warriors gained the edge by quick movement. Toohoolhoolzote, with a small group of men, secured a position behind some rocks and held the soldiers at bay until the full force of the warriors could be mobilized and sent charging up the ravines. As a result, the soldiers lost the advantage of attack and were reduced to shooting down on the tribe from above.

Once again, the soldiers' inadequate training proved to be their undoing. Their weapons were in poor condition, and many of the men had received target practice of only three shots a month. At so great a distance, even a skilled marksman would have been hard-pressed to do any damage.

They tried dragging their howitzers to the edge of the bluff, but because these guns were essentially great heavy steel cannons held by gravity onto wooden frames, they could not be leaned forward to aim down into the village. Instead, they had to be shot upward, serving only to send shells high into the air to land randomly on the distant countryside or to explode harmlessly in the sky with no effect other than to frighten the Indians below.

The Indian men, meanwhile, were quite willing to engage. They had a camp full of women and children to protect, and the attack on Looking Glass's innocent village had galvanized their anger. The warriors were also brimming with confidence. With fewer than two hundred fighters and limited weapons, they had whipped the soldiers at White Bird Canyon and had routed every attack by volunteers while they had recrossed the Camas Prairie. Everywhere they had gone they had left the bodies of white fighters in their wake, but not a single fighter among them had yet been killed.

The men stripped for battle, removing all but their breechcloths so that any bullet strike would not push cloth or animal skin into the wound. Then they went on the offensive, riding up the ravines, hidden by brush until they reached the top and took positions surrounding the soldiers. It was a noose, loosely formed, but one from which there could be no easy escape. On the bluff side, the soldiers were hemmed in by the precipitous drop off the edge of the cliff. In their rear, a group of warriors had taken up protected positions on a small ridge. On either side, blocking access to the ravines, other warriors had barricaded themselves behind trees and small rock breastworks and were putting up a steady hail of rifle fire.

It was a classic encirclement maneuver, and the soldiers could not escape except by breaking through the Indian lines. But because the Indians were well hidden in the terrain and were crawling through the brush on their bellies, camouflaged by grass tied to their heads, no one knew exactly where they were, so no one knew exactly how to attack.

Instead, the confused soldiers began firing in all directions, shooting some of their own men in the process. The Indians kept up their fire until the howitzers and Gatling guns were hauled back from the bluff and turned on them. On level terrain with an enemy right in front of them, these once again became effective weapons, and the Indians were driven back.

By nighttime, it had become something of a stalemate. The Nez Perce held their positions but had not advanced. To get to the soldiers, they would have had to cross a broad, open field hundreds of yards wide. Also, and for the first time, they had experienced real casualties. One of their warriors had been killed, and two others had been wounded. After darkness fell, some of the women crept up and rescued one of the gravely wounded men and carried him back to camp. But he too soon died. Death was beginning to visit the Nez Perce.

Fighting resumed the next day. Many of the warriors had moved back down to the camp under the cover of darkness. But many had spent the chill night on the bluff, shivering behind their small stone rifle barriers clad only their loincloths. But they knew that if they could endure the night, another scorching hundred-degree day was coming, and the soldiers, without access to water, could not survive for long. All they had to do was keep them from the spring at the top of one of the ravines.

The greater problem the warriors faced was that they were not of a common mind about the wisdom of this fight. While some of them saw this as an opportunity to entrap and defeat a large body of soldiers, others saw it as a waste of time and effort. The soldiers had not attacked the village, and there was an easy escape route for the people along the river's edge and back into the hills, so in their minds there was no need to risk death in a fight that was not necessary.

Accusations of cowardice were hurled, met by counteraccusations of stupidity. But the end result was that the warriors did not act in concert. Nez Perce warriors were trained to fight on horseback in moving battles, with quick strikes and withdrawals. The idea of setting a siege behind small rock barriers was not comfortable to many of them. It was not a tactic that allowed them to exhibit individual bravery, and it did not allow them to use their skills at horsemanship to good advantage. This was a soldier way of fighting, and many of them did not wish to fight like soldiers. So some of the warriors simply refused to fight and repaired to a rock-rimmed "smoking pit" that had been constructed at the base of the bluff for the old men to gather in and hold council.

When the Gatling guns and howitzers were turned on the few Indians still holding the siege, filling the sky with thunderous noise and an impenetrable cloud of smoke, it became obvious that the advantage could not be maintained. The warriors who wished to continue the fight became so disgusted with what they felt was the cowardice of the others that they abandoned their positions and began heading toward the ravines. They could see no good reason to die when their skills at fighting and protection would likely be needed again in the future.

When the soldiers realized that they were receiving no return fire, they broke for the Indian lines. The warriors who had remained on the bluff were soon in full-scale retreat. They scrambled down the ravines, with women who had come to assist on the battlefield trailing, terrified, behind. Above them they could hear the cheers of the pursuing soldiers mixed with the booms of the howitzer shells exploding over their heads.

Once in the valley they grabbed what they could and ran. Some of the chiefs tried to rally the men to make a stand, but there was no common will. The women in the camp were already fleeing with the children and the elderly. Pots of boiling meat were left gurgling on the fires, and almost all the camp goods had to be abandoned in hastily constructed caches.

Normally, Joseph and White Bird, in their capacity as camp chiefs, could have prepared the people for an orderly withdrawal. But the unexpected suddenness of the warrior retreat and the chaos and confusion that resulted allowed only the gathering of such goods as were at hand. People were running for their lives.

Yellow Wolf, a young warrior of twenty-one, was one of those who had stayed on the high bluff holding back the soldiers. When he finally found his horse and escaped down the ravine and across the river, the camp was almost deserted. But he could hear a woman crying amid the din of the howitzer explosions and rifle shots of the pursuing soldiers. It was Joseph's wife, Springtime, carrying their infant daughter, now only several weeks old. Springtime was trying frantically to control her horse, who was terrified by the explosions of the howitzer shells. The animal was bucking wildly, making it impossible for her to mount while carrying the infant on its cradle board.

She shouted out to Yellow Wolf that she was afraid for her baby.

Yellow Wolf held the infant while she mounted her horse, then the two of them rode off together to catch up with the other fleeing members of the camp. Joseph was somewhere far ahead, trying to lead and control the frightened and disorganized families in their retreat. But this apparent abandoning of his wife and child in the face of fierce fighting did not go unnoticed.

Finding the Nez Perce gone, the soldiers and citizen volunteers poured into camp and began looting everything they could find. They took jewelry, small pouches of gold dust, and silverware that the Nez Perce had gotten in trade years before. Everything that was not of value they burned, while other settlers scavenged the area, poking into the earth with the ramrods of their muskets in hopes of finding caches of Nez Perce goods. Soldiers who tried to claim booty for themselves had it stolen when their backs were turned by settlers who had ridden up in wagons when they had heard the shooting in the distance.

The Nez Perce, meanwhile, were moving ever farther ahead, aiming toward the Christian Nez Perce settlement of Kamiah a few miles up the river past the site of Looking Glass's ravaged village. There they could commandeer the boats owned by the Christian Nez Perce and make their way across the Clearwater River and up into the safety of the Weippe Prairie in the foothills of the Bitterroots. Sadly, this crossing would be easier than their last river fording at the Salmon, for most of their household goods, much of their food and clothing, and many of their horses and cattle were still back in the campsite they had just abandoned, being ransacked, burned, and appropriated by gleeful soldiers and settlers.

Though insignificant as a military battle, the fight at the Clearwater was, in fact, a watershed event. Howard was quickly becoming the subject of much scrutiny and public derision after the devastating defeat at White Bird Canyon. Every braggart settler anywhere in the Plateau region, and indeed in the entire West, was convinced he could do better, and each was quick to make those declarations publicly and repeatedly. The residents in the areas that had been touched by the Nez Perce conflict, faced with the realities of murdered neighbors and the rumors of Indian atrocities, were justifiably upset by military failures such as those at White Bird Canyon and now were loudly demanding better military protection and more competent military leadership.

Howard was not insensitive to these criticisms, so he was anxious to put a good face on any military success. With his newfound friend, Sutherland, available to post glowing dispatches about his bravery and leadership, he had found his chance in the skirmish at the Clearwater.

Howard knew that a strong enemy makes an opposing commander look good, and a great opposing general makes the victorious general look even better. Every time he had been called into the Plateau country, it had somehow involved an issue with Joseph. He had heard the man's eloquence and seen the way that the other nontreaty chiefs had deferred to him on matters concerning the Wallowa. So he erroneously assumed that this imposing, charismatic, formidable chief was also the energetic, charismatic, formidable military leader of all the nontreaty bands.

As a result, in his reports and in the dispatches from his friend, Sutherland, his military campaign was depicted as a struggle with the masterful war chief, Joseph, whose brilliant leadership and field strategies and tactics only served to make Howard's victory seem even greater. Taking Howard's lead, Sutherland referred to the Nez Perce as "Joseph's people" and soon adopted the military shorthand of making observations such as "Joseph is in full retreat." In the public's mind, the Nez Perce were rapidly becoming "Joseph's people," and every military action was becoming an engagement between the Civil War general, Howard, and Joseph, the Nez Perce general and leader of the Nez Perce people.

Meanwhile, the Nez Perce were anything but Joseph's people. They were not even united among themselves. It had been all the chiefs could do to get everyone moving in a single direction. Even questions of allegiance still had not been sorted out. Many families included members who lived among the treaty factions as well as among the nontreaty bands. This had never presented a problem because all knew that a person or family could cross back and forth between sides if they decided that the Christian way or the traditional way was better. But now, with bullets flying, lines were hardening. In fact, in the Clearwater skirmish, one of the treaty Nez Perce fighting for the soldiers and even wearing a blue soldier's jacket learned that his father had been killed while fighting on the nontreaty side, so he raced across the ground between the two factions, enduring fire from both camps, threw off his coat, and led a charge of the nontreaties against the soldiers he had just abandoned.

Others changed sides in the opposite direction. They were uncomfortable with the rampaging and killings committed by the young warriors and knew some of the whites who had died for no cause other than the color of their skin. Others saw what was coming and did not want to be forever divided and exiled from their families. Many were simply afraid.

Broader questions too were coming into high relief, especially for the fleeing bands. It was now clear that they were not acting with common purpose, and this was costing them dearly. It was failure to control the young men at the campsite in Camas Prairie that had involved them all in this fight; it was failure to have a common military purpose at Clearwater that had resulted in the surprise retreat that had forced them to flee unpacked and unprepared. The time had come to become one people under strong command or to scatter and go their respective ways.

But before any such decision was made, one last unified military action would be attempted. If Howard could be beaten in a standing fight for which the Nez Perce were prepared, perhaps a good end to the situation could be achieved. After all, the killings had been done by only a small group of young men raging out of control. Perhaps, if Howard could be stopped, there would be time to explain. The fording place at the Nez Perce village of Kamiah presented this opportunity.

Kamiah sat on the edge of the Clearwater River, nestled in a deep valley about twelve miles from the site of the Clearwater skirmish and a slightly lesser distance from Looking Glass's now-devastated village. It was among the most successful and Christianized of the Nez Perce settlements. It had a wooden church with a tall, pointed steeple, a small schoolhouse, and fields of corn and vegetables. White missionaries had been living at Kamiah since shortly after the arrival of the Reverend Spalding at the Lapwai, and it was the traditional home of some of the most influential of the Christian Nez Perce—men like James Lawyer and James Reuben. The Nez Perce here were devoutly Presbyterian, and they did not want to be drawn into the conflict with the white soldiers.

But Kamiah was also the site of the Heart of the Monster, the great land mound where the Nez Perce people believed themselves to have been created. If there was a place of sacred power from which the fleeing bands could draw spiritual nourishment for a final fight, this was it. It also was a strategic spot for battle, since it necessitated another river crossing by the soldiers. The Nez Perce warriors, well positioned, could destroy the soldiers as they struggled to cross to the other side.

Though the fleeing bands had suffered the loss of many of their possessions and had been forced to scatter in disarray, they were neither hurried nor frightened. Their misfortune had been the result of poor preparation and miscalculation, both things that could be corrected. They paraded single file down the hills toward the village of Kamiah, confident that they could finish their business with the soldiers one way or another at this destination.

The Kamiah Nez Perce, in their white people's clothing and short hair, wanted nothing to do with the nontreaty Nez Perce, resplendent in their beaded buckskin, "heathen" braids, and Dreamer forelocks. They refused the nontreaties the use of their boats, and they commanded their children to remain in their houses, far away from their brothers and sisters and cousins who still lived in the ways of spiritual darkness.

But if their concern was spiritual, it was also practical. They were a peaceful people, and they had been appalled at the alcohol-crazed actions of the young warriors gathering across the river. They did not wish to be seen as aiding the Nez Perce who had done such unnecessary killing and burning, and they were not at all interested in incurring the wrath of the military for aiding and abetting an enemy. Nonetheless, they could not deny that the people massing across the river were their brothers and sisters. They hoped to persuade them to give up their warring ways so all the Nez Perce could live in peace with the American government.

But the nontreaty people were of a different mind. They set up their lodges across the river from the Heart of the Monster and began constructing buffalo skin bull boats to ferry themselves and their remaining goods across. Their strategy was simple. The families would ford the river and begin moving very visibly into the foothills of the Bitterroots just to the east. The warriors would remain out of sight on the near side of the river to await the soldiers, who would see the fleeing families and come rushing after in hot pursuit. When the soldiers reached the river, the warriors would ambush them in a hail of rifle fire. The military would be decimated and the pursuit brought to a halt.

The next day, when the soldiers appeared on the crest of the distant hill, the warriors put this plan into action. As the cavalry came riding down toward the river, the men opened fire from their hiding places. The assault was withering. The warriors now had a number of repeating weapons, which allowed them to fire rapidly upon the troops. They also had single-shot, breech-loading weapons, which rejected the spent shells and could refire as quickly as another shell could be inserted. These were a far cry from the muzzle-loading rifles that many of them had been raised with, which required a fighter to stop, tamp powder down the barrel of a his gun, insert a ball, and then fire it with minimal accuracy in the rough direction of the desired target. Though some men, like Toohoolhoolzote, still clung to the old muzzle-loading weapons, most of the Nez Perce were now equipped with rifles that were the equal of any possessed by white soldiers and settlers. And they were skilled in using them.

The barrage of fire caught the cavalry unawares. They jumped from their horses in a panic and quickly retreated to cover several hundred yards back from the river, where they awaited instructions on how to proceed.

The Nez Perce kept goading them to attack. But General Howard did not wish to engage on these terms. He knew that his cavalry was no match in either horsemanship or bravery for the Nez Perce, and his infantry, though courageous, could not do the job alone. So instead he attempted a ruse. The route back to Fort Lapwai lay directly along the Clearwater. If he could make it seem that his troops had given up the fight and were returning to the fort, perhaps he could cross the river on a log ferry that he knew was tied up farther along the river and circle in behind the Nez Perce. He was unsure if the hostiles were intending to head north to enlist the aid of other tribes to initiate the long-dreaded, Plateau-wide Indian war or were moving toward the Weippe Prairie and the start of the trail over the mountains. In either case, they would likely encamp in the Weippe because it was a traditional stopping place and one of the few spots where they could find forage and campsites enough for all their horses and people. If he could beat them there, he could drive them backward toward his own troops who remained at the Clearwater and finish them off in a pincer move.

Making a public show of changing direction, he turned his cavalry north, as if he intended to return to Fort Lapwai. But the Nez Perce were not so easily fooled. They sniffed out Howard's ploy and sent a band of warriors to cut the guy rope that was used to haul the flat, log ferry across the river, leaving the raft banging helplessly against the shore in the swift current. If Howard truly intended to cross, he would have no choice but to return to his camp near Kamiah, where he would have to force his balky horses across the river in a time-consuming and difficult fording.

In the meantime, the remaining Nez Perce did indeed head up the narrow trails out of the river valley into the high meadows of the Weippe. They had not succeeded in wiping out Howard's troops, but they had one final trick for the general. While he was executing his sham march north, the Nez Perce sent word through the Christian Nez Perce that Joseph wished to discuss surrender. The Wallowa chief, they said, was at odds with the other chiefs and did not wish to subject his people to further difficulties. He was far from his homeland, and many of his people were without food and household goods after the caching at the first Salmon crossing and the attack at the Clearwater. He wanted only fair justice for his people, and then he would willingly lead them to the Lapwai and accept life on the reservation.

When the treaty messengers caught up with Howard and delivered the message, the general hurried back to begin the negotiation. But he found no Joseph, only a warrior named No Heart standing across the river shouting toward the soldiers and Nez Perce scouts. No Heart said he was a messenger from Joseph and wished to agree to terms of the surrender. Joseph, he explained, had been forced by the other chiefs to continue his flight but was prepared to turn in himself and his people under the right circumstances.

Even though he had been hoping to speak with Joseph himself, Howard was excited by this apparent turn of events. He was not willing to negotiate anything beyond unconditional surrender, but he promised an honest tribunal overseen by nine men that he would handpick for their fairness. No Heart continued pressing for conditions, and the discussions went back and forth for hours, with Howard getting more and more frustrated. Eventually, someone fired a shot, and No Heart turned his backside to Howard and slapped his buttocks—a sign of complete contempt—and rode off.

Howard feared he had been tricked, but he decided to wait until morning to see if Joseph truly would turn himself in. Fording the troops would be difficult and time consuming, so it was worthwhile to wait. Perhaps his terms would be relayed to Joseph, and the chief, so concerned about the well-being of his people, would see the offer as fair and desirable. With Joseph in his hands, the other bands could cross the mountains or be hunted down at Howard's leisure. He would have the prize most sought, the public criticism of his military would die down, and the dangers to the people in his area of command would be over.

But Joseph did not show the next morning. Instead, a band led by a man named Red Heart emerged. They had been returning from buffalo country and had run into the fleeing Nez Perce in the Weippe Prairie. Wishing nothing to do with the war, they had proceeded down the trail to the crossing at the Clearwater. There they encountered Howard. Though they knew nothing about the fighting and wished to stay as far from hostilities as possible, their long hair and traditional dress marked them in the soldiers' minds as belligerents. They were taken prisoner and stripped of their horses and saddles, then marched sixty miles through the stifling July heat to Fort Lapwai, from which they could be shipped to Fort Vancouver to be held in captivity.

If Howard could not have Joseph, he could at least show success by capturing and incarcerating thirty Indians, even though over half were women and children and none had shown any signs of belligerence or involvement with the fleeing bands. At a distance, and with proper crafting of his reports and the able assistance of Sutherland's dispatches, none would know the difference, and few would even care.

The actual Nez Perce he had hoped to capture were now up in the Weippe Prairie, fifteen miles away, at the very spot where the three boys had first encountered Lewis and Clark seventy years before, and the place where one of the two major Indian trails across the difficult Bitterroot Mountains began.

The climb had been difficult and wearying. The Clearwater River, like all the rivers in the area, was a wide flow in the bottom of a deep canyon carved out of the landscape over hundreds of thousands of years. The trail up to the Plateau where the Weippe stood was steep and arduous, sometimes too acute to be walked directly, and able to be ascended only by narrow switchback trails of rock and mud. Where it was a direct climb, much of the path lay in a narrow gully filled with deadfall and boulders. By the time eight hundred people and all their horses had traversed this trail, it was little more than a slippery mush of mud and horse manure. The soldiers who had to follow were confronted with a climb of utmost unpleasantness and difficulty.

In the Weippe, far from the pursuing soldiers, the Nez Perce were gathering to make the most momentous decision they had faced. They could not go on divided in intent and lacking in common purpose. Looking

Glass, who had assumed an attitude of authority, insisted that the wisest course was to travel across the Lolo Trail, which led off from the Weippe over the Bitterroot Mountains to the territory the white men called Montana. It was a journey of almost two hundred and fifty miles, but it was a journey he, as well as many of the other Nez Perce, knew well. Though the Nez Perce lands ended at the top of the Bitterroots, his band had spent much time across the mountains, and the Flathead people on the other side were almost like brothers to them. Many of his men had married Flathead women, and many Nez Perce women had married Flathead men.

The whites in that country were friendly too. Looking Glass knew many of them and had often purchased supplies at their stores and left his horses to winter with them while he continued east to buffalo country. There was even a friendly Black Robe priest who gave medicine to the sick Nez Perce as they traveled through. These white people would know that the Nez Perce were not hostile. In fact, they would welcome them. They would sell them supplies and allow them to pass through to buffalo country, where Looking Glass and his warriors were something close to heroes to the Crows because of assistance they had provided several summers before in a war against the dreaded Lakota.

Crow country meant fewer whites and the presence of good friends, plenty of buffalo, and a place where they could live at peace until issues in their home country settled down. And if it came to a fight, the Crows were willing warriors. They had sworn to help the Nez Perce in battle with the whites if they were ever needed.

The respected warriors Five Wounds and Rainbow supported Looking Glass. They too had spent much time in buffalo country and in fact had been returning from there when they had met up with the other bands after the fighting in White Bird Canyon. What Looking Glass said was true, they said. It would be a good place to go.

If for some reason the tribe still did not feel safe, they could go north across into the British territory in Canada to join with Sitting Bull and the Lakota, who were now living there under the protection of the government. Though the Nez Perce were not close friends with the Lakota, they had agreed to cease warring with each other. And even at their worst, the Lakota hated the whites more than they disliked the Nez Perce. Anyone opposing the white soldiers would be welcomed as a friend.

The other chiefs found these arguments compelling. White Bird and

Toohoolhoolzote, who had no time for white promises and white justice, were easily convinced, though White Bird initially had favored going north to meet with Sitting Bull immediately after getting across the trail. Only Joseph was unsure. There was something too final and wrong about crossing the mountains. His people were not buffalo country people. Perhaps it would be better to live on the reservation or, if not, to die in their own country.

"What are we fighting for?" he asked. "Is it our lives?"

To him it was not. It was the land the Creator had granted them, the land where his father was buried, the land that had given him life and whose soil he wished to nourish with his bones. He preferred to send the women and children into the mountains and then to double back into their own country and die fighting for the land where the Nez Perce people had always lived. If it was honor the young warriors sought, this was the way to achieve it, not by running or by getting drunk and slaughtering innocent people. Once they gave up and crossed the mountains out of their own country, they were people without a home.

Joseph's position, though respected, was not well received. Only the strongest believers in the old ways—men like Wottolen and Two Moons—were open to his impassioned plea to stay true to their land. He was outvoted and reminded, in no uncertain terms, that the people had agreed to stay together. If he chose to leave, not only would he lose respect, he would lose trust as well.

In a final vote, Looking Glass was chosen to take command of the bands and lead the people over the mountains. They would travel away from their homeland to find peace in buffalo country.

On the morning of July 16, 1877, this uncertain assemblage of eight hundred people, almost three thousand horses, and hundreds of dogs set out into the Bitterroot Mountains along the rocky, deadfall-laden Lolo Trail. Joseph's band was the last to leave. Their hearts were in the Wallowa, and this flight gave them neither joy nor hope. The man who the whites thought was in charge of Nez Perce strategy was at the end of the group. His voice, if ever it had been heard in matters of war, was now barely listened to at all.

9

"The Most Terrible Mountains I Ever Beheld"

THE LAND INTO WHICH the Nez Perce were entering was some of the most impenetrable in the American West. It had almost killed Lewis and Clark, causing one of their men to note in his journal that these were "the most terrible mountains I ever beheld," while Clark himself observed that there were "high rugged mountains in every direction as far as I could see."

Few whites ever traversed this country, preferring to use more manageable passes far to the south and the north. This land was truly *terra incognita*—a jumble of jagged sawtooth peaks, diagonal tree-covered slopes, and deep impassable ravines with impenetrable brush thickets growing to the very edge of fierce, rushing rivers. Far more than the Rockies, these Bitterroots served as a barrier to physical passage between the East and the West. The only way through them was on one of three trails that the Nez Perce had forged over generations by following paths made by animals and connecting them through their own efforts into trails by which people on the Columbia Plateau could make their way to and from buffalo country.

The Lolo was the most northerly of these trails. Though the Nez Perce had traveled it frequently and knew it well, it was in no way an easy journey. Wind and rain constantly blew trees across it; boulders blocked the path in many places; and there were precipitous ledges that had to be navigated with care. Generations of horses had worn stretches of it into a deep furrow, and these frequently became filled with deadfall and scree. In addition, it tended to follow the ridgetops, so there were constant sharp descents and ascents, which became slippery and treacherous when snowmelt or rains turned them from dirt to mud.

Nonetheless, with enough time and proper preparations, it could be a tolerable, even enjoyable, passage. But this was not such an occasion. With so many people and so many animals, this crossing would quickly become an arduous, muddy, dangerous trek. Care could be taken, but only to the extent that it did not slow the group's journey to the next broad meadow and camping place. This meant forcing animals over fallen trees and between tight rocks that had been dislodged onto the trail. But the need to find forage for so many horses and camping areas with water enough for so many people forced them to travel without regard for hardship.

Looking Glass did not expect the soldiers to follow them into the mountains. Howard had been left tarrying at the Kamiah crossing and had shown no sign of pursuit. The Nez Perce presumed he had lost interest after the people had headed toward Montana country. To them, tribes were tribes, no matter whether white or Indian. Howard's tribe was the Idaho and Washington tribe. The Nez Perce had no quarrel with the Montana white tribes and no reason to think that Howard would continue to care about them after they had left his lands. But, still, it paid to be careful. Many feeder trails led into the Lolo, and the Christian Nez Perce knew them all. If the people were not vigilant, it was possible for their Christian brothers who were scouting for Howard to lead his soldiers in on one of these routes.

So Looking Glass ordered a group of five warriors to form a rear guard. They were to linger behind for three days to watch for soldiers, and if any were sighted, two of the men were to ride ahead to warn the full group while the other three were to fight as much as necessary to slow the soldiers' pursuit. Among these five volunteers was Sarpsis Ilppilp, one of the three boys who had started the fighting and now was reveling in his newfound warrior status.

Looking Glass's caution proved to be merited. Soon several scouts for General Howard were discovered in a heavily wooded area just up from the Weippe. These men included James Reuben, the Presbyterian Nez Perce leader from Kamiah who had tried to convince Joseph to come on the reservation; Captain John, who had become something of a real estate dealer by selling Nez Perce lands to settlers and whose daughter was traveling with the nontreaty bands; and Horse Blanket, known by the name of

Sam Morris, who had the same father as Yellow Wolf, the young warrior who had rescued Joseph's wife during the retreat from the Clearwater.

The rear-guard scouts were incensed. They captured the men and berated them. "We are your relations," they scolded. "Your skins, your hair, your bodies, everything is the same as ours. The Americans, your great friends, have marked our land with the blood of your relatives. The white man has been spilling Nez Perce blood for years, and our chiefs have put their nerves between their teeth to keep peace with these whites."

They told the men they were sick of giving the treaty Nez Perce chances to prove their loyalty to their own people. They would let the men go this one last time if they promised to return to their homes and never again raise a hand against their brothers and sisters who were fleeing with Looking Glass. "The next Nez Perce scouts we capture acting under General Howard," they said, "we will kill at once."

The captured men retreated gratefully and promised never to aid the soldiers again. But in no time at all movement was heard again in the underbrush. The scouts recognized the voice of Captain John.

"Here are some fresh tracks," he said. "Let us turn back."

But before they were able to do so, the rear-guard scouts opened fire. Because of the thick brush, all the men escaped except Sheared Wolf, who had taken the Christian name of John Levi. Levi was not killed but was badly enough wounded to be unable to flee. As the scouts approached him, he pleaded for his life.

"I have news to tell you," he said.

"You may tell it in the spirit world," one of the scouts responded, and shot him through the head.

It was now apparent that the soldiers had not completely given up the chase. But the sad discovery that James Reuben, Joseph's nephew and one of the foremost nontreaty leaders, had been the lead scout for the soldiers was especially disheartening. Individuals might change sides or decide that the flight was too difficult or even choose to stay with the Christian way. But joining the soldiers against your brothers and sisters was a betrayal that cut to the heart. The Nez Perce were now truly a divided people. They would never again be able to look at each other without seeing the blood on the ground between them.

Other sadnesses too had begun to darken the journey. One woman, traveling with her baby, had been unable to keep the infant from crying. All through the evening the infant had sent up a piercing squall, filling the quiet night with its cries. The warriors pleaded with her to find a way to calm the child.

"You must quiet the baby," they said, "or the soldiers will find us."

But the baby would not cease crying.

Soon the warriors came again. "You have to quiet that baby or we'll all be killed," they pleaded.

The woman did what she could, but the baby could not be comforted. In desperation she took the infant and killed it by striking it against a tree. All mourned this horrible loss, knowing the unspeakable sacrifice this mother had made to protect the safety of the people. This turned their hearts even darker against the soldiers and treaty bands who had forced them into this cruel journey far away from their homes and the lands they loved.

General Howard, as the warriors had presumed, was not inclined to pursue, but not because the Nez Perce were leaving his territory. It was the terrain that concerned him, and reports of the condition of the trail had given him pause. Its almost endless tangle of deadfall, along with trees on either side of the trail growing so tightly together that a man could barely pass between them, meant that his artillery and supply wagons could not make a meaningful chase.

This same trail that had almost killed Lewis and Clark would surely not admit of the quick passage necessary to capture the fleeing bands. Besides, he had a whole territory of frightened settlers to protect on his side of the mountains. There was no guarantee that the other tribes of the Plateau were not readying to fight; no guarantee that Joseph and his followers would not double back; no guarantee that he would be able to catch them even if he decided to follow. When reports started arriving of flare-ups between Indians and settlers in his own jurisdiction on the Idaho side of the mountains, he decided that pursuit was out of the question.

But his superior, General Sherman, did not see it in that way. The celebrated Civil War general, now elevated to the head of the army, did not take kindly to the idea of renegade Indians wandering unmolested over the mountains into the settled areas of Montana. General Howard might be in charge of only the Department of the Columbia, and the border between his command and the Army of the Missouri might lie along the ridge of the Bitterroot Mountains that the Nez Perce were now crossing, but the Indians making that journey were from his area of command and thus still his responsibility.

So Sherman ordered Howard to follow. Sherman had not achieved his military successes by being weak-kneed; his march through Georgia had been ruthless and decisive in breaking the will of the Confederacy. He expected the same or greater ruthlessness and decisiveness from his western forces in breaking the will of the belligerent Indian tribes.

Howard was well aware of his superior's approach. Sherman's order eleven years ago regarding the Sioux could not have been clearer: "We must act with vindictive earnestness," Sherman had declared, "even to their extermination, men, women, and children." And though there was no proof he had said it in so many words, his current attitude was well expressed in the statement often attributed to him that "the only good Indian is a dead Indian." Howard knew that Sherman saw his job as creating "good Indians" and that his immediate objective was Joseph. There would be no more massacres under Sherman's watch, no more Little Bighorns. Any movements of tribes that spoke of possible consolidation and uprising would be opposed with the utmost vigor and malice.

This order to pursue went against all of Howard's instincts. He did not like wanton loss of life. His memories of the deaths of young men during the Civil War still haunted him. He did not wish to subject his men to undue hardship and possible death when equally effective alternatives were available. It was his intention to wait until reinforcement troops made their way into the area from other parts of the country, then to block the Lolo at the back end with one group, use another group to shadow the Nez Perce by traveling parallel to them on the Mullan Road, a more northerly route on which wagons and artillery could travel, and leave a third group to quell any disturbances and keep peace in this western country while the actual pursuit took place.

But reports trickling in from the Weippe and Kamiah areas soon caused him to abandon this strategy. Lootings and burnings were still taking place among the settlements back in Idaho. Howard could not be sure if these were the acts of a few hostile bands that had doubled back into their home territory or if, perhaps, the Indians had not actually left.

The only way to be sure that the hostiles were truly crossing the mountains was to pursue them himself.

He ordered his men into readiness and prepared to leave as soon as the necessary reinforcement troops arrived from other posts. When these new soldiers were in place to protect the settlers on the Idaho side of the mountains, he personally would lead his men up the Lolo Trail and drive the Nez Perce into Montana Territory, where they would be out of the jurisdiction of the Department of the Columbia and become the problem of other commanders.

The retreating bands, however, had no intention of returning. The burnings and lootings still taking place in the Weippe and down toward Kamiah had been the work of a rear-guard group trying to gain more horses and supplies. Most of the people were already well on their way across the Bitterroots.

The trail wound high along the ridgetops and saddlebacks. In many places it was barely wide enough to walk; in others it was a braided tracery of small paths over uneven and difficult terrain. There were precipitous drops, rendered even more perilous by ground made slippery by heavy rains. The winds blew sharp, and the people were traveling without lodge poles for teepees. On some nights they could make only brush shelters by hanging skins and canvas against rocks or over branches. Many of the buffalo skins used for lodges had been left behind at the Clearwater, so shelter was minimal, making cold, rainy nights difficult, especially for the infants and the elderly.

Though they were now traveling in smaller groups to take advantage of the more numerous smaller meadow camping spots, the sheer number of travelers had a cumulative effect on the trail. Those in the rear often had to walk through slop, and when the weather was warm and the earth dry, animals in front kicked up a cloud of choking dust for those who rode behind.

Nonetheless, they traveled the trail in eleven days, coming out of the high mountains into the broader, gentler valleys in Montana just as Howard was finally preparing to begin the journey into those same mountains on the Idaho side. Howard had delayed his departure until the reinforcements had arrived in order to mollify the settlers in his Idaho jurisdiction, who by now were awash in rumors of Indian massacres and uprisings and had no wish to see the military depart their area to pursue renegade Indians off into Montana Territory. In delaying, he had opened himself to severe and mocking criticism in both the local and national press. Despite Sutherland's glowing accounts of his pluck and heroism, other newspapers were posting stories accusing the general of tarrying and bungling and having no stomach for Indian pursuit.

The smaller newspapers in more isolated towns were especially critical. They had the most to fear from renegade Indians and felt the most need for military protection. They were also the most susceptible to rumor. The *Fort Benton Record* in Fort Benton, Montana, wondered aloud if "the white people of Montana" were "forever to remain in danger of plunder and murder . . .?" while one paper's claim of Indian atrocities made it all the way to the East Coast and *Harper's Monthly,* where it was diligently reported that "on the 10th of July Joseph's band . . . massacred thirty Chinamen on the Clearwater River."

When Howard finally did begin moving over the trail, fully two weeks after the Nez Perce had undertaken the journey, he was faced with terrain that had been stripped clean of pasture and forage by the Nez Perce horses, and was ill suited to his pack mules and horse-drawn artillery pieces. He had to send men ahead with axes to clear the logs and stumps and widen the trail, and even then could travel no faster than his large contingent of foot soldiers allowed. He was less willing than the Nez Perce to drive his animals to exhaustion, and even had he been willing to do so, he did not have the luxury of a herd of fresh ponies to use when his regular mounts and pack animals got tired. So he was often forced to rest when he really did not wish to do so. But he wanted to spare his troops and his animals any unnecessary hardship.

His men pressed ahead through this unfamiliar mountainous country, traveling by day through blinding, cutting rain and shivering by night in their thin military coats while the waters in the high mountain meadows and passes crusted over with ice. On occasion they were forced to make camp on slopes so angled that the men had to dig out flat spots in order to keep from rolling down the hills during their sleep. More than one soldier commented that this was the most difficult trail, and these the most broken mountains, that he had ever seen. Those who had known the Adirondacks and mountains back East now took to referring to those as "picnic" mountains. One man noted simply that these mountains were "grand, gloomy, and peculiar." It was a description with which none would disagree.

But for the Nez Perce, to whom these mountains and trails were familiar, the mountains were the least of the difficulties. There had been tragedies, like the sad death of the child at the hands of her mother, and there had been logistical problems of finding resting and grazing places for so many people and horses. But the great problem was what to do once on the other side.

There was talk that Joseph and White Bird wanted to finish the journey across the Lolo, then travel south and take the southern trail back across the mountains to their homelands. There was also the issue of keeping the young men under control if and when white soldiers or settlers again appeared. Looking Glass spoke strongly in this regard, stating in no uncertain terms that no harm was to come to white settlers they met, and this meant no stealing, no looting, no killing. The war was over, he said. They were to leave all anger and confrontation behind.

Eventually they completed the crossing and descended into the broader valleys of the low Montana foothills. Here there were wide, flat meadows with meandering creeks and good grass for pasture. It was easy country to travel and country that offered easy rest. They still assumed that Howard would stop at the summit and break off his pursuit; in their minds the soldiers and the war were left far behind. They could now move leisurely down the remaining trail to the land of their Flathead friends, purchase goods from the stores in the white settlements, and proceed unmolested to buffalo country, if that was the course they chose.

But this sanguine outlook was shattered when one of the advance scouts came riding in with a desperate message. "Soldiers are in front of us building a fort. They are heading us off. In a little while we will see soldiers. They know our camp."

This made no sense. The war had been left behind.

Leaving the camp and the people, Looking Glass, Joseph, and White Bird went down to see this white fort and consider the situation. What they found was a small group of soldiers and settlers hunkering behind a barrier two logs high. These logs had been hastily cut and laid across a narrow spot in the trail. By leaving open spaces between the logs, the soldiers had created a makeshift breastwork with firing channels. It was hardly more than knee high and was anything but a fort.

Upon seeing it, Looking Glass laughed, calling it a "soldier corral." It presented no significant military impediment to their journey, but it did raise the question of who these soldiers were and why they had built such a barrier. More disconcerting still was the presence of Flathead warriors wearing white armbands and white scarves on their heads. Such things were not part of traditional Flathead dress. They could mean only one thing—the Flatheads were expecting hostilities, and wanted the soldiers to be able to differentiate them from the Nez Perce when fighting started. Their friends—the people they considered a brother tribe and from whom they had counted on gaining assistance—had joined with the military. And they were dressed in a manner that spoke of war.

But still, there was hope of resolution. The Nez Perce meant no harm to the Montana people. They wanted only to pass through peacefully. The whites in the Bitterroot Valley were their friends and had been for a long time. A proper explanation could set things right.

Joseph, White Bird, and Looking Glass continued down to meet with the soldier in charge of the barrier. The man introduced himself as Captain Rawn. He had with him an interpreter known to the Nez Perce as Delaware Jim, a Flathead warrior who was married to a Nez Perce woman.

The Nez Perce explained that they did not want trouble. "We do not want to fight," they told him. "If you allow us to pass, we will pass peacefully. But we are going to pass."

Rawn listened carefully. He was not here by choice. At the command of his superiors, he had hurried down from Fort Missoula thirty miles to the north and had hastily constructed the barrier. Howard had begged for assistance at the Montana end of the Lolo Trail, asking that troops be sent to delay the Nez Perce until he could catch up to them from the rear and engage them in a final battle. Rawn had been given that assignment.

He had done his part, but his heart was not in it. His "troops" consisted of about twenty-five regular soldiers, one hundred fifty to two hundred settler volunteers, and twenty or so Flathead warriors. The regulars had arrived in the area just several weeks before to help with the construction of Fort Missoula and knew nothing about the people and the terrain.

His settler volunteers too were problematic. Rawn was a military veteran. He had dealt with volunteers before. They always thought they were smarter and stronger than the army and that they would set things right when they got the chance. It was true that they usually knew the country better than the soldiers because they lived on the land they had volunteered to protect. But they were undisciplined and untrustworthy. Their motives ranged from foolish arrogance to a frightened desire to protect their families to a selfish greed for the spoils of battle. They could never be organized for troop movements and they could not be counted on to fight more than was necessary to achieve their own private ends. The best you could hope is that they would form skirmish lines and hold their ground or that they would be willing to charge when called upon to do so. To expect them to hold their fire as part of a larger, overall tactical maneuver or to operate in controllable formations was foolhardy. If they had bravery, that was all you could expect. Discipline in the face of fire was beyond reasonable possibility.

Rawn's current volunteers were clearly cut from this mold. About fifty of them had come down with him from the area around Fort Missoula, and they were filled with the customary bluster and swagger. They were itching to "eat Indians for breakfast," as they were fond of saying. The other volunteers were from the little settlements right at the base of the Lolo Trail in the wide Bitterroot Valley. Some of them too had grandiose visions, but many were friends with the Nez Perce and had engaged in trading and horse racing with them. They knew each other by name and were not anxious for fighting. Had it not been for the horrible reports of savagery that had filtered over from the Salmon River country and the fact that their families lived in the direct path of the Nez Perce travels, they would never have joined in such a dangerous and foolhardy venture. All they wanted was to protect their homes and wives and children.

Then there was the issue of the Flathead warriors. They too had no real heart for the fight. They had joined with the soldiers only because they did not want to incur the wrath of the white government. Many were friends and family of the Nez Perce. Neutrality was the most Rawn could expect from them. Even though the Flathead, like all tribes, coveted the Nez Perce horses, that was probably not inducement enough to make them fight fiercely against a people they had long regarded as brothers.

Overall, it was not a force with which a seasoned commander like Rawn felt comfortable going into battle. He would discuss issues with the chiefs and try to hold them as long as possible so Howard could come up from the rear. But he was not interested in a full-scale engagement.

During the discussions, Looking Glass wandered off and spoke with some of his friends among the volunteers. He told them he and his people would pass through quickly and without incident. The Nez Perce, he explained, were on their way to buffalo country, and this passage would be as peaceful as all their other journeys.

This was all the local volunteers needed to hear. Why start an Indian war when one of the Indian leaders you knew and trusted told you that he and his people were simply passing through? Relieved and reassured, they picked up their arms and went home.

This left Rawn with only twenty-five unseasoned soldiers, fifty undisciplined volunteers, and twenty warriors of suspect loyalty—not a force to stand against the tide of warriors he believed was massing against him farther up the trail. Aided by liberal amounts of whiskey, he decided that discretion was the better part of valor, and after a halfhearted attempt at negotiations, he agreed to let the tribe pass unchallenged.

He really had little choice. The army had concentrated all its forces and forts farther to the east to protect them against the Sioux, so he could not count on prompt or adequate reinforcements. And the battles with those very Sioux had provided graphic examples of what happened to armies that lost engagements with hostile Indians. If saving lives and property was his purpose, acquiescing to the Indians' request was the surest way to achieve that end. It also, incidentally, was probably the only way to stay alive and keep all your body parts attached to one another.

When the actual passage of the Indians began, any remaining fighting sentiment among the soldiers dissipated almost entirely. The sight of the mounted Nez Perce dressed in their beautiful beaded shirts and leggings, coming in unknown numbers and carrying weapons equal to or better than those possessed by the troops and remaining volunteers, made Looking Glass's promise of peaceful passage seem like an offer only a fool would refuse. And any last flicker of ardor for combat was quickly doused by a continuous, dreary drizzle. Soon the last of the volunteers had packed and headed back down the canyon toward their homes, and the remaining soldiers were left with the realization that a fight would surely result in their annihilation.

Meanwhile, the Nez Perce had stationed warriors on the ridge high above the valley where the log "soldier corral" had been constructed, and had begun moving their people along the back side of the ridge out of sight of the troops. The few army regulars looked up from their huddled position behind their two-log barrier to see mounted, armed, Nez Perce warriors high above them flanking their puny defenses and well positioned to shoot down directly into their pitiful compound. They fired off a few token shots, but only for show. The Nez Perce proceeded unopposed down into the valley of the Bitterroot.

Despite the disquieting issue of why some of their brother Flathead had stood with the soldiers, and the unanswered question of why this Captain Rawn had attempted to stop them, Looking Glass was pleased. He had led his people peacefully across the mountains to the country where they were friends with both the Indians and whites. In the process, he had reached an agreement with a soldier chief that there should be no more war. Truly, he had achieved his objective. The fighting was now behind them, and they could now take the time to decide, once and for all, what course of action to follow to bring this unfortunate situation to an end.

The Bitterroot Valley, which the Nez Perce now entered, was a very different place from the Salmon River country from which they had come. While the Nez Perce side of the Bitterroot Mountains was carved and furrowed with deep, almost impassable canyons, the eastern side was made up of broad, intramontane valleys that stretched in a long north-south corridor from the plains of Canada to the deserts of the Southwest. Soft, pellucid, Pacific hazes had been replaced by bright blue skies of crisp, sharp-edged, high-mountain clarity.

Without the ocean to soften temperature swings, this long string of valleys saw sweltering heat swoop up from the south during the summer and frigid, snow-blown cold sweep down from the north in winter. Though there was the daunting range of the Rockies yet to cross before a traveler reached the buffalo plains, those mountains did not offer the formidable barrier formed by the jagged, forested Bitterroots through which the Nez Perce had just come. Once they were on this side, the east and the great plains beckoned, and travelers, both Indian and white, moved easily on several well-known trail passages to and from the land of the buffalo.

This had not been the case while the Nez Perce were snaking along the narrow Lolo Trail. There they had been without options. Once they had embarked on the Lolo, their only choices had been to proceed or turn back. But now, having reached the end of the Lolo and entered into the wide, long, north-south corridor of the Bitterroot Valley, they found themselves confronted with several choices and faced with a significant decision.

It would be an easy journey to turn north and proceed up the broad, open valleys to the British possessions they knew as the Old Woman Country. They could also take a broad, easy route directly east across the Rockies onto the buffalo plains. A third route followed the Bitterroot Valley south for about sixty miles then turned east across a low pass into a great open expanse called the Big Hole, or "the place of ground squirrels," and from there across the land of the geysers into the southern buffalo plains and the country of the Crow. A last option would be to travel those same sixty miles south but then turn west and double back into the Bitterroots on another of the narrow Nez Perce mountain trails in order to return to their homelands.

Each of these choices had its virtues and liabilities, and each had its proponents and detractors. But whatever they chose would shape the future of their people, so they set up camp at a creek near the house of a friendly white man named McClain and set about making this momentous decision.

The original intention as determined in the Weippe had been to cross the trail then continue on east to buffalo country. This was still the preference of Looking Glass. But as they were camped, three Nez Perce came riding in from the north. They had been scouting for the U.S. government against the Sioux and knew something of the forces and situation in the surrounding territory.

"You are fools to go to buffalo country," they said. "Too many settlers. Too much military. Better to go north to the Old Woman Country. There you can be safe."

White Bird, Toohoolhoolzote, and most of those who were not intimately familiar with buffalo country took this counsel to heart. They listened intently as one of the newly arrived scouts, named Grizzly Bear Youth, explained what he had learned about where the whites had established the border between the Americans and the Old Woman Country. It was a 240-mile journey over easy country from where they were camped. The route to buffalo country was much longer and across much more difficult terrain.

But others were quick to point out that a turn to the north would take them right past the new soldier fort being built at Missoula and into

Blackfeet country. No tribe was more hated and feared than the Blackfeet, and no tribe was less trusted. With the women and children and elderly, the Nez Perce would be too vulnerable to hostile attack.

Even if the many settlers who were filling the valleys to the north let them pass, even if the soldiers let them travel in peace, the Blackfeet would force them to fight. The route might be easy in terms of terrain, but it was fraught with perils in terms of potential human enemies. Also, what were they to do for food and blankets if they went north? They had lost at least half of their goods when they had been forced to run from the Clearwater. Without the meat and buffalo blankets they would obtain in buffalo country, they would soon find themselves living in cold country without adequate shelter and provisions.

These people spoke up for the route to the buffalo plains. Some preferred the route directly east. This broad passage had the virtue of ease of travel. But it too was filling up with settlers and miners. Looking Glass, who had recently been to the buffalo plains, preferred to drop south then take the trail across through the Big Hole valley and the land of the Bannocks. It was not much more physically demanding, he claimed, and it surely was less populated and less likely to offer up surprises. It also would bring them directly into the land of the Crows, their friends and allies.

Pile of Clouds and some of the other warriors agreed with this assessment, but they did not like the idea of traveling into the open Crow country. The people were traveling with thousands of horses; their group included hundreds of women and children and elderly. The Crow country was mostly open, rolling plains that offered little protection and hiding place for the people if they had to engage in battle. Better, they felt, to travel down the valley, as Looking Glass proposed, but to turn west on their southernmost trail through the Bitterroots, then move back into the safety of the steep, forested mountains where the timber and terrain would be their allies in the event of further conflict with the military.

In the end, after heated debate, Looking Glass's position won out. He had already been appointed leader, and he was probably the most familiar with both the buffalo country and the Crows. He had also been present at the conversations with Captain Rawn and was most friendly with the white settlers through whose country they would have to pass. If he thought the war was over and the southern route to their Crow allies was the best decision, the others would go along with it. White Bird, however, issued a caution. "If the white men fire on us," he said, "we will burn their fields and take their scalps. Their life will be no better than ours."

Joseph said nothing. When asked for his position, he did not even rise to speak. "Since we have left our own country," he said, "it matters little where we go." In his mind, they were now a people in exile. No choice they made would lighten the burden in his heart.

With their course of action determined, the concern now turned to what sort of welcome they would receive from Chief Charlot and his Flathead people as they passed through their lands. The Nez Perce had never doubted the friendship of the Flatheads. But the presence of Flathead warriors with Captain Rawn had raised questions about the strength of that friendship.

On July 28, Looking Glass and a few warriors went ahead to meet with Charlot while the rest of the travelers retrieved some camping goods from one of McClain's outbuildings, where they had been cached on a previous journey to buffalo country. All made sure not to disturb or take anything that was not their own. Then they settled in and established the first truly relaxed camp that the weary people and animals had experienced since leaving the Weippe.

Soon Looking Glass returned, dark with anger. He had met with Charlot and extended his hand in friendship. Charlot had refused to accept it, saying he did not wish to touch a hand that had spilled white man's blood. Looking Glass had responded angrily. Yes, he had spilled white men's blood, he said, but only because he had been attacked. "Your hands are as bloody as mine," he'd told Charlot. "I did not come to talk about blood. I came to ask you the best place to camp."

Looking Glass's chiding had bothered Charlot. He was in an impossible situation. The Nez Perce were indeed his friends, but the survival of his people depended upon his continued good relations with the whites who had settled in his country. A military fort was being constructed only thirty miles north near the town of Missoula, and Missoula itself had already grown to be a community of five hundred white people. Peaceful coexistence with these newcomers was more important to the welfare of his people than assisting a brother tribe that had already decided to fight.

"All right," he told Looking Glass. "You may camp here. But if you raise a hand against any white person, we will drive you out."

This was not the bond of friendship and support for which Looking Glass had hoped, but it did at least tell him that the Flatheads would not oppose him as he led his people through the valley so long as no violence occurred. With this assurance, he arranged for the bands to break camp the following morning and move south to set up camp on Charlot's land.

The new camp was right outside the town of Stevensville, a small settlement of about 150 men, women, and children. Stevensville had originally been settled to meet the supply needs of miners in the area and was a thriving little mercantile community with a single main street bordered by wooden buildings. Looking Glass had been here many times and had traded with the people, as had other Nez Perce traveling across the Lolo on their way to buffalo country. It was here that the local Black Robe priest, Father Ravalli, gave medicine to the Nez Perce through a little window in his house when they rode up and asked for assistance. They had every reason to expect a friendly reception when they rode into town the following day.

But the stories of the Salmon River killings had preceded the people across the mountains, and the local residents were not inclined to greet them with open arms. Indians might be friendly as individuals, but the experience of the Salmon River and Slate Creek settlers were reminders of what could happen when things went bad. As far as the settlers here knew, the people murdered in the Salmon River had been every bit as friendly to the Nez Perce as they themselves had been here in the Bitterroot Valley. Who knew what sort of dark grievances those Indian people carried in their hearts and what sort of dark crimes they might be capable of committing?

So when the Nez Perce arrived, hoping to purchase goods to make up for those they had lost in their rapid flight from the Clearwater, they discovered an empty town of locked doors and shuttered stores, while the white families and shopkeepers huddled behind the walls of nearby Fort Owen, an abandoned adobe trading post that they had fortified with chunks of sod. Some had already been barricaded there for almost three weeks, not wishing to be caught by surprise by these Indians they had considered their friends but who apparently had gone on a murderous rampage in towns like theirs across the mountains in Idaho.

But Looking Glass's promises of peace had given them a measure of relief. A few of the tradesmen, having dealt with the Nez Perce often in the past, ventured back to their stores to sell the Indians the supplies they desired. They knew the Nez Perce as a wealthy and fair people. If they wanted goods, were willing to pay, and truly intended to pass through peacefully, the Stevensville merchants were more than willing to assist them in their passage while making a few dollars in the process.

Looking Glass made the Nez Perce position clear to the tradesfolk. There would be no killing or stealing. The Nez Perce had gold dust and gold coins as well as silver and horses to trade, and their women had American greenbacks tied in their braids. They would pay fairly, would pay what was asked. "But if you will not sell," he said, "we will take what we need. We will not leave our women and children hungry."

The Indians' needs were simple: flour, sugar, coffee, tobacco, some dry goods, some cloth. They also wanted bullets, and some of the young men wanted whiskey. The townspeople were quick to oblige except for bullets and whiskey. They could see that the older tribal members were trying to keep order but that the young men were on the edge of violence. It would take only one shot fired by either side and the battle-hardened Nez Perce with their repeating rifles and strong horses would overrun the town and make the Salmon River massacre look like child's play. If there was one commodity likely to set off that shot, it was whiskey.

Nonetheless, one of the merchants could not resist the lure of easy money. He began selling whiskey from a barrel until some of the other townsfolk stopped him. There was a clamor to hang the man for his greed and stupidity. But such a public event might incite the Nez Perce, so he was merely separated from his supply of whiskey at the point of a gun and sent back to the fort where he could cause no more trouble.

The Indians too sought to keep tensions down. Looking Glass sat on his horse in the middle of the town's main street, keeping his whip ready to strike anyone who stole or destroyed property not his own. When one of the young men insulted a white woman, the chief grabbed him and sent him back to the Indian camp. No indiscretion, however small, was to be tolerated.

It was a tense but ultimately peaceful day. With stern faces and severe decorum, the chiefs and elders kept tight rein on the situation. Though the merchants were charging exorbitant prices—Joseph was forced to give up his powder horn just to get a bit of milk to give to the children—conflict needed to be avoided at all costs. Charlot had meant what he had said about expelling the Nez Perce by force if any raised a hand against a white man, and he had his own warriors patrolling the streets along with the Nez Perce chiefs and elders. No one wanted to see that first shot fired because all knew that any confrontation would come to a tragic and bloody end.

The next day, after breaking camp, the Nez Perce passed by Stevensville one final time before proceeding south. The townsfolk looked on in amazement as the tribesmen and -women rode past arrayed in their finest clothes—white tanned buckskin shirts and dresses covered with beadwork and ermine tails; shell breastplates; colorful blankets. Their horses had elaborate beaded bridles, and the men carried their rifles in beaded gun sheaths. Babies slept soundly on cradle boards beaded with sky blue swirls and intricate floral patterns. Even their riding quirts were beaded. No opportunity for adornment had been overlooked, from the braids in the women's hair to the saddles and bridles of the horses. Looking Glass himself had a mirror framed in a leather star hanging from his wrist, and Joseph wore a red coat covered with small mirrors. The residents of Stevensville watched with relief and awe as the regal procession with its hundreds of families and thousands of finely bred horses passed by right across the river. One man estimated that the parade stretched for five miles. It took more than an hour for the whole group to pass.

Once through Stevensville, only a few isolated settlements remained before the Nez Perce reached the place where the trail turned east toward buffalo country. No opposition was expected. The little town of Corvallis held no more than a hundred inhabitants, the town of Skahalko, no more than seventy-five. Outside these towns, homesteads were widely scattered in the valleys and hillsides, often separated from each other by miles of open country. The last military post lay far to the north at Fort Missoula, where Captain Rawn had come from, and they had made peace with Captain Rawn.

The Nez Perce settled down to a leisurely pace of twelve to fifteen miles a day, breaking camp late and setting up camp early, just as Looking Glass had always done when traveling to buffalo country. As always, each band and family was free to travel in its own most comfortable fashion, some leaving earlier than others and each taking whatever route suited its fancy. At night they would gather in a common camp.

One evening, the young men of Toohoolhoolzote's band burst into camp boasting. They had found a white man's house where nobody was home. They had gone inside, tossed a few things around, and taken several hundred pounds of flour and coffee for the people.

Looking Glass was incensed. Toohoolhoolzote's band was always the hardest to control. They had been among the bands most cruelly treated by the whites back in their own country, and they all still smarted from the insult done at the council where General Howard had imprisoned Toohoolhoolzote and dressed him in the clothing of a bride. They were proud of their belligerence and took every opportunity to express it.

Looking Glass made the men go back to the settler's house and leave seven horses in payment for the goods they had stolen and the damage they had done. He even insisted that the men take the settler's branding iron and mark the horses with the settler's brand so there would be no misunderstanding about the purpose and intent of the gift. As long as he was in charge, there would be no harm done to white men, no insult done to white women, and no damage done to white property.

Beyond this incident, there were only a few minor break-ins and thefts by unruly young warriors and a few cattle killed to provide food for the travelers. But for the most part, the passage remained peaceful. This was now no different from any journey to buffalo country except for the great number of travelers.

Several lodges of Nez Perce who lived in the valley even joined up with the procession. Some families from the band of Eagle from the Light, who had left the Clearwater River Valley years before in disgust at the behavior of white miners, decided to travel with the group. Poker Joe, a half-breed buffalo hunter who loved gambling and had a rough command of English, was among them.

Near the little town of Corvallis, the travelers found the townsfolk huddled inside a hastily constructed sod pen. Since many of the Nez Perce knew the settlers from previous travels, they rode up to the edge of the enclosure and shouted for the people to come out and visit. No one would be hurt, they said. The war was finished, the fighting over. The tribe was just passing through on its way to buffalo country.

Cautiously, a few of the settlers came out and were greeted warmly by the Nez Perce. They shared a pleasant meal and sat together around common campfires. Word soon passed that the Nez Perce were traveling peacefully, as they always had done, and before long, wagons with supplies were arriving from nearby communities, and merchants all up and down the Bitterroot Valley were making a tidy profit selling the Nez Perce food-stuffs and camp goods to augment those purchased at Stevensville. There were even reports that some Indians were willing to pay a dollar a shell for replacement ammunition. The reign of terror and bloodshed that the white settlers had been led to expect was nowhere to be found.

While the Nez Perce were moving peacefully down the Bitterroot Valley, lurid newspaper articles and exaggerated military reports were telling a very different story. "Joseph's Indians," as they were now called, were being accused of every atrocity imaginable. Sutherland was not the only person writing about the Nez Perce journey, though he was the only one on the scene. Most of the small towns in the West had their own papers—little one- and two-person operations that printed whatever information they could glean from local sources. Anyone within a day's ride of the Nez Perce was quick to share stories of close calls with Joseph's dangerous savages, and the newspapers were more than willing to pass along these overblown and incendiary accounts. The *Weekly Missoulian*, hearing of the approach of the Nez Perce on the Lolo Trail, had been so convinced of an impending Indian massacre that it put out a special edition with a banner headline imploring, "Help! Help! . . . Come Running!" The *Fort Benton Record*, published two hundred miles away in isolated Fort Benton, stated, "all the tribes of Montana are ripe for revolt. . . ." The *Helena Independent* reported that the Indians coming down the Lolo Trail had "stampeded square over Rawn's rifle pits."

Such hysteria, and the stories that engendered it, quickly assumed the authority of truth. In the wide, lonely spaces of the West, where families might go for weeks without seeing even their nearest neighbor, rumors took on the weight of fact, and the ever-present threat of Indian uprising made the slightest sign of Indian activity a source of fear and anxiety. Stories of even the most dubious veracity were recounted and embellished and conflated and exaggerated, and then, through the miracle of the recently laid telegraph lines, transmitted to an Eastern press that knew little of the realities of life in the West and was hungry to provide its readership with accounts of this distant and exotic area of the country. Joseph's savages were on the loose, and all across the nation people were beginning to watch the chase with breathless interest.

But in the Bitterroot Valley itself, most of the settlers were simply counting their money and breathing a sigh of relief that the Indians had passed. A few men, mostly well fortified with liquor, still made bold talk about pursuing and finishing off the redskins. Many of these were the same men who had been quick to abandon their posts at the Lolo barricade but now were once again proclaiming their desire to eat Indians for breakfast.

Generally speaking, however, the Nez Perce passage had done little more than whet the local residents' appetite for profits. Area settlers knew they could petition the government for compensation for losses of goods and cattle to the renegade Nez Perce, so they were happily fabricating outrageous claims. And there was much talk around kitchen tables about the wealth of weapons and horses and fine clothing the passing Indians had displayed.

Men whose families owned nothing more than crude clothes made of rough cloth spoke covetously of the fine, highly decorated buckskin garments of the Nez Perce men and women. Ranchers with worn and weary horses thought fondly of the beautiful, perfectly formed mounts in the Nez Perce herd. And the high-quality, repeating rifles carried by many of the Nez Perce had not escaped the notice of settlers who seldom could afford anything other than a single-shot weapon and in some cases had nothing more than old ball-and-powder muskets, which had so little accuracy that any shooting became as much an exercise in luck as in skill.

All throughout the valley, in houses, at tables, and around bottles of whiskey, discussions were taking place about how the settlers could get some of these goods for themselves. In their minds, there was nothing unsavory in this. Most of the horses and guns, they believed, had been stolen from settlers and taken from the bodies of soldiers. They would simply be reclaiming ill-gotten gains.

So when a soldier named Gibbon came marching down the valley in pursuit of the Nez Perce, the same men who had accepted the friendship and money of Looking Glass and his people were happy to join up if they could be promised the right to keep the spoils of victory for themselves. Some even had designs on specific shirts and rifles they remembered.

Gibbon, though not excited about increasing his numbers with rash, untrustworthy volunteers, was willing to oblige. He was Rawn's direct superior in charge of the armies in the Montana Territory. After Rawn's failure he had started down from his post at Fort Shaw, a small garrison 150 miles northeast of Rawn's post at Missoula. His orders were to support the laggard General Howard and put an end to this Nez Perce escapade.

Like all frontier armies, his was made up of ragtag, ill-trained, and poorly supplied soldiers, many of whom were immigrants or criminals on the run from the law. Their numbers were so small as to be laughable. In his case, the force he had mustered totaled only 146 fighting men. With numbers like this, he and other beleaguered commanders were expected to keep peace and provide protection in the vast, roadless West.

In reality, their forces were spread so thin that they could offer little protection to anyone other than people in the immediate vicinity of their garrisons, and the second they moved their few men away, the settlers in the area would complain loudly of being abandoned by the military and the government. It was such complaints that had caused Howard to delay his pursuit of the Nez Perce, and now men like Gibbon and Rawn were being asked to pay the price of Howard's well-intentioned efforts at accommodating the outcries of the settlers in his area of jurisdiction.

Gibbon was in charge of the Seventh Infantry. A year earlier, they had arrived at the Little Bighorn a day after the Custer massacre and had been responsible for burying the mutilated, bloated bodies of the dead soldiers of their sister group, the Seventh Cavalry. It was they who had seen the men with their hearts cut out and their heads beaten to bloody pulp by repeated bludgeonings with rocks and rifle butts, they who had been forced to pick up severed arms and legs and try to match them with the torsos scattered around the battlefield. They had a score to settle, but they also had a healthy fear of what they were likely to confront in the event of another Indian engagement. They were more than happy to have their numbers increased by volunteers, no matter how raw and undisciplined.

Gibbon himself was ambivalent about the involvement of the locals. During the Civil War, he had been in charge of a group of volunteers known as "the Iron Brigade," and they had been the equal of any fighters in the regular army. He still smarted from the criticism he had received for his tardy arrival at the Little Bighorn battlefield and had even endured accusations of cowardice. Though he would have preferred a larger group of regulars, these volunteers did know the country, and they had observed the passing Nez Perce. If he could keep them under control—a dubious proposition at best—their assistance might be enough to allow him to bring this Indian affair, and the questions about his skill and bravery, to an end.

Soon Gibbon was traveling through the Bitterroot Valley with a force of 45 volunteers augmenting his 146 regulars, which included Rawn's men, whom he had picked up back at Fort Missoula. Howard was still working his way over the Lolo pass and had sent word that he would arrive in support as soon as he could make his way through the mud and deadfall. But Gibbon's concern was with catching the fleeing Nez Perce, not with keeping track of the clumsy movements of General Howard. By commandeering wagons at Missoula, Gibbon had been able to move his tired foot soldiers twice as fast as the Indians he was pursuing. He could see the remains of their camps at about twelve- to fifteen-mile intervals. If he traveled twice as far each day, it was only a matter of time until he overtook them.

The Nez Perce, however, were completely unaware of this pursuit. With General Howard and Captain Rawn behind them, the settlers befriending them, and country many of them knew well in front of them, Looking Glass was moving slowly in order to allow the horses and people maximum time for rest and rejuvenation.

Many of the people were happy and relieved at this pace, but some of the chiefs were not. At one point, White Bird sought out Looking Glass and confronted him.

"By the way you're acting, you seem to anticipate no danger," he said. Looking Glass responded with a shrug. "What are you so worried about?" he countered. "We have traded with the settlers, made peace with the volunteer soldiers, and been allowed to pass unharmed by the government soldiers at the Lolo barricade. This should be enough to calm your fears."

White Bird, however, was unmoved. "It does us no harm to be prepared," he said. "We were told in the Bitterroot Valley there were soldiers and volunteers all over the country."

He pointed out that even though Rawn had allowed them to pass, he had first asked them to turn over their horses and weapons. Simply because he did not mount a vigorous protest when they had refused to comply did not mean that all danger was past.

But Looking Glass was adamant. "War is quit," he said. "Our fight was with the people in Idaho. We are not fighting the people of this country." While he was in charge, they would travel at his pace and he would make the decisions.

Joseph remained wistful and quiet. They were almost to the place where the southern Nez Perce trail started up into the mountains to the west. Once they turned east toward the buffalo country, that trail would be in their rear. All hope of return to their homeland would be gone.

10

"In a Dream Last Night I Saw Myself Killed"

WITH NO RECOURSE other than breaking up the tribe, which none wanted to do, White Bird and the others who entertained doubts about Looking Glass's leadership kept their concerns to themselves.

But the fears did not go away. As they moved down the tightening valley and the jagged, gray mountains to the west loomed up as a silent barrier between them and their homeland, an air of foreboding began to overcome the camp. Many of the older people and those with strong medicine power began to sense that something was wrong. Even leaving gifts at the medicine tree where all travelers placed offerings for the spirits did nothing to change their uneasiness. They were now out of their country, and it was as if the land were no longer listening to them.

One morning, when light was just beginning to show over the edge of the eastern hills, the voice of Wahlitits, the young warrior who had started all this, could be heard rising above the lodges.

"My brothers, my sisters," he shouted, "I am telling you. In a dream last night I saw myself killed. . . . We are all going to die."

Lone Bird, another young warrior, also spoke up.

"My heart is shaking," he said. "Trouble and death will overtake us if we do not hurry through this land."

These were brave, if impetuous, young men. Since the beginning they had placed their lives in danger to protect the people on their journey. If they had fear, it was not from cowardice.

Everywhere in camp a feeling of foreboding began to afflict the people. They petitioned Looking Glass to speed up their movement so they could escape this land that brought such discomfort to their spirits.

But Looking Glass refused to change his pace. If there was danger, he said, he did not fear it. If there were premonitions, he did not feel them. The people were strong, the horses were gaining health, and all war was far behind them. The buffalo plains, a place he knew so well, beckoned them like a coming sunrise.

For many, the fear subsided somewhat when they finally turned eastward toward the wider, more open area of the Continental Divide. The gray Bitterroots had looked like jagged animal teeth while the mountains in front of them, though high and difficult, were not so forbidding and unwelcoming.

By the time they had moved through the rugged pine hills and arrived at the traditional stopping place called "the place of the ground squirrels," the feelings of foreboding had almost disappeared. Only the warriors and some of the elders with strong medicine power were still concerned.

This new country—the great, broad expanse known to the whites as the Big Hole—was a grand, high-country prairie rimmed by distant, snow-covered mountain ranges. The people had been stopping here for years on their journeys to buffalo country. Here they could find good grass for grazing, abundant game for hunting, and small, winding fish-filled streams. Like the Wallowa, it was too cold and snowbound in winter to admit of any year-round habitation, so there was no white settlement. But now, during the gentle days of early August, camas flowers carpeted its floor, water flowed gently through its twisting creeks, and birds darted among the willow bushes that grew low along the water's edge. It made a fine resting place for travelers.

The people made camp along a meandering stream several yards wide. They set up crude lodges near its banks, placing them a few feet apart and arranging them in the shape of a V aiming north, like the pattern of migrating birds. Then the women set to work digging pits for drying camas and went off to the nearby forested hillsides to gather and peel lodge poles. The men readied themselves for the enjoyable task of hunting the antelope that bounded freely over the wide prairie.

Under Joseph's guidance, the older boys took the horse herd to a broad, sloping hillside on the other side of the creek while the young boys and girls splashed in the shallow stream and played hide-and-seek among the willow bushes. The people would remain in this camp for several days until the new lodge poles had dried. They could hunt, repair their clothing, gather and dry camas, and let the very young and old build their strength for the long eastward journey before them.

The first night was spent under brush shelters, as the freshly cut pine trunks were not yet dry enough to use for lodge poles. But by the second night, teepees had been erected, a tent for the sick had been established, and a special maternity lodge had been set up for the newborns and their mothers. Joseph, who was now firmly in charge of the organization and well-being of the camp, made sure that the horses were well cared for and that all the people were comfortable and safe. At last, they were camped without the shadow of pursuit hovering over them.

But, still, some were uneasy. The young warriors could not forget the feeling of dread that had overtaken them back in the Bitterroot Valley. And Wottolen, one of the men with strongest medicine powers, had continued to see visions of soldiers in his dreams. To put their minds at ease, the warriors decided they should form a party to back-scout the trail across to the Bitterroot Valley. They needed only fresh horses to make the journey possible.

Ten or twelve of the young men approached the chiefs and told them of their plan. Looking Glass became exasperated and told them to give up their thoughts of war and concentrate their efforts instead on helping the people in the things of peace. But the young men were not mollified. They went to old Burning Coals, a wealthy man with a large herd of good horses. If he would loan them several of his racing horses, they could move quickly over the back terrain to see if they were being followed.

Burning Coals, however, felt much like Looking Glass. He liked his horses, he told them, and wanted to give them rest. If the young men wanted to do back scouting, they should use horses of their own. But the young men were not wealthy enough to own extra horses, and their own mounts were too worn-out from the journey. Since good scouting required fast, fresh horses, they abandoned their plan. Instead, they settled down with the rest of the group to spend a relaxed evening of games, footraces, and song.

With the teepees erected and the comforting smell of freshly picked camas roots baking in the fire pits, concerns and premonitions were soon a thing of the past. The young boys played the bone game, and the old men smoked contentedly by the warm glow of campfires, while the rest of the camp laughed and sang and told stories long into the night.

One by one, as exhaustion overcame them, the people went off to their teepees to sleep. Soon silence lay over the entire camp. Only the occasional pop of a coal in a fire and the gentle gurgling of the murmuring creek broke the quiet of the star-drenched night.

But while the people slept, there was movement on the other side of the creek. Gibbon had marched his men hard, keeping track of the Indians' progress. When his advance scouts had returned with a report of this camp in the Big Hole, he'd decided that this was his chance to end the Nez Perce flight once and for all.

Like all seasoned Indian fighters, he knew that surprise was his best ally. Indians did not fight well when they were on the defensive, and there was no better way to put them on the defensive than to surprise them in their sleep. His troops were now sneaking up close and taking positions just across from the camp.

He had equipped each of his men with ninety rounds of ammunition and a day's food rations and sent them forward under the cover of darkness. He instructed them to form a line high above the camp and to advance as close as possible in formation, then to wait until they heard the first shot. Then they were to charge the camp and finish the job that Howard and Rawn had been unable to complete.

By the time the first lines of daylight were limning the distant eastern mountains, Gibbon's soldiers were settled into positions not more than a few hundred yards from the sleeping Indians. They were wet and shivering from crawling through dew-covered grass, but their efforts had brought them into perfect position for a surprise attack on the campsite. Slowly they began their advance across the marshy creekbed, wading chest deep in the frigid, mountain waters toward the eighty-nine lodges of sleeping Nez Perce.

Across in the people's camp, an old man named Natalekin was unable to sleep. He decided to cross over to the hillside to visit his horses. The sky was still dark, and his eyesight was poor, so he depended on his horse to guide him.

As he approached the soldiers, they became convinced they were about to be discovered, so one leveled a shot. Almost instantly three other shots were fired, and Natalekin fell from his horse, mortally wounded.

In their teepees the Nez Perce heard the sound, unsure whether it was a dream or gunfire. Many had been asleep for only a few hours and were still groggy with exhaustion from their late night of games and singing and dancing. But when the few sporadic shots were followed by a fusillade of gunfire, they knew they were under attack.

The men, half awake, groped in the darkness for their clothing and rifles. The young children rolled over and rubbed their eyes, wanting to know what was happening. Infants began squalling, and the camp dogs were thrown into a barking frenzy. Outside, the horses that had been kept in camp began to snort and kick.

Quickly, the women grabbed the children and pulled them by their arms to get them up and out of the teepees. Many of the little ones, slumbering comfortably under the heavy robes in the warmth of the lodges, just rolled over and snuggled deeper into their blankets. Then bullets began ripping through the hides and canvas of the teepees.

The whole camp quickly descended into chaos. The crack of rifles mingled with the shouts of warriors and soldiers. The air filled with the choking smoke of gunpowder, making it impossible to identify the shadowy figures running between the lodges. The heavy-booted footsteps of soldiers could be heard amid the howling of dogs and the frantic shrieks of terrified horses.

The women who could escape ran toward the safety of the creek and the willows, dragging the screaming children behind them. The sick and old, unable to move quickly, tried to find their clothing and make their way into the brush or into some low, hidden spot near the creek bottom. Horses ran through the camp knocking over lodges and trampling cooking gear and clothing.

Suddenly, the sky was alive with flames. The soldiers were lighting the teepees on fire. The camp filled with the acrid smoke of smoldering animal skins and the sickening sweet smell of burning human flesh. The cries and moans of elders and the infants trapped in the burning teepees cut through the dawn.

Many of the Nez Perce warriors were half dressed and without their rifles. They had run out of their lodges and found the soldiers splashing up the creek bank into the camp. They had fought back with their hands, with rocks, with sticks, with war clubs, any way they could. They had jumped on the soldiers' backs, pulled them down, beaten them with stones—anything to protect the women and children.

The soldiers had now overwhelmed the camp and were shooting everywhere, aiming low into the lodges to kill the children and those still sleeping. They fired into the teepee for the infants, the teepee for the sick people. The piercing cries of the newborns could be heard amid the desperate wails of mothers trying to shelter their wounded and dying infants.

From the midst of the chaos, the voice of White Bird rose up. "Since the world was made, brave men fight for their women and children," he shouted. "Are we going to run to the mountain and let the whites kill our women and children before our eyes? It is better that we should die fighting." Hearing these words from the mouth of a seventy-year-old man, the men who had panicked at the outset of the fighting turned and headed back into the camp.

Looking Glass shouted out to Wahlitits and the other young men who had started the war with the attacks in the Salmon River, "These men are not asleep as those you murdered in Idaho. . . . Now is the time to show your courage and fight. . . . I would rather see you killed than the rest, for you started this war. . . . Now fight!"

The battle quickly spread throughout the camp. Wahlitits took up a position in a small depression by the edge of the creek, with only a small log for a barrier. He fought like the warrior he had dreamed of being, holding off soldiers who emerged from the creek until they overwhelmed him and killed him. His wife, soon to give birth, then picked up his rifle and continued shooting, until she too was felled by the soldiers' bullets.

Five Wounds, the strong warrior who had joined the travelers earlier on their journey, was killed in the fighting, as were Rainbow, Red Moccasin Tops, and others of the best, most willing warriors.

The carnage was frightful. Small children suffocated or burned to death in their teepees. Women were shot in the back as they tried to run. Potsikonmi, an old woman, was hit by a soldier's bullet as she crawled desperately on her hands and knees in search of a hiding place; Halpawinmi, only eighteen, was shot while trying to dress the wounds of the injured with mud from the creek. Illatsats, a young boy of only seven or eight, was left lying bloody and lifeless on the creek bank. A newborn, shot through the arm, sucked helplessly at its dead mother's breast while its arm hung from its shoulder by a thread of shredded flesh. The daughter of Wottolen, the man of strong medicine powers who had foreseen the coming of soldiers in his dream, lay dead near her lodge.

Everywhere the camp was filled with death and terror. The women huddled in the creek amid the willows, trying to keep the children quiet so they would not be found. When soldiers heard the whimpering and splashed across with their rifles poised, the women held their infants out in front of them, pleading for mercy. The gurgling waters, which only a day before had been so clear that the children could see the stones on the bottom, now ran red with blood.

In the midst of the fighting, a small girl was seen walking resolutely across the ground between the lodges and the creek. She had broken away from her mother and was striding determinedly back to their teepee, stopping every few feet to swat at bees around her head. When she emerged from the teepee carrying the small doll she had gone back to retrieve, she walked confidently back to the creek, where her desperate mother was frantically gesturing for her to get down. She was barely able to get to the safety of the willow bushes before the bullets that she had mistaken for bees began cutting into the branches and snapping the twigs above their heads.

On the far end of camp, Five Fogs, one of the Palouse Dreamers of Hahtalekin's and Husis Kute's band, was seen shooting arrows at the soldiers coming from the creek. He was a man of only thirty but believed in the old-time ways. He got off several arrow shots before the soldiers were able to cut him down.

Wounded Head tied on his wolfskin headband, seeking to claim the spirit power that his animal spirit guide had given him. Other men sang out their medicine songs, seeking help from their *wayakin* power. The niece of old Kahpots begged him to use his medicine power to hold back the soldiers. "I have tried," he said, "but my power has no effect. I feel helpless. You better look out for yourself. Go farther down the creek."

But all were not without power. Wahnistas Aswetesk, a very old man of great medicine, called upon his *wayakin,* then sat down before his lodge and calmly smoked his pipe while the soldiers riddled him with bullets. Only steam came from his wounds. He continued to sit, unharmed, as the battle took place around him. Many others fought fiercely, surviving bullet wounds to their bodies because their *wayakin* powers had given them the gift of surviving all shots that hit below the neck.

The Nez Perce were frantic and confused. They did not know where these soldiers had come from, and they had not been prepared to fight. They did not have time to get to their horses and were not used to hand-to-hand ground fighting. As men saw their wives and children fall from bullet wounds or heard the screams of dying children from within their teepees, they were torn between continuing the fight and saving their families. Joseph was seen huddling near the creek bank. "I have no gun to defend myself," he shouted to Two Moons. He was cradling his infant daughter in his arms.

The attack lasted no more than twenty minutes. Somehow, the Nez Perce warriors were able to regroup and drive the soldiers back across the creek and up the hill into a grove of pines. Joseph succeeded in getting the young boys across the creek to protect the horses. Whatever this attack had been, and wherever it had come from, it was now over, at least for the time being.

While the warriors held the soldiers at bay in the distant grove of pines, the people remaining alive in the camp crawled out from their hiding places and began to survey the carnage. Wounded horses lay screaming and writhing. Teepees were tipped over or smoldering. In the maternity lodge, which had been set up a few paces away from the camp, a woman lay dead with her newborn in her arms, its skull crushed and bloody from being smashed by a rifle butt or a soldier's boot.

All through the campsite there was horror beyond anyone's imagining. A wail rose up from the women loud enough to be heard by the barricaded soldiers far up on the distant hill.

Slowly, numbly, the survivors began to clear the camp. People dragged their relatives to the creek bank and pushed dirt over them to bury them as best they could. In the hollows they found old women—mothers and grandmothers—lying lifeless in pools of blood. Little boys and girls, holding shattered arms and oozing blood from bullet wounds, wandered whimpering through the camp, looking for parents who were lying still and empty-eyed on the earth near their lodges. Dolls, cooking pots, clothing—all lay scattered. Some of the dead lay in the smoldering camas pits, where their flesh burned and baked with the roots that had been cooking there since the previous night.

With the assistance of some of the young boys, Joseph brought the remaining horses down from the distant hillside. By running up to the herd at the first chance during the fighting, he and No Heart and the young boys had kept the soldiers from stampeding the pack animals during the confusion. Now he needed to get the people packed and moving before the soldiers broke through and attacked again. But many were too stunned to move. They simply sat, empty-eyed and moaning, looking at their butchered friends and children and staring at the bodies floating in the blood-filled stream.

But Joseph knew there was no time for grieving. The warriors could not hold back the soldiers forever, and others might be coming up from behind. The dead had to be buried as quickly as possible, and such belongings as remained had to be gathered and packed. Perhaps there would be time to come back later for proper burials. But now, the people had to be saved.

Slowly, as the sun rose higher and the smoke drifted up into the growing morning light, he assisted the decimated and traumatized remnant in loading their few remaining belongings onto the backs of horses and helping into their saddles the wounded who could still ride. Those too injured to stand were tied into blankets and placed on hastily constructed travois litters made from the lodge poles the women had cut the day before. Then the weeping, wounded survivors picked their way through the bodies of their horses and dogs and hastily buried wives and husbands and parents and children and rode aimlessly and hopelessly toward the mountains far to the south.

Above them on the hill, they could see the remaining warriors trying to set the grass on fire to burn into the trees where the soldiers lay hiding. Perhaps these soldiers might soon know some of the same horror and agony that they had visited on a people who had meant them no harm and who wanted nothing more than to find a place where they could raise their families in peace.

As if in a dream, the stunned people, led by Joseph and White Bird, moved across the cruel emptiness of the sweltering August Big Hole plain. The travois pole ends bumped harshly across the uneven ground, causing the injured to cry out in agony. Wounds broke open, shattered bones ground against each other, bullet holes stuffed with pieces of cloth oozed blood onto the grass and dust.

Joseph was like a man no longer living. His wife was wounded; his newborn infant daughter clung desperately to life in the relentless summer heat. Yet, as a camp chief, he could not focus on his own concerns and sorrows; it was his sacred duty to care for all the people and to do his best to calm their fears.

While a thin cordon of remaining warriors protected the perimeter of the moving procession, he moved among the injured and dying, offering such comfort as he could. As the wounded died, he assisted in their burials, standing by while the relatives sang death songs over the shallow graves. He then made sure the horse herd was driven over the ground so the graves could not be found and dug up by soldiers or Indian scouts intent upon scalping or thieving or desecrating the bodies.

When the wounded and elderly, unable to bear the bouncing of the travois and the jostling of the horses, begged to be left behind, he made sure they were left with food and water and the best blankets. Then he did what he could to console the families as they rode away, leaving behind the loved ones they would never see again in this life.

That night, camped on the edge of a small lake, the people began to take stock of the day's horrifying events. None knew where the soldiers had come from. One young boy confided that the night before the battle he had seen two men wandering near the fires wrapped in blankets. In the glow of the flames, he had seen that they had white foreheads. But he had been too afraid to tell anyone.

Others recounted the bravery of the men and women who had died. A few told of strange soldier kindnesses, where they were let go by men who easily could have killed them. But most remembered only the killing and the screaming and the settler fighters from the Bitterroot Valley who only days before had sold them goods and acted like their friends.

Joseph tried to assist the grieving and the wounded, but there was little he could do. He stood by helplessly as life ebbed out of Fair Land, his brother Ollokot's wife. He went through the camp making sure there were families to care for the little children whose parents had been killed. He assisted in the grisly task of doing a death count. Until the warriors returned, they would not know for certain how many they had lost. But by talking among themselves, the people were able to identify at least fifty women and children and elders who were no longer with them.

On the following morning, to the great relief of all, the few warriors who had not returned during the night began to trickle in. They had pinned down the soldiers in the grove of trees on the hillside and killed as many as they could. But the wind had kept the fire they set from catching the trees, so many of the soldiers had escaped death. They would have stayed longer and killed all the soldiers, but one soldier, trying to trade information for his life, told them that General Howard was close behind.

When they heard a cheer go up from inside the grove of trees, they thought it might be Howard and his troops coming up from the rear, so they had chosen to leave. It had been a hard decision. If they had stayed they could have killed all the soldiers. But they knew that each soldier who fell would eventually be replaced by another while each warrior who fell would be one less man available to protect the women and children. With so many of their best fighters now dead, it seemed better for those who remained to save their lives than to die fighting when their protection would be needed in the days to come. But one good had come from their siege—they had managed to capture a great amount of ammunition and had picked up many guns.

Their hearts were now dark with rage. They had held back all across the Lolo and all through the Bitterroot. They had listened to Looking Glass's claims that the settlers were his friends and that war had been left behind. Now it was clear what kind of friends these white men were and how much faith was to be put in the words of soldiers and settlers. War was not behind them; it was all around them. All white men were now their enemies, and all would be made to pay.

The anger in the camp now turned toward Looking Glass. He had always been held in the highest regard, but now he had lost much respect. It was his arrogance that had caused the people to move slowly, as if on parade. It was his claims of friendship with the whites that had caused them to reveal their goods and money to the settlers in Stevensville. He was the one who had refused to allow back scouting and had not listened to the vision warnings from the men with strong spirit powers.

He had never been willing to listen to anyone's ideas unless they coincided with his own. Now almost ninety of their people were dead, the best warriors were lost, and every family was grieving. Because of his pride, coyotes were digging up the bodies of their fathers and mothers, little children who should be playing happily were lying, half buried, in an unmarked creek bed, and Flatheads and Bannocks were parading around holding their grandparents' scalps.

A council was held to determine what should be done. Joseph spoke again for returning to their own lands, but this idea was rejected because it meant going back through lands controlled by whites. The chiefs knew the people could never get their wounded and elderly through the angry settlers whose fathers and brothers lay dead by Nez Perce hands. Charlot too had sworn to fight them if they raised weapons against the whites. His Flathead warriors would swell the numbers of the settlers and the army. There would be no Nez Perce left alive long before any of them ever set foot again in their own country.

Instead, the council voted to take leadership from Looking Glass and give it to Poker Joe, who had joined them in the Bitterroot Valley. He knew the country; he knew the Montana people. He could speak a little English, and it was thought that with his part-white blood he might be able to understand something of the white man's mind. All who had fought by him or hunted with him knew he had no fear, and he was familiar with the locations of the soldiers and the way to buffalo country. He was lucky in gambling, and gambling success spoke of strong ties to spirit power. It was felt that he would give them the best chance to get through to the Crow and the buffalo plains.

Looking Glass was insulted, but he could not resist. It was the people's will as decided in council, and he had to accept it, just as the others had been bound to accept his leadership when the council had granted it to him. Like Joseph, he must either go along or separate from the group and go on his own.

With Poker Joe in charge, the whole pace changed. Everything was now geared to escaping from an unseen enemy. The people rose at first light, ate a cold breakfast that required no fire, then rode without resting until late morning, when they stopped and cooked their only warm meal of the day. Their afternoon march began at two and extended far into the evening, sometimes almost until midnight, even though the shortening days of mid-August meant that much of that travel had to be done in the dark.

There was no scrimping on scouting now. Parties of warriors moved in front and behind and ranged in all directions around the group. Women and children were kept at the front where they could be protected. At night the people regathered into family groups, but while traveling the only concern was safety. It was no longer a procession but a flight, and all decisions were directed toward protecting those least able to protect themselves.

Joseph's task now became much harder. There were many wounded and many children without parents. Most of the lodge poles had been burned or shattered by bullets at the Big Hole. Those that remained had been commandeered for use as travois sticks to drag the wounded, so shelter once again was reduced to skins and blankets draped over trees and bushes. Many of the buffalo robes that the families had used for cover had also been lost, as had a great deal of their clothing. Much of what remained had been torn up and used for bandages and slings.

Because they had been forced to leave so quickly, food too was in short supply. The women had counted on the camas bulbs they were harvesting and drying, but those had been left in the ground when the people ran from the soldiers' attack. All foodstuffs that they had purchased in Stevensville had been lost or left. They were reduced, now, to hunting. And when hunting parties were not successful, it became a hard choice between feeding those who were still strong, and trying to nourish those who were weakened by injury.

Emotions in the camp were fragile. People were angry and frightened and confused and grief-stricken. Each band wanted to protect its own, and each had different feelings about the journey. Some of the people wanted to trust the chiefs, some wanted to trust the medicine visions. Toohoolhoolzote's and White Bird's men remained belligerent, while Joseph's people, farthest from their homes, were becoming increasingly heartsick. The Palouse, who had joined the Nez Perce bands near Clearwater, turned increasingly toward their faith in the Dreamer way. And through the entire camp, people struggled with the memories of death and suffering and grappled with the hard truth that their medicine powers had not been able to protect them against the guns of the soldiers.

Joseph did his best to keep order while they moved. But Poker Joe's pace was hard on everybody. With each body buried in a shallow grave, with every grandmother or grandfather who had to be left behind, the spirit of the people dimmed. And with each loss, the anger and unruliness of the young warriors grew.

These young warriors now began clamoring for leadership. If this was a war, they were the warriors. It was the peace people, the trusting people, who had gotten them into this situation. They could have ambushed all the soldiers back in the Weippe; they could have attacked and killed soldiers at the mouth of the Lolo. But in each case, their hands had been stayed. Now the people were without food, without shelter, without cooking gear, without clothing. Because of the peace-talking chiefs, the once-proud Nez Perce were running for their lives. Because of the peace-talking chiefs, they were being haunted by the spirits of the dead.

They began going out each morning on raiding parties. There was no fear about expending ammunition now because they had captured thousands of bullets from the soldier supply wagon at the Big Hole. They would get what the people needed by robbing white settlers. If they chose to, they would kill these white settlers or burn their houses and harvests. No supplies would be left behind for any soldiers who might be following.

At one ranch, they killed four white men, then tore up the mattress covers to make fresh bandages for the wounded back in camp. At another, they took more than a hundred head of horses. All this was done in the name of helping the people and stripping the land of anything valuable to soldiers. But it was done with dark anger and cruel hearts. In one case some of the warriors made handprints around a settler's cabin with the murdered man's blood. Other warriors, upset at such barbarities, covered the bodies of the slain with blankets.

All along the route of their flight the warriors broke into the homes and stores of white settlers. It no longer mattered to them that these people were not fighters. The people in the Bitterroot had not acted like fighters, either. All white people were now like snakes, harmless only when dead.

The chiefs tried hard to keep the journey peaceful. They would ride ahead into the small towns and talk to the white settlers, telling them that no trouble would come to them, that the Nez Perce fought only soldiers and that they intended to pass through without incident. But then the young warriors would follow, breaking the trust that the chiefs had established, stealing horses and food, saying they acted for the good of the bands.

Soon word of the Nez Perce depredations began to filter out. From these small, isolated towns, where people locked themselves in courthouses and cabins—in one case, even locking the children in the bank safe—stories of Nez Perce cruelty were carried by courier to nearby towns, then by telegraph to distant places, confirming the worst fears of nervous white settlers. The Nez Perce were on the warpath; they were killing innocent people and destroying whole communities; they were on their way to join with Sitting Bull to start the great Indian war that would leave all the struggling settlers and their families mutilated and dead. Even the *New York Herald,* on the distant eastern seaboard, carried a dispatch stating that unless Joseph could be driven back, "he will be reinforced by sufficient numbers to keep the Northwest in terror for some time." A general panic began to spread across the West.

Along with this panic came a growing anger at the military. It did not matter that the post–Civil War cutbacks had left Gibbon with fewer than 150 instead of the 600 men he would have had if the Seventh Infantry had been funded to full strength. It did not matter that Howard's men were traveling with two pairs of socks apiece and were living on pork fat and hardtack biscuits, some of which were left over from the Civil War. What mattered was that the Nez Perce were killing white settlers and escaping unpunished. The clamor for retribution was exceeded only by the scorn being heaped upon military leaders who seemed unable to exact it.

As a result, military reports from the field became more and more skewed. Battles became fiercer, the adversary more bloodthirsty and cunning. Victories were overstated, and skirmishes became battles. In his report on the Big Hole fight, Gibbon stated that he had killed eighty-nine Nez Perce. He did not mention that more than fifty of the dead were women and children and that many had been killed in their sleep.

Joseph too was now firmly established in the public mind as the leader of the Nez Perce, and in public depictions he became both fiercer and greater. To those in the West, who saw each confrontation and Indian escape as another bloody step toward their own extinction, he became the embodiment of all that was dark and cunning in the Indian character. For those in the East, who rankled at the cruelty and ineffectiveness of the government's Indian policy and were not in harm's way from Indian actions, he became a heroic symbol of noble resistance—the father figure of a beleaguered band of men, women, and children who were accomplishing a brilliant escape from the relentless pursuit of the bumbling U.S. military.

The man who was spending his days trying to move lodges and herds of horses and his nights worrying over a newborn infant and a wounded wife was being elevated in the public imagination to the status of a red Napoleon or red fiend; and he was becoming the lightning rod for a national debate on the justice and sufficiency of the government's Indian policy.

On the trail, however, the issues were much less abstract and much more dire. The warriors had little fear of pursuing soldiers because they knew that most were on foot and had proven cowardly when forced to fight armed men rather than sleeping women and children. They shared mocking stories of how the soldiers in the grove of trees had cried like babies when they were trapped, and they formed teepee-shaped piles of horse dung on the trail behind as a signal of derision to any troops who might be following.

But the chiefs, trying desperately to protect a dispirited, grieving group of people, sensed a gathering storm. It was true that the warriors' raids were gaining them much-needed provisions and were depriving the pursuing soldiers of forage and fresh mounts, but these endless attacks on innocent settlers were sure to bring the wrath of the whites down upon them. Though the warriors were killing no women or children, the settlers could not know that. All men will fight more fiercely to defend their homes and families than they will when alone in the field. If these settlers formed together or were joined with a strong soldier force, the Nez Perce would be faced with a battle they could not easily win.

In a last effort to gain allies, and perhaps the ear of sympathetic whites, Looking Glass and White Bird led a group of warriors into the small mining town of Junction to talk with Chief Tendoy of the Lemhi Shoshone. Though the Shoshone and Nez Perce had a long history of enmity, it was hoped that their common skin color would elicit sympathy and support. But Tendoy, like Chief Charlot, had chosen the route of conciliation and wanted nothing to do with a tribe that was at war with the U.S. military. He told the Nez Perce that they would get no assistance from him and that they should leave. Reluctantly, they agreed to do so. But their mere presence in the town had so unnerved the white populace, who had taken refuge in a hastily built log stockade, that many were convinced the renegades had come to attack the barricade. It was only through the townsfolk's fortitude and solid preparation, they believed, that the murderous red men had been kept at bay. Soon another story of heroic white resistance to Indian savagery was making its way by courier and telegraph to the outside world.

But not far outside that town, an act of true savagery and terror was taking place. While the Nez Perce families were struggling along in the relentless August heat, a small caravan of freight wagons appeared in the distance. The wagons were making their way through the dust and sagebrush with supplies for the scattered white settlements in the area. The chiefs, hoping to trade, rode up to the wagons and made conversation. The wagoneers were nervous and offered food as a gesture of friendship. Though the goods they were transporting were not theirs to distribute, the frightened freight haulers willingly exchanged bags of flour for Nez Perce gold dust, hoping the trade would mollify the Indians and send them on their way.

While this was going on, some of the young warriors discovered two Chinese miners who were traveling with the wagon train. Full of their newfound power, the warriors made the terrified miners get down on all fours and buck like horses to save their lives. When the warriors tired of this sport, they tried to make the white wagoneers do the same.

But the white men refused to do so. An altercation ensued, and the wagoneers were quickly overwhelmed and murdered. Then the warriors discovered ten barrels and a few random bottles of whiskey on the wagons and proceeded to drink themselves into a stupor. One of the nondrinking warriors, named Ketalkpoosim, became upset and tried to stop them. "If soldiers come," he said, "you will not be able to fight, not be able to ride."

The drunken warriors paid him no mind. When he tried to restrain them they took out their guns and shot him. He had been among the bravest fighters at the Big Hole, helping to capture an army cannon and dismantle it and risking his own life to save the lives of the women and children. Now he was mortally wounded at his own brothers' hands.

Looking Glass, White Bird, and Joseph were furious. They made the warriors pour out the remaining whiskey. But the drunken warriors simply got down on all fours and ate the mud.

Everything seemed to be disintegrating. They were in hot, desolate country. Every tribe they had counted on for friendship had turned against them. Internal divisions were surfacing everywhere, and the young warriors were out of control. The hard pace—the pace they knew they needed to keep—was killing the weak and the wounded. It had become a daily occurrence to see families singing death songs while gathered around a dying mother or father or child, then hastily sewing the body and a few precious possessions into a blanket before laying it in a shallow grave scraped from the dry earth by grieving hands and shovel bayonets taken from the ends of dead soldiers' guns. And now, with the death of Ketalkpoosim, they were dying at each other's hands.

Ollokot tried to exert some control over the warriors. Even though he was held in high regard, and all knew he had fought bravely at the Big Hole and had lost a wife in the battle, he could not control men drunk on alcohol, blood, and anger. With each death on the trail they became less willing to listen, more undisciplined while out on their scouting expeditions, and more willing to kill or die.

Meanwhile, Joseph and White Bird struggled to maintain the people's spirits. The land had turned from a broad, rolling prairie to a thirsty sink of sagebrush and sharp rocks. The pace was breaking even the strongest wills. Camp was often nothing more than a blanket draped over a pile of rocks, and food was whatever they could put together out of their dwindling supplies. Their horses were tired and worn down, and their own bodies were chafed and sore. Many of the families had never been to this country, and none knew where they would end up. Not a family among them had been left untouched by death.

Poker Joe and Looking Glass tried to console them with the knowledge that the place of the geysers was not many days ahead, and after that they would be near buffalo country. But each night brought dark memories of the soldier attack and fears that it could happen again. None could escape the horror of knowing that behind them the Bannocks and other soldier Indians were killing the old ones who had been left on the trail; and all knew that the bodies of the dead were being dug up and insulted, with the bones left lying to be dragged away and gnawed upon by coyotes.

There was also concern about troops that might be following. The people had looped far south after the battle, following a path that would keep them near the cover of foothills and out of the vicinity of major white settlements. Any soldiers who might wish to cut them off had only to travel the easy route straight across from the Big Hole to intercept them when they turned back north to pick up the trail. The chiefs knew that Howard's men were slow and had shown no real heart for fight. But they knew also that it was Howard's way to send men ahead to set traps so he could squeeze the people from behind. By taking the easy, straight route, he could easily send soldiers to lie in wait for the families as they moved toward the place of the geysers.

In order to protect against this, scouts always ranged far ahead and behind. This kept the people safe, but it left the young warrior scouts to their own devices. Men like Yellow Wolf, who could smell white men at a long distance and read the flights of birds and the distant shapes of shadows, could be trusted. But men like Otskai, whose mind was known not to work right, could not. There was no certainty that the young warrior scouts would not bring trouble on the people by their rash actions. Many had short vision and often were more concerned with bravery and vengeance than with the overall good of the people.

But there was no time to worry about these difficulties. The people needed to get across the searing heat of this dry sagebrush sink and into the safety of the hills and folds of the place of the geysers. Fearing the soldiers, fearing the settlers, fearing the crazed actions of the young warriors, they moved as fast as they could toward the strange otherworldly landscape of tall-shooting waters that had just been declared America's first national park.

II

"Pursue Them to the Death"

A FTER A DAY of weary, heat-choked travel, the people came to the place known as the dry creek. It cut like a knife wound through the flat sagebrush landscape, invisible to any but those who approached its edge. But once there, travelers could see that it stood as an impassable barrier, twenty feet deep and wider at its narrowest place than a horse could jump, with sheer, craggy rock sides, impossible to get down except in several places many miles apart. At these breaks, where the rock cliff sides gave way to sloping banks, white men had set up small shacks to serve as freight stations. The white man's "talking wire" ran along the far side of this cut in the earth, as did a wide wagon trail, known as Corrine Road, that the whites used to bring supplies and gold back and forth from the Union Pacific railroad in Utah to the settlements in Montana. If Howard had gotten ahead to block their progress, this is where he would be.

They wandered along this cut in the earth searching for the best place to cross. Eventually they found a place near a crossing known as Hole-in-the-Rock that seemed to suit their purposes.

A quick reconnoitering found no sign of Howard or any other white men. The men who operated the station had been alerted by the talking wire and had gone to a nearby cave in the hills to hide. From their vantage point, they watched as the Nez Perce procession made its way down the rocky, sloping opening and up the other side. One of the station men later guessed that it had taken almost five hours for the whole group to pass.

Once on the other side, the Nez Perce cut the "talking wire," disconnecting the people of Utah from the people of Montana Territory. This loss of communications caused the imaginations of the settlers to run wild. People had heard stories of the Big Hole fight, and stories of the murder of settlers abounded. There had been sightings of the Indians as they had passed through the sparsely settled countryside, so all knew that the Nez Perce were in the area. But no one was exactly sure where they were or what they intended to do.

This had caused Howard no end of difficulties in his attempts to head off the hostiles. He was indeed traveling in a straight line across from the Big Hole to the Corrine stage line route, with the intention of beating the Nez Perce to the dry creek and the road on the other side.

However, whenever he and his men came near a community that lay in the possible route of the Nez Perce, they were beseeched to provide protection to the terrified settlers and were abused in person and in the press when they did not. Never sure where the Nez Perce were going, and feeling sympathy for the fears of the settlers, Howard often listened to these entreaties and either split his troops or lost precious time traveling to protect communities the Nez Perce had already visited and left.

As a result, he managed to squander his chance to cut off the Nez Perce by traveling directly from the Big Hole to the stage crossings at the dry creek and instead ended up camped at one of the crossing points on the stage road forty miles north of the Nez Perce, who were leading their ponies and their people through the opening down near the Hole-in-the-Rock station.

This was the closest his soldiers had come to the Indians since the battle on the Clearwater. When he received confirmation from his scouts that the Nez Perce were only a short distance ahead, he knew that with a strong push he could overtake them and put an end to their flight. But it was a difficult decision. He had pushed his men hard. His infantry soldiers were now footsore and depressed. Many lacked socks and had been reduced to wrapping their feet in rags to protect against the sharp-edged volcanic rocks covering the landscape. The cavalrymen too were exhausted. Unlike the Nez Perce, they did not have extra horses to spell their own mounts, and many of their animals were too tired to do more than plod along with their heads down. Many of the men could not remember when they had last spent a night sleeping with their boots off.

Nonetheless, he pushed on, eventually closing to within eighteen miles of the escaping bands. But here the fatigue caught up with his men. Even the few volunteers that had managed to make it down from the north had been in the saddle for two days and a night, some almost falling off their horses as they had tried to stay awake during the ninety-mile forced march from the mining town of Virginia City.

The next day he tried to push them again. But the heat was overwhelming and the Indians' horses had trampled and eaten all the forage. By midafternoon he had reached the campsite the Nez Perce had just left, but his men were at the point of collapse.

A few miles ahead, the Nez Perce too were struggling with exhaustion. The trail had been hard, the weather hot. They had been forced to leave two more of their weary and wounded behind at the dry creek crossing. They had managed to have a good night camping at a low-lying oasis called Camas Meadows, where the sagebrush and volcanic rock gave way for a short time to an area of good grazing grasses and fish-filled streams. Now they were better rested and moving ahead again. But they were in no condition to move quickly. Their back scouts had discovered Howard's presence and were monitoring his movements from the low volcanic hills. It seemed like the battle they had tried to avoid was now inevitable.

But Howard had made his decision. Though his chief Bannock scout, Buffalo Horn, had reconnoitered the nearby Nez Perce camp and had tried to convince him that this was the moment to strike, he had decided not to do so. He was convinced the Nez Perce were heading down the wide valley toward Henry's Lake and the new Yellowstone National Park and had sent a group of forty men ahead by a different trail to hold off the Indians as they approached the pass that would give them entry. He was confident that this time he would trap the renegades in a pincer and be able to roll them up from behind. He wanted his troops to be rested and well fed and his animals as strong as possible for any mounted attack. So instead of pursuing an enemy that was only a half-day ahead, he instructed his men to make camp at the same Camas Meadows site the Nez Perce had left only that morning.

This mystified the three Nez Perce scouts who were watching from the nearby hillsides. They had been keeping an eye on the pursuing army through a telescope they had procured, and from the moment they had seen the large dust cloud in the distance, they had assumed that a major attack was about to be launched. One of the young men had even ridden ahead to camp to tell the warriors to prepare for battle. Now, while the warriors in the Nez Perce camp were readying for attack, General Howard and his men were setting up tents and tethering their horses. It was only midday. General Howard was impossible to understand.

When the news of General Howard's halt was relayed to the Nez Perce camp, the chiefs too were mystified. Howard was now only a short day behind. No one could understand why he would drive his troops so hard but be so afraid to fight. Yet he would not stop coming, would never give the people rest. They could keep running, but it was taking a devastating toll on their bodies and spirits. Perhaps it was time for them to take the offensive and bring on the decisive battle that Howard seemed so unwilling to undertake.

Black Hair, who had been wounded at the Big Hole, spoke up. Because of his wound, he could not sleep well. The previous night, while waiting for sleep, he had been given a vision by his *wayakin,* the great bird that lives in the clouds. With his bird's eyes he had seen Nez Perce warriors capturing soldiers' horses and other animals he could not identify. But he could identify the place. It was the same spot where the Nez Perce had stopped and the soldiers were now camped.

This gave many of the warriors hope. They had not heeded the visions at Clearwater, and they had lost much of what they had owned. They had not heeded the visions at the Big Hole, and many people had died. If Black Hair had seen them capturing horses in his vision, this time they would listen. They would attack the soldier camp and at least take the horses.

The men discussed the plan among themselves. It was a dangerous action. If they failed, the women and children would be left without protection, and all would fall into the hands of the soldiers and the their Indian scouts. But if they succeeded, the soldiers would be without horses and unable to follow. The time seemed right, and the young warriors needed the chance to fight or they would soon rage completely out of control. Eventually the decision was made. They would attack. They had to make this work.

They decided on a nighttime raid, when the soldiers were asleep. The men would ride back the eighteen miles on their horses, then gather together to make a final plan before attacking.

About thirty men were sent on the journey, including Looking Glass, Ollokot, Wottolen, Toohoolhoolzote, and all the good fighters, while the others remained in camp. The raiders made their way back through the sagebrush, traveling quietly in the moonless night. There was to be no loud talking, no smoking, nothing that would alert a sentinel or scout to their presence.

Moving slowly and carefully, they arrived above the soldier camp well after midnight. Here the older men, who had been in many battles, gathered everyone together to form a plan of attack.

Wottolen, whose daughter had died at the Big Hole, wanted to sneak into the camp on foot and kill Howard and the leaders. But Looking Glass said no, they should instead attack on horseback. The younger warriors concurred. They did not like to be far from their horses in battle.

Next came the question of whether to mount a full-scale attack or only steal the horses. Many liked the idea of attack. Everything was in their favor. They knew the land, having camped there only the night before. The soldiers were asleep, and it was a perfect avenging of the nighttime attack on the sleeping people at the Big Hole.

But others pointed to Black Hair's dream. In his vision, he had seen only the capture of animals. There had been no vision of battle. Though it would be good to stay and kill soldiers, it was better to follow the vision, to get the horses and leave the soldiers on foot, unable to follow. Then the warriors could get away without suffering more losses in battle. An army without horses in this country was as good as dead, anyway.

The discussion went back and forth as the night wore on. Finally, Ollokot became frustrated with the wrangling. Dawn was coming, he said, and if they waited until the sky lightened they would lose all advantage. He rode off toward the soldier encampment, announcing he was going after the horse herd. The others, acknowledging his wisdom, soon followed.

As they drew near, they slowed their horses to a walk so as to not alert the soldiers with the sounds of hoofs. Meanwhile, other warriors sneaked into the herd on foot to cut the tethers and bell harnesses from the pack animals.

It was a quiet night, and very dark, with stars but no moon. Howard had been so convinced of the safety of the location that he had not taken full battlefield precautions when setting up the camp. The Nez Perce had never yet attacked except in defense, and the open space with its surrounding emptiness and sight lines made an ambush almost impossible. So he had posted the minimal number of sentries and encouraged the rest of the men to bed down comfortably.

The troops had responded enthusiastically. For the first time since the Clearwater battle many of them would sleep with their boots and trousers off. Their few ragged clothes could air out, and they could get a good night's rest before pushing on after the fleeing Indians. The volunteer fighters from Virginia City were camped across the creek.

By two in the morning the camp was in restful silence. The quiet, dark, and chill night air was broken only by the howl of a distant coyote and the occasional shuffling and snorting of one of the tethered horses.

Suddenly, from just outside the camp, a shot rang out. The soldiers and volunteers leaped up and scrambled for their clothes and weapons. The Nez Perce too were taken by surprise. It was Otskai, the Nez Perce whose mind did not work right, firing his gun for no apparent reason.

All plans were now off. The Nez Perce, who were waiting in the darkness, rode screaming into the herd, cutting at the tethers and making war whoops and cries. They knew that soldier horses were afraid of Indians and would run if stampeded by shouting and gunshots. Other warriors rode among the soldiers' tents making as much noise and confusion as possible. The soldiers, unable to find their pants and boots, ran in all directions, and the civilian volunteers came splashing across the creek into the protection of the soldiers' camp carrying each other's boots, the wrong gun belts, and only half their clothing, shouting, "We are white men! Don't shoot!"

The Nez Perce drove the frenzied horses forward, gathering any animals they could as they passed. With gunshots and shouts they herded them toward the east, leaving a small group of warriors to hold off any pursuing troops.

The animals were slow and balky and difficult to drive, but the warriors pushed them hard through the dark. When they had finally outdistanced the soldiers and the sun was tracing the edges of the morning hills, the warriors slowed to examine the herd they had captured. To their disgust and astonishment, they discovered that they had captured mostly mules. Somehow, in the dark and confusion, they had missed the horses and gotten the pack animals.

The warriors were angry and embarrassed. How could such a thing have happened? What Nez Perce did not know mules from horses? Then they remembered Black Hair's vision. These were the animals the great *wayakin* bird could not identify. In the darkness, the warriors too had been blinded by the same power.

But there was no time for talk or recriminations. The soldiers were coming behind, some running, some on the horses that the warriors had failed to capture. The land now was almost all sagebrush and low hills, offering no cover and no identifying landmarks. Without some kind of rearguard action, the soldiers would soon overtake the balky mule herd and reclaim their lost animals.

Abandoning the most recalcitrant of the animals, the warriors pushed forward, driving the mules with shouts and whoops. A few of the men stayed behind and took positions behind the hump of a small ridge, intending to hold back the soldiers while the others got away.

When the soldiers came into view, this rear guard opened fire. The horse soldiers quickly dismounted and built tiny rock walls to protect themselves from harm. While they were barricading themselves and returning fire, the Nez Perce sneaked around their flanks and flushed them from their tiny earthen depressions. The soldiers retreated like deer into a small ragged aspen copse and huddled there behind hastily constructed stone breastworks barely a foot or two tall. From these pitiful barricades they exchanged fire with the Nez Perce for several hours while the warriors with the captured mules caught up to the weary families and moved toward the relative safety and cover of the land known to the whites as Yellowstone Park.

The warriors were chagrined at their mistake, but the people had no such feelings. The mules were distributed among the families according to their need, and the fact that Howard was now without pack animals gave them a feeling of security. They set up camp on the edge of a large, mountain-rimmed lake right on the edge of the pass into the land of the geysers. They were unaware that the forty troops Howard had sent ahead to block their passage had just left the area, convinced that the Indians they had been sent to stop had already passed by.

The lake, known to the whites as Henry's Lake, was a traditional camping area for Nez Perce hunters on the way to buffalo country. It offered good grazing, good fishing, and fine berry picking. It was a pleasant respite for the people after the harsh sagebrush and sharp stones of the country through which they had just passed.

But the high country nights were now getting cold, and the days were getting shorter. There was no need for undue haste, but the weather, as surely as the military, was gradually becoming their adversary. They needed to get such rest as they could while keeping an eye to both the changing seasons and the pursuing soldiers.

The raid on the horse and mule herd had given the people a palpable feeling of relief. Not only had the soldiers been slowed, perhaps even stopped, by the loss of their pack animals, the warriors had come face-to-face with Howard's troops for the first time since the Clearwater and had found them wanting. They were disorganized, poorly equipped, and no match for Nez Perce fighters. If the people could keep from being taken by surprise in night raids or ambushes, Howard's troops did not present any real obstacle. Only the teepee dog Bannock scouts presented any real danger, and they were interested only in Nez Perce horses. With proper vigilance the camp could move comfortably across the place of the geysers and over the mountain passes to their final destination in buffalo country.

This place of the geysers, long known to the Indians, had only recently gained the interest of whites. Years before, a man from the Lewis and Clark expedition had chanced upon it on his way back from the Pacific, and ever since, miners and trappers had wandered through its mountains and canyons in search of gold and furs. But most of white America knew it only through fantastic newspaper accounts of bubbling sulfuric pits, a towering two-stage waterfall, and spouts of steam shooting hundreds of feet into the air. It had even been dubbed "Coulter's Hell," after the man from Lewis and Clark's expedition who had made the first report of its wonders.

Another traveler had dropped a plumb line from the top of the lower falls to measure its height and had reported it to be twice the height of Niagara. The upper falls, it was observed, added another Niagara to its height. Such stories had inflamed the public imagination and prompted Congress to declare the area a national park, the first such designation of any place in the country.

Still, few non-Indians had actually seen the place. It was in one of the wildest, most unexplored regions of the nation, surrounded by almost impassable mountains and situated hundreds of miles from the nearest railroad line. To get there, a person had to journey for days on narrow mountain trails while navigating rock slides, braving unpredictable weather, and dealing with bands of roving Indians.

Nonetheless, each year a few hundred intrepid souls made the difficult journey from civilization to see what had so captured the imagination of previous visitors. At any given time, this vast, trackless wilderness might be playing host to a tiny collection of traveling Indian bands, prospectors moving from the Black Hills to the gold fields of Idaho, curious soldiers on leave from their western posts, and the occasional tourist who had decided to enter this welter of mountains and rivers and geysers and hot springs in search of adventure.

Even General Sherman, head of the entire United States Army, had just completed a camping visit to the country. He had entered the park on a trail "so sharp and steep that every prudent horseman will lead instead of riding his horse" and had waxed poetic about the scenery of "the boldest mountain character." Though he had been informed that the Nez Perce were heading this direction, it had caused him no concern because he was convinced Indians avoided this country because they associated geysers and hot springs with demons and hell.

In fact, the Nez Perce made no such associations. Their buffalo hunters had traveled through this area many times and were intimately familiar with its marvels and its complex and spectacular terrain. They had even learned to use its hot springs to cook their food. So after a day of camping at Henry's Lake, the people resumed their travel on this last difficult leg of their journey to the buffalo plains. They knew nothing about this new "park" designation, nothing about their near encounter with General Sherman—indeed, that such a man even existed—and nothing about the forty troops that General Howard had sent to ambush them at Henry's Lake. They knew only that they were now in country that formed the last barrier to the vast, rolling buffalo country and sanctuary among the Crows.

For General Howard, now two days behind and stripped of his pack mules, the situation was far more complex. His ambush at the pass into the park had failed because his forty soldiers had stayed only forty-eight hours, as they believed they had been instructed, then returned to the main body of troops before the Nez Perce even arrived. His Bannock scouts, now swelled in ranks by recent arrivals, were giving him problems. Never a trustworthy bunch, they were becoming unruly because of his army's slow pace and were causing him trouble by their horse thievery and butchery of wounded and elderly Nez Perce left along the trail. Without mules, his troops were not able to move quickly and were footsore and dispirited. Their clothes were torn and thin and completely unsuited to the growing cold of the high mountain nights. The screws that held the soles of their shoes to the uppers were breaking through and lacerating their feet. Many did not have to worry about this problem because their shoes had fallen apart, and they had now become accustomed to the morning ritual of wrapping their feet in rags in order to undertake their daily marches.

Their meals too had become a source of frustration as much as of nourishment. They were a monotonous repetition of fried pork fat, burned coffee, and hardtack biscuits so inedible that the men often soaked them in water overnight to make them soft enough to fry in pork grease. Many of the men were without blankets and spent the nights curled up and shivering on the frost-covered ground. They had not had an opportunity to wash their clothes for over three weeks.

Adding to these difficulties were the acrimonious telegraph exchanges between Howard and his superiors. While his men were resting at Henry's Lake, he had ridden seventy-five miles north to the small mining settlement of Virginia City in an attempt to procure more horses, mules, clothing, and supplies for his troops. There he had communicated by telegraph with General Sherman and with General McDowell in San Francisco, who, as head of the Army's Division of the Pacific, was his direct superior.

The condition of his troops had prompted him to ask for assistance from other forts to head off the Indians as they moved farther east. Sherman, more and more irritated with Howard's ineffectual pursuit, was unsympathetic. He was less concerned with the plight of Howard's men than with the ever more raucous ridicule being heaped upon his military in the press. The *Fort Benton Record,* discussing the capture of the mules, had surmised that the stolen animals might have been laden with newspaper accounts critical of Howard's soldiering and that the Indians had been forced to fight only because they had dawdled so long reading the press clippings they had captured.

Such damning press, coupled with Sherman's increasing impatience with Howard's plodding ways, caused him to issue a sharp rebuke to Howard's request for assistance. In pointed words, he questioned the general's stamina and implied that perhaps Howard was too old for Indian chasing and might want to consider giving over command to a younger man. He also pointedly instructed Howard to quit whining about conditions and supplies and to prepare to live off the land, as the Indians did and as troops had done during the Civil War.

Howard, stung to the quick by the challenges to his stamina and military skill, wrote back that he and his men were quite capable of continuing the pursuit "to the death," as Sherman had requested. He resisted pointing out that living off the western land was quite a bit different from living off the gardens and orchards and pigs and cattle of southern families, as Sherman had done on his march from Atlanta to the sea, and that the Nez Perce had already stripped the land of any usable forage—facts that Sherman knew but conveniently had chosen to ignore. Instead, Howard pushed his men forward, trying to keep their spirits up while struggling to get the most out of his unwilling and untrustworthy Bannock warriors who were more interested in gaining Nez Perce horses and plunder than they were in actually catching the Nez Perce.

The land of the Yellowstone was difficult country, where mistakes had dangerous consequences. The ground around the bubbling springs was unpredictable and unstable, trapping any horse that broke through into the muck that lay right beneath the thin, brittle, earthen crust. The hillsides were almost vertical and covered with forests of lodgepole pines so dense that a man, much less a horse, had a difficult time passing between them. There were tight canyons covered with boulders and scree, and paths that ended at precipices and cliffs. A wrong choice of route, and travelers would find themselves trapped in a situation from which they could not easily escape.

None of this would have concerned the Nez Perce if they had been willing to take the broad Bannock Trail, which formed the traditional crossing into buffalo country. This trail was well known to all because it was used by all the tribes traveling to and from the plains of the buffalo. But it was also the route most likely to bring them into contact with troops and miners and hostile tribes. If there were soldiers, Bannocks, or anyone else in this country, it was on these well-known trails that they would be traveling.

So instead, the Nez Perce decided to move on less-traveled hunting trails that looped to the south. Poker Joe knew these trails, though not well. They were narrow, difficult passages, ill suited to the movement of large groups of horses and people but even more ill suited to the movement of troops and artillery. By sticking to these routes, the Nez Perce could maintain their advantage over Howard and minimize their likelihood of contact with hostile forces.

There was some discussion about the wisdom of subjecting the sick and wounded to such difficult travel, but in the end Poker Joe's decision was trusted. He knew this country better than anyone else. He was even rumored to have a house in a nearby town. His knowledge offered the people the best chance of safe passage across this difficult landscape.

Because of the people's concern about hostile forces and their uncertainty about the land, scouting parties were sent out daily in all directions. They were to watch for soldiers and also to identify and define the trail because Poker Joe, though familiar with the various trails, did not know them well.

As a result, the Nez Perce soon found themselves encountering some of the strange assortment of travelers who also had eschewed the well-known routes and were wandering in this wilderness. The first was a white miner named John Shively, who was returning to Idaho from a mining expedition to the Black Hills. He had lost his pack animals and had set out into the backcountry to search for them. The scouts chanced upon him as he was chopping wood for his campfire.

Some of the warriors sneaked up behind and grabbed him. He did not seem afraid, so they asked him if he knew where they could find the trail to the buffalo country. Since he had just come through the buffalo plains, he was familiar with the route. The warriors asked him to travel with them to show them the trail and promised him a good horse if he would do so. Somewhat reluctantly, he agreed. He put up a brave and amiable front but kept his eyes open for the first chance to escape.

Soon other scouts spotted a campfire in the distance. Creeping up close, they discovered seven white men and two white women dancing and playing music by a campfire. A quick council was held to decide what to do. Some of the young warriors, remembering the Big Hole, wanted to kill them outright. To them, all whites, whether men or women, were enemies because all had tongues and all could provide information to soldiers. It was their belief that any white person encountered had to be silenced.

Others opposed this course. Why kill now? they asked. We did not kill soldiers when the mules were stolen. And we have done no killing except when blinded by whiskey or when resisted or attacked. If we begin to kill women and innocent children, we are no better than the soldiers who are following us.

Yellow Wolf, who was leading, favored murdering the campers. But when he approached the group and one of the men greeted him with a handshake, he had a change of heart.

The campers asked to see Chief Joseph. This surprised and confused the scouts. They did not understand why the white people should know about Joseph or want to see him. But the campers had been reading the newspaper accounts, and in their minds the Nez Perce were all under the command of Joseph. It only made sense to them to ask to see the man they believed to be in ultimate control of the tribe.

The scouts discussed this development among themselves but ultimately decided to bring the people back to the chiefs. The leaders could decide whether these people should live or die. However, before leaving, the warriors decided to help themselves to the food the campers were preparing.

One of the campers, wishing to secure the good graces of the warriors, started to hand the Indians sugar and flour and bacon. But another became angry and tried to stop him. This angered the warriors and almost resulted in the instant murder of the entire party. But in the end, the warriors decided to abide by their initial decision to bring the white people to the chiefs and led them forward toward the main encampment.

During the journey, more trouble erupted. The campers and scouts encountered another group of young Nez Perce warriors, maybe sixty in number, who had been reconnoitering on their own. This group was more hostile and aggressive. They tipped over the white campers' wagons, rifled their goods, and began breaking up the wagon wheels to make whip handles. One grabbed some mosquito netting the campers carried and tied it to his horse's tail. Another made a turban out of a piece of cloth that the women had been carrying.

Soon the warriors became belligerent toward the white men and began moving toward the women. At this, one of the male campers tried to stop them. He was the husband of one of the women and the brother-in-law of the other, who was a child of only thirteen. The belligerent warriors quickly turned on him. One of them raised his gun and shot him, then began beating his head with a rock. His wife ran to her wounded husband and threw herself upon him to protect him from the warriors, and it was only with great difficulty that the other warriors who did not want more trouble were able to control their aggressive brothers. During the confusion, all but three of the campers were able to escape.

Eventually, the remaining three people were gotten to camp. They had asked to see Joseph, and to the warriors who wanted no trouble, this seemed like a good idea. Joseph and Poker Joe were the most positively disposed to whites and the least likely to allow their killing. Other chiefs, like White Bird and Toohoolhoolzote, might not be as generous and lenient.

The campers were ushered to the lodge sites of Poker Joe and Joseph, who told them to stay close. Poker Joe, with his broken English, tried to explain that the warriors were not all of a common mind and that the safety of the campers could not be assured if they fell into the hands of the wrong bands.

Meanwhile, the more belligerent young warriors were running about the camp shouting and making war cries. They were ready to take their anger out on these white people. It made no difference to them that these were not combatants. They could not be carried along, and they could not be allowed to escape and inform the soldiers of the Nez Perce whereabouts. This left only one option in the young warriors' minds, and it was an option they were more than willing to exercise.

Joseph was silent and somber at the violent turn events had been taking, but now he became angry. Some of the young fighters were no more than sixteen years old and had no proper sense of what it meant to be a Nez Perce warrior. They confused killing with protecting and revenge with honor. Events had made them like dogs that had tasted blood.

He took the older woman and her brother into his camp. It was nothing more than a piece of canvas draped over some bushes, but he did his best to make the man and woman comfortable, smiling often, offering them food, and even giving the woman a Nez Perce infant to hold, hoping that this gesture would show them his good heart and serve to calm their fears. For sleeping, he brought the people close to the fire and provided them with blankets. They slept with his family, rolled in their blankets with their feet close to the warmth of the fire, in the traditional Nez Perce way.

They awoke the following morning to a freezing drizzle. Since the captives had few warm clothes, Joseph insisted that the woman be provided with a blanket to cover her shoulders. His wife made some willow tea, camas porridge, and fry bread, but the woman would not eat, and the man would eat but little. Ice was almost an inch thick on the water in the nearby ponds.

The belligerent young warriors were again milling around in a threatening manner. Poker Joe tried to keep them at bay by telling them that he knew all the whites in the territory and that the Nez Perce would be chased forever if they harmed white women. Joseph too did his best to protect the campers, and the campers themselves tried to play upon the warriors' fear of magical powers by making the sign of the cross whenever someone approached them in a threatening manner.

Eventually the young warriors turned their attention elsewhere. The camp was getting ready to travel, and their responsibilities as scouts took precedence over any anger or desire for personal revenge. They also had been informed of another group of whites in the vicinity, and many of them had ridden off to find and confront this new potential threat. The prisoners were left to travel with families who wished them no harm.

When the moment was right, these sympathetic families gave the captives new moccasins, bedding, jackets, bread, and matches and helped them slip out of camp. Poker Joe led them on two old horses he provided for the women. He did not wish to provide a third horse for the man because he did not want the group to be able to travel too quickly once they were released. He knew that they would eventually meet up with soldiers and provide information about the Nez Perce's location and direction of travel. Best to leave them to their own devices in the wilderness, knowing that they had been well supplied and well cared for. By the time they reached white soldiers or white settlements, the tribe would have moved ever farther into the confusing landscape of the Yellowstone, and any information the captives gave the soldiers would be of little value.

But before setting them free, Poker Joe made an impassioned plea for them to tell the whites that the Nez Perce wanted no more fighting, that they wanted only peace. The captives listened impatiently while he struggled to make himself understood with his limited English; then they rode off in the direction he pointed them, hoping they would reach Bozeman before being caught by some of the more hostile Nez Perce who were not so disposed to allow them to escape.

The Nez Perce then turned to the task of moving farther into the high mountain country. They still had the old miner, Shively, with them, as well as a white soldier they had recently captured. They were moving now on small trails, not well known to the Nez Perce, and covered with fallen trees and large boulders. Poker Joe made the miner and soldier clear a trail with axes, but even so, many injured horses had to be left behind.

In some places travel was easy, taking them across wide meadows with curving streams and grass good for grazing. These places, with their abundance of elk and fish, reminded the Nez Perce of their home country in the Wallowa and Clearwater. They stopped in these clearings as long as possible to give their people and stock a chance to build up strength and to savor the bittersweet feeling of being in land similar to their own.

August was drawing to a close, and high summer was now long past. Each day they watched as more of the aspen leaves turned yellow, and each morning they awoke to thin ice on creeks and frost on their buffalo robes. Snow was descending lower on the high mountain peaks, often shrouding them in a distant, wintry mist. The cold of winter was beginning to be felt on the winds.

Every morning the scouts went out at first sun, traveling far in all directions. Unlike the camp chiefs, they had no compunction about killing white people they encountered. If they had their way, there would be no white eyes left to see, no white tongues left to talk.

Their reports at night were a conflicting welter of information and boasting. It had been assumed that General Howard would have to slow his pursuit while he sent for more horses and pack mules, but none had counted on the confusing collection of white people they would encounter in this odd, rugged country. They had seen settler volunteer soldiers riding in groups, and regular soldiers with new clothes and new guns. There were packers, miners, and campers. They had seen Indians too—mostly Bannock, but maybe even Crow. All that was known for certain was that the soldiers' Indian scouts were killing the elderly and wounded whom the people were forced to leave behind when the rigors of the trail became too difficult to endure.

In the face of such confusion, the people redoubled their efforts to get to Crow country. They were trusting in Looking Glass's promise that the Crow would welcome them, that they would be able to join together with their Crow brothers and sisters into one great village of a thousand lodges, with good horses and many guns. It was their fervent hope that, once united, the tribes would live together in peace, hunting the buffalo, trading with friendly white settlers, returning to a normal life of sweats and feasts and dances and song carried on under skies not darkened by the constant cloud of war.

The long journey had made them weary in body and spirit. They longed to see their children playing, their elders smoking, their horses grazing and growing strong rather than falling wounded from being driven too hard. They wanted to teach the young people the ways of life, not just the ways of war; to send them on their *wayakin* quests, to show them the skills of the camps, and to teach them the stories of Coyote and the ancestors. They longed once again to bury their dead in the proper way, with proper songs and rituals, not quickly in unmarked graves, leaving their spirits without rest and their bodies to be picked at by animals and insulted by enemy bands in unfamiliar land.

But shadows lay at the edges of these bright hopes. The possible presence of Crow warriors among the soldier scouts had been very upsetting. There was concern that maybe the Crow, like the Flathead and the Bannock and the Shoshone, had cast their lot with the soldiers. So Looking Glass rode ahead to meet with his Crow friends to learn their hearts. He had no concerns about their loyalty because the Crow had sworn their friendship to him after he and his men had fought beside them in their battle against the Sioux. He knew that a few scouts with the soldiers meant nothing. Those scouts were likely river Crow, a tribe more friendly to the whites than the mountain Crow, who were Looking Glass's friends.

Besides, as all Nez Perce knew all too well, each warrior was free to act in accord with his own heart. If tribes were able to control all their warriors, the killings on the Salmon and Slate Creek would never have happened, and the Nez Perce would not now be wandering through unfamiliar mountain passes in an effort to evade the U.S. Army. The Crow scouts, if indeed there were any, were probably young men who had chosen on their own to work with the soldiers and the U.S. government. But Looking Glass wanted the people to feel at ease, so he undertook this journey to calm their fears.

With two warriors he rode off to meet the Crow and tell them of the Nez Perce's arrival. They could give him information on the best routes and perhaps even send their own warriors to help if there was any danger of a white soldier attack. The rest of the tribe would move slowly until he returned so as not to arrive too quickly in the open country on the eastern side of the mountains. Once they were in open land, all advantage went to the soldiers because they could move quickly, and the Nez Perce would have no place to hide the presence of hundreds of Indians and thousands of horses.

In camp, Poker Joe continued to lead with a strong hand. Each morning he would ride in a circle around the lodges, shouting orders for the day. With a voice as loud as a buffalo bull's, he could be heard all across the camp, even though he was still nursing a cruel stomach wound received at the battle of the Big Hole. Under his guidance, the people had traveled a difficult route through the Yellowstone, passing through dense forests and down hills so steep that the horses literally had to slide on their haunches. The women and young boys had spent their days whipping the mules and horses in an attempt to urge them forward, hitting their noses with sticks when they became wedged between trees, and pushing them over logs and boulders until the flesh on their bellies and flanks was scraped bloody and raw.

Now they were in high country, where the nights were cold and the winds were cutting. The surviving animals, like the surviving people, were tired and weak, despite the stops in meadows and grasslands. A few days' rest could not make up for the months of harsh travel they had all endured. They moved with a weariness that was worn into their hearts and bones.

The people now split up and traveled in different groups, hoping to confuse the soldiers and find trails too difficult or obscure for soldiers to follow. At night they slept on frost-covered ground, and during the day they were often pelted by rain and slushy snow. The children now were always cold, always crying. It seemed that every morning another elder awoke too weak to travel and was helped to the woods or the nearby rocks and given blankets for comfort, then left behind. The group moved on to the haunting sounds of their loved ones' death songs receding in the distance.

All around now there were only mountains—high, jagged, snow-covered peaks stretching into the far distance. The wind blew constantly across the great spaces, and from the promontories a person could see many days' journey in all directions. Ascents were steep, descents precipitous. Sometimes they had the protection of thick forests, other times they were forced to move across naked, exposed ridges.

The scouts kept returning with sightings of soldiers moving on distant hillsides and through distant valleys. It was hard to know who they were or where they came from. The soldiers had many guns, including cannons. Thoughts of the Big Hole were in everyone's mind.

The chiefs were now faced with hard choices. Should they keep moving around in the high country, waiting in the cover of the mountains for Looking Glass's return, or should they move quickly onto the rolling plains to join with their Crow brothers and sisters before the arrival of the soldiers and the coming of the snows? Should they continue to divide and travel separately in an attempt to confuse the soldiers' scouts? Should they stay together to remain strong in case they were ambushed and needed to fight?

Perhaps most important, which route should they use to travel this last part of the journey into buffalo country? They were at the peak of the final range, and from here all dropped off toward the great, open plains. Ahead of them, three long canyons stretched off toward the sunrise like the space between fingers, each canyon separated from the next by a high, spiny range of mountainous rocky bluffs and vertical cliffs.

Each canyon had a trail through it—well known to all the tribes and all the Indian scouts. If the soldiers or their scouts saw the people begin their descent, they could send messengers ahead to alert other troops to block the trail at the bottom. By now it was clear that this was General Howard's method—to set traps in front, then try to close in from behind. If he succeeded in this instance, they would be caught. And once they had made the choice of a trail, they could not turn back.

The men met in council to consider the dilemma. The young warriors had, for the moment, turned their thoughts back to the people rather than to clearing a path by killing whites. They joined the discussion to offer their opinions and knowledge. Escape would be hard, they said. They had seen Indian scouts across a valley and had called out to them that the people wanted no more fighting, that they were all brothers and should speak together as friends. The scouts had called back that they did not wish to talk in words but only with their rifles. The young men had been unable to tell if they were Bannock, Snake, or even Crow. But it did not matter—whoever they were, they no longer had the hearts of brothers. Their hearts, now, were the same as soldiers'.

Worse still, some of the scouts had ridden ahead to the highest promontories, from which they could see far out onto the plains. In the distance they had seen many small fires, like a soldier camp, flickering in the darkness. It was as they had feared—General Howard had set another trap, just as he had done at the soldier corral. But this time there were no ridges for the people to use to circle around. And this time, the soldiers would not be settlers with weak hearts for fighting.

In counsel with the young warriors, Poker Joe formulated a plan. They needed to trick the soldiers and convince them to block the base of the wrong canyon. So they arranged for all the people to move toward the trail down into the canyon that opened farthest to the south. When they were safely ahead of the soldiers and their scouts, the warriors would take all the mules and horses and ride in circles to make a great confusion of hoof-prints. Then they would drag branches behind so dust would rise up, making it seem to anyone observing from a distance that the whole group of people was moving in that direction.

While the warriors were doing this, the people would turn north and move up into the heavy timber of the high mountain ridge that separated the south canyon from the next canyon. They would proceed along this ridge through the forest until they could find a way down into this next canyon. The soldiers would see the dust and commotion and assume that the people had taken the easy trail down into the canyon to the south and would set up their blockade at the bottom. Meanwhile, the people would make their way down into the next canyon and escape into buffalo country.

Poker Joe was convinced this would work. He knew the canyons, knew the trails. He knew that even if the soldiers followed the people, the narrow gap that he was proposing to use to descend into the north canyon was too steep for soldier horses and too narrow for the soldiers' supply wagons. The people would be able to escape even if pursued so long as the soldiers at the bottom did not realize the deceit and return to block this more northerly trail.

Joseph spoke against this plan. He wanted to go the third way, the easi-est, most frequently traveled way, up the valley called the Yellowstone. He knew there were mining settlements there and that the soldiers might easily find them, but he did not think the children and elderly could endure the difficult route that Poker Joe and the warriors were proposing.

He was willing to risk confronting the white settlers. He was even will-ing to consider surrendering if necessary. He wanted no more suffering, no more weeping and dying, no more spirits of the unburied dead wandering in the other world waiting for rest, no more elders insulted and mutilated when left behind to wait for death. Almost 150 people had died since this flight had begun. The time had come to say, "no more fighting." It was time to think about the lives of those who remained, to do what was necessary to let them return to their homes and the land that they loved.

But others vehemently opposed this plan. They had come this far, and Crow country lay just ahead. They did not want to live on government reservations, like white men's cattle in white men's pens. Better to be like the buffalo, running free until shot down, living in the way the Creator had shown them.

The people even discussed the possibility of each band's going its own way and doing what it thought best. But returning scouts announced that soldiers were everywhere, as well as miners and other white people. They did not think surrender was a possibility. Too many white people had been killed, and too many had not been soldiers. It was their belief that all the people who could not escape would be massacred, and this would mean the oldest and weakest. Soldiers did not take Indian prisoners, and the Bannocks did not allow the people to die without torture and insult.

With uncertain hearts, the people agreed to Poker Joe's proposed plan of escape. Joseph remained silent. He knew that the council was right: they would not see their homes again. Too much blood had been spilled. The killings and burnings and lootings by the young warriors had sealed their fate.

So Poker Joe put his plan into action. He led the people across a high meadow into the timber while the warriors rode in circles, dragging branches tied to their lariats. With the riders raising what would seem from a distance to be the dust of a thousand horsemen, the people squeezed their way among the trees and ledges until they came to the narrow crevasse that Poker Joe had chosen for the descent into the more northerly valley. It was as deep as three men and barely as wide as a horse. The whole gully was filled with loose rock and scrabble and was so steep that it was easier to slide down than to walk.

With their horses falling against each other and scraping themselves raw on the deadfall and rocks, the people dragged their wounded and elderly down this half-mile, almost vertical, defile and out into the bottom of the valley.

Howard continued his distant pursuit, heading toward the dust and commotion made by the circling warriors, while the soldier waiting at the bottom blocked the end of the wrong canyon, just as Poker Joe had hoped.

12

Alone in a Strange Country

THE SOLDIER waiting at the bottom of the wrong canyon was Colonel Samuel Sturgis, a Civil War veteran with a checkered career, who had lost a son in Custer's rash debacle at the Little Bighorn only a year before.

He had been given orders by his direct superior, Colonel Nelson A. Miles, to ensure that the Nez Perce did not link up with Sitting Bull and his renegade Sioux, who were living across the national boundary in Canada, out of reach of the American military. Initially, this had meant patrolling the area of the northern buffalo plains near the Canadian border to provide a military presence to confront the Sioux if they came south or the Nez Perce if they turned north after exiting the mountains of the Yellowstone. But word had come that the Nez Perce were still in the mountains of the Yellowstone region and perhaps could be struck a fatal blow as they emerged. So Sturgis had come down from the buffalo plains at the instruction of his superiors and was nervously trying to outguess the Nez Perce as to which canyon they might take in their descent from the mountains.

Like all the soldiers now in the field in the West, Sturgis was hungry to be the man to catch Chief Joseph and these renegades. But like all the others, he was rapidly falling victim to the confusing military chain of command that had resulted when General Sherman told Howard to pursue the Nez Perce to the death, no matter where they went.

General Sherman was head of all the U.S. armies and so most answerable to political pressures generated in Washington and the press. He had a well-earned reputation for ruthlessness and decisiveness, and though he greatly respected the military skill of the Nez Perce, he did not intend to allow them to make a laughingstock of his military in the public mind. Neither did he wish them to join up with other tribes or even to give other tribes false hopes of success against the U.S. military. He knew that such a linkage, or even the perception of such a linkage, would cause a wide-spread panic in the West and a furor in the eastern press. His already ma-ligned and underfunded military would be further gutted in the resulting political firestorm. He intended to catch the Nez Perce and deal with them in the most severe manner so as to make an example of them and to raise the rather bruised status of the military in the minds of the politi-cians who controlled the funding and the public who controlled the politicians.

Right below General Sherman in the military chain of command were commanders of separate jurisdictional regions, called divisions or armies, of which three were directly involved in the pursuit of the Nez Perce—the Army of the Pacific, which stretched from the western ocean to the Bitter-roots, and included all of the Pacific Coast and Alaska; the Army of the Missouri, which covered most of the plains and Midwest; and the Army of the Atlantic, which covered the eastern seaboard, Appalachians, and origi-nal colonies.

General Irwin McDowell, based in San Francisco, was commander of the Army of the Pacific. The Army of the Missouri was commanded by General Phil Sheridan, based in Chicago.

When Sherman ordered Howard to follow the Nez Perce to the death and to do anything necessary to catch them, he was ordering Howard to cross from the jurisdiction of General McDowell into the jurisdiction of General Sheridan. It was unclear how much this order gave Howard the right to make demands of troops in General Sheridan's division in terms of deployment, supplies, and command.

Sheridan was quite happy to have the capture of the Nez Perce take place within his jurisdiction, but he was not disposed to have a com-mander from a different division operating with a free hand in his terri-tory, and he was certainly not disposed to let this commander determine where his troops should go, how supplies should be distributed, and how a battle with the Nez Perce should be conducted when his entire area was still alive with Sioux and Cheyenne warriors who had been only partially controlled and pacified. He also wanted any glory for the capture to come to him and his men.

The divisions themselves were divided into departments, each responsible for a smaller geographic area within the division. General Howard headed one of these smaller areas, the Department of the Columbia in the Army, or Division, of the Pacific. It included Washington, Oregon, and Alaska. His equivalent officer across the mountains in the Army, or Division, of the Missouri was General Terry, who was in charge of the Department of the Dakota, responsible for maintaining order on the northern plains and the upper Rocky Mountains. Terry and Howard had recently crossed swords over an issue of seniority, and neither was fond of the other.

Within the departments were districts, which were still smaller geographical units with their own commanding officers. General Gibbon, who had attacked at the Big Hole, was in charge of the District of Montana, one of the subregions in the Department of the Dakota. Just to his east lay the District of the Yellowstone—also in the Department of the Dakota—under Colonel Nelson Miles. Both men were under the command of General Terry.

Below the districts were the actual fighting units—regiments, battalions, companies, brigades—organized around their special responsibilities of artillery, infantry, and cavalry.

Sturgis was the leader of the Seventh Cavalry unit of the District of the Yellowstone. His orders came from Miles, Miles's orders came from Terry, Terry's orders came from Sheridan, Sheridan's orders came from Sherman. Once Sherman had confused the issue by sending Howard across into Sheridan's territory with the mandate to pursue the Nez Perce to the death, men like Sturgis were caught in a snarl of jurisdictional disputes and political intrigues at which they could only guess.

Sturgis and his Seventh Cavalry of 360 men had originally been heading to the Judith Basin in the northern buffalo country close to the Canadian border. General Sherman had ordered Sheridan to assist Howard in his efforts to stop Joseph, and Sheridan had passed this order down to Terry, who had passed it down to Gibbon and Miles. Miles had taken it upon himself to send his man, Sturgis, onto the buffalo plains to effect a blockade. If the Nez Perce did indeed head north toward Sitting Bull, any transit would have to take place through this broad, open, high plains country.

Meanwhile, Gibbon, who commanded the District of Montana, just west of Miles's area, was sending his own men into the field to engage in the pursuit. All across the northern tier, from the Rockies to the Dakota high plains, men were on the march in an effort to surround, engage, or otherwise forestall the Nez Perce people, who were still wandering in the high mountains of the Yellowstone.

The whole buffalo plains region north of the Missouri River—the country where Sturgis had been heading—was a sort of no-man's-land between settled America and the British possessions in Canada. American troops patrolled its gigantic open spaces as needed to keep such order as they could.

Since the buffalo plains were the hunting area of many tribes, it was not uncommon to see hunting parties of Sioux, Assiniboine, Gros Ventre, Cheyenne, and others moving across their vast empty expanse. No one had been too concerned about this until Sitting Bull had retreated across this territory into the British possessions and set up camp under the protection of the British crown. Now the northern buffalo plains were seen as a potential staging area. Sitting Bull, with his hatred of whites and his mounted warriors reported to number in the thousands, was considered to be the match that could ignite the tinderbox of Indian dissatisfaction, and the prospect of his moving south with his warriors was the greatest single fear of all the military and settlers in all the central and northern regions of the West.

Since the buffalo plains lay within Miles's jurisdiction, the task of keeping Sitting Bull at bay fell to him and his men. When he had sent Sturgis toward Judith Basin, the one great, broad valley that provided a north-south transit from the plains to the country below, he had been trying to put in place a loose blockade that would keep Joseph and Sitting Bull from unifying their forces.

But Gibbon, who was closer to telegraph lines and thus privy to better intelligence and information, had received word that the Nez Perce were still in the mountains of Yellowstone Park. Since this was the most current information available, and Sturgis's Seventh Cavalry was the nearest significant military force, he countermanded Miles's orders and instructed Sturgis and the Seventh to turn south to try to form their blockade at the base of the mountains that formed the boundary of the park.

Now Sturgis was camped at the base of the high, rugged Absarokas—

some of the tallest and most impenetrable mountains on the continent—under orders to stop an indeterminate number of Indians with indeterminate weaponry and to hold them back until they could be rolled up from behind by a general about whom he knew little and an army about which he knew even less. All he knew was that Gibbon had ordered him to establish this blockade, and it was up to him to make it work.

Because the Nez Perce had killed all the scouts who had tried to bring communications down from Howard, Sturgis lacked any meaningful intelligence. He was left to his own devices to determine which pass out of the mountains to block. He had ruled out the route Joseph had sought—north down the Yellowstone through the area of white settlements. That left only the two other canyons—the Clarks Fork and the Stinking Water. Both were deep, U-shaped glacial valleys flanked by granite walls thousands of feet high.

The Stinking Water appeared to be the easier of the two to descend. But Sturgis did not wish to take chances. He had given some thought to splitting his 360 troops so he could cover both possible canyon exits. But his sketchy information said that the Nez Perce warriors numbered over 400, and the stories of their ruthless fighting at the Big Hole and White Bird Canyon made him wary of confronting them with inferior forces. So instead of dividing his troops, he stationed them all near the Clarks Fork at a place where the two rivers lay only about forty easy miles apart, and he sent scouts out in both directions, figuring he could move south to the Stinking Water if either his scouts or a message from General Howard indicated that as the place where the Nez Perce would emerge.

In fact, the Nez Perce now had only slightly more than 100 surviving warriors—a number that Sturgis might well have been able to overcome even if he had split his troops. He surely could have held the people at bay until Howard managed to close on them from behind. But his lack of reliable information left him at the mercy of hearsay and his own dark memories of the Little Bighorn and the death of his son. He preferred to keep his troops together and take his chances.

Word soon arrived from some advance scouts that the route from the mountains into Clarks Fork canyon was impassable and that great clouds of dust had been seen on the route to the Stinking Water. So he quickly moved all his troops south toward that canyon escape route. Meanwhile, the Nez Perce slid and scrabbled their way down into the Clarks Fork canyon and easily made their escape from the mountains toward the land of their friends and allies, the Crow.

But if their escape from the army trap gave the Nez Perce any feelings of relief or excitement, those feelings were quickly dashed when Looking Glass returned with somber news. He had met with his friends, the Crow, and told them of the Nez Perce's desire to join with their people. They had greeted him warmly and spoken strongly of their deep friendship with the Nez Perce and of how they carried that friendship close to their hearts. But since the killing of the long-haired General Custer, the U.S. government had brought in more guns and built more soldier forts. Now, they said, soldiers were everywhere, and white settlers had moved everywhere into their land. They dared not help the Nez Perce for fear of starting a war with the white soldiers. There was talk among the whites, they told him, that the Nez Perce were trying to join with Sitting Bull to start a great Indian war. If the Crow helped the Nez Perce, they would be seen as part of this, and all would be killed, even women and children.

They admitted to Looking Glass that many of their warriors were now fighting on the side of the soldiers. It made their hearts heavy to do so, but they felt they had no choice. But if there was ever a battle, they promised they would shoot over Nez Perce's heads.

When this information reached the Nez Perce camp, everyone's spirits sank. None had expected that the Crow, who had sworn friendship and assistance, would turn their backs on their friends. It was because of the Crow promise that they had made this hard journey. It was because of the hope of sanctuary with the Crow that the people had kept their spirits strong.

Now they were alone in a strange country. They had no lodge poles for making shelter. Their horses were injured from hard travel and worn down from a sickness that made their wounds ooze and fester. The weather was becoming cold and blustery, with days of rain and snow and nights with winds that cut like the edge of a knife. Their people were sick, and soldiers were coming at them from all directions. Their own people and the people they had once considered friends were helping track them and trying to steal their horses. The land was getting flat, with no good places to hide and no good places to fight.

The chiefs and warriors again met in council. Their only chance, they believed, now lay with Sitting Bull, far to the north in the Old Woman

Country. But it was not a good chance. Only several years earlier Looking Glass had led Nez Perce warriors against Sioux warriors in the battle between the Sioux and the Crow. The Sioux and the Nez Perce had since met and made a pact of peace for all time. But it was clear to all that the pacts made between tribes could no longer be trusted. None knew if this Sioux promise would be stronger than the pacts of friendship made by the Flathead and the Crow, but it was known that Sioux hearts were black toward the white man and that they at least had not become teepee dogs for the white soldiers. On this slender hope, the chiefs decided to put trust in the Sioux promise and head north toward Sitting Bull in the Old Woman Land.

Poker Joe argued for continuing to move quickly. Much time had been wasted staying in the high mountains waiting for word from the Crow. This had given General Howard time to resupply and come up close behind, and winter was coming fast, as the days of rain and sleet attested.

Joseph remained quiet. He knew now that escape would be hard. The people were tired. Their clothing was worn. They had little food, and for shelter at night they huddled in gullies or hung blankets over bushes. Ahead lay only more days of cold rain and snow and freezing wind. This was no good life for the elders, for the small children and the newborns, for the sick and the wounded. Too many of the people had already been buried; too many more would have to be placed in shallow graves before the bands found their way to safety.

The pace was taking its toll on everyone. One young boy had become so exhausted on the trail that he had fallen asleep in his saddle, then slipped to the ground unnoticed. Only when his mother saw his horse with no rider did she go back to find him. He was still asleep on the ground where he had fallen.

The elders too were losing the strength to go on. Old women, old men, some blind, some with eighty winters of life, were telling their families to leave them behind. Sad and tearful good-byes were said, and the caravan moved on while the elder would huddle in a blanket to wait for certain death.

Looking Glass felt the burden heavily. His trust in his friends had brought the people to this point. Chief Charlot, Chief Tendoy of the Lemhi, the young chieftain son of his Crow friend, Double Pipe—all these he had trusted, and all had betrayed him. Now the people were suffering. He still stung from the dishonor of having been replaced as trail chief after the Big Hole. He still believed it was wrong to drive the people so hard. He would not have allowed this escape to become a death march.

But Poker Joe paid no attention to such concerns. His job was to save the people. If some had to die so others could live, this was how it had to be. He would lead them north, driving them hard, so they could get safely to Sitting Bull and the Old Woman Country. He did not want them to get caught either by soldiers or by the coming snows.

The land now had begun to flatten out. It was rumpled and furrowed—no longer mountainous but not yet the great open country of the buffalo plains. Buttes and mesas rose from the low sagebrush, offering good places for ambush. Vigilance now had to be total. Not only soldiers and the Bannocks but the Crow as well were arrayed against them. And this was the Crow's home country. They knew its landscape, its gullies and rivers and safety and danger, were closest to its spirit powers. They also were the best horse thieves of any tribe, able to sneak into the most heavily guarded camp and escape unnoticed. If the Nez Perce were not attentive at every moment, they could find themselves surrounded, cut off, or stripped of their horses, which were their only remaining possession and their only remaining hope.

Once again, the young warriors took it upon themselves to act as the protectors of the people. Any white person seen was killed, often brutally, often wantonly. One prospector was later found with a miner's pick driven through his neck.

Meanwhile, Sturgis was trying doggedly to catch up. It was his error in judgment that had allowed the Nez Perce to escape from the trap at Clarks Fork. When he and Howard had closed their noose and discovered that it contained no Nez Perce, Sturgis had become so upset that he swore he would go after the hostiles by himself if necessary and even if he had to do it on foot.

Howard, noting the spring in the step of Sturgis's fresher men and horses and sensing that their embarrassment might provide them with increased motivation, had assigned fifty of his best men and some extra artillery to Sturgis's command and sent them off in pursuit of the fleeing Indians. He would move his own tired, footsore, and dispirited troops more slowly behind them.

Sturgis was indeed filled with shame and determination. He raced off on the path the Nez Perce had taken, driving his contingent of 400 men relentlessly through the rain and cold. By the time they stopped for the first night, their clothes were soaked and their boots were filled with water. To a man they were exhausted and chilled to the bone. They had traveled over sixty miles, but they had not overtaken the Nez Perce.

The next morning Sturgis tried to get them to resume the pursuit with the same intensity. But the horses were stiff and sore, and his men were weary and listless. He pushed them hard for a while, but when they had to ford the cold waters of the Yellowstone River, it was clear that they had no more will for this hard travel. Reluctantly, the colonel ordered them to dismount, unsaddle, and tether their horses. It did no good to catch up with the Indians if the men who caught them were too cold and exhausted to fight. These Indians were a formidable foe. To attack them when your men were tired and dispirited was to risk another Little Bighorn. He did not want to lead other men's sons into the same tragic death his son had experienced because of Custer's false bravado.

So he allowed his men to stop and abandon the pursuit. The Nez Perce had gotten away. Much as he had wanted to catch them, that accomplishment, if it was to belong to anyone, it was to fall to someone else. That someone else was likely to be Colonel Nelson Miles, his commanding officer, who at that moment was camped 150 miles to the east at a crude collection of log buildings called the Tongue River Cantonment.

Colonel Nelson A. Miles, the commander of the District of the Yellowstone in the Department of the Dakota in Phil Sheridan's Army of the Missouri, was the man who had sent Sturgis off toward the Judith Basin before Gibbon had ordered him to change course.

Sturgis did not like Miles. He thought him arrogant and ambitious. It did not help that Miles looked upon Custer, the man who had cost Sturgis's son his life, as the very model of what a good Indian fighter should be. But Sturgis had concurred with Howard's conviction that Miles should be alerted after the pincer movement at the base of the Clarks Fork had failed.

So General Howard had sent messengers ahead to Miles at the same time he had sent Sturgis on his pursuit. He knew that a failure by Sturgis would leave nothing but three hundred miles of open country between the Nez Perce and the safety of Canada. He also knew that if they crossed into Canada, they would cross at the very place where Sitting Bull was now camped, out of the reach of U.S. soldiers. The linkup that the entire West feared, and that he had been charged with preventing, would take place. If Sturgis could not overtake the hostiles, only Colonel Miles remained to keep them from making the border.

Howard knew Miles well, and he respected him. Miles had served under him during the Civil War and had been with him at Fair Oaks when Howard had lost his arm. There was no doubt in Howard's mind that Miles was a good and capable soldier. There was also no doubt in his mind that Miles was extremely ambitious. The colonel had married the niece of General Sherman and had done everything possible to rise in the ranks, despite his lack of a West Point pedigree.

In the Civil War and post–Civil War army, generalships were almost always reserved for graduates of the military academies. Howard knew that a general's star was the single, overriding goal of Miles's military career and that a success like the capture of Joseph would more than make up for Miles's lack of military pedigree. If someone else was to have the glory of capturing Joseph and the Nez Perce, Howard would be pleased to have it be his old subordinate.

But his thinking was not altogether altruistic. He was also well aware that Miles's ambition might be the single greatest asset they had in their final push to catch these elusive hostiles. Miles's hunger for that general's star would make him drive his men without compromise. If anyone could accomplish the impossible task of overtaking and bringing the Nez Perce to account, it was Miles. After all, he had brought the Sioux and Cheyenne to bay by attacking them in winter when no other soldier in the West dared undertake winter campaigns, and he had been so single-minded in pushing his men that on one occasion they had attacked the Sioux while badly outnumbered, simply to get to the food stores they knew the Sioux possessed. Such a man could perhaps accomplish what thus far had proven impossible and thus assist in fulfilling Sherman's command to Howard to capture the Nez Perce no matter what the cost.

Miles himself was fully cognizant of the opportunity that was slowly presenting itself. He knew how crucial this capture was for both the reputation and political prestige of an army that had fallen out of favor in the eyes of the public. The man who brought down Chief Joseph would be the toast of the military and the pride of the nation. He wanted to be that man.

But he also had been loathe to take his eye off Sitting Bull. The growing national obsession with Joseph and the Nez Perce was real, but it was nothing compared to the nation's obsession with Sitting Bull. Though the pursuit of the Nez Perce was galvanizing the nation's attention, sympathies ran both ways. To some, Joseph was still the ruthless, escaping savage, while to others he was the heroic leader of a desperate band of innocent people being mercilessly hounded for nothing more than wanting to live in accord with their traditional way of life. Some of the public was now rooting for his escape, while others clamored for his capture.

About Sitting Bull there was no such ambivalence. He was the murderer of Custer, the desecrater of bodies and committer of unspeakable abominations on corpses. He was every dark terror in the breast of every American who dreamed of seeing the land pacified and the nation linked from coast to coast. In press accounts he was the leader of a thousand warriors with long-range rifles, ready to swoop down from his Canadian refuge into the sparsely settled West, taking scalps and inciting fifteen thousand Indians to rise up against the scattered settlers. Since that Canadian refuge lay directly north of Miles's jurisdiction, Miles had been unwilling to commit all his forces to the pursuit of the Nez Perce while Sitting Bull was poised directly above him. Capturing the Lakota chief, or at least holding him at bay, remained his most important task.

But the message from Howard and Sturgis had changed his focus. Sturgis's Seventh Cavalry had been the one line of defense preventing a linkup of Joseph and Sitting Bull. Now that word reached him that Joseph had gotten past Sturgis, he realized that the Nez Perce were moving unimpeded toward the unification with Sitting Bull that everyone feared.

With his old commander, Howard, fairly pleading for his military assistance and the prospect of a major Indian fighting force being created to threaten his jurisdiction, he had all the reason he needed to take to the field himself. He would have a chance at the capture that would make him the toast of the nation, and in so doing he would secure the safety of the entire northern plains. This was exactly the kind of opportunity for which he believed he had been born.

Miles had dreamed of being a soldier from his earliest days as a grocery clerk in Boston. He had even hired an elderly French army veteran to tutor him in the skills of military drill and discipline. He had enlisted as a volunteer in the Civil War and had distinguished himself with both his skill and bravery, even earning the prized Medal of Honor. When he had heard of the debacle at the Little Bighorn, he had requested posting to the West and had set himself immediately to the task of studying the Indians and their ways. He made his men establish camps outside in the winter because he felt that if Indians could live and thrive in such conditions, so could his men. He studied the Indian character closely. And he spent long hours analyzing the strategic realities of warfare on the great, open buffalo plains.

The buffalo plains were unlike any other place in the West. A vast, undulating earthen sea of blowing grasses and hills and swales, they admitted of little natural cover for moving troops or large groups of people. A man on a promontory—whether a soldier or an Indian—could easily see for fifty miles. A campfire—by its plume of daytime smoke or its flicker of light in the midnight darkness—could reveal the location of a person a day's journey away.

Military maneuvers on such a landscape required a whole different mind-set and range of tactics than fighting where there was cover. One had to use the natural features to advantage—starting fires for diversions and cover, keeping behind hills and promontories when moving groups of men, knowing how to distinguish the tiny specks of distant buffalo herds from similar specks of distant enemies, keeping the dust clouds from your horses to a minimum, and knowing where good campsites and sources of water could support your troops. Skills in scouting, establishing effective supply lines, and understanding angles of pursuit were also essential. A commander who could move his men without being noticed, keep them watered, fed, clothed, and armed, and position them intelligently could accomplish much in this terrain.

Miles believed he was such a commander. He had proven it many times since his arrival in the West. It was he who had driven Sitting Bull north of the border, and it was he who had contained and pacified the Sioux and Crow and Cheyenne. Like his old friend Custer, he believed he understood Indians and their ways, and like Custer he was fearless in his leading of men. But unlike Custer, he knew the line between courage and rashness. He had full confidence that his reputation as the best of the army's Indian fighters was well deserved. The chance to capture Joseph was exactly the kind of opportunity he had been seeking to solidify that reputation and earn himself the general's star he believed was his due.

If Howard was too slow and Sturgis too timid, he himself was neither. He would move his men with speed and decisiveness across the 150 miles from their garrison into the path where Joseph and his people were traveling. If he was not too late, which he feared he already was, he would get ahead of this group of hostiles and use his military skills to bring this chase to an end.

He had received Howard's message by courier at 6:00 p.m. on the night of September 17. With hardly a pause to reflect, he had begun outfitting his forces and establishing the supplies and weaponry he would need for the pursuit. By sunrise the next morning, he had outfitted thirty-six supply wagons and two ambulance wagons, readied his pack mules, horses, and field artillery, and ferried all these goods and troops across the Yellowstone River in preparation for a morning departure. He had also sent off messages to his superior, General Terry, regarding his intentions, and had arranged for more supplies to be sent by steamer and dropped off at the Missouri River halfway to where he expected the Nez Perce to be.

Before the sun was barely over the horizon, his contingent of horses, wagons, pack mules, and more than 500 men was winding its way up bluffs on the far side of the Yellowstone. His intention was simple. He would march them without compromise until they either met the Nez Perce or received word that the hostiles had achieved their goal and made it across the border into Canada.

While Miles was receiving Howard's message, a very different scene was unfolding 150 miles up the Yellowstone. Sturgis's worn-out men were camped on the riverbank, drying their clothes and trying to fortify themselves on the meager rations they had carried. Howard was limping his footsore, dispirited troops north in slow and labored pursuit of Sturgis, and the tired, despondent Nez Perce, who had only recently crossed the river themselves, were camped a few miles ahead of Sturgis in a wide canyon that formed a broad passageway from the river to the high, open buffalo plains. None knew the location of the others.

For the Nez Perce, the journey had reached a point of crisis. The young men were once again killing wantonly, convinced, often with good cause, that all whites were eyes for the military. The people were almost too tired to move, but they knew it was too dangerous to stop. The horses were so exhausted and worn-out that many had to be left behind. Nerves were frayed; tempers were flaring. All the latent tensions between the bands were beginning to surface.

Joseph, who until now had remained quietly in the background, began to speak up for the health and welfare of the people. The ceaseless killing by the young men was getting them nowhere, and as many of their people were dying from the hard marches as from encounters with the soldiers. His band had not sought this flight and had not countenanced all this killing. They had wanted peace. If White Bird and Toohoolhoolzote wanted revenge and killing, that was fine for them. He was more concerned with tired bodies and weary spirits than he was with angry hearts and warrior pride.

But the young warriors were once again beyond listening. It was necessary that they go out each day and scout a broad perimeter around the people, but once out of camp they could not be controlled. They burned white people's camps, burned their houses, burned their hay bales, burned their corrals. Smoldering ruins were greeting the soldiers all along the line of pursuit.

The place where the people had camped was a flat-bottomed, mile-wide dry creek bed of sagebrush and alkali, known as Canyon Creek, that ran like a corridor up from the Yellowstone River to the open buffalo plains six miles to the north. With high, chalky escarpments on either side, it was a dangerous place for ambush, made all the more so because the cliff walls came close together at the far north end where the canyon gave way to open country.

But the people were not concerned. They knew General Howard was still far back beyond the Yellowstone and that the river crossing would slow him even further. He offered no threat to them in this camp. The warriors had even taken to mocking him, calling him General Day-and-a-Half-Behind. They would keep good watch, but they had no fear of ambush at his hands.

But even without strong pursuit from the soldiers, the camp was now a hard place. Many elders were sick and blind, their health failing rapidly, and many small children had lost their parents. Most of these children had found shelter with uncles or aunts or other families, but there were still too few blankets, and many children, as well as many of the elders, were constantly cold and hungry. The women had all they could do to keep everyone warm and fed. It also fell to them to prepare the dead for burial and to aid the old and blind who could not take care of themselves.

The hard daily pace meant that the people barely had any time for rest between setting up camp late at night and breaking it early in the morning. Firewood too was becoming difficult to find, and the water was alkaline and not good for cooking and drinking. If the men brought back no game from hunting, food was scarce. All knew that the warriors must eat first because it was they who protected the people. Oftentimes, after the warriors and the elders and children had been fed, there was nothing left for the women themselves.

The young boys too were having a difficult time with the horses. The herd had developed a sickness that kept their sores from healing, and it was not easy to find good grass for them to eat. Getting them to move each day was becoming harder and harder. When the spirit of the horse gave out, the spirit of the Nez Perce would give out.

Only the young warriors were taking any pleasure in the current situation. They left in the morning and roamed through the hills, looking for any white settlers or any sign of possible trouble. On this morning, after backtracking down the canyon, they found a stagecoach standing near a small log building on the trail that ran beside the river. There were no people around, but the horses were grazing in a nearby corral, and bags of mail and the passengers' luggage were still on the stage. Not concerning themselves with the whereabouts of the passengers or station master, the warriors lit the building and some haystacks on fire and rehitched the horses, then crowded on top of the stage and rode at breakneck speed back toward the main camp, scattering pieces of mail and clothing all along the canyon.

In the distance, some of Sturgis's scouts, who had just crossed the river a few miles farther down, saw the plume of smoke and raced to see what was happening. They caught a glimpse of the retreating stage with its Nez Perce riders heading up the flat sagebrush canyon bottom. Far ahead, maybe four miles up the valley, they could make out the entire retreating Nez Perce party.

They sent messengers riding full speed back to the river where Sturgis and his men were just beginning to unsaddle their horses and accept the reality of their humiliating failure to overtake the Nez Perce. The cries of "Indians, Indians!" brought them back to life and sent them running for their mounts. Perhaps they yet would be able to overtake and capture the hostiles.

But Sturgis's scouts had not gone unnoticed by the Nez Perce. Their own scouts had seen the riders watching them from behind. They did not know who these soldiers were—Howard should have been far back on the other side of the river—but they were well aware from past travels to the northern buffalo plains that this canyon was gradually narrowing and that whoever arrived at the narrow mouth first could control the exit. Whoever these soldiers were, they could not be allowed to beat the people to this opening. If they did, they could set up a few riflemen on the bluffs and create a blockade from which there could be no escape.

The day was cold and rainy, with strong, sharp winds. The people had just finished packing when they saw their back scouts giving the blanket signal for imminent attack. Knowing they dared not lose the race to the canyon mouth, they lifted the wounded and sick onto travois and began their desperate run north up the canyon. Some of the elders were almost too weak to ride, and many of the women had to travel with an infant strapped to their back and a toddler holding on for dear life around their waist. But there was no time to worry about comfort. They had to beat the soldiers to the narrow gap where the canyon opened out onto the buffalo plains.

Joseph rode among the people, trying to organize the departure to make sure that no children or horses were left behind, while the warriors whipped their horses up the side of a tall, flat-topped mesa that rose in the middle of the canyon. From that vantage point they would be able to shoot down on any pursuing soldiers, holding them at bay while the people and the horses moved along the canyon floor.

Soon the soldiers were sighted coming up the canyon several hundred strong. They were mounted men, not foot soldiers, and would be able to overtake the people if they were not held off. From their hiding places on the mesa, the Nez Perce shot the soldiers off their horses one by one. The sound of the gunfire echoed off the canyon walls, making it difficult for the soldiers to identify the number or the location of the snipers. Poker Joe added to the confusion with his heavy fifteen-pound rifle, which had a concussion so loud that the soldiers thought perhaps they were being fired upon by a cannon.

Uncertain how many warriors they were confronting and the nature of the weaponry being arrayed against them, Sturgis's commander, Major Lewis Merrill, ordered his charging cavalry to dismount, form a skirmish line, and advance on foot. The act amazed the Nez Perce, who feared men on horses far more than foot soldiers. But it made their task easier. They now had only to hold these men down while the people made good on their escape.

Leaving a few warriors behind to keep up sporadic firing, the others rode back to join the fleeing families. Every time the soldiers came too close, the Nez Perce shooters retreated, leaving the exhausted soldiers no one to fight when they finally climbed the buttes or made their way up to the rocky promontories from which the shooting had come.

The dismounted soldiers followed the escaping Indians as best they could through the rain and cold, but the terrain was rutted with hillocks and folds and washes and ravines. The Nez Perce easily outdistanced them while the soldiers managed only to march themselves into a state of exhaustion. They were only one day removed from their forced march of sixty miles, and they were still cold, hungry, and tired. Many of them were young and confused and frightened by this confrontation with an unseen foe. The veterans among them were almost tearful with rage that they had been forced to dismount when a real confrontation and possible capture had been only minutes away.

But Sturgis also had recognized the strategic realities of the situation. In an attempt to head off the fleeing Nez Perce, he had sent another group of mounted soldiers along the bluff on top of the canyon wall in an effort to secure the canyon mouth before the Nez Perce got there. But his forces were now spread too thin. There were too few men on the ridgetop to pose any threat to the Nez Perce by themselves, and since the men in the bottom of the canyon had dismounted and were now on foot and unable to catch up, the men on the top of the canyon wall finally had to withdraw.

Eventually, Sturgis gave up the pursuit. This had been his one best chance. But his men were tired and wet, he had outraced his supply wagons, leaving his troops with nothing to eat and nothing to drink except the alkali-laden groundwater, and he now had wounded he needed to tend and transport. Once again, the Nez Perce had beaten him in a footrace. They had made it to the narrow canyon mouth. He would take up the chase again when his men were rested. But for now, the Nez Perce had made their escape.

For the Nez Perce, it had been a strange encounter. They had not expected these soldiers, but neither had they felt threatened by them. The soldiers had shown no stomach for a fight and no intelligent plan of attack. A few well-placed riflemen had easily been able to hold them at bay. But it was unclear who they were or what their intentions had been.

Nonetheless, to stop any further pursuit, the warriors pushed boulders across the narrow mouth of the canyon and blocked the trail with stumps and brush. Since there was no easy way up the canyon wall, they knew that the soldiers would have to either turn back or remove the rocks and brush before continuing. If a few warriors remained high up among the rocks of the canyon, they could snipe at any soldiers who tried to remove the brush. That would slow any pursuit until the people were safely onto the high, open buffalo country. Even if the soldiers did break through, the Nez Perce knew that pursuit would not be strong. White men had to have three meals a day or their spirits became weak. They would not follow hard until their supply wagons caught up. By then the people would be far ahead. Only the bluffs and badlands along the Missouri, several days' journey ahead, could now slow their passage into the Old Woman Country.

With the soldiers blocked behind them and warrior sharpshooters poised in the rocks above the narrow canyon mouth, the Nez Perce spent a comfortable night in preparation for the next leg of the journey. Though they were not well supplied with food, they knew that it was only a short journey to the buffalo plains where the warriors would be able to catch enough buffalo and antelope to keep them fed. They could also make new robes and blankets from the hides of the animals the warriors killed. The children and elders would again be warm; the people would again be well fed and comfortable.

The next morning they awoke to another day of cold, driving rain. The Missouri was only several days ahead, and Canada only several more after that. Yellow Wolf, Ollokot, and several warriors stayed behind to scout the back trail and hold off any advancing soldiers trying to make it through the canyon gap.

But soon another threat revealed itself. On the adjacent hillsides, far behind, Yellow Wolf noticed groups of Indians moving among the scattered pines. He assumed they were Snake or Assiniboine, the people the Nez Perce called "Walk-Around Sioux." Both frequented this country on buffalo hunts and were likely to be in the area. But upon closer approach, Yellow Wolf saw that these were Crow warriors. With their pasted-on hair, sometimes so long as to touch the ground when they walked, and their war lances adorned with eagle feathers, they were easily recognized.

The chiefs and warriors were upset. They rode up and confronted the Crow. The Crow responded that they were not really fighting—that the Nez Perce should travel slowly and the Crow would soon come ahead and join them. But none of the Nez Perce believed that this was anything more than a ruse. These men were clearly scouting for the soldiers and hoping to have a chance to steal Nez Perce horses.

There was a brief skirmish, with a bit of halfhearted shooting, before the Crow galloped off, leaving the Nez Perce to return to the main camp and tell the people it was as Looking Glass had said—the Crow were no different from the Flathead, the Bannock, and the Shoshone, other tribes that had promised friendship but had sold their honor for a life of safety and white-man ease.

But it was the Crow skill as horse thieves that most concerned the Nez Perce. Crow warriors could move silently through the grass, sneak in among the herd, and cull animals without even being noticed. If they were now riding with the soldiers, a whole new level of vigilance would be needed.

With this new dark knowledge in their hearts, the remaining Nez Perce continued into the growing northern cold. They had already been forced to leave many lame and worn-out horses on the side of the trail, cutting their hooves so they would be of no value to the soldiers or their Indian scouts. Other animals wandered off each night and had to be left behind because there was no time to search for them before the morning departure.

The Crow could be seen riding on the distant ridges, numbering sometimes in the hundreds, often with the Bannock at their side. At night they would sneak down and steal the resting horses, just as the Nez Perce had feared. During the day, they milled about at a distance, sometimes coming down from the ridges and scaring the women. The Nez Perce warriors would chase them away but dared not pursue. They needed to stay near the horses so other Crow would not sneak in and steal from the herd while it was left unguarded. But even so, many healthy horses were lost.

This continued loss of horses wore at the spirit of the people. The herd was their wealth; the herd was their hope. When the horses were strong, the people were strong. When the herd was weak, sick, and lame, the people were weak, sick, and lame. Little by little, their legs and heart were being taken from them.

The journey had been going on for almost a hundred days now. It had started in early summer when the waters in the rivers ran high. Now the time of the snows was coming near. At night, the water in the buffalo wallows was skimming with ice; in the morning the hills were blanketed with frost. On the far mountains the snow line was descending, and many days they rode through a steady downpour of wind-driven rain mixed with slush and snow.

The country through which they were now passing was broad and empty, made up of grassy hills that rolled endlessly toward a distant horizon. Sometimes, in the distance, herds of buffalo or antelope could be seen moving like small dots across the hills and plains. When the sun came out it was weak and without heat, and many days the skies were heavy bellied with gray, threatening clouds.

The scouts watched the buffalo herds closely. In this country, the buffalo could give them many messages. A group of soldiers moving behind hills could cause the buffalo to stampede. And the thickness of the hair on the buffalo could tell them about the nearness and depth of the coming winter.

The Crow and other soldier Indians were always a worry. They continued to raid the camp at night, thinning the herd. One night the Nez Perce caught a young Crow boy trying to steal a horse. They cut his hair, placed him on a worn-out mount, and sent him back to his people with the message that the Crow were old women and cowards and that the Nez Perce neither feared nor respected them.

In one instance, they encountered a group of river Crow out hunting buffalo for the winter. They killed some of the hunters, stole all their horses, and took as much of the dried buffalo meat as they could carry. They allowed the chief, Dumb Bull, to escape. His shame would be more fitting punishment than death, and all his people would know that the Nez Perce did not even consider him worthy of being killed.

Eventually, pursuit by the Crow and the other Indian scouts lessened. Their numbers were fewer, their raids more halfhearted. Many had gotten enough horses to satisfy themselves; others had no stomach for fighting with the desperate and angry Nez Perce. They had done their part for the soldiers; now they would go home. One by one, they dropped back, then disappeared altogether.

The soldiers, who were plodding along far behind, were also weary. The infantry was poorly equipped for the growing cold. They had only their summer jackets, and many now were without boots and socks. The cavalry was not faring much better. Their horses had developed a hoof disease, so they too were reduced to crossing this great open country on foot, leading their horses behind them. The Nez Perce or some other tribe had burned the prairie, leaving no grass for the horses to forage and no easy way to track the movements of the hostiles. Many of the men were sick from drinking the alkali water, and the enemy was nowhere to be seen. They had no more heart for this pursuit.

The white scouts that Howard had retained were mostly seasoned civilians who knew the country well, and they were disgusted with the army's sluggardly pursuit. They were convinced that Howard was a fool and that Merrill's timidity back at the canyon bottom—ordering his men to dismount rather than to charge—had cost them their best chance at catching the Nez Perce. Many were on renewable one-month contracts, and rode off as soon as their time was up, proclaiming that Uncle Sam's men weren't fast enough, smart enough, or brave enough for Indian fighting.

With his Indian scouts gone, his white scouts leaving, and his own troops almost too worn-out to travel, Sturgis brought his men to a halt. They were so sore and tired that they were strung out over ten miles, with those in the rear not arriving in camp until long after dark. Since their confrontation in the canyon, his men had never encountered another Indian other than their own scouts.

They set up camp on the banks of the slow, winding Musselshell River, thankful to be able to rest near water that they could drink without getting ill. There they subsisted on horsemeat, half rations, and tart berries picked from bushes near the riverbank while waiting for General Howard to arrive with supplies and reinforcements.

Soon some of Howard's men did arrive, carrying five hundred pounds of beef the general had sent forward when his advance scouts had informed him of Sturgis's predicament. Howard himself had detoured to a nearby fort to drop off his wounded and pick up more supplies for his own and Sturgis's worn-out men.

By the time he and the rest of his troops finally caught up to the group, it had been a week since Sturgis had encountered the Nez Perce in the dry canyon. Neither of the men held out any hope that they would be able to catch the fleeing Nez Perce before they made it to Canada, now only 180 miles due north. But Howard had sworn to Sherman that he would chase the hostiles until they were caught or managed to get across the border, and this was what he intended to do. It was possible that they had already made it to the border. In any case, he no longer looked upon this pursuit as a preface to military engagement but rather as a herding action designed to make sure that the hostiles really did leave the country. Indeed, there were those among his men, and many higher up in the military as well, who claimed that this was the outcome they should have sought in the first place.

Howard decided that his best course was to advance with a small group of men made up mostly of Sturgis's troops, who, though exhausted, were still fresher than his own foot-weary soldiers, who had been on the trail for almost five months. His own men would go back by river and ultimately by rail to their home posts in Oregon and Idaho. Many were now privately expressing sympathy for the courage of the Nez Perce, and many others were expressing open disdain for the task they had been assigned. They had not signed up to get trapped in a 40-below-zero winter on the high Montana plains.

Howard did not take Sturgis to task for his decision to rest, and it was not simply out of respect for the men's exhaustion. Both he and Sturgis had come to the hard realization that the Nez Perce sped up their travel when the army sped up its pursuit. By slowing their own pace, they believed they perhaps could keep the hostiles in the country until Colonel Miles, marching vigorously on his diagonal line from the distant Tongue River encampment, could overtake them and pin them down. Howard could then come up from behind with his men, and he and Miles could share the glory of the capture, if indeed there was to be any capture at all.

The question now was whether capture was even possible. Miles himself had stated that he held out faint hope for success, and Howard, by his decision to send many of his troops home, was making his feelings on the matter clear. However, he still clung to the slight possibility that success was possible. He had even turned to prayer, beseeching God to grant the expedition success, "even at the expense of another's receiving credit. . . ." But with or without God's help, he would persevere. As a military man, it was his only honorable choice.

13

"Our People Are Hungry and Weak"

A HUNDRED MILES farther ahead, the Nez Perce sensed the weakening pursuit. Attacks by the Crow and Bannock had dwindled to almost nothing. The rear scouts saw little in the way of soldier movements to concern them. Their struggle now lay with the great emptiness of the buffalo plains.

Within the camp some felt that their spirit powers had saved them. Warriors like Yellow Wolf, who had received a vision in his youth that he could not be killed by bullets, had survived direct attacks by soldiers and the Crow. Old Wahnistas Aswetesk, whose body had been riddled by bullets in the battle of the Big Hole and had emitted steam rather than blood, not only was still alive but had healed. Many others too had been kept alive by their *wayakin*s. Though the trail was littered with the graves of their dead, the medicine power of the people still seemed to be working. Their good fortune at finding the camp of Dumb Bull with its horses and store of dried meat had increased this feeling. There was more talk that the time had come to slow down and let the people rest.

But Poker Joe was insistent. He knew the soldiers, he knew their ways. Until the Nez Perce crossed the border into the Old Woman Country, they should not feel safe. As long as he was leader, they would not have easy rest.

The vast empty spaces allowed the groups to travel separately, each leaving when it saw fit and taking the route it chose. Many among them knew this country well, and the distant landmarks of low-lying mountain ranges and lines of hills allowed them to designate camping places where all would gather at the end of the day. By moving in small groups, they could hunt more effectively and find better forage for their horses as well as confuse any pursuing soldiers. But it also increased the divisions that were beginning to show in the hearts of the people.

The one constant was Joseph, who been steadfast and unwavering in his role as camp chief. The bands could disagree about the wisdom of the young warriors' actions; they could differ on the leadership of Poker Joe and the speed with which he was driving them; they could be for or against the way Looking Glass had led them. But none could fault the steady hand and calming influence that Joseph had exercised in guiding the young boys to care for the horses and in making sure that the orphaned children were cared for and the elders clothed and fed.

All knew that he had opposed this war, and many now shared this feeling. They were moving north into unknown land to join with a tribe they did not know well and with whom they shared no strong bond. The peace that had been made between their people and the Sioux was a peace of warriors, not a peace of camp friendship. They were unsure how they would be received and what they would find. All the promises of safety and sanctuary had come down to joining with a tribe very different from themselves and with whom they shared little except a common refusal to turn to white ways.

Joseph's constant calls to turn back to their own country—calls that had been discounted by the other chiefs in council decisions—now seemed like the voice of wisdom. His wish had become the wish of many of the people. Though the dream of return was no longer possible here in the high buffalo plains, with soldiers behind them and winter in front of them, none forgot whose voice it had been that had spoken so strongly and fondly for remaining in their home country. If they must die, would it not have been better to do so in land that would accept their bones rather than in unknown country, where coyotes and Bannocks insulted the dead and disturbed their spirits? Would they not have done better to listen to Joseph than to the chiefs with their grand promises of sanctuary and to the young warriors with their hollow boasts of honor?

Joseph himself remained a calm, quiet presence, caring for the camp and doing what he could to keep up the people's hopes and spirits. All knew that he understood their burdens. He had an infant daughter only several months old and an older daughter just moving into womanhood. He knew how fragile young lives were and how important it was to protect the helpless. He had helped bury his brother's wife and had shared in grieving for the dead. While other chiefs had been off scouting or fighting, he had stayed among the families and assisted in the frantic packing and frightened retreat. He had helped distribute food and had seen the hunger in the faces of the sick and the elderly. He was not blinded by false dreams of honor or bitter feelings of revenge. His eyes were always on the people, and his heart was always open to their suffering.

With uncertain hearts they moved toward the last great barrier that stood between them and the border to the Old Woman Land. It was the fractured landscape and turbid river known as the Place of the Caves of the Red Paint. Once across this difficult terrain, they would find only rolling high plains for the remaining eighty miles to the border.

The river, known to the whites as the Missouri, wound brown and muddy through the bottom of its own canyon, which cut like a deep furrow into the rolling flatness of the buffalo plains. Travelers approaching from either side, accustomed to the vast distances and hypnotic emptiness of the high plains, were suddenly confronted with a complex welter of hillocks and dry washes that extended downward for miles until it ended at the twisting, brown ribbon of river far below. Seen from the rim of the plains, these descending hills looked like a rumpled maze of dry mud mounds and sand spires dropped upon the earth by a giant, careless hand. In reality, they were tall, peaked cones and pyramids of desiccated rock and earth, sculpted into fantastic shapes and layers by eons of erosion as the river had ground its way downward into the earth. Passage through them meant navigating a labyrinth of tight draws and canyons on trails barely wider than horse paths.

It was a confusing, barren, inhospitable landscape, relentlessly hot in summer, frigid in winter, and slick and mucky and nearly impassable after even the slightest rain. The white men called this country the "dreaded badlands," or the Missouri Breaks, and anyone wishing to descend from the plains to the tiny ribbon of river or ascend from the river to the plains high above had to make their way through it in order to reach the buffalo grasslands on either side.

Nez Perce buffalo hunters had forded this river many times on their way to and from the great northern hunting grounds. The spot where they always forded lay at a bend in the river where several cottonwood-studded islands provided shade and rest. It was also the only place shallow enough

for the people to cross on foot and horseback without stopping to construct bull boats to ferry themselves and their goods to the other side.

But this shallowness had made this bend a significant spot for the
white travelers as well. The Missouri was the mother river of the West—the
river into which all the others fed and the route that could be followed all
the way from St. Louis into the little-known western interior. It was the
route of exploration, the route of supply. As settlers had moved to the interior, and as soldiers had been sent to protect them, it was the Missouri
and its tributaries that had carried them. As travelers and supplies came
up from the growing settlements at Council Bluffs and Bismarck, it was
the Missouri and its tributaries that brought them. Troops were ferried on
it, goods were carried on it. Steamboats, flatboats, and all manner of wa-
tercraft navigated its muddy, brown flow during times of high water.
Sometimes as many as forty steamboats could be traveling its wild, uninhabited upper reaches here in Montana Territory.

But though it was the mother river, it was also the river that looped farthest to the north and so was less hospitable than some of its lesser tributaries farther to the south. Aside from Fort Buford, which lay almost 300
miles to the east in the Dakota Territory, and several smaller military encampments, the few stopping places in this upper Missouri were mostly
rude log huts or temporary encampments of tents—lonely, widely separated embarking and debarking points for troops, goods, and the occasional settler moving to or from the interior. The closest thing to a
meaningful settlement on this upper river was Fort Benton, 120 miles to
the west from the wide bend where the Nez Perce intended to cross. Between Fort Benton and the crossing point there was nothing but the
turbid, murky river running between uninhabited banks of rocky outcroppings and woolly scrub.

Fort Benton, like many western towns, was a huddled outpost that sat
lonely and isolated in a vast, forbidding landscape. It had grown from a
converted military fort into a thriving commercial settlement of more
than 600 residents because it was the end point for steamboat travel up the
Missouri and the beginning of the Mullan wagon road, which bumped its
way for 600 miles to the settlements of eastern Washington. Unfortunately
for the town's residents and for the military and far-flung settlers who
relied on the town for supplies, the Missouri was not a cooperative river. It
was so full of shallows and shifting sandbars that the steamboats that

plied it had to be equipped with large, insectlike, hydraulic arms that could be extended from their sides to lift the boats out of the water and over spots too shallow to be navigated.

But even with this mechanical assistance, and despite the constant efforts of teams of soldiers to dredge channels and remove snags and deadfall, there was a point beyond which steamboat travel could not take place when the water level in the river fell too low. This point was Cow Island, the wide, shallow bend in the river toward which the Nez Perce were heading.

As a result, the Cow Island landing had become a supply drop where goods were offloaded and kept under tarps until their owners, whether military or settlers, could arrange for their transport. Clothing, bedding, foodstuffs, cooking utensils, fabric, medicine, tobacco, alcohol—whatever the people in Fort Benton and beyond needed—had to be left on this unprotected, uninhabited riverbank 120 miles from their destination. And since hauling anything other than the most minimal goods up the narrow trails through the ravines of the badlands was almost impossible by horse-drawn wagon, a lively commerce of what were called "bull trains" had sprung up.

These bull trains were series of heavy, groaning wagons hooked together like train cars and pulled by teams of oxen, sometimes sixteen strong. They would load up at river's edge, then slowly creak their way up the narrow trails through the breaks to the plains high above. From there they would proceed through the rolling buffalo country to Fort Benton.

Their passage along the narrow trails up through the badlands was so slow as to be almost painful. Passengers who had taken the steamboat on their way to the settlements often walked to the top and waited rather than suffer through the slow, agonizing climb at the pace of the bull-drawn wagons.

On the day that the Nez Perce arrived on the ridge overlooking this great valley of badlands, a bull train of fifteen heavily loaded wagons had just begun its climb from the river flats to the plains, and the remaining piles of goods on the riverbank had reached over twenty-five feet in height. Normally, only a few men who worked for the steamboat line stayed camped at the river drop point. But on this day, there happened to be a contingent of twelve soldiers, eight of whom had been stationed there to protect military goods and four who had come down the river from the direction of Fort Benton to pick up rations for a group of men who were trying to clear a channel a few miles upstream.

Upon descending through the narrow trails of the breaks, the lead men of the Nez Perce looked across the river and saw the small collection of military tents and tall piles of goods that stood directly in their path. The five lead chiefs called their men together for a discussion. There was no other good place to cross. If they were to move to the other side and continue on to the Old Woman Country, it had to be done here.

It was agreed that there should be no fighting if at all possible. Enough people had been hurt, and the wounded were suffering enough from the cold. These few tents did not speak of many soldiers. Perhaps if the warriors did not shoot first, the soldiers would not be inclined to fight.

The chiefs sent an advance group of twenty warriors across the river to stand between the soldiers' tents and the people as they crossed. A strong show of strength might stop the soldiers from taking any rash action.

The warriors rode calmly across the half-mile-wide expanse of brown, slow-moving water and set up a picket line. The people then began crossing the river behind them. Though the piles of goods that the soldiers were guarding were covered with tarps, it was possible to see food, cooking gear, and cloth protruding from around the edges.

Since the raid on the camp of the River Crow, the people had eaten only dried buffalo meat, and most of their camp goods had been lost along the trail. It did not go unnoticed that these piles contained much of what they would need to make it comfortably to the Old Woman Land and to start a new life among Sitting Bull's people.

Carefully scrutinizing the piles as they passed, the people moved across the shallow river as the soldiers observed them from the safety of shallow trenches they had dug around the edges of their tents. No one from either side fired, though rifles were kept at the ready.

Once the people were safely across, several of the chiefs went forward to ask the white men for food. The people, they explained, were tired, and the children were hungry. It did not seem much to ask for some small gift of supplies from piles so great as these.

One of the civilian men advanced to meet them. He tried to make indications of friendship, but when the chiefs found he was not a soldier they refused to talk to him. It was the soldiers who were their potential adversaries, so it was the soldier leader with whom they wished to speak.

Cautiously, the group's leader, a Captain Moelchert, came forward. He and his men had been informed upon their departure from the channel-clearing brigade that there was some chance they might confront the Nez Perce, who were known to be somewhere in the area. His men had responded with typical soldier bluster, saying, "Let them come. We are here first," and he had applauded their bravado.

But the sight of the warriors and their numbers had given him pause. He shook hands with the Indian leaders and accepted their declarations of friendship but steadfastly refused to allow them to approach any closer to his men, who were lying in the trenches around their tents a hundred yards downriver.

The young civilian who had first tried to communicate with the Indians was convinced that the men with whom they were dealing were Joseph and Looking Glass, the chiefs they had been reading and hearing about. He tried to serve as interpreter, but the Indians dismissed him. They did not need the assistance of this young man to make their wishes known.

They asked again for food, explaining that the people were tired and hungry and weak. If they could have some supplies, there would be no fighting and no raids on the goods. They only wished to pass peacefully and to obtain enough food to keep their people fed.

Captain Moelchert again refused, explaining that the goods were not his to disburse.

The Indians brought out handfuls of gold and silver and offered to pay for anything he gave them. But he still would not give them goods that were not his to sell.

Finally, after much pleading, the Nez Perce emissaries managed to convince him to give them one bag of hardtack and one bag of bacon. Though it wasn't what they had hoped, they accepted it and returned to the camp.

When they arrived with their meager bags of goods, the young warriors were incensed. This was hardly enough to feed 650 hungry people. From the time of their ancestors, hungry people, especially women and children, had never been refused food. These bags of hardtack and bacon were more an insult than a gift. It was once again white men being stingy, as they had been since the time of the Reverend Spalding, as they had been in all things at all times involving Indian people.

The warriors looked at the piles of goods as tall as a white man's house. The chiefs' admonition to avoid fighting now meant nothing to them. They would take what was needed, then they would show these white men not to insult Nez Perce and leave their women and children with empty bellies.

Some stripped down to their breechcloths and moccasins and began moving down the riverbank toward the soldiers. When the soldiers in their distant trenches saw this, they knew that a fight was near. They dug down deeper behind the barricades and prepared to open fire.

The Nez Perce had established their camp several miles on the up-stream side of the piles of goods. The soldiers' tents and trenches were on the downstream side. The goods were in a kind of no-man's-land between the two, piled up under the overhang of a bluff. The warriors believed that if they could keep the soldiers pinned down in their trenches, the people could sneak up to the back side of the pile and take what they wanted, keeping the pile between them and the soldiers' line of fire.

At first it seemed likely that the raiding could take place without vio-lence. But soon a shot rang out, then another, and a sporadic engagement of long-distance sniping began. The Nez Perce warriors had hidden them-selves well in the creases and folds of the eroded landscape, and the sol-diers were well protected by their earthen fortifications. There was little chance that either could do much damage to the other unless there was a charge. The dozen frightened and outnumbered soldiers were certainly not going to attempt anything so foolhardy, and the Nez Perce warriors were more interested in sport than warfare. For them, the encounter was essen-tially a chance for long-range target practice while the women from the camp hurried up to the back of the pile and helped themselves to whatever their families needed.

The standoff continued past sunset, with the warriors squeezing off an occasional shot and the women running back and forth between the pile and the camp carrying sacks of flour, rice, coffee, sugar, hardtack, beans, and various pots and pans and household goods. After everyone had taken what they wanted, a few of the warriors decided to light the piles on fire. Any goods—even those clearly intended for civilians—could be comman-deered by troops or used to give aid and comfort to the soldiers. Though the chiefs counseled them against it, they proceeded to ignite the remain-ing goods.

Since the piles contained cloth and wooden implements and hundreds of bags of greasy bacon, the fire soon rose dark and smoky into the evening sky. Some of the warriors had found liquor in the pile and, under its influence, were becoming more and more intrigued with the idea of attacking the soldiers. But the rising flames illuminated anyone who tried to move across the open river bottom, so they had to keep their distance, contenting themselves with alcohol and the occasional gunshot while watching the fire cast unearthly dancing shadows on the bluffs and mounds and making the river itself seem as if it flowed with flames.

The chiefs had remained back in camp with the people, where a feast was being prepared with the goods that had been taken from the pile. The sound of gunshots and the sight of the fire down the river did not please them. It meant that the ones they called the "bad boys" had been at work again. They sent a messenger down to tell the warriors to stop the fighting. No one had been killed, and the camp had the food it needed. They were not going to succeed in killing soldiers dug in behind earthen banks, and there was nothing to be gained even if they did. Leave them there and come back to camp.

The older warriors, more inclined to listen to the counsel of the chiefs, agreed. Slowly, the fighters made their way back to camp, keeping up sporadic rear-guard fire. By the time they had all returned, the sky was lightening with another high plains morning, and the whole camp had packed to move.

As the morning grew, the people began the climb along the narrow trails through the breaks and badlands toward the buffalo plains above. The going was difficult, but hearts were light. They now had food supplies and camp goods, and the border to the Old Woman Country was only several days' journey ahead. The country through which they had to pass was well known to the buffalo hunters among them, including Poker Joe and Looking Glass, and Howard was far behind, facing the almost impenetrable terrain of the breaks. Though the weather was cold and winter was on the edge of the wind, for the first time since they had left the Big Hole they felt truly secure.

Early in the afternoon they came upon the bull train that had left the Cow Island landing the previous morning. It was camped at the top of the breaks in a clump of trees near a small creek. This was good fortune beyond anything the Nez Perce had hoped. These were civilians with no military guard, and their thirteen wagons of goods would surely contain any provisions that the people had not been able to obtain in their hurried raids on the tarp-covered piles at the river's edge.

Their big hope was for ammunition, since that was the one commodity they needed most. Many of the older men still had a good supply of bullets for their guns, but the younger warriors, quicker to the trigger, had expended most of theirs. The rounds that had been captured at the Big Hole were almost exhausted, and without bullets, the warriors were severely limited in their capacity to hunt and to protect the people.

The problem was compounded by the fact that the people now were carrying many different kinds of weapons. They had built up a substantial arsenal by stealing settlers' weapons and stripping guns from the bodies of soldiers and volunteers killed along the way. But these were of various calibers and makes, and ammunition was not always interchangeable. So this opportunity to go through the wagons unmolested and unchallenged in search of ammunition was a rare stroke of good fortune.

Since these bull trains brought goods to the military posts throughout buffalo country, the Nez Perce were certain at least that there would be ammunition to fit their military rifles. Once resupplied with bullets, they would have the three things they needed to remain self-sufficient in the Old Woman Country: horses, functional weaponry, and camp goods. They would not have to impose or depend upon the good graces of Sitting Bull and his people, who themselves were living in exile and surviving on limited means.

Once again, the chiefs sought to get these supplies without violence. But they knew that the young warriors were impatient and unpredictable. So Poker Joe took the lead in trying to keep the encounter amicable.

The wagon drivers were justifiably nervous, watching a group of what they guessed to be 800 Indians gradually overtake and surround their unprotected wagons. But Poker Joe, using all the knowledge of English at his command, spoke to the men in a friendly and relaxed manner. He asked them if they knew of any soldiers in the area and if they knew of any good places for the horses to graze. The men responded civilly but kept a close eye on the young braves, who were examining the contents of the wagons with great interest.

Poker Joe continued his friendly banter, expressing the Nez Perce friendship for the whites and casually mentioning that his scouts had just reported the presence of 300 Sioux warriors a distance away on the other side of a low range of mountains. It would be wise, he said, if the wagon men abandoned the bull train and hid themselves, for the Sioux warriors would surely attack during the night and kill them all.

The wagon men were skeptical, but the merest mention of Sioux warriors struck fear into their hearts. They knew that this area north of the Missouri River was a kind of neutral zone between the American and Canadian territory, so military presence was small and freedom of movement for Indians was great. It was possible that Sitting Bull and his men were indeed ranging this far south from their sanctuary across the border. This was, after all, the best remaining buffalo hunting country, and winter was coming on.

So the wagon men took this information under advisement, all the while trying to keep on the good side of the remaining Nez Perce warriors, who now were asking if they would be invited to stay for dinner. The wagon men replied that they could offer food to some but not to all. This penurious gesture did not sit well with the warriors, who immediately assumed a decidedly unfriendly demeanor, then rode off.

With the distant, though probably fictional, threat of the Sioux, and the immediate threat implied in the irritation of the young warriors, the drivers decided that they had best follow Poker Joe's advice and move away from the wagons. They quietly went off to spend the night in the nearby hills, hoping the Indians would take what they wanted and leave the rest of the goods alone.

In the morning, they made their way cautiously back toward the wagons. The Indians, who had camped nearby, seemed indifferent and preoccupied with packing for departure. But the drivers found it unnerving that their return was announced by a shrill whistle from one of the young boys and that this signal, whatever it meant, was picked up and sent along through the entire campsite as they passed by on foot.

Soon they heard one of the chiefs yelling out commands and saw the warriors stripping for battle. Convinced that they were now to be killed, the men again ran off into the brush. From their hidden vantage point they watched the activity in the camp, until suddenly they heard shots, then saw Indians tearing the sheets off the bull wagons and setting the goods on fire. Knowing that the wagons were beyond protection, they jumped into a ravine and scrambled down the breaks toward the river and the small contingent of soldiers they knew to be camped there.

But it was not the wagon men who had drawn the attention of the Nez Perce. While the young men were clambering over the wagons, a new group of soldiers had been sighted. The warriors had just discovered barrels of whiskey and had begun to celebrate their good fortune when some of the scouts reported that white men with guns were coming up the trail from the river. It did not seem likely that these were part of Howard's army, which was still several days behind. They must be a new force arrived from somewhere else. But the warriors reported that, like the men at the river, these soldiers did not appear to be interested in attacking. So they held them at bay with long-range fire while the rest of the camp finished packing and began to move north. Then the warriors ignited the wagons and rode off to join their people.

The soldiers who had been making their way up the trail were a small group of volunteers under the command of a Major Guido Ilges, who was in charge of Fort Benton. He had heard of the Nez Perce arrival and had ridden down to help protect the goods at the Cow Island landing. When he had arrived and seen that all was destroyed, he and his men had moved up the trail from the river toward the high plains in an attempt to protect the bull train and its supplies. It was then that the Indians had seen him and opened fire.

Ilges was a seasoned commander and immediately recognized that his numbers were inferior and that his position below the Indians was good only for defense. His men too were only volunteers and had been frightened even before encountering the Nez Perce. So he ordered his troops to retreat to the river and leave the Indians to whatever looting and destruction they saw fit to commit. The most he could do was pass information on to Miles, who was still eighty miles to the east, making his way toward the Cow Island crossing.

14

"I Think We Will All Be Caught and Killed"

W HILE ALL THIS was taking place, Miles was camped on a small
creek that fed into the Missouri River a short distance from a confluence where the Musselshell and the Missouri met in a T. He had
marched his men hard through wild, open, high plains country that held
little water, and they had suffered for it. Here at this campsite they had finally been able to rest in a protected setting with abundant water for cooking and drinking.

But Miles was now faced with a difficult decision. He could cross the
Musselshell, which ran north and south, and continue directly to the west
along the south side of the Missouri, hoping to intercept the Nez Perce
before they crossed the Missouri farther up. Or he could try to cross the
Missouri here and be prepared to intercept them on the north side of the
river as they made their last dash toward Canada. He believed from his
scouts and his calculations that the Nez Perce were still at least seventy-five
miles south of the Missouri, but he could not be sure. He had sent scouts
out every day, some of whom traveled two hundred miles before returning,
and almost all of whom ranged at least twenty-five miles ahead, sweeping
in all directions, searching for signs of the Nez Perce. But thus far they had
encountered nothing.

His dilemma was this: If he crossed the Missouri, he might be far
ahead of the Nez Perce but could easily miss them as they maneuvered
their way through the complex, rumpled landscape of the Missouri
Breaks on the north side of the river. But if he crossed the Musselshell and
stayed to the south, they might get past him and cross the Missouri at

some point unknown to him. He would be forced to slow his pursuit while his men undertook the difficult task of fording the roiling Missouri. An added complication was that his direct superior, General Terry, commander of the Department of the Dakota, still begrudged Howard the victory that the Christian general had won during their seniority battle and was not inclined to give significant support to Howard's ineffectual efforts to catch the Nez Perce.

Terry could not openly snub Howard's requests for support. After all, Howard's pursuit of the Nez Perce was being carried out under General Sherman's direct instructions. But he did not have to commit his entire command to Howard's impotent pursuit. In fact, he had strongly hinted to Miles that he should not devote all his troops to Howard's support but keep men available for Terry himself, who was 150 miles to the west and marching toward Canada from Fort Benton to parley with Sitting Bull. Miles did not wish to disregard his superior's "strong suggestion," but neither did he wish to lose his chance at the Nez Perce. So he made a decision to split his troops. Some would cross the Missouri and march to the northwest toward Terry, staying close to the edge of the badlands that bordered the river to make sure that the Nez Perce had not moved across at some unknown ford and begun their last run toward Sitting Bull. The others would cross the Musselshell and continue to the west on the south side of the river, hoping to encounter the Nez Perce before they made it out of the open country and down into the badlands and the river bottom.

However, neither of these crossings was going to be easy. The Missouri at this point was no small river, even in autumn. It was a wide, dark, muddy expanse that roiled and churned with a powerful current. Just the day before, one of his experienced scouts had been swept away trying to ford it on his horse. But he knew of no good crossing place between here and Cow Island sixty miles farther on, so this had to be the place to move his men and equipment to the other side.

The Musselshell, though not as dangerous to cross, was bordered by a particularly onerous stretch of the dreaded breaks, which made travel so difficult that wagons often overturned simply trying to navigate the crevasses and canyon trails. However he did this, it was going to be a challenging and time-consuming task, and time was the one thing that Miles did not feel he had on his side.

But Miles did have good luck on his side. As he was making his plans, one of his scouts returned with news that a steamer was coming down the river from the direction of Cow Island. This was the boat that had dropped off the goods that the Nez Perce had looted and burned and, as it happened, was the last scheduled steamer of the season. It had started on its return trip down the river before the Nez Perce had arrived, so the captain had no information to pass on to Miles. But it did offer Miles the opportunity to cross the river by boat rather than by an arduous and treacherous fording.

Miles took advantage of this bit of good fortune to move his one group of men and supplies across to the north side of the Missouri, a task that otherwise would have slowed him greatly and possibly cost him the lives of some of his horses and soldiers. He then used the steamer to ferry artillery and a complement of men across to the west side of the Musselshell. When he no longer needed the steamer, he released it to its captain to continue on its journey.

While he was preparing his one group of men for their march along the south side of the Musselshell, a small rowboat was sighted coming down the river. In it were two wounded men floating down from Cow Island in hopes of reaching a fort where they could get medical treatment. The men told Miles about the looting at the landing and that the Nez Perce had already crossed the river and were on their way north toward Canada.

This information changed Miles's plans completely. There was now no need to continue on the south side of the Missouri. It was imperative that he get his remaining men across to the north side of the river as quickly as possible and begin moving northwest on an angle to intercept the fleeing bands.

Miles looked frantically for the steamboat, which was churning out of sight down the river. His men tried shouting and hailing, but the distance was too great to catch the boat captain's attention. Some of his men, however, had an idea. They turned a cannon in the direction of the disappearing steamer and began lofting shells in its direction. The booming reverberations echoing off the bluffs along the river soon caught the attention of the steamer's captain, who realized that something was wrong back at the camp. He turned the boat around and quickly churned back to Miles and his troops, who stood cheering and waving on the riverbank.

The rest of the men and supplies were then ferried across the Missouri to join their comrades, and they all marched off, in high spirits, toward an anticipated rendezvous with the Nez Perce and great military victory.

. . .

The Nez Perce, by now, had made their way out of the breaks into the great openness of the last northern buffalo range. Nothing stood between them and the border except the cold, blowing grasslands of the high, windswept plains. Off to the left and the right, in the far distance, they could see the outcroppings of two small, snow-covered mountain ranges. Directly between these lay the route to Sitting Bull and safety.

The people felt no real fear now, only anticipation and exhaustion. They had new supplies, the plains were filled with vast herds of antelope and buffalo, and the soldier resistance had dwindled to almost nothing. Since the Big Hole, army attacks had become less and less intense. A few warriors with rifles were all that had been needed to stop the men in the dry canyon, and the soldiers at the supply piles and at the oxen train had not even had the courage to advance once they were fired upon.

The Crow too had withdrawn to their own country, leaving the Nez Perce with no more warriors and horse thieves to fear. They sometimes saw a few Cheyenne or Walk-Around Sioux chasing after a herd of buffalo in the far distance. But these men were not enemies, just hunters seeking food for the rapidly approaching winter. Only the heavy gray skies and cold winds were now threatening them.

They had traveled only a few miles since the river crossing—just enough to get up out of the badlands and into the high open plains. But no one had minded. The people were gaining strength and the horses were beginning to heal. Only Poker Joe was bothered. He knew the white man's ways and did not yet feel secure. He also feared the coming winter. He urged the people onward, insisting that they continue to travel at his rigorous pace. But he had little support. The people now had supplies and food, and there was only open country in front of them. They had no heart for more difficult days.

Looking Glass and the other chiefs sensed this. They watched as Poker Joe goaded and demanded, shouting out orders in a voice that could be heard across the entire camp. They realized that the whole fabric of the group was fraying and that Poker Joe was slowly losing control of the people. Finally, Looking Glass spoke up. He had never made his peace with being replaced as trail leader after the massacre at the Big Hole. In their own country, back across the Bitterroots, he had been among the most respected war chiefs. To be replaced by a buffalo hunter who was only half

Indian was an insult. He knew this country as well as Poker Joe, and he knew his people better. It was time to reclaim the lead.

In council, Looking Glass made his case. He berated Poker Joe for driving the people too hard. The elders were tired; the children were tired. General Howard was far behind, with weak horses and men who had no stomach for fight. The Old Woman Country was only a few easy days' journey ahead of them. Short days and long camps would build the people's strength, he said. The old people would have time to rest; the wounded would have more chance to heal; the horses could graze in the waist-high buffalo grass and gain strength for the winter. The hunters would be able to kill more buffalo, and the women would have more time to dry the meat and tan the hides to make blankets and buffalo robes.

The children too would have time to rest. Many had been crying almost constantly from cold and hunger, and many were sick. With the new cooking pots and food taken from the wagon trains and pile of goods by the river, the women could prepare better meals and the children could fill their empty bellies. They would also have time to sew new warm clothes and winter moccasins.

Poker Joe listened patiently but would not bend. Now was not the time to slow the pace, he said. Had Looking Glass not seen how soldiers arrived unexpectedly from unexpected directions? Did he think that white men would sit by quietly when they received word of the burned wagons and piles of goods?

But Looking Glass did not waver. Soldiers did not like to fight in the winter. Their horses were slow and unable to find forage in snow. No soldier leader would risk bringing his men into this open country with winter this strong in the air.

The other men listened carefully. Both men had spoken well. But Looking Glass knew the heart of the people. If there was no need to fear soldiers, then there should be no need for hurry. One by one the men made their positions known, some speaking, some giving the blanket sign of covering their shoulders when their feelings had been well expressed by another. In the end, when all had said their peace, leadership was given back to Looking Glass. Poker Joe was unhappy, but he accepted the will of the council.

"All right, Looking Glass," he said. "You can lead. I am trying to save the people, doing my best to cross into the Old Woman Country before the soldiers find us. You can take control, but I think we will all be caught and killed."

His words were enough to give some of the people pause. Looking Glass's prideful ways had gotten them into trouble at the Big Hole and had been responsible for their false hope of assistance from the Crow. It was not hard to be skeptical about his judgment. But he had spoken well, and his words had made sense. They were inclined to give him the benefit of the doubt.

With Looking Glass back in the lead, the people moved out into the broad, open plains. The scouts ranged far in all directions, watching for movement, keeping an eye on the behavior of the buffalo herds. People once again began traveling in smaller groups, with each leaving when it saw fit and all joining together at known camping places at night.

Slowly, the people began to feel that, finally, all danger was past. The scouts could ride to the tops of hills and buttes and see for miles in all directions, so any army—even a small group of soldiers—would be discovered. If they were, they easily could be attacked. This was horse country again, wide and large, where men on fast mounts could fight in the warrior way, while the slow-footed white men with their heavy wagons and heavy horses would be surrounded and cut down, as they had been in White Bird Canyon.

But there were no soldiers to be seen—only a few Walk-Around Sioux and Gros Ventre warriors, riding through distant buffalo herds hunting meat for the coming winter. A few Cheyenne too were observed riding along the hilltops. These the scouts confronted, asking them through signs if they were working for the soldiers. When the men said they were not, they were welcomed in camp and fed fry bread.

The feeling of relief was palpable. The people had food, the hunters were having success, and there was plenty of buffalo manure for cooking fires. Short days meant easy travel. When the weather got too cold and rainy or the children got too chilled, Looking Glass would call a stop and the women would make camp in a low place on the prairie or against the bank of a grassy draw, safe from the cutting edge of the hard, northern winds. The journey that under Poker Joe's guidance had felt like a desperate retreat had once again begun to feel like normal camp travel.

They began their days early with a warm breakfast. Then scouts rode off to establish a perimeter around the group while the women strapped the shelter skins and clothing into bundles on the packhorses and the young boys gathered the horses from pasture and prepared them for movement. Dogs moiled around the campsite looking for scraps of food. Young children were strapped tightly on the gentlest pack animals; the adults and older children climbed on their trail horses, and the camp slowly made its way forward, with the herd of horses and packs of dogs moving along beside.

Sometimes the hunters who had left early would return with news that they had killed a buffalo or a deer, and the women would ride off to skin and dress the animal and carry the meat back to camp. The hides would be given to the old women to cure and tan. Though there was no time to soak them in the manner of a home camp, once the group stopped for the day there would be time to scrape the flesh and smoke the skins enough that they could be used for shelter or cover. It was still not like home. But it was more like the life they had left behind than anything they had known since the time of running from the Big Hole. For this short moment, they felt again like a people on a journey, not a people engaged in a flight.

But the normality of the routine could not compensate for the debilitating effects of the weather. People's clothes were torn and ragged, and everyone was constantly dirty and wet. On the night after Looking Glass took over there had been a heavy storm, and the camp had awakened the next morning to a raw, cutting wind that blew their camp goods around and stung their faces as they packed to move.

The following day had been better, but the day after had again brought heavy winds and a driving rain. Even the short journeys of just a few miles were becoming difficult, and the camps were being made with soaking goods and little shelter other than pieces of canvas or buffalo hides hung over small prairie bushes. When there was not enough room under the shelters, the men would sleep in the open rolled up in buffalo blankets. Such moccasins and gloves as the people had were not able to dry, so in the morning they rode off with frozen hands and soaking feet and little to comfort them other than the hope that this bitter journey would soon be over.

But if the Nez Perce were having a difficult time, Miles's men were not faring much better. What had begun as a festive march up from the ferry crossing at the Missouri had deteriorated day by day into a cold, dreary push toward an unknown enemy. While the weather had remained warm,

the men had delighted in flocks of ducks and the great buffalo and antelope herds that moved like clouds across the plains in front of them. But
as the nights had gotten cold and the troops had outdistanced their supply
wagons, their thoughts had turned to the more pressing realities of survival. Their situation was made even worse by Miles's announcement that
there could be no hunting because he did not wish to risk having a gunshot stampede the buffalo—a sure sign to any Indian scout that soldiers
were near.

The troops rode and marched for hours in wet boots on mushy and
frozen ground, seeing only the empty, rolling landscape in front of them.
They spent their nights rolled up in their coats under icy skies because
their tents were far behind in supply wagons that were still laboring along
the narrow trails through the Missouri Breaks. Hot food was scarce because there was no wood, and the men were not skilled at starting fires
from wet buffalo dung. Such fires as they could make had to be fully extin-
guished before dawn so no telltale smoke would rise into the daytime skies
to alert the fleeing Indians. Water too was hard to find and often had to be
dipped from pools so filled with mud that it had to be strained before it
could even be boiled for cooking and drinking.

Despite these hardships, Miles drove the troops relentlessly, not stopping to camp until shortly before midnight, then waking the men at three
in the morning so they could be back on the trail by five or six. He intended
to catch these Joseph Indians, and a bit of privation for his soldiers was a
small price to pay for the honor that would come with the capture.

Part of his strategy was to keep up a constant scouting sweep, with men
ranging for miles in all directions and taking sightings from any high
point they encountered. He was confident that in this way any movement
by the large group of Nez Perce through this broad, open country would
be observed and reported.

He knew he had good scouts. Several were mountain men who were
well experienced in Indian tracking, and others were Sioux and Cheyenne
who had signed on to work for the military. The warriors regarded the soldiers as slow and weak, slaves to the need to eat and drink at regular intervals. Nonetheless, they were willing to sign on for short-term scouting
assignments because working for the military meant good food, good
guns, and an opportunity to live once again in the old warrior way, riding
free over open country rather than sitting around forts with nothing to do

but wait for rations. It also meant white man's pay and the chance to gain Nez Perce horses if the hostiles were captured. They also harbored no great love for the Nez Perce, so it was no hard thing to take arms against them. Still, working for the soldiers was not a life they fancied, but it was the best available to them since their leaders had surrendered to the soldiers the autumn before.

The warriors, however, did rankle at Miles's demand that they operate under a white commander. They told him that the warrior way was for each man to ride freely and make his own decisions. They had no desire to be like white soldiers, who moved slowly and relied on the commands of leaders. But Miles insisted, and reluctantly they agreed.

They were happiest when sent ahead to scout. They could read trails better than any white man and thrilled at the sensation of ranging free over open country in search of an enemy. While they were out on scouting missions they felt alive, like in the old days. But when they were forced to return to the camps and ride with the soldiers, they plodded along, sleepy-eyed and indifferent, staying near but keeping to themselves. Still, they always carried their war dress with them and kept their fast war ponies tethered beside them, anticipating the moment when the chance might come to break free to engage in a chase or a fight.

By now, Miles had gathered enough information to determine the approximate route the Nez Perce were taking. He knew where and when they had crossed the Missouri and the approximate speed at which they were moving. If his calculations were right, his men were on a diagonal to intercept them.

He knew that the Nez Perce were as likely to be scouting his movements as he was to be scouting theirs, so he decided to march his troops behind a small mountain range that poked up from the plains and separated him from the route of the hostiles. This range, known as the Little Rockies, was not much more than a series of tall hills that ran north and south for about fifty miles, then faded back into the rolling high plains just short of the northern border. With good fortune, he could travel his men unnoticed on the opposite side of these small mountains from the Nez Perce, come around the top just south of the Canadian border, and either block their passage or hit them in the flank.

Everything depended upon speed, surprise, and stealth. He knew that Indians did not fight well in pitched battles and that once dismounted they were reduced to the status of uncoordinated, individual snipers. In his dealings with the Sioux and Cheyenne, he had learned that the best attack was a hard charge, executed at dawn, that scattered the warriors and sent them fighting in retreat. This same tactic had been successful in the Civil War against the South, but it was even more successful with Indian tribes, which were burdened with women and children. It was cruel and devastating and resulted in the loss of innocent lives. But it broke the spirit of the enemy, and war was about winning, not about kindness. If he could outdistance the Nez Perce and catch them unawares, it was his intention to charge hard, disperse the warriors, surround the camp, and do what was necessary to force a quick surrender. But first he had to find the Indians, and he had to do so before they found him.

The Nez Perce were now five days out from the place where they had looted the wagons. The weather had alternated between mild warmth and wet, bone-chilling cold. In the far northern distance they could catch glimpses of the low line of hills that they knew as the Wolf's Paw and the other tribes called the Bear's Paw. Just north of it you could see the silhouette of the mountains that looked like an old man lying on his back. This marked the line between the United States and the Old Woman Country the whites called Canada. The people only had to pass to the right of the Bear's Paw and beyond the Old Man, and they would have safety. American soldiers could not follow them there, and Sitting Bull's many warriors were living just over that line.

With the Bear's Paw within reach, Looking Glass called a stop to set up camp in a hollow known to all buffalo hunters as the Place of the Manure Fires. It was a broad, wide depression in the plains surrounded on three sides by low bluffs and cutbanks, with a small creek winding like a snake through its center. Hunters of all tribes had long used this as a stopping place during journeys in search of buffalo because it offered protection from the relentless high plains winds and provided them with good water for drinking and plenty of buffalo chips for fuel.

The advance scouts had killed several buffalo at this spot and left them for skinning. Since no soldiers had been seen either in front or behind, Looking Glass knew this would be a good place to make a final, relaxed camp before pushing on to the border two days' journey ahead.

The day before had been filled with low clouds and rain, and this day gave the promise of worse. The snow line had already dropped low on the mountains, and a wet fog was obscuring everything with a fine, gray mist.

The halt was called, and Joseph began the process of organizing the campsite and making sure that the people's needs were met. The hillocks surrounding the site were not high—maybe fifty feet—but they formed a perfect three-sided bowl in which to camp. The people would be out of the remorseless winds, and there would be plenty of fresh water and fuel.

On the fourth side, a long, slow rise sloped off to the west. It offered an ideal spot for the horses to graze. Though it lay across the creek, the creek itself was only several yards wide and could be crossed easily without getting too wet and cold. He could send the boys over to tend the grazing horses, and the whole herd could be kept in easy sight of the camp.

The creek, with its many tight bends and curves, created an ideal camping site. The land along its banks was flat and low so families could be close to water, and the low-lying clumps of willow that bordered its edges could be used for kindling and to support the crude blanket and canvas shelters the people were now using against the cold and rain. It would have been good to have poles for teepees, but those days were far behind. Not since the Big Hole had the people actually had lodges that protected them. The rest of the journey had been made either sleeping in the open or in such makeshift shelters as these, created by draping blankets over stumps and bushes or whatever deadfall was in the area. At least at this site they would be protected from the wind. And if they needed greater shelter, the bottomland itself was furrowed with deep gullies. They could burrow dugout shelters into the earth if the weather got too bad.

Looking Glass announced that this would be their stopping place until the following morning—long enough to skin the buffalo, cook warm meals, and get much-needed rest. In the morning, the groups could leave as they wished, but all should be on the trail before midday.

By the time the people had set up camp, the weather had worsened. By midafternoon, the winds had picked up and the rain that pelted the camp was rapidly turning to snow. It fell in large, heavy, wet globs that weighed down the shelters and leaked onto the children and elderly huddled underneath. The buffalo manure too was getting soaked, making the fires hard to start and harder to keep burning. On the hills to the south the snow line was continuing to move lower. With each day's journey they had moved farther north, and with each mile traveled, the winds and rains had gotten colder. Now they seemed to be in the very grip of winter, with skies the gray of gun barrels and snow piling to several inches on the ground.

They could see the steam rising from the horses in the distance, and the creek was skimming over with ice. But this was the price they had to pay for rest. The freshly killed buffalo gave them food, and the hollows gave them shelter from the worst of the rain and snow and wind. And if this was hard for them, it would be even harder for General Howard, wherever he might be.

Most of the people had almost ceased worrying about the one-armed soldier chief. They were sure he had given up the pursuit. The scouts, though, remained concerned. The day before, while riding to the east, they had seen a group of figures in the far distance. They had been too far away to be identified as any more than dots moving across the rolling plains. But they had moved like people, not like animals.

Some of the warriors had wanted to back-scout to make sure this was just another tribe and not a group of soldiers. They had told Looking Glass about their discovery and proposed that he keep the people moving north while they rode back to determine what these strange figures were. But Looking Glass would have none of it. Everyone knew that Howard was at least two days behind, if he was following at all, and that he would be traveling on the same trail the people were using. Those dots the warriors had seen were far off and to the east. They were probably hunting parties from the Gros Ventres or Sioux or maybe even Assiniboine or River Crow. This buffalo land was shared by many tribes; it would not be unusual for a group to come in large numbers to hunt for meat and skins for the winter. The people were still not strong; the horses' hooves were still sore. A hard march could undo the healing that the slow easy days had begun to allow. The chiefs had chosen him to lead. Now they needed to let him do so.

The disagreement became heated, and tensions that were rife within the group quickly rose to the surface. Poker Joe still had his supporters, and many in the camp still doubted Looking Glass's wisdom and judgment. In the end, Looking Glass, supported by Joseph, prevailed. It was the suffering of the sick and the elderly and the children's weariness that carried the day. This place would be their camping spot. In the morning they would begin their move toward the border crossing into the Old Woman Land. But nothing could assuage the strange uneasiness some among them felt in their hearts. There was something unsettling about the distant movements of the animals, something not right about the movements of the birds. They felt a strong nervousness, like animals before a storm or birds in the days before the long winter flight.

The warriors too were uneasy. They were uncomfortable about the camping spot Looking Glass had chosen. It was a good place for protection against the winds but not good for protection against attack. It put the people in a bowl where they could easily be surrounded on three sides. They had no long line of vision except toward the broad slope to the west across the creek where the animals grazed. And all skilled fighters knew that you did not willingly abandon the high ground. Without good scouting, they could be surprised like they had been at Big Hole. None had expected soldiers there either.

Torn by this confusing welter of sentiments, the people bedded down under their buffalo robes and ragged canvas shelters in the chill high plains night. The snow had stopped, the air had cleared, and the sky was a dark, icy vault filled with distant, brilliant stars.

Fifteen miles away, on the other side of the low hills of the Little Rockies, Miles's men too had bedded down. But their night was even less comfortable than the Nez Perce's. The supply wagons carrying the tents still had not caught up, so they were forced to scrape away the snow from the ground and make do with only their own coats for cover. Miles had awakened them at 2:00 a.m., unable to get decent cooking fires going from the wet buffalo chips. By 4:30 they were loading up their wet packs and moving forward, wet to the core, hungry, and unsure of when, or if, they would ever meet any enemy.

By dawn the wind had changed and the snow had started to melt. But this did not make travel any easier. The ground now became a morass of ice and mud, seeping into the shoes and soaking the feet of the infantrymen. Reports had come in last night that the Cheyenne scouts had picked up the Nez Perce trail. But the soldiers' greatest fear was that they were moving ever closer to the dreaded warriors of Sitting Bull. Fighting a group of fleeing Nez Perce burdened with women and children was one thing; meeting a group of two thousand Sioux warriors bearing down on them with good weapons and fast horses was quite another. They had to hope that the reports from the Cheyenne scouts were true and that confrontation with the Nez Perce and only the Nez Perce was about to take place.

Their hopes were soon realized when a Cheyenne scout came riding in, shouting that the Nez Perce camp had been found. A group of warriors wearing the striped blankets of the Nez Perce had been seen chasing down buffalo. Then, while scanning the horizon through field glasses, the Cheyenne had spotted a plume of smoke rising in the distance and had followed it to a ridge. Though the ridge had obscured their view, and they had dared not move too close for fear of being observed, they had seen the great herd of horses grazing on a nearby hillside and knew that the camp of the Nez Perce had to be directly below.

This news quickened the hearts of the discouraged men. The dreary march through the early morning darkness suddenly had a sense of purpose. They picked up their step and moved forward toward the fresh trail the Cheyenne scouts had found. They were ready to meet the enemy.

15

"Soldiers Are Coming"

MORNING AT THE Place of the Manure Fires came slowly for the Nez Perce. Overnight the weather had turned colder. The creek was skimmed with ice, and the rolling plains were a sea of frost-covered grasses beneath gray and wintry skies. But at least the air was clear. Cold and bitter winds they could endure, but the days of sleet and snow were taking too great a toll on the children and the elders.

The early risers had begun gathering their pack animals from the hillside across the creek, and many of the women were already fanning buffalo chips into low cooking fires. There was less concern about smoke trails rising into the sky than at other camp stops because there was little fear that Howard was anywhere within range to see them, much less within range to strike.

Many of the children were already up, running along the creekside and playing games of tag by flipping balls of mud at each other with the ends of sticks. The scouts had packed and mounted and ridden off into the hills to kill a few more buffalo before the camp departed. Groups of women were following behind, prepared to skin any animals and pack the meat back to camp.

The people were anxious to get moving. Many among them would not feel secure until they had reached the safety of Sitting Bull and the Old Woman Land. Others simply anticipated the journey's end and did not wish to delay the conclusion any longer. It had been more than a hundred days since they had left their homes, and they had seen too much death and suffering. It was time to come to a stop and begin to establish some kind of normal routine for the families, even if it was in an unfamiliar country among unfamiliar people.

Joseph too looked forward to the rest. He had supported Looking Glass's decision to move slowly these last few days, but now it was time to finish the journey. He had done his best to keep the camp together during their ordeal and had counseled peace at every opportunity. Now, at last, a kind of peace was at hand.

He still held out hope that there were those in the white government who would listen to reason once tempers cooled. From the safety of the Old Woman Country perhaps they could open dialogue with the white law chiefs to explain what had happened. Perhaps, with the calming effects of time and distance, those law chiefs could be made to understand that it had been the young, rash warriors who had done the killing and that the people themselves had never killed wantonly but only when attacked. They could point out the humane way captives had been treated and how the people had resisted the temptation to strike back at innocent women and children, even though their own women and children had been brutally murdered at the hands of the soldiers. Even the rash young warriors, with the exception of their raid on the settlers of the Salmon River country, had neither killed nor violated white women. What white army could say the same about its soldiers' treatment of Indian women?

If there were good men among the white men, and he believed there were, surely some reasonable resolution could be found, and the Nez Perce could return to their own country without fear of reprisal. At a minimum, he hoped they would be permitted to return to the reservation toward which they had been heading when the hostilities had broken out. But in his heart he still dreamed of the Wallowa.

He surveyed the activity in the early morning camp. The smell of coffee and roasting buffalo meat sweetened the chill morning air. Packing was going well and spirits were high. After a good breakfast, the people could begin this final journey over the wintry plains toward Sitting Bull and his people.

With his elder daughter, Noise of Running Feet, he crossed the creek to the horse herd. Joseph was proud of his daughter. She was just twelve but well able to do a woman's work. He would leave her to bring their horses back across the creek while he made sure that the rest of the people found their mounts and got their families moving along the trail.

They had just begun to ready the horses when they heard a strange strident sound rising from back in camp. It was Wottolen, walking among the lodges shouting loudly. He had just awakened from a dream that had disturbed him deeply. In his sleep he had seen the very place where they were camped. The sky had been dark with the smoke of battle, and the waters of the creek were running red with blood. He had even dressed and walked out to see if this was the place in his vision. All was exactly as he had dreamed. Surely they were soon to be attacked.

Wottolen's message caused a commotion in the camp. He was a man of strong medicine, and he had seen a vision before the battle at the Big Hole and the fight at the Clearwater. In both cases, his warnings had been ignored. And in both cases, death and suffering had followed. Now he was warning the people again.

But Looking Glass was having none of this. He quickly mounted his horse and rode among the lodges instructing the people to stay calm. "There is no need to rush," he shouted. "Build fires. Cook breakfast. Give the children time to eat. Afterward we will pack up and start moving."

The camp was now filled with confusion. A man with strong medicine power was telling them to hurry while the man they had chosen as their leader was telling them to go slowly. Many of the women began gathering their pots and blankets and tying them onto the pack animals. Other families splashed across the creek to gather their horses. Even if there was nothing to fear, this was sign enough that the time had come to get moving.

In the midst of the confusion, two scouts came riding into camp at full run. They had spent the night camped out in the open country with a group of Walk-Around Sioux hunters.

"We have just seen buffalo stampeding," they shouted. "Soldiers are coming."

This message confused the people even more. Some quickly gathered up their remaining camp goods and began hurrying up the draw toward the north. Others resisted, unwilling to interpret the movements of the buffalo as a sign of approaching soldiers. Perhaps the animals were just moving north to escape the mountain snows. It did no good to alarm the children over nothing.

But the young warriors were not about to ignore such a warning. They had been wary of this campsite from the beginning. A few clambered up the bluff to the south to take up positions of defense. There would be no repeat of the Big Hole massacre while they were alive.

Order in the camp was now fragmenting rapidly. Children, awakened by the commotion, were running about in excitement. The horses, ever sensitive to the emotions of the people, were kicking and snorting. Dogs barked wildly and ran among the shelters and campfires.

In the midst of the commotion, another scout came riding at full run from the south. He reined to a stop on the rise above the camp, fired his rifle, and began shaking his buffalo blanket and riding in tight circles. There was no mistaking this message. It was the signal of an imminent attack.

People shouted for their children and grabbed what they could. Wottolen's dream had been right. Somehow, troops were upon them. There was no time to wonder who they were or where they had come from.

Joseph ran back from the horse herd to the edge of the creek. He could see the panic in the camp. "The horses! The horses!" he shouted. "Save the horses!" Clothes and cooking utensils they could do without. But if they lost their horses, they would be helpless here in open country.

More people splashed across the creek toward the herd. Those whose horses were already in camp threw their possessions into packs, gathered their families, and headed up the gullies to the open plains toward the north.

But while they were packing, a strange sound rose up in the far distance. At first it seemed to be thunder, or a herd of stampeding buffalo. But instead of passing, it grew louder, until the whole ground was shaking.

Suddenly, with almost no warning, a sea of blue uniforms poured around the bluff to the south and headed toward the plain where the horses were grazing. In the lead were Indians stripped for battle and wearing long, feathered war bonnets.

The few remaining warriors who had not yet taken positions on the hillsides dropped everything and raced up the bluffs to firing positions. Some had not even had time to dress. They knew it was up to them to hold off these attackers and give the people time to escape.

Joseph ran back to the center of the herd and began shouting orders. The soldiers' intentions were clear: they were trying to scatter the horses. If they succeeded, the people would be left on foot to be hunted down and shot like animals. He threw a rope to Noise of Running Feet and told her to catch any horse and head toward the Old Woman Country with the others.

All around him the horses were shrieking and rearing. While he was struggling to calm their panic, Indians on horseback and painted for war came charging full speed into their midst, followed by soldiers screaming and shouting and firing their weapons. Some rode past in pursuit of the escaping families, while others rode into the center of the herd and slapped at the animals' flanks to scatter them into the hills.

He could hear shouts from the men across the creek and the voices of women calling for their children. Dogs yelped and howled, and horses bolted through the camp, trampling shelters and destroying the camp goods. The air was filled with the screams of women and infants, and the smoke from gunpowder hung low in the air, burning the eyes and stinging the nostrils. On the bluff to the south, Joseph could see flashes from rifle barrels and hear the cries of warriors and soldiers. Nothing was clear except that they were under attack. Not since the Big Hole had it been like this.

He turned quickly to the north to see if Noise of Running Feet had caught up with the others, but could make out nothing through the smoke and haze. His heart was sick as he thought of her riding frantically across these snow-covered plains, pursued by soldiers and Cheyenne warriors. He knew what they would do to a twelve-year-old girl if they caught her. But she was now beyond his help. It was his wife and his infant daughter he had to protect.

Like a man in a trance, he jumped on his horse. Calling to his *wayakin* for protection, he headed toward the creek through the fire of the soldiers. If his spirit power was strong, he would make it to his family. If not, he would fall.

Bullets cut through his clothing and grazed his flesh. They whistled by his head and thudded into the soft ground near his horse's feet. He rode crouched over, trying to present as small a target as possible. His felt his horse flinch as a bullet dug into its side. But he was not being harmed. His *wayakin* power was with him.

He splashed through the frigid creek and up the small bank to the crude shelter where his wife was huddling with their infant. She handed him his gun and shouted, "Here is your rifle! Go and fight!" Then she crawled back into her shelter to comfort their terrified infant.

Joseph had not willingly engaged in combat since the battle at White Bird Canyon. But the end was near if they could not drive these soldiers back. For the first time since the Big Hole, his anger was greater than his sorrow. He took his rifle and ran up the hill toward Ollokot, who had dug in with the other warriors. There was a time for peace, but that time was gone. Now they had to fight to save the lives of the women and children.

Across the creek to the west he could see soldiers driving the horses off toward the hills. To the east other soldiers were riding hard along the bluffs around the campsite. Their strategy was becoming clear. The group that attacked the horses would scatter the herd, then secure the broad plain to the west. The other soldiers would surround the camp on the bluffs. Once they had the camp boxed in, they could mount a charge from the weakest point. If they were able to break through the defense of the warriors, the foot soldiers could rush in and slaughter everyone left in camp. If not, they could set up a siege and slowly starve the people to death.

But the situation was not without hope. Last night, despite Looking Glass's insistence that they were beyond the reach of the soldiers, Ollokot and the other warriors had surveyed the land to determine the best way to protect the people if they were attacked. A quick view of the terrain had convinced them that the camp, though vulnerable to attack, was well situated for defense. The bluff to the south was too steep for cavalry to ride down, so soldiers approaching from there would have to dismount and attack on foot. A few well-armed warriors in fortified positions near the crest of that bluff could hold an entire army at bay.

There was a low draw in the hills to the east. Soldiers on horses would be tempted to attack the camp through this crease. But it was narrow and long. Troops attacking there could be funneled to an easy death at the hands of a few well-placed riflemen.

Soldiers trying to move around the outer perimeter of the bluffs would have to travel across open, treeless hilltops without benefit of cover. They too could be held off by well-positioned warriors with steady aim and accurate weapons. It was all a question of achieving strategic positions and holding them. And, from what Joseph could see, the warriors had gained those strategic positions.

The warriors also were now well schooled in fighting white soldiers. All remembered the lessons learned in White Bird Canyon—that bluecoats panicked when they were leaderless. So the warriors knew to focus their fire on anyone who wore stripes or raised his voice in command. Once those giving orders were killed, the troops would disintegrate into a directionless mass, and the fight would become man against man. No Nez Perce feared a U.S. soldier in hand-to-hand combat.

It was the Cheyenne they needed to fear most. Like all Indians, the Cheyenne were used to fighting alone and communicating almost by instinct. They knew how to exploit weak spots, and a single man could do as much damage as a whole brigade of white soldiers if he found the point of advantage. But even if the Cheyenne did not intend to kill Nez Perce people, they would surely seek to steal the Nez Perce horses. With their skills at movement and strong spirit powers, they were a threat that could not be ignored.

Joseph looked to the north of the camp, where a small group of the best horses had been hidden in a draw. With the rest of the herd being run off by the soldiers, these remaining mounts needed to be protected at all costs. He raised his rifle in salute to the few warriors who had taken up positions on a point of rocks directly above these remaining horses. They were the farthest from the camp, and their situation was the most perilous. But they understood their mission. They saluted back, then returned to firing against the soldiers and Cheyenne who were rapidly surrounding them on the hillsides.

The battle was over in less than an hour. The camp was in shambles. Pans and clothing and children's dolls lay strewn about the ground. The soldiers had been beaten back, but they had gained the high bluffs that encircled the camp. The horses had been scattered, and the people had been split. Some had made it away toward the north, and the others who had not been able to gather their families or find their horses were now pinned down in the broad hollow of the campsite. It was impossible to know which warriors were still alive in the rifle pits on the hillsides and who had been killed. No one was even sure who had been among those who tried to escape and if they had outdistanced the soldiers or if they had been caught and slaughtered. The clear air of the morning was turning cold, and the children were hysterical. No one was sure what to do.

Most of the people had retreated to one of the deep folds on the far north end of the bowl. There they could keep out of the direct line of the soldier's fire, but they were backed into a corner. The warriors in the rifle pits on the hills above them would have to hold off any attack, or they could be slaughtered like animals in a pen.

The situation was desperate. Many of the children were only partly dressed, and many of the people were wet and shivering from running through the creek to escape the fighting. The old women had placed the frightened children beneath the buffalo robes and were trying to keep them calm and warm, while the younger, stronger women had begun digging shelter pits into the hillsides.

Joseph and the others who had not retreated to the gully or were not in fighting positions on the hills remained out in the open near the creek, piling saddles and camp goods around the perimeter of hastily dug rifle pits. They knew that the soldiers were just regrouping. They could hear their shouts and the snorting of their horses from the bluffs above. Another attack could come at any minute, and it was up to the remaining men to keep any charge from making it to the huddling women and children in the gully.

Soon a hail of bullets rained down on the camp from the east, and several dozen foot soldiers poured over the steep bluffs and out of the ravines to the south, shouting and waving weapons. From their rifle pits the Nez Perce shot them one by one, though many of the soldiers were able to dodge between the rocks and gullies and advance toward the camp.

A few made it all the way across the open creek bottom to the old campsite where Joseph and the others were barricaded. The men fought fiercely, shooting from behind the piled saddles at every uniformed figure who came into view. From the draw to the east they could hear fearsome screaming and firing but could not determine what was happening. Husis Kute, the Palouse chief, fearing the Cheyenne more than the soldiers, took it upon himself to focus his firing at their warriors. Through the smoke and mist he took aim at any warrior he saw, shouting, "I got one!" each time he saw an Indian fall.

At one point, one of the Nez Perce men yelled out to the attackers, "Who are you? We don't want to fight." The only answer was the sharp snap of a rifle shot and the terrifying percussion of a heavy shell tearing into the ground on the edge of camp.

Darkness came none too soon. The people had withstood the attack, but they were deeply shaken. One by one, the warriors crawled back into camp, frightened, wounded, shivering from the cold. They needed warmth, but there could be no fires because the glow would provide easy targets for the soldiers on the hills.

The people huddled together under buffalo skins and passed around the few bits of cooked meat left in their stores. The warriors sat silently, refusing food so that the children could eat. Everyone was exhausted and numb.

In the cold darkness they tried to take stock of what had happened. Some of the young boys who had been playing by the creek said they had seen Indians in war bonnets riding on the ridge early in the morning but had been afraid to tell anyone. Warriors reported that they had seen Cheyenne the day before and had even eaten with them, but the men had said they were only hunting and were not working for any soldiers.

But there was little time for conversation. They had to use the few hours of darkness to their advantage. The wounded had to be retrieved and the bodies of the dead brought back to camp and buried. Weapons and ammunition had to be stripped from the fallen soldiers. They needed to bring water from the creek to slake the thirst of the injured and the dying, and the dead horses had to be skinned and dressed to replenish the dwindling food supply.

It was decided that the rest of the camp should move to the tight draw on the north edge of the hollow where the women and children had retreated after the first attack. There the women could dig better shelter pits into the banks and keep the people out of the line of fire. The draw also gave them a better chance to protect the camp from direct attack because the area was less exposed to charges from the cavalry and better situated to be defended by a few warriors strategically situated on nearby promontories.

Moving quickly and with as little noise as possible, they dragged their few remaining possessions across the several hundred yards of frozen ground to the narrow ravine. Some of the women were already digging into the earth with bowie knives and pots and pans while others were crawling out into the battlefield, ministering to the wounded and stripping guns and ammunition from the dead soldiers. One white soldier, too injured to crawl, kept crying out that he was thirsty. Some of the women brought him water in a buffalo horn and placed a blanket under his head. They had sons and husbands too and did not wish to increase his suffering.

The men who were strong enough to do so used the cover of darkness to scale the northern bluff and begin digging rifle pits with knives and the broad, flat-ended bayonets they had taken from the soldiers at the Big Hole. These pits would have to be deep and wide enough to contain several fighters, so fire could be leveled in all directions at once if necessary.

They worked hurriedly. Some pits were hollowed out to the depth of a man's waist; others were little more than depressions in the ground, barely deep enough to offer protection to a single fighter. Stones were then piled around the edges, with small cracks left in between, so the warriors could peer out without having their heads vulnerable to direct shots.

Everyone knew another attack would come at daybreak. White soldiers did not have the courage to attack Indians at night. But even in the darkness they had to be alert to the presence of the Cheyenne. Every animal sound, every shift in the wind, had to be listened to with caution. Indian warriors had no fear of darkness and could call upon spirit powers for assistance. And they did not move with heavy footsteps like white soldiers.

Huddled in one corner of the gully, old Alahoos was listening to the people recount their experiences of the day. It was he who had been chosen to keep track of the dead and to carry the story of the fight in his memory. One by one, people gathered around him to tell what they knew.

What they told him was numbing. Ollokot, Joseph's beloved brother, was dead. Toohoolhoolzote was dead. Pile of Clouds, one of the bravest fighters who had joined them in the Bitterroot, was dead. Husis Kute, who had been heard shouting out each of his kills, had made a terrible mistake. He had tragically confused Nez Perce fighters with Cheyenne warriors and had accidentally shot Lone Bird and two other warriors who had taken up positions near the soldiers' lines. Poker Joe had also fallen to a Nez Perce bullet.

When all the deaths were counted, Alahoos reported at least twenty killed, including many of the best warriors and several elders who had been doing nothing more than trying to hide from the bullets. Of the families who had escaped toward the north, he had found out little. Yellow Wolf had crept back into camp after holding off the soldiers who had chased after the families, but he could tell them nothing more than that the soldiers had gotten most of the horses but ultimately had been turned back. Whether the people had made it the forty miles to safety at the border, he could not say. He knew nothing of the fate of Noise of Running Feet. Nor was there word of the hunters and women who had left early in the morning to catch and skin buffalo. Perhaps they had been captured; perhaps they were hiding in the hills. Perhaps they had joined the fleeing families. Perhaps they were all dead.

As to the soldiers, no one knew what losses they had sustained or even who they were. No one knew how many Cheyenne they had on their side or how they were connected with General Howard. All anyone knew was that they had been wearing winter boots and heavy coats, not the skimpy torn capes and worn-out shoes last seen on Howard's men.

Other things too were brought forth to Alahoos. Young Elahweemah, so small he could barely get on a horse by himself, had been seen riding to the north with his little brother holding on tightly behind him. A soldier was chasing after them, shooting. One of the soldier's bullets had cut so close that it clipped one of the braids from the younger boy's head.

Two Moons told of seeing Grizzly Bear Lying Down throwing signs to one of the Cheyenne warriors, saying, "We have red skin, red blood. Why do you fight us?" The Cheyenne had signaled back that he would only shoot over the Nez Perce's heads. But Two Moons had seen that same Cheyenne kill a Nez Perce woman only moments later. The Cheyenne himself had escaped unharmed; he must have been a man of strong medicine because bullets could not touch him. Grizzly Bear Lying Down had soon been killed by a shot from a soldier's gun.

As the night deepened, the weather worsened. The wind picked up, and rain turned to sleet, then snow. The elders and the children huddled together beneath their buffalo blankets, listening to the moans of the wounded and the sporadic gunfire from the soldiers. The Old Woman Country now seemed like a distant, hopeless dream.

By morning, the stark reality of the situation had revealed itself. Most of the horses were gone. The soldiers had taken positions on all the bluffs as well as out on the plain to the west, and had them surrounded. No one knew if Sitting Bull had been alerted or even if he would come. The whole camp was covered in several inches of wet, heavy snow. They were alone and encircled in a vast, empty landscape.

The men huddled together in council. Some thought they should wait until nightfall and try to sneak the rest of the camp through the soldiers' lines. It would not be hard, they said. The soldiers were spread thinly, and there were great gaps in the line.

But Joseph was against this. He pointed to the wounded and the elderly and the women with young children. "They will never make it through," he said. "And even if they do, what will happen to them? The ground is now covered with snow, we have few horses, and the people have no shoes."

Yet they could hardly stand and fight. Their best warriors were dead. Fewer than a hundred men young and strong enough to carry on a good fight remained. The rest of the camp was made up of old men, barely able to see, and women and children. With the exception of some of the younger women, they surely could not be expected to take up arms.

Occasional gunshots cut through the gray dawn. A big gun boomed and roared in the distance. From up on the bluffs a voice shouted down telling them to surrender. One of the remaining young warriors shouted back contemptuously, "Come and take our hair." It was a cruel and bitter challenge: in fact, a soldier had been seen the day before scalping one of the warriors who had fallen during the fight.

Joseph spoke for giving up. There was no way to continue the flight, he said. Whoever this new commander was, it would be better to talk to him than to wait for Howard, who had shown the rifle at the meeting in Lapwai and was probably following a day and a half behind. Perhaps this new soldier chief was a man of greater honor or was more important. He was surely a better general, and his men were better fighters. Perhaps he was a man with whom they could make an honorable peace.

White Bird and Looking Glass disagreed. White men's promises were never to be trusted, and besides, they still held out hope. During the night six men who knew the land had been sent through the soldiers' lines to contact Sitting Bull. At least one of them was sure to get there. Perhaps some of those who had escaped during the confusion of the first attack had already contacted Sitting Bull's scouts, and the Lakota chief was on his way. If he and his two thousand warriors arrived, it mattered little if this new soldier held the high ground or if Howard arrived with his men. The blood of the bluecoats would cover the ground, and the Nez Perce could travel in peace to the Old Woman Country.

In the end, the chiefs decided that the camp should hold out. The children were well protected in earthen hollows and pits dug in the sides of the draw. The warriors were positioned under buffalo robes in their rifle pits and were well supplied with weapons and ammunition that had been taken from the wounded and dead soldiers during the night. Though the people were low on food, and the earth in which they were hiding was damp and frigid, they still had their lives. They would stay in their shelters, huddled against the snow and freezing drizzle, and wait for Sitting Bull to arrive.

16

"Colonel Miles Wants to Meet with Chief Joseph"

O N T H E S O U T H E N D of the battlefield, on the hill above the Nez
Perce camp, the soldiers too were huddled against the snow and
wind, trying to stay warm in the early morning cold while Miles mapped
out another strategy. His attack had been a failure. The Indians had not
scattered as he had expected but had dug in and held their ground. He had
succeeded in pinning down the Nez Perce, something no other commander had been able to accomplish, but almost seventy of his men had
been killed or wounded—a number that might be acceptable if it had resulted in surrender and defeat but a numbing total when nothing more
had been achieved than placing the Indians under siege. If a siege was all
he had sought, it could have been achieved with no loss of life. This was
not the kind of result that would gain him a general's star.

The night had been hell for his men, especially his wounded. The pack
train with the tents had not arrived, so they had spent the dark hours shivering under thin blankets while their frozen clothes stuck to their bodies
and their blankets became soaked from the snow and blood.

One by one the injured had succumbed to the wet and cold, dying with
cries, curses, and desperate tearful pleas for mercy. His remaining men had
been unable to bury the dead because of fears of the Nez Perce sharpshooters. Many of them had never been in combat before, and even the most experienced had never confronted a foe that shot with such deadly accuracy.
Some claimed that they had seen Indians firing from as far as a thousand
yards away, almost always hitting their target.

Louis Shambow, the white man in charge of the Cheyenne scouts, said that he had spent the day pinned down behind a rock, and every time he placed a small stone on top of it to see if the Nez Perce were still out there, it had been blown off by a direct hit from a bullet.

All the brave talk about avenging Custer had long since ceased. Each man now had to face the dark possibility that perhaps Custer's defeat at the hands of Sitting Bull had resulted not from bad strategy but from the superior fighting skills of the warriors who had opposed him.

All night men had fired randomly into the dark at any unusual sound, and there had been constant frightened reports of someone seeing shadowy movements on the hillsides. None wanted to contemplate what would happen if Sitting Bull's two thousand warriors, with their known penchant for torturing and mutilating, were to sweep down from the north to join these Nez Perce, who already had fought the troops to a standstill.

Miles shared their fears. A siege took time—maybe enough time to allow Sitting Bull to arrive. He knew his depleted forces were no match for the seasoned Sioux fighters. He did not want to see his men's throats cut and bellies slit. He did not want to be this year's Custer.

At the same time, he did not relish the arrival of his old commander, General Howard. He knew he had the Nez Perce trapped and that Howard was coming up behind, albeit with a small force. He had great personal fondness for Howard, but he desperately wanted this capture for himself. If Howard arrived and claimed command, the victory that Miles's men had suffered so greatly to achieve would be credited to the senior officer.

As he listened to the moans of his wounded, he knew that whatever he did, it could not be another direct attack. His loss of a fifth of his fighting force had been unacceptable—and his remaining troops, now fewer than three hundred, were demoralized and frightened. He had expected that a direct charge would result in a quick surrender, as it had with other tribes. But instead it had only increased the Nez Perce resolve. He was now faced with a dug-in foe that shot with uncanny accuracy. None of his soldiers was anxious to risk taking a hit from a Nez Perce bullet when they had seen that the wounded were being sorted into groups of those being left to die and those being given medical attention that amounted to little more than a quick bandaging followed by a swig of brandy laced with opium. And the prospect of field amputations—a terrifying practice employing knives to cut through the skin and muscle and a dirty saw to cut through the bone— dampened the battle enthusiasm of all but the most hardened fighter.

In addition, the weather had turned against them. Miles had used the mists and low-lying fog to his advantage as cover while he had approached the Indians along the far side of the Little Rockies. But these plummeting temperatures and this wet heavy snow now made his situation miserable. His men were well equipped with long underwear, buffalo hide greatcoats, and the newest-issue rubber-bottomed arctic overshoes. But still, they were soaked to the skin from sloshing through the mud and lying on the wet ground. Men who were wet and cold too easily lost their fighting will. A call for another charge would be met with something between indifference and mutiny. He needed a different strategy. He needed to find a way to force Joseph's immediate surrender or capture.

All night he had pondered how best to achieve this. Now, in morning light, he had a plan. After his men had eaten their meager breakfast, he ordered shelling to begin again. He did not want his troops to exhaust their ammunition; even when the supply trains and Howard's and Sturgis's men eventually arrived, they would need every gun and every bullet if they were to survive a possible attack by Sitting Bull's warriors. But he wanted the Nez Perce to realize that they were trapped and that there would be no escape.

He summoned the men who had arrived the previous evening with the Hotchkiss gun. This weapon was a new army prototype that was like a small cannon—a French-manufactured successor to the clumsier mountain howitzer that troops had used during the Civil War and in Indian battles such as at the Big Hole. Like the howitzer, the Hotchkiss could be broken down into pieces and packed on three mules, then reassembled on wheels and maneuvered easily in the field. It had a range of fifteen hundred yards—enough to pin down an enemy like the Nez Perce at a distance far too great for them to offer any meaningful return fire.

Unfortunately, as Miles found out, it suffered from a design flaw: its barrel position could not be raised or lowered sufficiently to allow for high trajectory firing or to allow it to shoot downward onto an enemy dug in below. If he left it at its normal trajectory, it would lob its shells far beyond the Nez Perce shelters. If he tipped it forward far enough to aim down at the Nez Perce encampment, it would fall on its nose.

Miles ordered his men to dig a pit for the yoke of the gun so it could be leaned backward and used to lob shells into the sky, like a mortar. Though it could not be aimed accurately in this fashion, the shells would make a fearsome noise and a frightening percussion whenever one landed. Even if only an occasional round hit its intended target, random terror from the sky would eventually wear down the will of even the indomitable Nez Perce.

With this weapon of terror in place, he set his plan for capturing Joseph into motion.

Meanwhile, in the Nez Perce camp, all was gloom and despair. The wet snow that had fallen most of the night had soaked the people and their few possessions. A raw wind was whistling and howling among the draws and gullies. The few warriors remained defiant, and young boys, striving to be men, spoke bravely of avenging the deaths if they were given weapons. But most had lost their heart for the struggle. The cold and hunger and sadness of families separated and loved ones left unburied had become almost too much to bear. The bodies of the dead lay scattered throughout the campsite, covered by only a ghostly layer of snow. The shells from the soldiers' guns were shaking the ground, threatening to collapse the shelter pits and bury the children inside. It was like a nightmare from which they could not awake.

The wait for Sitting Bull had become an obsession. Men anxiously scanned the northern horizon for signs of movement. Between gunshots they strained their ears against the worsening wind in hopes of hearing the sounds of hoofbeats from approaching horses. But there was only the snow and the gunfire and the great howling gales of the cold northern plains.

At one point, Looking Glass thought he saw a Sioux warrior approaching in the distance. He stood up in his rifle pit to get a better look and immediately was felled by a bullet through the forehead. The chief who had brought them to this place, who had been so sure that he could lead them to freedom and safety, had now too gone to the camp of the dead.

Throughout the camp, talk continued about giving up. All through the previous day the soldiers had been yelling down to them from the hills, telling them to surrender. A few of the Cheyenne scouts, hoping to save the lives of the women and children, even rode up to the gully to ask the Nez Perce to consider the army's offer. Three Nez Perce met them with handshakes and a beaded necklace that had been made by one of the young girls. The people would listen, they said, but no more. The Cheyenne peered into the pathetic hollow filled with crying children and snow-covered bodies, then rode back to deliver the Nez Perce response to the soldiers.

About noon, a voice came echoing down from the hills above. The speaker was using Chinook, but the message was clear: "Colonel Miles wants to meet with Chief Joseph." The request was accompanied by a white flag, indicating a desire for a truce.

The request threw the Nez Perce into a state of confusion. They did not all have confidence in Joseph, especially those who were opposed to surrender. They knew he had been against this flight from the earliest days in Camas Prairie and that his heart was for saving the people, not for fighting. Many doubted that he would have the courage to refuse a surrender offer from the soldiers.

But Joseph tried to calm their fears. They should agree to the meeting, he said. He would make no decisions but only hear what this Colonel Miles, whoever he was, had to say.

White Bird, however, remained opposed. He feared that Joseph's heart would be swayed as he heard the crying children and death songs of the elderly while he sat in council with this new soldier chief. Besides, it was men of White Bird's band who had killed the settlers on the Salmon River and Slate Creek. As their leader, he would surely be hanged if he gave himself up.

They discussed why it was that Joseph had been singled out. Perhaps Howard had told this new commander that Joseph's resolve was weak. Perhaps his was the only name the commander knew. It did not matter, Joseph said. His ears would be closed to talk of surrender. Any action that bought time while they awaited the arrival of Sitting Bull was an action worth pursuing.

In the end, the others agreed. Joseph would meet with this Colonel Miles. If nothing else, he could count the soldiers' numbers and see their fortifications and weapons.

They raised a piece of white bunting on a stick, indicating their desire for truce, and sent Tom Hill, who spoke some English, across to the soldiers' camp to arrange the meeting. The people peered anxiously from their hiding places as Hill rode his horse through the corpse-littered snow to the soldier camp behind the far southern bluff. Few were confident that he would emerge alive.

After a long while he came walking into view with a soldier at his side. The man had a large mustache and long side-whiskers. He wore a heavy fur hat and a long coat with a fur collar. At this distance he looked more like a bear than a man. He walked with an air of authority and showed no fear in the face of the Nez Perce, who were training their weapons on him from all vantage points. This, they realized, must be Colonel Miles.

The two men walked to a rise halfway between the camps. Then Tom Hill called to Joseph to come across, but to come armed. Slowly, Joseph stood and prepared to approach. The soldiers peered down from their places on the bluff, equally anxious to see this Chief Joseph about whom they had heard so much. From what they understood, it was he who had led this unlikely retreat, he who had outsmarted and outmaneuvered Howard, he who had fought off Gibbon's surprise attack at the Big Hole, he who had tricked Sturgis at Clarks Fork. They had experienced firsthand the marksmanship of his warriors and had seen firsthand the toughness of his people. The thought that he could outrun and outfight the best the U.S. Army had to offer while traveling fifteen hundred miles with old women and children made him seem like a giant in their minds.

So the man who stood up and walked toward them came as something of a shock. He was just a man like themselves. He was broad and solid, about six feet tall, and wore his hair long, with a small braid on either side of his face. He had no war paint, no feathers, wore no warrior dress. What struck them most was his air of intelligence and calm. They had expected a creature of sinister demeanor and animal cunning. What they saw was a man with a warm smile and dignified bearing. Though he was obviously weary, he carried himself with great presence. He walked slowly toward them, carrying on a quiet conversation with the several warriors who accompanied him. As he approached, they could see that his shirt and blanket were riddled with bullet holes.

He crossed the body-strewn, snow-covered bottomlands and made his way up the rise to where Miles and Tom Hill were waiting. As he and Miles met, Joseph reached out his hand as a sign of friendship and peace. In full sight of the two camps, the men shook hands, then conversed a bit with the help of Tom Hill before walking together up the bluff toward the colonel's tent.

The sight of the handshake and the two men walking side by side under a flag of truce seemed, for the moment, to change the whole feel of the battlefield. Slowly, people from both sides stepped from behind their barricades. Keeping a wary eye on each other, knowing that rifles were poised on them from both camps, they moved cautiously down into the hollows and coulees in search of their wounded and their dead.

It was a poignant and surreal moment. The soldiers could hear the Nez Perce babies crying from their frigid dirt shelter pits in the nearby ravines. The Indian women looked in the faces of the soldiers and saw young boys no older than their brothers and sons. For a moment, time and the war stood still. Then they all set themselves to the grim task of brushing the snow from the corpses and dragging the bodies back to their respective camps.

On the hill above, in the warmth of Colonel Miles's tent, Joseph listened warily as this new soldier chief told of how he wished no more war, of how General Howard and Colonel Sturgis would soon arrive with more men, of how, as a man, he wished to avoid more unnecessary killing.

Joseph responded that he too wished to end this killing. His brother had been killed. Other chiefs had been killed. His people were cold and hungry. He would gladly end this fighting and wanted nothing more than the return of his horses and to be left alone. But he spoke for no one other than himself, and there were many among the Nez Perce who preferred to wait for Sitting Bull, whose warriors would surely overwhelm any forces that the colonel could mount against them.

He told Miles of White Bird's fears, of the people's concern about being hanged and exiled as had happened to the Modoc when they had surrendered. He asked what would happen if the Nez Perce were to lay down their arms, whether they would be allowed to return to their homeland or whether they too would be punished with exile or death.

Colonel Miles assured Joseph that the people would be returned to their homeland, though such a journey would have to wait until spring when the mountain passes had cleared. In the meantime, the army could accompany them to a place in the Yellowstone country where they could camp for the winter. They would have to turn over their weapons, but their needs would be met.

At this, Joseph balked. He might be willing to propose to the people that they give half the weapons to the army, since many had been obtained in raids and from the bodies of soldiers. But the others they would need to keep so they could hunt during the winter.

This was impossible, Miles explained. Surrender would have to be unconditional, and all weapons would have to be turned over.

Again, Joseph balked. I am not talking about surrender, he said, I am talking about an agreement to stop fighting. We have no surrender to make because there has never been any war. If there had been a war, the Nez Perce could easily have killed all the soldiers many times over. Only the soldiers have treated this as a war, killing women and children. To his people, this had been a journey to find a place where they could live in peace and have a fair chance to talk to the white chiefs about returning to their homes. They had fought only as much as was necessary to continue their journey and to protect themselves from discovery. Any wanton killing had been done by out-of-control young men, often drunk on white man's whiskey. Even Miles must understand that young men cannot easily be controlled. As to their journey, the people could continue it even now if they waited for the arrival of Sitting Bull, which he and the other chiefs were quite willing to do. There would be no talk of surrender.

The two men measured each other. Neither was willing to compromise. Finally, Joseph stood up and extended his hand to Miles. There was no further need for discussion. He would return to his people and tell them what had been said. Each side would have to await the arrival of the supporting forces to see who would prevail.

He and Tom Hill then left the tent and began to walk from the camp. But before he had gone more than a few steps, Tom Hill was called back, and several armed soldiers blocked Joseph's way. Joseph looked at them, then at Miles. Miles stared back, revealing nothing. Joseph nodded sadly and returned to the tent. The others had been right. The white man could not be trusted.

On the battlefield below, the strange lassitude and passivity were continuing. The sorrow at death seemed greater than the anger of war, and all were occupied in removing their dead and wounded to places of rest and refuge behind their respective lines. The soldiers pulled and carried the bodies of the men up the side of the hill and lay them in a long depression like pieces of cordwood. The Nez Perce dragged the bodies of their fallen sons and fathers and brothers back to the coulee and laid them out on buffalo blankets. Neither side could bury their dead in a manner that did them honor.

The snow continued to fall, covering the corpses of horses and ponies until they seemed less like animals than strange, boulderlike forms. The distant hills and mountains were lost in the mist, and the wind blew and swirled with an empty moan. The people gradually retreated to their gully, and the soldiers slowly made their way back to the bluff. The few soldier sentries posted on the circling hills huddled in their hastily dug pits. Both sides searched the snow-blown distances for signs of Sitting Bull or Howard.

On occasion, a thin line of movement would appear on the distant plains, striking fear and excitement into the hearts of those who saw it. But always it turned out to be a distant herd of buffalo walking in almost military precision against the blowing snow and cold.

Each side knew that the fighting was now at a stalemate. The Nez Perce, without their horses, could never hope to escape with children, elderly, and wounded across these cold, windblown plains. The soldiers knew they did not have the horses or wagons to transport their wounded to safety. There was nothing either side could do but wait and hope that the meeting between Joseph and Miles could bring some conclusion to this situation, which was breaking everyone's spirit and sapping everyone's will.

Tom Hill's return dashed the Nez Perce's hopes. They watched anxiously as he made his way alone down the bluff and back across the battlefield to their hollow, hoping that he brought word that Joseph and Miles had reached some kind of understanding. Instead, he told them that Joseph had been taken prisoner by Miles and that he himself had been sent back as a messenger to demand their surrender. He went from shelter pit to shelter pit, telling the people that the time had come to quit fighting; that Joseph was held in the soldier chief's tent; that the soldier chief had promised they could return to their own country if they quit fighting and gave up their arms.

This was exactly what some of the people had feared and exactly what others had hoped to hear. But all were angry that Joseph was being held against his will by the soldier chief. They had met under a flag of truce. Now that truce had been shown to be a lie. This new war chief Miles was a man of two tongues, just like all the other white soldiers and government men. This, said White Bird, is what comes of trusting in white man's promises.

As the Nez Perce huddled against the sleet and cold, trying to decide what to do, they noticed a strange figure emerging from the swirling snow of the battlefield. It was a soldier in a long, yellow raincoat, moving casually on horseback among the snow-covered corpses and making his way toward their camp. He exhibited no fear. In fact, he seemed almost curiously indifferent. Accompanied by several Cheyenne scouts, he rode directly into the hollow where the Nez Perce were dug in, wandering leisurely through the campsite and peering into the shelter pits and the rifle hollows.

The Nez Perce were amazed. What was this man doing? Was he reconnoitering? Checking to see if they were caching weapons? Was this part of some larger strategy by this new soldier commander Miles on the hill?

Yellow Bull went up to the soldier and grabbed the reins of his horse. White Bull then pulled him out of the saddle, announcing, "I'm going to kill this man."

But others stopped him. "Why don't you kill soldiers when there is fighting?" they said. "We who do the real fighting don't want to kill him, so why should you?" White Bull was well known among the tribe as a man whose courage was all in his mouth, and this was exactly the kind of rash act they could not afford at this dire time when one of their few remaining chiefs was being held in captivity.

Wottolen and Yellow Bull immediately realized the value of the man and ordered that he be kept in camp and treated well. He appeared to be a commanding officer, and he was their insurance that Joseph would be returned alive. His presence would also protect the camp from sneak attack. Even white soldiers did not cause the certain death of their own men.

All night the people watched the hilltop where this Colonel Miles had his tent. There was no word from Joseph or the soldiers. Yellow Bull even approached the soldiers' camp under the flag of truce and asked to see the chief. His request was refused, though he was allowed see the tent where he was told that Joseph was being kept.

Meanwhile, the Nez Perce treated their strange hostage like a guest. They gave him water and such food as they had and allowed him to keep his pistol and walk around, so long as he didn't go beyond the edge of the camp. When it was time to sleep, they placed him a shelter pit with about a dozen of their own people. But they soon had to move him for his own safety, as there were many who still wished to see him dead. He spent the remainder of the night under guard in a different shelter pit, sleeping on a buffalo robe and covered by two blankets.

Morning dawned to three inches of new wet, heavy snow. The camp was now soaked, and the bodies of the dead were now simply lumps under the shroud of white that covered the land. The buffalo chips that the women had used for fires were buried under the fresh snow and had to be found by foot. Even when they were discovered, they were almost too wet to light. The children were whimpering. The elderly were singing their death songs. It had been two days since the first attack, and still there was no sign of Sitting Bull and his warriors.

The Nez Perce leaders were now adamant. They wanted to know what had happened to Joseph. Late in the afternoon the day before, their scouts had heard the cheering of soldiers as the supply wagons of the army had come rumbling in, and now the people were forced to huddle in the cold and wet, uncertain of the fate of one of their two remaining chiefs while the aroma of fresh coffee and warm meals wafted down from the bluffs above.

The soldier too was hungry. He asked for warm food, but the Nez Perce had none to give him. They did give him some of their best remaining buffalo meat, but their food stock was limited. The warriors themselves had not eaten for days so the children could be fed. They told the man that if he wanted warm food, he should send a note to this Colonel Miles asking for some to be sent down.

The soldier sat down and wrote a note to his commanding officer. He said that he was being treated well and that he hoped Joseph was being treated in the same manner. The Nez Perce read the note as best they could to verify its contents, then sent Red Wolf's son to carry it to the tent where Colonel Miles was quartered.

Miles received the note with dismay. The captive soldier, Lieutenant Lovell Jerome, was known for his bravado. Miles had been aware of Jerome's foray and subsequent capture but had been hoping that the lieutenant could escape during the night. This note showed that his lieutenant was still in the hands of the hostiles. His brash subordinate had given the Nez Perce exactly what they needed—a hostage of significance. Miles had no choice but to agree to a prisoner exchange.

Reluctantly, he ordered Joseph to be readied for transfer and sent word to the Indian camp that he would release their chief when they released Jerome. The Indians replied that they would not release Jerome without proof of Joseph's release. Finally, it was agreed that there would be a meeting at a central point where the prisoners would be exchanged in full view and under the armed vigilance of both camps.

Miles instructed his Lieutenant Maus to affix a white flag to a staff, and at midmorning, he and Maus and Joseph advanced through the sleet and snow across the frozen hollows toward a buffalo robe that had been laid between the two camps to designate the point of exchange. Maus kept a cocked revolver under his coat to use on Joseph if any treachery took place.

As Miles and Joseph advanced, three Nez Perce men set out from their camp with Lieutenant Jerome. Riflemen from both camps lay on the snow-covered hilltops with weapons aimed and ready to fire if there was unusual movement or any sign of betrayal.

The walk was tense and grueling for all. The cold winds buffeted them, the wet sleet cut their faces. No one knew if a hothead or skittish fighter on either side might fire the shot that would result in a mass carnage of all involved. But there were no incidents. Joseph and Jerome met at the blanket, shook hands, and walked off toward their respective camps. Both sides kept their rifles poised until each man was safely back behind his own lines.

Once back in the Nez Perce camp, Joseph was surrounded by his people. How had he been treated? What terms had he been offered? How strong was their camp? What was the condition of the soldiers?

Much hinged on his answers. The people were desperate. Sitting Bull was nowhere to be seen, and the children were crying constantly from hunger. They could not go on this way. Some wanted to charge the soldiers. Others wanted to surrender. White Bird was nervous about what sort of agreements Joseph had made.

"I made no agreements," Joseph said. "The soldier chief, Colonel Miles, is the one who wants to quit. But then I was held against my will, like Toohoolhoolzote by General Howard. This man is like the others. His promises are no different from lies. We must continue to fight."

Tom Hill had heard enough. It was he who had been used by Miles to arrange a false truce, he who had been tricked by the colonel into bringing Joseph into camp. He shouted to the warriors that the time had come to charge and fight face-to-face. He started to run toward the soldiers, but only two men followed him. The people looked at each other, confused and uncertain. Then they slowly went back to their rifle barricades and shelter pits to contemplate the hopelessness of their situation.

The remainder of that day was a bleak, freezing standoff. The Nez Perce stayed barricaded in their shelter pits, and the soldiers huddled in their tents and at their rifle posts. Neither side wanted to waste their ammunition, and neither side wanted to charge. The battle had become as shapeless as the wintry, windblown landscape. The soldiers sent a wagon off to the distant hillsides to look for wood while the Nez Perce warriors, who had known almost no rest since the first attack, lay back and tried to catch a few moments of sleep to ward off the deep weariness and hunger that were quickly overtaking them.

Now and then a shot was fired into the cold and mist by one side or the other. But these were lackluster efforts, designed more to keep up the illusion of combat than to inflict any real damage on the enemy. The true adversary had become the cold and snow, and the only true hope of victory lay in the arrival of support for one side or the other.

Occasionally, words were shouted back and forth between the two camps. One Nez Perce warrior who could speak some English heard a soldier voice shout, "Charge them to hell!" from his post on the hilltop. The warrior quickly responded, "Go ahead and charge, you sons of bitches. You're not fighting the Sioux this time," a pointed reference to the Sioux willingness to flee or surrender when cornered. But mostly, there was only the desultory and sporadic gunfire of men weary of war and unsure of how to bring a bloody, hateful battle to an end.

Gradually, the bleak, gray day gave way to a chill, wintry dark, and all that had been accomplished was that each side had dug in deeper. The Nez Perce women had spent the day fighting the sleet and cold, digging in the wet, loamy earth with their camas hooks and butcher knives and removing the dirt with frying pans in order to enlarge the shelter pits. Now, at nightfall, enough shelter pits were dug deep enough to offer protection to everyone, and furrows had been hollowed out between some of the pits so that people could move from one to another in case of shelling or attack.

The warriors also had deepened their fighting pits by gouging the earth and throwing out the dirt as best they could. The soldiers had fortified their firing positions by piling up rock barriers behind which to hide. Every effort was made more difficult by the stinging wind and wet snow, which numbed the hands and froze the feet. Some of the soldier wounded had already lost their feet to frostbite, with the camp surgeon performing his dreaded amputations with an icy saw, using only a shot of brandy for anesthesia. The warriors, who fought stripped to the waist, were almost torpid from the cold and hunger. Many had not eaten for over three days—since that fateful breakfast before the first attack. Even their rigorous childhood training of long fasts and swimming in cold rivers had not prepared them for circumstances like these.

In the shelter holes the children cried softly. The old people sat empty-eyed, saying nothing or singing their death songs, while the infants squalled from hunger and cold. There was almost no food to cook. People's minds drifted deliriously back to their days in the Wallowa and along the Clearwater and Salmon until it was hard to know which was real and which was a dream. All thought constantly of the women and children who had ridden off from the battlefield on that first day, and wondered if they were still alive or if they had perished in this cold, harsh land.

Soon time too began to lose all meaning. They became indifferent to day and night, wishing only for some release. All night they could smell the sweet lingering scent of wood smoke drifting down from the soldiers' camp, mocking them with memories of heat and warmth. In the daylight the rich smell of boiling coffee and frying meat tortured them with its distant promise of nourishment and an end to their cutting hunger.

The men met in constant council, trying to decide what course of action to take. Hopes for assistance from Sitting Bull were fading rapidly. Each line of distant figures that proved to be buffalo, each sound that proved to be nothing more than the howling of the wind, dashed their hopes further. It had been days since the first group of people had escaped and almost as long since the first scouts had been sent. Surely at least one of them would have gotten through. It was time to face the hard truth that the promise of help from Sitting Bull might have been as great an illusion as the promise of help from the Flathead and the Crow.

White Bird spoke again for escape. The soldiers' siege line was so porous that they could easily sneak through unnoticed, and the scouts had observed that the soldiers often fell asleep at their posts. The murder of one or two would open a gap wide enough to assure easy passage. With the rain and snow and mist, all sound was muffled and sight was reduced to a few feet. They could surely make their escape under the cover of darkness and be almost to the Old Woman Land before the soldiers noticed.

"But what of our women and children?" Joseph countered. "Do you see horses to carry the wounded? Moccasins to cover the feet of our elders? Do you think we can walk through the snow in the dark far enough to escape the pursuit of soldiers on horseback when they discover we are gone? And what of the Cheyenne? At least we are dug in here, safe from them and the bullets of the soldiers. I do not wish to leave our wounded. I do not wish to leave the bodies of our dead unburied here in this hollow. I do not want to see the blood of our children reddening the snow. If you choose to go, you are free to do so. I will remain here with those who cannot travel. I have never heard of a wounded Indian recovering in the hands of the white man."

Many of the warriors also spoke for holding out. White soldiers were weak, they said, and this weather was cruel to the spirit. If the Nez Perce waited long enough, the soldiers might charge. Already, the braves had been taunting them, shouting across that soldiers were too cowardly to attack when warriors stood against them. They had also been firing their guns infrequently so the soldiers would believe they were low on bullets. Let those soldiers charge, they boasted, then we will show them our bullets. We are ready to destroy them. Then we can reclaim our horses and move on to the Old Woman Country.

But all this changed on the cold, dreary morning of the fourth day after the first attack. Miles had sent word that there must be surrender by the middle of the morning or his men would resume firing in earnest. This gave the warriors hope. Perhaps the foolhardy soldier charge they sought would actually take place. But as the deadline came and passed, a terrifying noise, like a clap of thunder, filled the air, followed by a fusillade of artillery fire that crackled like raindrops all through the camp. This was followed by another great explosion. The sound was so powerful, so terrifying, that the women and children jumped screaming back into the shelter pits and the dogs were thrown into a frenzy of yelping and barking. The soldiers had brought some new and horrible weapon onto the battlefield, and they were aiming it right into the ravine where everyone was hiding.

The percussion from this great gun shook the ground and caused explosions in the air above their heads. No one knew what it was or what horrible damage it might do. All they knew was that the soldiers had moved around to the west and that they were now in possession of a terrifying weapon that could fire from a great distance directly into the people's camp.

Joseph was despondent. This was the result of his meeting with Miles. Only the man in the yellow raincoat, for whom he had been traded—the man who had been allowed to wander into camp under the flag of truce that Joseph had wanted—could have identified so accurately the location of the places where the people were dug in. Surely it was he who had carried this information to Miles.

Perhaps the whole meeting with Miles had been a ruse, and Miles had sent the strange soldier in the yellow coat into camp to gain knowledge, knowing that the warriors would trade him for their chief. Was he, Joseph, responsible for the suffering and terror that were now being visited upon his people? And what sort of person was this Colonel Miles, that he would order his men to fire into shelters that held only women and small children and old men and wounded?

The great cannon shells continued to explode above the camp. On occasion, the firing would stop and the people would begin to hope that perhaps there was no more ammunition for this horrible gun. Then, just when they were beginning to feel secure, another thunderous concussion would rip the sky above them, showering chunks of steel down upon their heads.

Terror was now coming at them from all directions. The earth shook, knocking dirt loose from the walls of their shelter pits. The sky was filled with cracking gunfire, and shells cut randomly through the air in their camp. The snow continued to fall, melting under the warmth of their bodies, then freezing again as it settled on the cold earth, turning their shelters into damp, slushy tombs of water and ice. People began to see visions of their ancestors calling to them. There was nothing to do but wait for death.

Night brought some relief but, again, no assistance. The snow let up somewhat, and the women were able to crawl down to the creek to collect water in their buffalo horn cups.

The disagreements between White Bird and Joseph had now intensified. Two chiefs who for months had been in charge of the camp were now in charge of the war. White Bird's distrust of the soldiers and white justice ran deep. He had seen his valley overrun by miners, his people killed, his women raped, his elders cheated, and his efforts at all honest dialogue used against him. Every meeting with every white official had resulted in greater injustice and ruin for his people. Any surrender would be no different. Had Joseph not seen the way he had been used by Miles? This was the way white people acted. They sought no honor, only advantage.

Joseph could not disagree. But he could not lead the women and elders and wounded and children to certain death, cruelly delivered. One more day, and if Sitting Bull's warriors did not appear, he would give up the fight and try to find a place in the hearts of the white men where he could meet them with honesty and compassion. His father, Tuekakas, had once believed in these men and their ways. He too would take that chance, though he knew well that all efforts up to this point had turned to dust in their hands. Until that time, he would continue the resistance.

Other camp members were doing their own soul-searching. Many had relatives who had taken flight when the soldiers attacked and now were somewhere on these snowy plains, either meeting a harsh death or an uncertain welcome from the tribes with whom they sought refuge. Some in the camp wanted to do whatever was necessary to have a chance to find their lost loved ones. For others, fighting to the death was a question of honor and a gesture of respect to those who had already died. Still others held strong to their faith in their old ways and the old powers and would not betray that faith for something so small as their own personal survival.

If it came time to choose, each person, each family, would be free to make its own decision. But until that time, they would stay as one people, hoping for assistance from Sitting Bull, hoping for strength from their *wayakin* powers, hoping for some foolhardy act on the part of the soldiers that would let them gain the advantage and resume their flight to freedom.

But as the day dawned, none of these arrived. Instead, the shelling resumed, with great thundering bursts from the new gun mixing in with the sharp reports of constant rifle fire. The clouds were still low and the air was still cutting and raw, but the sky had cleared somewhat. After days of snow and sleet, the people were able to gaze across the landscape to see the reality of their situation.

All around them lay a great sea of snow, stretching as far as the eye could see. The high mountains behind them were still shrouded in mist, and the thin lines of distant ranges to the east and the west were almost invisible against the gray, wintry sky. The tall buffalo grass sticking up through the snow rattled and hissed in the relentless high plains wind. In the clear air, rifle reports from the entrenched soldiers seemed sharper, and in the far distance the people could see the great gun on the open plain beyond where the horse herd had been grazing. It was lined up to fire directly into the open end of the ravine that held the shelter pits.

In the rifle pits on the ridges above, the warriors were offering sporadic fire in response to shots coming from the soldiers. There was nothing to target, since all men on both sides had dug in. Except for the horror of the cannon, neither side could do damage to the other.

In midmorning, another thundering concussion from the great cannon filled the sky. Suddenly the earth in the ravine split open in a shower of dirt and mud. People screamed and ran to the place of the explosion. It was the shelter pit where little Aspiteen, only twelve years old, and her grandmother, Inetah, had been resting with three other women and a little boy.

The women grabbed their frying pans and camas hooks and dug frantically. They could hear choking and muffled screams beneath the dirt and see the struggling movement of partially buried bodies. Throwing dirt aside with their hands, they were able to grasp the arms of the little boy and the three other women and pull them free, but they could not get to little Aspiteen or Inetah in time. By the time they scraped the dirt and mud from them, their eyes were empty and their bodies lifeless. The soldier guns were now killing old women and children.

With two more dead, even more heart went out of the people. They knew now that their earth shelters were no protection against the shells of the great soldier gun far across the creek on the distant hillside. At any moment, another shell could land, killing the newborns or ripping the arms and legs from their tired mothers and fathers.

All afternoon they scanned the horizon for signs of Sitting Bull and waited for the explosion that would end the lives of more of their people. But neither Sitting Bull nor the explosion came, only the occasional concussion in the sky above them and the empty keening of the high plains wind. Then, as the thin afternoon light began to wane, scouts shouted down that the one-armed general had been seen riding in with a few of his officers. His troops could not be far behind.

The Nez Perce peered out into the purpling twilight in one last desperate search for any sign of Sitting Bull and his warriors. But there was nothing to be seen. Miles had won the waiting game. Any remaining hope for the people had disappeared. They had only three choices: try to escape, surrender, or fight and die.

17

"It Is Cold and We Have No Blankets"

WHEN WORD REACHED Miles that Howard had been sighted approaching from the south, he was both relieved and upset. With Howard's reinforcements he could mount an attack and end this siege, or at least his men could be spelled and get some much-needed rest. And the odds were now tipped at least slightly more in their favor should Sitting Bull and his warriors appear.

But Howard's arrival also meant that command would now turn over to the senior officer. Miles, who had done all the work and had lost all the men, would be relegated to a subordinate status. The capture would belong to Howard, while Miles would be left to answer the question of why so little had been accomplished at such a great loss of life. He could see the generalship he so desired slipping from his grasp.

Accompanied by several aides and soldiers, he rode out onto the snowy plain to meet Howard. The general greeted his younger comrade with a hearty handshake. "Miles!" he said. "I'm glad to see you. I thought you might have met Gibbon's fate. Why didn't you let me know?"

Miles responded with a military formality that was quite out of keeping with the friendship the two men had established while serving together during the Civil War. "I have the Indians corralled down yonder," he said, and offered little more.

They proceeded to a vantage point where Howard could assess the situation. He looked down into the snow-covered bowl with the narrow creek winding through it. Miles pointed to the broad plain to the west, where the cannon was barricaded far out of range of any Nez Perce rifle fire. He pointed to the hilltops that surrounded the bowl on three sides and showed where his men were situated. Then he gestured to a narrow gully in the center of the bowl. "There are your hostiles," he said.

Howard stared in amazement. This is what was left of the eight hundred people and thousands of horses that he had begun pursuing three months ago. Whether by luck or by sheer force of circumstance, Miles had accomplished what he and Gibbon and Sturgis and so many others had not been able to do. He had reduced the Nez Perce to a pitiful remnant, no longer able to flee or fight. It was only a matter of formality to effect a capture, so long as Sitting Bull and his warriors did not arrive.

Night was descending rapidly, and the whole valley was quickly disappearing into wintry darkness. Miles led Howard to the warmth of his command tent, where the two men could fashion a conclusion to this long, bloody campaign.

Inside the tent, Miles continued his forced formality. Howard watched with bemused detachment. He knew the colonel well. He had observed him closely during the Civil War campaigns and had even arranged for Miles to receive his first regimental command. He knew his young associate's military ambitions and his hunger for a general's star.

After allowing Miles to continue in this awkward, forced manner for a while, he smiled at his young colleague. "I did not come to rob you of any credit," he said. "I know you're after a star, and I will stand back and let you receive the surrender. I'm sure that will come tomorrow." At this, all Miles's stiffness fell away, and the younger man's manner brightened.

General Howard's aides stood by in shocked silence. Their men had pursued these hostiles for three months, living on almost no rations, walking on blistered feet through wet, wintry plains and mountain passes, sloshing through creeks, sleeping under thin blankets, and suffering almost unheard-of privations while receiving little or no pay. Many of them had suffered wounds and injuries that would burden them for the rest of their lives. Now, their commanding officer was giving away the one prize that would have made all the hardship worthwhile.

Howard's aide, Lieutenant Wood, began to protest. Howard put his hand on Wood's shoulder and said, "Miles was my aide-de-camp in the Civil War. I trust him as I would trust you."

Wood fell silent and looked away in disgust. The surrender would go to a well-fed, upstart army that had shown up a few days ago and done nothing more than surround a group of worn-out and dispirited Indians who had been chased into exhaustion by the very troops who were to be denied the capture. But the general had made his decision. While Wood looked on, Howard and Miles sat down to plot the strategy by which the surrender would be effected.

Howard had with him two treaty Nez Perce whom he employed as herders and horse handlers. These men, Captain John and Old George, each had daughters who had married into the families of the hostiles and were somewhere down there among them, if indeed they were alive at all. Captain John was also one of the scouts who had first reconnoitered for Howard as the nontreaties left the Weippe Prairie. These men wanted nothing more than to see the Nez Perce surrender so they could find their daughters and bring them to safety.

Howard had made sure that the two men were well aware of how many troops were coming up behind and were prepared to communicate this fact to the hostiles down below. He also had with him a volunteer named Ad Chapman, who had lived near the Nez Perce in White Bird Canyon and fired the first shot of the war, and who spoke Nez Perce with almost native fluency. Between the three of them, they could make both the situation and the surrender terms known to the Nez Perce.

Tomorrow morning, after he and his men had gotten some much-needed rest, Howard would send the two Nez Perce fathers forward under a flag of truce.

The night passed drearily for the Nez Perce. The imminent arrival of Howard's troops meant that death was now only hours away. Some sang their medicine songs, hoping for power; others, having given up hope, sang their death songs in preparation for the journey into the spirit world.

Far over the distant bluffs, sparks rising from the soldiers' fires mocked them with visions of warmth. Now and then a shot rang out, causing the children to whimper in their sleep. This had ceased to be a war; it was now a dream—Wottolen's dream—from which none could awake.

Toward dawn, the battlefield fell strangely quiet. The firing subsided, then stopped altogether. The Nez Perce peered from beneath their buffalo robe blankets. Bands of pink painted the eastern horizon. The white peaks of the distant Bear's Paw glowed beneath a blue, cloud-wisped sky. For the first time since they had made camp, the day held the promise of sun.

In the distance, in the direction of the soldier camp, far out of firing range of their rifles, they could see several men standing on a crest overlooking the battlefield. Some were soldiers, others appeared to be Indians dressed in white man's clothing. Soon two other soldiers approached the group. One looked to be Colonel Miles, the other they recognized as the one-armed Howard. After a short discussion, the two Indians raised a tall pole with a white flag and began walking slowly down the hill toward the Nez Perce camp.

The Nez Perce gathered on the edges of their shelter and rifle pits. They could hear the men talking as they approached; it sounded like they were speaking Nez Perce. As they got nearer, one of them shouted, "All my brothers, I am glad to see you alive this sun." He kept calling out, saluting the Nez Perce in their own language. Soon the two men got close enough to be recognized as Jokais and Meopkowit, known as Captain John and Old George.

White Bull wanted to shoot them as they approached. They were worse than the white soldiers, he said. They were traitors to their own people. They had scouted for the white soldiers, and Jokais had even sold Indian land to white miners for money. They deserved to die.

But the others grabbed White Bull's gun and told him to be patient. "Let us hear what they have to say," they said.

When the men got within a few yards of the camp, Captain John spoke up. "We have traveled a long ways trying to catch you folks," he said. "We are glad to hear you want no more war, no more fighting. I am glad because all my sons are glad to be alive."

Old George added, "We have come far from home. Now you see many soldiers lying down side by side. We see Indians too lying dead. We are all not mad. We think of you as brothers."

One by one the people in the camp stood up and looked at the men. Both of them were weeping. A few of the warriors advanced and shook the men's hands, telling them that their daughters were still alive. "We are glad to shake hands with you," Captain John said. "I am glad to catch up with you and to find my daughter alive too."

But not all were swept up in the emotion of the moment. These men commanded no respect. Among their own people they were known by the names "Lazy" and "Know-Nothing." Why should they now be trusted? They had fought with the soldiers against their own people. They spoke the white man's words. Many times a flag of truce had been raised; each time it had hidden a serpent's truth. Promises from the white soldiers, even when spoken from an Indian tongue—especially these Indian tongues—amounted to little.

Captain John continued to address the group. "Listen well to what I have to say. I have been with General Howard. I heard General Howard saying, 'When I catch Joseph, I will bring him back to his own home.' General Miles is an honest-looking man. He said, 'Tell Joseph we do not want to have any more war.'"

Despite their reservations, this was enough for some of the people. Tom Hill announced he was ready to quit fighting right then and there. But others were not so sure. Let us discuss this, they said. These men and their words count for nothing.

They sent the two men back to the soldiers while Joseph and White Bird and the head warriors met in hurried council. The discussion was full of strong words. Joseph said he needed to consider this offer, not for himself, but for the elders and wounded and women and children. Yellow Wolf confronted him. "If you go with General Howard, he will hang you. You know how he destroyed our homes and took all we owned."

Others agreed. There were white men back in their own country who would convince Howard to hang them all. When had the white soldiers and white law ever listened to Indians? They reminded him of Looking Glass's words: "I am older than you. I have my experiences with a man of two faces and two tongues. If you surrender, you will be sorry, and in your sorrow you will feel rather to be dead."

But Joseph was adamant. He had never agreed to surrender; he never would. Those who accused him of such things spoke falsely. He believed they should try to make an agreement to be paid for the lands that had been stolen from them and to accept terms that would return them to their homeland. If they could achieve this, he said, they should cease fighting. The soldier chiefs knew the people could escape if they so chose. They knew Sitting Bull was likely to arrive any day and that even with Howard's troops, the soldiers were no match for the warriors of the Nez Perce and Sitting Bull joined together. This would not be surrender; it would be an agreement to quit fighting and to settle their differences in peace.

As the silence from the Indian camp dragged on, Howard grew impatient. He shouted across, demanding to know why they were not coming.

"See?" the warriors said. "He does not show kindness. His face is not good."

They reminded Joseph of Howard's impatience at the council of Lapwai, where he had insulted Toohoolhoolzote and thrown him in prison.

"It is to Miles that I will hand over my weapons," Joseph responded, "not Howard."

"A man who betrayed a flag of truce," others reminded him.

The discussion was interrupted by movement on the hillside. Old George and Captain John were approaching again.

"General Miles wishes to speak to Chief Joseph," they said.

Joseph was upset. "It is we who will decide what to do," he said. He did not like being singled out. It made him look like a conciliator.

The men continued to council, allowing Captain John and Old George to remain among them. Soon Captain John spoke up again. "Those generals said to tell you, 'We will have no more fighting.' They say that they have sent many messengers but that some of you have not seen the truth. They said to tell you that they will have no more war."

These were the words Joseph was waiting to hear.

"See?" he said to the others. "It is as I told you when I returned from Colonel Miles's tent. I did not say, 'Let's quit.' Colonel Miles said, 'Let's quit.' Now General Howard says, 'Let's quit.' I did not say, 'Let's quit.'"

The warriors discussed this among themselves. If it was the soldiers who asked to quit, this was no surrender. There would be no punishment, just an end to the fighting. They could gather their wounded and return to their homes.

One man spoke for the group. "Yes, now we believe you," he said. "We should tell Colonel Miles that we will quit."

Joseph was relieved. This was the ending for which he had hoped. There would be no more killing, no more death. Now discussions could take place about how to get the people back to their own country. Perhaps he could yet honor the promise he had made to his father to never give up the land that held his parents' bones.

He called Old John and Captain George to him and instructed them to listen carefully, for they must relay correctly what he was about to say.

"Tell General Howard," he said, "that I know his heart. What he told me before, I have in my heart. I am tired of fighting. Our chiefs are killed.

Looking Glass is dead. Toohoolhoolzote is dead. The old men are all dead. It is the young men who say yes or no. He who led the young men is dead. It is cold and we have no blankets. The little children are freezing to death. My people, some of them, have run away to the hills and have no blankets, no food; no one knows where they are—perhaps freezing to death. I want to have time to look for my children and see how many of them I can find. Maybe I shall find them among the dead."

Then he turned toward White Bird and Yellow Bull and Husis Kute and met their eyes with his.

"Hear me, my chiefs. I am tired. My heart is sick and sad. From where the sun now stands, I will fight no more forever."

He looked quietly at the ground. He had spoken his will.

Then it was White Bird's turn to speak. Joseph was a fool to trust these men, he said. It was offering the people up for death. He, White Bird, did not choose to die in this way. He had come back to aid his people after leading the first group out of range of the soldiers on the first day of the attack. Now he would take the rest who wished to make their escape and head toward Sitting Bull. If they were caught and killed, better to die like a wolf than a sheep. What Joseph said to Miles and Howard was all right. But he, White Bird, had nothing to say.

Old John and Captain George committed the words to memory and went back across the snowy hollows to the hill where Howard and Miles stood waiting. With tears in his eyes, Captain John recited the words he had heard. Ad Chapman then repeated them to Howard and Miles in English. Lieutenant Wood, Howard's adjutant, wrote them down in pencil on a sheet of paper as Chapman spoke. The long, hard war was coming to an end.

All that remained was to agree to the conditions by which the fighting would cease. Joseph, with good cause, had no faith in the promises of safe conduct by General Howard or Colonel Miles. He was not about to enter into the soldier camp to discuss terms. So a buffalo robe was laid on the ground on a rise halfway between the ravine where the people were dug in and the bluff where the soldiers stood. This spot, in open view of all and with a clear line of fire from each camp, would be the place of meeting.

When the robe was in place, men from each side stepped forth under the blue winter sky and made their way through the wet snow toward the rise. Miles and Howard were accompanied by Chapman to translate for them. Joseph, who did not trust Chapman, brought Tom Hill to serve as his interpreter. Though Hill's English was not good, he would speak truthfully and not twist words. Joseph also brought several warriors to serve as witnesses to any agreements that were made. White Bird remained behind.

The men met at the buffalo robe and sat in a circle. Joseph insisted on the safe return of his people to their own country, with no punishment for crimes committed in the past. Miles agreed, saying that he could guarantee their return to the reservation. Joseph also spoke of payment for the lands taken and was concerned for their horses and their weapons.

Howard held back, allowing Miles to conduct the surrender negotiations. But Joseph's constant restating of conditions irritated him, and he began to speak loudly in a threatening manner. Miles tried to maintain calm. "I think General Howard will soon forget all this," he said to Joseph. "I will take you to a safe place for the winter; then you can go to your old home."

Joseph was wary of Howard. But Miles seemed to be in charge and taking the lead on all issues, so he agreed to the words that had passed between himself and Miles.

"Miles is a head man," he stated, "and we will go with him."

Still, he wanted assurances that his people would be fed and treated well. Miles was quick to agree. "From this sun, we will have a good time on both sides, your band and mine," he said. "We will have plenty of time for sleep, for good rest."

Howard, sensing that an agreement was near, concurred. "The war is finished. From now on we will have time to rest." Then, satisfied that Joseph was indeed going to turn himself over, he spoke warmly to him, like a man speaking to a brother from whom he had been too long estranged. "You have your life. I am living. I have lost my brothers. Many of you have lost brothers, maybe more than on our side. I do not know. Do not worry anymore. While you see this many soldiers living from the war, you think of them as your brothers. Do not worry about starving. We have plenty of food left. Anyone who needs a sack of flour, anything the people want, come and get it. All is yours for the asking."

Despite Joseph's mistrust of Howard, these words spoke to his fondest hopes for the suffering people. Finally, the children would eat, and the shivering elders would have warmth and peace.

The participants stood up and stepped forward, sealing the agreement with handshakes all around. The Indians then lifted their hands toward the sun, indicating that from the place where it now stood, this agreement was a solemn bond.

With the conditions established, each side went back to its camp, stunned, exhausted, and almost disbelieving of what had just occurred.

The next few hours brought a strange combination of sadness and elation to both camps. The soldiers were proud that they had been present when the great struggle with Chief Joseph had come to an end, though they grieved for the loss of their comrades and the wounds so many had suffered. General Howard's officers still smarted from the way their leader had given away the victory to troops who had done no more than pick the fruits of their three months of hard labor. Still, the thought that there would be no more wet marches and cold nights and deaths from snipers' bullets made the surrender a moment of sweet celebration.

In the Indian camp, fear of the unknown mixed with the sadness of mourning and deep relief that the children and elders would now be fed. Some held out hope that this new soldier chief Miles would return them to their homeland and that they could return to their old way of life. Others doubted his word and feared that the hangman's noose awaited them all. But none could deny the feeling that a great burden had been lifted from their hearts.

Joseph and White Bird discussed how best to proceed. White Bird had already established that he would not give himself over to the two-faced white men and would seek refuge with Sitting Bull across the border. Those who chose to make peace with the white soldiers would follow the lead of Joseph, while those who wished to flee could leave with White Bird.

Joseph agreed that he and his people would turn themselves in slowly, leaving time for White Bird and those who wished to go with him to cache weapons and prepare for escape. If they could extend their coming forth well into the night, the absence of White Bird's people would not be noticed until the following morning. By that time those who chose to escape should have the lead necessary to make it across the border to Sitting Bull. Joesph also agreed to provide food and hiding places to the wounded who were not able to travel but did not wish to turn themselves over to the army.

For those who chose flight, it was going to be a perilous journey. They would have to travel on foot across frozen, wind-whipped country. Most had no warm clothes. Some were without shoes and could do no more than wrap strips of blanket around their feet. Almost all had sustained injuries in the course of the journey. Some were so badly wounded that they would need assistance while traveling. The soldiers would surely come after them, and hostile tribes roamed the hills between this campsite and the security of Sitting Bull. It was in many ways a doomed effort. But they had made it this far; they would not give up their dreams of freedom to the promises of men whose hearts were filled with lies.

As Joseph prepared to bring his rifle to Miles as a gesture of peace, families discussed what course of action each would take. Some of the elderly, too weak to flee and well aware of the burden they would present, counseled their families to leave without them. Other families decided to send their younger and healthier members with White Bird, while the rest would turn themselves over along with Joseph. All knew that whatever course they took, they were leaving their dead in this unmarked ground far from the land of their birth.

As the sun moved past its high point in the sky, Joseph mounted one of the few remaining horses. Flanked by five warriors on foot, he made his way across the bottomland and up the hill toward the Plateau where Colonel Miles and General Howard stood waiting beside a buffalo robe that had been spread out to mark the spot of the surrender. He rode slowly, with his eyes cast down and his rifle resting across his knees, speaking quietly with the warriors as they walked.

His hair hung in two heavy braids on either side of his head, and his scalp lock was tied back with otter fur, in the manner of the Dreamers. He wore buckskin leggings and a striped blanket riddled with bullet holes. Bullet holes also peppered his shirt and leggings. He wore no war paint. The men accompanying him kept their hands on him, as if offering him solace or power. Howard, the Christian soldier, could not blind himself to the symbolism of the action unfolding before him.

Joseph rode slowly up from the shadows of the gully onto the rise where the two men were waiting. Their aides, with the interpreter Chapman, stood at a respectful distance behind. Still farther back, a courier waited next to his horse, ready to carry a message to Fort Keogh announcing the official surrender.

As Joseph reached Miles and Howard, he dismounted and straightened himself. Meeting the gaze of the two men with a look that was strong and clear—almost defiant—he walked toward Howard. He exchanged a few words with the general, then proceeded directly to Miles. Standing before Miles, he pointed to the sky and said, "It is finished. From where the sun now stands, I will fight no more against the white man." Then he handed over his rifle. The two men regarded each other, then Miles accepted the gun and shook Joseph's hand. One by one, the other soldiers stepped forward. Joseph smiled sadly and shook each of their hands in turn.

When the formalities were finished, Howard turned to his adjutant, Lieutenant Wood, and said, "Mr. Wood, take charge of Chief Joseph as a prisoner of war. See that he is made comfortable and in no way is molested or troubled." Wood led Joseph to a large tent that had been prepared for his arrival and ushered him inside.

At the sight of Joseph's turning over his weapon and shaking hands with the soldiers, other Nez Perce began to emerge from the gully. In groups of twos and threes they made their way out of their shelter pits and up the hillside. They were dirty and ragged and covered with wounds. Many were elderly; a few were blind and unable to walk without assistance. There were hollow-eyed, shoeless children and old men who needed to be supported as they tried to climb the hill. One woman carried an infant only several days old.

Howard and Miles stood mutely as this haggard group of people, who had eluded the best that the armies of the West had to offer, struggled across the snow-covered ground to the soldiers' camp. The soldiers who awaited them were shocked as well. This was not an army; these were starving men, women, and children.

As the sky darkened and the cold winds of evening picked up, the flow of refugees slowed to a trickle. Those who had been waiting for a chance to surrender had come forth quickly. Others needed time to decide or to say their good-byes to the relatives who were planning to escape under cover of darkness. Still others were assisting the wounded who did not want to surrender but were too weak to travel. They gave them food and weapons and helped them hide in the remaining shelter caves, covering them with earth and leaving only small air holes through which to breathe. Those who were planning to flee with White Bird gathered all the weapons and ammunition they could find and wrapped their feet in strips of blankets against the snow and cold.

With tearful good-byes, White Bird's people began moving quietly up the gullies and draws toward the north. Their friends and relatives watched them go, then turned and began their slow climb up the southern hills toward the distant campfires of the soldiers.

On the hill above, Joseph sat quietly in his tent, listening to the low talk of soldiers. His brother was dead, his twelve-year-old daughter was wandering somewhere on the wintry plains, and the bodies of old women and children he had sworn to protect lay buried in shallow graves on foreign land. Their horses were gone, their lodge poles and hunting guns were gone. His people were divided, and none knew who remained alive and who was dead. He had delivered his wounded to a man who had lied to him and an army in whose hands no wounded Indian had ever been known to survive.

The words of Looking Glass would not leave him: "If you surrender you will be sorry, and in your sorrow you will feel rather to be dead."

Part Three

A Time of Betrayal and Exile

18

"You Will Be Returned to Your Homeland"

THE DAYS IMMEDIATELY after the October 5 cessation of hostilities were filled with both relief and confusion. Those among the soldiers who had not developed a fundamental hatred for all things Indian found themselves strangely fascinated by their captives. Most had expected something close to animals—subhuman beings with skin as tough as horses' hooves and an amazing threshold for pain, who lived more like wild beasts than humans. They had been fully prepared to receive the surrender of a pack of creatures only marginally less unruly and dangerous than wolves.

Instead, what had emerged from the draws and the gullies was a steady stream of women and children helping the wounded and elderly and treating each other with a touching tenderness. They were not animals, they were simply 418 cold, dirty, wet, frightened people, just like themselves. It was hard for the soldiers not to see echoes of their own grandmothers and grandfathers in the white-haired elderly who made their way up the hillside on unsteady legs, supported by their children and grandchildren; hard not to feel a twinge of sadness and guilt as the women dragged up their pitiful tattered sacks of clothing and cooking utensils and the children stared with fear and fascination at their captors and their weapons.

But it was the stories told by their wounded comrades that most softened the soldiers' hearts toward this ragged group of captives. To a man, the wounded who had fallen in the battlefield had lain in terror as night descended and shadowy figures moved among them in search of weapons. Well steeped in the horrors of the Custer massacre, they had expected to be flayed alive or have their testicles staked to the ground if the Indians found them. The best they could hope for was to be killed before the abominations began. Those still in possession of their weapons had even prepared to take their own lives rather than submit to the tortures they knew were sure to come.

Yet their treatment had been anything but brutal. As they had been discovered, the Nez Perce had comforted them and provided them with water, placing blankets under their heads. One young soldier had been comforted by a woman who said, "Poor boy, you're too young to die." Another had been told, "Don't worry, we're not after your hair, only your weapons." Not only had they not been mutilated like the soldiers who had fallen into Sioux hands, they had been treated with kindness and civility, more like unfortunate comrades than like enemies.

Most amazing of all was Lieutenant Jerome's story of his time in the Nez Perce camp. While held prisoner, he had been given food when the Indians themselves were doing without and had been permitted to walk about the camp carrying his own pistol. The warriors who spoke a little English had even bantered with him, saying that if the weather didn't improve, they'd have to go back to fighting just to keep warm. At night he had been offered a warm buffalo blanket and would have slept soundly and comfortably had his own army not kept him awake by firing down upon the Indian camp in direct violation of the truce.

In many ways, these Indians had behaved with more honor than the soldiers. One of the enlisted men noted that the only scalping that had taken place during the battle was by one of their own men who had decided to get himself an Indian trophy. This, while the Nez Perce were providing food and blankets to prisoners and offering water and comfort to the wounded soldiers in the battlefield.

Most impressive of all was their leader, Joseph, who since handing over his rifle had spent his time walking among his people, speaking gently, calming their fears, and trying to buoy their spirits. He showed no rancor toward his captors and carried himself with a quiet dignity. The soldiers had heard about his deep grief at the loss of his daughter, who had taken flight at the time of the first attack and was now wandering somewhere in these icy hills with only a thin blanket for protection. Yet here he was, quelling his own grief in order to comfort his people and meeting his captors with dignity and respect. It was hard to equate this calm, soft-spoken, powerful figure with the wily savage general they had been led to expect.

Since the surrender, Joseph and Colonel Miles had seemed to develop a kind of camaraderie. They were about the same age; they had been through a common hell, and each man carried the burden of the dead upon his shoulders. They could be seen walking together on the wintry hillsides, talking not like victor and vanquished but like two generals charged with the common task of caring for the weary and the wounded. Ad Chapman stayed near their side to serve as translator; Tom Hill had chosen to cast his lot with White Bird and had disappeared into the snowy darkness during the previous night.

Slowly, the two groups began to take on the attitudes of their commanders, developing a grudging understanding, even a wary respect. The Indians fascinated the soldiers with their self-reliance and good humor; the soldiers impressed the Indians with their willingness to provide warm food and medical treatment for people with whom they had engaged in such deadly battle. The children especially took a liking to their captors. They gathered around the soldiers, touching their beards and uniforms. The soldiers, for their part, built their captives warm fires and prepared food for them. For everyone, it was a great relief to sit before warm, roaring fires, listening to the laughter of children rather than to the cries of the dying and the sharp cracks of rifle fire in the night.

All during the day following the surrender, the two groups engaged in the grisly task of picking their way among the bloated, putrefying corpses of the horses to retrieve their dead from the battlefield. It was a strange experience to be so close to an enemy who had caused these deaths yet to feel the kinship of grief.

The soldiers dragged the rotting bodies of their comrades to the top of the ridges, where they buried them in a mass grave, while the Indians placed their dead in the shelter pits and hollows in the creek banks and covered them with layers of soft, loamy earth. The smell of death hovered over the entire battlefield, and the wails of the Indian women wove a haunting descant into the high plains wind.

For the soldiers, this was their first chance get an up-close look at the actual battlefield. They wandered among the coulees and gullies, marveling at the extent of the fortifications the Indians had constructed. There were over a hundred shelter pits, many five feet deep and twice as wide. It was hard to imagine that these people had dug such holes with only knives and frying pans while being fired upon from the surrounding hills. One man noted that trained army engineers could not have designed more sophisticated fortifications.

The soldiers also unearthed caches of weapons and food and clothing. Rumors spread about a great fortune in gold dust that some of the Indians had buried, but none was found, though many of the caches contained saddles and robes and foodstuffs like flour and beans.

In one of the shelter pits, soldiers discovered a small breathing hole in the earth extending away from the pit itself. Upon digging into it, they found a warrior with a broken hip who had been supplied with a gun and food enough to survive until his escaped comrades could come back for him after the army left. The soldiers extracted him and brought him up the hill to join the other captives.

Much to the troops' disappointment, few weapons of any consequence were discovered. The long-distance accuracy of the Nez Perce marksmen had convinced them that the Indians possessed high-quality rifles with scopes, and many of the men had hoped to procure one for themselves. But these, it was determined, must have been taken by White Bird and his people, who had escaped on the night of the surrender.

This escape was the one great source of tension between the Nez Perce and the soldiers. Howard, particularly, was incensed by the disappearance of White Bird and his band. He had turned the specifics of the surrender over to Miles, and Miles, not wanting to lose any of his men to ambush, had allowed the Nez Perce to trickle in all through the afternoon and into the night. He had assumed that allowing the Indians to come forth at their own pace would make them less burdensome and more compliant as captives. But neither he nor Howard had expected White Bird and many of the best remaining warriors to use this as an opportunity for flight. Every Indian who escaped was an Indian who could join up with Sitting Bull. Howard saw it as a violation of the terms of the surrender, and he told Joseph so.

Joseph remained unmoved, even defiant. There had been no surrender, he said, only a laying down of arms. And it was only he and those who had come with him who had chosen to do so. White Bird, like all others, had been free to make his own choice. There could be no violation where there had been no agreement. No Indian was ever bound by the promises of another, and he could no more speak for White Bird than Lawyer had been able to speak for Joseph's father when he had claimed to sell the Wallowa to the whites in the thief treaty of 1863.

A modest effort was made to seek out the escapees. Search parties were sent out into the hillsides, and a few injured Nez Perce were found and returned. Couriers rode off to the surrounding tribes to tell them that the government would look favorably upon any efforts they made to impede the flight of the escaping Nez Perce.

Considering the small number of able-bodied warriors that had come forth with Joseph, there was ample reason to think that many of the best fighting men had chosen to leave and head for Canada with White Bird. They had left with a good knowledge of the strength of the armies and the nature of their weaponry. The escape of these men, and their capacity to join up with Sitting Bull, meant that the potential for continued trouble could not be ignored.

This constant threat of the Sioux sat like a shadow over efforts to secure the battlefield. The dead needed to be buried and the wounded readied for transport, but all due haste had to be exercised so as to get out of range of a possible Sioux attack. Once across the Missouri River, a week's journey away, they would be safe. But until that time, the possibility of an engagement with Sitting Bull's warriors loomed large.

All through the day following the handing over of the rifle, Joseph and Miles continued to talk. General Howard remained with the party, but his concern lay elsewhere. His charge from his superiors had been to pursue the Nez Perce as far as necessary to effect their capture, and he had done so. He and Miles had determined that the captives would winter with Miles near Fort Keogh, then be returned to the Lapwai in the spring. Now he had to finish the administrative tasks of dealing with the troops he had left behind and reporting to his superiors. He would travel to Chicago to brief Sheridan about the long pursuit and the capture and to explain the proposed disposition of the hostiles. Then he would return to Portland and his command of the Department of the Columbia.

The pursuit of the Nez Perce had been his responsibility. Their transport and maintenance belonged to others. He left these tasks to Miles and turned his attention to hurrying back to the Missouri in order to catch a ferry east before the river froze.

But for Joseph and Miles, the task was more human and personal. It was up to them to bring this cruel and brutal war to a humane and

workable conclusion. While their people were out on the battlefield burying the dead and bringing in the wounded, they tried to shape a plan by
which all could arrive safely at a location where they could spend the
winter before the Nez Perce returned to their homeland in the spring in
accord with the agreed-upon plan.

Miles explained that he would escort them to Fort Keogh, several
weeks' journey away on the banks of the Yellowstone. There the army
would be able to provide for the Nez Perce's needs until the snows of the
winter melted enough to allow them to be escorted back west through the
mountain passes.

Joseph was satisfied with this arrangement. His people knew how to
live in winter in buffalo country. If Miles returned their guns and horses,
they would be able to care for themselves until it was time to embark upon
the journey home. Miles listened patiently but steadfastly refused to give
the Nez Perce their rifles. The handing over of arms had been a condition
of the surrender, and it was not negotiable. The army would provide sufficient rations to ensure their survival until spring.

Joseph was upset, yet he had no choice but to comply. The soldiers were
treating them well, and his first task had to be to care for his people, who,
despite their brave demeanor, were broken and heartsick. Many had said
good-bye to children and families as the stronger and healthier had chosen
to leave with White Bird, and all had buried fathers and mothers and husbands and children on the battlefields and along the trail. Though to the
soldiers they appeared to be relieved and in good spirits, it was only because that was the Nez Perce way. In truth, their hearts were heavy with
grief.

Joseph could not expect Miles to see this, or even to care. Miles was a
soldier, and as long as he was honorable in dealing with the people, Joseph
would do his best to convince the people to go along with his wishes. Still,
it rankled him that Miles had spoken of this as a surrender. To him and his
people, it was just an agreement that would allow them to regain their
strength and health before returning home in the spring.

Early in the afternoon on the second day after the handing over of the
weapons, under a mountain-blue sky filled with high, running clouds, the
soldiers and their captives left the battlefield on the plain of the Bear's Paw
and set off toward the southeast. To the scouts and the outriders looking

down on the scene from the surrounding hills and ridges, it appeared like a grand and colorful spectacle—the Nez Perce in their multicolored blankets and the soldiers in their blue coats, followed by wagons and pack trains and the great herd of the captured Nez Perce horses, all moving in solemn procession across the high, rolling, snow-covered grasslands. Now and then a cloud would pass in front of the sun, causing shadows to race like giant birds across the landscape before disappearing over the pine-steepled, snow-covered mountains rising in the distance. More than one soldier commented on the beauty of the scene and how this would be a good place to make a home when the Indian wars were finally ended.

But from within the procession the scene was anything but beautiful. The Nez Perce's clothes were torn and ragged; their moccasins were worn through, exposing their bruised and lacerated feet to the sharp grasses and frozen snows. Their wounded were slumped over on horses or laid out on makeshift travois and litters that shifted and jolted as they bumped across the uneven ground.

Many of those who had been injured in battle were close to death, and the lame and the elderly, who had been further weakened by their time in the shelter pits, were having great difficulty keeping up. Almost all had suffered some frostbite during the battle, causing an agonizing burning in their fingers and toes from which there was no relief.

The wounded soldiers were faring no better. They had been placed in hay- and grass-filled wagons, but this was not enough to keep the jostling from ripping apart sutures and jarring loose hastily set fractures. The bodies of two officers who had been killed in battle were being carried along for delivery to their families back east, and despite their being wrapped in blankets, the smell of their carrion flesh forced those directly downwind to cover their faces to block out the stench.

The captured horses too were faring poorly. The Nez Perce herd was still afflicted with the disease that caused cuts and scrapes to fester rather than heal. Their suppurating wounds made them nervous and skittish and increased the rankness in the air. Only the children seemed oblivious to the hardships, and their laughter and play provided a stark counterpoint to the suffering going on around them.

Joseph rode at the front with Miles. He knew that this journey was his best opportunity to communicate his understanding of events and to present the case of his people. He did not entirely trust Miles. After all, the

man had kept him captive against his will after claiming to meet with him
under a flag of truce. But since the end of the fighting, Miles had shown
himself to be honorable and a man of his word. He had fed and warmed
the people; he had used his own limited medical supplies and personnel to
treat the Nez Perce wounded; he had shown great kindness to the children;
and he had always spoken clearly and directly about his intentions. Joseph
recalled having seen him ride unprotected on the hilltops among his soldiers on that first day of fighting. A man who had courage in battle could
be counted on to have courage in peacetime, and Joseph desperately
needed the aid and support of a man who spoke honestly and had the
courage to stand behind his words.

So he took the chance of opening himself to Miles. He spent much of
the journey recounting the flight and trying to make Miles understand the
Nez Perce side of the war. He told of the crimes that had been committed
against his people while they were still in their homeland, of the murders
by whites that had gone unpunished, of the government promises left un-
fulfilled and the graft of the Indian agents. He explained how he and his
people had been preparing to go on the reservation, but the young men's
rash acts while the people were camped in the Camas Prairie had forced
them to join the flight. He gave his version of the battles of Clearwater and
the Big Hole and told of his people's sufferings along the way. He explained that he had always sought to protect the lives of white settlers they
encountered and that alcohol had been at the root of the atrocities that the
young Indians had committed.

All of this was relayed by Ad Chapman, who rode between the two men,
interpreting from one language to the other. Joseph did not trust this
craven little man with the sunken eyes and drooping mustache. White
Bird's people had spoken of him as a cowardly bully back in their home
country. They recounted stories of how he had whipped young boys who
broke into his melon patch and how he had stolen Nez Perce horses yet
had not possessed the courage to admit it when confronted. They told of
the times he had bound young Nez Perce children and thrown them into
corrals of wild horses, allowing them to be terrified as the horses raced and
reared around them.

But all the Nez Perce who could speak passable English had either been
killed or had fled with White Bird, so Joseph had no choice but to count
on this spineless little rancher to pass his words along accurately. It was

imperative that Miles be made to understand that not all the Nez Perce who had been part of this journey had wanted war and that those who had started things were now dead. Rumors and fears were rampant among the families that they were all soon to be killed. He needed to have Miles's word that there would be no hangings and that the people would be well cared for during the coming cold winter on the plains. Chapman was the only means he had to make himself understood and the only way he could gain the assurances he needed.

Miles listened patiently as Joseph spoke. He understood a leader's grief and a leader's responsibility. It was his conviction that history had doomed all native peoples to an inevitable extinction if they did not change from their primitive ways, but he felt obligated to accord this chief a fair hearing. Since the surrender, he had developed great respect for the way Joseph conducted himself and looked after those in his care. And as the journey progressed, and he heard more of Joseph's story, he became ever more convinced that he was in the presence of an extraordinary leader and an extraordinary group of Indians.

He retained his contempt for many of the cultural practices of the Nez Perce, such as the way the men allowed the women to do all the work while they sat around smoking and talking and playing cards. But he was well able to see the kindness with which the Nez Perce parents raised their young, the good behavior of the children, and the touching way the healthy cared for the elderly and the wounded. These were clearly Indians of a different order than any he had confronted before.

He marveled at the beautiful decoration on the Nez Perce clothing and saddles, and more than once his men commented on the strategic cleverness shown by the children as they engaged in mock battles using mud balls thrown by sticks. And all the men noted the unfailing good humor of this people who were clearly suffering and had every reason to be surly and uncooperative and morose.

Through it all, Miles observed that Joseph maintained peace and order by the sheer force of his personality. He seldom raised his voice, but could communicate more with one stern glance than many men could with an hour of haranguing and speechmaking. He was solemn but not severe. He seldom smiled but seldom expressed exasperation or sadness. The overall impression he communicated was one of great calm and self-control, and this attitude seemed to pervade the attitude of all the people under his command. Miles understood leadership, and it was rapidly becoming apparent to him that in Joseph he did not have a dangerous adversary so much as a worthy ally in bringing this unfortunate chapter in the Indian wars to a safe and honorable conclusion.

For almost two weeks the soldiers and the Nez Perce traveled together over difficult terrain, sharing the bounty of the soldiers' hunts and watching each other bury their comrades who died in the course of the journey. With each passing day, Miles became more convinced that the civil, uncomplaining Nez Perce people and their quiet, dignified leader were far superior to any Indians that he and the rest of the military had previously encountered. They surely bore no resemblance to the bloodthirsty Sioux with whom they were frequently linked, and they deserved better treatment than the harsh punishment bordering on extermination that was destined to be meted out under General Sherman's Indian policies. He did not share Sherman's purported belief that the only good Indian was a dead Indian; rather, he believed that the only good Indian was a changed Indian, and he saw in these people the capacity not only for change but also for becoming valuable participants in American civilization.

By the time they had completed their five-hundred-mile journey to Fort Keogh, he had determined to help his captives as best he could and, as much as it was in his power to do so, to be their champion in dealing with the complexities of the United States governmental system.

What Joseph did not understand—and what Miles failed to fully take into account—was the power of the great forces swirling far above their heads as they made their lonely journey across the high wintry plains of the Montana Territory.

The U.S. government, still reeling from the devastating human and economic cost of the Civil War, was engaged in a heated debate over the future status of the army. Some wanted it built up further so civil and external strife could never again threaten the strength of the union. Others wanted it pared back to save money and correct the excesses and graft to which it had become prone during the Reconstruction period after the war. Still others were concerned about the idea of institutionalizing a standing army during peacetime and wished to see the whole military apparatus disbanded and absorbed into a more peace-oriented Department of the Interior, while opponents of this saw the idea of combining military and civilian affairs under a single department as a dangerous step toward militarizing the entire United States government.

Added to these concerns was a lack of appreciation in the populous East for the problems people were facing in the sparsely settled West and a complete misunderstanding of what would be required to keep an effective standing army in such a vast and underpopulated landscape.

The whole Indian question too had come to the forefront of the national agenda. While Joseph saw the Nez Perce struggles with the United States as a disagreement between sovereign peoples and expected it to be treated as such, the U.S. government had come to see all Indians as part of a single problem and each tribal conflict as the equivalent of the individual battles in the War Between the States.

The Nez Perce were just the latest skirmish in the great sweep of the U.S. military across Indian-held territory. The Kiowas and the Modoc and Comanches and a host of other tribes had been pacified through resettlement and containment. The Nez Perce were just the next in line. Once they had been addressed, the government could turn its attention to the next tribe that stood in the path of the growth and progress of the expanding nation. No more energy and focus would be expended on one tribe's situation than were necessary to put it to an expeditious rest.

At the same time, the question of what to do with conquered Indians had become part of a national policy debate. The financially strapped military did not want to incur the costs of housing, feeding, and providing medical treatment for a perpetual prisoner class; they had enough trouble just paying and maintaining their own men with the penurious appropriations Congress was approving. There were even those in the military establishment who spoke privately about the benefits of complete extermination—dead Indians cost nothing to maintain—or the wisdom of driving all the tribes into Canada and Mexico, where they would be the responsibility and wards of another nation. But if the hostiles had to be captured and maintained, all agreed that they were to be passed along to other branches of the government or society as quickly as possible. While they remained under military jurisdiction, they were to be dealt with in whatever fashion minimized the costs involved in their maintenance.

But national sentiment complicated the issue. White America had always been decidedly ambivalent toward the native inhabitants of the land. On one hand, these indigenous people were seen as indolent savages who raped, pillaged, and violated all standards of civilized behavior. On the other, they were seen as children of nature, unspoiled by the ways of cities and civilization. This fissure in the American consciousness had only deepened as the East had become settled and the Indian situation in the West had become more dire.

The easterners, steeped in literary lore of men like Fenimore Cooper and Longfellow and no longer directly threatened by hostile Indian tribes, were quite willing to mythologize the Indians and elevate them to the status of noble children of the plains and forests. This attitude was further strengthened by the claims from Christian churches that the Indians were simply untutored innocents who had not been afforded the opportunity for conversion and salvation. Treating them as prisoners and bloodthirsty savages rather than as helpless children in need of Christian care and teaching in order to advance in the ways of civilization was seen as callousness bordering on criminality.

Meanwhile, in the West, where fledgling settlements were springing up on traditional tribal lands, the Indians were seen in a far different light. Their cultures appeared cruel and violent, their people showed no willingness to stay put and accept the rule of law and property, and their numbers compared to those of white settlers were frightening and in some cases overwhelming. When they felt wronged, which they often did, they rose up in varying degrees, and failing to get justice or even fair hearing in the frontier judicial system, they visited violence upon the towns and settlers with indiscriminate fury, as the Nez Perce had done in their raids and murders along the Salmon River and Slate Creek.

Whenever such violence occurred, rumors abounded and reality was embellished until the worst abominations became the expected. Any sentiment toward Indians as other than dangerous, wily, untrustworthy savages likely to kill and steal without provocation was seen as a weak-kneed, naive fantasy of the rich and comfortable in the East. When tribes became restless, the whole thinly settled West was gripped with the fear that the many tribes would join together and sweep across the land, killing and raping and burning and maiming until all settlers were driven off or exterminated and the land had been reclaimed for the savage lifestyle that the white people so despised and the Indian people seemed so unwilling and unable to give up.

The telegraph too had become a significant factor in the country's intellectual and political landscape. Information about Indian activities and the Indian wars had become a part of the daily discourse of all newspaper-reading Americans, wherever they happened to live.

The *New York Herald* and the *Chicago Tribune*, which had been following "the Indian problem" for years, had reporters in Montana Territory with General Terry at the time of the Nez Perce surrender. These reporters sent couriers to the nearest telegraph station at Helena with reports of the events taking place on the snowy plains of the Bear's Paw. *Harper's Weekly* published field sketches purporting to depict the battle site and siege. Soon people sitting at their kitchen tables in Boston and San Francisco and New York and Chicago were avidly following the ongoing national drama of the conflict between the Indians and the military.

Through such chroniclings, feelings for and against the Indians were both escalating and hardening, though in many cases the reports were being created secondhand or even fabricated entirely from hearsay and anecdotes gathered by whiskey-drinking layabouts who spent their time sitting at the bars of hotels in frontier towns rather than observing any actual battles.

Even in the diligent press, conflicting biases were resulting in conflicting pictures. The western press was quick to focus on savage actions of the various unconquered Indian tribes and to see every conflict as the potential harbinger of the dreaded pan-Indian uprising, while the eastern press openly suggested that the Indian policy of the United States was a bumbling, economic failure as well as a cruel and wrongheaded attack on people whose crimes often were no greater than wanting a little bit of justice and the chance to live unmolested and unharassed on their traditional tribal lands. The *New York Times* minced no words on the matter. It called the pursuit of the Nez Perce "a war which, on our part, was in its origin and motive nothing short of a gigantic blunder and a crime."

With regard to the Nez Perce, papers everywhere took to chronicling the ongoing misadventures of the U.S. military in its efforts to catch and subdue the hostiles, and General Howard, with few exceptions, was vilified and ridiculed as an incompetent laggard. Headlines such as the *Bismarck Tribune*'s "Howard Fizzles Again" were commonplace, and every editor and letter-writing armchair general had a better idea of how the general should have fought and how the Nez Perce could have been captured. Meanwhile, the fleeing Nez Perce, who initially had been portrayed as a restless group of marauders committing depredations on innocent settlers in the deep folds of Oregon and Idaho, slowly metamorphosed from violent savages into a beleaguered group of refugees who, through personal bravery and masterful military strategy, were outwitting the entire U.S. military and, in the process, costing the military and the U.S. government money that could be better spent elsewhere. After the capture, some writers waggishly suggested that the United States should enlist Nez Perce warriors to serve as lieutenants in their army since they were clearly far more competent militarily than those currently in command.

Perhaps most significant of all, and completely unknown to the Nez Perce, was the elevation of Joseph in the public consciousness to the status of sole chief and strategist for the entire retreat and military campaign. Howard's incessant efforts to put the face of Joseph on the war and the willing adoption of the phrases "Joseph's war" and "Joseph's Indians" by other military leaders and civilian correspondents had combined with Joseph's presence as the surrendering chief at the Bear's Paw to create the impression that he had been responsible for every act and decision that had taken place during the entire long, tragic journey.

His explanation to the other chiefs as to why he was giving up had been embellished into a surrender speech by General Howard's aide, Lieutenant Wood, an aspiring author, and had been transmitted across the country. His solitary ride up the snow-covered gullies of the Bear's Paw and his subsequent handing of his rifle to Miles had been depicted ornately by correspondents vying with each other to offer the most epic and dramatic portrayals of the events and the participants. Typical was the *New York Herald* correspondent's florid description of the chief at the moment of surrender to Miles: "His eyes, black brilliant, and as piercing as an eagle's, rested on those of Colonel Miles with an expression once melancholy and reserved."

Thus, with no effort or knowledge on his part, Joseph had become, in the public's mind, the great general, the master of strategy, the charismatic leader of all the Nez Perce people. And the contrast of the behavior of his Nez Perce people, both during and after the campaign, with the behavior of the Sioux, whose battles had been equally well chronicled the year before, made his stature as a great and compassionate leader grow to almost legendary proportions.

In him, the public that sought the noble savage and wise child of nature had found its man, while the voices of those who wished to see him hanged and held responsible for Indian atrocities grew more and more faint, until they amounted to little more than a squeak from the tiny frontier towns and newspapers scattered across the sparsely settled intermountain and high plains West. Joseph, the camp chief, leader of one isolated band in the great Nez Perce nation, had become, in the American public's mind, a military genius of Napoleonic proportions, a national symbol of the Indian plight, and the flash point for a fierce moral, economic, and political debate.

As he and Miles rode side by side down the steep trail to the few wooden buildings that constituted Fort Keogh, greeted by salutes of cannon fire and the musical offerings of the assembled post band, he had no idea that he and his people were quickly becoming a cause célèbre. For him, it was just the end of a sad journey that had begun almost four months earlier on the Camas Prairie, and the beginning of a long winter's wait before he could lead his people back across the mountain passes to the land where the Creator had always intended them to be.

But in the distant Washington offices of General Sherman, things were seen quite differently. The real financial costs of the Nez Perce war were coming to light, and the public and the politicians were not happy. If the military was to have any hope of upgrading its personnel and equipment, not to mention expanding its scope and scale to meet the challenges facing the nation in the post–Civil War era, it needed to show an absolute control over its budget. Quartering captive hostiles at sites of their choice, even if based on promises made by field commanders, was not the way to demonstrate that control. If the Nez Perce could be wintered more economically at a location closer to supply lines from the East, that was what should be done.

Sherman was also fundamentally opposed to the idea of the military getting involved in nonmilitary activities. He looked upon his army as "the sheriff of the nation," not its court or its jailer. His army had caught the Nez Perce, and that was all it had been charged to do. Let some other agency incarcerate them, and let them do it on its own budget.

So while the Nez Perce were setting up their camps in a grove of stately cottonwoods on the east bank of the Yellowstone and preparing to survive the approaching winter in government tents with government rations,

Miles was receiving notification by courier that his captives should be moved farther east to Fort Lincoln, near the new town of Bismarck in the Dakota Territory. Bismarck was the terminus for the rail lines from the East, so supplies could be transported there more cheaply and the Indians could be quartered and cared for more economically. There, in the shadow of the house where General Custer had lived, they would await further disposition, probably to the Indian Territory in Oklahoma.

Miles protested vigorously. His captives had suffered enough. Among their number were wounded who could not survive another move. Fort Lincoln was three hundred miles to the east but an eight-hundred-mile journey by river. He could look out from his quarters at Fort Keogh and see the Yellowstone River filling with ice, and he had experienced firsthand the snow-filled gales that were blowing across the frozen prairies. To make the tired and injured Nez Perce travel further was inhuman.

Sherman, however, was quite happy to subject his captives to inhuman conditions. He had not changed his basic stance about warfare since the march through Georgia and the burning of Atlanta. Opposition must be crushed in body and spirit, rendered incapable of and unwilling to ever fight again. And all who might entertain thoughts of opposition in the future must be made to bear witness.

In Joseph and his people he found the example he had been seeking. He admired the Nez Perce as fighters and strategists. After all, burdened with elderly, women, and children and, eventually, substantial numbers of wounded, they had managed to defeat Perry at White Bird and Gibbon at the Big Hole, to elude Rawn and Sturgis and Howard, and to hold Miles to a virtual stalemate. Such tactical and strategic skill, he said, rivaled any in the history of warfare. But he would never allow them to look like anything other than a defeated foe. He would place the boot to their neck, and do so publicly. After he was finished, any other tribe would think hard before resisting government policy.

This would also serve to silence the political drumbeat from the increasingly influential West. Voices there were demanding that the Nez Perce never be allowed to return to Idaho and Washington. Under the guise of protecting them from inevitable retribution, Sherman could send these people into an exile that would effectively erase them from the public consciousness while pleasing the western legislators and teaching the Nez Perce and all other potential hostiles a lesson. He could save the army money, increase the military's public prestige and political influence, disimbue all other tribes of any ideas about resistance, and silence the popular pro-Indian outcry that was galvanizing around the Nez Perce and their leader. He could also move them out of the jurisdiction of the military and into the jurisdiction of the Department of the Interior.

It was a solution too perfect to resist.

19

"You Must Move Again"

MILES FOUND JOSEPH walking among his people in the camp by river's edge. It was a healthy setting with abundant water and large, sheltering trees, and Miles had been heartened by the progress his captives had been making in establishing a normal camp life. They were still complaining about the loss of their weapons and horses, and they had been angered by Miles's decision to award each of his Cheyenne scouts a choice of five Nez Perce horses as a reward for faithful service. But overall they seemed as happy as could be expected after only a week in this setting, and Joseph seemed to have taken control of the camp with a firm and decisive hand. Miles knew that the message he was about to deliver would undo all the goodwill that had been building up slowly during the long journey from the battle site at the Bear's Paw.

He broke the word as gently as he could. "You must move again," he told Joseph, "to a fort many days' journey to the east. There it will be cheaper to house and feed you for the winter."

Joseph listened silently. "You must not blame me," Miles continued. "I have endeavored to keep my word. But the chief who is over me has given the order, and I must obey it or resign. That would do you no good. Some other officer would carry out the order."

Joseph knew that Miles was speaking the truth, but it was small consolation. If a nation sent a man to fight another man, then would not stand by the word of the man who had done the fighting, by whose words would it stand? If Miles's promise to winter the Nez Perce near the Yellowstone was so easily broken, what other promises might be broken in the future?

Joseph knew he had to keep his people calm. They were well aware of the white man's penchant for going back on his word. It had been a big part of the discussions about whether or not to cease fighting at the Bear's Paw. Now they were being told to move again, and this time to a place even farther from their homeland and the graves of those they had buried along the trail. How would he explain this new order to his people who had trusted him and were already filled with doubts about the wisdom of the surrender and fear of the white man's justice?

He went throughout the camp, gently informing the people that they must move one more time. The people looked at him with disbelief and incomprehension. Why could they not stay here? Had they not been promised this? There was room enough and they would bother no one. The river was already flowing with ice. How would they survive such a journey?

Already they were grieving the parents and children and relatives who had fled toward the Old Woman Land. Now they were being moved even farther away. Would they ever see their families again? Would they ever touch the earth of their ancestors? Would they even live to see the melting of the snows, or were they simply being taken away to be hanged?

Joseph could not give them answers. But he dared not show his own doubts. He instructed the people to break camp and prepare for this new journey.

No one moved quickly. They did not wish to travel again. This might be unfamiliar land under unfamiliar sky, but in their short time at that spot they had begun making their peace with it, putting up lodges and shaping their days into a comfortable camp routine. The wounded were healing, the old men were whiling away their time gambling and playing cards, and the children were running about and playing as children should. Though their hearts were heavy and their spirits weary, this encampment had given them hope. They had only to survive one winter in this place, then they could travel back over the mountains to the hills and valleys of their homeland. Now they were being told to gather their belongings for another journey.

The soldiers kept prodding them to hurry. Though the weather here was not so bitter as it had been on the high plains of the Bear's Paw, the temperature at night was now dropping below freezing. Already on some days they had awakened to a ground covered with snow. The river too spoke of impending winter. Its edges had begun to freeze solid, and its center was running heavy with slush ice coming down from the north. The journey had to begin at once.

Colonel Miles had brought up fourteen flat-bottomed boats made of heavy, sawn timber—little more than rafts with low, protective sides. The sick and the wounded and the elderly and the very young—all the people who might slow the pace or fail to survive on an overland journey—would travel in these, along with some of the women who could care for the others. Those who were strong enough to travel by land would cross the country with the soldiers. They would all meet at a fort several days' journey farther along the river.

Joseph protested vehemently. He did not wish to leave the women and children and the sick and the elderly. He had been charged by his father to protect his people. Those were the people who most needed his protection.

But Miles was adamant. It has to be this way, he explained. We do not have enough boats to carry all your people and their provisions. And even our own sick and wounded are always transported by water when possible. Would you not rather have your weak and injured carried on the smooth, fast surface of the river than being jolted and jarred across frozen ground?

Joseph could not argue, and even had he wished to, he had no choice. Miles's word, or the word of those who commanded Miles, must be obeyed. So, reluctantly, he said his good-byes to the sick and the elderly and promised that he would see them soon at the new fort farther down the river. Then, on the morning of October 31, he set out with the soldiers and the other strong and healthy among his people on this new journey across these cold and unfamiliar plains.

The weather had taken on the character of early November. On good days, the travel was easy, though cold. On bad days, when the snows and sleets of the approaching winter cut into their exposed flesh, it was a journey almost too painful to endure.

Joseph was profoundly upset that the people were being hauled in wagons and that all their horses other than the few they were riding had been left behind. He had not agreed to give up his horses when he had handed over his rifle. First it had been their weapons, now it was their herds and their saddles. How were they to survive? Without guns and animals, they were as helpless as children.

The soldier Miles had placed in charge had no answers. He was instructed only to deliver the captives to the place where the Yellowstone and

Missouri Rivers met. There they could speak to men with more authority. Until then they must accept their situation and do what they were told.

Several days into the journey, Joseph and the others saw one of the boats coming up the river behind them. It beached nearby, and Colonel Miles, who had stayed behind to oversee the launchings, stepped out wearing a long, blue, caped coat and high leather boots. He announced that he would travel the rest of the way with the overland party.

While the transfer was being made, Joseph had time to speak with his people who had been traveling on the boat. There had been a frightening rapids early on, they said, and one of the other boats had been lost, killing many of the people. One of the young mothers with her child on her back had bent over the side of the boat to get a drink and her baby had fallen in. When she had jumped in to save it she had been lost along with the child. But by and large, they had been treated well. They were allowed coffee to drink and salt pork and sugar and beans and rice to eat. The white man in charge of the boat was not a soldier, and he had been very trusting, even allowing the boys to steer and row and one of the old men to use a rifle to go ashore and hunt.

The remaining boats were still far behind because the white men had decided to make a race of the journey. Since their boat was curved toward the front and the back, and because their young boys had proven to be such strong rowers and polers, they were now in the lead. The others would be coming up soon.

Joseph listened with sadness. It was good that his people were being fed and that the young boys were able to find some pleasure and satisfaction in this endless journey. But more of his people were now dead, and he had been powerless to help them.

Soon the boat pushed away, and the tired party of overland travelers resumed its eastward journey across the increasingly cold and alien plains. With each mile, the weather grew colder and the journey more difficult. The land still felt like buffalo country, but the grass was shorter and the hills were becoming lower and fewer. The sky had turned from blue to empty gray, and the winds were often filled with driving sleet and snow.

For more than a week they traveled this way. Colonel Miles had assumed command, and he forced a rapid pace. The people's mood was once again descending into hopelessness and despair. Even Miles was saddened to see them suffering so as they made their way silently through these cold, empty lands. The men longed for their families and spoke of all who had been lost through flight or death during the long journey. No one knew if the boats on which the others were traveling would be able to navigate the ice-filled waters or if the injured could survive the numbing cold.

Hardest of all was their uncertainty about their impending fate. Just a few weeks ago they had been free people, willingly though sorrowfully walking forth to meet with the soldiers in a common armistice. Now they were captives, divided and herded like white men's cattle, being driven to a place they did not know in a country they did not understand. Their weapons had been taken from them, their horses and saddles had been claimed by the white soldiers and Cheyenne, and the man to whom they had entrusted their fate seemed to have no authority to keep his own promises. They were moving into a white man's world where no man was master of his own word and no Indian seemed able to long survive.

The journey to the meeting place, which the soldiers called Fort Buford, took ten cruel, cold, and wintry days. The only thought that lifted the people's deep sadness and growing gloom during the travel was the promise of being reunited with their brothers and sisters.

When they finally reached the fort, they were relieved to discover that the boat travelers had arrived two days earlier. Their journey had been hard and cold, they said, but it had not been unbearable. Almost all were alive, except for those on the boat that had capsized, the mother and child who had fallen overboard, and one man who had died just before they had arrived at the fort. And they had learned much from the white boatmen during their travels.

They had been told about Washington, the strange, mysterious white settlement to which the soldiers and government people were always referring. So many white men lived there, the boatmen said, that people had to fight for space to live and air to breathe. They also had been told of huge boats that traveled over all the waters of creation and of a great, fire-snorting iron horse that lived on wood and water and could outrun the fastest Nez Perce pony.

All agreed that the white boat leaders had been good to them. They had fed them well and let them pray in their own way. They had shown them new birds and animals that were good to eat and had even let the boys hunt with bows and arrows. The women had been permitted to go ashore to pick berries, and they had found many that they knew from their own country.

At this soldier fort too they had been treated well. They had been provided with firewood and allowed to sleep in an empty soldier building, even though there had always been white soldiers positioned nearby as guards.

They said there had been much arguing between the soldiers and the boat leaders, and the soldier chief of the fort had taken the boat leaders and put them under arrest. The argument, they believed, had something to do with the boat leaders' not wanting to travel down the new river that joined where they were now camped.

The people could understand the boatmen's concern. This new river was brown and wide, and its whole surface was covered with fast-moving slush. The boatmen said that it was the same river the people had crossed back at the place where they had raided the piles of supplies—the river the white man called the Missouri. But here it was a winter river, giving off steam as it passed and moving with a constant, ominous hiss.

Neither the people nor the boat leaders wanted to get back on this river. They knew that some morning soon the slush would stop moving and the river would freeze, trapping the boats and the people in a sheet of solid ice. But the soldiers did not care. They had received orders from the Great Chief in Washington, and the boats were to resume their travel as soon as the foot travelers arrived.

Again, Joseph asked Miles what was to become of his people. Miles told him that he would allow them several days' rest, then they would begin the journey to another fort far down the ice-filled river. The people again would be separated, with the healthy men continuing their travel overland and the weak and elderly again traveling in the boats. At this new fort they would be kept for the winter before being allowed to go back to their own country when the snows melted in the mountain passes.

This did not please Joseph; it left too much unknown. But if it were true, at least his people would be together, and he could keep his promise to care for those who had chosen to stay with him and remain under his protection.

After several days at the fort the people were instructed to prepare to leave quickly. The river, they were told, was within days of freezing solid.

The women hurried to the small buildings that housed white women who did laundry and made bread and cookies for the soldiers. There they bought bread and cakes and pies with some of their remaining coins and American dollars.

The boats soon pushed off into the slush-filled river, leaving behind the men, who were to travel overland by horse and wagon. The soldiers informed them that the trip would take about another ten days.

As before, Joseph remained with the overland travelers. Once again, it was hard to see the people separated; surely more would die on this leg of the journey. Hardest of all was the realization that they were now entering country that none of them knew. Since the deaths of Poker Joe and Looking Glass and the escape of the remaining healthy warriors with White Bird, there were none among them who had ever traveled to this eastern edge of buffalo country.

It was a strange, bleak landscape with a very different spirit from the land in which they had been traveling. The rolling hills had flattened out into long, open prairies with thinner light and heavier air. The smell of the wind was different, and the light from the sun seemed weaker and more filtered. There were different birds, different animals. Even the wind had a different sound. This was not country that seemed good for Nez Perce people.

The people traveled for days through this land, settling into an attitude of despair and gloom. The travelers on the boats were able to look up and see platforms with Indian corpses in the trees—a practice they knew from some of the eastern tribes but that seemed harsh and alien to a people who felt that the bodies of the dead should be returned to the bosom of their mother, the earth. Soon Indians appeared on the riverbanks fixing rifles on the passing boats. The boatmen were able to keep the people from harm, but none felt safe in this new country where even the people seemed turned against them.

After a while the telltale smell of a white man's fire cut through the air, and a fort came into sight on the distant bank. It was not the fort where they were to spend the winter but another fort, only partway along on their journey. The boatmen called it Fort Berthold.

About 300 Indians were standing about at water's edge. The people recognized some of the tribes—Arikara, Hidatsa, and Mandan, along with a few Sioux and Cheyenne and Crow people the Nez Perce had known and even dealt with in some of their travels. But something about them had changed. They did not seem like free men and women. They stayed near the fort and behaved like camp dogs, milling around waiting to be fed.

These people had heard about the Nez Perce and how they had fought the soldiers, and they were curious to meet the strangers from far over the mountains. When the overland travelers arrived, Joseph gathered all these strange Indians together in a great circle and stood in the center, telling the story of the journey using the language of the hands. He told them of the war, of how his people had been chased by soldiers from the time of first flowers to the time of first frosts; of how they had fought with the army many times and had lost many of their people. He told of the capture and the promise made by Howard and Miles and the separation of his people. He told of the soldier chiefs and the hard trek they were making.

The white men at the fort stood back, watching him speak in signs to this assembled crowd of hundreds of Indians. They were amazed at his power to communicate without words and the rapt way he held an audience that used its eyes to listen.

The experience was good for Joseph. It allowed him to tell his story to people of his own kind, even if they were strange and listless in their ways. He was gradually becoming aware that the white government looked upon all people with skin the color of his as the same and did not see them as different people with different beliefs and different ways of life and different gifts from the Creator. It was one more insight into the ways of the white men who now held the fate of his people in their hands, one more bit of knowledge he might be able to use to help his people.

While they were camped in this flat land of cold skies and thin light, he had a chance to speak again with the others who had been traveling by boat. They had docked at the fort while the boatmen picked up food and blankets, and they told him something very troubling. There had been a white man at the last fort—a very strange man with long, greasy red hair who spoke in a language the people were able to understand. He had seemed to have a bad spirit and wanted always to be near the Nez Perce women. The soldiers had tried to keep him away, but before they did, he told the people that the soldiers were taking them to a place where a great gun shoots twice, and there they would all be hanged. This had darkened the people's spirits and filled them with a heavy gloom.

Joseph knew nothing about this and was not able to give them any peace beyond what Colonel Miles had told him. He did not know who this white man was or if he had some power of far sight. He could only reassure the people that they would soon move again to a fort down the river where Colonel Miles had promised they would be safe until the snows melted and they could return to their homes. But white man's promises, even those of Colonel Miles, had begun to have a very hollow ring.

20

"When Will These White Chiefs Begin to Tell the Truth?"

THE NEZ PERCE on the boats reached Bismarck before Joseph and the overland travelers, and it was an arrival filled with anguish and terror. As they approached, they heard a cannon shoot twice, as the strange man had predicted. Not only did it bring back all the terror of the great gun on the final battlefield and the memories of the death that had rained from the sky, but they were convinced that it signaled their impending hanging. They fell moaning and screaming into the bottom of the boats, certain that their end was near.

They could not know that this was the white soldiers' way of signaling riverboats to stop at Fort Abraham Lincoln for inspection. To them it was simply a signal of death. And their fear was made greater by the earsplitting screech of a locomotive steam whistle and the heavy, metallic groan of its wheels as it backed down the tracks. Short of thunder and buffalo stampedes and the roaring of the rivers and falls in their own country, these were the greatest sounds any Nez Perce had ever heard, and they seemed to contain everything terrifying about the white world of metal and noise.

Most of them had never seen anything like Bismarck. The three forts where they had previously stopped or camped—Keogh, Buford, and Berthold—were little more than huddled collections of wooden buildings, built in the strange fashion of the white man and standing lonely in the great openness of the empty landscape. The white towns they had known, like Stevensville, were nothing more than a few buildings set on either side of a single street.

But Bismarck was a place of a different order. A strapping young frontier town, it boasted a railroad connection, a telegraph line, blocks of two-story buildings with boardwalks and signage, and streets filled with stagecoaches and men and women in eastern attire. Though to the rest of America it was little more than a scrawny frontier outpost, it was to western settlers the first city of the East, connected by transportation and technology to the larger cities of St. Louis and St. Paul and, by extension, to the growing metropolises of mid-America and the eastern seaboard.

Its rawboned activity and mechanical clamor stunned the Nez Perce. As they moved along the river amid the bustle of the ferries and railroad clamor, the people huddled on the floor of the boats and sang their death songs. The young boys would not even assist the boatmen in bringing the boats to dock.

Eventually, the boats were moored at the landing at Fort Lincoln just downriver from the town, and the people were mustered across a gangplank and up the bank to a field, where they were ordered to set up tents on bottomland at the edge of the river. Two of the wounded had worsened on the journey and were carried by ambulance wagon to the post hospital building.

The overland travelers had not yet arrived. They were a day behind, camped in a thicket called the Painted Woods, preparing to march through Bismarck to their place of encampment at the fort. But the newspaper accounts had preceded the prisoners. Colonel Woods's florid embellishment of Joseph's short surrender message had been communicated as his actual surrender speech, and the chief was in rapid ascent in the public mind. The *Bismarck Tri-Weekly,* in a piece written by a correspondent for the *New York Herald,* described him as having the "figure and mien of as gallant a warrior chieftain as ever confessed himself fairly beaten at the game of war."

Even Howard himself had been quoted in the Bismarck papers a month before as calling Joseph an "intelligent and very good Indian," who, he believed, had been inclined to surrender far sooner but had been held back from doing so by other chiefs and warriors.

His people were characterized as uncomplaining, kind, and "far superior" to other Indians; his warriors as the best of any horsemen and marksmen; his war as a masterful retreat. And no reader, especially those in the frontier towns and the land that had been terrorized by Sitting Bull and the Sioux, could fail to appreciate the significance of the fact that Joseph's Indians had done no scalping or mutilation. This exalted reputation, combined with Miles's status as a military hero for his capture of this great warrior and his brilliantly elusive people, made the entry of Joseph and Miles into Bismarck a triumphal moment for the local populace.

The mayor and leading citizens went out to the Painted Woods to meet the noble chief and his captor while the town itself prepared for the entry as if for a great civic event. The band from Fort Abraham Lincoln was positioned along the main street, and the general populace gathered with foodstuffs to offer to the arriving soldiers and captives.

As the line of travelers appeared on the top of the hill, the band broke into the "Star-Spangled Banner." Women and children pushed through the troops and rushed up to the captives. The sad-eyed, haggard Nez Perce watched with amazement as the townsfolk surged toward them, offering them dishes of hot food.

Joseph rode at the front along with Miles—the two men who were seen as bringing this tragic chapter of American warfare to an honorable close. The cavalry and infantrymen followed behind, sullen and morose. They were tired from the journey and tired of the prevarications and financial evasions by the military. Many had not seen pay for seven months. Some were riding with their pockets turned inside out to underscore their poverty.

But none of this mattered to the townsfolk of Bismarck. They stood on the sides of the streets cheering and waving. This was the greatest event their growing western settlement had ever seen, and they were reveling in their young community's day in the sun.

No one was enjoying it more than the city fathers. The presence of these two great leaders was a coup for the town, and they intended to make the most of it. It was their chance to showcase themselves in the national press and to gain advantage in the struggle among small western settlements to attract residents and businesses.

Right now, Bismarck was bustling because it was the end of the railroad line and the jumping-off point to the frontier West. Everyone disembarked here, purchased goods here, spent money here, and returned here after their forays farther west. But the tracks would soon move past them, and other communities would spring up to compete with them, just as they themselves had sprung up to compete with cities like Jamestown and Fargo farther along the railroad line to the east. The massacre of Custer and the continued threat of Sitting Bull had cast a pall over their prospects, reinforcing their image as a dangerous outpost in unsecured Indian territory.

The presence of Joseph and Miles could change that. They could herald the coming of a new era, a new peace, a new chapter in white-Indian affairs. Most of all, they could be the start of a new civic image. They could provide Bismarck a place at the table of urbane American cities and remove the stigma of being a lawless, rough-and-tumble town born in the grit and greed at the end of a railroad line.

Miles was immediately invited to a banquet at the Sheridan House, a stately three-story hotel that stood by the side of the railroad tracks and dominated the town with its massive, ornamented grandeur. He graciously accepted, expressing all appropriate humility that he should be so honored when he had only been doing his job. But in fact, this was exactly the sort of adulation that he sought from this victory. He had even doctored the surrender message he had sent out from the battlefield, changing it without Howard's knowledge to remove all significant references to meaningful participation by Howard and his soldiers. This had resulted in a firestorm of controversy within the military, but it had served its purpose as cementing Miles's popularity among a public hungry for a genuine military hero.

So that evening, while the Nez Perce sat in the cold confines of their tent camp by the river and his troops bivouacked nearby in their own campgrounds, Miles was feted with a reception, dinner, and celebratory ball at the Sheridan. He used the opportunity to compliment the citizens on their culture and refinement and to praise the Indians now under his stewardship. He recounted many of the abuses that the Nez Perce had suffered at the hands of unscrupulous Indian agents back in their home country, citing the incidents Joseph had told him about while they rode together on the overland journey to Fort Keogh.

He told of how their government agent had taken $200,000 that had been allotted for the people and had provided almost no services in return. He explained how Joseph had not wanted this war and had been forced into it by the unscrupulous behavior of the whites. He praised Joseph's kindness and generosity in dealing with soldiers who had been wounded in battle, pointing out that the wounded were never killed and were even assisted and given succor. He finished by saying that the Nez Perce had conducted one of the most humane military campaigns in the history of the country.

In light of the citizens' all-too-recent experience with the treatment of wounded soldiers at the Little Bighorn by the Sioux and the pitiful condition of the refugees that the people had seen paraded through their streets that morning, these comments from a military hero only deepened their sympathy for the guests who were making their five-year-old city such a center of national attention and excitement.

By the time Miles had finished, the residents of Bismarck were convinced that they had in their midst a completely different order of Indian—one that could help erase the bloody memories of the past and help their fledgling city take its rightful seat at the table of civilization.

That evening, as the city fathers listened to Miles's story, they determined to make an effort to bring this new era to pass. They would provide another banquet for the other great leader of this most noble of Indian wars, Chief Joseph. It would take at least a day to set the planning into motion, but it was worth the cost and effort. After all, what other city had ever had the opportunity, and been so greathearted and broad-minded, as to honor opposing combatants on the same civic stage only days apart?

The following morning, Miles and Joseph met in a formal session, well attended by correspondents and journalists, to discuss the status and disposition of Joseph's people. Joseph expressed himself with an oratorical solemnity befitting the gravity of the occasion. In the course of his travels, he said, he had come to know the heart of the soldier chief Miles, and he now trusted him and believed him to be a good man. They had fought each other like warriors and now stood side by side as friends. His people had been poorly treated back in their homelands, and that had been the cause of the war. The agents assigned were bad men who stole the people's money, once taking $18,000 in a week for fences that had been built only on paper. Now his people were far from their home, and they were tired and sad. They loved their homeland like they loved their mother, and they wanted to go back. This, he believed, the soldier chief Miles would help them to do.

Miles listened approvingly then spoke in response, praising Joseph and his people again for their character and conduct during the war. He too valued his new friend, Joseph, and wished to see his people and the white people of America live in peace.

The conversation went on in this manner, duly observed and noted by the correspondents and reporters issuing dispatches to the newspapers back East. After a break for lunch it resumed in much the same fashion. But in the afternoon session, Miles delivered a surprise announcement. He would be leaving for St. Paul on that evening's train in order to meet with his superiors to give a report on the battle and its aftermath.

Joseph was visibly upset. This was a bad omen. He had handed his rifle to the colonel and had placed himself and his people in his care. At Miles's word he had allowed his people to be brought to this strange and unfamiliar country. He had spoken well of the colonel, praising him as an honorable man, and had given his people assurances that Miles was a man of his word. Now the colonel was leaving.

What was to become of his people when the man in whom they had placed their trust was no longer present? Though the people of Bismarck had been good to them, and their campsite seemed healthy, how could they be sure that the people would treat them so well after Miles left? How could they be sure that after he departed they would not all be hanged?

Miles assured him that there would be no hanging, but he refrained from telling Joseph the truly difficult news that he had learned from Sheridan's headquarters in Chicago: that the Nez Perce, though not to be executed, were also not to be allowed to stay at Bismarck and Fort Abraham Lincoln. In short order they were to be moved by train to Fort Leavenworth in Kansas to await final disposition to a place of the government's choice. The army did not wish to have them in such close proximity to Sitting Bull, and quartering them would be cheaper at Fort Leavenworth. This would also place them close to Indian Territory, where, if they could be so assigned, they would be out of the military's hands and off the military's payroll and thereby become the problem and the expense of the Department of the Interior.

With this unspoken knowledge heavy on Miles's mind, the formalities continued far into the afternoon.

While Joseph and Miles were speaking, and the correspondents and other dignitaries were sitting in rapt attention, many of the other Nez Perce were tentatively venturing up from their campsite into town. Few had ever seen a city of this size. With the exception of Stevensville in the Bitterroots, some had never seen a white city at all. The stores and goods amazed them, and they wandered among them, greeted by the townsfolk and shopkeepers with the same curiosity and good humor that had been exhibited toward them the day before.

Many of the Nez Perce still had money to spend. Some of the women had American currency they had plaited into their hair at the start of the journey, and some of the people still had gold dust they had carried with them from Idaho. The shopkeepers were more than happy to make sales to these exotic visitors. They could charge exorbitant prices and gain the story of a lifetime in the process.

By the end of the following day, every storekeeper and saloonkeeper had such a story, and they ranged from the likely to the absurd. One saloonkeeper claimed an argument had broken out in his establishment over a game of cards, and an errant shot fired by one of the participants had passed between the arm and the body of a Nez Perce man who happened to be in the saloon at the time. The Indian, he reported, had not even moved but had merely lifted his other arm to show bullet holes in his shirt that had been made by other gunshots he had encountered during battles on the retreat. Such things, the warrior had said, were common and not worth getting concerned about so long as they didn't hurt.

Another store owner spoke of conversing with a Nez Perce in sign language for twenty minutes before the man asked, in perfect English, by what measure the people of this town sold their flour.

Most of the stories were fanciful or fabricated, and almost all were embellished. But all who encountered the Nez Perce on their forays through the town agreed that they had never seen Indians of this sort before. They had money, they were well behaved and civil, they did not steal, and they did not drink. All this contrasted not only with their previous experience with Indians but also with the soldiers themselves, who had entered the town dirty and rambunctious and, despite their lack of pay, had proceeded to prevail upon the good offices of the saloonkeepers to get so drunk that many had to be carried back to their barracks.

Such stories were happily grabbed up by the newspaper stringers, who were thrilled at last to be in a place where bars and eating establishments were readily available and great stories, whether verifiable or not, were to be had for the asking. They crafted flowery dispatches and sent them out across the telegraph lines, where the stories quickly made their way into the newspapers in Chicago and New York and other major cities in America. The feeds filtered down to the smaller papers, and soon what was being seen, reported, and fabricated in Bismarck was being discussed and recounted as truth at kitchen tables and in parlors all across the country.

Among these stories were descriptions of Joseph, the noble leader, dressed in embroidered moccasins and a buckskin shirt heavily decorated with red, white, and blue beads, wandering from store to store, making purchases with money of which he seemed to have an endless supply. He was depicted as "cutting an elegant figure," with white ermine-tail tassels hanging from his shirtsleeves and a wolfskin sash, lined with red cloth, suspended from his hip. He was said to have carried a medicine bag slung across his chest, and he wore a string of large white beads around his neck.

Some descriptions had his hair adorned with white paint, others his forehead and ears decorated with red paint. These portraits in writing made him seem every inch the regal warrior, and, accurate or not, became his indelible image in the American reading public's mind. He was, as the papers said, one of Cooper's "good Indians"—a noble savage, innocent of the wicked ways of modern society, worthy of respect and even admiration, but doomed by the inevitable tide of civilization to be washed out of exis-tence unless he and his people could adapt to the changes in the world that no one, red or white, could resist or control.

The following morning, with Miles already in St. Paul, Joseph was pre-sented with the invitation to the banquet that the city fathers had planned in his honor. It was addressed to "Joseph, Head Chief of the Nez Perces" and read:

> *Sir. Desiring to show you our kind feelings and the admiration we have for your bravery and humanity, as exhibited in your recent conflict with the forces of the United States, we most cordially invite you to dine with us at the Sheridan House, in this city. The dinner is to be at 1½ today.*

It was signed by the leading citizens of the town, including the mayor, George Sweet, and Dr. H. R. Porter, who had been the only surviving battle surgeon after the horrifying massacre of Custer's Seventh Cavalry at the Little Bighorn.

Joseph received it with pleasure and respect. It indicated that the town would not turn on him and his people now that Miles had departed, and it showed the kind of respect that he valued in the interaction between people. He would be pleased to attend, and he would return the honor by bringing some of the other head men as a sign of appreciation.

At noon he, Husis Kute, Yellow Bull, and several of the other men made their way from the tent camp up the hill to the great, looming Sheridan House hotel. They were greeted warmly under the grand wooden portico and were ushered into a high-ceilinged parlor, where the women and children of the town, dressed in their finest clothes, were waiting for an audience.

The Nez Perce leaders formed a reception line and received the guests graciously, shaking each of their hands and expressing thanks for the kind treatment that the Nez Perce people had been accorded by the white citizens of this fine town.

One woman was so overcome at being in the presence of these noble men of nature that, upon being introduced to Joseph, she could not resist kissing him. Others were more reserved, but all treated the guests with a deference usually associated with royalty, which, in a sense, the townsfolk believed these chieftains to be.

At the table, after receiving an official welcome in which the formal invitation was read as if it were a proclamation, Joseph and the others were treated to a meal of roast beef, fish, potatoes, cabbage, beans, pies, and pudding. They ate using knives and forks, which amazed and gratified the onlookers, who apparently had expected them to eat with their hands, never stopping to think that the average Indian probably had more experience and dexterity with a knife than any white man or woman. Most amazing of all to the onlookers was the fact that Joseph wiped his mouth with a napkin rather than on the end of his sleeve.

The meal was followed by a round of speeches. Mayor Sweet spoke at some length, welcoming the guests and proclaiming them friends. He told them that the wise men of the white race had dug down into the rocks of the earth and uncovered the truth that the earth has been occupied by many races of living beings, each succeeding the other, and each a little higher than the one before.

As a result, the white race had now ascended to a controlling position on the globe, and the Indian race, though good, had to change its habits and live in the manner of the white race in order to flourish. The buffalo, he said, were like the red race and were now being supplanted by the fields and cattle of the white race. Such was the way of nature, and such was the fate of the Indians if they did not change their way of life and become cultivators of herds of cows and sheep.

After Sweet's speech, Husis Kute spoke, saying he was thankful for the words of the white chief and that sharing dinner, like shaking hands, was an act of friendship. He hoped, he said, that the white people and Nez Perce people could be friends and that their children could grow up together. Joseph, when called upon to speak, was slow to express himself and seemed to be having difficulty controlling his emotions. He did not speak long, saying only that he tried always to entertain good sentiments in his heart and that he entertained them at this moment. All people, he said, should have good sentiments and express them. If all did so, there would be no trouble all the world over, for those who live with good sentiments never have trouble. For his part, he wished only to speak well of others.

The audience was grateful but a bit disappointed. People had expected something more extensive, something with more woodland eloquence. They attributed his halting words to his discomfort at speaking in the confines of a room rather than outdoors under the shade of great oaks, as at a grand Indian council. And when, at the end, he came near to tears and fell silent, they attributed this not to sadness or loneliness but to the overwhelming emotion he felt for the kind treatment he had received at the hands of his white brothers and sisters.

Almost unnoticed during this whole period was the quiet ascendance of Ad Chapman, who on this afternoon was standing at the side of Husis Kute and Joseph, serving as their interpreter. He had assumed this role after the surrender and had become increasingly essential as the Nez Perce and the whites were forced to try to communicate with each other.

Tom Hill, the man Joseph had trusted to communicate his thoughts to Miles and Howard during the negotiations at the Bear's Paw, had been sent out by the soldiers after the capture to search for the fleeing Nez Perce and had taken the opportunity to escape. This had left Chapman, the lying, cowardly, bullying rancher, as the sole person who could speak both languages well enough to serve as an intermediary between cultures. With their limited English, and no other white person around who spoke their language, the Nez Perce had no choice but to rely on him and trust that he reflected accurately both what they were saying and what was being said to them.

And in fact, to a great extent this was what Chapman was doing. Though a scoundrel and braggart, he was not a fool. He recognized opportunity when he saw it, and the chance for a government paycheck certainly qualified as an opportunity. From the moment of the surrender, he had stuck close to Miles and Joseph, making himself indispensable as a bridge between languages. Now, with Miles gone, he had attached himself completely to the chief. He willingly embellished his prior relationship with the Nez Perce in Idaho, conveniently ignoring its acrimony, and soon was so closely identified with Joseph that the correspondents were describing him as the chief's "bosom companion" and "old neighbor and life-long friend."

For Joseph it was a precarious situation. Chapman had become his tongue and his ears. A man who was willing to eradicate a brand on a Nez Perce horse to claim it for his own, as Chapman had been known to do back in Idaho, was not above eradicating the meaning of a Nez Perce word to turn a situation to his own advantage. But Joseph knew that, properly controlled, Chapman could be a great asset in pleading the people's case for return to their beloved homeland.

At the banquet, the arrangement seemed to work well. But later that evening, Chapman was put in a position to use his interpreter's skills in a less than comfortable mission. He was called upon to communicate the contents of the dispatch that Miles had received about the transfer of the people to Fort Leavenworth. He accompanied the soldiers with the orders down to Joseph's tent and spoke the words that Miles himself had not had the heart to say.

Upon hearing about the new move, Joseph put his head down and murmured, "When will these white chiefs begin to tell the truth?" Chapman did not have to interpret his words to the soldiers in order for them to understand what was in the tired chief's heart.

For the remainder of the night and into the early morning, Nez Perce men and women met in council to discuss their situation. They did not want to leave Bismarck. They had been treated well in this white people's town, and it was here that the soldier chief Miles had promised they could stay. Now they were being told to leave again.

How did they know this was not one more lie? How could they know what this new place would be like? How could they know they were not to be killed? They did not wish to travel in that great snorting metal beast that moved on rails, and they did not wish to move farther to the east. They wanted to stay here until spring, then return to their homeland.

Joseph listened, but he knew that in the end the people would have no choice but to comply. Their only hope was the promise, given by the soldiers and conveyed by Chapman, that they would see Miles again in the white man's city of St. Paul. Maybe there he could provide them with some understanding. Maybe there he could bring them news of their families who had escaped with White Bird. Winter was getting strong, and their fear and sadness were growing.

The following morning the people were moved up near the railroad yards from their camp by the river. The women had spent the night and early morning cooking the four days' ration of beef the army had given them and packing it together with the two days' supply of hardtack they had been allotted. As much as possible, they were ready for the journey.

They stood watching anxiously as the great belching black engine surged and backed its way into position. The army had assembled a special transport train out of eleven dilapidated coaches and several freight cars. It wheezed and surged and snorted acrid, choking smoke as the frightened people loaded their supplies and packs of clothing and household goods into the cars. Then, amid a crowd of townsfolk who had gathered to see them off, the Nez Perce climbed on board the strange, frightening metal beast, assisting their children and wounded and physically carrying a number of soldiers who had been assigned to accompany them but were too hung over to stand or walk.

Joseph sat on one of the wooden seats, staring out the open window at the assembled townsfolk who had come to see them off. Before leaving, he had been forced to sell the beloved horse that had carried him on this long and difficult journey. He had wanted to take the horse with him, but the government had informed him that it would not be responsible for feeding and transporting the horse to the new destination many miles away. Reluctantly, he had sold it for $35, receiving white man's money in exchange for an animal who had been his Nez Perce legs and part of his Nez Perce spirit. He was now little different than the Indians sitting around the buildings at Fort Berthold—a man without freedom, without hope, and dependent for survival on white man's money and white man's goods.

As the train pulled away, he nodded and waved to these citizens of Bismarck who had treated his people so well and with whom he had hoped, at last, to be able to stay. The people in the crowd waved back, sorry to see the departure of this good Indian and his good people—people who had brought money, excitement, and a national spotlight to their little frontier town.

Orlando Goff, the photographer who had been fortunate enough to have Joseph sit for a photograph upon his arrival, was already selling cards with pictures of the great chief. The man who had purchased Joseph's horse was besieged with at least twelve purchase offers, some almost doubling his money. But he was holding out for higher profits. There were, he believed, "millions" to be made from Joseph's ponies if they were allowed to multiply.

The marketing of Joseph had begun in earnest.

21

"Is It Possible That the Noble Red Man Is Not a Myth?"

FOUR HUNDRED FIFTY miles farther down the tracks in the more urbane city of St. Paul, there was great curiosity about this celebrated chief. The citizens had been keeping up with the story of the Nez Perce through the telegraph dispatches printed in their local paper, and they were having a hard time believing what they were reading.

The residents of Bismarck, though raw and somewhat naive frontier folk, were anything but naive when it came to Indians and Indian affairs. They had lived through Sitting Bull and the Custer massacre and resided right at the edge of country where Indians still roamed without restraint. They were not likely to be taken in by fantasies of Fenimore Cooper's noble savages. But the dispatches from the *Bismarck Tri-Weekly Tribune* made it obvious that the citizenry of Bismarck, almost without exception, had not only been charmed but impressed and deeply moved by these Nez Perce and their Chief Joseph, who had just spent four days in their town. Far from being treated as captives or refugees, they had been treated as honored guests and, by all reports, had behaved accordingly.

The St. Paul editors determined that the claim of a "banquet" for the chief attended by "all the citizenry of Bismarck" was only so much self-serving frontier puffery. In fact, their sources suggested, it had been nothing more than a good meal attended by some of the city's elite. But there was, nonetheless, something almost incomprehensible in the citizens' warmhearted embrace of these heathens who had fought with and killed so many American soldiers in the course of the last five months.

The *St. Paul Pioneer Press,* voicing the unspoken feelings of its citizenry in an editorial, raised the almost unthinkable possibility: given the "golden opinions" of the residents of Bismarck regarding Joseph, "which are altogether inexplicable upon the supposition that he is the average dirty, sullen, uninviting savage . . . Is it possible that the noble red man is not a myth. . . ?" The people of St. Paul could hardly wait for the arrival of the train so they could finally see for themselves.

The Nez Perce, however, were feeling anything but noble. The train on which they were traveling terrified them. It was louder than anything they had ever heard and was moving at a speed beyond their comprehension. It rocked back and forth like a wagon about to fall over and screamed across the land like a wounded animal. The air inside was filled with coal cinders from the train's smokestack, and the wood stoves provided no heat to the drafty centers of the cars. The screeching of the wheels and the bumping on the track made sleep difficult and conversation impossible.

They rode through the cold November night in stark terror, huddled on the wooden seats, cradling their children and fearing for their lives. The soldier in charge showed them the toilet hole in the small room at the end of the car, but they could see through it to the tracks flying by below and were afraid to use it. So they held themselves as best they could, but when they could wait no longer, relieved themselves on the floor.

The train had received clearance to travel day and night on unimpeded tracks, so the only stops it made were to take on water for the boilers. At these, the desperate people ran out and relieved themselves or drank thirstily from water in nearby ponds. Joseph received no special treatment, but he did have the advantage of being under the care of a Captain Johnstone and Colonel Reed. They had traveled with the people on their overland march and were familiar to the chief. By staying near them and asking questions, he was able to glean some information about what was going on and what his people were confronting.

At the small town of Jamestown, a hundred miles east of Bismarck in the Dakota Territory, he and several other of the head men accompanied these officers to a local boardinghouse to eat dinner while the boilers were

filling with water. After a quick meal the men hurried back to the departing train. But as it moved away from the station and built up speed, one of
the Indians came running back through the cars, talking excitedly in Nez
Perce. Chapman was quickly summoned, and it was learned that Joseph
had not reboarded the train.

Colonel Reed pulled the bell cord to signal an emergency. The train
screeched to a halt, then began backing toward the town. Through the
window they could see Joseph running desperately up the tracks toward
them. As he reached the train and climbed on, loaves of bread dropped
from under his blanket. On the way back he had seen a house with bread
displayed in the window and had stopped to purchase some for his family.
While he was doing so, the train had begun to pull away. He had run as fast
as he could and was lucky the train had stopped, or he might have been
separated from the people he had sworn to care for and protect. The soldiers joked that if he had run so fast during the pursuit, Miles would never
have caught him. But beneath the joking was the awareness that this chief
cared so much for his people that he took a train's untimely departure as a
crisis of separation rather than an opportunity for escape.

Though the train was a fearful experience for the Nez Perce, it was a
learning experience for their chief. Its speed was beyond the fastest horse;
its power to travel without rest beyond that of the fittest animal. At one
stop, soldiers pointed out the telegraph wires and told Joseph that white
men could talk through these. The chief was skeptical and challenged the
men to talk to someone at the next stop and tell them to bring him a glass
of water and call him by name. The men passed this message to the sta-
tionmaster, and he sent the instructions ahead down the line. At the next
station a woman came out asking for Joseph. She held a glass of water in
her hand.

Joseph understood immediately. This was how the soldier armies had
located the people during their flight. This was how they could keep
coming at them no matter how fast they traveled or how well they covered
their path. The white man, indeed, did have power beyond anything the
Indians could imagine. They could move words faster than the fastest
Indian courier could ride.

This growing awareness of the power of white society hit Joseph full
force in the great city of St. Paul. As the train made its way into the city in
the deep November darkness, he could see flickering lights on the hillsides

in all directions. There were shadows of large buildings—hundreds of them—far larger than the building where he had shared the feast with the people of Bismarck. And these buildings were made of stone, not wood. One street was lined on either side by small fires on tall poles. They gave off a pale greenish light that made the buildings seem like small mountains.

People were everywhere. They stood in front of the tracks, crowding so closely that the train could barely move through them. They pounded at the train windows and shouted out Joseph's name.

The Nez Perce cowered in the cars and stared out the windows at the shouting, waving people. There must have been thousands of them. Joseph, realizing what was happening, moved to the rear car and stepped onto the platform to a great cheer. He began shaking hands with the people, who chanted his name and surged forward to touch him. He shook hands until his arm ached and he had to quit, all the while hoping to see Colonel Miles, as he had been promised by the soldiers before he left Bismarck. But Colonel Miles never came.

The train left St. Paul at ten in the evening. The frightened people had been mobbed by the white citizens as they had stepped out of the cars to get air. They had been prodded and touched and crushed in upon until they could hardly breathe. By the time they were back on board and moving again, the iron horse seemed almost as much a refuge as a fire-snorting object of terror.

They rode on through the night, uncertain where they were going or what was to become of them. The sparks from the smokestack of the train flew by the windows like fireflies. The following morning they awoke to a feeling of gloom and despair. The sky had changed, the land was different. The trees were lifeless sticks with no leaves, and the air was strangely heavy in an unhealthy way. They passed white towns that seemed almost numberless, as many as there were Indian villages in their own country but larger, with more people, all crowded together. At each stop, the white citizens pushed against the train and peered in the grime-smoked windows, cupping their hands against the glass and shouting for Joseph.

The chief tried to oblige. While the train was stopped he would step out onto the platform of the rear car and wave. People would rush forward, presenting him gifts and asking him to speak. He tried to be respectful and show gratitude for their kindness, but his spirits were low. Often he would say only a few words, then fall silent or retreat to the inside of the car while the white faces continued to press against the windows.

The citizens who had gathered were mildly disappointed. They wanted to be like the woman they had read about who had given the chief her wedding ring at a reception line in Bismarck or the people who had been treated to his heathen eloquence at the banquet given in his honor. But the melancholy, sad-eyed man who stepped forth onto the platform of the train and greeted them with a winsome smile and polite handshakes seemed distant and disengaged, anything but a master strategist and a woodland orator. And his black, pointed hat with its green and black headband seemed somehow out of place on a Napoleon of the high plains.

He accepted their gifts graciously, even lighting up a cigar that was handed to him, but his heart was not in it. His concern was not to make white people happy, but to find a way to help his frightened people, who were huddling in the drafty, cinder-filled coaches, worrying about their lost friends and families and wondering if they would ever again be able to set foot on the earth that they once had called home.

22

"A Good Country to Get Rid of Indians In"

LATE ON THE AFTERNOON of November 27, 1877, the train snaked around a bend and moved along a wide river bottom at the base of a rolling, tree-studded bluff. In the distance Joseph could see a gathering of people and a group of soldiers standing in formation by a wooden railway station. Off to the left, toward the river, was a small city of white canvas teepees arranged in straight rows like a soldier camp. The guards on the train explained that this was Fort Leavenworth, and these teepees were where Joseph and his people were going to live.

As the train came to a stop, Joseph stepped off and looked up at the buildings that lined the top of the bluff. There were far more than at Fort Lapwai, far more than at the fort where they had camped near Bismarck. And, like the buildings of St. Paul, they were made of stone, not wood. The light was strange, the air heavy and damp. This did not feel like a good place for the Nez Perce people.

Slowly, the others emerged from the train and gathered around him. They stood in the cold awaiting his instructions while the curious towns-folk pushed toward them. Their packs and goods were nowhere to be seen.

Joseph led the frightened people to a grassy spot on the side of the bluff. He insisted that all communications with his people must go through him. When orders were issued, Chapman would interpret, then the chief would pass the word on to the families. He was still in charge of the well-being of those traveling with him, and he would allow nothing to take place without his knowledge or approval.

After several hours of waiting, the sick and elderly were put in wagons and taken down to the tents while the others walked across the cold, marshy, mile-wide field toward the place that was going to be their home.

The townsfolk who had come to witness the arrival milled about in the cold. They tried to speak to Joseph using first English, then French. But he did not understand. His physical appearance came as something of a surprise. He was squarer and heavier than they had expected. The newspapers had led them to expect an Indian of the sort they had imagined from Fenimore Cooper and Longfellow—noble, regal, perhaps wearing feathers and war paint.

This man had none of that. He wore a black hat and had a striped blanket draped over his shoulders, and he seemed weary and intensely human. They returned to their homes curious and a bit perplexed. But they would have more chance to get to know him in the following months. This tent camp was only a short buggy ride down the hill from the town, and they would be able to visit and observe the famous chief and his people whenever they wanted.

Joseph was escorted to the hospital tent where a section had been quartered off from the medical area by a canvas partition. This was to be his residence until a private tent with a floor and a stove could be erected for him nearer the camp of the guards. The rest of the people were assigned to the white canvas teepees that stood in formation along this marshy bottomland. Many wanted to remove the canvas and use their own skin lodge coverings, but the soldiers explained that their packs were on a different train and would not arrive for several days.

The weather was cold and the land boggy. A large river ran by the side of the camp, but it was brown and silty and not good to drink.

For the next several days, the people wandered around looking for bushes and medicine plants they recognized, but found none. The river seemed to have fish, but they were not like the salmon from their own country. There were many birds but few animals. It would not be a good place to seek the food with which they were familiar.

Nonetheless, if this was to be their home, the people were prepared to make the best of it. They set about constructing sweat lodges on the edge of the river and sent the young boys off in search of rocks to heat to make steam. Some of the children cut saplings and made bows and arrows. The women cleaned the campsite and washed the clothes.

Joseph took to the task of running the camp and serving as the spokesperson to the visitors who began frequenting the camp. He met with the soldiers and curious citizens in the confines of his tent. His wife and infant daughter stayed close by, as did the other head men. He was gracious and polite and always forthcoming with his answers about how the war had taken place. At every opportunity he expressed his desire for his people to return to their own country, as had been promised by General Howard and Colonel Miles.

Reporters took in his every word. Though Leavenworth was a sprawling town of almost fifty thousand, this chief and his Indians were its most fascinating story. The newsmen swarmed about him, noting his "well formed head," his "well modulated voice" and his "frankness of features." They described his "richly ornamented buckskin suit," which they characterized as his "court costume," and they depicted his audiences as something out of fantasies of the Orient, with the chief "reclining gracefully on a huge couch made of furs of wild animals," surrounded by an entourage of his leading men.

Soon the townsfolk, fascinated by the stories and rumors, were streaming down from the their city on the hill to see this celebrated red man and his people. Within a few weeks, the number of visitors had increased so greatly that the major in charge of the camp was forced to restrict visits to Wednesdays and Sundays between the hours of one and four. Otherwise, he said, the crowds were so large and constant that it was impossible to keep the area clean.

On one Sunday, it was estimated that five thousand people made the trip down the bluff from the city to the teepee village by the river, almost all of them intent upon seeing the chief himself. They came in their Sunday finery—the men in their dark suits with silk handkerchiefs, the women in their long dresses with French lace collars. If they were not inclined to walk and had no transport of their own, they were able to purchase rides on Mr. Hall's omnibus, which departed at nine and returned at noon, making numerous stops along the way to pick up passengers wishing to see the Indians practicing their native way of life.

Eventually, the Nez Perce became such a curiosity that visitors were traveling from Kansas City and St. Louis for a chance to see the captives. The newspapers speculated that over half the people in the territory had made the visit to the river bottom and the native camp.

Joseph and the people did their best to accommodate the guests and even to take advantage of their presence. Young boys used their sapling bows and arrows to shoot nickels out of the forks of small branches in exchange for the right to keep the coins they hit. Women made gloves out of antelope skins purchased from hunters and sold them to the townswomen, irritating the local merchants, who were losing sales because their gloves could not compete in quality or style. Joseph himself tried to greet every visitor personally, shaking hands until he was too weary to do so.

But away from the visitors, life in the camp was an exercise in tedium and depression. The men, having no horses to ride and no animals to hunt, whiled away their hours playing cards or smoking. The women occupied themselves with such domestic tasks as sewing and cooking. Only the children found any pleasure in this strange, marshy landscape and the constant stream of white visitors that came and stared at them like animals in a pen.

It was possible to have sweats, but their deeper spiritual hungers remained unmet. This was not their land; their *wayakin* animals and spirits were nowhere to be found. Children could not be trained in the old ways, and the kouse and camas and berries and salmon did not live on these lands and waters. There were no buffalo, no elk, no beaver. The only way they could get hides was to buy them, and the only way they could get the wild meat they liked to eat was to trade their beef for it.

They waited each Saturday for the soldiers to hand out their rations. But the pickled pork, bread, and beans were not pleasing to them and did not feel like food from the hand of the Creator. The canvas tents leaked, and their few skin tent coverings, which had arrived with their goods, were frayed and torn. Each day their hearts grew heavier, and loneliness for their home country deepened. The wounded were not getting well, and the healthy were giving up hope.

On Sundays they would gather to perform their longhouse ceremonies as they had been taught by their ancestors. Each day they would heat the rocks and perform the cleansing sweats. They would sing the songs to their spirit guides, make the prayers they had been taught. But the Creator seemed to have turned his back on them. They were now in the world of the whites, and it appeared that only the white way possessed any power.

Joseph saw his people's failing spirits and did his best to keep their hopes alive. He continued to meet every white visitor who came to the village, even when he had no heart to do so. He knew that the task was upon his shoulders to tell each visitor the story of his people and to plead for their return to their homeland, as had been promised by General Howard and Colonel Miles. Perhaps if he found the right person, something would be done.

He signed autographs, scrawling a rude approximation of the words "Young Joseph," as he had been taught over thirty years before at the Spaldings' mission in the Lapwai. He spoke constantly of his good feelings toward the white people and his hope that his people and theirs should remain friends forever.

He shared the pipe with visitors, though many recoiled at the prospect of touching their lips to the same pipe that had touched the lips of a savage. At all times he kept Ad Chapman at his side to make sure that his words were understood and his feelings were passed along clearly.

The white townsfolk tried to show kindness, but it was always with gestures of hospitality, not actions that would help return his people to their homeland. They even presented him with a special invitation to a concert up in the town, where it was felt that the soaring tones of Mrs. Jackson's soprano arias would uplift him after a lifetime of hearing only the "wild echoes of his song on the plains." But at the last minute the army refused to allow him to attend, stating that it was against regulations for prisoners to leave the camp area, thus providing a stark reminder that the freedom he and his people experienced in the river lowlands was ultimately an illusion, and that, despite their humane treatment, they were in fact prisoners of war.

Nonetheless, Joseph continued his unceasing efforts to force the army to uphold the agreement made by Colonel Miles. One time he and seven other head men enlisted the aid of a sympathetic officer, Captain George Randall, to draft a petition to General Sherman asking for their return to their homeland, as they had been promised.

Sherman's response was swift and direct. "These Indians are prisoners," he wrote, "and their wishes should not be consulted." He had no interest in angering the western congressmen by reintroducing a troublemaker into their midst, and he had no interest in incurring either the cost or the problems that the relocation of these prisoners would entail. Randall was reprimanded, and the request was refused. Joseph and his people would remain where they were until Sherman determined how best to dispose of them.

Long into the winter Joseph fought for his people in every way he could. Every chance to speak he took. Every offer to meet with white citizens he accepted. He acted the gracious host, complimenting those he met and reminding them gently of the failure of the U.S. government to deliver what it had promised. While his people sat in the cold winter damp, falling deeper into depression and despair, he continued to reach out with professions of appreciation and friendship, hoping that someone with whom he spoke might have the power and influence to release them from this shapeless existence that was sapping their strength and killing their spirits.

As spring approached and the frozen earth of the bottomland began to thaw, the true squalor of their situation became clear. The Nez Perce sewage filtered into the groundwater, and spring runoff brought the waste from the town of Leavenworth flowing in their direction. The humidity spoiled their meat, and the river water, brown with silt, was almost undrinkable. They dug down into the marshy earth hoping that fresher water would filter up, but this too was foul and unhealthy.

With no resistance to white illnesses, the people began falling ill in alarming numbers. There was sickness in their stomachs, sickness in their lungs. White medicine could do nothing. Their own medicine men could do nothing. Those who had been clinging to life lost their will and died. Others who had arrived healthy fell ill and passed on to the spirit world.

The people constructed a small graveyard in the manner of their ancestors, surrounding it with fresh saplings. But the ground was marshy, and the bodies could not be well buried. Even Joseph's infant daughter, who had been born on the Camas Prairie, was stricken. He closed his teepee and brought those with strong medicine in to perform the healing ceremonies, but the sickness was slow to leave. All the while, white visitors gathered around the tent, remarking on the strange-sounding music and hoping that the chief would soon come out so they could get his autograph or maybe shake his hand.

By summer, conditions were almost unbearable. The arrival of the heat brought mosquitoes and new illnesses. The air was so heavy that it seemed impossible that birds could even fly. Terrifying thunderstorms with deafening lightning strikes cracked the sky in two. The canvas tents blew down or leaked profusely through the seams, soaking the people's clothes and spoiling their food. Soon almost half of the four hundred remaining people were too sick to move and spent their days lying in a delirium that the military physicians attributed to diseases ranging from whooping cough to malaria to influenza to tuberculosis.

Joseph continued to speak out, but his efforts had no effect. The Nez Perce were like a forgotten race. Aside from the small complement of soldiers assigned to guard them, and the streams of visitors that came down each Sunday and Wednesday to buy crafts and see the Indians in their "native habitat," there seemed to be no one who even cared if they existed. No government person came to assist them in their quest to get home; no one even explained what, if anything, was going to happen to them.

Then, in mid-July, word came that the people were to be moved again. They were to depart on a special train and travel 150 miles south to Indian Territory. There they would be settled next to the Modoc, who had been sent there five years before. It was intended that the Modoc, who were from the same part of the country as the Nez Perce and showed promise in adopting white habits and customs, would have a positive influence on the Nez Perce and assist them in adapting to a civilized way of life.

The summer of 1878 had already become one of the hottest on record, with daily temperatures reaching well into the nineties and humidity so oppressive that it was almost impossible to get a full breath of air. People all across the Midwest were being felled by heatstroke and dehydration. Deaths in cities numbered in the hundreds.

On July 19, with the mercury hovering near one hundred degrees, the Nez Perce were herded across the broad open field from their campsite and up to the Fort Leavenworth railroad station at the base of the bluff a mile away. They had to drag their tent poles and goods, and the sick and the elderly were forced to make the journey without assistance through the unforgiving heat and sun.

The train cars that had been requisitioned for them had not yet arrived, so the people were forced to spend the night huddled under mosquito-ridden bushes and curled up on the empty siding near the station. Many of them had been weakened by heatstroke, and the humid, breathless night air offered little relief.

When morning came and the train had still not appeared, their situation became desperate. The sun was rising into an empty sky, and they had no cover under which to protect themselves. They sat by the rail siding, staring down the tracks into the shimmering heat for signs of an approaching engine. But no plume of smoke rose in the distance; no rhythmic chuff of an approaching engine cut the still, fetid air.

By noon the sun was an angry bead burning down on them with merciless indifference. The elderly lay in the bushes, trying to find any shade they could. The weak fell sick from the heat, and the children, already weakened by the poor water and diseases of the river bottom, began to fade into a lethargic torpor.

The few healthy among them tried to do what they could, but there was no way to offer relief. Joseph's wife fell ill, as did Chapman. One infant, unable to endure any longer, died in its mother's arms while she tried desperately to fan it and wet its brow to keep its body temperature down.

As the day darkened into evening, the train had still not arrived. By the following dawn, when it finally steamed into the station, the people were so weak that they could barely make it into the coaches. The doctor who had been assigned to travel with them went from car to car, ministering with such medicines as he had. But the military, in releasing the people to the Department of the Interior, had provided only minimal medical supplies, and the people were already too overcome by the heat to recover easily. Most slumped in torpor and delirium as the train slowly moved out from the Leavenworth station on its fifteen-hour journey south to Baxter Springs on the border of Indian Territory.

The train was scheduled to make few stops—and those only long enough to take on water. But news of the Indian transport train had been flashed along the telegraph wires, and residents of the towns along the rail line began gathering at their local stations in hopes of catching a glimpse of the famous chief Joseph and his legendary band of Nez Perce as their train passed through.

In Fort Scott, seventy-five miles south of Leavenworth, the townsfolk began lining up at one o'clock in the afternoon. The heat was relentless, and the station itself was soon filled with citizens in their Sunday finery, trying to keep cool while awaiting the Indians' arrival. An unscheduled "extra" that steamed past gave them a momentary surge of excitement, but when it was determined that this was not the train carrying Joseph, they settled in beneath the station overhang and in the few shady spots nearby, determined to stay as long as necessary to see the chief and his exotic band of savages.

By three, the crowd had swelled to several hundred. Men stood on the tracks peering into the hazy heat, hoping to be the first to announce the arrival of the transport. Eventually, the sound of a whistle rose up in the distance, and soon after, the train steamed into the station. The townsfolk rushed forward and surrounded the cars as the train ground to a stop. They were not going to miss their chance to see Joseph.

Inside, heatstroke had rendered most of the Nez Perce helpless. Two more children had died, and their mothers held their lifeless bodies close as the townspeople pushed up to the windows and peered in demanding a glimpse of the famous chief. Others of the Nez Perce were lying on the seats and floor, fevered and sick and incoherent. Even with the windows open, soot and heat from the engine had rendered the cars almost uninhabitable, and now, at this station, there were suddenly well-dressed white people sticking their heads in, crying out, "Where's Joseph?"

Some of the Indians would point one way, some the other—anything to keep these strange, ghoulish gawkers away. But the crowds would not relent. They climbed onto the platforms at the ends of the cars and pushed their heads in through the open windows. Once Joseph was discovered, they all surged toward his car, clambering onto the platform and trying to push their way inside. He slammed the door, but they pushed around to the windows and pounded on the doors. His wife was near delirium, and the families of the dead children were grieving and in shock. But the crowds would not back off. They had come to see the famous chief, and they would not leave until they had done so.

Soon, despite the sweltering heat in the car, Joseph ordered the windows closed and the blinds pulled down. The townsfolk grumbled and backed off, disappointed that the chief was so ungracious. This was not the noble red man they had been led to expect.

A few healthy Nez Perce came out and filled buckets with water for the rest of the passengers and were immediately surrounded by the townsfolk. Some of the young boys sold bows and arrows to the onlookers, and some of the women sold beads.

The townsfolk happily purchased their treasures and held them aloft. Though Joseph had not been the courteous and gracious host they had anticipated, the Sunday excursion to see the Indians had been a success. All could say they had seen the notorious captives, and the town now had enough authentic Indian bows and arrows to supply its numerous, growing archery clubs. They hurried back to their houses clutching their souvenirs, filled with stories of their sightings of the famous chief and proud to live in a city that offered them such opportunities for excitement.

The train continued south, passing through a strong windstorm. By 7:00 p.m. it had arrived at Baxter Springs, the southernmost town in Kansas and the end of the rail line.

The Modoc, with whom the Nez Perce were to be settled, had been assigned the task of meeting the train and transporting the newcomers across the border into Indian Territory. They were waiting patiently with their wagons when the train pulled in. But the lateness of the hour and the condition of the people made the journey impossible. They stood by quietly while the Nez Perce climbed down from the train, buried their three dead children in shallow graves, and curled up on the ground to rest. The Modoc then went among them with potatoes, corn, tomatoes, and other foodstuffs. It was the traditional Indian practice to share food with hungry travelers, but the Modoc were trying to learn the ways of the whites. So instead of giving food to the suffering Nez Perce, they sold it to them.

Since their departure from Fort Leavenworth, the Nez Perce had been in the charge of Mr. Hiram Jones, a Quaker agent who had traveled north from Indian Territory several days earlier in order to accompany the exiles on their journey. His presence among them was a result of President Grant's strange, well-intentioned, but utterly disastrous Peace Policy, the same policy that had placed Monteith and Presbyterians in charge of the Lapwai back in Idaho.

At the close of the Civil War, when the nation had resumed its western expansion and faced the great military problem of pacifying the various Indian tribes who stood in the way of settlers streaming west, many argued that the Indians could not simply be defeated, they had to be removed, eradicated, or otherwise made to disappear from the lands they claimed as their own. Several courses of action had been considered. The more draconian of the military leaders and policy makers believed that extermination was the only realistic answer, since the nation, they said, could not afford to house and maintain a perpetual prisoner class. Others called for permanent exile—driving the hostiles into Canada or Mexico where they would be the problems of some other government—or warehousing them all on some undesirable tract of land.

But Grant, under the influence of more humane thinkers, had opted for a third course. Like most Americans, he believed that the march of civilization was an inevitable progression from wandering savagery to settled, Christianized civility and enlightenment. Perhaps there were indeed good people among the lower orders of humans, but they were doomed to extinction by the natural course of history and human affairs. Assisting these unfortunates in their ascent from savagery to civilization was the only policy that a compassionate and enlightened nation should pursue.

So he had instituted his Peace Policy, whereby the military would round up the Indians roaming the West and deliver them to specified sites, called reservations. There the tribes would be placed under the control and guidance of various religious denominations, which would take responsibility for training and educating them in the ways of civilized life.

Ideally, these reservations would be in the home territory of the captured Indians because it was believed that Indians, like animals, had specific habitats to which they were accustomed and in which they were most likely to thrive. But in the event that a tribe could not be kept in its own country, either because there was not sufficient room available after white settlers had arrived or because feelings between settlers and local Indians were too volatile and acrimonious to allow peaceful coexistence, an area called Indian Territory had been set aside in the barren flatlands between Kansas, Arkansas, and Texas. This great expanse was believed to be sufficient to quarter all Indians that might require resettlement, so long as they gave up their wandering ways and turned to the more efficient and productive lives of agriculture and settled living. It was divided up into administrative areas called agencies, and these, like the individual reservations, were assigned to various religious denominations.

The Quapaw Agency, where the Nez Perce were being sent, lay on the very northern edge of Indian Territory and had been placed under the jurisdiction of the Quakers. The agent currently in charge was Hiram Jones.

Jones was a cruel and venal man who flew in the face of every image the public had of Quakers as peaceful, caring people. He was unabashedly corrupt and unapologetically self-serving. Most of the money he received for the Indians he siphoned off into salaries for his family, and he regularly short-weighted rations and withheld food and medicine from the tribes under his care. A nearby neighbor to the Quapaw Agency had referred to him as a "missionary with a cloven foot."

But he had managed to "civilize" the equally troublesome Modoc who had been exiled to the Quapaw from their original country just south of the Nez Perce homeland in the West, so, from the administrative distance of Washington, D.C., he seemed like a successful agent and an ideal candidate to achieve the same positive results with the renegade Nez Perce. Little notice was paid to the fact that a third of the Modoc had died since they had been entrusted to Jones's enlightened care.

General Sherman, as head of the Department of the Army, was completely indifferent about where the Nez Perce would be taken or to whom they would be assigned. All that mattered to him was that, once they had boarded that train in Fort Leavenworth, they were the responsibility of the Department of the Interior and off his budget. He had determined long ago that sending them back to the Lapwai reservation in their own country was only asking for trouble, despite any promises that had been made by Miles or Howard or anyone else.

Returning them to the Lapwai would likely cause friction with the Indians already living there or, worse yet, foment rebellion among the pacified Nez Perce. It would surely incite violence among the local white settlers, who held all the exiles responsible for the atrocities that had been committed prior to the flight. Quelling any rebellion and keeping the peace would become the problem and expense of his army, and he had no interest in devoting further time or resources to these obstinate, renegade Nez Perce. Besides, sending Joseph and his followers to Indian country would teach them, and all other Indians, a lesson. He had happily sent them off with agent Jones to whatever fate awaited them.

The land of the Quapaw Agency, where the Nez Perce were being sent, was unique in Indian Territory. Most of the vast tract that had been set aside for Indian resettlement was rough, flat country, raked by bitter winds and vicious storms. But the Quapaw lay on a small stretch of beautiful, rolling, oak-studded hills, resplendent with hickory and berry bushes and laced with clear, spring-fed streams. Hay grew abundantly, making it good country for horse and cattle raising.

The quality of the land was the reason Baxter Springs, where the Nez Perce disembarked, had become the first real cow town in Kansas. Its white residents cast covetous eyes on the verdant hardwood and meadow country of the Quapaw, hoping that the government would one day open it to settlement or that they at least could sneak in and cut its fine hardwoods or even build a small cabin and live on it as if it were their own. But it was also land of intense humidity, oppressive heat, violent summer storms, dangerous tornadoes, and unpredictable winter freezes. For all its physical beauty, it was a place of unforgiving climatic brutality. If you lacked adequate preparation and shelter, it was land that could kill.

Almost a dozen tribes had been moved there, mostly from the Midwest and East—tribes like the Peoria, the Ottawa, the Seneca, and the Wayandotte—all small remnants, none numbering more than 250, altogether totaling only 1381. The only western tribe among this number was the Modoc, who had been brought to the Quapaw four years earlier, handcuffed and chained in cattle cars. After losing over a third of their people to sickness and disease, they had decided that adapting to white ways was better than extinction.

Like the Nez Perce, they too still dreamed of their homeland. But they had done what was necessary to survive, and this meant adopting the white manner of dress, building wooden houses, fencing gardens, working as teamsters and hotel workers in nearby Baxter Springs, and living by the economic rules of American society. They were not rich, but at least they were alive, and even though their chief called the agency "good country to get rid of Indians in," the Modoc had managed to stabilize their small tribe and had actually begun to prosper.

When Jones had gone north to accompany the Nez Perce on their journey, he had instructed the Modoc to harness their wagons and be waiting at the Baxter Springs railhead to transport the arrivals to their new home fifteen miles south in the Quapaw Agency. They were to serve not only as the teamsters and haulers but also as the temporary host people and model of successful acculturation for this new western tribe, which thus far had resisted adapting to civilized ways.

So while the desperately ill Nez Perce had been traveling south in the heat and humidity toward the rail terminus at Baxter Springs, the Modoc had been bumping their wagons north across the unfenced grasslands of Indian Territory to meet these arrivals with whom they were expected to share the small plot of land they so diligently, and at so great a human cost, had turned into a tolerable living situation for their few remaining people.

In the morning following their arrival at Baxter Springs, the Nez Perce awoke to find that the pigs roaming near the tracks had unearthed the bodies of their dead children and begun to eat them. In horror, they reburied the little bodies and did what they could to protect their graves.

But Jones had little patience for such niceties. He needed to get his new wards down to the agency as quickly as possible. He set the Modoc to the task of helping the sick Nez Perce into the wagons and driving them south. The people's goods and tents and tent poles would have to remain behind to be picked up later.

The move took all day because almost all the Nez Perce were too sick or too weak to walk. It was also slow going because they had to ford the wide Spring River, which ran between the railhead and the campsite. By the time all the Nez Perce had been transported, the wagons had made over forty trips between the railhead and the agency.

The Modoc Reserve where the people were to be quartered was only two and a half miles square. The place that was to serve as their campsite, a broad open field known as the Modoc Prairie, lay at its southern edge. The Modoc had built houses for themselves in the white man's style on the surrounding hills, and the valley itself, which had a small, meandering yard-wide creek passing through it, was open land used as a common grazing pasture for their cows and pigs.

The hundred surviving Modoc were not happy about having to share their small reserve with more than four hundred newcomers. So the Nez Perce were unloaded in the field and left there to fend for themselves. They had no tents, no cooking supplies, no fresh clothes, and almost no food. Most were too still too sick to move, so they once again huddled up as best they could and settled in for another long and difficult night.

That evening a violent storm arose, drenching the entire camp and turning it into a sea of mud and manure. Without shelter, the people were helpless to protect themselves. Three more of them had died on the wagon journey from Baxter, and others were fading quickly. They lay shivering on the soaking ground, hoping they would have the strength to survive until morning.

The following day when the sky had cleared, the people tried to return to the railhead for their goods. But the downpour had turned Spring River into a wild, surging torrent too strong to be forded. When, after several days, the river had receded enough for them to return for their possessions, they found that all their tent poles and packs had been stolen. What remained had been ruined by the rains. The people who had left Idaho with several thousand head of horses, gold dust, American dollars, buffalo skin lodges, guns, camp goods, and the finest clothes and blankets of any tribe in the West, were now without clothing, shelter, and anything more than the few personal items they had carried with them on the wagon journey from Baxter Springs.

As their leader, Joseph was heartsick. This was the result of the promise Miles had made to him at the Bear's Paw, the promise on which he had convinced his people to lay down their weapons and trust in the white man's good faith.

The time at Fort Leavenworth had been bad, especially toward the end. They had been curiosities, gazed at like animals in a pen, and had been left with nothing to do and no shape to their lives. But at least they had been given food and white medicines.

Here, sickness was everywhere, and nobody knew or cared. Each day more of their children died; each evening more of their dead were buried in unfamiliar lands. The pigs of the Modoc roamed everywhere, trying to unearth the bodies, and the water in their small stream was made filthy by the cattle and hogs that wallowed in it. The mosquitoes were frightful, and the few canvas shelters that they were given rotted and leaked.

All through the camp the moans of the dying could be heard; all night the drumming and singing of the people filled the air as they tried vainly to heal the sick before giving them up to the spirit world. There was no white leader to speak to, no white man to ask for medicine other than the corrupt Agent Jones. And they had no faith that any medicine he might offer would not be in fact a poison that increased their illness. This is what the Modoc claimed that Jones had done to them, and the Nez Perce had no reason to doubt that they would not suffer an identical fate.

Day by day their position deteriorated. They no longer cared about good housing; they no longer cared about proper rations. Memories of their long lodges and the clear waters of the Snake and the Salmon and the Clearwater seemed like distant, impossible dreams. They were a people without hope, living in the daily shadow of death.

On August 14, three weeks after their arrival, the Nez Perce looked up from their squalor and lethargy and saw several well-dressed white men arriving

with Agent Jones. The white men were introduced to Joseph as Mr. Stickney and Mr. Fisk. They explained that they had come from the government
and were there to assist him in choosing land of his own so he and his
people would no longer have to live among the Modoc. With good land,
they said, his people could begin their journey upward toward civilization.
They proposed that he join them the next day to search for a place on the
agency that was more to his people's liking.

Joseph resisted. The only journey he and his people wished to take was
back to their homeland far across the western mountains. This Quapaw
place, he said, might be fine land for a white man, but it was land that
killed the Nez Perce. The air, the strangeness, the sicknesses were all signs
to him that this was not earth that was meant for his people. He wished to
remain where he was until he was allowed to go back to his homeland as
he had been promised. He instructed Chapman to read the visitors an extract from the report in which Miles had promised him and his people the
right to return to their home country after the snows had melted. Then he
refused to accompany them on their journey.

Stickney and Fisk were at a loss. They could see the conditions in the
Nez Perce camp, and they were appalled. The people were living in flimsy
tents among the Modoc pigs and cattle, drinking water that had been polluted by human and animal waste. Many of them were too sick to stand,
and they were dying at an alarming rate, sometimes as many as four a day.
The camp area was filthy, and the Modoc were antagonistic and accusa-
tory. At all times, wails could be heard coming from the tents of the dying,
only to fall silent, then rise again from another tent somewhere else in the
camp. By every indication, they were a people simply waiting to die. Nonetheless, Joseph was refusing to consider a move.

In an attempt to change the chief's mind, Stickney arranged for a
telegram to be sent from A. E. Hayt, Commissioner of Indian Affairs, explaining that Joseph and his people were being permanently resettled in
the Quapaw and that they would have to find a way to make the best of it.

This telegram was the first official notice Joseph had received indicating that he and his people were not to be returned to their home, and it affected him deeply. When the next day came, and Fisk and Stickney came to
begin the search for a new campsite, the chief sent word through Chapman
that he was too sick to travel and would remain in his tent. The telegraph
message from the highest law authority telling him that he must live in

this place forever had wounded his heart. He would not take part in any search for a new home camp.

Unable to persuade the chief to go, Chapman, Stickney, and the others of the commission set off on their own to select a new home site for the Nez Perce. After surveying various locations, they selected a beautiful piece of land, seven thousand acres in extent, several miles from the Modoc encampment. It was rolling, verdant hill country, dotted with berry bushes and graced with groves of great canopied nut trees. A wide, clear, spring-fed stream meandered through its center. There was open prairie for grazing cattle and sufficient timber for houses and firewood. It was among the choicest land in the entire Quapaw, better than almost any other land in all of Indian Territory. Any white man within a hundred miles would have been ecstatic to have owned it for himself and his family.

But Joseph wanted nothing to do with it. Even after the land was purchased and his people were moved there, he insisted that the soil was poor, the timber scarce, and water insufficient. He would grant no good to any piece of land if it meant giving up the dreams of returning to his home and the land the Creator had given them.

Meanwhile, Chapman was gaining firsthand insight into Jones and the way he ran his agency. An unapologetic opportunist himself, Chapman was well acquainted with using the U.S. government to personal advantage. But Jones's behavior went beyond anything even he could conceive. Jones withheld Nez Perce rations, refused them medicine, charged the government for corn that was never provided, and allowed his personal friends to come onto the reserve and charge the Indians exorbitant prices for foodstuffs and supplies while keeping honest traders out.

He short-weighted the rations given the Nez Perce and provided them with mealy, tainted flour. Chapman saw the beef that Jones was providing, and as a man who had raised cattle back in the West, he could easily estimate the hoof weight of an animal. The amount the agent actually delivered was less than half of what he claimed. Some of it was so unhealthy that the white man in charge of the cattle said it was unfit for human consumption. And all this while Jones was accepting kickbacks from traders and building himself a beautiful two-story house with oak floors and walnut newel posts.

Two years earlier, when he had lived on his ranch in Nez Perce country, none of this would have bothered Chapman. But since the capture he had traveled with the exiles, lived with them, spoken for them, even fallen ill with them. In some strange way, he had developed a sympathy for them that he had never felt while living near them in the steep canyon country of the Snake and the Salmon. The man who had beaten Nez Perce youth back in Idaho and fired the first shot in the war was now, slowly, becoming their champion.

He refused to rent a room in Jones's home and stayed instead in a tent in the Nez Perce camp. In addition, he began a vociferous writing campaign against Jones and on behalf of the Nez Perce. On August 29, barely a month after the Nez Perce had arrived, he sent off letters to distant newspapers exclaiming, "I have never heard of so much suffering among the same number of people in all my life . . . and nothing to eat but beans and bread. Mothers dying, leaving children six and eight months old to be taken care of, and no milk or anything else to feed them on. . . ." With Joseph's blessing, he took advantage of the nearby telegraph offices and newspapers to mount a relentless attack on the corruption of the Quaker "man of God" who was systematically exterminating the very people he was supposed to be protecting.

Jones's practices had been suspect ever since his appointment as agent in 1872. The government had even sent an investigator to assess his superintendency on several occasions, but all the claims against him had been hearsay, and his ability to keep the tribes pacified had constituted sufficient success for him to avoid any real censure.

But with Chapman's arrival, hearsay turned to direct witness. Chapman could not be dismissed as a disgruntled trader or some local harboring personal animosities. He was, in fact, a government-salaried interpreter. So when he began barraging the local papers and Washington officials with chapter and verse of Jones's graft and cruelty, it not only caused governmental officials to take notice, it also gave heart to Jones's local critics, who had been complaining for years about his practices. They joined in the outcry, haranguing the Secretary of the Interior through their own letters, pointing out that the Nez Perce were dying from "cruel unmitigated neglect—having been unprovided with medicines for days, weeks—forced to live on damaged insufficient rations—left to die like sheep with the rot."

For the next several months, Chapman and the angry locals kept up this deluge. They pointed out that Jones charged a dollar more per pound of flour than was being paid only three miles away; that he was selling bacon for sixteen to eighteen cents a pound that could be bought for twelve cents a pound at the local store; that he gave the Nez Perce meat so tainted that it was not fit to eat; that he was selling the Nez Perce worn-out ten-year-old wagons purchased from his friends for the same price as brand-new wagons in town. They cited the fact that almost all the money allocated for maintenance of the Indians was going to salaries of the agency personnel and that eleven of twelve agency employees were related to Jones in some way.

All of this, of course, outraged Jones. He had always operated without any meaningful scrutiny. Baxter Springs, fifteen miles away, was little more than a rough cow town occupied with its own concerns. And it had no jurisdiction over him anyway, since Indian Territory was under federal control and the nearest federal oversight sat 150 miles north in Fort Leavenworth. His Quaker superiors were an equal distance away in Lawrence, Kansas, and were headed by his sympathetic brother-in-law. And to administrative entities measuring success by the lack of problems with which they had to deal, his agency was operating quite efficiently. He had kept his Indians from creating disturbances and had managed to convince many of them to take on the trappings of white civilization. That he had done so by depriving them of food, medicine, and their health did not show up on official reports. To a distant eye, he was a successful agent employing an effective "straightening-out process" to bring the Indians upward from savagery to civilization.

So when Chapman brought the harsh glare of official scrutiny upon him, Jones fought back with a vengeance. He accused Chapman of moral turpitude and impregnating a Modoc woman. He claimed that the townsfolk who spoke against him were simply unhappy at having lost bids for goods and services. He claimed that Chapman was seeking to supplant Jones and feather his own nest—a claim that may not have been entirely without merit, since Chapman, in fact, had taken to calling himself "acting agent, hospital steward, commissary sergeant, interpreter, and superintendent of farming" and even was seeking an appointment as an agent of a life insurance company.

Eventually this battle of scoundrels could no longer be ignored. The government was forced to turn its attention to the goings-on in this small, previously peaceful corner of Indian Territory. Arden Smith, the investigator for the Indian Bureau, reopened his dormant inquiry into Jones's practices, and a congressional joint commission was sent to take testimony as part of its ongoing assessment of whether civilian oversight of Indian affairs was really superior to the more efficient, more accountable oversight that had been provided previously by the Department of the Army.

All of this Joseph observed with interest. In the year since his people had been tricked into laying down their weapons, he had learned more and more about the workings of white society. On the train from Bismarck he had seen that the telegraph could outrun the horse, and he had seen how messages sent on this talking wire reached people in all the white cities all across the country. A few days before leaving Fort Leavenworth, he and Yellow Bull had been invited to the newspaper office in town and shown how white writing could be put on papers and copied thousands of times so it could be carried to every white house and family. He had even been shown a new machine that a person could talk into and be heard a far distance away, and he and Yellow Bull had sung into a horn and then had their own voices played back to them on a wax cylinder. It was clear to him that whites had the power to capture words and send them where they wanted faster and farther than any Indian had ever imagined.

He had also seen how white citizens flocked to him and wanted him to speak. It had been this way since Bismarck and had only increased on the train journey and in the camp at Leavenworth. They wanted to hear him, and they wrote down what he said and sent it out to other white people in the papers and on the talking wire.

All this knowledge led him to form an idea in his mind. If he could not fight for his people with guns, perhaps he could fight for them with words. Chapman, his onetime enemy, would serve as his mouthpiece.

When the congressional joint committee came south to hold its hearings, Joseph and Chapman traveled to nearby Seneca, Missouri, so he could provide testimony. Asked whether he thought Indians were better served by being under the control of the military or the Department of the Interior, he replied, through Chapman, that it did not matter which branch of government was over them because land should be free like the sun—equal to all—and that all men should be free to come and go when and where they pleased. He did acknowledge that he might prefer to live farther west and might even be willing to farm and raise crops if a suitable location could be found. But he much preferred to return north to healthier country and, ideally, to his own homeland, as had been promised.

The congressional committee was impressed by the chief. After hearing his testimony along with the testimony of the Modoc and the complaints of the various local merchants and farmers, they returned to Washington convinced, just as Stickney and Fisk had been, that Jones was indeed corrupt and that the situation in the Quapaw was seriously in need of redress.

The commission had corroborated many of the claims and complaints made by Chapman and the locals, but Joseph knew that the government would quickly forget its concern if the matter were not kept in the public eye. So he encouraged Chapman to continue his barrage of letter writing and telegraph dispatches.

Eventually, the complaints and reports and articles convinced Commissioner Hayt that he himself needed to get involved. Accusations and counteraccusations were continuing unabated, there was concern about white whiskey traders and timber thieves sneaking onto Indian lands, and pressure was mounting from white claims leagues insisting that the land be opened to white settlement. The letters from the local residents had even hinted at possible Indian uprisings if something wasn't done to improve the Indians' plight.

So Hayt traveled from Washington to assess conditions for himself. He immediately recognized the volatility of the situation and determined that perhaps there was some wisdom in resettling the unhappy Nez Perce on a different piece of land farther from the controversy and farther from the claims and counterclaims of corruption and negative influence.

After meeting with the Nez Perce, he arranged for Joseph, Yellow Bull, Husis Kute, and Chapman to accompany him on a journey deep into the far western reaches of Indian Territory to seek out a piece of land that the Nez Perce people might be more willing to accept as a permanent home.

Joseph was willing to go, but only with hesitation. It was a chance to talk man-to-man with the head of Indian Affairs as he had talked man-to-man with Miles on their long ride. And perhaps there was something to be said for finding a more isolated place in which to settle while they fought for their right to return to their own country. But he made it clear that he had no intention of accepting any place in Indian Territory as a final destination for his people.

On a sunny mid-October morning they set out on their long journey across the brushy inhospitable prairies of what eventually would become Oklahoma. After several days of riding, they came upon on a flat, windy strip of land at the bend of a silty, slow-moving river. Joseph surveyed the landscape and announced that he found it to his liking. Though the decision made no apparent sense in light of the rolling, verdant country he inhabited at Quapaw, Hayt was more than willing to accede to the chief's wishes if this would keep him satisfied. Perhaps more open space, 180 miles from the corrupt Jones, and under the supervision of a different agent, was what Joseph needed to finally allow him to make peace with his situation.

They returned to the Quapaw, with Hayt convinced that he had finally found a solution to the seemingly intractable problem of the Nez Perce. He immediately began making arrangements for Joseph and his people to move to this new country out west as soon as it would be practical, most likely the following spring.

But the public furor raised by Chapman and the other letter writers had spread beyond the halls of government. While Joseph and Hayt were traveling over the western prairies in search of new home for the Nez Perce, a special correspondent from the *New York Times* had made his way to Quapaw to report on their condition. He gave a description of the Nez Perce camp and its operations, noting the frequent medicine ceremonies being conducted over the dying and observing with a kind of compassionate contempt how the Indians had been reduced to living a life of "sulky scorn" in a land of "deadly fever and malaria." He ended with the haunting question as to whether there was a place for them in American civilization, even if their children were turned into well-scrubbed, proper students of mathematics, spelling, geography, and the Bible.

It was a question that none could easily answer.

23

"I Have Heard Talk and Talk but Nothing Is Done"

THE ONSET OF THE WINTER of 1878 brought increasing horror and suffering to Joseph and his people. They had made the short move to the better land chosen for them by Stickney and Fisk, and they knew that they would be making the move farther west in the spring. But the change in location did not create any fundamental change in their situation. As long as they were in the Quapaw, they remained under the control of Jones, who had returned to his corrupt ways as soon as the investigators had left. Freed again from any meaningful scrutiny, he immediately resumed withholding medicines, short-weighting rations, and providing tainted and substandard food.

The people were also faced with surviving a cruel and cutting winter with no decent shelter and no way of supporting stock. Their move had come too late in the season to allow them to put up any hay, so they could not raise cattle for food or horses for trade and were reduced to relying on Jones for any assistance they needed. In their weakened physical and spiritual states, they could not easily survive a winter under Jones's hand.

Joseph knew that he had to act. Chapman's letter writing and telegrams were having some effect, but not enough to save his people. It was time to do whatever necessary to make his voice heard. He decided he needed to travel to Washington, D.C., where he could plead his case directly to the government officials.

He had always found a willing audience when he spoke to those who had visited his camp in Leavenworth, and he had gradually reduced the situation of his people to a story that he could tell succinctly and fairly whenever anyone took time to listen. With his skill at speaking and the apparent white interest in his people's plight he believed that if he could speak for himself and not have his words twisted by others, he could find men of influence who would give him and his people fair hearing. He also wanted to talk to the president himself to make sure that a move to the land Hayt had found would not mean that he and his people could never return to their homeland.

But his requests for a trip to the capital were turned down. So Joseph determined to do the next best thing. With the prospect of a winter of illness and starvation looming before his people, he arranged to have Chapman visit Washington in his stead. The people took up a collection of their few remaining dollars and traces of silver and gold and bought a ticket to send their enemy-turned-champion to the nation's capital to be their voice. Then they waited with faint hope for word that the government would honor the promises that Miles had made and that something would be done to deliver them from the cruel, killing ways of the Christian agent Hiram Jones.

But Jones himself was not standing still. In addition to mounting a vigorous justification of his own actions through a barrage of his own letters and explanations, he had quietly made arrangements with the Presbyterian agent, John Monteith, at the Lapwai reserve in Idaho, to have several nontreaty Nez Perce sent down to Oklahoma in an effort to supplant Chapman's influence and undermine Joseph's standing among the exiles. It was his hope that the Nez Perce were ripe for a conversion, if not to Christianity, then at least to a different regime under a more pliable leadership.

In fact, his scheme was not without merit. With their faith in the goodness of the earth as their mother and their strong belief in the power of the earth to heal and protect them, the nontreaty Nez Perce had experienced exile as a deep wound to their hearts and spirits. As Joseph himself had said, the Creator seemed to have turned his back on them. The earth was providing them with sickness, not health; their medicine men were powerless to ward off the deaths and diseases that were claiming their young and their elderly. Their seven-drum ceremonies were not gaining the favor of the Creator, and their *wayakin* spirits seemed to have lost their power to assist them in times of need. In the hearts of some, the hard question had started to rise up as to whether, indeed, the white people's way might not, in fact, be the chosen way of the Creator.

And if religious doubts were not sufficient to pry the wavering Nez Perce from Joseph's grip, Jones willingly assisted their conversion by withholding rations from those who stayed faithful to the obstinate chief and his old ways, and he increased the rations of those who converted to Christianity and embraced the new way of life that was being practiced so successfully by the Modoc and other tribes under his control.

The Christian Nez Perce back in Idaho were more than happy to assist Jones in his mission. In their eyes, their exiled relatives were lost sheep. Many of the people who had fled to Canada with White Bird had found life with Sitting Bull and the Sioux harsh and difficult and had begun to trickle back to the Lapwai reservation. From these returning families the treaty Nez Perce had learned of the suffering that their brothers and sisters had experienced during the flight. And though there was still great anger toward Joseph and the others who had caused this misery by their actions, they wanted to assist in any way they could to bring the exiled people back to their homeland. When the opportunity came to send three of their own number to Oklahoma to aid in this effort, they were only too happy to oblige.

James Reuben, the Kamiah leader who had been one of Howard's scouts and was proud of the fact, was chosen to go as interpreter. He was reputed to have been among those shot at by the escaping warriors near the Weippe Prairie, though it was unclear whether he had been shot there or whether he had been shot in the back while trying to run away from the Clearwater battle. Nonetheless, he had proven his loyalty to the government, and his Christian zeal had gained him this opportunity to travel to Indian Territory to try to arrange for the freedom and return of the exiles.

Archie Lawyer was to travel with him as schoolteacher and minister, and Mark Williams was sent along as chief farmer. That they were being used by the U.S. government and Indian agents was less important to them than that they were being used by the Lord to bring their brothers and sisters back to the flock. The agency life in Idaho was good; they were self-sufficient and prospering in the white manner, and the gifts they had received from the Lord had shown them that the spiritual path they had chosen was right for the Nez Perce people.

In early November 1878 they set out by train to the Indian Territory to begin their work for the Lord. They were accompanied by a number of White Bird's returning stragglers, who were being sent into exile so they would not create problems with either the treaty Nez Perce or the still-angry white settlers in the area.

The group arrived in Baxter Springs on December 6, while Chapman was still in Washington. Jones immediately installed James Reuben as official interpreter and set Williams and Lawyer to work trying to convert the Nez Perce who were already wavering in their faith in the old ways.

The three men took their status as civilized, Christian men very seriously. They arrived dressed in black suits and white shirts, their hair cropped short. They took up lodging in Jones's house rather than staying among their nontreaty brothers and sisters in their camp two miles away. They insisted on proper wages, proper respect, and proper treatment in all things, just as would have been accorded white visitors in their capacities.

Joseph, however, accorded them little respect. He was occupied with the suffering of his people—a young boy he had taken as his son was on the verge of dying—and his families were now almost indifferent in their despair. The arrival of these nontreaty Christian Nez Perce who had fought against him and his people was an affront and insult. He had come to rely upon, if not entirely trust, Chapman and was not about to give over the power of his voice to a man like James Reuben, who had taken up arms against his own people. He continued his resistance, refusing to be party to the efforts of Reuben, Lawyer, and Williams to offer assistance to the tribe.

But others among the tribe were not so adamant. Husis Kute, who had always been a spiritual man, was beginning to waver in his faith in the old ways and rankled under the constant designation of Joseph and Yellow Bull as the head chiefs. He had been allowed to accompany Hayt to look for land to the west, but it was clear that he was not accorded the respect given to Joseph. He did not see why he should always be placed third on government rolls and listed behind Yellow Bull, a subchief, when he, in fact, was a full chief of the Palouse people.

Others too were beset by doubts and desperate to find a spiritual power that would deliver them from this exile. Still others simply wanted full rations so they could maintain their strength and ward off the illness that was claiming the health and lives of so many in the camp.

When Joseph refused to sign for rations in Chapman's absence, not trusting Reuben and not wishing to place his name on a white document that he did not understand, Husis Kute stepped up and signed in the people's behalf, further dividing hearts and allegiances. Soon Reuben,

Williams, and Lawyer began making allies and converts among the suffering people, becoming exactly the wedge that Jones had hoped for.

When Chapman returned from Washington and found the three Lapwai Nez Perce living in Jones's house, he knew immediately what Jones had been up to, and in his mind it had nothing to do with religion. These three Indians, with their white clothing and white ways, were here to take his authority and, equally as important, his job.

He also knew that these men would be tools of Jones, who would use them to continue his oppression and exploitation of Joseph and the others who would not adapt to the agent's ways. During his stay in Washington, three more children had died, including the young boy Joseph called his son. The people had run out of rations, the cattle allotted for future slaughter had gotten so thin that the white man in charge doubted that more than ten of the fifty could even survive, and the healthy cows that had been weighed into the herd before Chapman's departure had mysteriously disappeared. In addition, the weather had turned snowy and bitterly cold. Once again, death and starvation were descending in full force upon the suffering Nez Perce people.

Chapman immediately shot off a new fusillade of letters and telegrams to officials in Washington describing the situation, vilifying Jones, and promoting his claim as the legitimate translator. Jones responded with counterclaims, and Reuben, Lawyer, and Williams chimed in on their own, indignant at their poor treatment as civilized men and requesting more funds to cover the cost of their stay in Jones's house. All the while, the Nez Perce sat in their leaky canvas teepees amid snow and frigid rains, hoping for an answer, or at least a ray of hope, that would deliver them from their increasingly hopeless and seemingly endless situation.

Joseph realized that the situation was now perilous. Chapman's visit to Washington had succeeded in keeping the issue of the Nez Perce before the public eye, but he could not be sure exactly what Chapman had done, and on whose behalf, during his visit. But whatever Chapman had done, it had not resulted in any significant lessening of his people's suffering. It also had allowed Reuben, Williams, and Lawyer to gain a foothold with the people. Sickness and despair were now being joined by divisiveness and doubt. He needed to get to Washington himself.

The one person who could help him was his longtime acquaintance, Colonel A. B. Meacham, who had once been the Superintendent of Indian

Affairs in Oregon and since had begun writing a pro-Indian newspaper in Washington called the *Council Fire*. Though Meacham himself had earlier pleaded with Joseph to accept the truth of history and begin living in the white manner, he had always held Joseph in high regard. He also was a confidante of Chapman, and he had previously visited the Nez Perce encampment and seen their pitiful situation. When Chapman and Joseph pleaded with him to assist them in saving the Nez Perce from a slow death at the hands of Jones, he willingly agreed to take up their cause. Through his influence, Commissioner Hayt and Secretary Schurz of the Department of the Interior finally granted permission for Joseph to travel to Washington to present his case. If there was a chance that Joseph could change people's hearts and minds, this was it.

On a cold, wintry day in January 1879, Joseph, Chapman, and Yellow Bull set off for Baxter Springs to catch the train to Kansas City. From there they would proceed to St. Louis, then on to Washington, D.C.

The three men tried to travel unobtrusively, but they were unable to avoid public attention. Neither Joseph nor Yellow Bull had ever become comfortable in white man's clothes, so they continued to dress in their traditional outfits. The presence of Indians in full tribal regalia created excitement wherever they went, even if no one knew the true celebrity of the barrel-chested, self-possessed Indian they saw sitting silently next to them in railroad coaches and at restaurants.

In St. Louis, they caused a great stir at the grand three-hundred-room, six-story Lindell Hotel when they walked into the dining room along with the thin, scruffy Chapman. They took a table in the corner of the room and tried to keep to themselves, but two Indians with shoulder-length hair wearing moccasins and red, white, and blue blankets were not easily ignored. The other diners began whispering animatedly about these exotic creatures who had glided noiselessly among them and now were eating adjacent to them, skillfully using knives and forks and the other utensils of civilization.

After the strange group finished and left the dining room, a reporter for the *St. Louis Globe Democrat*, who had happened to be dining there that evening, rushed up to the front register and asked about the identity of the unusual visitors. When he was informed that it was the famous Chief Joseph along with one of his subchiefs and an interpreter, the reporter im-

mediately sent his card up to the room, hoping he would have the unbe-
lievable good fortune of getting an interview with this legendary war
chief.

Joseph was more than willing to meet the man. A reporter, especially
one whose work was distributed in this great, astonishing city of St. Louis,
was exactly the kind of quarry he had hoped to catch in his hunt for public
support. And, truth be told, he had actually begun to enjoy the celebrity
status that white American was according him. He quickly arranged to
have the man invited up.

When word passed that this strange party of diners had included the
legendary Joseph, everyone of any note in the hotel began asking for a
chance to meet the chief. Informed that he was holding an audience in
room 200, they rushed up the stairs to become part of this once-in-a-
lifetime event. Before long, the room was filled to overflowing with citizens
hungry for the opportunity to be in the presence of the man who was rapidly becoming the most famous Indian in America. Among the assembled
was a man who had served in the military at Lolo Pass and Fort Lapwai,
and even a lieutenant who had been Miles's quartermaster.

Cigars were brought up and offered around, but Joseph demurred, indicating that he preferred to smoke his own pipe, which was wrapped in a
beaded deerskin bag slung over the back of a nearby chair.

Chapman too was enjoying the notoriety. He had installed himself in a
seat across the room and was engaged in a long, self-serving exposition of
the history of Joseph's people and the retreat they had conducted. It was
fundamentally accurate in its specifics; Chapman, after all, had heard and
repeated the story many times as a translator in the last three-quarters of a
year. It reflected the story as Joseph was now telling it in various venues—
with reference to the threats and treaty violations that started the problems, the various battles that had been fought during the retreat, and the
betrayals by the government of the promises issued by Miles and Howard
at the time of the surrender. But it placed Chapman at the center of the
action and underscored his supposed long friendship and loyalty to the
Nez Perce. It also continued the growing tradition of placing Joseph in a
position of leadership throughout the campaign, referring to his masterful acts of generalship and his centrality in all decision making. But, for all
these distortions, it offered a compelling case regarding the breach of faith
by the government and a plaintive plea for fair treatment of the Nez Perce

people, who had been so misled and mistreated since the time of the surrender. The people in attendance listened with rapt fascination.

All this the reporter dutifully copied down, along with wide-eyed physical descriptions of the two chiefs. He described the men's clothes, the slopes of their foreheads, and the shapes of their noses. He reduced their nods of assent to "ughs," but he also noted Joseph's generous responses to the assembled audience. He even captured some of Joseph's short speech to the group, as translated by Chapman.

"I think I am a true man," he reported the chief as saying. "There is nothing deceitful about me. I always try to be open in everything I say or do. I will never forget you, nor any remarks you may make. I have good feelings toward you, and I hope that you have the same toward me. Although we may never meet each other again, and although we will part at a distance, we will think of each other in good feeling. I am very thankful to meet you here this evening. That is all I have to say."

The people in the room gave Joseph a standing ovation after he had finished, and this too the reporter dutifully noted. He concluded with a description of the chief's meeting a young boy who also had the name Joseph, and an elaborate recounting of sharing in the smoking of Joseph's pipe of peace. He then followed the three men out of the hotel as they caught one of the horse-drawn streetcars and went off to the station to continue their trip east.

It was indeed a scoop for the reporter, and it made for great copy. But it also served Joseph's purposes perfectly. He had once again raised his visibility in the eyes of the white public and placed the story of his people in the forefront of their minds. Additionally, he had learned a new and valuable fact about white culture. The reporter had been taking his notes in shorthand, and when Joseph had been shown that the scrawlings captured his words exactly, he realized that he now had the power to make himself heard throughout white America, even if his speech was not transmitted by telegraph or telephone or captured on the odd wax cylinder that could hold and replay a person's voice. He now knew he was able to speak to any assembly that contained a reporter and that his words would be transmitted to white people anywhere. If he could get the audience he desired in Washington, perhaps he could finally get his people the fair hearing they deserved.

———————

On the evening of January 17, 1879, an excited audience gathered in Lincoln Hall in Washington, D.C., to see and hear the man who indeed had become the most famous Indian in America.

Though the government and the military had done their best to quiet the furor over the hapless Nez Perce exiles, the legend of their leader had continued to grow. In *Harper's New Monthly* just a few weeks before, a poem entitled "Joseph, the Nez Perce" had been published, in which the author had demanded:

> *Let the nation in its glory*
> *Bow with shame before the story*
> *Of the hero it has ruined and the evil it has done.*

The poet had gone on to write of Joseph's noble journey, noting how the chief had traveled for months over "continental ridges" and "tottering torrent bridges by the verge of black abysses," chased from behind by one army while another crouched in wait ahead, until, "burdened by his weak and wounded," "like a lion," he "stood at bay." And all simply because this "chieftain of the Northland" had possessed the temerity to seek, in the author's words, "the home the good God gave him . . . the shelter of his children," and "the right to be a man."

With such sentiments moving among the populace, it was small wonder that the Lincoln Hall audience packed the auditorium early that evening, excited to hear the story directly from the mouth of the great chief himself.

And Joseph did not disappoint. He entered the room to tumultuous applause that did not let up until the entire entourage of Indian leaders and dignitaries was seated. When he was introduced and walked up on the stage, the applause cascaded forth again and redoubled when he paused to take a drink of water.

He was dressed in full Nez Perce regalia. His forelock was flipped back, as befitting a follower of the Dreamer way, and his long side braids were ornamented with beads. He wore a blanket coat adorned with skins and furs, and his moccasins were heavily decorated with beads. His carriage and bearing were solemn and self-contained, causing many in the audience to whisper that he seemed to be the very embodiment of Fenimore Cooper's noble savage.

When he began to speak, this image was only enhanced. His voice, clear and unwavering, filled the entire hall. In unhesitating words, translated almost simultaneously by Chapman, he unfolded the story of his people and the plight they had endured. "Some of you think an Indian is like a wild animal," he began. "This is a great mistake. I will tell you all about our people, and then you can judge whether an Indian is a man or not."

He proceeded to speak for an hour and twenty minutes, recounting the history of his people, from the laws passed down by the ancestors to the arrival of Lewis and Clark and the fur traders and Spalding.

He told of the tribes' troubled dealings with the whites, from the meetings with Stevens to the two treaties to General Howard's ultimatum and the great chase that had ended in their exile. He told of the difficulties his people had suffered in Leavenworth and the Quapaw and of the many promises that had been made, first by Miles, then by others in the government, all issuing in nothing.

He closed with entreaties mixed with excoriations and visionary hopes for the brotherhood of all people, where "we shall all be alike—brothers of one father and one mother, with one sky above us and one government for all."

It was a masterful performance, honed over many months of telling and retelling, and in its presentation he and Chapman functioned almost as one. By the time they had finished, the audience had heard, for the first time and with stunning clarity, an exposition that made the long, confusing Nez Perce saga into an understandable narrative. And what they were left with was the firm conviction that Joseph, the eloquent, regal embodiment of the Fenimore Cooper noble Indian who stood before them, had led the Nez Perce on their tragic, perilous flight and led them still as they sought nothing more than the opportunity to be removed from the unhealthy squalor of their distant exile and returned to the land from which they had been so unjustly removed.

It had not been Joseph's intention to minimize the importance of the other chiefs or to raise himself into a position of sole leadership. He simply had recounted the decisions made by his own band and, after the surrender, referred to those who remained with him as "my people." In Nez Perce fashion, not wishing to speak for another, he had not voiced the opinions of Looking Glass, White Bird, or any of the others and had kept his narrative grounded in his own personal experience.

But the audience, unfamiliar with the band structure of the Nez Perce and hungry to impute greatness to the man before them, took his words to mean that he was solely responsible for the journey, the surrender, and the care and protection of those who remained in Indian Territory.

They also gained a fuller picture of the man about whom they had heard so much. If his appearance had underscored their belief that he represented the noblest of red men, his words had convinced them even more. Reaching back to the distant teachings of the Reverend Spalding and his Book of Heaven, he had told them that "the Great Spirit sees and hears everything, and He never forgets; that hereafter He will give every man a spiritual home according to his deserts." He had challenged the morality of the white leaders, wondering aloud how a government could send a man out to fight, as they had done with Miles, and then refuse to uphold his word.

"Such a government has something wrong about it," he said. Then he had shamed them with his indictment that "I have heard talk and talk, but nothing is done. Good words do not last long unless they amount to something. Words do not pay for my country, now overrun by white men. They do not protect my father's grave. They do not pay for all my horses and cattle. Good words will not give me back my children . . . will not give my people good health and stop them from dying . . . will not get my people a home where they can live in peace. . . ."

Indeed, all the good words seemed to belong to this man, and the cause of right seemed to be on his side. As they filed out that evening, the audience of dignitaries, cabinet members, congressmen, and ordinary citizens—many of whom had never seen an actual Indian before—took with them a picture of a man who represented everything good they wanted to believe about the red man and everything bad they wanted to believe about American policy and treatment of a people who had committed no crime other than wishing to live in peace in the way that their Creator had intended.

The evening was a stunning success for Joseph, and it became an even greater victory when he was given an audience with President Rutherford B. Hayes, Secretary Schurz of the Department of the Interior, and other important officials. He, Chapman, and Yellow Bull returned to the Quapaw hopeful that the government would now act fairly and uphold the promise it had made to allow the people to return to their homeland or, at least, to move to a healthier land farther north.

But their chance for celebration was short, for upon their return to the Quapaw they discovered that there was now even greater dissension among the people. Taking advantage of the absence of Joseph and his interpreter, Jones had begun spreading stories that Joseph was in Washington making deals to move some of the people back north while leaving others behind in the Quapaw. Husis Kute, who once again had been left out of the official delegation, had turned his allegiance toward Reuben and Jones, and many of the people, desperate for full rations, had done the same. Reuben's presence had also given them new hope. Here was another Nez Perce voice, familiar with their home and their people, who was promising them a better life and even holding out hope of a return to the homeland if they accepted the new Christian ways. Many among them even began asking the hard question of whether Reuben's Christian God might not truly have more power and speak of a more favored relationship to the Creator.

The tribe, once divided by missionaries, then separated by war, was now being divided again.

24

"I Know What Is Good for You Now, Mr. Indian"

T HE WINTER DRAGGED on, and the anticipated positive governmental response to Joseph's Washington visit never materialized.
Western congressmen, under heavy pressure to keep Joseph and his people
from returning west, blocked every effort to allow the Nez Perce to return
to their home country. They did not want the charismatic chief among the
other tribes, and they did not want the troubles that would come from re-
opening the wounds with the settlers who had suffered so greatly during
the time of the first killings. The army, not wishing the expense of keeping
peace in the distant, expansive regions of the West, was quick to concur.
All the goodwill that Joseph thought he had created during his Washington trip had come to nothing.

But, in fact, the trip was bearing slow fruit. Though the government resisted Nez Perce relocation, public sympathy was building once again for
the Nez Perce cause. Joseph's eloquence and charisma had rekindled the
public's imagination, and he and his people were slowly gaining the status
of tragic victims. Joseph himself was being elevated ever higher as the very
embodiment of the noble man of nature that the nation had decimated on
its relentless march across the western expanses of the continent. When a
widely read journal called the *North American Review* published what was
understood to be a transcription of his Lincoln Hall speech, his fame
spread even further and his reputation as America's premier Indian was cemented even more.

At the same time, another force was slowly coming into play, one that
emerged from a very different source than Joseph's eloquence and

charisma. Ever so subtly, the consistent righteous indignation of the clean-cut, civilized, English-speaking Reuben was beginning to make inroads with people who measured Indians not by the greatness of their past but by the promise of their future.

The issues that seemed so crucial up close—the dissension between Chapman and Reuben over who would serve as translator and thus serve as the voice of the Nez Perce, the constant bickering between Chapman and Jones, and even the struggle in the people's hearts between the old way of the seven drums and Dreamer faith and the new way of Christianity—were of no concern to the distant observers in whose hands the fate of the Nez Perce ultimately lay. What they saw, from their respective positions, were two men, one embodying the best of what the Indian had been, and one embodying the best of what the Indian could be.

Joseph's personal eloquence and persona were giving a public face to the Nez Perce struggle, while Reuben's Christian fervor was giving it a political base. Jones's decision to bring the Presbyterian Nez Perce down to subvert the influence of Joseph and Chapman had produced the unintended consequence of bringing the formidable political influence of the Presbyterian Church into play. When Reuben spoke, the Presbyterian establishment was there to listen, just as the American press listened when Joseph spoke. Together, these two men—the obstinate, charismatic chief and the self-righteous, clean-cut Christian minister—were unwittingly creating a potent mix of political power and public opinion that had the potential to do what neither man was able to do alone.

But this congealing of forces was the furthest thing from the minds of the Nez Perce themselves. They were engaged in a struggle that ran far deeper than any of the white observers understood. It was the same struggle that had taken place back in the Lapwai forty years earlier when Spalding preached the gospel and told the people to honor the old gods no more, the same struggle that had divided the tribe after the Treaty of 1855, the same struggle that had found part of the tribe assisting the whites after the outbreak and another part trying to escape over the mountains. It was the struggle over how to be a Nez Perce in the face of the new and overwhelming power of the intruding white nation and how to live in the manner that best reflected the wishes of the Creator. In short, it was a struggle for the Nez Perce soul.

When Reuben, Lawyer, and Williams had arrived, they had brought with them the whole weight of that struggle. They were the inheritors of Spalding, the offspring of the treaty Nez Perce, the embodiment of the successful transition that had been made since the first Nez Perce had spread boughs on the ground before the Reverend Parker on the journey back from the rendezvous. They were the living presence of the success that had accrued to those who cast their lot with the spiritual powers of the Christian way. But, with their short hair, white man's clothing, and white man's ways, they were also the embodiment of all that the Nez Perce had lost in embarking on the Christian path.

What Joseph saw when he looked at them were men who had betrayed the sacred trust of the ancestors and violated the laws of the Creator; men who dug into the earth and disrespected the spirits and set the children on a path away from the teachings of the grandmothers and grandfathers. What they saw when they looked at Joseph was a misguided adherent to a discredited past who clung obstinately to a backward stage of cultural and spiritual development, a man who had failed to grow in accord with the new knowledge revealed by the Creator. In their own minds, they were simply shepherds coming to gather the lost sheep and bring their brothers and sisters up from darkness and into the light.

So while the white public was slowly being drawn back into a sympathetic awareness of the Nez Perce plight by the potent combination of a romanticized Fenimore Cooper noble savage and a successful, Christianized, "civilized" Indian, the men who embodied these two visions of Indian identity were engaged in a struggle for the hearts and minds and spirits of the suffering tribal members they were both trying to serve.

It was a struggle that Joseph could not easily win.

Over the winter the tides ebbed and flowed. Jones succeeded in driving a wedge between the people by issuing two separate sets of rations: one for the followers of Joseph and his ways, another, more plentiful, for those who cast their lot with Reuben, Husis Kute, and Christianity. Sometimes he gave the followers of Joseph no rations at all.

He claimed publicly that the money Joseph and his people had collected to send Chapman to Washington had actually been extorted from them, and when Joseph traveled over to the nearby town of Seneca, Missouri, to engage a notary to witness that the money had been given of the people's own free will, he pointed out that the person translating the document Joseph signed was none other than Chapman himself. He even told the Nez Perce that those who continued to side with Joseph would be sent farther south while those who accepted the Christian ways would be allowed to return to their homeland.

Joseph, for his part, continued with Chapman's help to send telegrams to Washington complaining of Jones's cruel practices. They rode on the tide of sentiment growing throughout the country that the only real solution to the Indian "problem" was to remove corrupt agents and place the responsibility for disbursing funds and goods in the hands of military paymasters, who at least were accountable and able to keep honest records. Joseph even proposed exchanging his old country in Oregon for land farther to the west in Indian Territory and a quarter of a million dollars in government bonds so they would have their own funds and not be dependent upon the whims of the agent.

Meanwhile, the winter deepened, and every day more of the heartsick, hopeless, frightened people died. The wet climate, poor food, and lack of medicine allowed diseases to run rampant, killing almost all the elderly and the newborns. Stillbirths were common, and miscarriages even more so. Even Jones's more liberal allotment of rations to the Christian Nez Perce could not save the people from death. And all of them lived in fear of what the agent would do next—send them farther south, poison their medicines, or withhold their rations altogether.

Eventually, the Quakers and the government could no longer avoid the truth of Jones's regime. The Bureau of Indian Affairs ordered him removed, and in early May 1878 he left in disgrace, owing the government more than $38,000 and leaving in his wake a devastated, disheartened, and divided people.

With Jones's departure, and no other agent yet in place, Joseph moved his people back up to the Spring River near the place they had first crossed when they had been transported by the Modoc from the railhead at Baxter Springs. The campsite was on a flat piece of land at river's edge, graced by towering canopied oak and abundant with nuts and berries. But, more important, it was only several easy miles from Baxter Springs, so the people could walk to town to trade the gloves and other hide goods they had made and purchase goods with their government cards.

The Arden Smith joint congressional commission of the previous fall had been so disgusted with Jones's practices that they had ordered the Indians be provided ration cards that they could use with any merchant they pleased. But Jones had easily circumvented this by allowing the tribes access only to his trader compatriots, who brought their wagons into the Indian camp and sold supplies at exorbitant prices. With Jones gone, the possibility of free trade opened up. Joseph knew that the site near the edge of Indian Territory offered his people the best opportunity to engage in this trade. It also kept them nearer the white settlements and white oversight in case the new agent proved to be as cruel and corrupt as Jones. And in the event that he and Chapman needed to send or receive telegrams, they were now only a short journey from the towns where this could take place. Slowly, Joseph was moving his people out of the hellish exile into which they had been thrust since their arrival in Indian Territory over half a year earlier.

But their exile was not over; it was only entering a new phase. Jones might be gone, but the sickness and sadness and internal division remained. And there was still no prospect for return to the home country, only the hope that the harsh, killing conditions might lessen and that the people might have a better chance to survive.

When the new agent arrived, he was indeed a better man than Jones. His name was Haworth, and he was a man much more in line with the best of Quaker beliefs and values. He immediately set about preparing the Nez Perce for the move west to the land that Joseph had chosen the previous fall on the ride with Hayt and Yellow Bull and Husis Kute. He knew that time was of the essence, because in little more than a month the killing heat of summer would descend in full force, bringing with it the thunderstorms and flash floods that would make the passage almost impossible.

He issued twenty wagons to the anxious Nez Perce and purchased forty broodmares to pull them. He helped the Indians mate the horses in suitable teams and gave them a quick day's lesson in how to drive the horses in harness, something that the expert Nez Perce horsemen had never done before. He outfitted them with bacon, medicine, and flour for the journey and secured the employment of several locals to travel along with them to keep the wagons in good repair. When early June arrived, the people were ready to travel to their new homeland 180 miles farther to the west in Indian Territory.

The departure was not easy because most of the people were too sick or weak or simply refused to walk, and the number of wagons was not sufficient to carry them. So Haworth had to have an extra thirty-nine wagons sent down to the campsite on Spring River to assist the people on their journey.

But despite the problems, on the morning of June 6, 1879, almost a year after their arrival in the Eekish Pah, or "hot place," which had claimed so many of their friends and family, the Nez Perce, led by Chief Joseph on horseback, set out in fifty-nine wagons for a new, unknown country and a new, uncertain life. Of the 800 people who had begun the journey in the Camas Prairie, only 370 now remained.

The journey took nine days, most of it on a rough wagon trail that had been made thirty years before by an army surveying crew. It wound through open, rolling, tallgrass prairie laced with many small creeks. The Indians, including Joseph himself, were constantly having to drag rocks and deadfall off the trail or assist in pulling the wagons up and down the banks and across the streams.

They began each day early, getting on the trail by five and stopping by two in the afternoon to avoid the heat of midday and the vicious, sky-splitting thunderstorms that often rose up in the afternoon and early evening. Even so, one woman died on the journey and was buried along the trail, and many others lay sick in the wagons as they lurched and bumped over the rough prairie landscape.

Haworth had appointed Chapman master of the wagon train, so it fell to Reuben to serve as Joseph's interpreter. The relationship between the two was distant at best, though Reuben was, in fact, a relative of Joseph's. But Reuben's Christianity, as well as his role as Howard's chief scout during the war and his subsequent friendship with Jones, had made Joseph wary of the man and distrustful of his integrity as an interpreter.

Nonetheless, Joseph wanted to stop in any town they passed and go into the newspaper office to tell his story. So while Chapman was guiding the wagons, Joseph and Reuben were visiting editors and recounting the struggles and broken promises the Nez Perce had endured.

Joseph, as always, painted the picture of a people betrayed and ex-pressed hope that the government might see fit to make things right. He spoke of his good feelings toward white people and his hope that all races might live together under common laws and a common sky. He would end by leaving his signature, a rough scrawling of the words "Young Joseph," which always delighted the recipient and pleased the chief himself.

But Reuben, as an interpreter, had very different intentions from Chapman. He would tell Joseph's story but would add that the Nez Perce now had among their numbers a substantial number of Presbyterians, a fact that was not significant to Joseph but that helped to advance the cause of the Nez Perce among a sympathetic Christian population.

The people arrived at the site of what was to be their new home at two in the afternoon on the fourteenth of June. The country that Joseph had visited in November, when the temperature was in the sixties and the grass as high as a saddle's pommel, was now sweltering in the summer sun and thick with black flies. It was flat and formless as far as the eye could see, and the river that was to provide their water ran slow and torpid and brown with silt. Above them, ponderous cumulus clouds rose miles into an empty sky, and the wind blew hot and breathless and without relief.

Agent Haworth, who had accompanied the people on their journey, turned them over to the new agent, a Mr. Whiteman, who was to take responsibility for their settlement and well-being in their new country. Whiteman had been instructed to meet the people with supplies and medicines. But the instructions had come too late for him to gather the required provisions, so he had no assistance to offer them. Haworth then departed for his home in the Quapaw, and the Nez Perce were left alone in an empty land with a few days' rations, a confused and unprepared agent, and no knowledge of what to do or how they were to survive.

Fortunately, their situation was not as dire as when they had arrived at the Quapaw. Whiteman was a man more in the mold of Haworth than of Jones, and the people had arrived with tent poles, shelter, broodmares, and livestock. Nonetheless, the country was cruel and unforgiving in a way that the Quapaw had never been.

The Quapaw had been a land of gentle hills with hickory and sumac and sheltering, towering oaks. The water, when not polluted by livestock, had been good. But this new country was a place of a different order. Though in some ways it reminded the people of the great openness of the buffalo plains, even to the extent of having an occasional herd of bison roaming across its vast open grasslands, it was in all other ways a harsh and merciless land. The rolling banks of cumulus clouds that filled the summer sky quickly darkened and turned to fire-spitting thunderheads. Torrents of rain, driven by slashing, cutting winds, blew down shelters and turned streams into rushing, uncrossable floodbeds. And swarms of flies and mosquitoes tormented the flesh of humans and animals alike. On some days the air would grow still and breathless, turn the green of an animal's eye, then unleash a fury of swirling wind that snapped off trees and ripped tents from their moorings. The air was so hot and wet that it kept the weak and elderly from ever getting a full breath.

The Nez Perce had never experienced such a place before. It seemed more like the hot place spoken of by the Reverend Spalding than like the kind and gentle mother in whom they had been taught to believe. Truly, they seemed to have been forgotten by the Creator.

When Colonel Meacham visited the people less than a month after their arrival, Joseph minced no words in his assessment of their situation. "You come to see me as you would a man upon his deathbed," he told the colonel. "The Great Spirit above has left me and my people to our fate. The white men forget us, and death comes almost every day for some of my people. He will come for all of us. A few months more and we will be in the ground. We are a doomed people."

Meacham could not but agree. All through the camp the air was filled with the constant haunting death wail that announced the impending passing of yet another member of the band.

Yet the people persevered. Broken in body and defeated in spirit, they gave in to the demand to work the earth to save their lives. The season was too advanced to allow for the planting of crops, so Agent Whiteman provided them tools and assistance in putting up hay to feed their stock for the winter. The people who had refused to cut the hair of their mother in the home country were now reduced to doing so in order to survive.

But despite Whiteman's best efforts, progress came slowly. By the time the icy gales of winter began to blow, only a commissary shed had been constructed, and this was little more than a crude construction of rough-hewn cottonwood planks with batting boards nailed over the cracks. The people were forced to spend another winter in canvas tents, shivering against the high prairie winds and living off the meager rations that the agent was able to provide.

By the time spring came, the canvas on the tents had become so rotten that they could no longer keep out the rain, and the people were sleeping on mud and trying to keep warm under soggy, soaking blankets. Because they were unable to keep warm and dry, consumption and diseases of the lungs moved among them, filling the camp with coughs and wheezing and claiming the people one by one.

As their leader, Joseph was able to do little. He was visited frequently by well-meaning government officials—some promising to help him move to a healthier land in the north, others promising to help him if he would accept the white man's ways and make a life for himself and his people in this country. But none of their promises ever came to anything.

Slowly, the hopelessness of the situation and the deep sadness of the people were wearing down their spiritual as well as their physical resistance, and the Christian teachings of Reuben, Lawyer, and Williams began to take solid root. It was not just the power of the Christian religion; it was the simple requirements of survival. Here, no one could survive without tilling the earth. No stock could endure the winter unless the hay was cut. The old sanctions not to gouge the mother's flesh and not to cut her hair seemed impossible and, in their impossibility, became distant spiritual echoes for all but the strongest believers. Even the most devout wavered, slowly abandoning their grandfathers' faith as they slowly abandoned their grandfathers' dreams.

By spring, even Joseph was preparing to plant a field of corn, and he and Yellow Bull had become frequent visitors to the white settlement of Arkansas City across the northern border of Indian Territory into Kansas. In an attempt to survive, the Nez Perce had begun planting fields and working as teamsters, hauling goods from the railhead at Wichita to the agency. Many of them had adopted white clothing and white names along with white religion. A few crude houses were going up, though they amounted to little, since the supplies promised by the agent were slow in coming and the amount being allotted for each house was only sixty dollars, compared to the four thousand dollars that the Quakers had appropriated for the house Jones had built himself back on the Quapaw Agency. Still, it was a movement toward civilization and away from the old ways. The Nez Perce seemed to be learning the lessons of survival that the Modoc had learned at such a great human cost back in the Quapaw.

Joseph too had begun to lose his voice among the people. Chapman had committed one too many indiscretions and had been driven off. With his absence, Reuben had become the prime spokesman for the tribe. His command of English and his connection with the Presbyterian Church allowed him to move quickly to the forefront of power and influence.

Reuben's goal was to get the people back to Idaho where they could be reunited with their Nez Perce brothers and sisters at Lapwai and where they could learn to live freely in the Christian way. By this time he also had the complete allegiance of Husis Kute, who had transferred his deep spiritual convictions from the ways of Smolholla to the ways of the Christians.

Together these two men formed a formidable spiritual presence: the impressive, pious, "civilized" Nez Perce from the successful, nonbelligerent branch of the Nez Perce in Idaho, and the once-adamant follower of Smolholla and the ways of the Dreamers who had served as spiritual leader of the exiles and now was beginning to walk in the light of Christian truth.

Reuben began appearing at Presbyterian meetings in Arkansas City and took to pleading the Nez Perce cause before any who would listen. His message was always the same, focusing on the injustices the Nez Perce had suffered and the progress they were making on their march upward from savage ignorance toward civilization. In one of his most eloquent pleas in Colonel Meacham's *Council Fire* journal, he told the Nez Perce story with a poignancy and bitterness that both buttressed and stood in stark counterpoint to the stately, measured, recounting that Joseph had made the previous year in the *North American Review.*

"White man has wronged the red nations in every respect," he wrote. "He has moved on to his camping places without his consent; he has swindled him out of his home by cheatings and sharp practices; he has abused him and he regarded him as beasts of the mountains and did treat him accordingly. . . . White man stands up and says, I know what is good for you now, Mr. Indian, get up now, move your foot off that last piece of ground, for I want it and am going to have it. . . . Indian packs up his bundle and away he goes, he turns to take a last look of his old home and cast a last glance upon the graves of his fathers; he utters no cry, he sheds no tears, he heaves no groans."

Reuben continued in this vein, recounting with undisguised rancor how whites pursued Indians wherever they went, taking whatever they wanted and, when challenged, cried to Uncle Sam for assistance. He then turned to the current Nez Perce situation and pointed out how he himself had come among them of his own free will and sought nothing more than common human justice for the tribe, which, by right, would include returning them to their homeland in Idaho.

He concluded by excoriating the white government for disrespecting the Indians' rights to life, liberty, and the pursuit of happiness, and calling upon the government to "treat Indians like people." For such, he said, "would be a glorious thing."

Such eloquence naturally drew the confused and frightened Nez Perce to him and raised the possibility, however faint, that his voice and his path would be the one to possibly lead them out of this shapeless exile and back to the land of their ancestors.

When he started a school in the back section of the drafty plank commissary building, his influence increased even further. Even many who were not sure of these new ways came to believe that the way of the future belonged to the whites and that the children should be taught white ways and language so that they might not suffer the same fate as their parents and grandparents.

Soon, thirty-eight people were attending Reuben's classes, including a few adults. Archie Lawyer, whose kind and caring manner had won the favor of many of the exiles, opened them further to the Christian faith with his preaching and ministering.

Joseph put up no resistance. He had fallen sick, and his young daughter, born on the eve of the outbreak of violence back in the Camas Prairie, was now among the dead. If following the Christian way would get his people food and medicine and give their spirits hope, he would not speak against their new belief. He even enlisted Reuben's aid in composing a letter to General Howard, begging him to use his influence to get the government to fulfill the promise that had been made at the Bear's Paw. "I want you to know now I am going to be a Christian man," he said.

But Howard offered no assistance. He wrote back a response expressing pleasure at Joseph's apparent decision to become "a real Christian" but said that he had never promised to return the people to Idaho, and he counseled the chief to accept his situation and "make a garden of the land."

It was left to Reuben to carry the people's cause forward. Joseph could speak to visitors and make the case for his people, and he always did so. But it was Reuben and his zealously public Christianity that was having the greater effect.

Unlike the Quapaw, which had been mostly isolated from white contact, this new location, called the Oakland agency, was in direct and frequent contact with the outside world. Missionaries and government inspectors often passed through the country, and though for long periods the agents themselves were absent, the people were visited regularly by physicians, philanthropists, and others who felt concern for the Indians.

As the most vocal and civilized of the Nez Perce, Reuben quickly made his presence felt. He cut a figure of imposing gravity and piety and was able to speak to the visitors in English. He was quick to point out that he was in Indian Territory of his own accord and had accomplished much as a teacher and practitioner of the Christian ways, always without government support. In all manners he comported himself as a dignified man well conversant with the ways of white society and was a constant visitor to the churches across the border in the white town of Arkansas City.

He showed an interest in white learning and culture, and he had a white man's concern with financial affairs, insisting constantly on proper compensation for his work and keeping a strict accounting of moneys owed him. He also was adamant in his opposition to alcohol, even testifying before government officials against liquor peddlers on the reservation. To white observers, he was everything that a converted Indian should be. He embodied what the red man could become if he accepted the gifts of civilization and abandoned his savage and backward ways.

So when Reuben entreated the Presbyterian leaders in Arkansas City to visit the reservation to help establish a church, they were ecstatic. They quickly made arrangements for the visit, and on October 20, 1880, a small entourage, including a minister and a church elder, set out on the nine-hour wagon journey south from Arkansas City to the Nez Perce encampment.

Reuben's Nez Perce followers greeted the visitors with a piety that took the white men aback. As soon as the group had been ushered into the crude commissary building and the Arkansas City pastor and the accompanying church elder had been seated in the building's only two chairs, a procession of Indians filed in and took their places around the sides of the room. In orderly and dignified fashion the children entered, followed by the women, then the men, until 125 Nez Perce were seated quietly in a ring around the visiting white officials. The children sang a Presbyterian hymn in their own language, then joined together in reciting the Lord's Prayer. When they were asked questions about their faith, their answers, translated by Reuben, were spoken with clarity and certainty.

The visitors sat in stunned silence. Before their eyes they were seeing the very fulfillment of the biblical prophesy that things hidden from the wise and prudent would be revealed to the hearts of the innocent.

In the course of the next three hours, fifty-nine Nez Perce made a profession of faith and asked for baptism. More would have done so, but the hour was late and the Arkansas City pastor needed to be present the following morning at the laying of a cornerstone for an residential school on the Ponca reservation fourteen miles away.

Reluctantly, the delegation left, convinced that they had seen the spirit of the Lord moving among this poor, beleaguered people. They promised that they would return on the first Sabbath in November to administer the last supper and complete the baptism of the children.

As they rode away, Chief Joseph stood outside watching. He had declined to enter the building to be part of the church service but had remained among the crowd of observers, bearing witness and showing silent support for the efforts of his people to find a way to heal their hearts and gain the favor of the white leaders who might somehow help them in their efforts to escape this exile and return to their homeland.

The next day, at the laying of the cornerstone, the missionaries were surprised to see wagonloads of Nez Perce arriving for the ceremony. By the time festivities began, two hundred Nez Perce were present, far more than from any other tribe. Among them was Joseph.

The ceremony opened with hymns and proceeded with speeches. Reuben stood at the front of the Nez Perce delegation and, when the time came for testimony, told how Joseph's people had come down to this country in an almost savage condition but now sought to embrace Christianity and walk on the good path.

Tom Hill, who had been Joseph's first interpreter at the surrender and had been sent to Indian country after his return from the land of Sitting Bull, made an impassioned confession of his previous sins and bitter heart and spoke of how he believed there was no hope for Indian people unless they adopted the white man's beliefs and ways, as he himself had done.

When the time came for the actual laying of the cornerstone, a tin box was brought forth in which those present could place what the agent and missionaries referred to as "mementos," which would allow people of the future to know the savage manner in which Indians had lived a thousand years before. People stepped forth and dropped in knife cases, beaded bracelets, and even a Sioux scalp. Reuben deposited a history he had written of the Nez Perce since the time of Lewis and Clark, and some of the women contributed a kouse root they had carried with them from Idaho. Then the box was placed in a hollowed-out rock, and the cornerstone was mortared into place.

Another hymn was sung, this time in English, and the ceremony was over. The people returned to their homes, having cemented their past into a rock on which the promise of a Christian future was to be built. As a gesture of unity with the others, Joseph had placed a small finger ring in the box before it was buried.

Joseph's quiet acquiescence to the ascendancy of Reuben was having an effect. By giving tacit support to the people in their Christian fervor, he was keeping the division between the Christian and non-Christian factions from breaking into the same open acrimony that had sundered the people back in the Lapwai.

But despite his claims in his letter to Howard, his own declared willingness to convert to Christianity did not run deep. When the pastor and the other Presbyterian elders returned in November for the promised baptism and last supper, he sat in a front seat wearing a white man's suit but not participating in the singing and prayers. While Tom Hill made another grand public confession of his past spiritual blindness and Husis Kute gave testimony about his previous savage ways as a worshiper of spirits in the mountains of Idaho, Joseph expressed neither approval nor disapproval. But his presence inside the meeting sent a message that could not be misunderstood.

However, keeping unity was not an easy task. The Christian converts had become zealous in their new faith, and those who opposed Reuben were becoming progressively more enraged as his influence grew. Many who had been through so much to save the old ways were embittered by the newfound influence of this man who had fought against them during the war and had belittled them as fools afterward. Often his translations were called into question by other Nez Perce who spoke and understood some English. It was felt that he twisted words to raise himself up in the eyes of the white authorities and that he misrepresented what was said in order to make the Nez Perce look more devoted to Christianity than they actually were. He also acted imperiously toward the people who remained faithful to the old seven-drum and Dreamer ways, demeaning them and berating them and speaking to them as if they were children.

But Joseph did not engage in these arguments. It mattered little to him if Reuben twisted words for his own benefit. If Reuben had the skill to influence the whites and draw them to the cause of the people, Joseph was quite willing to stand aside. He would simply use the man as he had used Chapman. For him, Reuben—like Chapman, like the telegraph, like the newspaper reporters—was but one more tool by which to work for the single goal of returning the people to their homeland.

And in fact Reuben's activities, along with the honest piety of Archie Lawyer, were having an effect. Word was spreading throughout the Presbyterian congregations that the Nez Perce, so recently a wild and savage people engaged in a running battle with the U.S. military, were now rapidly being brought to Christ. They held prayer meetings each day and twice on Sunday. They greeted visiting tribes with prayer sessions rather than dances. And all of this without any formal spiritual guidance or training other than that provided by James Reuben and Archie Lawyer.

The Presbyterian congregation in nearby Arkansas City began promoting the Nez Perce cause to the Kansas synod, and the synod in turn began making the Nez Perce case to the U.S. government through a series of memorial messages submitted to Congress in the form of petitions to be read at the opening of each day's business.

But time was of the essence. The people were getting sicker, and despite their appearance as well-scrubbed Christian converts in the eyes of ministers and visitors, their depression had continued to deepen. All the children were being born dead or were dying shortly after birth. Diseases of the lungs were taking the lives of the sick and the elderly, and neither Christian prayer nor white-man medicine was saving them.

Even Yellow Wolf, the strong warrior who had seen all the death and sadness on the trail of the exodus, could not hide his melancholy. "All the newborn babies died," he said, "and many of the old people, too. . . . Everything so different from our old homes. No mountains, no springs, no clear running rivers."

Finally, one of the agents, Thomas Jordan, said what all knew but none had possessed the courage to say. "The tribe, unless something is done for them, will soon be extinct."

Urged on by such ominous predictions, the Presbyterians redoubled their efforts to have the people returned to their home country. With the earnest support of sympathetic agents such as Jordan, they continued to make the case to officials in Washington for the return of the Indians to their homeland in Idaho.

But western resistance was still strong. These warlike belligerents could yet foment rebellion among the peaceful Indians of the Northwest, and their presence would surely call forth retribution from the white settlers in the area. Yet even the most adamant among them could not make a case against the repatriation of the widows—who the government called "surplus women"—and orphans. So, in the spring of 1883, under intense pressure from the influential Presbyterian lobby, the government finally relented.

In June of that year, almost four years to the day after the Nez Perce had arrived in the empty flatlands of central Indian Territory, thirty-one widows and orphans and two elderly men set out under the care of James Reuben on the long journey back to their homeland. The government had refused to appropriate any money for the relocation, so the tribe paid for it themselves—the women by selling gloves and moccasins, the men by selling foodstuffs and contributing the wages they had earned as teamsters.

The refugees arrived in the Lapwai several weeks later, led by Reuben, dressed impeccably in a dark blue business suit and riding regally on horseback. They were met by a throng of more than a hundred waiting friends and relatives who grabbed them, kissed them, and shared in the tearful reunion that all had so long desired but few had ever believed would come to pass.

But the Presbyterian churches in Kansas who had seen both the faith and the despair of the Nez Perce firsthand were not yet mollified. They wanted to see the rest of the Nez Perce returned to their home country. They continued to petition their church authorities to take up the cause of this exiled remnant who even their own agent praised as a "brave, good, and generous" people.

Under the relentless pressure from their churches in southern Kansas, the Presbyterian General Assembly decided to send Dr. George Spining to assess the situation. Spining had spent much of his life among Indians and was thought to be a man whose observations and judgments could be trusted.

In November 1883 he made the journey south from Arkansas City to the area where Joseph and his people were residing. He spoke with the agent in charge, who informed him that he knew of no community of whites who were of such good character. "They do not steal, they do not drink, they do not swear, and they observe the Sabbath," he said.

Spining then went out to the children's graveyard with the minister, Archie Lawyer, to see for himself the extent of the tragedy the Nez Perce had suffered. Lawyer pointed to two small mounds of earth. "Those are mine," he said, sobbing. The graves contained two of his young children who had lost their lives since his arrival in Indian country, and a third was back at home clinging to life at that very moment.

Spining then began counting the graves. They numbered almost a hundred. A single bell tinkled mournfully above one of the small mounds as the men stood quietly in the midst of this burial ground of the innocents.

When the doctor looked up, he saw a solitary figure sitting silently on horseback, observing him. The man was dressed in white man's clothing. "Keep this in your heart," he said. "Tell it to the Great Father in Washington, that maybe his heart will be touched and he will take pity upon this suffering people."

The solitary figure was Joseph.

Spining was overwhelmed by his visit. He returned to the synod and issued an impassioned plea for aid to be given to the suffering Nez Perce people. They have no newspapers and few advocates, he said, and they have surely suffered enough, no matter what crimes they may have committed in the past. He noted how more than half of them had become Christian and that none had done anything in their time in the agency that had stood in violation of any of the laws of God or man. Almost all the belligerents, he said, had either been incarcerated or killed long ago, and those who remained were merely a pitiful remnant made up mostly of women, children, and the elderly. Surely Christian charity demanded the return of these people to their native land, or at least to a healthier climate somewhere in the north.

Spining's plea was widely distributed and touched the hearts of all who read it. The time had come to override the resistance of the western congressmen and other opponents of relocation and force the issue before the Nez Perce people perished to the last one.

"We Won't Be Responsible for Their Lives
24 Hours After Their Arrival"

MEANWHILE, THE REST of the Nez Perce exiles remained in Indian Territory, trying to survive as best they could. Joseph had quietly continued the tradition of the seven drums, holding services for the people on Sundays while the Christians were raising their voices nearby in song and prayer. He also had taken to leading groups of men to the sun dances held by other tribes, both to show respect and in order to build up the people's herd of horses. He knew that it was a widespread custom to offer gifts to visitors who honored you with their presence and that horses were the gifts most traditionally given. Sometimes he and the other men would leave their agency for months, traveling the length of Indian Territory, then returning late in the summer with a long string of ponies that could serve as the breeding stock to build up the herd that had been taken away from them by Miles at the time of surrender.

He also continued his efforts to use the white governmental system for the good of his people. When it was discovered that white ranchers were grazing their cattle on Nez Perce land, instead of appealing to the government to have them removed, Joseph worked to have the land leased to a white rancher who was willing to pay for the right to use it as pasture.

But it was the Presbyterian influence, more than Joseph's, that kept the Nez Perce cause alive in the halls of government. They wanted to see all the Nez Perce returned to their home country, albeit to the care and oversight of the Presbyterian agents in the Lapwai. In a petition submitted to the president several years before, and subsequently distributed to Presbyterian churches all across the country, they had declared, "These Indians today are simply prisoners of war, wrongfully held and dishonorably treated." They had noted that no Nez Perce had ever scalped a white person during the entire time of their flight and warfare and that the bulk of the Nez Perce were law-abiding, prospering people back in Idaho. Joseph, they said, "stands before the American people a victim of duplicity . . . his confidence wantonly betrayed . . . his people rapidly wasting by pestilence."

By the time Reuben had left for Idaho with his small contingent, this sympathy for the people had begun to spread throughout the nation's Presbyterian synods. By the following spring it had reached a zealous fervor. In a coordinated effort, the Presbyterian churches across the country began issuing their own memorial petitions to the Congress as statements to be read into the congressional record each day before the beginning of official business.

In formal language, and in the prescribed manner of governmental presentations, they outlined the wrongs that had been done to the Nez Perce, the promises made to them and never fulfilled, the great progress they had made in the ways of Christian civilization, and the rapid deterioration of the people in the hostile and inhospitable climate of Indian Territory. They concluded with the plea that the exiles be returned to their own native country, where they would be welcomed and cared for by their waiting brothers and sisters at no cost to the government, and where they could prosper in the Christian manner that they were so willingly and successfully embracing.

On April 21, 1884, a petition was received in Congress signed by "the citizens of Kansas." On April 29, petitions arrived from the congregations of Osage City and Derby, Kansas. On May 5, Eldorado, Kansas, and Lawrence County, Indiana, weighed in. On May 7, New Haven, Connecticut, was heard from; on May 12, it was Vincennes, Indiana. In unending succession, these petitions arrived, praying that Congress would return these wronged people to their homelands.

With such an outpouring of sentiment from such an influential and extensive part of the electorate, the politicians began to take notice. A petition from five hundred Ohio Presbyterians, claiming the backing of "4000 of the best citizens of Cleveland " was not to be taken lightly, especially when it was delivered by the widow of President James Garfield and was only one of many from a widely spread, interconnected group of people who all seemed to be of like mind about these exiled Indians. The complaints from western lawmakers suddenly began to sound fainter to the ears of vote-counting politicians, many of whom shared the sentiment that the U.S. Indian policy had been somehow flawed from the outset and who felt that, frankly, the government had more important issues on which to spend its time.

The last real reason for resisting the return of the people was the issue of keeping the peace in the West. Even if these Indians indeed had converted, the memory of their atrocities and belligerence still remained, and many settlers in Idaho and Oregon were not about to abandon their cries for justice and vengeance.

In this regard, the Nez Perce found themselves with a fortunate and familiar ally. In 1880, Colonel Miles's relentless self-promotion, along with his very real accomplishments as an Indian fighter and pacifier, had gained him his general's star. In 1881 he had parleyed this into an appointment as head of the Department of the Columbia, Howard's old post. Even before taking over the position, he had begun campaigning for the return of Joseph and his people to their home territory. He pointed out that no judicial investigation had ever been made to ascertain exactly which of the Indians had been responsible for the killings on Slate Creek and the Salmon and that all of the people, including women and children and wounded, had been held in virtual confinement since their capture.

When the Secretary of the Interior and others chastised him for being presumptuous and instructed him to hold his tongue and carry out the orders of the president, he merely pushed forward in his typical fashion, claiming, "I still adhere to my opinion that to banish a village of people, many of them innocent, is not in accordance with any law or just rule, and I therefore recommend that that portion of the tribe not charged with crime be allowed to return to their reservation."

From the pen of anyone else, this would have been but one more plea for leniency and compassion toward the Indians. But Miles was not only the preeminent Indian fighter in America; his new appointment would put him in charge of keeping the peace in the Plateau region. If he said that these people could be safely returned to their homeland, who was anyone to argue?

In July 1884, a year after the first group of widows and orphans had been allowed to return, and almost seven years after the outbreak in Camas Prairie, Congress authorized the Secretary of the Interior to return the Nez Perce people to their home territory.

But the issue was not yet finished. Miles's assurances notwithstanding, many remained opposed to the relocation, including the Presbyterian missionary in the Lapwai. "It is difficult for men and women to forgive and forget such hellish treatment as they were subjected to when their houses were burned, their property destroyed, their husbands and children murdered, and their wives ravished," the minister declared. The editor of the *Lewiston Teller* carried the threat a step further. "We won't be responsible for their lives 24 hours after their arrival," he wrote.

Even the confident assurances of Miles could not completely remove the unease created by such veiled threats of vigilantism. After all, he was based in Fort Vancouver, 360 miles away. These ominous words were being issued by residents who lived in the very towns and valleys where the exiles would be resettled.

The Commissioner of Indian Affairs instructed the local agent in Oakland to put the matter to the Nez Perce, explaining the situation. He encouraged them to separate into two groups to be relocated to two separate areas, one among the treaty Nez Perce, the other in a farther exile somewhere else in the Northwest. There were still warrants out for a number of specific Indians, including Joseph, and it was deemed best to keep this group far removed from the angry settlers who held them responsible for the killings. Even Miles thought it would be prudent for Joseph and the others with warrants against them to consider relocating, at least temporarily, to a spot outside the jurisdiction of the state of Idaho, where the warrants had been issued.

Joseph was angered and frustrated that he was seen as a belligerent. "If I could, I would take my heart out and hold it in my hand and let the Great Father and the white people see that there is nothing in it but kind feelings and love for him and them," he said. He had taken no part in any killings and had resisted hostilities from the outset. But he had long since learned that white people did not listen to the voice of Indians unless the Indians looked and lived as white people. He understood the wisdom, and even the necessity, of the proposed division. He did not want the safety of his people jeopardized by white rancor and animosity, even if it was unjustified and unfounded.

He was also concerned about the rights of those among the exiles who had not willingly or deeply embraced the Christian ways. Lapwai was Christian and had been so since the time of the Reverend Spalding. It was run by Presbyterians and overseen by Presbyterian agents. Many of the Lapwai Presbyterians were so opposed to the old ways that they had even gathered and burned clothing worn by their traditional brothers and sisters. It was not an environment conducive to the practice of the old ways and beliefs.

And he had one further concern. The Lapwai, though Nez Perce country, was not his homeland. It was to the distant Wallowa, among the bones of his ancestors, that he wished to be returned. He feared that if he accepted a place in the Lapwai, that would be seen as accepting the government's conditions, and he would never have a chance to return to the winding waters and snow-covered peaks that his band knew as home.

But in the end, the people reluctantly agreed to split. Joseph had been offered a home by his old friend, Chief Moses, on the Colville Reservation two hundred miles north of Lapwai near the Canadian border in the state of Washington. It was country similar to his own, and it was out of the jurisdiction of Idaho, so he and any others with warrants against them would not be subject to arrest and trial. There he and his people would be free to live in the old ways and to practice their own religion. And from there they could continue negotiations to return to the valley of the Wallowa.

Those who chose to go to Lapwai and live as Christians would receive a joyous welcome from their Christian friends and relatives, who would provide for them and assist them in rebuilding their lives. Any who still practiced the old ways but were willing to risk the dangers of being seen as a traditional in this land of Christians and angry white settlers would be welcome to go to the Lapwai too.

Only one stumbling block remained. In an attempt to accelerate the acculturation of the people, the children of the tribe had been sent to a recently constructed boarding school in Chilocco, several miles south of Arkansas City just inside the border of Indian Territory. The Chilocco school was run by Dr. H. J. Minthorn, one of the men who had been in the entourage that visited the Nez Perce when they had been petitioning to set up a church in the Oakland agency. The Chilocco school had been modeled on the famous Indian school in Carlisle, Pennsylvania, that had been dedicated to converting the Indian "in all ways but color into a white man." And in this, the school was making good progress. They had cut the children's hair, dressed them in suits and dresses, and taught them to read and cipher and practice the ways of blacksmithing, efficient farming, and domestic arts.

The Chilocco school wanted to keep these children in Oklahoma to complete their education. They would be the first true fruits of the labors of the Christian missionaries—children of the forests who had abandoned all vestiges of the past to become full participating members of American society. Their presence would also allow the school to continue to receive the government subsidies that were based on the number of children in residence at the school.

The people met in council to discuss the issue. They were of common accord that they would not leave their children behind. One by one, they spoke their peace, drawing nods of assent from the others that this was not a subject on which they could compromise. If they were to leave, their children must leave with them.

Finally, the government officials gave in. It was agreed that the children should meet up with the people at the station in Arkansas City, and together they would all be allowed to return to their homeland.

On the morning of May 21, 1885, in a steady mist and drizzle, the people turned their backs for the last time on the Oakland agency and began their journey to the railhead at Arkansas City, thirty-five miles to the north. The government had provided them with several wagons on which to carry their goods and a few of the weaker among them, but most of the men and women were forced to walk.

The man in charge of their move, a Dr. W. H. Faulkner, had come down several weeks earlier to oversee their transfer. He was a fair man but impatient, and he had told them that all their stock and possessions that could not be brought with them would have to be disposed of by the twenty-first. Once again, in a dark echo of General Howard's order to leave the Wallowa those many years ago, the people were forced to leave much of worth and value behind. Luckily, the local rancher C. M. Scott, who had been their friend since he had first escorted them from Arkansas City upon their arrival from the Quapaw, agreed to sell what they could not dispose of before their departure and send the money to them. Nonetheless, they had been forced to sell much of their stock at unfairly low prices and were leaving with little to show for their five years of labor in Indian Territory.

They had been allowed to visit the graves of their loved ones several days before the departure, and this had caused them great sorrow. Of the more than eight hundred people who had begun the journey over the Lolo eight years before, fewer than three hundred remained. The rest were scattered in alien earth along the trail, in the bottomlands by Leavenworth, in the hillsides of the Quapaw, and here in the cruel flatness of the Indian Territory, where more than a hundred lay buried. In leaving this dark exile, they were leaving a part of their heart, which could never be reclaimed.

For the entire day they pushed through the mud toward the railhead. The mist turned to rain, soaking everyone and making the ground a slick quagmire of ankle-deep muck. But except for a pause at midday to eat, they did not slow their pace.

Some were able to make the entire distance in two days, arriving soaked and exhausted at the Arkansas City station about midnight on the night of the twenty-second. The others straggled in the following morning. They were permitted to trade and purchase supplies in town but were told to return to the station by 10:00 a.m. to begin loading for departure.

The government had arranged for seven emigrant sleeper cars to carry the people west. These were passenger cars with few windows, lower seats that folded into beds—albeit without padding—and upper berths that hung from iron rods suspended from the ceiling. Traditionally they had been used for transporting emigrants to the frontier to seek their fortunes and were neither comfortable nor commodious. But to the Nez Perce, they were a lifeline to home.

All morning the people loaded their baggage and scanned the horizon for signs of the children who were supposed to meet them from the boarding school. None was willing to leave without them.

As departure time drew near, the situation became tense. But finally, right before the train was to pull out, the children arrived in the care of Superintendent Minthorn's assistant. Dr. Faulkner, however, refused to accept them.

Minthorn's assistant pleaded their case. Their parents, he said, had agreed to send the children to the school because it was seen as evidence of their trust and docility and commitment to the ways of civilization. Now

Faulkner was betraying that trust as well as breaking a promise that the children would be allowed to return with them.

Eventually, Faulkner relented. But once again, one final issue arose. The government wanted the Nez Perce to sign a document relinquishing the title to their lands in Indian Territory. Again, the people met in hurried council. This land had been deeded to them by the Cherokee two years before and was their last vestige of wealth as a people. Now they were being forced to barter it for their freedom.

Such a demand was cruel and unjust and without legal basis. But in the end, it was simply one more injustice visited upon them by a government that had betrayed them and treated them unfairly for as long as any could remember. So, with sadness and anger, the chiefs signed the document, making the people landless and homeless but freeing them to return to the country that they had been longing for in their hearts for the past eight years.

The people climbed on, the wheels began to move, and the train moved slowly away from the Arkansas City station. As the engine gradually built up steam, observers near the tracks heard a strange, keening wail coming forth from the cars. It was the cries of the people, lifting a last lament for the parents and grandparents and young children and infants whose bodies they were leaving in this strange and alien country, far from the land the Creator had given them and far from the land they believed was their home.

The journey did not go smoothly. At McPherson, Kansas, only 120 miles from Arkansas City, the station agent insisted that the people transfer to a Union Pacific train, in direct violation of their agreement with the government. Given the supplies they had been issued, along with their blankets and teepees and personal goods, their freight weighed almost eighteen tons. Though still exhausted from their long walk of the day and night before, the people were forced to take all their baggage from the first train and reload it onto a second, while curious citizens from McPherson crowded in on them, impeding their efforts and offering no assistance.

At midnight, after three strenuous hours of unloading and reloading, they were able to depart again on what they hoped would be an uneventful journey to a station near the Lapwai. But, again, they were wrong.

At the town of Pocatello, several days down the track, the station attendant announced that the train was to be divided. Those people going to the Colville would travel north on a rail line that went north into Montana then turned west to Spokane. The others would continue on a different rail line that ran on a northwest diagonal directly to Wallula, near the site of the Whitman massacre, and disembark there to be transported to the nearby Lapwai.

But Agent Faulkner balked. He had been charged with the responsibility of transporting all the people to the rail junction at Wallula, and he was going to do so. There would be no division of the families unless he received direct confirmation to this effect.

In order to clarify his orders, he went into the telegraph office and sent for instructions. But delay was dangerous. An edgy crowd was already gathering around the train, and there was word that a U.S. marshal was on his way to arrest Joseph for his supposed part in the killings back on the Salmon.

Faulkner became nervous. It was not impossible that this supposed change of orders was nothing more than a ruse to stall the train until the marshal arrived. He did not want to be responsible for a situation that went against the army's wishes, but neither did he want to resist an order that might indeed have come from official sources.

Finally, without waiting for a return message clarifying his responsibilities, he convinced the station agent to send all the people together to Wallula junction, and the train departed hastily before any of the potential confrontations or arrests could take place.

Stopping only to pick up some troops for protection, the train moved across southern Idaho on rails that now ran where once only Indian trails and wagon roads had been. From the window Joseph could look to the north and see the distant mountains that protected his Wallowa Valley. Then the tracks turned north and headed up toward the Wallula not more than 150 miles from the homes and villages the people had left eight years before.

But now came the difficult moment. It had been left until now for each person to decide whether he or she wanted to go to Lapwai and live as Christians or to Colville and live in their traditional ways. The interpreter came among them asking for their decision. Only Joseph was given no choice.

Those who by now had fully embraced the Christianity taught them by Reuben had no difficulty deciding. But for others it was not so easy.

Especially in the case of White Bird's people, who had been among the most belligerent and intransigent about accepting white people's ways, the decision was difficult. Lapwai was only several days' ride from their home country. But in order to live there peacefully they would have to look and act as Christians, even if they did not feel it in their hearts. The Christians in the Lapwai not only were opposed to the old ways, they feared those who practiced them, thinking that they might still have the old powers and could use them for harm. If any of White Bird's band or any of Toohool-hoolzote's people who still believed in the old ways wished to live in Lapwai, they would either have to hide their true beliefs or risk certain persecution.

Joseph's people had less difficulty. Their chief was being forced to go to Colville. Their home country in the Wallowa lay more than a hundred miles from the Lapwai across the deep canyons and treacherous waters of the Snake and Salmon—almost a different world. The Colville was on land filled with game and fish and wild berries and roots. It could easily support their traditional way of life. In addition, Chief Moses had extended a welcome to them, which was far different from the reception they would receive at the Lapwai. And by refusing to accept placement at the Lapwai, they would continue to demonstrate that they were a people in exile and could not be said to have relinquished their right to land in the Wallowa by accepting placement on the Nez Perce lands at Lapwai. Though saddened at the thought of further exile, they willingly chose the Colville Reservation as a destination, hoping that it would be but one more stop on their journey back to the land of their birth.

When the final counting was made, 118 people had chosen a reunion and reunification with their friends and families in Lapwai, and 150 had chosen to continue north by train to the sprawling Colville Reservation, where they would continue their life on land they did not consider their own.

26

"I Would Be Happy with Very Little"

THOSE FAMILIES WHO chose the Lapwai received a warm, joyful reception. They had been carried by steamboat from Wallula to Lewiston and by wagon and on horseback from Lewiston to nearby Lapwai. The whole reservation was waiting when they arrived, and both the exiles and the waiting families stood in ceremonious formality while a prayer was offered and welcoming speeches were delivered. Then they rushed forward and greeted each other, seeking out friends and relatives. It was only at the end of this hour-long reunion that the true tragedy of the exile began to be revealed. Now, for the first time, both those who had been gone and those who had remained were able to realize the great number of their friends and family members who were not present at this celebration. As the depth of the loss began to sink in, the tears of joy turned to mournful wails from those who had sought mothers and fathers, sisters and brothers, and were now standing alone, realizing that time or the trail or the harsh conditions of exile had cost their loved ones their lives and that the reunion they had so long desired would not take place in this life.

For Joseph's followers there was no such discovery because there was no such reception. Joseph's people arrived by train in Spokane Falls and were immediately transported by wagon to the Colville agency headquarters fifty miles to the west.

The Colville was a large reservation of mostly high, rolling country that stretched from the Columbia River north to the Canadian border. Governor Stevens had established it in 1872 as a kind of "Indian Territory" of his own devise, where he could place a number of tribes on common ground in order to open up their homelands to white settlement. As a location for living, it had much to recommend it. There were broad expanses of open meadow and prairie with ample grass for horse and cattle raising. It was crisscrossed by streams abundant with fish, and its forested hills teemed with game of all kinds. Many of the roots and berries that were central to the diets of all the people who had lived in the area grew on its hillsides and in its meadows. Except for its cold, snowy, high-country winters, it was an ideal setting to give people an abundant way of life.

But its great extent and diverse terrain were also a source of problems. Over the centuries, many tribes had roamed freely over this land in search of food and game. A number of them, including the San Poil and Nespelem, considered their homelands to be inside the boundaries of the Colville Reservation. Sharing its great expanse for seasonal hunting and gathering was one thing; sharing it as a living place was another. When the government began assigning other tribes to the Colville as their place of permanent residence, they were denying the primacy of those tribes who considered this land their own, and frictions quickly developed. The forced imposition of outsiders put a strain on the fish and game supplies, changed settlement patterns, and placed people side by side who had differing languages, differing beliefs, differing attitudes toward white culture, and long-standing histories of interaction that had not always been hospitable and amicable. Chief Moses, who had invited Joseph to live with his people, was one of these outsiders.

Joseph and Moses had crafted this arrangement quietly through a series of messages exchanged by courier. Moses was an old friend, eleven years Joseph's senior. His people, the Columbias, had once lived farther to the east near the Columbia River. He had spent time at Spalding's mission as a child and, much like Joseph, had striven to achieve a kind of distant accommodation with the whites, accepting those aspects of white culture that benefited his people but keeping a distance in matters of belief and manners of living. He had once been a very powerful chief among all the peoples in the Plateau and Columbia Basin, but his middle course had alienated many who strongly supported or strongly opposed accommodation with white culture, and his relocation to the Colville and lands previously occupied by the Nespelem people had increased tensions between his people and some of the other Colville tribes.

Nonetheless, he had managed to gain the favor of the white governmental leaders by convincing them that he was a voice of moderation and in this way had made himself the spokesman for all the peoples on the Colville, whether or not they approved of him. To the white observers and officials, this made him the *de facto* chief, and he was happy to look upon himself in that fashion.

But, as well as an astute politician, he was a hard-drinking, self-promoting individual who had his detractors among the white locals as well as among the tribes that did not consider him their actual leader. When Joseph arrived, supposedly as the guest of Moses, these underlying animosities and doubts rose to the surface. Joseph and his people became the objects of much of this resentment.

The Colville agent who took charge of the Nez Perce upon their arrival was not happy to have such a problem dropped onto his lap. He had no sympathy for Joseph and no respect for what he considered the weak-willed decision of those back East to send this group of renegades to his territory. He did not want them near the corrupting influence of what he considered to be a "whiskey Indian" like Moses, so he kept them in squalid conditions just off the reservation near agency headquarters, withholding their supplies and rations rather than sending them to be with Moses.

White shop owners and settlers, fearing that the proximity of the celebrated marauder, Joseph, would decrease the desirability of the area for settlers, derided the chief as a "large, fat-faced, scheming, cruel-looking cuss" and lobbied against his presence. The other tribes who shared the Colville were no more sympathetic, calling the people of both Joseph and Moses "horse thieves and murderers." The San Poil, on whose land the Nez Perce were initially placed, grew so angry at this imposition that troops had to be called in to keep the situation from escalating into violence. It was not a welcome calculated to make Joseph's people feel at home.

The new arrivals did their best but soon realized that that the situation, even if only temporary, was untenable. Joseph quickly began lobbying to be moved fifty miles west to the Nespelem Valley, where his friend, Chief Moses, resided with his people.

After a few tense months, the move was arranged. Unfortunately, since the Nespelem Valley was also the aboriginal land of the Nespelem tribe, they were no more interested in having Joseph settle on their lands than they had been to have Moses and his people settle among them. Joseph and his followers merely made a difficult situation even more difficult because the country was not well suited to farming, and the addition of more people with more stock simply put more stress on the grazing lands that all of them were trying to share. Though the Nespelems did not respond with the same fury as the San Poils, neither did they offer a warm welcome to the newcomers.

Joseph and his people did what they could to make Nespelem their home. There was no real agency presence there, just a subagent who had massive amounts of territory to administer. So the Nez Perce were left to their own devices, forced to forge an uneasy peace with resentful tribes and to establish such life as they could under the circumstances.

Once again, they had arrived too late to plant any crops, even had they wished to do so. So they were dependent on government rations and such trade as they could engage in with other tribes and the white settlers in the area. But here on the Colville, freed from the oversight of churches and agents committed to their Christianizing and civilizing, they were able to return to their old beliefs. As a result, they were able to live, at long last, in accord with the laws of the Creator, leaving the earth ungouged and the fields unshorn. But in so doing, they deprived themselves of the sustenance that came with a sustained practice of agriculture. They could hunt and fish and gather roots and berries, but without the freedom to travel across to buffalo country or to fish and hunt the places that their tribe had known best, they could not find the sustenance they needed. They tried to build up their horse herds, but this was not a quick solution. Slowly they descended further into poverty.

When the winter of 1886 arrived, bringing with it snows up to four feet deep and some of the coldest temperatures on record, the precarious reality of their situation truly revealed itself. The weak and elderly among them began to perish in alarming numbers. The following year, their situation was made even worse by a policy decision at the highest levels of the United States government. Grant's Peace Policy had been adjudged a failure, and since 1882 the agents in charge of reservations had been appointed directly by the government rather than through religious denominations. With this change it was hoped that agents would be selected for their business skills rather than because they espoused a particular belief. The result had been a notable change in business practices but no change in policy—the red race was still to be brought to the feet of civilization by being brought to its knees as Indians.

But in 1887 the Allotment Act, sponsored by Senator Henry Dawes, took the efforts at civilizing in a new direction. According to this act, the reservations would be divided into plots of land that would be distributed to individual Indians and families, who then would be able to work these plots for their own benefit. In theory, this would foster self-reliance, individual initiative, and a loyalty to home and family rather than to people and tribe. In reality, it opened up the possibility of a settler land grab on the reservations by allowing surplus land that remained after everyone had received an allotment to be sold to white settlers. It also resulted in Indians being duped out of their allotments by unscrupulous settlers and land agents who could manufacture trades of Indian lands for promises, services, or needed goods.

Some of the tribes—those who were inclined to accept the idea of individual ownership and white practices of animal husbandry and agriculture—prospered under allotment. Others, who either did not understand or did not wish to change their lifestyle, did not. In the case of Joseph's Nez Perce, the allotment policy created particular hardship. The people did not want allotments on the Colville because to accept Colville land meant they were giving up their claim to land in the Wallowa. Acceptance of allotments on the Lapwai would mean the same. Though some, like Yellow Bull, did relent and accept an allotment, others refused, effectively rendering themselves landless.

Joseph himself was offered an allotment on the Lapwai in 1889 but refused it. Passions had cooled enough for him to return safely to Idaho, but he knew that accepting land in the Lapwai would be interpreted by the government as relinquishing his right to land in the Wallowa, and this he would never be willing to do.

Instead, he redoubled his efforts to reclaim the Wallowa and to force the government to adhere to the conditions of the agreements it had made with him and his people over the years. With the help of white lawyers in Spokane, he began articulating the legal case for his claim to his homeland. He pointed to 1855, when his father had signed the initial treaty giving the government the land on which the Lapwai existed and nothing else. He pointed out that even the conditions of that treaty had never been fulfilled and that his father later had refused to sign the Treaty of 1863, in which the Wallowa was illegally given to the government by men who did not own it. He pointed out that Grant had put the Wallowa in trust for his people in

1873 and had abrogated this decision in 1875 with no legal authority to do so. He cited the fact that the Cherokee had given the Nez Perce land in Oklahoma and that the Nez Perce had never received fair compensation for it beyond the $18,000 that the government had appropriated for their transportation back to the Northwest. Since that land had been purchased originally for $300,000 from the Cherokee for the Nez Perce and later had been sold off to settlers for almost that much, he demanded an accounting of those moneys. He also pointed out that if the Nez Perce in exile were seen as part of the Nez Perce who stayed in Idaho, the more than $1.5 million that the Nez Perce had received for their lands should be distributed in some proportion or made available to the Nez Perce who had been incarcerated in Indian Territory.

Point by point, decision by decision, governmental action by governmental action, Joseph constructed an argument that allowed for no honest escape by the U.S. government. No matter what the government claimed, Joseph had legal grounds for refuting any argument that led to any conclusion other than that the United States owed the Nez Perce compensation for the various lands they once had inhabited.

His first hope, as always, was not compensation but the return of the Wallowa Valley. But if that were not to be, he wanted fair compensation so his people, like all other tribes, would have the annuities to allow them to become self-sufficient without turning to agriculture or continuing to rely on the whims and mercies of government handouts.

At the heart of his contention was the conviction that the Nez Perce were a people and should be compensated as a people, not as individuals with no collective identity or responsibility for each other. This was the one condition that the government, no matter what its sentiment toward Indian claims, could not accept. America was the land of free individuals, not a nation of subordinate groups that could negotiate for the collective good of their people. Joseph's claim to negotiate as the leader of a sovereign and separate people represented an antiquated, discounted point of view, and his claims, no matter how legally compelling, had to be disregarded.

But Joseph would not relent. He wanted to see the ancestral lands returned to his people as a whole; he was not interested in the distribution of individual plots to individual families. And if he could not get satisfaction through legal means, he would try to use his personal reputation to gain public support. Drawing upon the goodwill and reputation he had with the American public, he began traveling to Washington, D.C., in an effort to present his case to sympathetic authorities. His first visit there with Chapman and Yellow Bull in 1879 had been a great success. There was no reason to think that subsequent visits would be any different.

But in the intervening years, America had changed. When he had first traveled to Washington, the Indian question was still strong in people's minds. America was still coming out of the Civil War and struggling with the questions of how to deal with the people and spaces of the sparsely settled West. But in the few years since that first visit, the vision and focus of the country had shifted. Railroads now crisscrossed the continent, knitting East and West into a single nation. The telegraph now reached all corners of the country, making communication almost instantaneous. Cities had grown into teeming immigrant centers, and small wooden boardwalk frontier towns had turned into solid stone and brick communities, with banks and churches and newspapers and men and women as interested in the affairs of Europe as in the struggles of declining Indian tribes.

Men like Joseph, fighting to keep alive a vision of the past, were slowly becoming vestigial. They elicited curiosity, even a romantic nostalgia, but they did not fire public indignation with their stories of mistreatment and injustice. The closest most Americans came to an interest in Indians was attending one of Buffalo Bill Cody's traveling Wild West shows. Even the dreaded Sitting Bull, the scourge of the plains and the man whose ghostly presence had shaped both the escape route and the final battle of the Nez Perce people at the Bear's Paw, had been reduced to performing with Buffalo Bill, sitting onstage in front of a teepee while white barkers expounded on the spiritual nature of the Indian.

So now, when Joseph visited Washington, D.C., he competed for public attention with issues like the Standard Oil trust and construction of a canal across the isthmus of Panama. He was received politely, even given a presidential audience, then dismissed with the same kinds of vague promises that politicians made to all suitors and favor seekers. The business of America had become business, and anyone who represented any other type of concern was given civil hearing, then politely shown the door.

He also was fighting the tide of a reform movement that saw the "Indian problem" as an issue less of tribal sovereignty than of individual rights. The Indians' staunchest supporters both in government and society as a whole saw their primary task as bringing the Indian into the full status of American citizenship.

"Let us forget once and forever the word 'Indian' and all that it has signified in the past," said a participant at one of the Mohonk Conferences that were held annually in New York to help shape American policy toward the Indian, "and remember only that we are dealing with so many children of a common father."

Such an attitude fit perfectly with the less visionary attitude of more practical politicians. "Three hundred thousand people have no right to hold a continent and keep at bay a race able to people it and provide the happy homes of civilization," they declared. "We do owe the Indians sacred rights and obligations, but one of those duties is not the right to let them hold forever the land they did not occupy, and which they were not making fruitful for themselves or others." At its best, the issue of Indian rights had become an issue of human rights. Land claims, apart from individual property claims, were a thing of the past.

So when Joseph went before officials in Washington complaining about the treatment of the Nez Perce at Colville and pleading for the legal rights of his people to their old lands, he was received as a curious anachronism and met with almost patronizing indifference. The public as well as governmental officials were more interested in seeing the noble chief in his regalia than in dealing with him as an aggrieved plaintiff in a land dispute with the United States government.

He was still lionized by the public, but in a very curious way. In 1897, after a fruitless visit to Washington, he was invited to New York to participate in the great parade and celebration for the dedication of Grant's Tomb. On the day before the dedication, he was invited to Madison Square Garden to watch Buffalo Bill's *Wild West* show. Both General Howard and General Miles were visiting the city for the dedication and also in attendance. Upon seeing Joseph, each came over to pay his respects. When Buffalo Bill, mounted on his horse and directing the festivities, realized the chief was in attendance, he too rode over and paid his regards. The assembled public was provided with a treat even greater than the *Wild West* show's recreations of great Indian battles and feats of frontier marksmanship. There, in their own great arena in downtown New York City, America's most celebrated Indian had encountered two of its most celebrated Indian fighters and its most celebrated Indian scout, now turned showman and, by all appearances, had conversed civilly and congenially with each of them.

When the *New York Times* reported the event the following day, they referred to Joseph as the leader of his people's "romantic flight in 1877." The man who only a decade earlier had been viewed as the embodiment of America's unjust treatment of indigenous people had become instead the symbol of a bygone era and the embodiment of a romantic vision of America's past. The next day this image was emblazoned for all time on the public's imagination as Joseph, in full tribal regalia, rode alongside Buffalo Bill in the great parade honoring the deceased general and president.

Joseph returned home to the Colville an even greater hero in the public mind but no closer to achieving success in his quest to get his people back to the Wallowa. The American people, like the American government, were happy to lionize him as a symbol of the nation's exotic frontier past, but they had no interest in seeing him as a person with a legitimate legal dispute in the present.

There were still voices on his side. Miles, who had been promoted to Commander General of the Army, continued to advocate for the chief. He sometimes paid for Joseph's trips to Washington out of his own pocket, and he worked hard to make sure that the chief got fair hearing when he arrived. But he too was being swept up in the tides of change as the military was being forced to move from dealing with Indians and Mexicans and runaway slaves to offshore problems like the Spanish presence in the Caribbean. Howard made an occasional statement in support of Joseph, and Buffalo Bill Cody took up his cause. But by and large, the West of the Indian wars was receding into myth, and those who still represented that West were receding with it.

But in 1889 there seemed to be a glimmer of hope. Once again, Miles spoke up for the chief and arranged a visit to Washington, this time to include a hearing before the Indian Commission. The meeting went well, and Joseph had returned to the Colville convinced that he would finally be allowed to travel to the Wallowa to pick out the lands that he and his people would occupy.

The following spring, James McLaughlin was sent west to serve as inspector on Joseph's long-awaited journey to the Wallowa. He was to accompany the chief, assess the situation, and issue a report on which a determination would be made about allowing Joseph and his people to return to the land of their ancestors.

McLaughlin was a veteran of Indian affairs and fancied himself a friend of the red man. He had been the agent at Standing Rock Reservation in South Dakota when Sitting Bull had returned from his Canadian exile, and he had managed to work with the stubborn Lakota chief and even get him to practice some rudimentary farming. He was quite certain that he could assess the legitimacy and advisability of Joseph's claim to be returned to the Wallowa.

In the last week of June 1900 the two men, along with several other Nez Perce, made their journey to the Wallowa. The snows of winter had receded, and the valley was filled with greenery and birdsong. Joseph remembered every hill and stream, savoring the experience as he walked upon the earth that he considered one with his own body. He visited the grave site of his father and mother, where he wept openly. Some sympathetic white settler had fenced it and kept it in good repair.

On the following Saturday afternoon he was escorted to a meeting hall in the small Wallowa Valley town of Enterprise to present his case to the white residents of the area. A large crowd gathered to hear and see the long-exiled chief. Some of them had known him and counted him among their friends. Some were against the idea of even allowing him to speak at all.

He spoke through an interpreter, explaining that neither his father nor anyone else had ever sold this land and that he wished now to have the land near the forks of the creek where his father was buried, as well as the country around the lake and the distant Imnaha Valley, where his people had traditionally camped and which they had always held sacred. But the crowd jeered and made sport of him. He was asking for the best land in the entire valley.

At the completion of Joseph's speech, a Mr. Smith, who had lived in the area for years and had known both Joseph and his father, offered a long, patronizing response. He recounted the history of white–Nez Perce relations in the Wallowa and reminded Joseph that he had agreed to trade this country for land near the Lapwai reservation. Joseph vigorously denied ever having made such an agreement, which apparently referred to the ride he and White Bird had taken with Howard during the "showing of the rifle" council at Lapwai more than twenty years before. But his denials were to no avail.

In the end, the locals gave him no support. They denigrated his spiritual connection to the land as a simple fondness and looked upon his claims as antiquated and delusional. They expressed no willingness to allow him any land, even if purchased at fair market value. He left having received neither satisfaction nor respect. His only great joy had been to see the well-kept grave of his father and mother.

Nonetheless, he hoped that Inspector McLaughlin would write a supportive report. But two months passed, and the report had not been issued. Finally, Joseph enlisted the aid of a local teacher to write a letter to his white friend, Professor Edmond Meany, at the University of Washington, outlining his concerns and aspirations. "I told the inspector I would be satisfied with some land on one side of the river where there were only a few whites, and where creeks and mountains afforded good pasturage," he wrote. "I would be happy with very little."

But when McLaughlin's report finally arrived, it told a very different story. The land is "thickly settled by prosperous people," it stated. "It is enough that the white man has turned the desert into a garden that he should enjoy the profit of his enterprise."

In McLaughlin's view, Joseph was better off staying in the Colville.

The Indian Commission accepted his recommendation.

Meanwhile, the situation at Colville had worsened. The agent in place, Mr. Albert Anderson, was proving to be nearly the equal of Hiram Jones in his punitive practices. He was outraged at the Nez Perce's continued nomadic wanderings, the men's willingness to take in the wives of their deceased brothers, their fondness for horse races, and their refusal to engage in efficient agriculture.

"They are strictly 'blanket Indians,'" he wrote in his annual report in 1900. "They have no religion, believe in no creed, and their morality is at a low ebb." He advocated "abolishing the issue of subsistence and clothing to them" in order to force them to take up farming and other white pursuits.

Joseph in particular drew his ire because of the chief's insistence on living in his teepee even though a wooden house had been constructed for him. "He, with his handful of unworthy followers, prefers the traditional tepee, living on the generosity of the Government and passing away their time in a filthy and licentious way of living," he wrote. To Anderson, history had been partial to Joseph. "The appalling wrongs done by him are crying from the bloodstained soil of Idaho for restitution," he concluded.

He announced that Nez Perce children henceforth would be sent to boarding school at Fort Spokane, several miles across the Columbia River and outside the reservation, where a strong tradition of military discipline was imposed. Joseph recognized this as another effort to remove the children from their traditional language and practices, and he refused to send them. Anderson responded by stopping all rations and withdrawing privileges at the sawmill and blacksmith shop.

Though it created great hardships for them, the people stayed loyal to Joseph. They continued to revere him as the chief, in direct contradiction of the agent's efforts to break the tribal system and make all men equal in status. They built a longhouse in which they held their traditional seven-drum ceremonies. They refused to cut their children's hair or force them to learn the white people's language and adamantly refused to involve themselves in meaningful agricultural pursuits, even as the market for horses, their primary source of wealth and income, was beginning to dry up.

Joseph too persisted in the old ways. He would wear a white man's flannel shirt, but he preferred his Indian leggings and breechcloth and always wore moccasins. He went by his Nez Perce name of Hin-mah-too-yah-lat-kekht, and he accepted the deference that his status as chief accorded him. He always presided at Sunday breakfasts for his lodge, offering the prayers of thanksgiving before the meal, and took the lead in conducting the funerals of any who died in his tribe.

His tribe continued to consult him on all matters, even such insignificant issues as how to divide up a kill of venison. In all manners and actions, he remained every bit the traditional Nez Perce leader and chief—a man of grave and dignified presence with an air of unfailing calm and personal authority.

But the years were taking their toll. Though he was only in his early sixties, his body had begun to fail. His legs had become bowed, his back bent, and his body thick and heavy. His step was uncertain, and his energy had begun to ebb. Yet he continued to serve his people and advocate for their return to their homeland. In 1901 he wrote plaintively to his friend Meany, "My old home is in the Wallowa valley and I want to go back there to live. My mother and father are buried there. If the government would only give me small piece of land for my people in the Wallowa Valley with a teacher, that is all that I would ask."

But the government would do no such thing. Joseph might be a celebrity in the eyes of the American public, but to the local authorities he was indolent, obstructionist, the recipient of unfair publicity and privilege, and a bad influence on Indians who were trying to better themselves in the ways of civilization.

Isolated, ill with an undiagnosed malaise that sapped his strength and spirit, encroached upon by white settlers, and resented by the other tribes among which he lived, Joseph gradually declined, his life becoming a hollow shell of itself. He spent long periods sitting quietly outside his tent or looking at the photo of his one living child, Noise of Running Feet, who lived near Lapwai under the name of Sarah Moses and whom he had never seen or been permitted to visit since that day he had put her on a horse and sent her north across the snow-covered plains at the Bear's Paw.

In 1903 he undertook another journey to Washington. Gold had been discovered on the Colville, and the entire top half of the reservation had been taken from the Indians and opened to white settlement. The remaining southern half, where Joseph and his people lived, was being encroached on by white prospectors without regard for boundaries or legal restrictions. Even the agents and government employees charged with serving the people's good spent their spare time in the hills and streams panning for gold.

The blasts of miners' dynamite in nearby valleys shook the earth, frightening the Nez Perce horses and terrifying the old people, who remembered too well the explosions of the great cannon shells at the Bear's Paw. It not only reminded them of the death and suffering they had experienced, it seemed to repeat the great injustice that had befallen the Nez Perce people when gold had been discovered on their lands forty years before. Joseph wished to do what he could to stop it.

In Washington, he was permitted an audience with the new president, Teddy Roosevelt, who was known to be a great lover of nature and the land. At a buffalo dinner arranged by General Miles, Joseph pleaded his people's case and was promised by the president that someone would come to investigate the matter.

No one ever arrived. Joseph was unaware of Roosevelt's feeling toward Indians, that "I don't go so far as to think that the only good Indians are dead Indians, but I believe nine out of every ten are, and I shouldn't like to enquire too closely into the case of the tenth."

On his way home he stopped at Carlisle Indian Industrial School, the boarding school in Pennsylvania that had served as the model for the Chilocco School in Indian Territory, where the Nez Perce children had been taken from the Oakland agency. There he was reunited with General Howard, with whom he shared the stage as a speaker at the anniversary commemoration.

Joseph had never thought highly of Howard, either for his military prowess or his imperiously paternalistic Christian ways. Nonetheless, he graciously dined with the general and allowed himself to be photographed at the general's side. When he spoke to the audience, he said, "Ever since the war I have made up my mind to be friendly to the whites and to everybody. . . . I have lost many friends and many men, women, and children, but I have no grievance against any of the white people, General Howard or anyone."

He reiterated his long-standing belief that the Indian people should learn the white man's ways in order to mingle and do business with them but that they also should be allowed to keep their own ways and to live as they pleased. He concluded with the wish that he so long had expressed, "I want to be friends to everybody."

After he returned to his home, his health declined further. He spent long hours sitting alone, saying little. The agency doctor noted that he seemed listless. The agent in charge said that he complained of always feeling tired.

On September 21, 1904, Joseph lay quietly in his teepee. Most of the tribe was away in the Yakima Valley serving as casual laborers in white farmers' hops fields. Summoning his wife, who had remained in attendance with him, he requested that she get his headdress from the small wooden shed where he kept such items of value as his old rifle and the framed certificate he had received for participating in the parade at the dedication of Grant's Tomb. "I may die at any time," he told her, "and I wish to die as a chief."

While she was gone, he took his final breath.

Epilogue

"The Noblest Indian of Them All"

JOSEPH WAS BURIED in Nespelem on the Colville reservation in accordance with the wishes of his people. The Wallowa, where he had fought his entire life to return, was now completely in the hands of the white men, who had consistently denied him even the smallest plot of land, though they had named a town "Joseph" in order to capitalize on his fame and notoriety.

His father's grave, which had seemed so meticulously kept when Joseph had visited it five years before, had, in fact, contained only part of his parent's remains. His father's skull had previously been removed by souvenir hunters and was prominently displayed on the shelf of a dentist's office in the nearby town of Baker City, Oregon.

The nine children he had fathered in the course of his life were all dead, including Sarah Moses, or Noise of Running Feet, who was reported to have been pushed in front of a moving train while standing near the siding at the Lapwai mission.

Newspapers around the country took note of his death, usually mentioning him in regard to the epic journey his people had undertaken and praising him as a friend of the white people. The *New York Times,* in its short death notice, referred to him as "the Napoleon of Indians," later adding to that with a quarter-page article celebrating him as the "Noblest Indian of them all, the Washington of his people," and noting that "the world will hardly see his like again."

But Edwin Latham, the agency physician who had attended the chief during his last years, may have provided him with the most fitting epitaph.

"Chief Joseph," he said, "died of a broken heart."

It was an apt memorial for a man who had entreated the U.S. government, "Treat all men alike. Give them the same law. Give them all an even chance to live and grow . . . For this time the Indian people are waiting and praying."

That prayer had never come to pass.

A Note on Sources

In writing *Chief Joseph & the Flight of the Nez Perce,* I did not set out to write an academic treatise. As an Ojibwe elder once told me, "People learn best by hearing stories." And telling a story is exactly what I wanted to do.

But even a story, if told conscientiously, must adhere to the historical record. *Chief Joseph & the Flight of the Nez Perce* is undergirded by almost four years of research into primary documents, historical texts, scholarly articles, and personal interviews, as well as twenty thousand miles of travel across the United States to sites significant to the Nez Perce and their history. It is, to the best of my ability, accurate in its specifics and facts.

Nonetheless, choices had to be made. The historical record is rife with instances of substantial disagreement about numbers, facts, and interpretations. To take only a single example, here are but a few of the contested issues regarding the siege and surrender at the Bear's Paw:

Did the Nez Perce know the soldiers were coming?

Was Looking Glass killed before or after Joseph's parley with Miles?

Did the soldiers or the Indians raise the white flag for the first peace discussion?

Was there one instance of a white flag, or were there many?

Was Joseph bound and gagged during his detention or merely kept under guard?

Was Lieutenant Jerome's reconnaissance done on his own or at Miles's request?

Did Joseph hand his rifle to Howard or to Miles?

What did Joseph actually say at the surrender, and when did he say it?

A narrative that addressed each of these contested issues within the body of the text would cease to be a narrative at all. And this is what has happened to many of the best books on the Nez Perce and Chief Joseph. They have devolved into exercises in documentation, clarification, and qualification. They analyze well but read poorly.

Such books have their place, and I highly recommend them to anyone interested in weighing the pros and cons of disputed information. But I wanted to offer you a story with the pulse of life running through it. So, rather than interrupt the narrative with intellectual arguments and controversies underlying the text or break its momentum by littering the pages with footnotes, I made the best choices I could from the best materials available and presented them as part of the story as I have come to understand and believe it.

I cannot promise to be correct, any more than anyone else can promise to be correct. But what I can promise is this: At no point have I strayed beyond the historical record, whether written or oral. Each moment, each occurrence in this saga as I have recreated it, is as at least one participant or firsthand observer understood it to have happened. And the choices I have made reflect what in my estimation is the most plausible interpretation of disputed events.

Readers who wish to dig more deeply into the many fascinating questions about the Nez Perce's past should consult the copious endnotes of such fine historians as Alvin Josephy and Jerome Greene, whose works are cited below. There the questions of interpretation and controversy are laid bare for deeper analysis and discussion.

A final note: History is indeed a tapestry of individual stories imperfectly woven. It is my hope that, since I tried to tell the story in a way that preserves the heartbeat of human experience, others who have information—passed on by elders, in letters wrapped in ribbons in the attic, or merely held in memory from some distant source—will be encouraged to tell their stories as well. Only then will this tapestry reveal its full richness. Only then will this story, with its many faces and many voices, get the belated hearing in the American public that it so richly deserves.

Bibliography

The long sweep of the Nez Perce story has been told in various ways by various people. These retellings constitute important secondary sources that a researcher must keep by his or her side to serve as road maps to the journey. They all cover much of the same historical terrain, but each has a different emphasis and point of view. I note them in the individual note sections if they are especially relevant to that chapter.

The following list represents those works I found most interesting or valuable in giving a meaningful shape to this sprawling story. They do not all agree on either facts or interpretation, but each represents a worthy attempt to give a reader access to the story of the Nez Perce and their journey into exile.

Beal, Merrill. *I Will Fight No More Forever: Chief Joseph and the Nez Perce War.* New York: Ballantine, 1973. A no-nonsense, no-frills recounting of events, divided into many short chapters that locate the reader in the story better than any other account.

Brown, Mark. *The Flight of the Nez Perce.* Lincoln: University of Nebraska Press, 1982. Copiously researched with an unapologetic bias toward the U.S. government and military's point of view. Brings the reader closer to the military thinking than any other document.

Curtis, Edward. *The North American Indian,* vol. 8. Norwood, MA: Plimpton Press, 1911. Using personal conversations and sources within the Nez Perce community, the famous photographer presents a compelling picture of Nez Perce culture and the Nez Perce journey that is often at odds with other accounts.

Fee, Chester Anders. *Chief Joseph: Biography of a Great Indian.* New York: Wilson Ericson, 1936. Somewhat fanciful reconstruction of Joseph, with strong material about Joseph's boyhood and the world of the whites in the area at the time.

Greene, Jerome. *Nez Perce Summer, 1877: The U.S. Army and the Nee-Me-Poo Crisis.* Helena: Montana Historical Society Press, 2000. The best historical assessment of the war period; tries to give an honest appraisal of both military and Indian points of view. Used all available military, settler, and Indian sources to create a foundation document for the war period that is as essential as Josephy's work is for the prewar period.

Gulick, Bill. *Chief Joseph Country: Land of the Nez Perce.* Caldwell, ID: Caxton Printers, 1981. The only heavily illustrated history. Contains maps, photographs of participants and locations, and reproductions of newspaper accounts. Magazine journalism and style with solid historical grounding.

Haines, Francis. *The Nez Percés: Tribesmen of the Columbia Plateau.* Norman: University of Oklahoma Press, 1955. One of the best solid histories of the Nez Perce. Incorporates many direct quotes and integrates historical detail into a highly readable text.

Hampton, Bruce. *Children of Grace: The Nez Perce War of 1877.* New York: Holt, 1994. Along with David Lavender's work, the most readable historical account.

Howard, Helen Addison. *Saga of Chief Joseph.* Caldwell, ID: Caxton Printers, 1965. Often maligned for its overemphasis on Joseph's leadership role, it tries, more than any other, to bring the chief's story to the fore. Very readable and undervalued.

Howard, O. O., General. *Nez Percé Joseph: An Account of His Ancestors, His Lands, His Confederates, His Enemies, His Murders, His War, His Pursuit and Capture.* New York: Da Capo Press, 1972. Written by the general who pursued the Nez Perce, the account is obviously biased toward the military point of view. It is also heavily criticized for factual inaccuracy regarding the Nez Perce. But it provides a detailed and insightful assessment of the entire journey as understood, after the fact, by a key military player.

Joseph, Chief. "Chief Joseph's Own Story." *North American Review,* 128 (April 1879) 412–33. This is the text of the article published after Joseph's visit to Washington. It is purported to be an approximation of the speech he gave during that visit. It is the only account in Joseph's words of why his people fled and what transpired during their flight and exile. Whether because of the translator, the editor, or the chief himself, it has the problematic aspect of making Joseph the prime architect of all the events of the journey. As a result, it contributed greatly to the mythologizing of Joseph and the subsequent misinterpretation of events that has persisted to this day.

Josephy, Alvin. *The Nez Perce Indians and the Opening of the Northwest.* New Haven, CT: Yale University Press, 1965. The fundamental resource work for any study of the Nez Perce from a historical point of view. The only work that focuses primary attention on the preflight period.

Lavender, David. *Let Me Be Free: The Nez Perce Tragedy.* New York: HarperCollins, 1992. An engaging presentation of the time of contact with Lewis and

Clark to the Bear's Paw surrender. Perhaps the best written account, it rises to literature while still managing to be historically accurate.

McDonald, Duncan. "Through Nez Perce Eyes." In *In Pursuit of the Nez Perces: The Nez Perce War of 1877,* compiled by Linwood Laughy. Wrangell, AK: Mountain Meadow Press, 1993. Written by a reporter of mixed Nez Perce and Scots ancestry, this recounting is based on a series of articles written during the actual flight and published in the *New Northwest,* a newspaper published in Deer Lodge, Montana. It offers anecdotes and insight found nowhere else and hence cannot be corroborated. It keeps a journalist's distance while providing an insider's insight to the Nez Perce war and journey. Follows White Bird to Canada rather than Joseph to Kansas and Oklahoma.

McWhorter, Lucullus. *Hear Me, My Chiefs! Nez Perce History and Legend.* Caldwell, ID: Caxton Printers, 1983. As unapologetically pro-Indian as Mark Brown is pro-military. Developed from McWhorter's own correspondence with Nez Perce. The point of view and interpretation subscribed to by most Nez Perce.

McWhorter, Lucullus. *Yellow Wolf: His Own Story.* Caldwell, ID: Caxton Printers, 1940. This work was written from actual conversations with Yellow Wolf, who participated in the entire war experience. He escaped with White Bird at the time of the surrender and later rejoined Joseph's band in exile. Along with Joseph's recounting, it is the most compelling Nez Perce record of events, and McWhorter has endeavored to allow Yellow Wolf to speak in his own voice. An essential work.

Moeller, Bill, and Jan Moeller. *Chief Joseph and the Nez Perces: A Photographic History.* Missoula, MT: Mountain Press Publishing, 1995. A small book of color photographs that place the reader in the landscape of the entire Nez Perce journey.

Stadius, Martin. *Dreamers: On the Trail of the Nez Perce.* Caldwell, ID: Caxton Press, 1999. An earnest attempt to combine the author's personal journey of the Nez Perce Trail with a historian's recounting of the events along the way. Written in a conversational style, it endeavors to make the story of the exodus feel immediate. It ends abruptly with the surrender at the Bear's Paw.

Wilfong, Cheryl. *Following the Nez Perce Trail: A Guide to the Nee-Me-Poo National Historic Trail with Eyewitness Accounts.* Corvallis: Oregon State University Press, 1990. A large-format, mile-by-mile travelers' guide to the entire journey of the Nez Perce, including the flight of White Bird's band into Canada and the Leavenworth and Indian territory exile. Weak only on the Quapaw and

Oakland stays, and a bit sketchy on the post-surrender journey, it is by far the best traveling companion for the trail. It also contains well-researched quotes and illuminating photographs of the areas under discussion, allowing the armchair traveler and reader to stay well oriented in space and time.

Sources by Chapter

My chapter notes are meant to be a reader's guide to major secondary sources that are especially relevant for a particular chapter. They are, in effect, a reading list for the interested generalist, similar to one I might give students wishing to construct their own story of the Nez Perce history, flight, and exile. I have also confined my referenced works to those readily available to a general reader with access to a good public library or historical bookstore. The only exceptions have been when a particular article is especially salient or essential.

Part 1: A Time of Hope
1. "We Thought They Might Be Descended from Dogs"

The fine work of Alvin Josephy, *The Nez Perce Indians and the Opening of the Northwest* (New Haven, CT: Yale University Press, 1965), is the fundamental background work for any serious study of the Nez Perce. The photographer Edward Curtis, who was also an accomplished ethnographer, gives a clear, first-person view of Nez Perce culture in *The North American Indian,* vol. 8 (Norwood, MA: Plimpton Press, 1911). Herbert Spinden's *The Nez Percé Indians,* a monograph published by the American Anthropological Association (Lancaster, PA: New Era Print, 1908), offers an ethnographic assessment of Nez Perce culture and habits, as does Deward Walker's *Indians of Idaho* (Moscow: University of Idaho Press, 1978). Caroline James's *Nez Perce Women in Transition, 1877–1890* (Moscow: University of Idaho Press, 1996) uses oral histories and personal interviews to provide an inside look at the role and activities of women in Nez Perce culture and history. Lillian Ackerman's *A Necessary Balance: Gender and Power Among Indians of the Columbia Plateau* (Norman: University of Oklahoma Press, 2003), does the same, with a slightly wider geographic reach. The book *Salmon and His People: Fish and Fishing in Nez Perce Culture* (Lewiston, ID: Confluence Press, 1999), by Dan Landeen and Allen Pinkham, provides a deep understanding of the physical and spiritual role of the salmon in Nez Perce life. *Tales of the Nez Perce,* by Donald Hines (Fairfield, WA: Ye Galleon Press, 1984), presents many of the Nez Perce traditional tales and stories.

The initial years of white contact are discussed from the European point of view in the following sources: *Journals of Lewis and Clark,* edited by Reuben Gold Thwaites, *Original Journals of the Lewis and Clark Expedition,* 8 vols. (New York: 1904–05; reprinted, New York: 1959). *"Faithful to Their Tribe & Friends": Samuel Black's 1829 Fort Nez Perce Report,* edited by Dennis W. Baird (Moscow: University of Idaho Library, 2000); Washington Irving's *The Adventures of Captain Bonneville, U.S.A., in the Rocky Mountains and the Far West* (Norman: University of Oklahoma Press, 1961); Peter Skene Ogden's *Snake Country Journals* (London: Hudson's Bay Record Society, 1950); and Alexander Ross's *Adventures of the First Settlers on the Oregon or Columbia River,* edited by Reuben Thwaites (1849; reprint, Glendale, CA: Arthur H. Clark, 1904). Hiram Chittenden's two volumes of *American Fur Trade in the Northwest* (Stanford, CA: Academic Reprints, 1954) provide broad background into the fur-trading era. *Adventures of Zenas Leonard, Fur Trader,* edited by John Ewers (Norman: University of Oklahoma Press, 1959), offers a closer glimpse. Zoa Swayne, in *Do Them No Harm* (Orofino, ID: Legacy House, 1990), provides a fanciful reconstruction of the immediate postcontact period using Nez Perce oral accounts and the journals from the Corps of Discovery. Of the non-native historians, Francis Haines in *The Nez Percés: Tribesmen of the Columbia Plateau* (Norman: University of Oklahoma Press, 1955) is especially strong in this period.

Nez Perce historian Allen Slickpoo's *Noon-Nee-Me-Poo: Culture and History of the Nez Perces* (Lapwai, ID: Nez Perce Tribe, 1973) is fundamental to understanding the Nez Perce culture and history from within. The culture as it has been carried forward is well discussed in Horace Axtell's *A Little Bit of Wisdom: Conversations with a Nez Perce Elder* (Norman: University of Oklahoma Press, 2000). Lucullus McWhorter's *Hear Me, My Chiefs! Nez Perce History and Legend* (Caldwell, ID: Caxton Printers, 1983), drawn from his copious correspondence with native people, is as essential a groundwork as Josephy's.

The McWhorter papers in Washington State University, Pullman, Washington, provide incomparable insight into Nez Perce affairs. Internet users will find an invaluable resource at the National Park National Historic Trail Foundation Web site, http://www.fs.fed.us/npnht (accessed May 2005), where everything from a virtual tour of the trail to an annotated bibliography to a series of quotes from participants in the Nez Perce war can be accessed. I also relied heavily on personal interviews and conversations with individual Nez Perce, who shared their knowledge of their culture and history with me. For personal reasons, most have requested anonymity.

2. A Harvest for the Lord

Again, Josephy's *Nez Perce Indians* and McWhorter's *Hear Me, My Chiefs!* provide the historical skeleton, and Haines, *The Nez Percés*, gives a sound historical footing. The journals of Henry Spalding are covered in E. M. Drury's *Henry Harmon Spalding* (Caldwell, ID: Caxton Printers, 1936). *Where Wagons Could Go*, edited by Clifford Merrill Drury (Lincoln: University of Nebraska Press, 1997), presents the missionary point of view from the diaries of Narcissa Whitman and Eliza Spalding and offers insight into the spiritual mind-set of missionaries as well as into the feelings and experiences of two early frontier women. Drury also edited *Marcus and Narcissa Whitman and the Opening of Old Oregon* (Glendale, CA: Arthur H. Clark, 1973) and *The Diaries and Letters of Henry H. Spalding* (Glendale, CA: Arthur H. Clark, 1958). Rowena Alcorn's *Timothy: A Nez Perce Chief, 1800–1891* (Fairfield, WA: Ye Galleon Press, 1996) provides a sympathetic look at a Nez Perce who decided that there was goodness and wisdom in the white missionary ways. Kate McBeth's *The Nez Perce Since Lewis and Clark* (Moscow: University of Idaho Press, 1993), is a look at the Christian Nez Perce experience through the eyes of a missionary who worked among them. McWhorter's *Hear Me, My Chiefs!* has an appendix devoted to Tuekakas, Joseph's father.

Axtell's *A Little Bit of Wisdom* allows one to view through a prism the effects of Christianity on a traditional Nez Perce spirituality. James's *Nez Perce Women in Transition* provides insight into the role of women in all aspects of traditional culture. Gulick's chapters on the missionaries and the Book of Heaven in *Chief Joseph Country* are readable, informative, and well illustrated.

3. A Child of Two Worlds

Little is documented about Joseph's childhood. Chester Anders Fee's *Chief Joseph: Biography of a Great Indian* creates a plausible, if unverifiable, version. For the most part, it is necessary to construct a cultural context of Nez Perce childhood and fit Joseph into it. Eliza Spalding's references in *Where Wagons Could Go*, edited by Clifford Drury, provide some glimpses into the possible Christian influence on his childhood, an influence that some of Joseph's descendants have mentioned to me in conversations. Construction of Nez Perce culture is best done with the aid of James's *Nez Perce Women in Transition;* Spinden's *The Nez Percé Indians;* McWhorter's *Hear Me, My Chiefs!* (especially the appendixes); Ackerman's *A Necessary Balance;* and Landeen and Pinkham's *Salmon and His People.*

Naturally, all such reconstructions are clumsy and wooden, since they try to provide an analysis of something incandescent. The non-native person who made the best imaginative leap and succeeds most fully in animating the experience of Nez Perce belief is Curtis in *The North American Indian* (vol. 8, Norwood, MA: Plimpton, 1911); Ken Thomasma's *Soun Tetoken: Nez Perce Boy* (Jackson, WY: Grandview Publishing, 1990) is a children's book based on conversations with descendants of Joseph and has a ring of truth to it. The best emotional access to Nez Perce belief and traditional life perhaps is obtained by listening to *Nez Perce Words and Stories,* a recording published by Wild Sanctuary music, in which Elizabeth Wilson, a ninety-one-year-old Nez Perce elder, tells stories and sings songs from her tradition. This recording, made in 1972, offers the voice and memories of one who was raised in the old ways and whose life brushed against that of Joseph and the others involved in the flight and exile. Slickpoo's *Noon-Nee-Me-Poo* also offers a view of traditional life and childhood.

The Dreamer religion is addressed by Click Relander in his account of the Palouse Dreamers, *Drummers and Dreamers* (Seattle: Northwest Interpretive Association, 1986). Robert Ruby and John Brown present a more scholarly assessment of Dreamer religion in *Dreamer-Prophets of the Columbia Plateau: Smohalla and Skolaskin* (Norman: University of Oklahoma Press, 1986). Yellow Wolf explains his understanding of the *wayakin* quest in McWhorter's *Yellow Wolf: His Own Story.* Haines gives a cogent analytical explanation in *The Nez Percés.*

My best materials with regard to Nez Perce belief and child rearing came from conversations and interviews with Nez Perce themselves and from the extensive correspondence involving Wottolen in the McWhorter Collection of archival materials at Washington State University, in Pullman, Washington.

Matilda Sager Delaney gives a firsthand account of the Whitman killings in *The Whitman Massacre of 1847* (Spokane, WA: Ye Galleon Press, 1997). Josephy covers the aftermath thoroughly in *The Nez Perce Indians;* Haines's *The Nez Percés* is the most comprehensive and instructive in explaining the actual events and the reasons behind them.

4. A Tide of Laws and Men

Francis Paul Prucha's *The Great Father: The United States Government and the American Indians* (Lincoln: University of Nebraska Press, 1984) is the starting point and essential source document for understanding treaty relationships and realities. Josephy's *The Nez Perce Indians* includes extensive background materials on early governmental relationships between the Nez Perce and the United States as well as on all the mining and treaty periods.

The proceedings of the Treaty of 1855 are wonderfully documented in the first-person account of Lawrence Kip, "The Indian Council at Walla Walla," in *Sources of the History of Oregon,* vol. 1, part 1 (Eugene: University of Oregon, 1897). Gulick's *Chief Joseph Country* tells the story with narrative flair and historical accuracy, while Haines's *The Nez Percés* sets the proceedings in their broader political context. Landeen and Pinkham's *Salmon and His People* contains the entire treaty as signed, and Starr Maxwell's remarkable documenting of testimony of Nez Perce in 1911 in *Memorial of the Nez Perce Indians Residing in the State of Idaho* (Moscow: University of Idaho Library, 2000) reveals in the Nez Perce's own words what they thought they were agreeing to. This testimony also shines a bright light on the Indians' understanding of the subsequent Treaty of 1863.

Hazard Stevens's two volumes of *Life of Isaac Ingalls Stevens* (Boston: Houghton, Mifflin, 1900) gives us the government position on events of the time. McWhorter's *Hear Me, My Chiefs!* raises some interesting questions about Indian negotiating strategies and explains the Indian thinking on the treaties and the period surrounding them.

The world of the settlers and miners is revealed in *Conversations with Pioneer Men: The Lockley Files* (Eugene, OR: One Horse Press, 1996) and *Reminiscences: Incidents in the Life of a Pioneer in Oregon and Idaho,* by William Goulder (1909; reprint, Moscow: University of Idaho Press, 1989). Starting during the Gold Rush years of the early 1860s, newspaper accounts from the *Lewiston Teller* provide a daily picture of life in the area as well as a glimpse into the attitudes of the newcomers to the Nez Perce.

Further negotiations between the government and the Nez Perce are documented in direct testimony in a University of Idaho Library publication, *"The Treaty of 1855 Has Not Been Lived Up to and We Have No Faith That This Will Be Lived Up To": The 1867 Nez Perce Treaty Council,* edited by Donna Smith (Moscow:

University of Idaho Library, 2001). Here the Indians speak to the governmental officials in their own voices.

5. "We Will Not Give Up the Land"

Again, Prucha's *The Great Father* and Josephy's *The Nez Perce Indians* provide the historical groundwork for an understanding of this complex period. Gulick unpacks this period nicely in *Chief Joseph Country*. As always, Haines in *The Nez Percés* is strong at providing comprehensive historical information in a digestible manner.

At this point official correspondence begins to dominate historical accounts, which often include the reports of the various Indian agents such as John Monteith and letters between participants such as Howard and Monteith. General Howard, in *Nez Percé Joseph* and in *Chief Joseph: His Pursuit and Capture* (Boston: Lea and Shephard, 1881), provides first-person accounts of events, albeit from a military standpoint, while McWhorter, in *Hear Me, My Chiefs!* covers this period with thoroughness and clarity.

A small pamphlet, *The Death of Wind Blowing*, by Mark Highberger (Wallowa, OR: Bear Creek Press, 2000), gives an interesting account from local sources on the killing of Joseph's friend. Gulick, in *Chief Joseph Country*, gives a picture of the period drawn heavily from a local participant in the events.

6. "I Am a Man; You Will Not Tell Me What to Do"

General Howard in *Nez Percé Joseph* recounts the pivotal Lapwai meeting from his military perspective. McWhorter also covers it thoroughly from the Indian point of view in *Hear Me, My Chiefs!* Joseph's account in *Chief Joseph's Own Story* makes it clear that the Indians thought Howard was unreasonable and blundering in his negotiations. Hampton's account in *Children of Grace* offers a good narrative recounting of the treaty proceedings.

Emily FitzGerald's *An Army Doctor's Wife on the Frontier: Letters from Alaska and the Far West, 1874–1878* (Pittsburgh: University of Pittsburgh Press, 1962) allows us to watch the entire proceedings through the eyes of a woman living at the Lapwai post. Yellow Wolf, in McWhorter's *Yellow Wolf: His Own Story*, tells of the meeting from his point of view as a participant.

Part 2: A Time of War

7. "There Have Been Killings"

The secondary source that best recreates the outbreak is Hampton's *Children of Grace,* but the historical testimony of settlers is the most riveting. Much of my material came from interviews with descendants of the white settlers and family documents as yet uncataloged at the Grangeville, Idaho, museum. Among those that have been published, Norman Adkinson's *Nez Perce Indian War and Original Stories* (Grangeville: Idaho County Free Press, 1967) and Charlotte Kirkwood's *The Nez Perce Indian War Under War Chiefs Joseph and White Bird* (Grangeville: Idaho County Free Press) provide the most immediate glimpse into the minds of the locals at the time of the outbreak. McWhorter's *Hear Me, My Chiefs!* covers the outbreak with an even hand.

McDonald's "Through Nez Perce Eyes" tells of the acts in the camp that led to the warrior attacks. Wilfong's *Following the Nez Perce Trail* brings together many primary source quotes that give the an eyewitness view of the event.

John McDermott's *Forlorn Hope: A Study of the Battle of White Bird Canyon, Idaho, and the Beginning of the Nez Perce Indian War* (Boise: Idaho State Historical Society, 1978) is without peer in dealing with the events of the White Bird engagement. McWhorter, in *Yellow Wolf, His Own Story,* presents them from the Nez Perce point of view. As with all the encounters for which military records are abundant, Mark Brown's *Flight of the Nez Perce* is especially thorough.

8. "We Are Living Here Peacefully and Want No Trouble"

Greene's *Nez Perce Summer, 1877* and Hampton's *Children of Grace* offer short but fascinating chapters on the Clearwater battle. McWhorter's *Yellow Wolf: His Own Story* is especially impassioned on this series of events. Brown's *Flight of the Nez Perce* presents the military maneuvering in great detail. Francis Haines covers it well in *The Nez Percés.* An interesting document that becomes relevant for the first time here is Thomas Sutherland's war dispatches, published as *Howard's Campaign Against the Nez Perce Indians* (1877; reprint, Fairfield, WA: Ye Galleon Press, 1997).

Wilfong's *Following the Nez Perce Trail* again is valuable in bringing together many primary source quotes that give an eyewitness view of the event. McDonald, in "Through Nez Perce Eyes," offers the Indian point of view well. Gulick's *Chief Joseph Country* does an admirable job of making the entire first stage of the war come alive. McWhorter's *Hear Me, My Chiefs!* offers context and anecdote.

9. "The Most Terrible Mountains I Ever Beheld"

The Lolo crossing and the Bitterroot passage are covered by almost all writers to some extent. A valuable guide to the experiences of travelers on the Lolo itself is *In Nez Perce Country: Accounts of the Bitterroots and the Clearwater After Lewis and Clark,* edited and compiled by Lynn and Dennis Baird (Moscow: University of Idaho Library, 2003). Curtis, in *The North American Indian* (vol. 8), and McDonald, in "Through Nez Perce Eyes," offer evaluations that include anecdotes that do not appear in other accounts. Personal testimonies can be found in James's *Nez Perce Women in Transition.* Sutherland, in *Howard's Campaign,* and General O. O. Howard, in *Nez Perce Joseph,* provide the military perspective. *The Journals of Lewis and Clark* give the flavor of the terrain.

McWhorter, in both *Yellow Wolf: His Own Story* and *Hear Me, My Chiefs!* provides the Indian experience and point of view. Andrew Garcia's odd and delightful memoir, *Tough Trip Through Paradise, 1878–1879* (Boston: Houghton Mifflin, 1967), gives the first-person account of the flight across the Lolo by his Nez Perce wife, In-Who-lise.

Helen Addison Howard's book "Indians and an Indian Agent: Chief Charlot and the Forged Document" in *Northwest Trailblazers* (Caldwell, ID: Caxton Printers, 1966) offers insight into the Flathead decision to assist the army. Brown, in *Flight of the Nez Perce,* and Greene, in *Nez Perce Summer, 1877,* provide competent background, with Brown emphasizing the military strategy.

Much of the salient material here is archival, most of which is contained in the Montana Historical Archives in Helena, which contain perhaps the best collection of articles and testimonies on the West of the Great Plains and Rockies. Montana newspaper archives also come into play here, the most interesting being the *Helena Daily Herald* and the *Helena Independent,* the *Fort Benton Record,* and the *Missoulian.*

Harper's Weekly magazine contains many stories from this stage of the journey forward. Many were published months, even years, after the fact, but contain first-person accounts by men such as Colonel Gibbon as well as somewhat florid but always fascinating reconstructions of events.

I have also taken much of my material from personal contacts and conversations.

10. "In a Dream Last Night I Saw Myself Killed"

The entire period from the exit of the Lolo through the battle of the Big Hole is admirably documented by Aubrey Haines in *An Elusive Victory: The Battle of the Big Hole* (Helena, MT: Falcon Publishing, 1999). The Big Hole battle is thoroughly analyzed through artifacts and material culture in Douglas Scott's *A Sharp Little Affair: An Archaeology of the Big Hole Battlefield* (Lincoln, NE: J and L Reprint Company, 1994). Brown in *Flight of the Nez Perce* gives a dispassionate military overview.

Helen Addison Howard's fanciful and Joseph-centric *Saga of Chief Joseph* does the best job of making the battle dramatic rather than clinical. McWhorter's *Yellow Wolf: His Own Story* is by far the best Nez Perce–oriented source. It contains not only Yellow Wolf's story but also the recollections of many other Indian participants. Garcia's *Tough Trip Through Paradise* contains a haunting recreation of his wife's return to the site years later. The *New Northwest* newspaper out of Deer Lodge, Montana, did perhaps the best job of collating soldier testimony. Much telling testimony exists also in the newspapers of the time from Helena and Missoula.

It should be noted that the Big Hole battlefield is the most extensively researched and marked of any western battlefield other than the Little Bighorn. Exceedingly informative interpretive walks are available at the site, and a ghostly monument of skeletal lodge poles marks the places where the Indian teepees were pitched on the morning of the attack.

The post–Big Hole travels to the Dry Creek crossing are covered best in McWhorter's *Hear Me, My Chiefs!* and Hampton's *Children of Grace*, which gives a feel for the events of this stage of the journey. Brown's *Flight of the Nez Perce* is especially good on factual information. McWhorter's *Yellow Wolf: His Own Story* is sparse but telling in its details. For the entire Big Hole journey onward all the way to the Bear's Paw, Wilfong's *Following the Nez Perce Trail* is not only essential but also illuminating in its pithy compilation of first-person quotes from soldiers, settlers, and Nez Perce alike.

11. "Pursue Them to the Death"

Greene's *Nez Perce Summer, 1877* is good on the Camas Meadows encounter, as is Helen Addison Howard's account in *War Chief Joseph*. McDonald's "Through Nez Perce Eyes" analyzes the Indians' thinking. McWhorter's *Yellow Wolf: His*

Own Story tells how the raid felt and offers a distinctly contrary point of view to Howard's.

Brown's *Flight of the Nez Perce* is excellent on this whole period from the Big Hole to Yellowstone because it explicates the military issues beyond the battlefield. Beal too, in *I Will Fight No More Forever,* makes this period accessible.

The time in the park is brought alive by McWhorter's *Yellow Wolf: His Own Story.* David Lavender, in *Let Me Be Free,* presents a compelling explanation of the Nez Perce's slow movement through the park, as does William Lang in "Where Did the Nez Perces Go in Yellowstone in 1877?" published in the winter 1990 edition of *Montana, the Magazine of Western History.* Park historian Aubrey Haines presents a discussion of the Nez Perce journey in *The Yellowstone Story* (Niwot: University Press of Colorado, 1977).

The single most enjoyable document about the Yellowstone period, and one of the only real glimpses we get into the Nez Perce camp organization, comes in the remarkable book by Frank D. Carpenter, *Adventures in Geyser Land* (Caldwell, ID: Caxton Printers, 1935), in which first Carpenter and then Emma Cowan recount their capture and detention by the Nez Perce.

"The Journals of S. G. Fisher, Chief of Scouts to General O. O. Howard during the Nez Perce Campaign," *Contributions to the Historical Society of Montana,* vol. 2, 1986, presents the point of view of a scout for the military.

Much of the most interesting first-person material, including military letters and personal recollections, is either archival and unpublished or mentioned only in articles. Of special note, however, is the work of John W. Redington, a self-styled journalist who attached himself to the pursuit and wrote many journal entries that are both fascinating and self-serving. His work can be found in the magazines *Frontier,* vol. 3, 1933; *Sunset,* vol. 15, 1905; and The Archives of Lucullus McWhorter at Washington State University, Pullman, Washington.

As always, Beal's *I Will Fight No More Forever* is clear, lucid, and unadorned. Howard himself gives a detailed account of the Camas Meadows and Yellowstone events in *Nez Percé Joseph.*

12. Alone in a Strange Country

The complexities of military command structure are admirably simplified by Brown in *Flight of the Nez Perce.* Miles's role and actions are explained in *Personal Recollections and Observations of General Nelson A. Miles* (1896; reprint, New York:

Da Capo Press, 1969). Robert Utley's *Frontier Regulars: The United States Army and the Indian, 1848–1865* (Lincoln: University of Nebraska Press, 1988) provides essential background on the military. *Cheyenne Memories,* by John Stands In Timber and Margot Liberty (New Haven, CT: Yale University Press, 1967), looks at the pursuit through Cheyenne eyes.

McWhorter, in *Hear Me, My Chiefs!* provides a point of view that argues against Looking Glass's visit to the Crow. "Journal of S. G. Fisher, Chief of Scouts to General O. O. Howard During the Campaign against the Nez Perce Indians, 1877," reprinted from volume 2 of *Contributions to the Historical Society of Montana* (Boston: J. S. Canner, 1966), is insightful for the military scout's perspective. McWhorter's *Yellow Wolf: His Own Story* offers interesting anecdotes. Beal's *I Will Fight No More Forever* breaks this phase down into manageable conceptual blocks.

13. "Our People Are Hungry and Weak"

Here Indian accounts dominate, including McWhorter's *Yellow Wolf: His Own Story* and *Hear Me, My Chiefs!* and Duncan McDonald's "Through Nez Perce Eyes." Good secondary sources are those that lean toward literary reconstruction, including Lavender's *Let Me Be Free,* Hampton's *Children of Grace,* and Gulick's *Chief Joseph Country.* One exceptional article is from the *Havre Plain Dealer,* October 30, 1920, "The Battle of Cow Island: How a Platoon of Soldiers Held Off Chief Joseph's Band," in which Michael Foley, the freight agent at Cow Creek, provides a first-person account of his encounter with the passing Indians. The Moellers' photographs in *Chief Joseph and the Nez Perce,* which are always stunning, are especially helpful in understanding the Missouri Breaks and Cow Island crossing.

14. "I Think We Will All Be Caught and Killed"

The military aspects of this stage are best discussed in Miles's *Personal Recollections,* Brown's *Flight of the Nez Perce,* and Greene's *Nez Perce Summer, 1877.* William Zimmer, in *Frontier Soldier: An Enlisted Man's Journal of the Sioux and Nez Perce Campaigns, 1877* (Helena: Montana Historical Society Press, 1998), gives an unadorned, day-by-day account of the soldiers' lot.

Again, the most enjoyable secondary sources are those that involve narrative reconstruction: Hampton's *Children of Grace* and Gulick's *Chief Joseph Coun-*

try. McWhorter, in *Hear Me, My Chiefs!* and *Yellow Wolf: His Own Story*, also enriches the understanding.

Much of the relevant material here is archival or in reminiscences printed in regional newspapers and is not readily available to the general reader.

15. "Soldiers Are Coming"
16. "Colonel Miles Wants to Meet with Chief Joseph"
17. "It Is Cold and We Have No Blankets"

Miles's *Personal Recollections*, Zimmer's *Frontier Soldier*, and Captain Henry Romeyn's "Capture of Chief Joseph and the Nez Perce Indians," *Montana Historical Society Publications* 2 (1896), offer the best first-person military accounts of the Bear's Paw episode.

Chief Joseph in *His Own Story* and McWhorter's *Yellow Wolf: His Own Story* and *Hear Me, My Chiefs!* present Indians' views, *Yellow Wolf* perhaps best of the three. All secondary sources focus heavily on the siege and surrender, and each does well. Greene's *Nez Perce Summer, 1877* does the best job of sorting out the controversies surrounding this event.

Oliver Knight's *Following the Indian Wars: The Story of the Newspaper Correspondents Among the Indian Campaigners* (Norman: University of Oklahoma Press, 1960) offers interesting background to press coverage. The most interesting general press coverage is in *Harper's Weekly*, but accounts in the *New York Herald* and regional papers such as the *Bismarck Tri-Weekly Tribune* as well as local papers such as the *Benton County Record* and the *Helena Herald* offer fascinating insight into public attitudes and response. Sutherland's *Howard's Campaign Against the Nez Perce Indians* provides the general's point of view, as does Charles Erskine Scott Wood's *The Pursuit and Capture of Chief Joseph: A Story of the End of the Nez Perce War* (Wallowa, OR: Bear Creek Press, 2002).

General Howard's own interpretation can be found in *Nez Percé Joseph*. Insight into military equipment beyond that presented in Brown and Greene can be found in Randy Steffen's *The Horse Soldier, 1776–1943* (Norman: University of Oklahoma Press, 1978).

One of the most overlooked and important documents for the Indian point of view is Starr Maxwell's collection of first-person testimony in *Memorial of the Nez Perce Indians Residing in the State of Idaho*. Stands In Timber's *Cheyenne Memories* offers a Cheyenne point of view. Sitting Bull's situation is well covered in Robert Utley's *The Lance and the Shield: The Life and Times of*

Sitting Bull (New York: Ballantine, 1993). Duncan McDonald's "Through Nez Perce Eyes" follows the path of White Bird and his escapees, while Garcia's *Tough Trip Through Paradise* presents a haunting first-person account of the affair through the eyes of his Nez Perce wife, In-Who-lise.

Wilfong's *Following the Nez Perce Trail* is full of first-person observations and quotes and is of great value to the visitor to the Bear's Paw.

Though I have made it a practice not to cite individual informants among the Nez Perce, I feel comfortable noting the work of non-native Jim Magera of Havre, Montana, in collecting source materials and providing ongoing interpretation of the Bear's Paw battlefield.

Several final notes: The archival materials in the McWhorter Collection at Washington State University, in Pullman, Washington, are filled with Nez Perce accounts of this episode, and the small museum at Chinook, Montana, tells the story poignantly for those who visit.

Here I add a personal observation. For the immediate future, people who wish to have a physical experience of a historical event can do no better than to choose the confrontation at the Bear's Paw. The battle site is almost unmarked, untouched, and unchanged. It sits unnoticed on the side of a lonely Montana highway far from any major city and a good distance from any town at all. A few walking trails take you to small stakes that designate individual campsites and places where warriors fell. But there are no pavilions, no interpretive centers with dioramas and bookstores, no large expanses of asphalt with painted lines and designated RV parking. There are just the hills, the blowing grasses, and the ghosts.

It is a place where you can be alone with your thoughts, where you can touch a rock that bears the scars of a bullet strike, where you can see the impressions in the ground where the women dug frantically with knives and frying pans to create shelter pits for their families.

This is about to change. An interpretive center will soon be constructed there, and to my mind, it will be our national loss. No memorial we could construct, no interpretive center we could build, could make the experience of this battlefield more powerful or understandable. In its undeveloped state, it speaks with an eloquence that we cannot augment. There are places where the winds carry messages. This is one of them.

Part 3: A Time of Betrayal and Exile
18. "You Will Be Returned to Your Homeland"

Miles's *Personal Recollections* are essential reading for this sparsely documented period. Redington's "Scouting in Montana in the 1870's," *Frontier* (vol. 13, 1933), offers first-person insight, as does Zimmer's *Frontier Soldier*. The observations of Captain Henry Romeyn, published in *Contributions to the Montana Historical Society*, 2 (1896), also offer first-person experience.

The best secondary source for this period is Beal's *I Will Fight No More Forever*. Other than that, archived military recollections of men such as Henry Remsen Tilton, an example of whose recollections can be found in *Forest and Stream and Rod and Gun*, 9 (1877), provide the best picture.

19. "You Must Move Again"

Again, there is little documentation of this period with one significant exception: *Flatboating on the Yellowstone, 1877* (1925; reprint, Staten Island, NY: Ward Hill Press, 1998) by Fred Bond tells the story of the river journey from the point of view of one of the hired boatmen. Like Garcia's *Tough Trip Through Paradise* and Carpenter's *Adventures in Geyser Land,* this is the work of a nonprofessional chronicler and, with those other two, brings the period of the exile alive with an earthy flavor unmatched by any other non-native source. Like the other two, it is also fanciful in its interpretation and unreliable in its details.

20. "When Will These White Chiefs Begin to Tell the Truth?"
21. "Is It Possible That the Noble Red Man Is Not a Myth?"

The entire trek from Bismarck to Leavenworth is completely undocumented except for military reports and newspaper accounts, primarily in the *Bismarck Tri-Weekly Tribune,* the *New York Herald,* the *St. Paul Pioneer Press,* and to a lesser extent, in *Harper's Weekly.* Smaller newspapers along the route of travels carried local responses to the passing prisoners.

Miles conveys the feel of military rail travel of the time in his *Personal Recollections,* and the recollections of Colonel Hugh Reed, who accompanied the exiles on their journey, provide a close-up look at their travels.

22. "A Good Country to Get Rid of Indians In"
23. "I Have Heard Talk and Talk but Nothing Is Done"

There is, as yet, no comprehensive and reliable secondary source for the study of the Leavenworth incarceration. The time from the surrender on has been treated mostly as a burdensome but necessary coda by historians and writers. For now, the best picture of this essential period can be gained by perusing the archives of the *Leavenworth Times* of 1877–1878, where a picture of the life in exile can be gleaned secondhand.

The Quapaw period is covered briefly but accurately by Velma Neiberding in "The Nez Perce in the Quapaw Agency, 1878–1879," published by in the *Chronicles of Oklahoma* (Spring 1966). J. Stanley Clark's "The Nez Perces in Exile," *Pacific Northwest Quarterly* 36 (July 1945), is an excellent overview of the entire exile period. D. David Tate's "The Nez Perces in Eastern Indian Territory: The Quapaw Agency Experience," in *Oklahoma's Forgotten Indians*, edited by Robert E. Smith (Oklahoma City: Oklahoma Historical Society, 1981), is also extremely valuable.

A soon-to-be published book edited by Larry D. O'Neal, *The Nez Perce: An Anthology of a Tribe in Exile* (Moscow: University of Idaho Library, forthcoming), will consolidate the extant source materials on this period and begin a reassessment of the Quapaw exile, which will fundamentally change our historical understanding of this period.

24. "I Know What Is Good for You Now, Mr. Indian"

The Oakland agency period, again, is sparsely researched. *Chief Joseph's Allies,* by Clifford E. Trafzer and Richard Scheuerman (Newcastle, CA: Sierra Oaks Publishing, 1992), discusses the Palouse in this period. Clark's "The Nez Perces in Exile" gives a solid accounting, as does "Nez Perces in Indian Territory: An Archival Study" by Berlin Chapman, *Oregon Historical Quarterly* (vol. 50, 1949). A recent work by J. Diane Pearson, "Numipu Narratives: The Essence of Survival in Indian Territory," *Journal of Northwest Anthropology* (Spring 2004), breaks new ground in the study of this neglected period and offers the possibility of a rich reassessment of the Oakland relocation. Her work builds upon that done by Archie Phinney in *Nez Perce Texts* (New York: Columbia University Press, 1934).

Beal in *I Will Fight No More Forever* gives a quick and accurate overview, as does McWhorter in *Hear Me, My Chiefs!* Government documents, including agents' annual reports, provide factual data about Nez Perce adaptation to their Oakland Agency life. Documents from the Presbyterian churches show the changing public perception and the influence of Reuben and the Lapwai Christians. Of special interest are the letters written by James Reuben. The archives of the *Arkansas City Gazette* are most instructive about the interaction of the agents, the citizens, the churches, and the tribes.

Last, Kate McBeth's work, *The Nez Perces Since Lewis and Clark* (1908; reprint, Moscow: University of Idaho Press, 1993), offers a look at the return of the exiles to Lapwai.

25. "We Won't Be Responsible for Their Lives 24 Hours After Their Arrival"
26. "I Would Be Happy with Very Little"

The best books on the period in the Colville and the Lapwai after the return from exile are Steven Evans's *Voice of the Old Wolf: Lucullus Virgil McWhorter and the Nez Perce Indians* (Pullman: Washington State University Press, 1996); Mick Gidley's *Kopet: A Documentary Narrative of Joseph's Last Years* (Seattle: University of Washington Press, 1981); and Gidley's *With One Sky Above Us: Life on an Indian Reservation at the Turn of the Century* (New York: Putnam, 1979).

Robert Ruby and John Brown discuss the overall situation on the Colville reservation in *Half-Sun on the Columbia: A Biography of Chief Moses* (Norman: University of Oklahoma Press, 1965).

Last, and of particular note, is Erskine Wood's *Days with Chief Joseph: Diary, Recollections, and Photos* (Portland: Oregon Historical Society, 1970), in which the son of General Howard's aide records his experiences as a boy during summers spent with Joseph in Colville.